ARCHITECTURAL DRAWING

ARCHITECTURAL DRAWING

A Visual Compendium of Types and Methods

Second Edition

Rendow Yee

JOHN WILEY & SONS, INC.

Published by John Wiley & Sons, Inc., Hoboken, New Jersey
Published simultaneously in Canada

For general information on our other products and services or for technical
support, please contact our Customer Care Department within the United
States at (800) 762-2974, outside the United States at (317) 572-3993 or
fax (317) 572-4002.

Wiley also publishes its books in a variety of electronic formats. Some
content that appears in print may not be available in electronic books.

Library of Congress Cataloging in Publication Data:

Yee, Rendow.
    Architectural drawing: a visual compendium of types and methods / Rendow Yee.—2nd ed.
      p. cm.
    Includes bibliographical references and index.
    ISBN 0–471–05540-9 (paper : alk. paper)
     1. Architectural drawing—Technique. I. Title.

NA2708.Y439 2003
720'.28'4—dc21   2002072715

Printed in the United States of America

10 9 8 7 6 5 4 3 2

Dedicated to each student studying this book

past and present—

Always a source of insightful and innovative ideas.

To my parents—

Always a source for inspiration.

Contents

Preface to the Second Edition

There are two important new features in the second edition. The first feature is the addition of a drawing and drafting exercises section at the end of the book. This will allow professors of architectural graphics and design communications to glean ideas for formulating fundamental drawing/drafting exercises to suit their own classes.

The second feature is a supplementary web site chapter, "Conventional and Computerized Representation in Color," which can be found at www.wiley.com/go/yee. This overview chapter covers traditional color media such as watercolor, gouache, pastels, colored pencil, markers, airbrush, and mixed media. Various aspects of the potential of digital media are also discussed. In addition, typical student and professional solutions for the many drawing exercises in the textbook are shown on the web site. These solutions are available to course instructors upon request at www.wiley.com/go/yee or by contacting your local Wiley college representative for details.

Finally, the topics of diagramming and conceptual sketching have been condensed into a single chapter with more explanatory text, and the chapter on presentation formats has been expanded to include professional competition drawings from notable offices.

Acknowledgments

I am very grateful for three insightful critiques of the first edition. All chapters were reviewed by Professors Dick Davison and Stephen Temple; and Professor Owen Cappleman reviewed the chapter on diagramming and conceptual sketching, as well as the web site chapter. I would also like to express my gratitude to all of the office professionals who contributed work in a very timely manner. In addition, I am deeply indebted to the strong support team from educational institutions that supplied me with exceptional examples of drawing exercises. A warm thanks to the following architecture schools and professors who contributed projects:

Dr. Samer Akkach, Adelaide University (South Australia)
Professor Jonathan Brandt, Texas A&M University
Professor Owen Cappleman, University of Texas at Austin
Professor Rich Correa, Yuba College (California)
Professor Dick Davison, Texas A&M University
Professors Hank Dunlop and Mark Jensen, California College of Arts and Crafts
Professor Jane Grealy, Queensland University of Technology (Australia)
Professor Bob Hansman, Washington University in St. Louis (Missouri)
Professor Patrick Houlihan, California College of Arts and Crafts
Professor Chang-Shan Huang, Texas A&M University
Professor Karen Kensek, University of Southern California
Professor George S. Loli, University of Louisiana–Lafayette
Professor Fernando Magallanes, North Carolina State University
Professor David Matthews, Ohio University
Professor Valerian Miranda, Texas A&M University
Professor Dan Mullin, University of Idaho
Professor Bennett Neiman, University of Colorado
Professor Douglas Noble, University of Southern California
Professor Arpad D. Ronaszegi, Andrews University (Michigan)
Professor Thomas Seebohm, University of Waterloo (Ontario, Canada)

Professor M. Beth Tauke, State University of New York at Buffalo
Professor Stephen Temple, University of Texas at San Antonio
Professor Thomas L. Turman, Laney College (California)
Professor Mohammed Saleh Uddin, University of Missouri–Columbia

A special thanks to the following people who assisted me: Justin Ip, Brian W. Quan, Felix Ma, Lawrence Mak, Corvin Matei, and Hedy Hing Yee. I am very grateful for my superb editorial production team at John Wiley and Sons. Especially notable is the hard work and help I got from my editor, Margaret Cummins. She was always there to answer any questions I had. I also appreciate the coordination work of her editorial assistants, Kim Aleski and Rosanne Koneval. Finally, I would like to commend the fine work of the managing editor, David Sassian, and the copy editor, Lisa Story.

Preface to the First Edition

In the visual world of design education and the design professions, message (design) and language (graphics) are so interrelated that they cannot be separated. The design process always includes graphic skills to clarify and communicate the issues in question. This book's goal is to communicate a broad range of design-drawing methods; it is not intended to be a handbook on acquiring design skills.

People learn to communicate through language at an early age. They learn to speak, read, and write. The primary type of communication in any kind of design work, whether fashion or building, is drawing. To communicate our design ideas to others, we must learn how to draw. We must draw with enough facility to make our ideas clear. Furthermore, we need to be able to communicate graphic ideas to ourselves because, as we work on any design, our ideas are constantly changing and evolving.

The language of graphics requires the use of all aspects of the brain —analytical, intuitive, synthetic, and even emotional. The intent of this primer is to provide students and practitioners with graphic tools essential to visual communication methods in the design process. It will reinforce methods of perceiving existing reality in order to create an awareness of the visual world. It will also develop and build confidence in one's analytical and intuitive graphic skills and abilities.

It is quite common to find students with a wide range of backgrounds in drawing upon entering a beginning course in architectural drawing/graphics; some students may have had numerous courses in middle school and high school mechanical drawing and art; other students have never used or been exposed to drafting or sketching equipment. There are also students who show a strong potential on aptitude tests related to spatial visualization; but, for one reason or another, they have never had an opportunity to develop this potential. This book can be used by those who have little knowledge of geometry or basic mathematics. However, it is also designed for intermediate and advanced students in architectural drawing. Students and practitioners with a prior knowledge of pictorial drawing or perspective will find this book to be a convenient reference guide for presentation work.

The first four chapters, including "Representational Sketching," are basic to the study of architectural graphics and provide the necessary framework to pursue the major areas of two- and three-dimensional pictorial drawings. The chapters on paralines, perspectives, and shadows illustrate the most common manual methods in current practice with detailed but simple explanations on the theory behind their use. The use of these procedures will help both the student and the professional in communicating and presenting design ideas. The remainder of the book is devoted to a brief introduction to the topics described by chapter titles "Delineating and Rendering Entourage," "Diagramming and Conceptual Sketching," and "Presentation Formats." The variety of drawings illustrates a large number of diverse styles; and the medium used, the original size, and the scale used (if applicable) are given for each drawing where this information was available. In this sense, the book acts as a springboard to stimulate readers to explore each topic in more detail by investigating the extensive bibliography. Many of the images included are residential building types, but a large variety of other building types are shown as well. In view of today's global culture, many drawing exhibits from outside the United S⁺ also included.

This comprehensive guide attempts to elaborate equally on each of the architectural design-drawing methods in current use. However, the last quarter of the twentieth century has seen an upsurge in the use of paraline drawings. This is due to their ease of construction and their impressive ability to allow the viewer to see and to comprehend the total composition of a design. For this reason, a large number of professional paraline examples are included. Architecture and other design professions have been expanding their expressive vocabulary to include the emerging methods of three-dimensional computer imaging, animation, film, and video. This visual compendium of diverse graphic images done in a variety of both traditional and avant-garde media is rich in its content. Many illustrations are supported by personal commentary from their originators to help shed light on why each type of drawing was chosen to express the design.

Both students and design professionals are continually striving to come up with new ways to represent and express their designs. The graphic image examples that I have chosen are by no means exhaustive. These examples are meant to extend basic techniques that the students learn to a more advanced level as well as to provoke their imagination. They are not meant to dogmatically lead students onto a narrow path of particular styles or "isms"; instead, their goal is to encourage students to start their own journey of discovery and exploration.

As a reference for precise graphic constructions the book is laid out in a simple, easy-to-follow, step-by-step format. Although mechanically constructed pictorials are emphasized, freehand visualization techniques are encouraged. Most architectural schools have courses covering architectural design-drawing in a time frame from one to three semesters. In many cases the material is covered as an adjunct to the design-drawing studio. This book can be used under any kind of flexible time schedule as a student text or a studio reference, or as an office reference for practitioners. The encyclopedic nature of the book encourages browsing and wandering. For ease of reference, design-drawing types have been categorized in such a way that both students and design professionals will find them handy for reviewing design-drawing methods or for obtaining and extrapolating ideas for their own creative presentation compositions.

Plan sketch diagrams: Mica Moriane, Official residence of the President of Finland
Mäntyniemi, Helsinki, Finland
Medium: Color felt pens
Courtesy of Raili and Reima Pietilä, Architects

Acknowledgments

This book on architectural drawing developed from an expression of need over many semesters by the architecture faculty and the students enrolled in the basic architectural drawing course at the City College of San Francisco.

I would like to express my gratitude to my fellow staff members in architecture, Lawrence J. Franceschina, Ernest E. Lee, Enrique Limosner, and the late Gordon Phillips, without whose help and advice the realization of this textbook would not have been possible. Gordon gave me the necessary encouragement during the early stages of this book. In particular, I would like to recognize Ernest E. Lee, who along with Julian D. Munoz reviewed the book in its preliminary format. The latest edition is a result of continual revisions derived from frequent consultations with colleagues:

Robin Chiang	Norman C. Hall	Harry Leong	Curtis Poon
Alexander Diefenbach	Robert L. Hamilton	Pershing C. Lin	Nestor Regino
Jim Dierkes	Patrick Houlihan	Jerry W. Lum	Will S. Revilock
Olallo L. Fernandez	Spencer Jue	Ryszard Pochron	Russell Wong

A word of special thanks to Bernard Kuan for endless hours of typing the preliminary manuscript, and to Tony Ho and Winnie Chun for endless hours of pasteup work. I have always appreciated ideas and feedback from my students. A note of special appreciation goes to the following group of students who assisted me in small but significant ways:

Henry Beltran	Randy Furuta	Wilson Lee	Ann-Marie Ratkovits
Ed Broas	Randa Fushimi	Clarissa Leong	Suheil Shatara
Woo Sok Cha	Dennis Hodges	Hedy Mak	Lily Shen
Jason Chan	James Ke	Amos Malkin	Carl Stensel
Keng Chung	Andrew Kong	Amy Man	Kwok Gorran Tsui
Ken Cozine	Kenneth Lau	Corvin Matei	Nguyen N. Trong
Fred Dea	Albert Lee	Henry Ng	Kam Wong

I am deeply grateful to *Architectural Record* and *Progressive Architecture* magazines for giving me permission to reprint many drawings that were originally published in these magazines. Other magazines that I used as rich sources for graphic images were *GA Houses, GA Document International,* and *World Architecture.* Numerous illustrations are from student work contributed by various schools of architecture. Those contributing included Washington University in St. Louis, the University of Texas at Arlington, the University of Texas at Austin, Savannah College of Art and Design, Southern University, Columbia University, the University of Virginia, Cal Poly San Luis Obispo, The Catholic University of America, the University of Maryland, Texas A&M University, Andrews University, and the City College of San Francisco.

Initial exposure to drawing and drafting came from my father, the late Rodney Shue Yee. Kindled interest in the field of architectural drawing techniques came from two former professors of mine, the late Professor Emeritus Alexander S. Levens of the University of California at Berkeley and the late Professor Emeritus Roland W. Bockhorst of Washington University. Also, I would like to thank Dr. Wayne D. Barton of the City College of Sacramento for sharing his teaching experiences with me in basic drafting and drawing courses, and I would like to acknowledge Professor Zenryu Shirakawa of Boston University for improving my writing skills during my high school and college years. A special note of gratitude goes to all those who contributed illustrations to this book. The process of contacting everyone was both an arduous and an enjoyable task.

I am deeply indebted to the exceptional architectural teaching professionals who have reviewed my book. Their suggestions have been constructive and positive in helping me to sharpen my focus on elements that may need improvement. I want to give my heartfelt thanks to Dick Davison for his most significant, extensive page-by-page review. Other major review contributors included Owen Cappleman and Thomas L. Turman. ⅤBenedict shared his excellent syllabus with me, and excerpts from it have particularly strengthened ⸍ters on linear perspective drawing and delineating and rendering entourage.

I am deeply indebted to the exceptional architectural teaching professionals who have reviewed my book. Their suggestions have been constructive and positive in helping me to sharpen my focus on elements that may need improvement. I want to give my heartfelt thanks to Dick Davison for his most significant, extensive page-by-page review. Other major review contributors included Owen Cappleman and Thomas L. Turman. William Benedict shared his excellent syllabus with me, and excerpts from it have particularly strengthened the chapters on linear perspective drawing and delineating and rendering entourage.

William R. Benedict, Assistant Professor, California Polytechnic State University–San Luis Obispo
Donald J. Bergsma, Professor, St. Petersburg Junior College (Florida)
Derek Bradford, Professor, Rhode Island School of Design
Owen Cappleman, Assistant Dean and Associate Professor, University of Texas at Austin
Ann Cederna, Assistant Professor, Catholic University of America (Washington, D.C.)
Rich Correa, Professor, Yuba College (California)
Dick Davison, Associate Professor, Texas A&M University
Phillip R. Dixon, Professor, College of San Mateo (California)
Jonathan B. Friedman, Dean and Professor, New York Institute of Technology
Robert Funk, Professor, Bakersfield College (California)
Todd Hamilton, Assistant Dean and Associate Professor, University of Texas at Arlington
Hiro Hata, Associate Professor, State University of New York at Buffalo
Steven House, AIA
Paul Laseau, Professor, Ball State University (Indiana)
Harold Linton, Assistant Dean, Lawrence Technological University (Michigan)
George Martin, Professor, Catholic University of America (Washington, D.C.)
Valerian Miranda, Associate Professor, Texas A&M University
David Pollak, Adjunct Professor of Design, Roger Williams University (Rhode Island)
Arpad Daniel Ronaszegi, Assistant Professor, Andrews University (Michigan)
James Shay, AIA Architect
Michael Stallings, Chair and Professor, El Camino College (California)
Paul Stevenson Oles, FAIA, American Society of Architectural Perspectivists–President Emeritus
Martha Sutherland, Assistant Professor, University of Arkansas
Stephen Temple, Lecturer and Architect, University of North Carolina–Greensboro
Thomas L. Turman, Professor, Laney College (California)
Mohammed S. Uddin, Associate Professor, Southern University (Louisiana)
Dr. Osamu A. Wakita, Chair and Professor, Los Angeles Harbor College
Lee Wright, Associate Professor, University of Texas at Arlington
Lindy Zichichi, Professor, Glendale Community College (California)

Acknowledgments would not be complete without paying tribute to the fine staff at John Wiley & Sons, notably editor Amanda L. Miller, associate managing editor Jennifer Mazurkie, and editorial assistant Mary Alice Yates, who transformed the preliminary manuscript into the final product.

The following illustrations were reprinted with the permission of *Progressive Architecture,* Penton Publishing:

Anti-Villa, Batey & Mack, Architects
Armacost Duplex, Rebecca L. Binder, FAIA
Casa Canovelles, MBM Arquitectos
Central Chiller Plant, Holt Hinshaw Pfau Jones Architecture
Church of Light, Tadao Ando, Architect
Clybourne Lofts, Pappageorge Haymes Ltd., Architects
Franklin/La Brea Family Housing, Adèle Naudé Santos and Associates, Architects
J.B. Speed Art Museum addition, GBQC Architects
Kress Residence, Robert W. Peters FAIA, Architect
Louisiana Department of Health and Hospitals, R-2 ARCH Designers/Researchers
Museum of Modern Art, Hans Hollein, Architect
Private Studio, William Adams, Architect
The Stainless Steel Apartment, Krueck & Sexton, Architects
Waterfront Development Plan, Koetter, Kim & Associates, Inc., Architects and Urban Designers

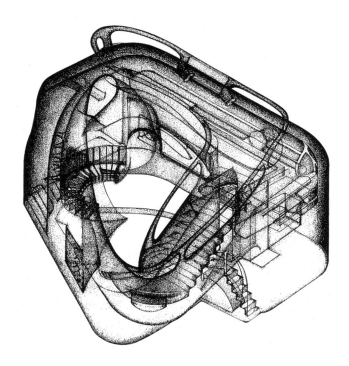

Drawing: Truss-Wall House, Machida, Tokyo, Japan
Transparent Isometric
Courtesy of Eisaku Ushida & Katheryn Findlay
of the Ushida-Findlay Partnership

1

Tool Fundamentals

Drafting tools should be treated with meticulous care with the goal of making them last a lifetime. Always purchase the best quality that you can afford. These tools are a necessity for clarity of graphical expression.

The intent of this chapter is to show the variety of instruments that are available, and how to properly use them.

In summary, following are some of the important skills, terms, and concepts you will learn:

How to use a drafting pencil
How to use drafting instruments
How to use different kinds of scales
How to set up a workstation

Contour lines
Contour intervals

Tool Fundamentals

Topic: Scales

Orr 1985.

Adler 1999.

Chapter Overview
In studying this chapter and doing the related exercises in the book's final section, you will learn how to use drafting equipment; how to measure with architect's, engineer's, and metric scales; and the meaning of contour lines.

A **metal drafting stand** is characterized by an adjustable table top, which can be fitted with a parallel straightedge (see p. 14).

A **four-post table** is usually made of wood or a combination of steel and wood. It has a tool drawer and a large shallow reference drawer. Concealed raising rods can prop the drawing surface to any comfortable drawing angle.

An economical **homemade table** can be made from a flush hollow core door placed on top of adjustable wooden horses.

Types of Drawing Table or Drawing Board Covers

1. **Plastic-coated Paper**
   A green paper underlay with ⅛" horizontal and vertical coordinates.

2. **Borco***
   A vinyl cover that is stain resistant, non-eye straining, and self-healing in the event of scratches or punctures.

3. **Illustration Board**
   A cover that should be hot press, heavy, white, and dense.

4. **Print Paper Sheets**
   Three or four sheets of print paper make a good cover that is not too hard.

5. **Rubber Pad**
   A pad with very little resistance or give.

Avoid drawing on hard surfaces such as glass or wood or hard plastic.

*Borco is a registered trademark of Safco Products Co., Minneapolis, Minnesota.

A highly recommended **drawing board** is one that is hollow with plywood faces or laminated white pine. The technology for types of drawing board and table covers is continually changing. Always check drafting supply catalogues for new surfaces being used. Likewise, there are many new designs for drafting tables that can be found in supply catalogues. Also use the catalogues as a guide for other important accessories such as lamps, chairs, plan files, and spiroll (attaches to drawing table or board to allow drawing to be rolled in to prevent working in cramped positions).

TABLE TYPES AND BOARD COVERS

Architectural drawings (drafted or sketched) are best produced by using leads in the grade range from 4H to 6B. Shown below are three equally good types of pencils that are commonly used. Experience each pencil type to determine which is most suitable for you. Cylindrical pencil leads are classified by a notation which ranges them from the smallest diameter (hardest—9H) to the largest diameter (softest—6B).

GRAPHITE DRAFTING PENCILS

PENCIL GRADE CHART

HARD						MEDIUM								SOFT		
9H	8H	7H	6H	5H	4H	3H	2H	H	F	HB	B	2B	3B	4B	5B	6B

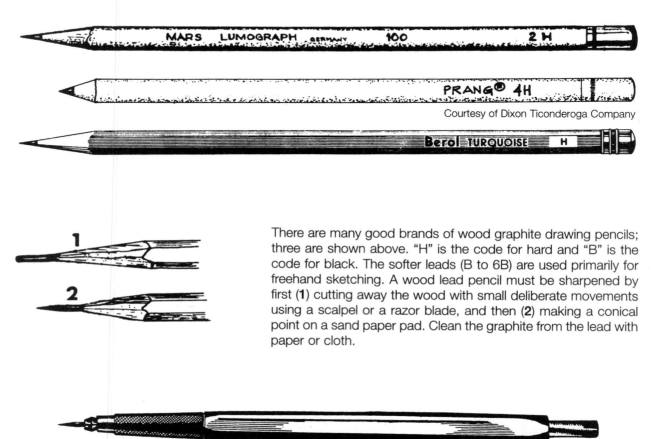

Courtesy of Dixon Ticonderoga Company

There are many good brands of wood graphite drawing pencils; three are shown above. "H" is the code for hard and "B" is the code for black. The softer leads (B to 6B) are used primarily for freehand sketching. A wood lead pencil must be sharpened by first (**1**) cutting away the wood with small deliberate movements using a scalpel or a razor blade, and then (**2**) making a conical point on a sand paper pad. Clean the graphite from the lead with paper or cloth.

A mechanical leadholder or clutch pencil is shown above. It uses a standard size 2-mm lead that can be drawn out or pulled back by the push-button on the end. Some variations include pocket clips and double end holders. Leads in most tone qualities can be interchanged to suit drawing conditions. Use a pencil pointer to sharpen the leads to a taper similar to a common wood pencil.

A fine-line leadholder with push button lead advance (propelling) is shown above. Using a 0.3-mm to a 0.9-mm lead that is protected by a sliding sleeve (0.5 mm is a popular size), this type of pencil does not need to be sharpened. This pencil type is used for drafting rather than sketching.

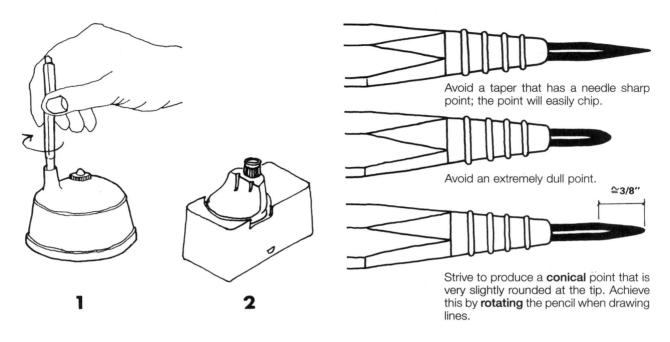

Avoid a taper that has a needle sharp point; the point will easily chip.

Avoid an extremely dull point.

≅3/8″

Strive to produce a **conical** point that is very slightly rounded at the tip. Achieve this by **rotating** the pencil when drawing lines.

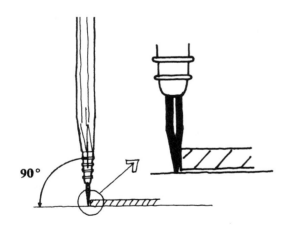

1   **2**

To sharpen your lead to a conical point, use either (**1**) a sandpaper desk-top pointer or (**2**) a cutting-wheel lead pointer. The sandpaper pointer works well with graphite lead but not with polyester lead. The sandpaper pointer sharpens by rotating your pencil-holding hand in a clockwise motion. The cutting-wheel pointer has one slot to give a sharp point and one to give a slightly dull point (for lettering). Electric pencil sharpeners cost more but are much faster.

90°

Always draw with a small space between the conical lead point and the straightedge (T-square, parallel bar, or triangle). This is best achieved by either keeping the pencil in a 90° vertical position, or tilting the pencil toward you at a slight angle from the vertical. Never tilt it away from the straightedge. Horizontal, vertical, or oblique (slanted or angled) lines are best achieved by leaning the pencil at approximately 60° from the drawing surface. The pressure should be adequate to give a dark and crisp line.

A typical sandpaper block is shown above. It is a piece of wood with sandpaper sheets stapled to one end. Rotate the pencil and move it in a side-to-side motion to obtain a tapered conical point. Apply minimal pressure to avoid snapping the lead. Also use this block to produce a tapered compass lead point (see p. 10).

SHARPENING AND USING DRAFTING PENCILS

ink cartridge　　　pen body　　　nib

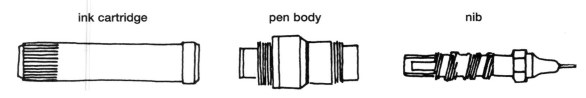

Technical pens are designed with a tubular point within which is a fine wire that controls the ink flow. The tubes are long enough to clear the thickness of drafting instruments. They give excellent control and consistency of line.

TECHNICAL PENS

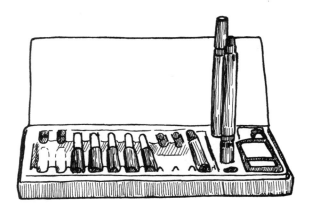

The most common problems encountered are clogging, drying up, touchdown blobs, leaking, and line feathering. Pens with good seals can prevent drying. New pen technology has made most pen brands virtually clog-free when not in use. There are also many brands of clog-free waterproof drawing inks. Waterproof inks will not fade if exposed to light, whereas most nonwaterproof inks will. Vertical storage should be maintained with the point up and the cap on.

6 x 0	
5 x 0	
4 x 0	
3 x 0	
00	
0	
1	
2	
2½	
3	
4	
6	
7	
8	
9	
10	
12	
14	

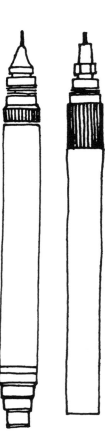

Technical pen sets come in a variety of sizes depending on the number of pen points desired. The primary advantage of technical drawing pens is that they produce clear even lines of constant width. 000 through 4 are the most commonly used pen points for freehand drawing, delineation, and drafting. The line widths shown can vary slightly depending on the type of surface or ink used, as well as the speed at which the lines are drawn.

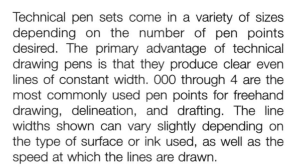
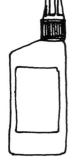

eradicating fluid　　　waterproof ink

A drafting duster with horse hair or natural bristle is used to keep the drawing surface clean and free of graphite.

Pounce powder is used to prepare a surface for ink or pencil. The pad absorbs dirt and powdered graphite. Skum-x dry cleaning powder keeps the surface clean while one is drafting.

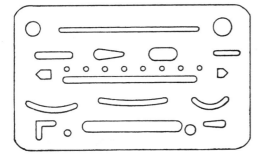

An erasing shield is a thin metal shield that protects lines in close proximity. Hold the erasing shield and erase the desired line or lines in small areas.

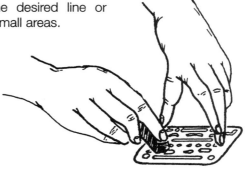

Also used with an erasing shield are electric cord style and portable cordless style erasers. They are very effective for ink drawings. The portable erasers are about 5½" long and use AA or AAA batteries.

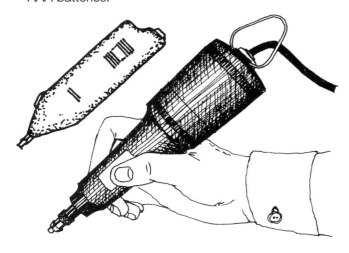

Soft erasers that are very pliable and smudge-free give the best results. Some excellent brands include Staedtler Mars and Koh-I-Noor, as well as Pink Pearl, Magic Rub, and Kneaded Eraser, all from Faber Castell. More dense than a soft eraser is the very effective plastic eraser. The Kneaded Eraser can be molded to any shape.

All of the small equipment mentioned in this chapter can be stored and transported efficiently in an art box or a fishing tackle box. Drawings (especially large sheets) should be transported using protective tubes, which can be commercially purchased.

CLEANING AND ERASING AIDS

TRIANGLES, T-SQUARES, AND FRENCH CURVES

Small triangles (4") are ideal for aiding vertical strokes in hand lettering.

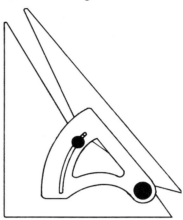

Plastic triangles can be clear or fluorescent with fingerlifts. The most commonly used triangles are 8" to 10" in their longest vertical height. Triangles can come with edges cut back for inking.

45°/45°/90° TRIANGLE

30°/60°/90° TRIANGLE

Triangles are used to draw vertical lines or lines at a specific angle (30°, 45°, and 60°) when used with a T-square or parallel bar. The adjustable triangle is extremely useful for drawing a variety of inclined lines at any desirable angle. A minimum 12" size is best.

T-squares come in lengths of 18", 24", 30", 36", 42", and 48". Good blades have a rigid head and are made of stainless steel or of wood with acrylic edges for visibility. 42" is an all-purpose length.

A flexible curve rule can be used to draw almost any curve by shaping and bending. The curve rule is made of plastic with a flexible core.

French curves are irregular curves that have no constant radii. Those made of hand-finished acrylic are best.

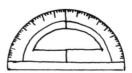

Protractors can be circular or semicircular. They are used to measure angles.

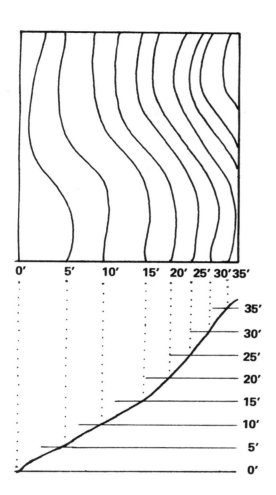

0'   5'   10'   15'   20' 25' 30' 35'

— 35'
— 30'
— 25'
— 20'
— 15'
— 10'
— 5'
— 0'

Contour lines are lines of constant elevation. Every point passes through the same elevation on the surface of the ground.

Contour intervals can be 1', 2', 5', or 10', depending on the conditions of the terrain and the size of the area being studied.

In the drawing on the left, note how the slope steepens when the contours become more closely spaced. It is less steep at the bottom since the spacing here is greater than at the top. Remember that contour lines should never cross one another.

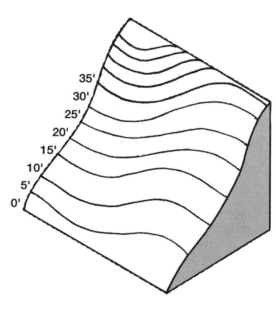

35'
30'
25'
20'
15'
10'
5'
0'

Contour lines can be drawn accurately by using a french curve. The french curve is used for noncircular curves. When fitting the curve through a series of points, be sure that the direction in which its curvature increases is the direction in which the curvature of the line increases. Tangents at each conjunction should coincide to avoid breaks and to allow for a smooth continuity. At sharp turns, a combination of circle arcs and french curves may be used.

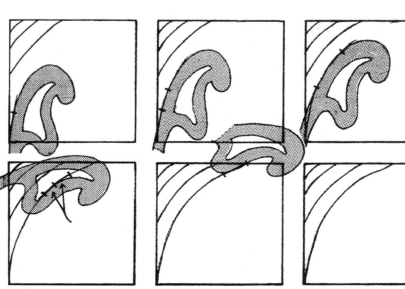

SITE TOPOGRAPHY/USE OF THE FRENCH CURVE

COMPASSES, DIVIDERS, AND THEIR USAGE

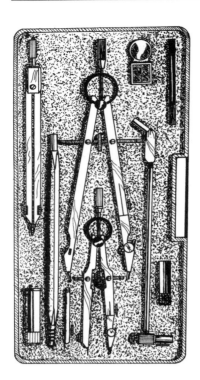

The divider and the bow compass are the major instruments in a drafting set. A **divider** divides lines and transfers lengths. A proportional divider is graduated for lines and circles. A **compass** is used primarily for drawing large circles.

A typical large drafting set includes the following:

1. Dividers
2. Large pen-pencil compass
3. Small pen-pencil compass
4. Mechanical leadholder pencil
5. Pencil pointer
6. Ruling pen handle
7. 6" extension beam
8. Lead holder
9. Lined protective case

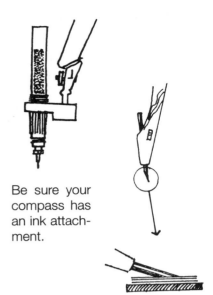

Be sure your compass has an ink attachment.

Keep a low angle when tapering the compass lead.

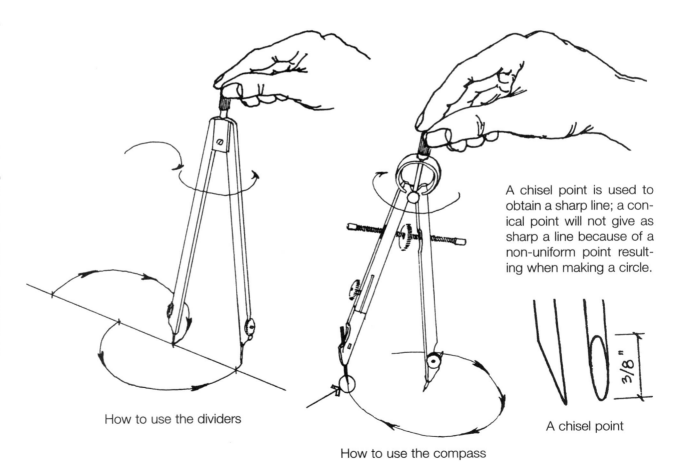

How to use the dividers

How to use the compass

A chisel point is used to obtain a sharp line; a conical point will not give as sharp a line because of a non-uniform point resulting when making a circle.

A chisel point

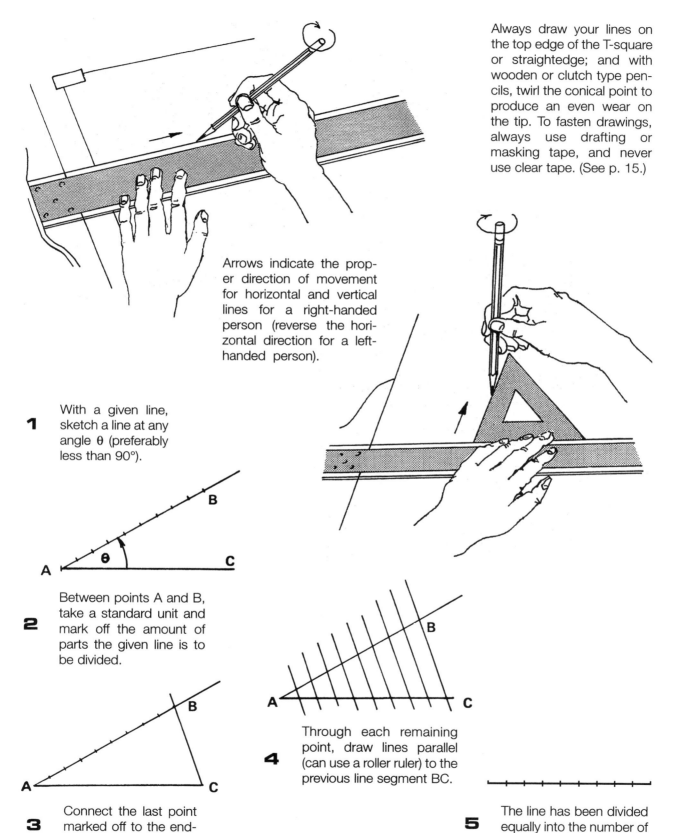

Always draw your lines on the top edge of the T-square or straightedge; and with wooden or clutch type pencils, twirl the conical point to produce an even wear on the tip. To fasten drawings, always use drafting or masking tape, and never use clear tape. (See p. 15.)

Arrows indicate the proper direction of movement for horizontal and vertical lines for a right-handed person (reverse the horizontal direction for a left-handed person).

1 With a given line, sketch a line at any angle θ (preferably less than 90°).

2 Between points A and B, take a standard unit and mark off the amount of parts the given line is to be divided.

3 Connect the last point marked off to the endpoint of the given line.

4 Through each remaining point, draw lines parallel (can use a roller ruler) to the previous line segment BC.

5 The line has been divided equally into the number of parts desired.

USE OF BASIC DRAFTING TOOLS

USE OF BASIC DRAFTING TOOLS

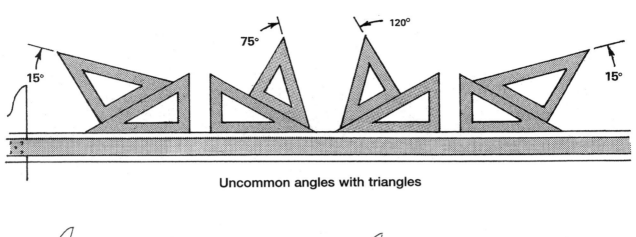

Uncommon angles with triangles

How to draw a line parallel to a given line

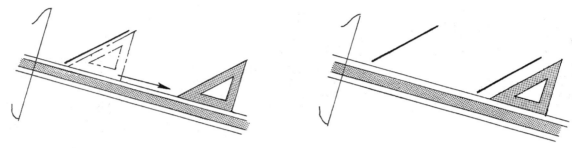

BISECTING AN ANGLE

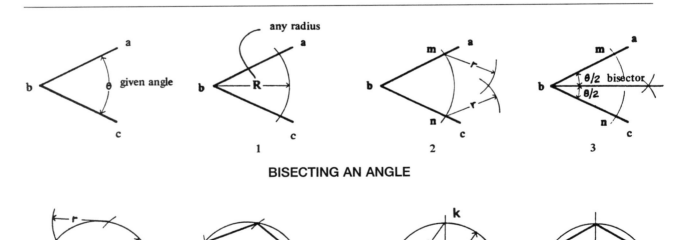

CONSTRUCTING A HEXAGON

Familiarity with drafting tools can be achieved by doing simple geometric operations and constructing various geometric shapes.

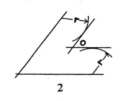 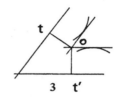 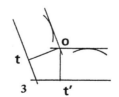
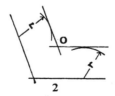 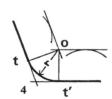 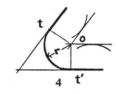

acute angle 1

obtuse angle 1

CONSTRUCTING TANGENT ARCS

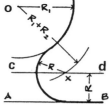 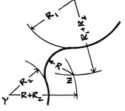 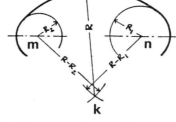 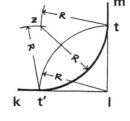
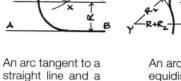

An arc tangent to a straight line and a circle. An equidistance is required.

An arc tangent to two circles. The arc center must be equidistant from both circles.

An arc tangent at a right-angle corner. An equidistance R is required.

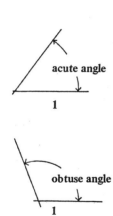
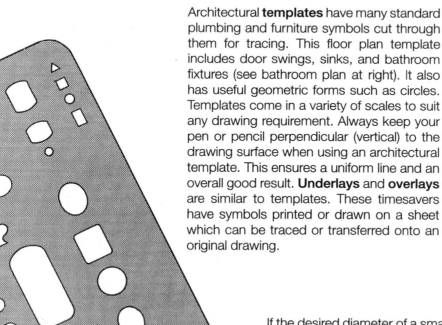

Architectural **templates** have many standard plumbing and furniture symbols cut through them for tracing. This floor plan template includes door swings, sinks, and bathroom fixtures (see bathroom plan at right). It also has useful geometric forms such as circles. Templates come in a variety of scales to suit any drawing requirement. Always keep your pen or pencil perpendicular (vertical) to the drawing surface when using an architectural template. This ensures a uniform line and an overall good result. **Underlays** and **overlays** are similar to templates. These timesavers have symbols printed or drawn on a sheet which can be traced or transferred onto an original drawing.

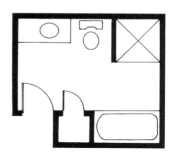

If the desired diameter of a small circle is known, a plastic circle template may be used in place of a compass. Other popular templates are classified as general purpose and elliptical.

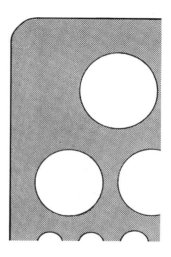

ARCHITECTURAL TEMPLATES AND OTHER TEMPLATES

The **parallel roller rule** with its effortless movement has made the T-square relatively obsolete. A slight push with either hand can glide the parallel rule into any desired position on the drawing board. Since it rolls on ball bearings, smudges on drawings commonly found with the use of a T-square are eliminated. It also has the advantage over a T-square of having both ends fixed; thus, a drawn horizontal line cannot deviate from its correct position. Special types of rules can have a built-in cutting edge.

When installing the parallel rule (also termed bar or straightedge), be sure that

1. Corner plates A and B are firmly attached with ½"-long screws.

2. The cable wire is parallel to the edge of the drawing board on both sides.

3. The cable wire passes between the clamping washer and the plate.

4. The spring is centered between A and B.

5. The cable wire is moved in the directions indicated below.

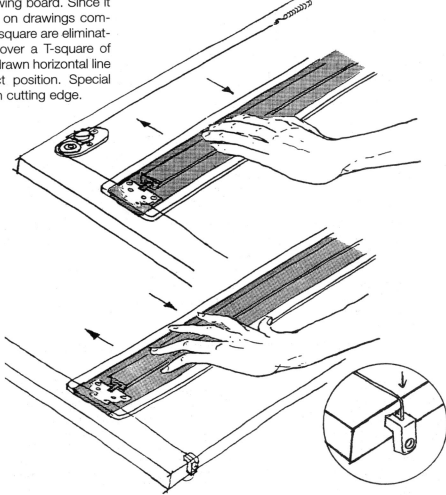

The cable wire is inserted through the hole on top of the stop and aligned with the slot on the rear of the stop. Trim excess cable, but leave enough for future adjustments.

Long, continuous, parallel horizontal lines are a frequent occurrence on architectural drawings. The rule can also be adjusted to many inclined positions slightly away from the horizontal. Rules come in lengths of 36", 42", 48", 54", and 60". Highly recommended is the 42" rule, which permits one to work on a 30" × 40" sheet.

THE PARALLEL RULE

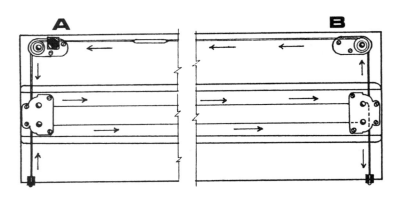

A   B

Provide yourself with a comfortable work space with adequate tack surface to pin up your work for reference. Architectural drawing is normally done in a sitting position, but it can also be done in a standing position. Avoid slouching; don't arch your back and collapse your abdominal regions. Sit erect and keep a good posture. Designing and drawing require long hours of sitting in one position. Poor posture will lead to a tired feeling, reduced drawing capacity, and a deteriorated physical state.

A tilted work table reduces the need to lean over the work surface. Most drafting/drawing tables can be adjusted to tilt at various angles. An adjustable stool is ideal for varying the seat height and the back rest. If possible, place one foot on a pile bar or footrest in order to raise one knee above the hips. Elevating one leg at a time helps to keep the pelvic region tilted forward. It also preserves the natural curvature of the lower lumbar region, preventing undue physical stress and fatigue.

Purchase the best quality table light source that you can afford in order to prevent eyestrain. An incandescent/fluorescent combination light is excellent. The light should have an adjustable counterpoise to give it flexibility to be positioned over your work.

Line up the drawing sheet horizontally and vertically using the T-square or parallel straightedge and triangle. It is best to apply the drafting tape as shown (broadside) to prevent slippage and movement of the drawing sheet. Drafting dots can also be used to secure drawings to a board or table. Try to make the T-square length match the board or table length. The head of the T-square should always be placed firmly up against the edge of the drawing board or drawing table. If the head is not firm, then there will be vertical movement at the end of the T-square. Also note that, with a T-square, it is common practice to use a metal angle to keep a true edge. A clean thin rag or towel can be used as a forearm rest and sheet protector for long drawing stints.

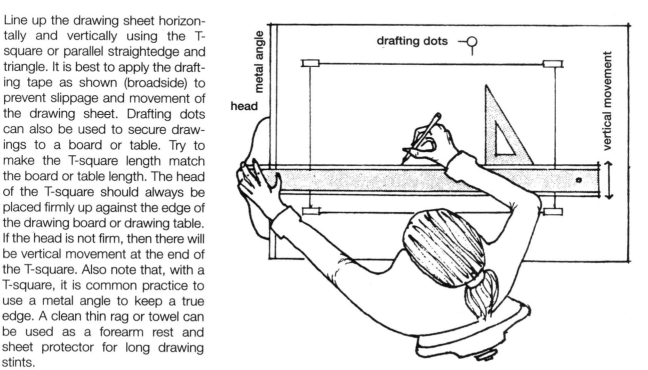

WORKSTATION SET UP: GETTING STARTED

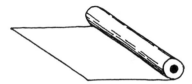

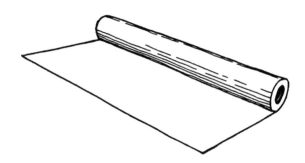

Light yellow or white tracing paper (termed flimsy or talking paper) is excellent for sketching with pencils or markers but not for erasing. It is used for rough sketches, overlays, and preliminary drawings.

TRACING PAPERS AND BOARDS

Tracing pad sizes are 8½" × 11", 11" × 17", and 17" × 22"

With a fade-out grid

Vellums are quality 100% rag tracing papers with excellent erasing qualities. They are available in either rolls or pads. Clearprint 1000H is widely accepted. Tracing papers are classified by weight, color, and rag content. Heavy and white are normally used for finished drawings. **Plastic film** from polyester (Mylar) gives the highest quality reproductions. It is wonderful for ink.

Both graphite and ink are used extensively with various types of architectural design-drawing methods. These media are frequently used on both translucent and transparent tracing papers. Rag is the cotton fiber in the paper. The higher the percentage of rag content, the better the quality. The peaks and valleys (fiber arrangement) on a tracing paper's surface are its "tooth" quality. Slick paper with less tooth is better for ink work, whereas paper with more tooth is better for pencil work. Sizes can vary from an 8½" × 11" pad to a 24" × 36" roll. Gridded paper is used to make the drawing of horizontals and verticals much easier. Other good qualities are (1) no harshness on the eyes and (2) no "ghosts" (grooves) showing after pencil lines are redrawn in the same location. Original drawings must "read" well in order to reproduce well for the use of others. Refer to the bibliography for sources that discuss the variety of reproduction processes (reprography).

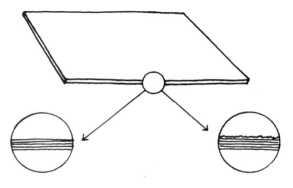

Hot press (less tooth)   Cold press (more tooth)

White **illustration board**, which comes in a variety of thicknesses, is heavier than tracing paper. This sturdiness makes it suitable for both finished drawing presentations and fine presentation models. Cold press boards have a more textured surface than the smoother hot press boards.

Preliminary study models are usually made of gray **chipboard**. Chipboard also comes in a variety of thicknesses. **Foamcore board** is a strong lightweight board that is excellent for modelmaking.

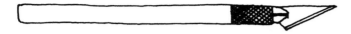

An X-Acto knife uses blades of several different shapes. The one illustrated is most commonly used. It is excellent for small detailed cuts (small apertures).

A utility knife is used primarily for long cuts on heavy materials such as thick illustration board, mat board, or cardboard. It is excellent for scoring. Stanley is a highly recommended brand (Stanley Tools, Division of the Stanley Works, New Britain, CT).

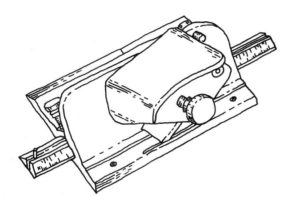

Good-quality cutters can cut a clean crisp 45° bevel. Highly recommended is a series 4000 Logan mat cutter, which has a built-in marking system. With a pivoting blade holder, it can be used against any suitable straightedge.

MODELMAKING AIDS

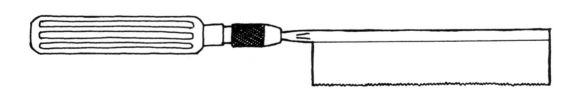

A razor saw with a thin blade and fine teeth is used for extrafine cuts on small pieces of wood such as balsa wood.

Adhesives or **glues** are used to fasten material together for modelmaking. A water-soluble glue is commonly used for cardboard. Rubber cement is excellent for collage work. Spray adhesives are most efficient for mounting drawings or photographs on cardboard, as well as for laminating porous smooth sheets together.

A basic cutting rule of modelmaking is **never** to make only one pass when cutting materials (especially thick cardboard). Make a series of light cuts. This will give better control and accuracy. Cutting on a soft surface such as illustration board or a self-healing plastic cutting surface will extend the life of your cutting blade.

The following are architect's scales:

12"=1'0"	1"=1'0"	¼"=1'0"
6"=1'0"	¾"=1'0"	3⁄16"=1'0"
3"=1'0"	½"=1'0"	⅛"=1'0"
1½"=1'0"	⅜"=1'0"	3⁄32"=1'0"

For architectural work, all of the above scales are used. Least used are the scales of 12"=1'0" and 6"=1'0". The scale is usually notated within the title block of an architectural drawing. It can also appear underneath the view of a particular detail. The choice of the proper scale size is dependent on the building size, the amount of detail to be drawn, and the size of paper used. Sometimes common practice dictates the size; for example, floor plans for residential buildings are normally drawn at ¼"=1'0". Construction details can use scales ranging from ½"=1'0" to 3"=1'0".

The actual size of the architect's scale. This scale is ⅛"=1'0"

The **architect's** scale is used primarily for drawing buildings, architectural details, structural details, and mechanical systems in buildings. The purpose is to represent large objects at a reduced scale to fit on drafting paper size sheets. The best quality scale is unbreakable plastic with color-coded, engraved, calibrated graduations. Scales come in three beveled types and one triangular type (see below). Choose the one most suitable for your needs.

The **civil engineer's** or **engineer's** scale is used primarily for site plans, location plans, and land measurements in map drawing.

The following are civil engineer's scales:
10, 20, 30, 40, 50, 60, or 80 divisions to the inch, representing feet, 10 ft, 100 ft, rods, or miles.

Be careful not to confuse "scale" and "size."
¼"=1'0" is referred to as "quarter scale" in the architect's language, whereas ¼"=1" is referred to as "quarter size."

OPPOSITE BEVEL
Easy to pick up and handle.

DOUBLE BEVEL
A good pocket scale.

FLAT BEVEL
Easy to keep flat to a board.

TRIANGULAR
The triangular scale has the advantage of having many scales on the same stick. Always observe the scale from directly above.

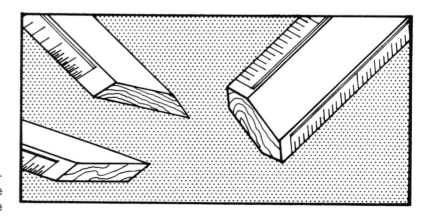

Remember to keep the scale clean, don't mark on it, and never use it as a straightedge!

SCALES

Determining How Much Each Subdivision Represents

The best procedure is to ask yourself the following question: Each subdivision represents what part of one foot?

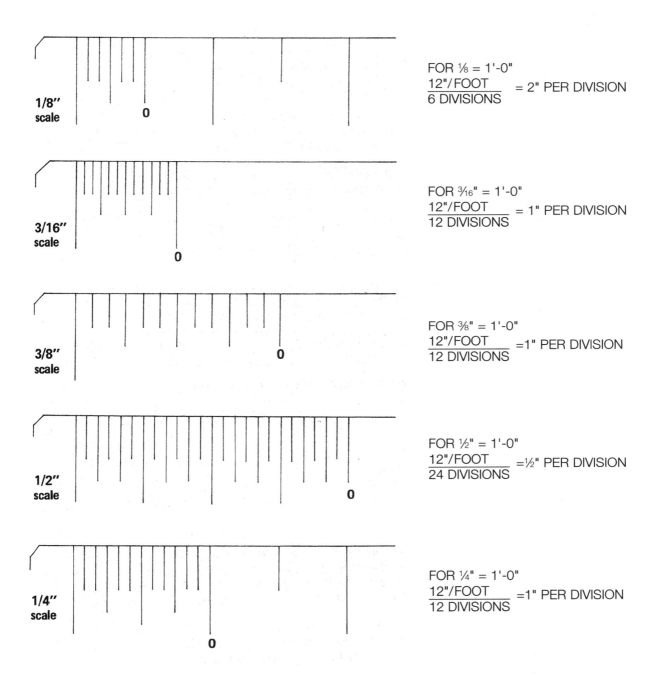

1/8″ scale

FOR ⅛ = 1'-0"

$$\frac{12"/\text{FOOT}}{6 \text{ DIVISIONS}} = 2" \text{ PER DIVISION}$$

3/16″ scale

FOR ³⁄₁₆" = 1'-0"

$$\frac{12"/\text{FOOT}}{12 \text{ DIVISIONS}} = 1" \text{ PER DIVISION}$$

3/8″ scale

FOR ⅜" = 1'-0"

$$\frac{12"/\text{FOOT}}{12 \text{ DIVISIONS}} = 1" \text{ PER DIVISION}$$

1/2″ scale

FOR ½" = 1'-0"

$$\frac{12"/\text{FOOT}}{24 \text{ DIVISIONS}} = ½" \text{ PER DIVISION}$$

1/4″ scale

FOR ¼" = 1'-0"

$$\frac{12"/\text{FOOT}}{12 \text{ DIVISIONS}} = 1" \text{ PER DIVISION}$$

THE ARCHITECT'S SCALE

Note that in all of the reduced scales, the major divisions represent feet and their subdivisions represent inches and fractions thereof. Therefore, ½ means ½ inch = 1 ft, not ½ inch = 1 inch.

To facilitate the counting of subdivisions, the above scales have been enlarged from their actual size.

THE ENGINEER'S SCALE

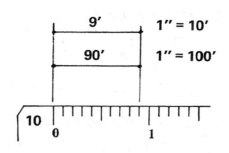

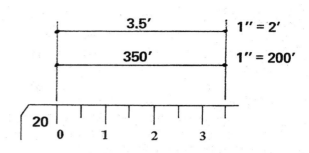

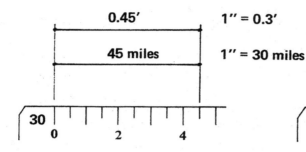

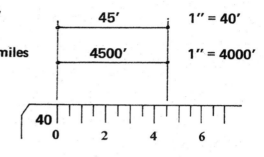

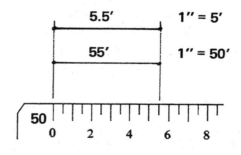

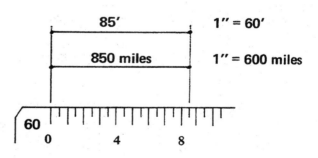

Shown above are the six standard scale units found on the **engineer's scale.** There are many possibilities for each scale unit since different lengths can be indicated for the scale unit. For example, in the case of a 10 scale, 1" can equal any one of the following: 0.1', 1', 10', 100', or 1000' (miles). Two possibilities are shown above for each of the six standard scale units. Divisions to the inch represent feet, rods, or miles.

Think of the scale number, such as 10, as the number of divisions per inch. Thus, 40 would indicate 40 increments or parts per inch. A 1" = 40' scale would have 40 increments, each increment being one foot. These incremental divisions are then continued along the full length of the scale. The engineer's scale is used primarily for site plans and location plans.

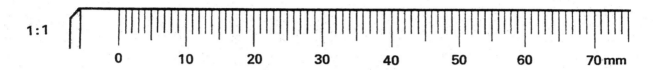

1:1

This metric scale has a 1:1 ratio and should be used for **full-size** drawings.

1:5

This metric scale has a 1:5 ratio and should be used for drawings **one-fifth full size**.

As with the architect's scale, the **metric** scales above have been enlarged for easier reading of the subdivisions. These scales are appropriate for architectural details (3"=1'0", etc.). The English system, which is still in use in the United States, is based on the inch and the foot. The **metric system** uses the **meter** (m) as its standard dimension; it has been accepted as the standard outside the United States and Great Britain. A meter is 3.281 feet in length. It is easy to manipulate because one only needs to add equal steps of 1000 parts to change to another multiple of the metric scale. For example, 1000 millimeters (mm) equals 1.0 meter (m). The metric scale is 150 millimeters long (about 6 inches). Architects use various metric scales for various types of drawings. For example, 1:500 is a common scale reduction ratio for site plans, whereas 1:100 is used for floor plans and elevations. Ratio reductions of 1:1 and 1:5 are seen frequently with architectural details. These examples show architectural drawings each requiring a different metric scale.

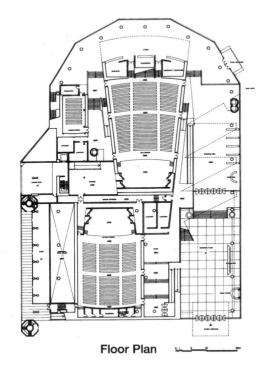

Floor Plan

Palazzo del Cinema, Venice, Italy
38 × 53 cm (15" × 20.9")
Medium: Ink on Mylar
Courtesy of Maki and Associates

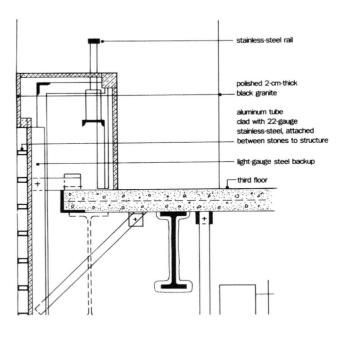

Partial section detail
One O'Hare Center
Rosemont, Illinois

Courtesy of Kohn Pedersen
Fox Associates, Architects

THE METRIC SCALE

2

Lettering, Typography, and Line Types

In drafting as well as in the design-drawing process, knowledge of line types, control of line quality, typography, and lettering are important. Well-executed hand lettering and proper line quality are needed for clear working drawings and design-drawings.

The intent of this chapter is to develop your ability first to recognize and ultimately to execute proficient lettering, typography, and line quality.

In summary, following are some of the important skills, terms, and concepts you will learn:

How to hand letter efficiently and properly
How to recognize line types

Presentation typography

Line weights
Line quality

Lettering, Typography, and Line Types

TOPIC: LETTERING

Ching 2003,179–181.
Lin 1993, 75–76.
Reid 1987, 43–45.
Sutherland 1989.

TOPIC: TYPOGRAPHY

Berryman 1990.
Burke and Wildbur 1999.
Carter, Day, and Meggs 1985.
Carter and Meggs 2002.
Craig 1990.

Chapter Overview

In studying this chapter and doing the related exercises in the book's final section, you will learn how to
execute good architectural hand lettering and good
line quality. For continued study, refer to Sutherland's
Lettering for Architects and Designers.

Precise architectural hand **lettering** for working drawings and presentations will be needed for the immediate future, despite the growing use of computer type styles in professional practice. Remember when doing hand lettering to work from the top to the bottom of the sheet; this prevents smudging. If it is not possible to move downward, then cover previously lettered lower parts of the sheet with some clean paper to prevent hand–graphite contact. The example below shows the lettering of a partial wall detail from a set of working drawings. Working drawings are the drawings used by a contractor to erect a structure.

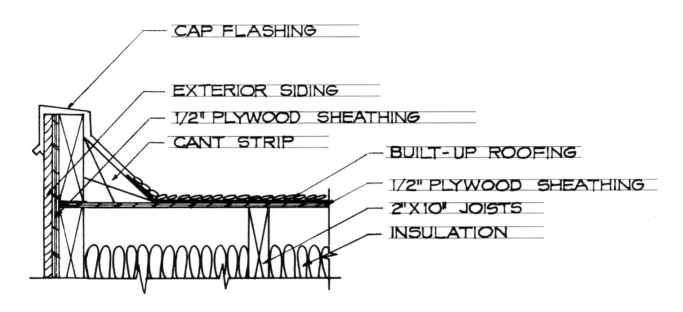

Evanston Public Library Design Competition

P E N I N S U L A   R E G E N T
BACKEN ARRIGONI & ROSS, INC.

Evanston Public Library Design Competition
Courtesy of Michael Blakemore/Sandy & Babcock, Inc.
Architecture & Planning

The Peninsula Regent, San Mateo, California
Courtesy of Backen Arrigoni & Ross, Inc.
Architecture, Planning & Interior Design

INTRODUCTION

An appropriate visual hierarchy of **typography** should be used for presentations. When we lay out a presentation, the drawings must be referred to using titles, heads, and text material in different styles, sizes, and weights. These bits of information are normally arranged in order of visual importance from heads to titles to text, in that order. There must be a hierarchy of heads and titles for any kind of presentation. Presentation drawings can use mechanical lettering methods such as stencils in the form of templates, pressure transfer lettering sheets, traceable sheets in a variety of scales, and traceable typefaces available in computers. Stencilled lettering can achieve a handsome uniformity for a series of drawings and is commonly used for titles. Stencils are cut in clear plastic templates so that guidelines can be viewed. Opaque color can be applied with brushes, flair pens, or ink pens. The highest quality computer type is attained by using PostScript or TrueType printers and fonts. The advantage of these fonts is that they can retain their sharp clear form at any scale size.

When architectural lettering exceeds a height of ½", use larger block typefaces. **Pressure transfer** lettering catalogs give a variety of excellent typefaces. This kind of typographic lettering comes in sheets that can easily be traced over to add a professional quality to drawings. They are divided into two major groups: **serifs** and **sans** (without) **serifs**. Serifs were originally the terminations of parts of a letter that were chiseled by the Romans.

Serifs and sans serifs are further divided into **light, medium,** and **heavy** weight types, as shown in the three samples below. Always use serifs or sans serifs consistently for any set of drawings.

PRESENTATION TYPOGRAPHY

dining SECTION

60 pt. l.c.   60 pt. CAPS   Helvetica Light

bath ELEVATION

54 pt. l.c.   66 pt. CAPS   Folio Medium Extended

A RESIDENCE

36 pt. CAPS   Microgramma Bold Extended

Some nicely proportioned lettering typefaces in both upper- and lowercase (usually easier to read) are Imperial Roman (serif), Bauhaus Demi (sans serif), and Katrina Heavy (serif.) Note these examples below.

kitchen DETAIL

48 pt. l.c.   72 pt. CAPS   Imperial Roman

Preliminary PLAN

48 pt. l.c.   60 pt. CAPS   Bauhaus Demi

storage NORTH

60 pt. l.c.   48 pt. CAPS   Katrina Heavy

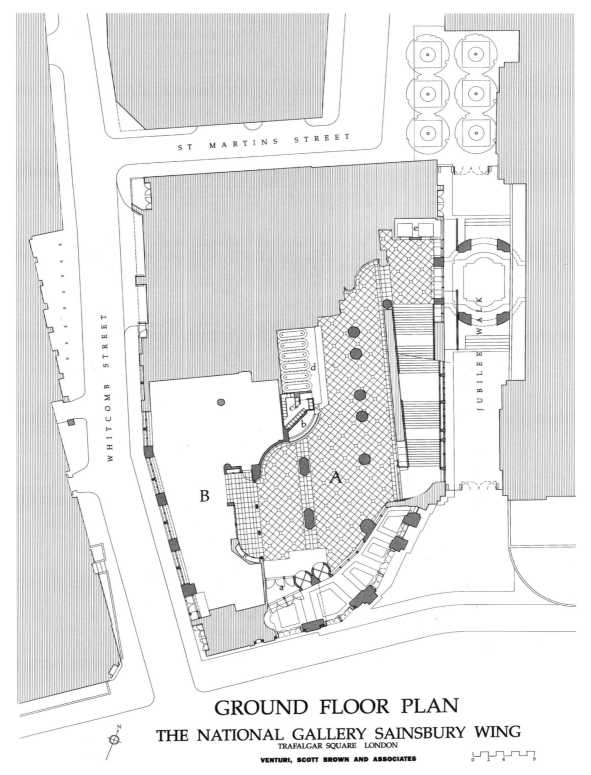

GROUND FLOOR PLAN

THE NATIONAL GALLERY SAINSBURY WING

TRAFALGAR SQUARE   LONDON

VENTURI, SCOTT BROWN AND ASSOCIATES

Drawing: Ground Floor Plan, The National Gallery, Sainsbury Wing. Trafalgar Square, London, England
Medium: Ink on vellum (CAD) 30.25" × 43.5" (76.8 × 110.5 cm)
Courtesy of Venturi, Scott Brown and Associates, Inc., Architects

Note the clear hierarchy of titles on this presentation drawing.

PRESENTATION TYPOGRAPHY

Architectural lettering is derived from uppercase Gothic letters; the relative proportions of each letter are easily seen using a gridded background. In actual practice a grid system is not used; try to "eyeball" the correct proportions for each letter. The suggested stroke order need not be followed; individuals differ in hand–eye coordination and may differ in the number of strokes needed to complete a letter. It is important to be consistent in forming an equally proportioned letter each time. For a left-handed person, the direction of the vertical strokes and curvilinear strokes remains the same, but the direction of horizontal strokes reverses.

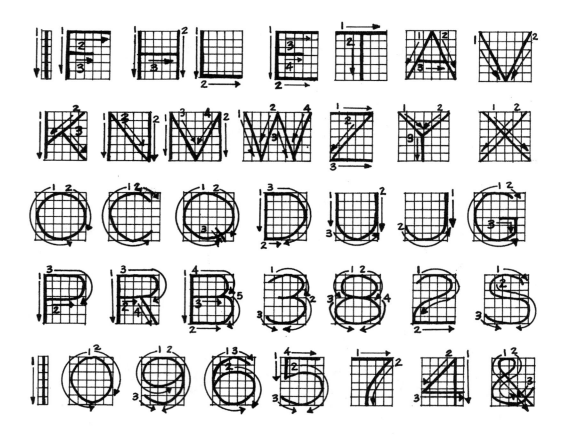

Notice that letters and numerals can be grouped in similar family types: the horizontal and vertical family (I through T); the horizontal, vertical, and angular family (A through X); and the curvilinear family (O through S). The numeral family has all the strokes. With time and practice, your overall goal should be to make controlled **quick, even strokes.** This is especially relevant to the rounded letters and numerals. Be sure the strokes are dark and crisp for good reproducibility. Good architectural hand lettering is the art of mastering basic motions: horizontal, vertical, angular, and curvilinear.

Lettering exercise: Become accustomed to the relative proportions shown for each letter by tracing or copying the letters and numerals on vellum. Repeat this exercise at two more heights: ¼" and ⅛".

The block lettering above is illustrated to help you develop your basic strokes. However, this type of lettering has the shortcoming of using too much space because it is very wide. In architectural work, a narrower proportioned alphabet, as shown on the subsequent pages, is more suitable.

HAND LETTERING

Lettering Examples

"I LIKE COMPLEXITY AND CONTRADICTION IN ARCHITECTURE. I LIKE ELEMENTS WHICH ARE HYBRID RATHER THAN "PURE," COMPROMISING RATHER THAN "CLEAN," DISTORTED RATHER THAN "STRAIGHTFORWARD," AMBIGUOUS RATHER THAN "ARTICULATED," PERVERSE AS WELL AS IMPERSONAL, BORING AS WELL AS "INTERESTING," CONVENTIONAL RATHER THAN "DESIGNED," ACCOMMODATING RATHER THAN EXCLUDING, REDUNDANT RATHER THAN SIMPLE, VESTIGIAL AS WELL AS INNOVATING, INCONSISTENT AND EQUIVOCAL RATHER THAN DIRECT AND CLEAR. . . . "

I LIKE COMPLEXITY AND CONTRADICTION IN ARCHITECTURE. I LIKE ELEMENTS WHICH ARE HYBRID RATHER THAN "PURE," COMPROMISING RATHER THAN "CLEAN," DISTORTED RATHER THAN "STRAIGHTFORWARD," AMBIGUOUS RATHER THAN "ARTICULATED," PERVERSE AS WELL AS IMPERSONAL, BORING AS WELL AS "INTERESTING," CONVENTIONAL RATHER THAN "DESIGNED," ACCOMMODATING RATHER THAN EXCLUDING, REDUNDANT RATHER THAN SIMPLE, VESTIGIAL AS WELL AS INNOVATING, INCONSISTENT AND EQUIVOCAL RATHER THAN DIRECT AND CLEAR. I AM FOR MESSY VITALITY OVER OBVIOUS UNITY. I INCLUDE THE NON SEQUITUR AND PROCLAIM THE DUALITY.

(VENTURI 1966, 16)

COMPUTER-GENERATED LETTERING

Architectural statement: Reprinted with permission from Robert Venturi's "Complexity and Contradiction in Architecture," 1977, 2nd edition, New York: The Museum of Modern Art

1. Computer-generated lettering: Tekton
   Used with express permission. Adobe® and Image Club
   Graphics™ are trademarks of Adobe Systems Incorporated.
2. Additional software from Handy by Epiphany Design Studio

BASIC GUIDES TO ARCHITECTURAL LETTERING

(1) ALWAYS USE LIGHTLY DRAWN GUIDELINES WHICH ARE THE UPPER AND LOWER LIMITS OF THE AREA BEING LETTERED.

(2) LETTERING SHOULD BE SIMPLE BLOCK VERTICAL CAPITALS.

(3) MINIMUM HEIGHT FOR ANY LETTERING IS 1/8".

MAJOR TITLES SHOULD BE 1/4" HIGH.

3/16" HEIGHT CAN BE USED FOR MINOR TITLES.

(4) MANY INDIVIDUALS ARE INVOLVED WITH THE PRODUCTION OF WORKING DRAWINGS. THERE IS A TREND TOWARDS THE ISSUING OF REDUCED DRAWINGS. THUS, A CLEAR UNIFORM TYPE OF LETTERING IS NEEDED. USE AN HB, H, OR F PENCIL LEAD WEIGHT WITH A ROUNDED CONICAL POINT FOR YOUR LETTERING.

(5) THE AREA BETWEEN VARIOUS ADJACENT LETTER COMBINATIONS IN ANY WORD IS BASED ON GOOD JUDGMENT. GOOD SPACING DECISIONS BETWEEN LETTERS IS AN ART.   AREA IS ~ EQUAL

	1/8"
	1/16" OR 1/8"
	1/8"
	1/16" OR 1/8"
	1/8"
	1/16" OR 1/8"
	1/8"
	1/16" OR 1/8"
	1/8"
	3/16"
DETAIL SCALE PLAN BRICK	1/4"
	3/16"
EQUAL SPACING IS BASED ON GOOD	1/8"
	1/16" OR 1/8"
VISUAL JUDGMENT.	1/8"

(6) EXAMPLE: ALPHABETS & NUMERALS

ABCDEFGHIJKLMNOPQRSTUVWXYZ

1 2 3 4 5 6 7 8 9 0

HAND LETTERING

THE USE OF A SMALL TRIANGLE TO KEEP
VERTICAL STROKES OF LETTERS VERTICAL
IS ACCEPTABLE AND IS COMMONLY DONE IN
PROFESSIONAL PRACTICE AS A QUICK
TECHNIQUE, HOWEVER, IT IS BEST TO
EXECUTE FREEHAND VERTICALS IF YOU HAVE
THE ABILITY TO KEEP LINES VERTICAL.

SLIGHT STYLIZATION OF LETTERS IS OFTEN
DONE IN PROFESSIONAL PRACTICE; ANY
DEVELOPMENT OF STYLE SHOULD ALWAYS
EXHIBIT CONSISTENCY IN SPACING, PROPORTION,
AND OVERALL APPEARANCE. FOR EXAMPLE,
THE LETTERS ON THE PREVIOUS PAGE CAN
BE STRETCHED HORIZONTALLY AND HORIZONTAL
STROKES CAN BE DONE AT A SLIGHT ANGLE
TO THE HORIZONTAL. "I" AND "J" ARE EXCEPTIONS
IN ATTEMPTING TO MAKE LETTERS AS
WIDE AS THEY ARE HIGH. SOMETIMES IT
TAKES YEARS TO MASTER THE ART OF GOOD
ARCHITECTURAL LETTERING; BE PATIENT
WITH YOUR PROGRESS.

HAND LETTERING

EXAMPLE: ALPHABET AND NUMERALS,

A   B   C   D   E   F   G   H   I

J   K   L   M   N   O   P   Q   R

S   T   U   V   W   X   Y   Z

1   2   3   4   5   6   7   8   9   0

Hand lettering (pp. 25, 30, 31, 33): Student project by Kam Wong
Medium: Pencil on vellum
Courtesy of the Department of Architecture
City College of San Francisco

A graph paper underlay is an alternative to guidelines (on translucent paper).

LINE TYPES AND LINE WEIGHTS

PENCIL LINES (for architectural drafting)	GRADE OF PENCIL TO USE
PROFILE LINE	H, F, or HB
VISIBLE/ELEVATION LINES	H, F, or HB
CONSTRUCTION/LAYOUT/GRID LINES	2H or 4H
SECTION LINE	H, F, or HB
SECTION LINING	H, F, or HB
HIDDEN/DASH LINES	H or 2H
CENTER LINE	2H or 4H
DIMENSION LINE EXTENSION LINE	2H or 4H

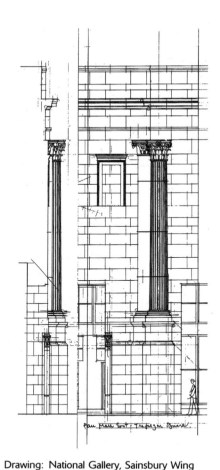

Drawing: National Gallery, Sainsbury Wing
London, England
2" × 26.5" (5.1 × 67.3 cm) Scale: 1:25
Medium: Ink on vellum
Courtesy of Venturi, Scott Brown and
Associates, Inc., Architects

Heavy slash marks and dots are alternatives to arrowheads for terminating dimension lines. Arrowheads are also commonly indicated by using a wide V shape with each leg approximately 60° to the dimension line.

Architectural drawing in the broad sense includes both architectural drafting and architectural sketching. Pencils are the simplest drawing medium in both areas. Pencil leads are made of compressed graphite and clay. The most common grades for architectural drafting work are 4H, 2H, F, H, and HB. To save time, it is common practice to use one lead and vary the pressure to give the desired line weight. An initially drawn line must be bold and uniform, not weak and tentative. Architectural sketching work (see p. 42) is commonly done with grades of 2B, 4B, and 6B, which are softer and allow for more expression.

Some drafting pointers:

Avoid corners that do not touch.

A very small overlap is permissible.

Keep an even line quality. See pages 89 and 94.

Just touching is the generally accepted correct procedure.

Pointing or slightly emphasizing the end helps to strengthen its presence.

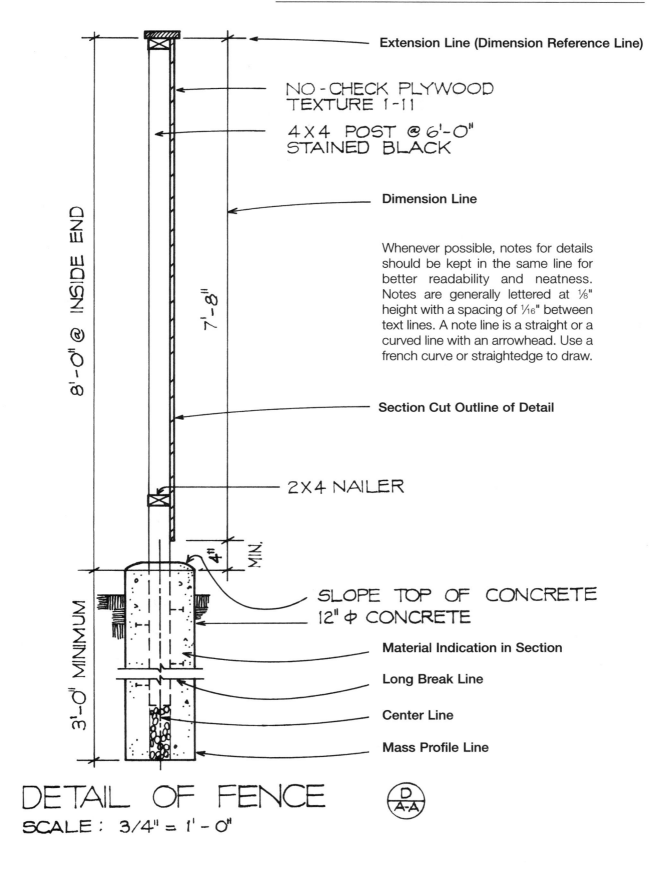

Extension Line (Dimension Reference Line)

NO-CHECK PLYWOOD
TEXTURE 1-11

4 X 4 POST @ 6'-0"
STAINED BLACK

Dimension Line

Whenever possible, notes for details should be kept in the same line for better readability and neatness. Notes are generally lettered at ⅛" height with a spacing of ¹⁄₁₆" between text lines. A note line is a straight or a curved line with an arrowhead. Use a french curve or straightedge to draw.

Section Cut Outline of Detail

2 X 4 NAILER

SLOPE TOP OF CONCRETE
12" φ CONCRETE

Material Indication in Section

Long Break Line

Center Line

Mass Profile Line

8'-0" @ INSIDE END

7'-8"

4" MIN.

3'-0" MINIMUM

DETAIL OF FENCE
SCALE: 3/4" = 1'-0"

D
A-A

LINE TYPES AND THEIR USAGE

LINE TYPES AND THEIR USAGE

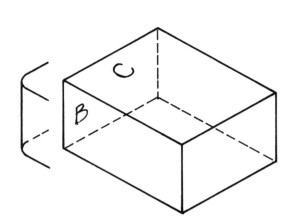

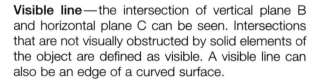

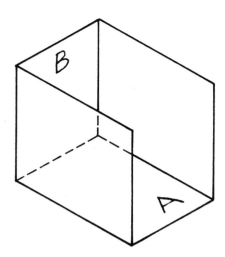

Visible line—the intersection of vertical plane B and horizontal plane C can be seen. Intersections that are not visually obstructed by solid elements of the object are defined as visible. A visible line can also be an edge of a curved surface.

Hidden line—vertical plane B and horizontal plane A intersect, resulting in an intersection line that cannot be seen from the observer's position. This is represented by a dashed line.

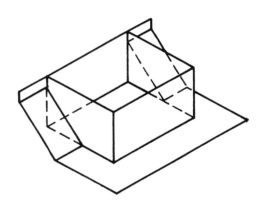

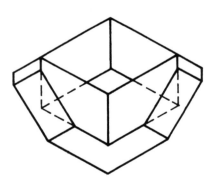

These pictorials (defined as pitch pockets) are part of construction documents for a contractor to use in the erection of a building. Note the use of hidden dashed lines to enhance the visualization of the details. When visible lines, hidden lines, and center lines coincide on a drawing, it is important to know which line takes precedence. A visible line takes precedence over a center line or a hidden line. A hidden line takes precedence over a center line.

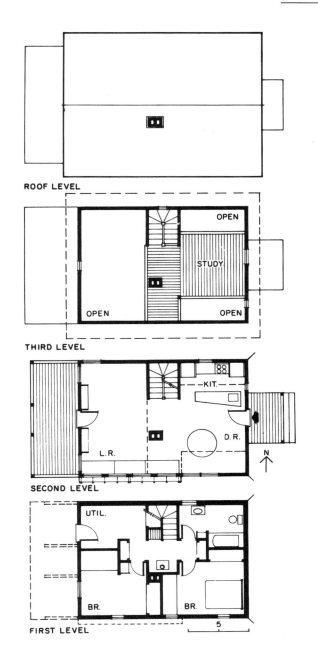

ROOF LEVEL

THIRD LEVEL

SECOND LEVEL

FIRST LEVEL

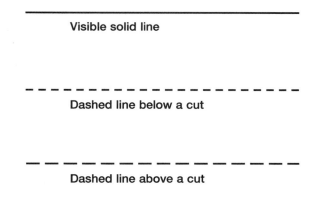

Visible solid line

Dashed line below a cut

Dashed line above a cut

Visible solid lines and dashed hidden lines are two of the most important lines in finished architectural drawings. These lines are drawn with H, F, or HB lead weights. HB drawn lines erase easily, but they also tend to smear the most. Note that the dashed line below a cut is proportionally smaller than the one used above a cut. Strive to produce a consistent spacing and length for each dash.

Drawing: Hog Hill House
12" × 30" (30.5 × 76.2 cm) Scale ⅛"=1'0"
Medium: Ink on Mylar
Courtesy of B FIVE STUDIO

LINE TYPES AND THEIR USAGE

Visible lines in architectural drawings can be used for the outline of plan or section cuts (see example above) and any other intersection of planes (wall intersections in plan or elevation, etc.).

Dashed lines in architectural drawings express lines above a plan cut that the observer cannot see, such as roof overhangs (see example above), roof perforations, and skylights; as well as lines below a plan cut that are obscured by the floor, such as partitions.

LINE WEIGHT AND LINE QUALITY

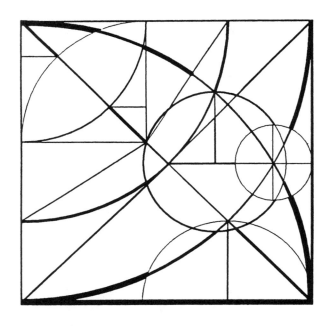

Drawing: Student project by Stephanie Slack
Medium: CAD
Courtesy of California Polytechnic State University, San Luis Obispo
College of Architecture & Environmental Design

Example Line Weights

Line quality refers to the crispness and the darkness (weight intensity) of a line. The darkness of a line is governed by the pencil used and the pressure applied. Inked lines generally have uniform value but can vary in width. It is extremely important to be consistent in drawing the same type of lines.

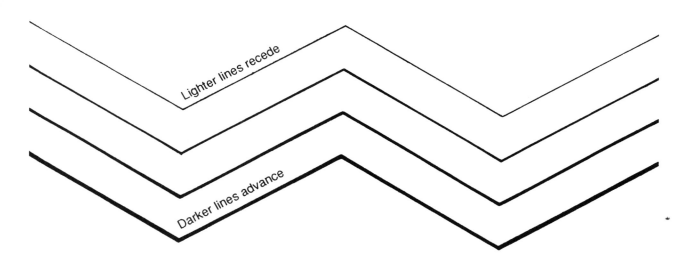

Lighter lines recede

Darker lines advance

As you develop your design-drawing skills, you will realize the importance of line weight and line quality in any composition. As line weights vary, so does their impact on any composition. Design parameters such as variety, spatial depth, and visual hierarchy can be affected.

 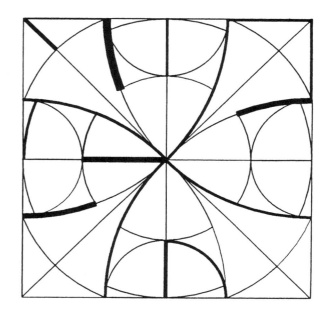

Drawings: Student project by Ben Ragle
Medium: CAD
Courtesy of California Polytechnic State University, San Luis Obispo
College of Architecture & Environmental Design

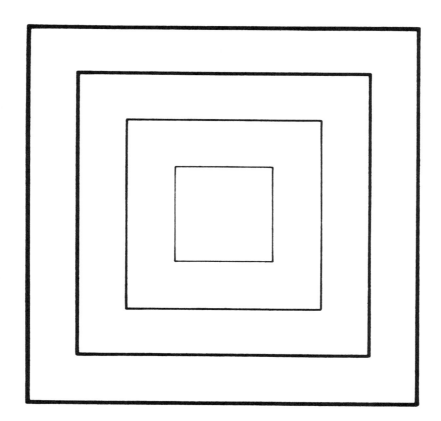

Emphasis is using line weight to create the illusion of space. The more variation of hierarchical line weight from thick to thin, the greater the implication of depth in the drawing.

EMPHASIS

3

Representational Sketching

Sketches of the built environment are analytical drawings that generally convey an overall image. We do these sketches to gain a greater understanding of the nature of the urban landscape. Such sketches must be executed quickly and accurately.

Geometric shapes are the foundation for all derived form. Environmental form and composition are an aggregate of simple and complex forms. These forms must be graphically expressed in a visually appealing manner, whether you sketch from "life" or from your imagination.

The intent of this chapter is to cover the basic aspects of freehand descriptive sketching, such as types of sketching tools, line, shape, proportion, and values, as well as to examine how to observe and depict encountered environmental elements. Another goal is to hone one's ability to sketch a subject in such a way as to describe it through the utilization of line and volume, as well as through proportional and perspective relationships.

In summary, following are some of the important skills, terms, and concepts you will learn:

Types of sketching pencils and the strokes they make
Types of sketching pens and the strokes they make
Sketching architectural elements like trees, cars, and buildings

Sighting	Blocking out	Construction lines	Contour drawing
Vantage point	Vignette	Focal point	Gesture drawing
Foreground	Middleground	Background	Balance

Representational Sketching

Topic: Contour Drawing

Chen 1997, 55–100.
Ching 2003.
Ching 1990, 42–45.
Dodson 1990.

Topic: Stroke Character

Ching 1990, 22–25.
Wang 1977, 18–28, 75–81.

Topic: Vegetation

Wang 1977, 44–56.

Topic: Drawing Methods

Crowe and Laseau 1986.
Goldstein 1989.
Hanks and Belliston 1977, 33–136.
Mendelowitz and Wakeham 1993.

Topics: Human Figures, Sighting

Bridgman 2001.
Wang 1977, 82–88.

Topic: Sketching with Markers

Linton and Strickfaden 1997.

Topic: Buildings/Travel Sketches

Ferriss 1986.
Ferriss 1998.
Fleck 1994.
Johnson and Lewis 1996.
Kliment 1984, 39–87, 105–113.
Leich 1980.
Oliver 1979, 83–130.
Pelli 1990.
Porter and Goodman 1988, 60–68.
Predock 1995.
Wang 1977, 70–74.
Wu 1990.

Chapter Overview

In studying this chapter, you will begin to develop skills in hand representational sketching. For continued study, refer to Ching's *Drawing: A Creative Process* and Wang's *Pencil Sketching*.

Drawing from life is essential to the development of the hand/eye/brain "loop." The more one draws, the more one becomes aware of the world in terms of vision. The more conscious architects, artists, and designers are, the more formidable their work will be. Often, when students begin to draw, they are anxious that what is drawn will not be "the right shape"; in other words, it will not have the correct proportions. One of the most fundamental tools for controlling proportion is called **sighting** (explained on pages 56 and 57). This method of using a drawing instrument held at arm's length as a measuring device (essentially simulating a picture plane) is highly effective in helping the beginner to make objects in the drawing "the right shape," as well as controlling distances and relative sizes in general. Looking and recording reality with the aid of sighting will strengthen the visual sense and bring confidence to the drawing process.

Drawing is a process that progresses from seeing to visualizing and, finally, to expressing. The ability to see gives us the raw material for our perceptions and, ultimately, for what we draw. Visual information seen by the eye is processed, manipulated, and filtered by the mind in its active search for structure and meaning. The mind's eye creates the images we see and eventually tries to express them in the form of a drawn image. Our ability to express and communicate relies on our ability to draw.

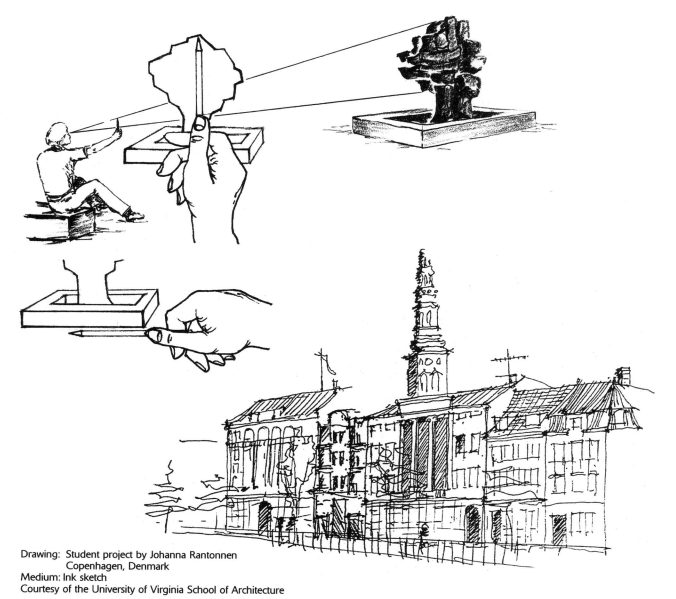

Drawing: Student project by Johanna Rantonnen
          Copenhagen, Denmark
Medium: Ink sketch
Courtesy of the University of Virginia School of Architecture

INTRODUCTION

FREEHAND SKETCHING PENCILS

As an introduction to sketching, this chapter will cover pencils, pens, and markers in terms of black and white and shades of gray only. Utilize the Bibliography to do your own investigation into the significant area of color sketching. Some of the many quality **sketching pencils** are shown on this page. In addition, experiment with charcoal sticks and Conté pencils. Also use different kinds of sketching **paper**. Beginners normally use inexpensive newsprint paper as their first drawing surface. Smooth (fine grain) sketching paper and coarse (textured) sketching paper are other popular surfaces.

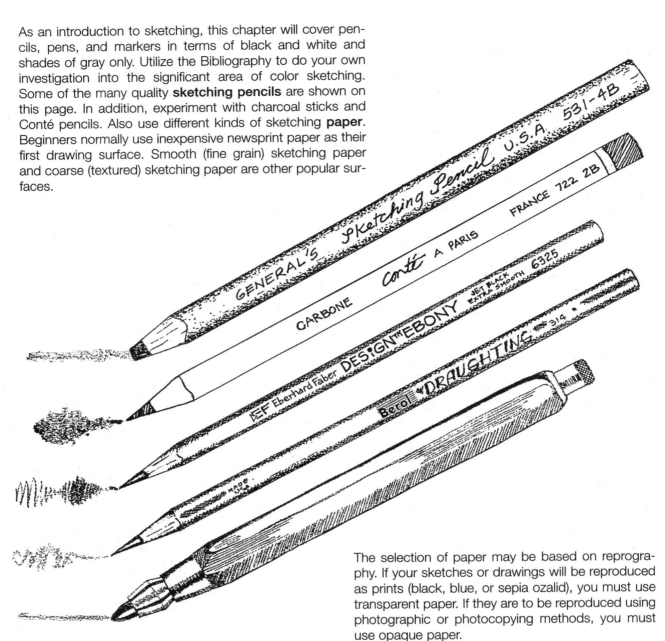

The selection of paper may be based on reprography. If your sketches or drawings will be reproduced as prints (black, blue, or sepia ozalid), you must use transparent paper. If they are to be reproduced using photographic or photocopying methods, you must use opaque paper.

Soft lead sketching pencils can have round or flat leads. A flat sketching pencil can be thick (carpenter's pencil) or medium thick (chisel pencil). Both must be sharpened by hand. Flat sketching pencils are mainly used in three degrees: 2B, 4B, and 6B. They are commonly used for covering large areas quickly, as when creating tonal indications for brick, stone, and wood. Conté pencils or sticks come in three grades of black, in four different colors, and in soft, medium, and hard. Both Conté and Ebony pencils give smooth lines. The Ebony pencil's soft core is slightly wider than that of a typical pencil. A good general-purpose sketching pencil with a soft lead is Berol Draughting 314. When round leaded pencils become too short from use, add length by using a pencil extender. An all-purpose mechanical leadholder clutch freehand sketching pencil can adapt its lead to almost any shape and is ideal for rapidly sketching over large areas. Other excellent brands include Derwent and Mars.

Sketch: Student project by Wan Othman
       Glass Study
Medium: Graphite pencil
Courtesy of Washington University
School of Architecture, St. Louis, Missouri

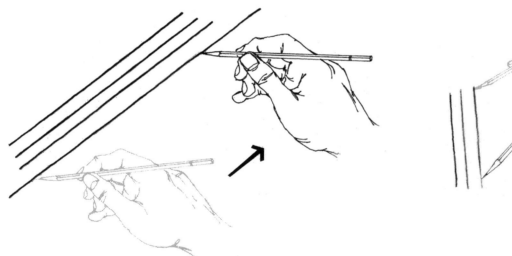

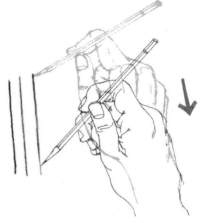

PENCIL STROKES

The quality of a freehand pencil stroke is determined by the hardness grade of the pencil lead, the character of the sharpened point, the amount of pressure applied, and the type of paper used. Compare parallel lines drawn on both smooth and rough sketching paper. Softer pencils work better with smoother paper, harder pencils with coarser paper. Architectural pencil sketching is most often done with grades such as HB, B, and 2B, though softer leads are not uncommon. Graphite and charcoal pencils can yield variable line widths and tone. Variable tone and value cannot be acheived when sketching with pens and markers. Lighting conditions resulting in shades and shadows are most accurately represented by using soft lead pencils, charcoal pencils, or Conté crayons. To prevent pencil work from smudging, cover completed sections of your drawing with tracing paper or use fixative sprays.

In the above illustration, the side of the little finger is resting on the drawing surface. The pencil should be held in a relaxed position; too tight a grip will cause hand fatigue. A wrist and arm movement will produce longer strokes. Use the wrist, elbow, and shoulders as pivot points. Attempt to master the control of sketching straight lines, curved lines, circular spirals, and circles. When sketching, use the whole page—draw big.

Using a pen or a marker as a communication tool allows the architect/designer to express a wide range of images, whether they be representational, like the hotel courtyard and the Austrian street scene, or conceptual, as with the Lloyd's of London sketch.

Sketch: The Garden Court of the Palace Hotel
           San Francisco, California
Medium: Ink pen
Sketch by Charles Moore, Architect
Courtesy of Saul Weingarten, Executor, Estate of Charles Moore, and
the Department of Architecture, UCLA School of Art and Architecture

PENS AND MARKERS

In addition to pencils, line and tone can be produced by a variety of pens and markers. **Markers** are available in a variety of halftones; but because of quick drying, mixing tones is difficult. Marker tips vary in size from fine to broad and vary in shape from pointed to chisel shapes. Finer tips generate more detailed fine lines, whereas broader tips generate wider lines and solid tones. Technical **pens** are commonly used for precise mechanical lines. Razor-point pens, cartridge pens, and fountain pens can generate loose sketching lines that are permanent. Fountain pens become quite versatile in their application of line weight simply by adjusting the finger pressure.

Sketch: Lloyd's of London, London, England
11.75" × 16.5" (29.8 × 41.9 cm)
Medium: Brown felt-tipped marker
Sketch by Laurie Abbott
Courtesy of Richard Rogers Partnership, Architects

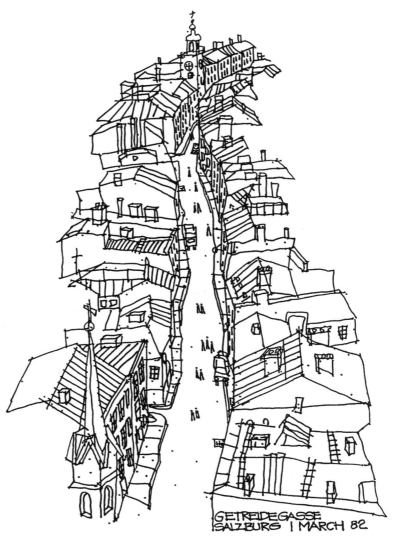

Drawing: Street scene, Salzburg, Austria
7" × 10" (17.8 × 25.4 cm)
Medium: Felt-tipped pen on paper
Courtesy of Steven House, Architect, San Francisco

Felt-tipped markers give a quick, loose, and very effective transparent method of presentation (similar to water-color) when time is a critical factor. One advantage of markers is that they very seldom smudge. They also come in a great variety of premixed colors in addition to black and gray. Markers are more suitable to smoother, harder, and heavier grades of paper. Pencils and colored pencils best accommodate medium-weight textured paper.

Ballpoint is just one of the many kinds of pen tips; others include felt-tipped, fiber-tipped, and roller-tipped. Ballpoint pens and rollerball pens can generate a variety of line widths. In general, all types of pens give steady, fluid, smooth-flowing lines without the need to apply pressure as one must with a pencil.

Pens and markers are perhaps best suited to drawing conceptual ideas (see Conceptual Sketching, Chapter 10). These tools give one the ability to "loosen up" to avoid inhibitions in the design-drawing process. See the Bibliography for books on sketching with pens and markers.

BALLPOINT PENS AND FELT-TIPPED MARKERS

PENCIL STROKES

Sketch: Texas Seaport Museum, Galveston, Texas, 1991
9" × 12" (22.9 × 30.5 cm)
Medium: Ebony pencil on paper
Courtesy of David G. Woodcock, FAIA, RIBA, Professor of Architecture
Texas A&M University, College of Architecture

The darkness quality of an Ebony pencil means that less applied pressure is needed when sketching. It can smoothly render any line width with its soft graphite and is acceptable for most slightly toothed paper surfaces. Pencil strokes can vary in direction (vertical, horizontal, angular) and pressure. Note in the above sketch the use of short angled strokes to create value. Try to experiment and discover new strokes as you sketch.

PEN STROKES

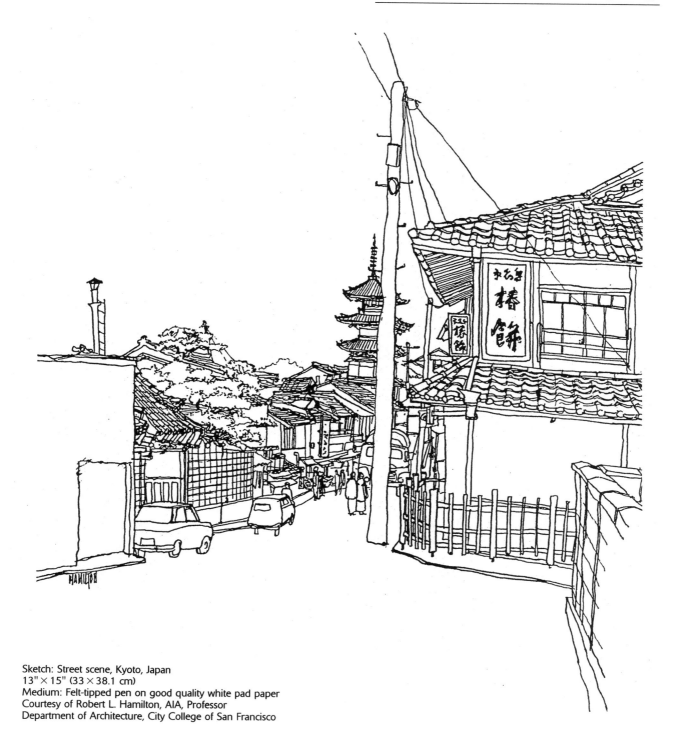

Sketch: Street scene, Kyoto, Japan
13" × 15" (33 × 38.1 cm)
Medium: Felt-tipped pen on good quality white pad paper
Courtesy of Robert L. Hamilton, AIA, Professor
Department of Architecture, City College of San Francisco

Like pencils, pens are a convenient medium when one is sketching quickly in an unfamiliar place. They do not require extra setup time as, for example, with watercolors. Graphite and ink differ in that ink is more permanent: Every mark and stroke is critical in the development of any drawing done with a pen. Pen strokes emphasize line work and the interrelationship of the compositional shapes. Street scenes in the cityscape are always popular travel sketches. Enliven building sketches by adding visible accessories like vegetation, people, and vehicular traffic in proper scale.

Sketch: Pomodoro showroom, New York City
35" × 24" (94.1 × 61 cm)
Medium: Black ink marker and sepia grease pencil
Courtesy of FTL Architects, PC

Lines in architectural sketches can be very disciplined, as in the sketch at right, or they can be very loose, as in the sketches below. Both approaches convey a different character to each sketch. All of the sketches on this page use pen and ink. With this medium, the controlled cumulative effects of the strokes are the most critical.

Pen strokes often simultaneously describe different drawing elements. For example, form and volume in the Barcelona sketch combine with value and texture. Line weight (the thickness or thinness of a line) can express the "quality" of line. This quality may have the express purpose of conveying form and/or shadow. In representational sketches, lines guide the eye by delineating shapes and enclosing spaces. In drafting, lines are drawn accurately to give a hardline representation of buildings. In conceptual sketches, lines are drawn freely and with rhythmic strokes.

STROKE CHARACTER

Sketch: Student project by Susan Pruchnicki
          Church of Sagrada Familia, Barcelona, Spain
10" × 12" (25.4 × 30.5 cm)
Medium: Pen and ink
Antoni Gaudí, Architect
Courtesy of Washington University
School of Architecture, St. Louis, Missouri

Sketch: Student project by Rosalino Figureras
          St. Louis, Missouri
3" × 7" (7.6 × 17.8 cm)
Medium: Felt-tipped pen on bond paper
Courtesy of Washington University
School of Architecture, St. Louis, Missouri

Sketch: Student project by Kathryn Korn
          Barcelona, Spain
3" × 7" (7.6 × 17.8 cm)
Medium: Felt-tipped pen on bond paper
Courtesy of Washington University
School of Architecture, St. Louis, Missouri

Sketch: Student project by Corvin Matei
　　　　　 Experimental train station for the D.A.R.T. (Dallas Rapid Transit Systems)
18" × 18" (45.7 × 45.7 cm)
Medium: 2B pencil on Strathmore paper
Courtesy of the University of Texas at Arlington School of Architecture

The drawing above shows precise controlled strokes of tone value within a mechanically constructed three-point perspective (see pp. 270–273). Subtle tone values are achieved much more readily with pencil than with ink pens (facing page). Here, the drawing fades from its detailed central image. Where there is less detail, there is a hint as to how the image might continue. This type of sketch is termed a **vignette** (see pp. 67, 71, 73, 76, and 83).

A soft 2B pencil was used to emphasize the parts of the drawing that are important in order to understand the spatial architecture. It has an unfinished look.
[ARCHITECTURE STUDENT'S STATEMENT]

STROKE CHARACTER

These two facing pages show a difference in stroke character based on the drawing instrument used. Felt-tipped or fiber-tipped markers and fountain pens usually encourage "looseness" in the hand and arm strokes, resulting in a more representational sketch (San Francisco sketches, this page) rather than a detailed copy sketch of what we see. A fine-point technical pen or a fine-tipped marker encourages more detail and a "copy" quality (Rome sketches, facing page).

Sketch: The Vedanta Society building, San Francisco,
         California
Medium: Ink pen
Sketch by Charles Moore, Architect
Courtesy of Saul Weingarten, Executor, Estate of Charles
Moore, and the Department of Architecture, UCLA School
of Art and Architecture

Bernard Maybeck, Architect
Medium: Ink pen
Sketch by Charles Moore, Architect
Courtesy of Saul Weingarten, Executor, Estate of Charles Moore,
and the Department of Architecture, UCLA School of Art and Architecture

Sketches: Student project by Corvin Matei, Rome, Italy
6" × 9" (15.2 × 22.9 cm)
Medium: Ink on Strathmore paper
Courtesy of the University of Texas at Arlington
School of Architecture

STROKE CHARACTER

These are simple **contour** drawings executed with a great economy of line. As minimal as they are, they clearly define positive and negative qualities of space. The stroke character of a contour line can convey an immense range of possibilites with respect to the viewer's sense of form, space, and light in the drawing context.

Drawing allows me to express the essence of a particular and dear quality of my design. This may be a play of light or color, a form or forms, a unique perspective, or most often, the relationship of my building with the sky.
[ARCHITECT'S STATEMENT]

Sketch: Boyer Center for Molecular Medicine, New Haven, Connecticut
6.25" × 9" (15.9 × 22.9 cm)
Medium: Pen and ink
Courtesy of Cesar Pelli, Architect, Cesar Pelli & Associates

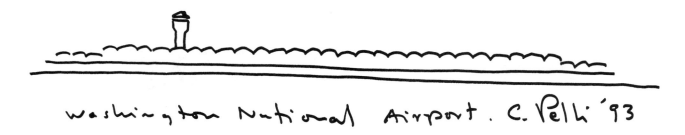

Sketch: New North Terminal Washington National Airport, Washington, D.C.
Medium: Pen and ink
Courtesy of Cesar Pelli, Architect, Cesar Pelli & Associates

Drawing: Petronas Towers, Kuala Lumpur, Malaysia
9.5" × 12" (24.1 × 30.5 cm)
Medium: Oil pastels on acid-free vellum
Courtesy of Cesar Pelli, Architect, Cesar Pelli & Associates

STROKE CHARACTER

These rapidly sketched strokes give the soft delicate character commonly found when pastels are used. Pastels lend themselves to compostions that are not very detailed, such as this value study. **Value** refers to the lightness or darkness of a surface. In this representational sketch, there is a high value contrast in the sense that an extremely light color (building form or figure) is placed adjacent to an extremely dark color (sky or background). A low value contrast occurs when either two (or more) light values or two (or more) dark values are placed next to each other. In the above example, this phenomenon begins to occur as the sky gradually becomes lighter toward the horizon to almost merge in value with the value of the base of the towers. Classic examples of this kind of value transition can be seen in the 1920s and 1930s work of Hugh Ferriss (see Bibliography). Architect Cesar Pelli is well known for using layered diagonal line strokes to control value and density. This expressive technique allows for qualities such as light and shadow, volume, surface, reflections, and transparency to appear.

Drawing is the essence of description.
Drawing connects the eye and the hand to define the world, both seen and unseen.
[ARCHITECT'S STATEMENT]

Representational sketching utilizes many basic elements, including line, value, texture, the massing of shapes and volumes, scale, and color (if color is used). A noncolored pencil or an ink pen will result in a monochromatic sketch. Working in any medium, one consciously manipulates either one element or any combination of the elements to produce a desired final composition. Sketches should exhibit a creative richness regardless of the technique and medium used. The goal of representational sketching should go far beyond accurately imitating what one sees.

REPRESENTATIONAL SKETCHING

Sketches: Manhattan, function and form
9" × 10" (22.9 × 25.4 cm)
Medium: Pen and ink
Courtesy of Hugh Hardy, FAIA, Hardy Holzman Pfeiffer Associates

TOWN PLAZA

Sketch: Alabang Town Center, Alabang, Philippines
17" × 11" (43.2 × 27.9 cm)
Medium: Felt-tipped pen on vellum
Courtesy of Architecture International and TAC, The Architects Collaborative;
Ayala Land, Inc.; and GF and Partners, Architects, Co.
Renderer: Lawrence Ko Leong

The choice of medium will affect a sketch's character. Establish the character or feeling by deciding which words would best describe your subject or your design. Will the word and feeling be formal or informal, soft or slick, etc.? Graphite, ink, and watercolor are just a few of the possible media that one can use in communicating architectural sketches. In the area of color media (see Web site, Chapter 12), there are many choices in addition to watercolor, such as colored pencils, colored markers, oil pastels, etc. Work with the medium (whether dry or wet) with which you feel most at ease. Be alert to other evolving media such as computers or computers combined with manual methods (mixed media). Mixing media can be an inventive challenge.

MEDIA TO REPRESENT SKETCHES

SIGHTING

Drawing: Sacramento State Office Building, Sacramento, California
Fisher–Friedman Associates, San Francisco, California

To properly establish accurate proportions in transferring what we see to our drawing pad, we must accurately compare relative lengths, widths, and angles.

1. Observe the subject/scene that you would like to draw.
2. Close one eye, hold your head still, and extend your arm to arm's length.
3. Holding a pencil or pen, make a basic unit length measurement on any part of the viewed scene, using the distance from your drawing instrument tip to the top of your thumb as a guide to proportion.

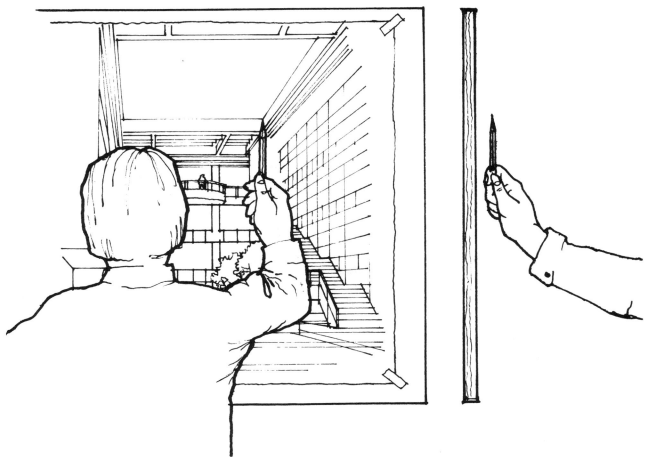

Drawing: Sacramento State Office Building, Sacramento, California
Fisher–Friedman Associates, San Francisco, California

SIGHTING

4. Other lengths and widths can now be measured based on the smaller unit length. All of these distances must reference the basic unit in terms of relative size.
5. The drawing instrument must coincide and align with any angled line to properly transfer the same angle to the drawing pad. Measure the angle with respect to a horizontal and vertical reference that corresponds to the edges of your pad.

Remember:

• that the plane of your eyes are must always be parallel to the plane of your drawing instrument, and
• to keep your drawing pad perpendicular to your line of sight so that your drawing instrument can lie in the same plane regardless of its orientation.

BLOCKING OUT AND CONSTRUCTION LINES

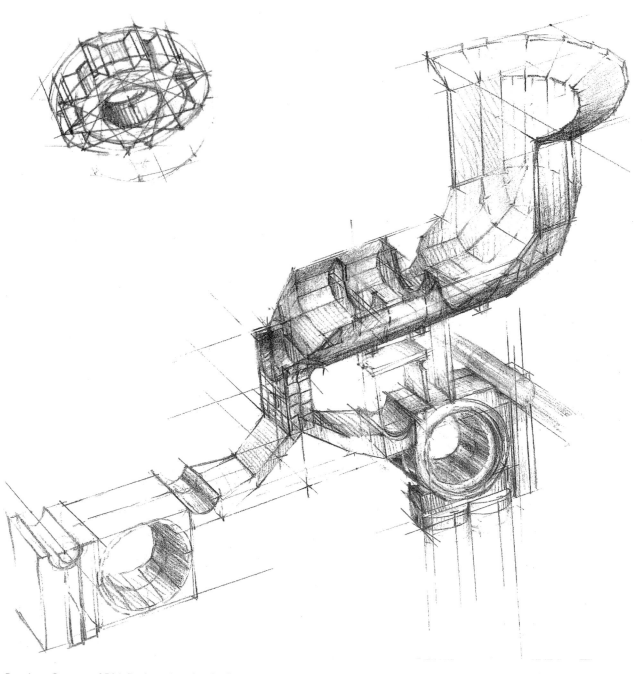

Drawing: Courtesy of Dick Davison, Associate Professor
18" × 18" (45.7 × 45.7 cm)
Medium: HB graphite pencil on Strathmore 400
Texas A&M University, College of Architecture

Objects in a composition should always be blocked out within a geometric envelope. Two-dimensionally, the shape can be a triangle, a circle, a square, or a polygon. Three-dimensionally, the basic element can be a cube, a sphere, or a polygon (3D). **Blocking out** helps to compose a drawing and gives us an idea of what the end product will look like. Once an accurate composition is drawn, line weights can be adjusted or values applied to complete and finalize the drawing. An HB pencil has a lead that is in the transition zone between hard and soft, and can achieve nice soft tone values halfway between white and black on a value chart (scale).

With any object, always begin to set up the proportions by using **construction lines.** These lightly drawn lines should envelop the object. The use of these lines is especially important with objects that are composed of nonlinear forms, as shown above. Straightedges can be used to assist with long straight construction lines if your instructor permits. On cylindrical or rounded shapes, be sure to locate the main central axis spine first. Long construction lines are most effectively drawn by holding the pencil beneath the hand with thumb and fingers.

Drawing: Courtesy of Dick Davison, Associate Professor
18" × 18" (45.7 × 45.7 cm)
Medium: HB graphite pencil on Strathmore 400
Texas A&M University, College of Architecture

BLOCKING OUT AND CONSTRUCTION LINES

STILL LIFES

1

2

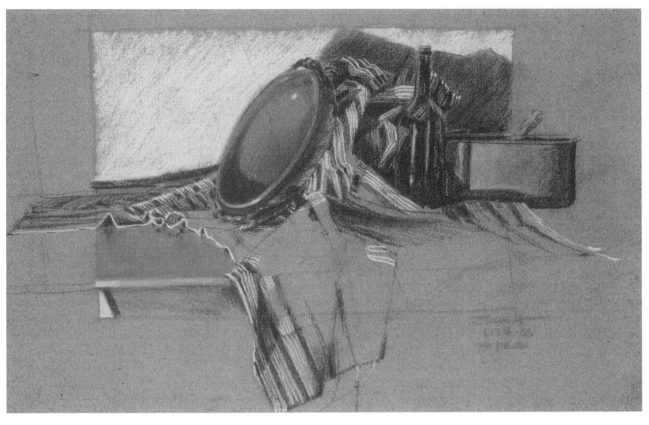

Still life: courtesy of Jonathan Brandt, Visiting Assistant Professor
Texas A&M University College of Architecture

(Opposite page)

(1) Still life: Student project by Alysha Haggerton
Courtesy of Jonathan Brandt, Visiting Assistant Professor
Texas A&M University College of Architecture

(2) Still life: Student project by Ryan Collins
Courtesy of Jonathan Brandt, Visiting Assistant Professor
Texas A&M University College of Architecture

When setting up a still life with three or more objects, it is important to symetrically or asymetrically **balance** (create a visually appealing arrangement of) the various elements, and to use techniques that involve "blocking out" and "construction lines." Correct proportions are set up by using construction lines. Light construction lines should envelop all the objects, as well as the total **composition.** Also important is a strong light source to explore the contrast of light and shade, and a background value, which will interrelate with the tone values in the composition. Vary the media and explore the results. For example, a different feeling is achieved when using charcoal as opposed to white chalk.

GESTURE AND CONTOUR DRAWINGS

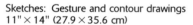

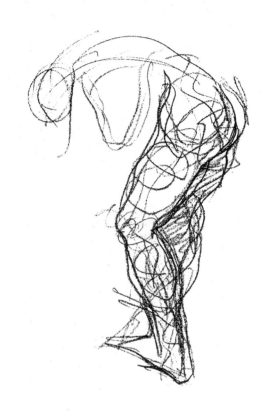

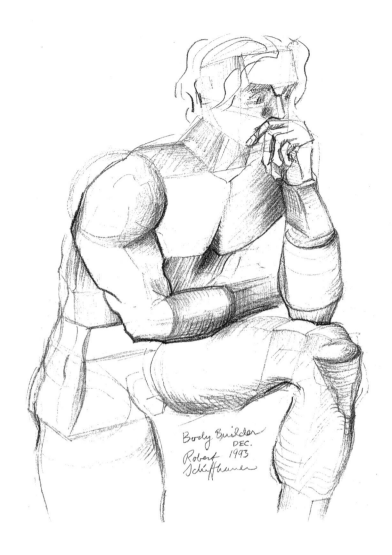

Body Builder
DEC.
Robert 1993
Schiffhauer

Sketches: Gesture and contour drawings
11" × 14" (27.9 × 35.6 cm)
Medium: Carbon pencil on cold-press drawing paper
Courtesy of Robert Schiffhauer, Associate Professor
Texas A & M University, College of Architecture

Gesture drawings are quick proportion and form studies that help to develop rapid hand–eye coordination. **Contour** drawings are more time-consuming and precise in nature.

The human figure is an excellent subject for both gesture and contour drawings. The human body is basically a composite of modified geometric solids. Note the cubic, conical, cylindrical, spherical, rectilinear, and wedge volumes in the human figure at right above.

All parts of the human body are composed of many wonderful contours. As the student explores the forms of exterior human anatomy, he or she is introduced to structural considerations in a most intimately understood manner. The artistic discipline of **life drawing** has been an adjunct to many architecture programs. Freehand representational sketching of the human body combines the intuitive fluidity of art with the geometric structural precision of architecture (see pp. 410–413).

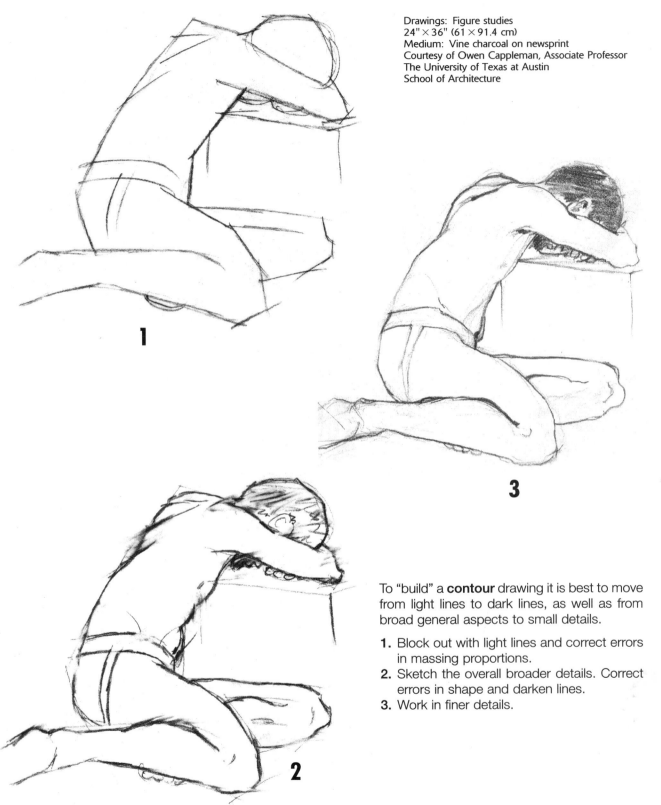

Drawings: Figure studies
24" × 36" (61 × 91.4 cm)
Medium: Vine charcoal on newsprint
Courtesy of Owen Cappleman, Associate Professor
The University of Texas at Austin
School of Architecture

CONTOUR DRAWING

To "build" a **contour** drawing it is best to move from light lines to dark lines, as well as from broad general aspects to small details.

1. Block out with light lines and correct errors in massing proportions.
2. Sketch the overall broader details. Correct errors in shape and darken lines.
3. Work in finer details.

By studying the proportions of the human body, we broaden our knowledge and understanding of how people fit physically with respect to the environment. This study is called **anthropometrics.**

BLIND CONTOURS

VIOLIN

Blind contours (clockwise from top left):
Student projects courtesy of Brian Blanchard
(Texas A&M University)
Dennis Martin, Amaza Lai Cheng Lam (City
College of San Francisco)

In the making of contour drawings, of which there are several varieties, the draftsman, artist, or architect attempts to use line in such a way as to express the essential form of the subject. In a good contour drawing, the line appears to wrap or traverse invisible volumes so that, as the eye follows the lines, the three-dimensionality of the subject becomes apparent. One approach is to draw the subject "blind"; that is, while looking only at the subject. The drawer attempts to supplant pencil with eye and "track" the surface of the subject. Concentrating and focusing on the subject allows one to be "loose" and relaxed while exploring the potential of the free-flowing contour line.

It is best for blind drawings to be done quickly, with a minimum of conscious thought. This results in contour lines that are more sensitive although not proportionally accurate. Note the concentrated small areas of dark tone in which many changes of line direction took place. This is the result of exaggerated and distorted lines, common characteristics of blind contour drawings. Blind drawings usually correspond very closely to one's visual perception.

Blind contours (clockwise from top left):
Medium: Pencil
Student projects courtesy of
Ebby Chu (City College of San Francisco)
Jennifer Sobieraj (Texas A&M University)
Dennis Martin (City College of San Francisco)

BLIND CONTOURS

Drawing: Triton Museum of Art, Santa Clara, California
Courtesy of Barcelon & Jang, Architecture

A large massing of trees can be loosely rendered and their foliage made highly suggestive. Often groups of trees have a wall-like effect. Landscaping vegetation such as trees, plants, and shrubs should always be complementary and secondary to the architecture to which they are adjacent.

SKETCHING TREES

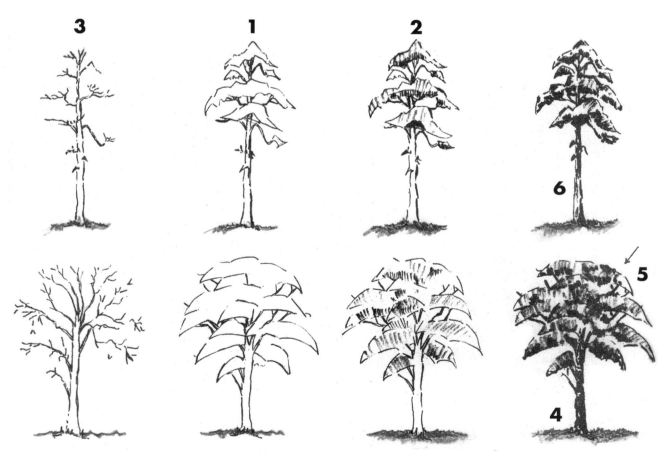

Each tree has a character of its own. When sketching or fabricating trees, one should always be aware of (**1**) the overall silhouette or shape (tall or short; bulky or thin), which is affected by gravity and wind; (**2**) the massing and pattern of the foliage; (**3**) the direction and pattern of growth on the branches, which is a clue to the tree form; (**4**) the manner in which the trunk flares or tapers off; (**5**) how the direction of light hits and penetrates various canopy shapes, producing shades and shadows; and (**6**) the texture of the bark. For pencil work, use 2B and HB for dark values and use 2H and 4H for contour lines and light values.

Sketch: Hillside residences, San Francisco, California
Sketch by Charles Moore, Architect
Courtesy of Saul Weingarten, Executor, Estate of
Charles Moore, and the Department of Architecture,
UCLA School of Art and Architecture

When you are doing rapid sketch studies at a site, the time factor often dictates that you may not have enough time to draw all the tree details (branches, leaves, etc.). In such situations, your objective should be to give a representational feeling of the essence of a tree or other landscape vegetation. Freehand trees can be abstractly simplistic. These quickly sketched suggestive trees are very effective. Sometimes it is what we leave out rather than what we put in a sketch that makes it highly expressive.

Sketch: Saitama Sports Arena Competition
Design offices: Takenaka Corporation, Tokyo, Japan
　　　　　　　　Cesar Pelli, Tokyo, Japan
17" × 11" (43.2 × 27.9 cm)
Medium: Prismacolor pencil
Courtesy of Lawrence Ko Leong, Architectural Illustrator

SKETCHING TREES

Drawing method: This was one of about 40 vignette sketches done using Prismacolor pencils and "eye-balling" a scale model. I used a light beige-rose pencil to outline the building, plaza, and entourage and used a soft blend of greens to maintain transparency and the canopy effect of foliage. A few bright spots of color were used to highlight the people and give liveliness to the composition.
[ARCHITECTURAL ILLUSTRATOR'S STATEMENT]

SKETCHING CARS

Sketch: Downtown Stockton, California
Courtesy of AIA and The Regional/Urban Design Assistance Team and Janice Filip, Architects

Cars range in length from approximately 14' (4.27 m) to 20' (6.1 m) and in width from 5.8' (1.77 m) to 6.3' (1.92 m). Tires range from 22" (55.9 cm) to 28" (71.12 cm) in diameter.

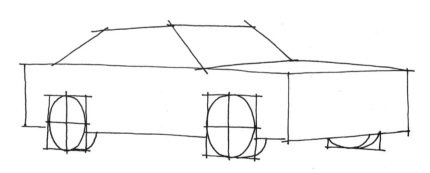

A car or any type of moving vehicle should be enclosed in an envelope of simple geometric shapes, such as a truncated pyramid, rectangular solids, and cylindrical elements. Boats are similar to cars in the sense that a boat can be skeletally set up as a rectilinear box with shaped ends and a specific center line. Graphite is the ideal medium for layout work.

After the basic volume and form are developed with light construction lines, structural details should be sketched with a contour outline technique. To keep it simple, only major details should be added, like headlights and bumpers. The drawing can be finalized with pencil or any other rendering medium (see pp. 418–419).

Drawing: Sybase Hollis Street Campus, San Francisco, California
18" × 12" (30.5 × 45.7 cm)
Medium: Sketch watercolor on mounted presentation blackline print of pencil drawing.
Robinson Mills & Williams, Architects
Courtesy of Al Forster, Architectural Illustrator

Cars in perspective should always be in scale with the rest of the drawing and secondary to major building elements. Contour outline cars are usually adequate for most architectural drawings. Add details and shaded tones in accordance with the complexity of the rendering. Keep in mind that the roofs of cars are slightly below the eye-level line. Also, add visual interest by showing cars turning as well as moving in both directions.

SKETCHING CARS

Drawing: Studio Durant (unbuilt), Berkeley, California
Medium: Computer-generated plot
Courtesy of David Baker Associates, Architects

SKETCHING BUILDINGS

Sketch: Student project by Leigh Stringer
           Movie theater
Medium: Pen and ink
Courtesy of Washington University
School of Architecture, St. Louis, Missouri

All objects can be broken down into simple **geometric solids.** For example, trees are basically spheres or cones on cylinders. Buildings are usually a combination of rectangular solids, cylindrical solids, spherical solids, and planar elements. On close observation of building forms, we see that line is in reality the joining of two surfaces or a darker surface against a lighter surface. The sketch on the left shows the buildup of line within an enclosed space to simulate texture or tonal value.

Drawing: Industrial façade, San Pedro, California
23" × 17" (58.4 × 43.2 cm)
Medium: Oil paint
Courtesy of Kanner Architects
Painted by Stephen Kanner

Sketch with rough thumbnail vignette: Iglesia de San Francisco, Javier, Cuatitlan, Mexico
5" × 8" (12.7 × 20.3 cm)
Medium: Black Pentel felt-tip, semi-dry
Courtesy of Lawrence Ko Leong, Architectural Illustrator

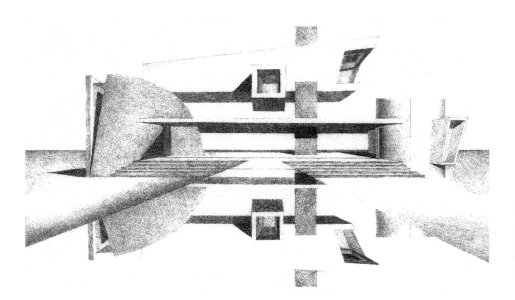

Sketch: House in Palm Springs II, Palm Springs, California
8" × 5" (20.3 × 12.7 cm)
Medium: Prismacolor
Courtesy of Kanner Architects
Drawn by Stephen Kanner

To create my drawings I lay the paper on glass, because it has a true, hard surface, and I draw and shade with the side of the sharpened point of a No. 2, soft, Ticonderoga pencil. The way to get an even texture is to squint or look obliquely, never directly, at one's work. To achieve hard edges, I draw against a straightedge (see p. 81).
[ARCHITECT'S STATEMENT]

SKETCHING BUILDINGS

BUILDINGS IN CONTEXT/FOCAL POINTS

Through the medium of lead or graphite, time is transcended as a contemporary Florence becomes transformed into a nostalgic moment from history.
[PROFESSOR'S STATEMENT]

Pencil stroke value on buildings and streets can be made broader by producing a flat surface on the lead. Using a flat surface, a uniform width and consistent value of stroke can be achieved. Best results can be attained by moving the arm at a constant speed.

In choosing subject matter for travel sketches like these street scenes, try to focus on a center of interest and then experiment with balance and composition. Elements on the street such as human figures should be detailed to add a **focal point** but not overly detailed to create a conflict of interest with other significant elements (e.g., buildings).

Travel sketches:
Left: Via Dei Rustic, Firenze, Italy
Above: Via Torna Boni, Firenze, Italy
Medium: Uniball pen on paper 1992
Courtesy of Professor George S. Loli
University of Louisiana–Lafayette

A study of a drawing technique called "perspective" (see Chapter 6), in conjunction with this chapter, will help you understand why the contours you draw instinctively in your representational sketches appear the way they are. We have seen that sighting skills give you an understanding of proportions in the viewed space. The theories of perspective will accurately verify these proportions. The sketch to the right is another good example of a sketch vignette. The continuation of the buildings is left to your imagination.

Sketch: Le Jardin Nelson, Montreal, Canada, 1993
9" × 12" (22.9 × 30.5 cm)
Medium: Ebony pencil on paper

Sketch: Galveston homes, Galveston Texas, 1993
9" × 12" (22.9 × 30.5 cm)
Medium: Ebony pencil on paper
Courtesy of David G. Woodcock, FAIA, RIBA,
Professor of Architecture, Texas A&M University,
Department of Architecture

Drawing on site is always a challenge for me, and I rarely spend more than twenty minutes on each sketch. As an architect my objective is to learn more about the subject, so I focus a lot of attention on form and materials. Ebony pencil allows me to explore shade and shadow quickly, and by keeping at least two pencils with sharp points I can still pick out critical details.
[ARCHITECT'S STATEMENT]

SKETCHING BUILDINGS

TRAVEL SKETCHING

Sketch: Student project by Margaret Stanton
        Pencil sketch of Vicenza, Italy
Courtesy of the University of Virginia School of Architecture

On-the-spot representational sketching done when traveling gives you a chance to fill your sketchbook with interesting subjects. The landscape is filled with exciting visual surprises, whether street scenes within a cityscape or mountainous roads in a rural village or panoramic beach views along a waterfront. Special events may be occurring and your goal may be to capture a sense of place and time. Unusual and interesting views should be sought. Perspective angles can vary from traditional ground eye-level views to bird's-eye or worm's-eye views.

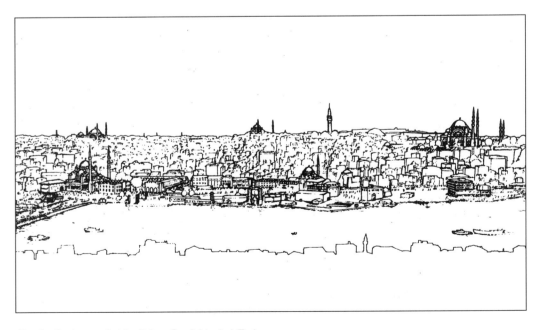

Sketch: Student project by Behan Cagri, Istanbul, Turkey
30" × 18" (76.2 × 45.7 cm)
Medium: Ink sketch on vellum
Courtesy of the University of Maryland School of Architecture

After the shape and proportions of an architectural subject are sketched, focus in and concentrate on the surface material textures of the structure or the building.

TRAVEL SKETCHING

Charcoal is a good medium for deemphasizing details. You have to work with broad strokes, so you can't be too fussy about details. Charcoal comes in both sticks and pencil forms and in a variety of grades. The long edge of the stick form is excellent for shading large areas.

Sketched images of China, Mexico, and Israel (clockwise from left):

Project by student James Ke, City College of San Francisco
3" × 4" (7.62 × 10.2 cm)
Medium: Charcoal

Lawrence Ko Leong, Architectural Illustrator
5" × 5" (12.7 × 12.7 cm)
Medium: Pentel felt-tipped pen

Brian Kelly, Architect, Associate Professor, University of Maryland
4" × 3" (10.2 × 7.6 cm)
Medium: Ink

TRAVEL SKETCHING

Sketch: Street scene, Miranda, Italy
8" × 10" (20.3 × 25.4 cm)
Medium: Felt-tipped pen on paper
Courtesy of Steven House, Architect, San Francisco

Sketch: Roofscape, Macau
5" × 7" (12.7 × 17.8 cm)
Medium: Pentel felt-tipped pen
Courtesy of Lawrence Ko Leong, Architectural Illustrator

Sketch: European travel sketch
Medium: Ink on paper
Courtesy of Lawrence Halprin, Landscape Architect

Sometimes the time factor will influence the character of the sketch. Detailed sketches like the Miranda, Italy, scene may need a couple of hours of your time, whereas the sketch to the left was rapidly done in a short amount of time. Small thumbnail, rapid sketches (vignettes) are needed when many studies of the same locale are required. A quick sketch lacking detail can be highly expressive.

Sketching and drawing are ways for me to have a dialogue with what I see and experience. In this interaction, I reveal my feelings about the world and my involvement with things and places and people. Sketches can influence my reactions of the moment and then lie dormant for future influences.
[LANDSCAPE ARCHITECT'S STATEMENT]

TAXCO 12·29·90

Travel sketching enables me to record the essence of time and place...with just a few lines a special moment can be captured forever.
[ARCHITECT'S STATEMENT]

Sketches: Taxco, Mexico
8" × 10" (20.3 × 25.4 cm)
Medium: Gray felt-tipped pen and watercolor on paper
Courtesy of Steven House, Architect, San Francisco

The examples above are serial sketches based on a visual progression or sequence through a site. Sketches done in this manner can function as a coherent group and allow for a more thorough spatial analysis of the built environment. This is analogous to the infinite number of serial views that can be called up in a computer-generated model.

TRAVEL SKETCHING

TRAVEL SKETCHING

Sketch: Resort Hotel, Mexico
17" × 11" (43.2 × 27.9 cm)
Medium: Black Prismacolor and thin Pilot razor-point Pentel
Shading was built up with a single-line thickness
Design Office: Sandy & Babcock, San Francisco
Courtesy of Lawrence Ko Leong, Architectural Illustrator

Sketch: Central Park Boat Basin, New York City, 1991
7" × 4" (17.8 × 10.2 cm)
Medium: Pencil
Courtesy of Stephen W. Parker, Architect

TRAVEL SKETCHING

Sketch: Abbey of San Galgano, Montesiepi, Italy, 1987
12" × 9" (30.5 × 22.9 cm)
Medium: Ebony pencil on paper
Courtesy of David G. Woodcock, FAIA, RIBA, Professor of Architecture
Texas A&M University, College of Architecture

The vantage point selected can affect the character and feeling of a building subject. Choice of viewpoint must be carefully considered, along with texture, lighting conditions, framing elements (like the foliage above), and the massing of forms. Studying the exact nature of light, shade, and shadow (Chapter 8) will help you understand lighting conditions as you sketch forms. Without any knowledge, your common sense and logic must help you interpret, for example, why the lighting effects on the cylindrical and prismatic forms above are quite different.

Also important in sketching the scenic environment is identifying the three "grounds" that one normally sees. These are the foreground (seen above as the curvilinear broadside sketched lines), the middleground (seen as the heavy vegetation), and the background (seen as the building). In this case, as with the views on the facing page, the middleground is emphasized to enhance the spatial quality.

TRAVEL SKETCHING

Sketch: Entry at 1816 Hickory
        Private residence, St. Louis, Missouri, 1992
3" × 9" (7.62 × 22.9 cm), 1992
Medium: Pencil
Courtesy of Stephen W. Parker, Architect

Sketch: Sacré Cœur Cathedral, Paris, France, 1995
4" × 9" (10.2 × 22.9 cm)
Medium: Pencil
Courtesy of Stephen W. Parker, Architect

Travel sketching has always been one of the joys of my journeys—and afterwards a truer memory than what a photo can evoke in me. I strive to capture the spirit of the moment and all that defines the experience of being at a certain place, at a certain time, in a certain light, in a certain season. And all the lessons I learn, the discoveries I make with my pencil, are brought back to influence my professional artwork—opening my mind's eye to new possibilities.
[ARCHITECT'S STATEMENT]

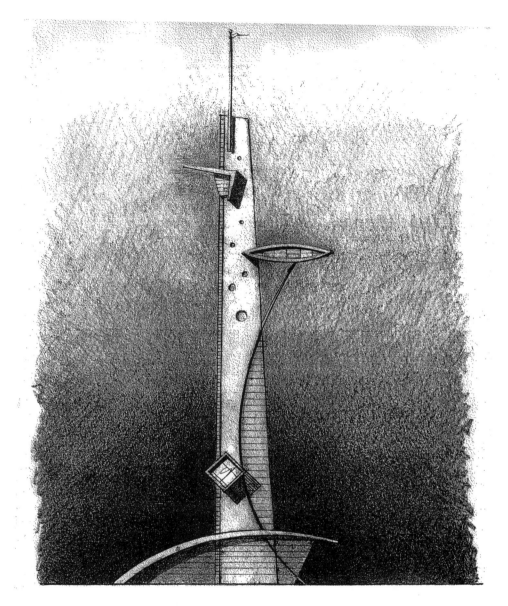

Drawing: Nan Jing Tower, Nan Jing, China
5" × 8" (12.7 × 20.3 cm)
Medium: Pencil
Courtesy of Kanner Architects
Drawn by Stephen Kanner

CONCEPTUAL SKETCH/IMAGE QUALITY

Conceptual sketches (see Chapter 10) are typically loose and free in execution. However, as the above drawing of a high-rise tower shows, a conceptual sketch can convey much more than one might expect—even having the appearance of a hard-edge representational drawing. In truly efficient drawings, every line conveys information about form, light qualities, and volume of space. Detailing may be suggested and surface qualities alluded to. A good conceptual sketch often will suggest possibilities that were previously unconsidered. In other words, the sketch can dictate the direction of the subsequent design. Architect Frank Lloyd Wright frequently did this kind of conceptual sketch (see pp. 7, 8, 99, and 141 in Pfeiffer's book listed in the Bibliography) by strategically using a straightedge. The result was a polished and authoritative look. He then developed the sketches into numerous preliminary studies and finally into presentation drawings (see p. 177).

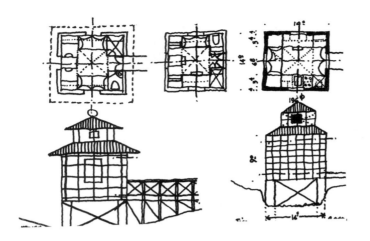

Sometimes travel sketches may not be what we see in terms of representational sketches. Some architects, such as Stanley Tigerman, often translate what they observe into many architectural graphic conventions. They may see a perspective view of a building; but in recording visual notes, they recode what they see into plan, elevation, section, or paraline diagrams.

STUDY SKETCHES

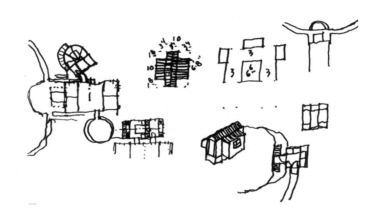

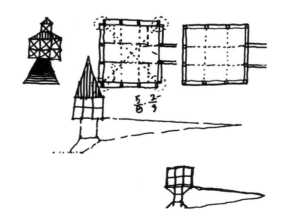

Travel sketches: Study for one-room house
                  Boardwalk, Michigan
3⅝" × 5¹³⁄₁₆" (9.22 × 14.76 cm)
Medium: Ink on paper
© Stanley Tigerman, Tigerman McCurry Architects
Sketches by Stanley Tigerman

My first thoughts are always recorded in my "Daler" sketchbook. I may draw anywhere from two or three up to twenty little sketches before they move to the next level.
[ARCHITECT'S STATEMENT]

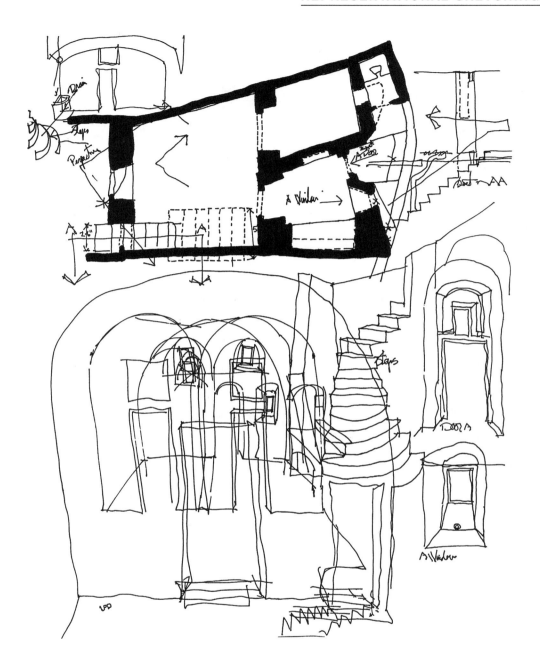

Drawing: House, Santorini, Greece
8" × 10" (20.3 × 25.4 cm)
Medium: Pen and ink on paper
Courtesy of Steven House, Architect, San Francisco

Travel sketching can offer spontaneous opportunities to document the environment. By drawing a plan view along with a series of corresponding vignettes, one can begin to capture the true essence of architectural space. These analytical studies can provide thoughtful insights into form and movement.
[ARCHITECT'S STATEMENT]

Multiple interior or exterior vantage points are common in study sketches. These superimposed sketches show a variety of perspective views taken inside a house with the direction of views indicated on the sketched plan. Travel sketches can sometimes be analytical studies.

4

Conventional Orthogonal Terminology

Scaled plans, elevations, and sections are drawings that depict a building or an urban landscape at a smaller size than true size. These drawings follow the principles of "orthographic projection" (see orthographic–paraline section) and help to depict an object in different but related two-dimensional views. Some other architectural drawing conventions (paraline, perspective) require detailed investigation, which accounts for their separate description in subsequent chapters.

The intent of this chapter is to introduce the potential and capabilities of these drawings and symbols and the kinds of information they can communicate.

In summary, following are some of the important terms and concepts you will learn:

Orthogonal	Orthographic projection	Plan
Section	Reflected ceiling plan	Elevation
Section arrows	North arrows	Graphic scales

Conventional Orthogonal Terminology

TOPIC: CONVENTIONAL ORTHOGONAL TERMINOLOGY

Ching 1990, 146–153.

Wang 1984, 16–28.

Chapter Overview

After studying this chapter, you will have a detailed understanding of drawing conventions such as plan, elevation, and section, as well as North arrows and graphic scales. For continued study, refer to Forseth's *Graphics for Architecture.*

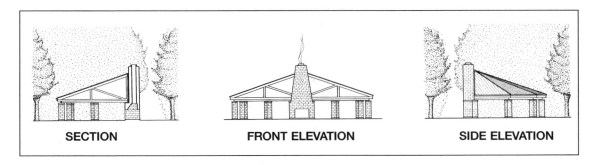

SECTION · FRONT ELEVATION · SIDE ELEVATION

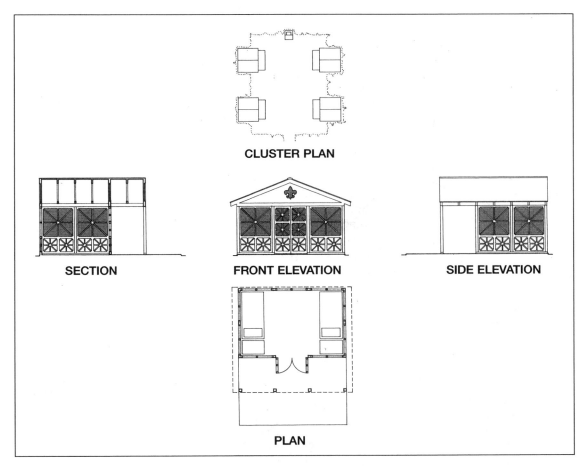

CLUSTER PLAN

SECTION · FRONT ELEVATION · SIDE ELEVATION

PLAN

Drawings: Hoover Camping Cluster in the Hoover Outdoor Education Center
Yorkville, Illinois
Medium: Ink on Mylar
Courtesy of Tigerman McCurry Architects

INTRODUCTION

Historically, buildings have been described using an **orthogonal** (right-angled) two-dimensional drawing system. The nomenclature used for the various orthogonal views is shown here. Popular architectural terminology such as "floor plan" is common knowledge for the layperson.

Small building types like residences are usually drawn orthogonally at a scale of ⅛"=1'0" or ¼"=1'0". A smaller scale (1/16"=1'0") can be used for larger building types such as hospitals and schools. A knowledge of orthogonal conventions and graphic symbols is necessary for architectural drawings and presentations. This chapter isolates and explores these topics in detail.

PRINCIPAL PLANES OF PROJECTION

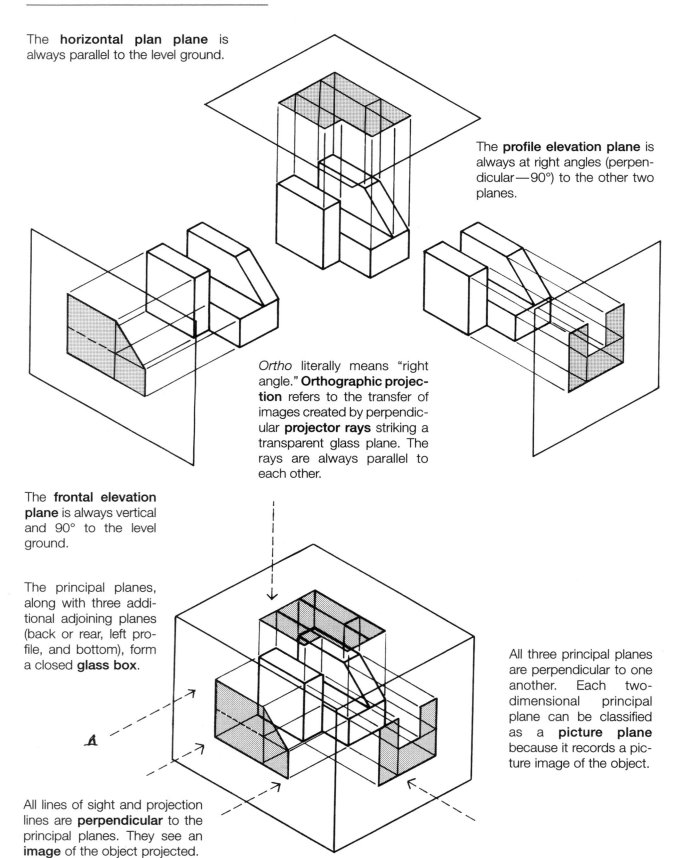

The **horizontal plan plane** is always parallel to the level ground.

The **profile elevation plane** is always at right angles (perpendicular—90°) to the other two planes.

Ortho literally means "right angle." **Orthographic projection** refers to the transfer of images created by perpendicular **projector rays** striking a transparent glass plane. The rays are always parallel to each other.

The **frontal elevation plane** is always vertical and 90° to the level ground.

The principal planes, along with three additional adjoining planes (back or rear, left profile, and bottom), form a closed **glass box**.

All three principal planes are perpendicular to one another. Each two-dimensional principal plane can be classified as a **picture plane** because it records a picture image of the object.

All lines of sight and projection lines are **perpendicular** to the principal planes. They see an **image** of the object projected.

The folding plane line is the intersection of any two principal planes. If a transparent glass box is opened on its folding plane or "hinge" lines, it will become a two-dimensional surface. The plan and profile elevation planes are rotated to become a part of the frontal elevation plane's extension.

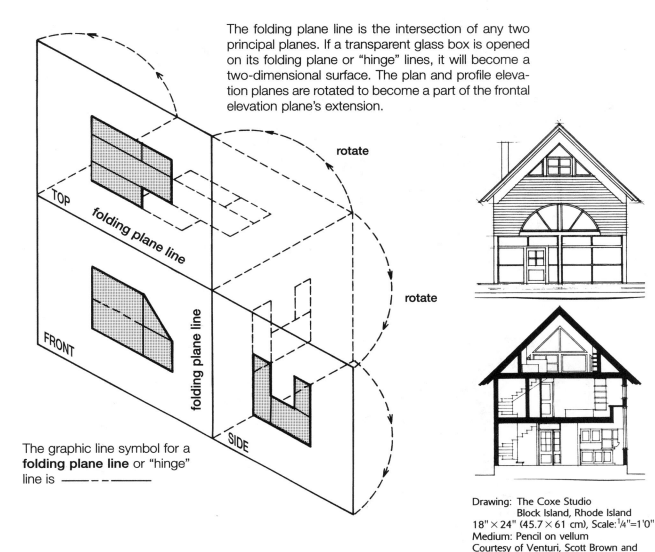

The graphic line symbol for a **folding plane line** or "hinge" line is ———— — ————

Drawing: The Coxe Studio
         Block Island, Rhode Island
18" × 24" (45.7 × 61 cm), Scale: $^1/4$"=1'0"
Medium: Pencil on vellum
Courtesy of Venturi, Scott Brown and
Associates Inc., Architects

The above example shows two true-size profile views (elevation and section). **Orthographic drawings** are true-size and true-shape views that are related on a two-dimensional surface. When two planes are perpendicular to a third plane, any point in space (such as **a**) will be seen twice an equal distance **K** behind the third plane where **K** can be any distance. In constructing related orthographic views, use a **45° diagonal line** from the intersection of the folding plane lines. Proper distances can then be transferred with projector lines from the top or horizontal view to the side or profile view. See an example of this process on page 615 and on page 19 of the web site's posted solutions.

ORTHOGRAPHIC VIEWS

ELEVATION/PLAN/SECTION

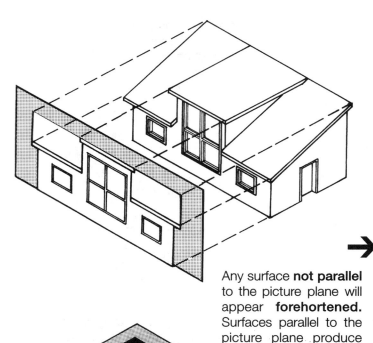

Any surface **not parallel** to the picture plane will appear **forehortened.** Surfaces parallel to the picture plane produce **true shapes.**

In an **elevation**, the image is projected onto a vertical picture plane. A building elevation shows vertical dimension relationships, the organizational massing, and the scale of the fenestration. It also shows also shows the location of doors and windows, as well as the pattern and textures of the construction materials (see pp. 398 and 399). Only the ground plane outside of the building will be shown as a solid cut line (see pp. 340 and 398) or a solid mass (see p. 102).

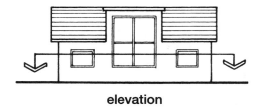

elevation

To help facilitate the understanding of viewer direction and location on sectional cuts, a line with labeled direction arrows (in this case B-B) should always be shown in the plan view.

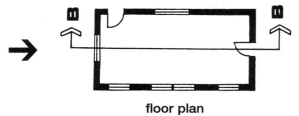

In a **plan,** a horizontal plane cuts through the building so as to remove that part of the building above the cutting plane. Floor plans express and communicate the intent of a design as well as the feasibility of a layout.

floor plan

Design sections normally do not show the foundation piers to reference the datum line, but rather show a toned or solid cut ground mass or an edge line between sky and ground.

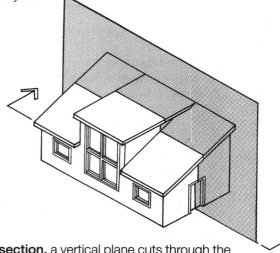

In a **section,** a vertical plane cuts through the building lengthwise (longitudinal) or crosswise (transverse) so as to remove that part of the building in front of the cutting plane.

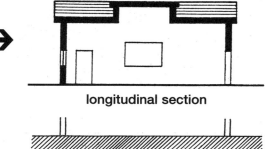

longitudinal section

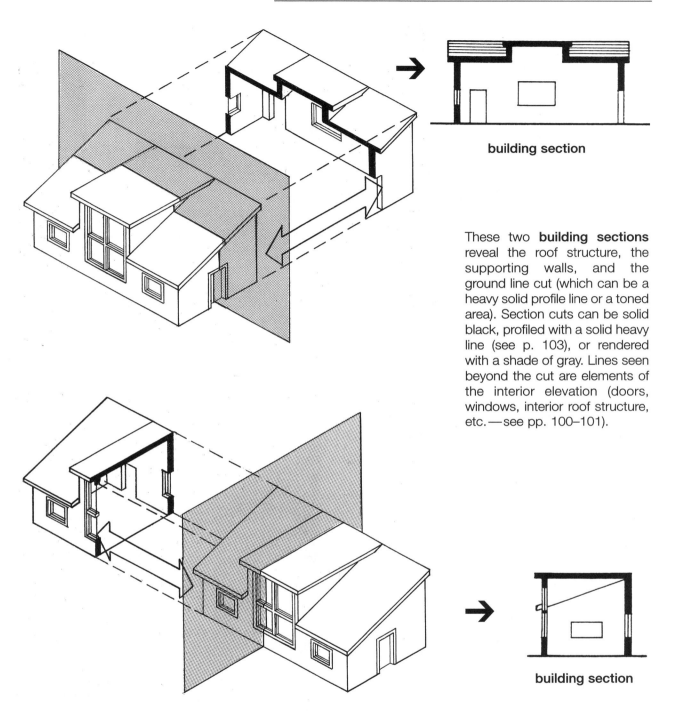

building section

These two **building sections** reveal the roof structure, the supporting walls, and the ground line cut (which can be a heavy solid profile line or a toned area). Section cuts can be solid black, profiled with a solid heavy line (see p. 103), or rendered with a shade of gray. Lines seen beyond the cut are elements of the interior elevation (doors, windows, interior roof structure, etc. — see pp. 100–101).

building section

BUILDING SECTION

A **building section** is analogous to the plan (horizontally cut section) except that the continuous cutting plane is **vertical.** Removing that part of the building in front of the plane reveals a cut section that allows us to glimpse the interior space. Logically, sectional cuts in architectural drawings are most often done parallel to walls in either the front or the side elevation. These sections are then properly annotated, as explained on the previous page. Other types of sectional cuts (such as offset cuts) tend to be more complex. The location of the sectional cut and the direction of view is left to the discretion of the architect/designer. Try to be most descriptive in showing the configuration and scale of the contained spatial relationships.

SECTION TYPES

The contour that defines where the sky (or space above) meets the building mass and the ground line determines the configuration of any **site section.** The primary function of a site section is to relate any building design to its **contextual environment.** It is quite common to see large site sections that show multiple cut sections of the building complex in combination with elevations of the same complex (see pp. 522–523 and 535).

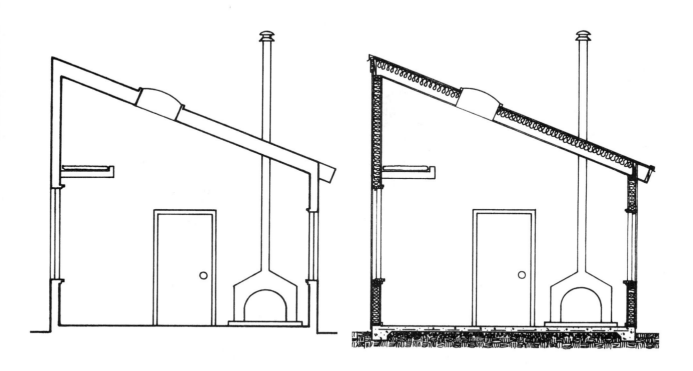

A **design section** shows no structural or construction details in the section area that is cut. The section is profiled with a heavy line to help define the interior spaces and overall form of the building. A **construction section** shows the details required to fabricate the building.

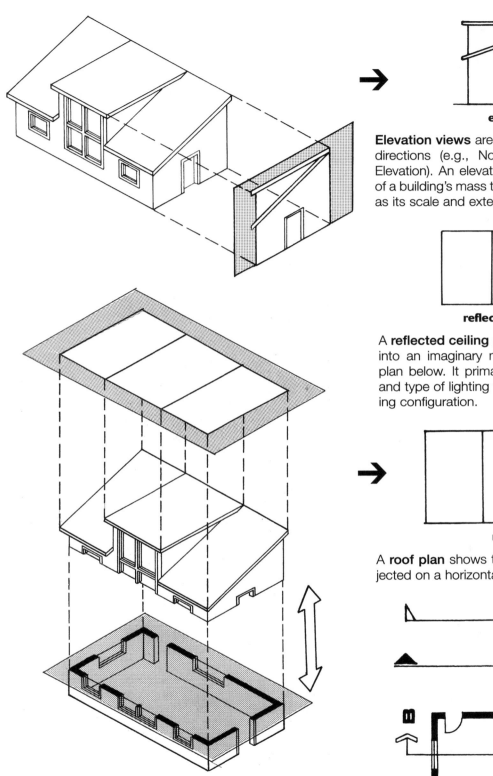

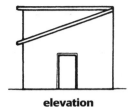

elevation

Elevation views are identified by the compass directions (e.g., North Elevation, Southwest Elevation). An elevation shows the relationship of a building's mass to the ground plane, as well as its scale and exterior material texture.

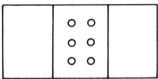

reflected ceiling plan

A **reflected ceiling plan** is the image reflected into an imaginary mirror placed on the floor plan below. It primarily shows the placement and type of lighting fixtures as well as the ceiling configuration.

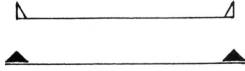

roof plan

A **roof plan** shows the roof configuration projected on a horizontal plane.

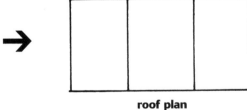

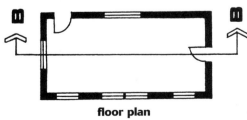

floor plan

A **floor plan** is represented best if the horizontal cut is taken through all openings (such as doors and windows) as well as important vertical elements (such as columns). The location of the cutting plane can vary, but normally ranges from 4' to 6' above the floor plane.

Section arrows shown in a plan indicate the observer's direction of sight.

ELEVATION VIEWS AND PLAN TYPES

DRAWING THE PLAN: STEP BY STEP

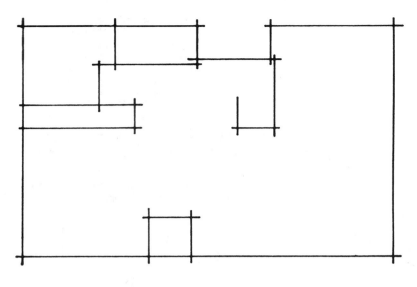

Pages 94 and 95 give a step-by-step process for drawing the plan. In general, the best procedure is to draw the building shell first, then all of the elements contained within the shell. Be sure to locate the center lines of all windows and doors.

1. Lightly draw the building outline with a single line. Again using a single line, lightly draw the center lines for interior walls.

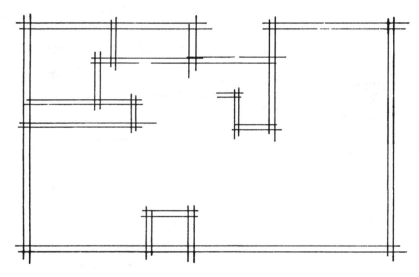

2. Add wall thickness for both exterior and interior walls.

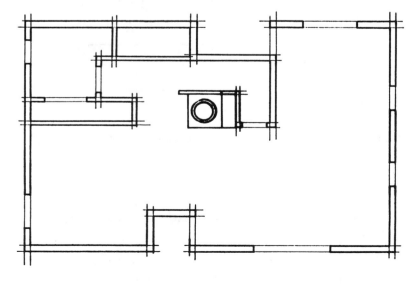

3. Locate and draw wall openings such as windows, doors, fireplaces, and stairs.

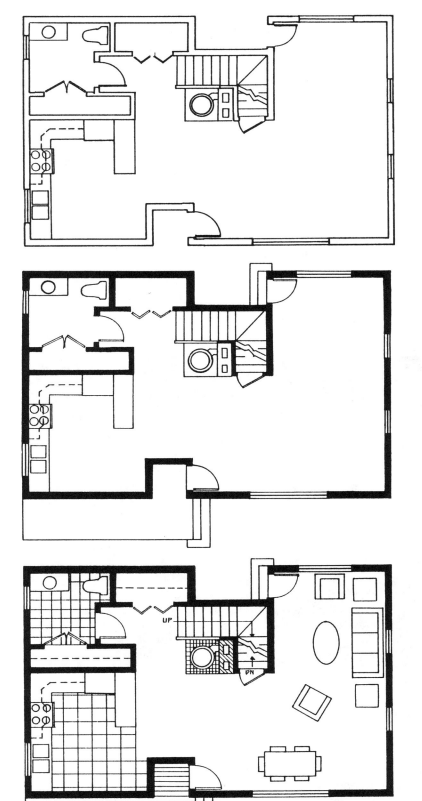

4. Locate and draw bathroom and kitchen fixtures, as well as plan details for doors and windows.

5. Draw any plan view wall indications with proper tone value (see p. 96). In this case the wall is toned solid black. If it were left white, the wall outline could be made heavier to make it read better.

Floor plans illustrate the location of walls, doors, windows, and stairs, as well as other elements below the cutting plane (countertops, toilets, etc.). Plan drawings are abstract views in the sense that physically at ground level we cannot see them.

6. Draw the proper material symbol (tone and texture) for the floors in each room.

This step-by-step procedure applies to both freehand and mechanically drawn plans.

The main purpose of including furniture and built-in elements (stoves, sinks, etc.) in the plan view is to show function and scale. For an accurate interpretation, the plan view, as with all orthogonal views, must have a constant scale.

DRAWING THE PLAN: STEP BY STEP

PLAN WALL INDICATIONS

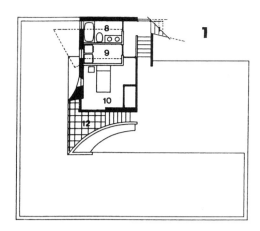

1

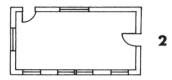

2

3

Drawing: The Hague Villa Project
The Hague, The Netherlands
8" × 10 (20.3 × 25.4 cm), Scale ¼"=1'0"
Medium: Pen and ink
Courtesy of Hariri & Hariri, Architects

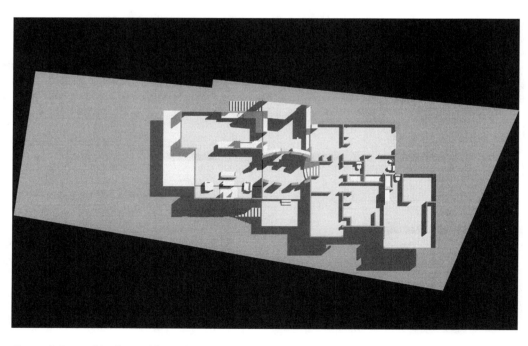

4

Plan study image: Nomikos residence, Berkeley, California
Courtesy of Inglese Architecture
Mark David English, Architectural Illustrator

Floor plan wall indications can be given different tonal values. In **1**, more contrast with the floorscape is desired; thus, the walls are toned solid black. In **2**, minimal contrast is needed; thus, the walls are left with no tone and a profile line. In **3**, a hatched tone is used for intermediate contrast (can also indicate the building material). In **4**, shadows are cast within the plan view to accentuate the walls and give added contrast. The shadows also give hints as to the heights of walls and other vertical elements.

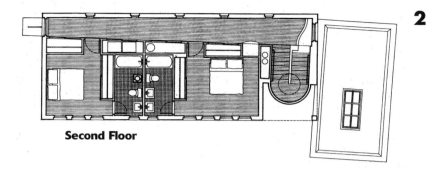

Second Floor

Ground Floor

Drawing: Son of Chang, Augusta, Georgia
24" × 24" (61x61 cm), Scale ¼"=1'0"
Medium: Ink
Courtesy of Anthony Ames, Architect

2

The patterns, values, and colors of floor finishes (see p. 393) are equally as important as plan wall indications. In Condition **2,** the outline of the plan cut is darkened to differentiate it from the floorscape texture. In Condition **3,** the plan wall indication for concrete block is strongly defined. In Condition **4,** a solid black wall easily contrasts with many floorscapes.

In multistory buildings, floor plans are commonly drawn in a vertical alignment (see pp. 147 and 494, and web site posted solution p. 44) with the lowest floor at the bottom. Plans can also be drawn in a horizontally related alignment with the lowest floor plan furthest to the left.

3

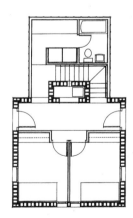

Drawing: Reid House
Johns Island, South Carolina
20" × 30" (50.8 × 76.2 cm), Scale: ¼"=1'0"
Medium: Ink on Mylar
Courtesy of Clark & Menefee, Architects

4

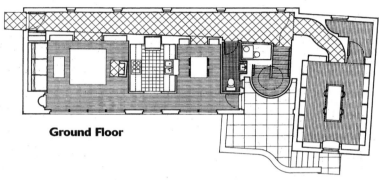
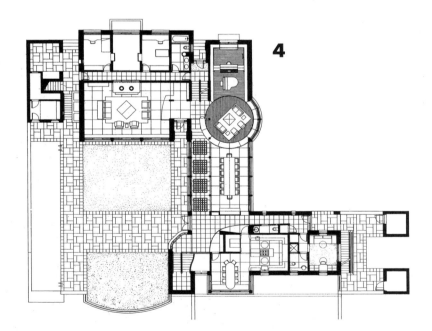

Drawing: Private residence, Zumikon, Switzerland
48" × 36" (121.9 × 91.4 cm), Scale: 1:50
Medium: Ink on Mylar
Courtesy of Gwathmey Siegel & Associates, Architects

INDICATIONS WITH FLOORSCAPES/FLOOR PLAN ALIGNMENT

NORTH ARROWS/GRAPHIC SCALES

SCALE

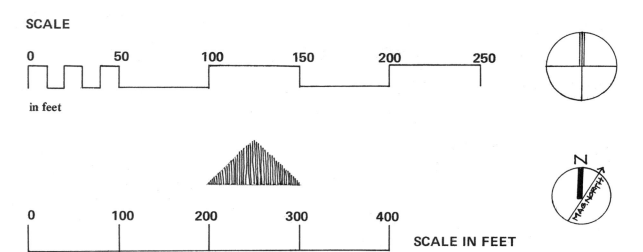

in feet

SCALE IN FEET

North arrows and graphic scales should be **clean, simple,** and **legible.** They should be placed adjacent to each other and next to the drawing they refer to in a presentation. These graphic symbols facilitate the understanding of the **orientation** and the **scale** of the building. Finally, they should never have fancy detail or be a distraction on a drawing.

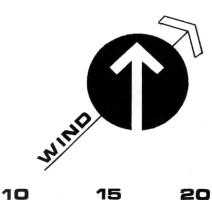

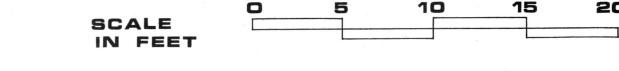

**SCALE
IN FEET**

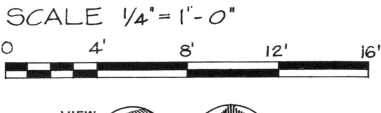

SCALE 1/4" = 1"- 0"

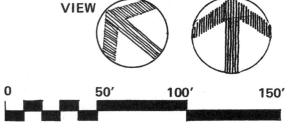

VIEW

The choice of a graphic scale size is dependent on the **size** and the **complexity** of the drawing. Note that 1" can be represented by whatever multiple you want to make it (e.g., 1" can be equal to 4' or 5'). For convenience, use 1"=1' unit of length regardless of the length represented.

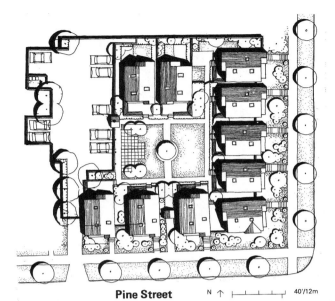

Pine Street   N ↑ |—|—|—|—| 40'/12m

Drawing: Pine Street Cottages, Seattle, Washington
Kucher/Rutherford, Inc., Developer and Contractor
Courtesy of Marcia Gamble Hadley, Designer

North Elevation

West Elevation

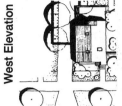

East Elevation

**South Elevation or
Pine St. Elevation**

If the front of a building faces north, then the proper notation is North Elevation, and likewise for any direction the various sides of the building may face (e.g., Southwest Elevation). An important site feature such as a major street or a body of water can be used in place of the direction.

Site plans show the orientation and the location of a building (below) or many buildings (above). They can be precise pictorial drawings as shown on this page or schematic drawings (see pp. 445, 454, and 455). They are commonly drawn at ⅟₁₆"=1'0" or at engineering scales such as 1"=20', 1"=40', or 1"=50'. The boundaries of the site, which should enclose all site elements as well as the building complex, must be clearly defined as shown below. Shadows help to reveal the building's height and its overall configuration (see pp. 379 and 392).

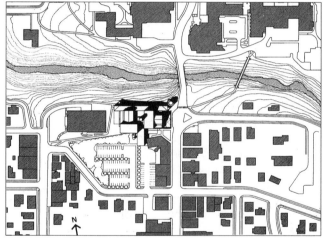

Drawing: Cornell University Center for the
Performing Arts, Ithaca, New York
Scale: 1"=50'0"
Courtesy of James Stirling Michael Wilford
and Associates, Architects

A **location plan** is a variation of the site plan that extends to include a broader, regional context. Important site features like transportation arteries, surrounding buildings, and the physical topography are commonly drawn. These environmental elements usually play a significant role in influencing the design of the proposed building.

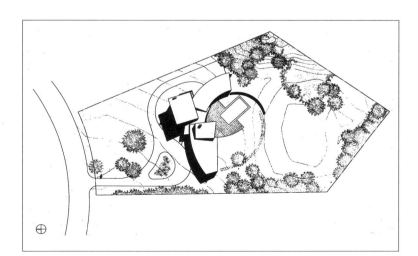

Drawing: Kreindel residence, Cresskill, New Jersey
Courtesy of Frank Lupo and Daniel Rowen, Architects

THE SITE PLAN

DESIGN SECTION: CUTS AND LIGHT STUDIES

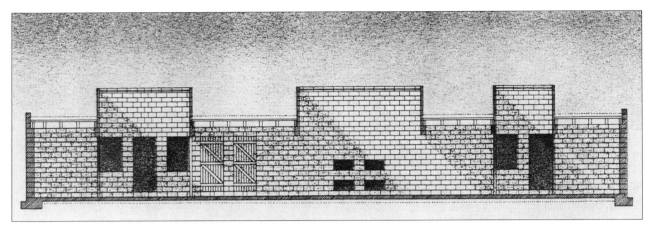

Drawing: Anti-Villa, Napa Valley, California
Medium: Airbrush
Courtesy of Batey & Mack, Architects

Section through hallway

A **building design section** must reveal design objectives as much as possible. To this end, slices are taken through important solids and voids. Light studies are frequently done to emphasize how directional sunlight comes through window or skylight openings. Human figures are also added to provide human scale to the drawing.

Sections are normally cut through (**1**) door and window openings, (**2**) circulation change of level elements (e.g., stairs and ramps), and (**3**) ceiling or roof openings such as skylights. Foundation elements may or may not be shown, depending on their significance in the overall design. Section cuts should never be made through columns.

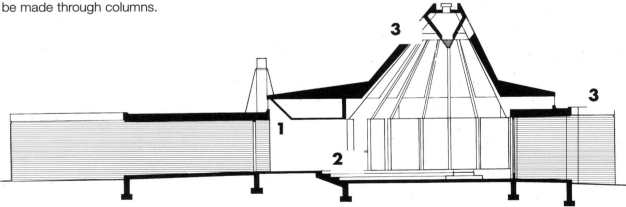

Drawing: Freeman residence, Grand Rapids, Michigan
30" × 20" (76.2 × 50.8 cm), Scale: ⅛"=1'0"
Medium: Ink on vellum
Courtesy of Gunnar Birkerts and Associates, Inc., Architects

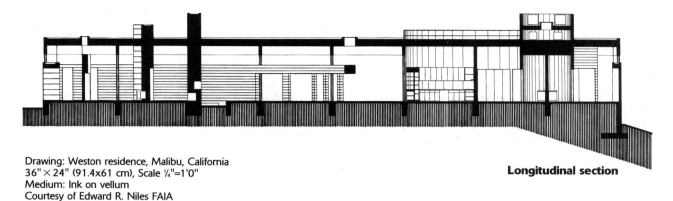

Drawing: Weston residence, Malibu, California
36" × 24" (91.4x61 cm), Scale ¼"=1'0"
Medium: Ink on vellum
Courtesy of Edward R. Niles FAIA

Longitudinal section

Lines within the longitudinal section showing the interior elevation (above) have slightly different line weight intensities to provide a greater sense of depth. Note the close spacing of vertical lines to indicate a cut ground section. Also note the unequal spacing of fine lines in the interior elevation to imply a curved surface (see p. 323).

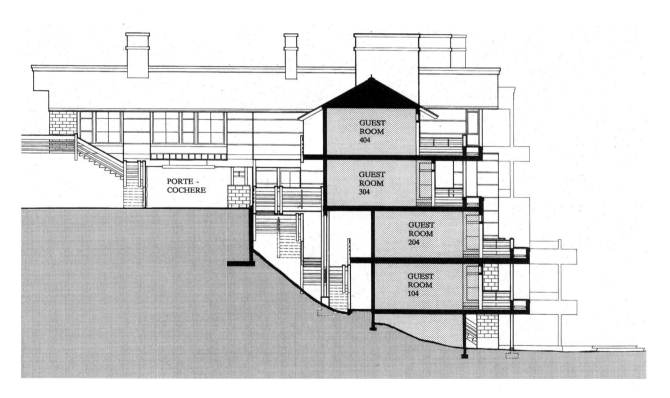

Drawing: The INN at Langley, Whidbey Island, Washington
Courtesy of GGLO Architecture and Interior Design

It is common to see a hierarchy of elevation lines in a design section. The elevation line weights diminish in intensity as the distance from the observer increases. This contrast in line weights is an excellent depth cue.

DESIGN SECTION: ELEVATION LINES BEYOND

SECTION/ELEVATION LABELING

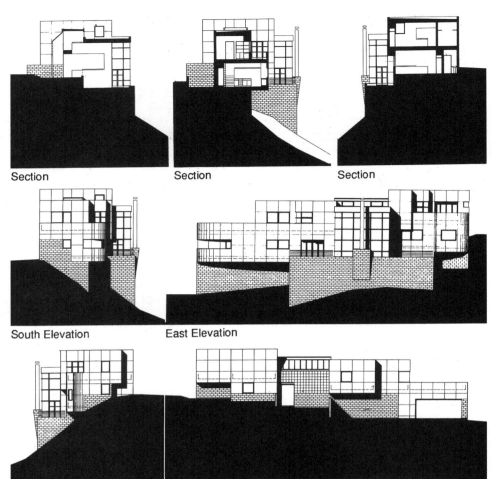

Section   Section   Section

South Elevation   East Elevation

North Elevation   West Elevation

Drawings: Naiditch residence
              Altadena, California
Scale: ⅜"=1'0"
Medium: Pen and ink on Mylar
Courtesy of Dean Nota Architect

In this compact presentation of sections and elevations, the sectional cut is toned solid black, which allows the viewer to see a clear relationship between the building design and the groundline. Drawings may be conveniently labeled and identified within or adjacent to this toned area.

Elevations are labeled based on the compass direction they are facing. In other words, the South Elevation means that the facade of the building is facing south (see p. 99).

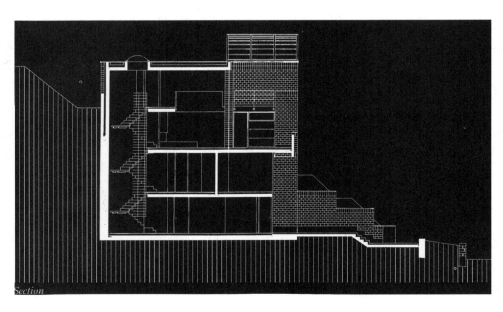

Section

Drawing: Single-family house, Daro, Bellinzona, Switzerland
Courtesy of Mario Botta, Architect, Lugano, Switzerland

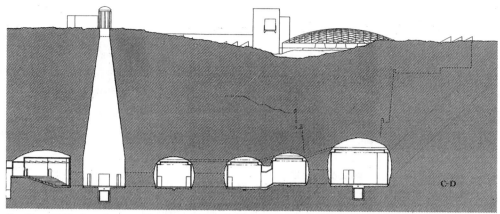

Section C-D showing auditorium, light shaft, and galleries

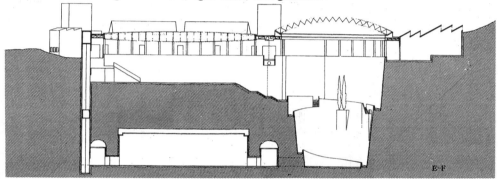

Section E-F showing "Sunk" and galleries

Drawings: The Guggenheim Museum, Salzburg. Salzburg, Austria
35.4" × 47.2" (90 × 120 cm), Scale: 1:50
Medium: Xerox print on paper
Courtesy of Hans Hollein, Architekt

The identifications of these sections are placed within the area of the section cut.

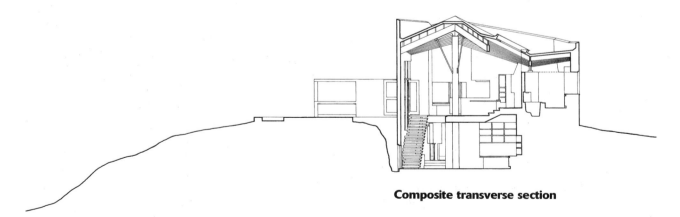

Composite transverse section

Drawing: Barnes House. Nanaimo, British Columbia, Canada
18" × 36" (45.7 × 91.4 cm), Scale: ¼"=1'0"
Medium: Ink on vellum
Courtesy of Patkau Architects

SECTION LABELING

COMPOSITE SECTIONS

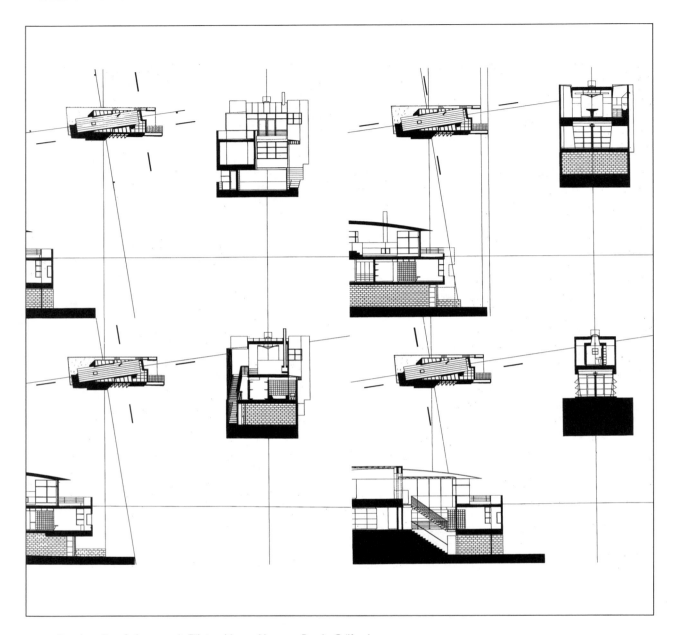

Drawings (two facing pages): Elliot residence, Hermosa Beach, California
Scale: ⅜"=1'0"
Medium: Pen and ink on Mylar
Courtesy of Dean Nota Architect

Webster's Dictionary defines *composite* as something comprising a number of distinct parts or elements (see composite drawings section in Chapter 11).

As shown above, the use of **composite sections** allows the viewer to examine a multitude of sections for a building. The cut sections are taken at selected intervals indicated in roof plan views. With the advent of computer-generated drawings, sectional cuts can be immediately examined at an infinite number of locations. This process is analogous to a CAT scan in medical technology.

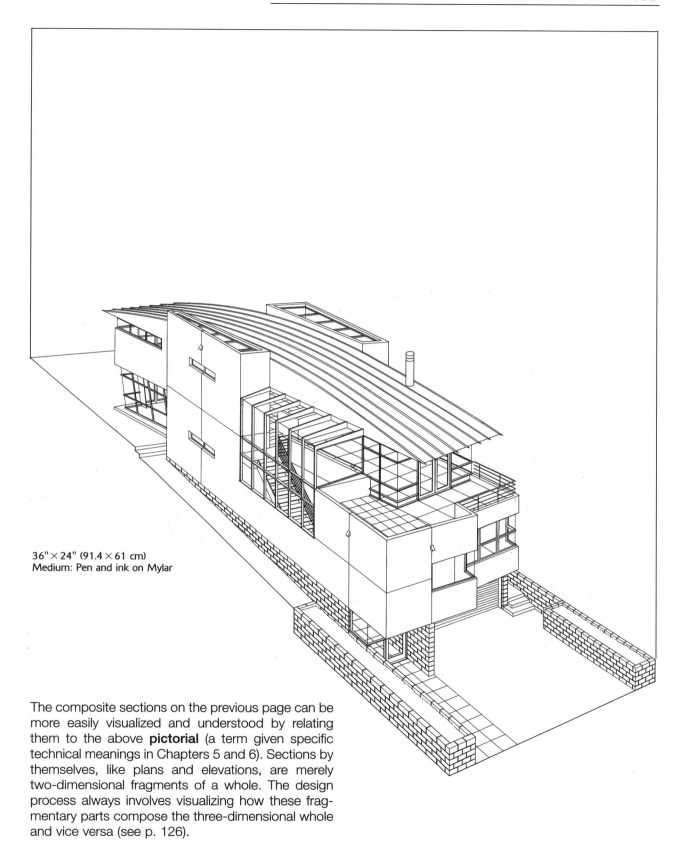

36" × 24" (91.4 × 61 cm)
Medium: Pen and ink on Mylar

PICTORIAL FOR COMPOSITE SECTIONS

The composite sections on the previous page can be more easily visualized and understood by relating them to the above **pictorial** (a term given specific technical meanings in Chapters 5 and 6). Sections by themselves, like plans and elevations, are merely two-dimensional fragments of a whole. The design process always involves visualizing how these fragmentary parts compose the three-dimensional whole and vice versa (see p. 126).

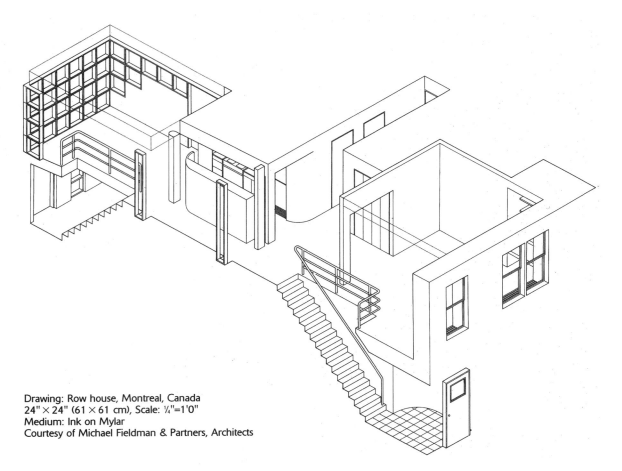

Drawing: Row house, Montreal, Canada
24" × 24" (61 × 61 cm), Scale: ¼"=1'0"
Medium: Ink on Mylar
Courtesy of Michael Fieldman & Partners, Architects

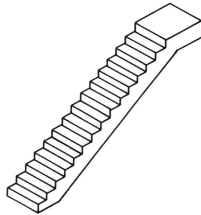

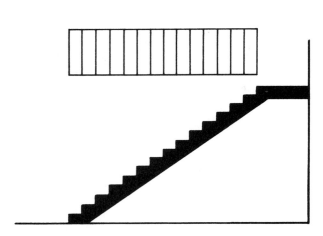

Straight run

A stair can be defined as either a single step with a tread (horizontal surface) and a riser (vertical piece or distance) or one of a series of steps providing access between two levels.

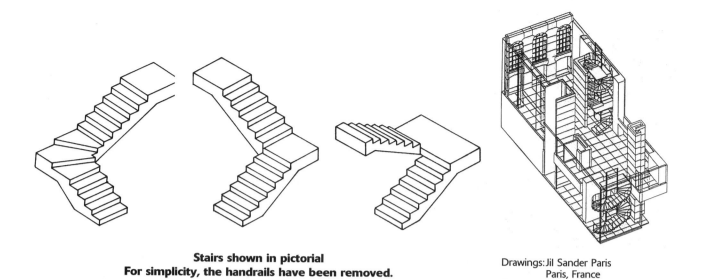

Stairs shown in pictorial
For simplicity, the handrails have been removed.

Drawings: Jil Sander Paris
Paris, France
Courtesy of Gabellini Associates

STAIRWAYS

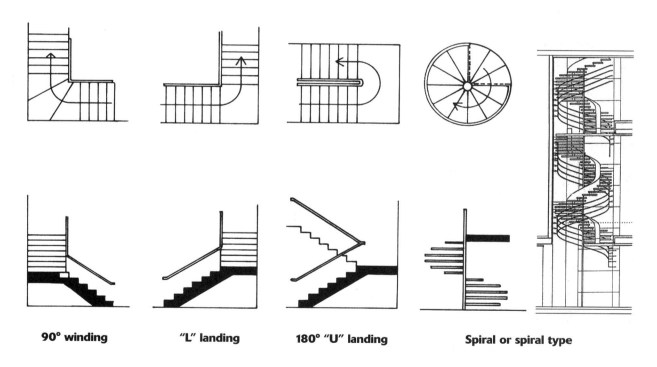

90° winding   **"L" landing**   **180° "U" landing**   **Spiral or spiral type**

Stairways are the sequences of steps that connect two or more floors in a building. The four examples above are typical stairway situations seen in plan and in section. Straight stairs are also common. In a floor plan, the up or down direction arrow is from the level of the floor plan.

WINDOWS

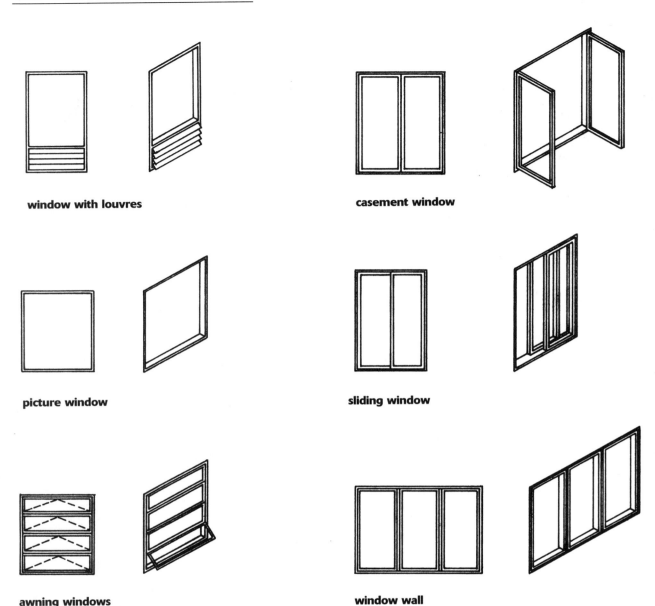

window with louvres

casement window

picture window

sliding window

awning windows

window wall

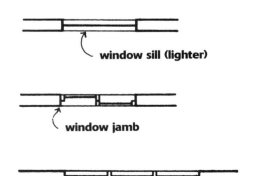

window sill (lighter)

window jamb

Six standard window types and five standard door types are shown in elevation and in pictorial on pp. 108 and 109. A plan window is the result of a horizontal cut through the window glass, its frame (jamb), and the wall on both sides.

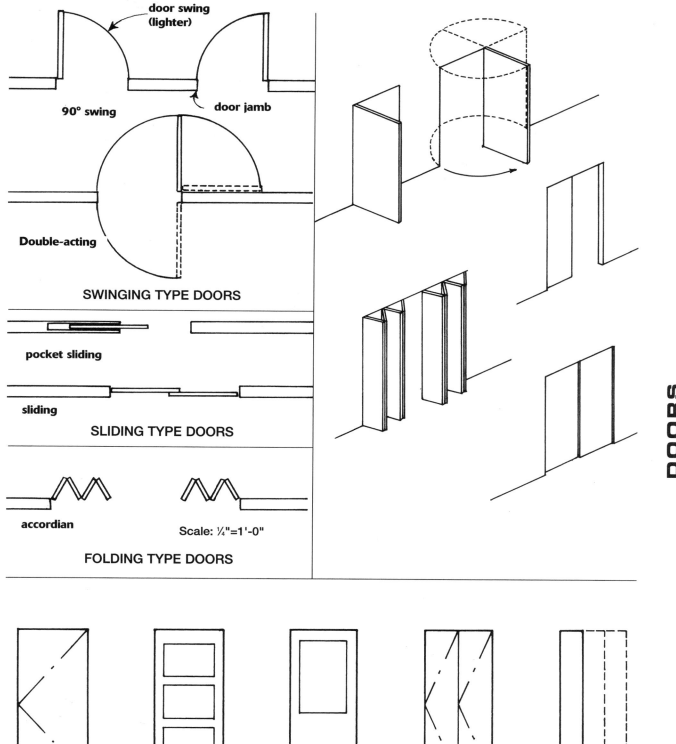

door swing (lighter)

90° swing

door jamb

Double-acting

SWINGING TYPE DOORS

pocket sliding

sliding

SLIDING TYPE DOORS

accordian

Scale: ¼"=1'-0"

FOLDING TYPE DOORS

DOORS

hinged   **panel**   **sash**   **bi-folding**   **sliding (pocket)**

STANDARD DOOR TYPES

5

Orthographic and Paraline Drawing

It is important that the student of environmental design develop the ability to visualize and graphically express forms and spaces in three dimensions. The design-drawing process begins with two-dimensional expressions in the form of orthographic sketches and drawings. These multiview drawings are the plan, elevation, and section vocabulary that an architect/designer uses. Also part of the process are the closely related three-dimensional single-view drawings termed paralines and perspectives. Single-view drawings depict volumetric forms by combining the parameters of length, width, and depth.

The intent of this chapter is to develop your ability to visualize and communicate form and space by relating orthographic drawings to three-dimensional paraline drawings such as axonometrics and obliques.

In summary, following are some of the important terms and concepts you will learn:

Orthographic drawings	Axonometric drawings	Plan oblique drawings
Paraline drawings	Isometric drawings	Elevation oblique drawings
Auxiliary views	Up views	Down views
Exploded views	Expanded views	Multioblique combinations

Orthographic and Paraline Drawing

TOPIC: ORTHOGRAPHICS

Ching 1990, 146–153.

Ching 2003, 24–28.

Cooper 1992, 125–132.

Forseth 1980, 21–75.

Wallschlaeger and Busic-Snyder 1992, 60–61.

TOPIC: PARALINES (AXONOMETRICS AND OBLIQUES)

Ching 2003, 28–30.

Ching 1985, 46–53.

Cooper 1992, 139–145.

Forseth 1980, 77–97.

Pérez-Gomez and Pelletier 1997, 266–280.

Wallschlaeger and Busic-Snyder 1992, 62–65.

PARALINES (THE AXONOMETRIC CALLED ISOMETRIC)

Numerous computer games offer an opportunity to play with isometric views with and without cast shadows. The following are good examples:

Without shadows: *The Sims House Party,* Electronic Arts Inc., EA GAMES.
With shadows: *Age of Empires,* Microsoft Ensemble Studios.

Chapter Overview

After studying this chapter and doing the related exercises in the book's final section, you will understand how to construct orthographic views, axonometric drawings, and oblique drawings. For continued study of the principles discussed in this chapter, refer to Uddin's *Axonometric and Oblique Drawing.*

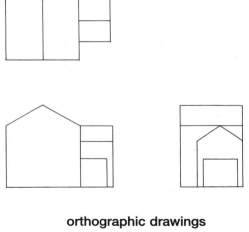

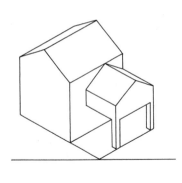

isometric

orthographic drawings

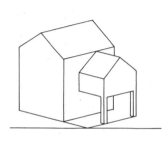

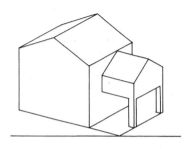

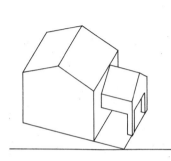

paraline axonometrics

INTRODUCTION

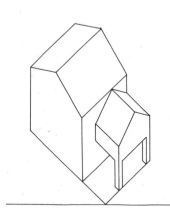

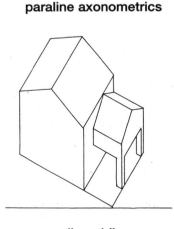

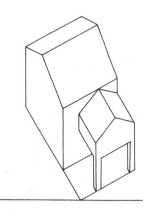

paraline obliques

Plans, elevations, and sections are **orthographic (multiview)** drawings (two dimensional). In **paraline (single-view)** drawings, sets of lines are infinitely parallel to each other, giving a three-dimensional character to the pictorial. The proper preparation for the study of **orthographic–paraline drawings** consists of a proven proficiency in handling drafting tools, lettering, and line quality. This, coupled with a brief introduction to drawing conventions, provides the essential background for a survey of these types of pictorial drawings. The family of **axonometrics** (includes **isometric**) drawings and the family of **oblique** drawings can be classified under the general term of **paraline drawings.** Paraline axonometrics are also termed **dimetrics** and **trimetrics.**

Any building form is composed of the basic elements of points, lines, and planes. We sometimes grasp intuitively why a shape appears the way it does. However, it is only through an understanding of how these geometric elements interact in orthographic projection that we can fully grasp what we see. The study of this interaction is called **descriptive geometry.**

In elevation, the building form displays true-length vertical lines (**1**), which can appear as either a point or a true-length line in the adjacent views. Likewise, true-length horizontal lines (**2**) also appear as either a true-length line or a point in adjacent views. True-length inclined lines (**3**) appear foreshortened in the adjacent views.

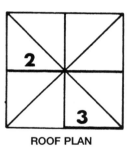

ROOF PLAN

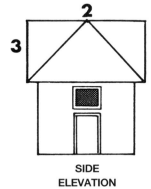

FRONT
ELEVATION

SIDE
ELEVATION

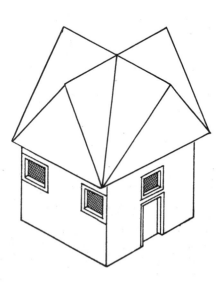

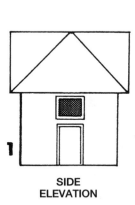

FRONT
ELEVATION

SIDE
ELEVATION

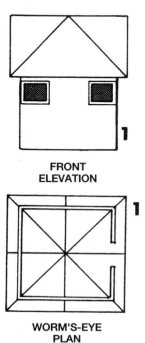

WORM'S-EYE
PLAN

In the drawing at bottom right, note that the edge view contains a true-length line (outer soffit line), which appears as a point. Edge views of a plane show the plane as true shape in the adjacent view. The concepts of a point view from a true-length line, edge view (true-length as a point), and true shape (true size) become readily apparent as one visualizes the roof structure of this house. Correlate the orthographic views with the pictorial (true shape is the toned area).

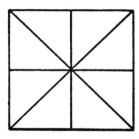

ROOF PLAN
(with four edge views)

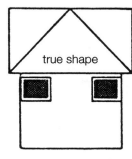

true shape

FRONT ELEVATION

SIDE ELEVATION

see edge view

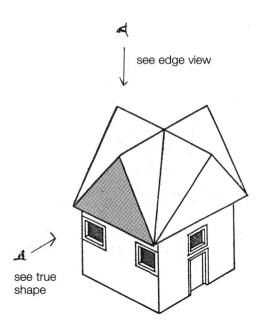

see true shape

edge view (true-length as a point)

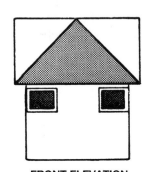

FRONT ELEVATION

SIDE ELEVATION

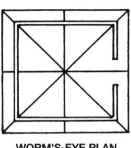

WORM'S-EYE PLAN

POINT VIEW/EDGE VIEW/TRUE SHAPE

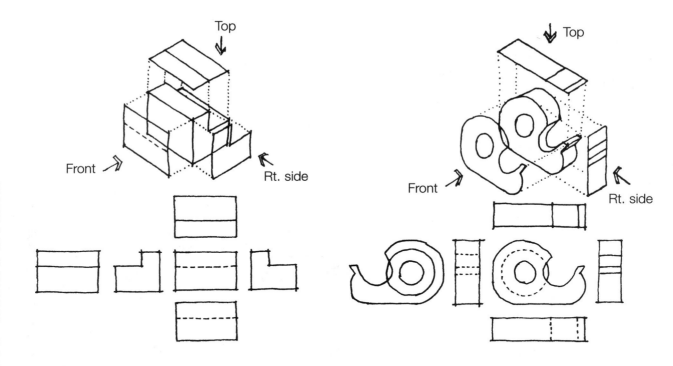

SIX VIEWS/VISUALIZATION SKETCHES

As we have seen in Chapter 4, architects and designers represent a three-dimensional building by utilizing "right-angle," or orthographic, views. The many orthographic images allow us to comprehend the totality of a design. These images are reproduced through a process of **visualization** and the consequent sketching of the visualized shape. This freehand graphic process begins with the sketching of a three-dimensional pictorial image, the pulling of the two-dimensional orthographic images away from the various surfaces of the object (or building) in question, and the transfer of these images to a two-dimensional orthographic drawing.

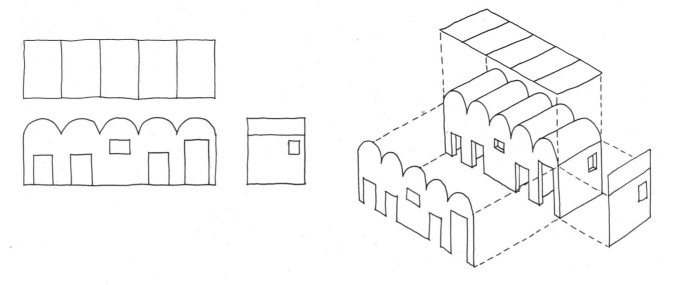

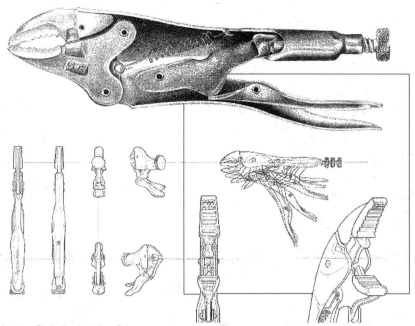

Drawing: Student project by Chris Ernst—Vise Grip
Medium: Pencil
Courtesy of the University of Texas at Austin
School of Architecture

Being confident and competent in this visualization sketching process requires a lot of practice. The mental visualization process can begin with objects that you can hold in your hand and rotate. An orthographic image by itself cannot be descriptive enough to give us clues as to the spatial composition of the three-dimensional form; but when many orthographic views are related to each other, they become a powerful tool in describing and deciphering the object in question.

Before you can develop the skill of visualizing objects that exist only in the imagination, you must hone your skills in visualizing real objects from several different directions.

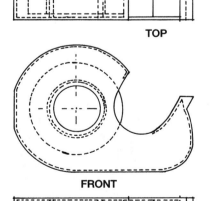

TOP

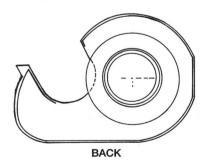

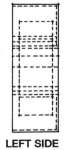

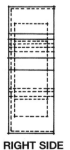

BACK   LEFT SIDE   FRONT   RIGHT SIDE

BOTTOM

Drawing: Student project by Jacquelyn Mujica—Tape dispenser
11" × 8.5" (27.9 × 21.6 cm), Scale ¾"=1"
Medium: Pencil
Courtesy of the City College of San Francisco
Department of Architecture

SIX VIEWS/VISUALIZATION SKETCHES

VISUALIZATION SKETCHES

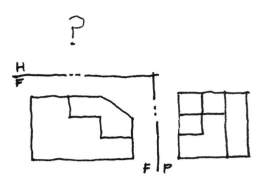

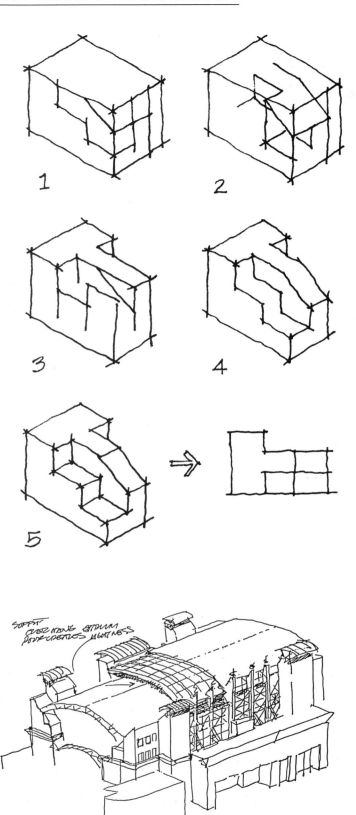

Design professionals often use paraline sketches as well as other types of sketches to help them visualize their designs. Refer to Chapter 3 in order to understand how conceptual sketching is used as a communications tool. The best way to develop your **visualization** skills is to practice seeing the relationship between orthographic and paraline drawings.

This example shows a missing horizontal (top) view. To resolve the missing view, sketch the front and profile planes as shown in sketch **1**. Project related points toward the interior of the rectilinear box. Start with the basic or rough forms as shown in sketch **2**. Proceed with more detailed parts of the object as shown in sketches **3**, **4**, and **5**.

The ability to develop **rough freehand sketches** in the orthographic-paraline conversion process will enhance visualization. When an impasse is reached in the resolution of the problem, it is much better to be "loose" than "stiff"; this helps to avoid communicative inhibitions in the design-drawing process that may develop later on.

Sketch: The redevelopment of Charing Cross Station
London, England
Medium: Black ink line with colored pencil
Courtesy of Terry Farrell & Partners

Honing your skills in the visualization of simple block forms will enhance your ability to understand the building forms shown in the latter part of this chapter.

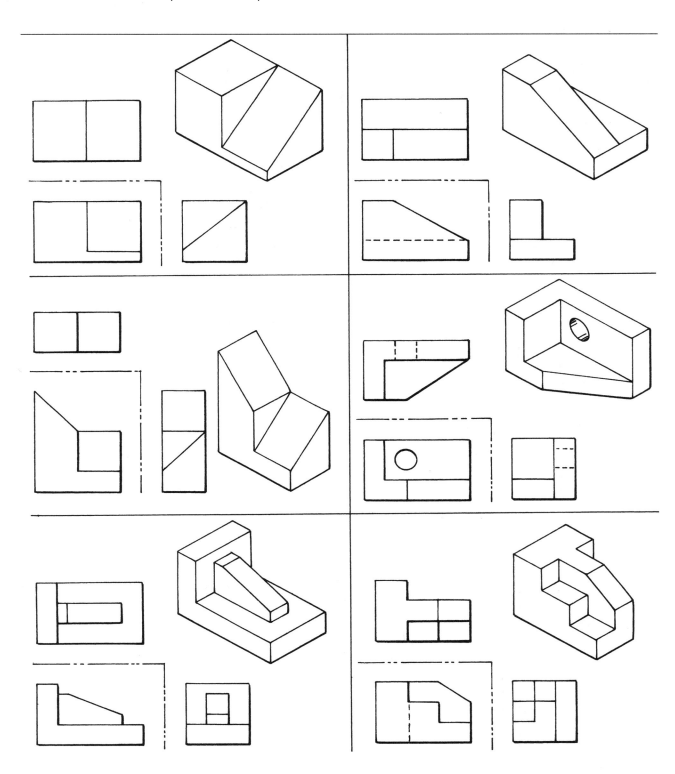

BLOCK VISUALIZATION

BLOCK VISUALIZATION

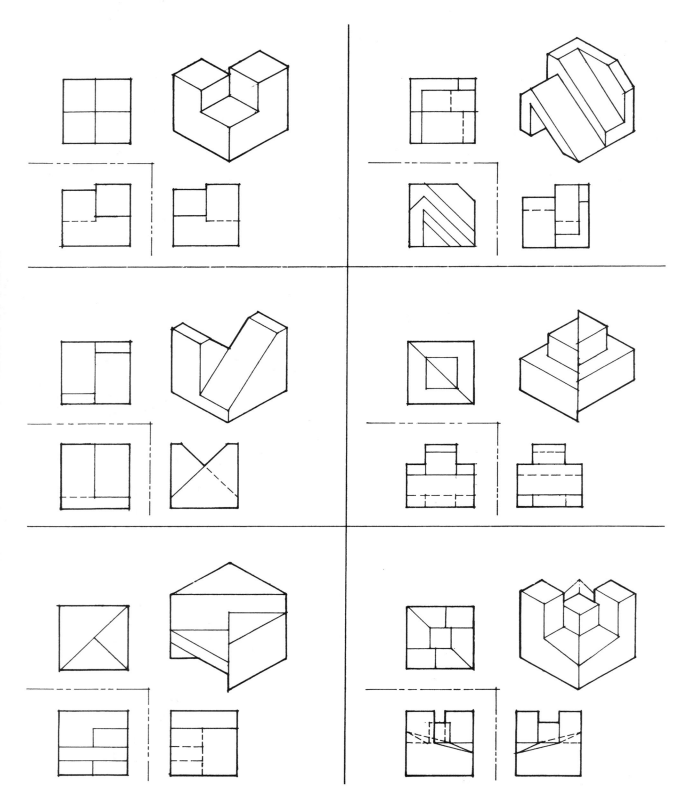

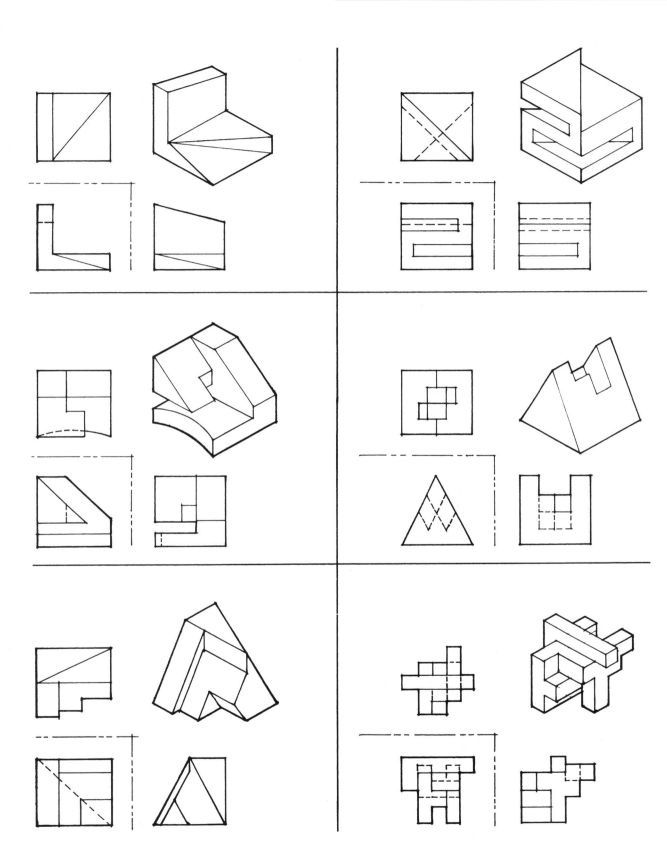

BLOCK VISUALIZATION

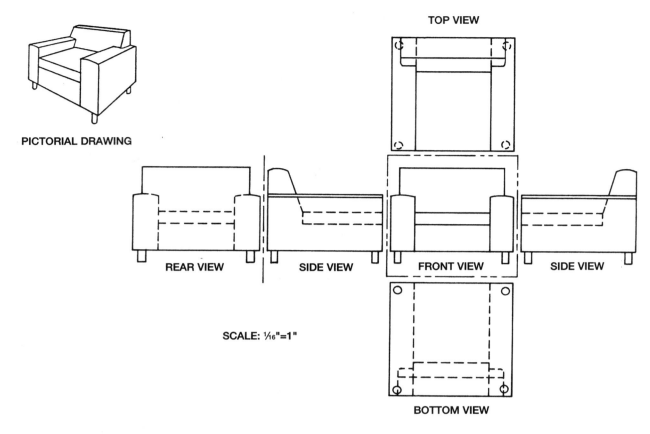

PICTORIAL DRAWING

TOP VIEW

REAR VIEW   SIDE VIEW   FRONT VIEW   SIDE VIEW

SCALE: 1/16"=1"

BOTTOM VIEW

ORTHOGRAPHIC DRAWINGS

SIX VIEW DRAWINGS

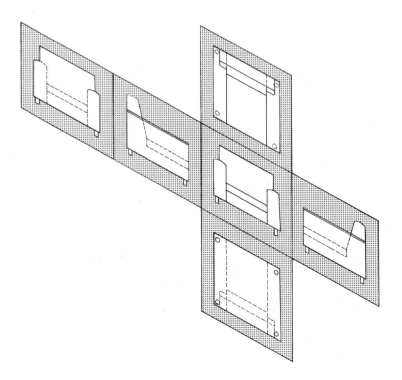

Pictorial and orthographic drawings:
Student project by Ellen Lew
Medium: Pencil on vellum
Courtesy of the City College of San Francisco
Department of Architecture

After drawing handheld-size objects, examine larger objects like furniture and small buildings and draw them with six or fewer views as needed. The drawing at left shows six views of a chair projected on the surfaces (picture planes) of an opened glass box. In orthographic projection we use a folding plane line to help understand how the six views are positioned in relation to each other. Henceforth, this line will not be shown between views because in actual architectural practice the line is not drawn.

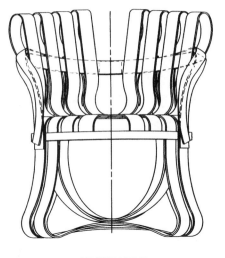

FRONT VIEW

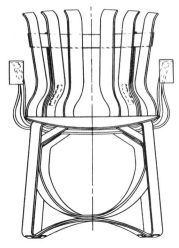

FRONT VIEW

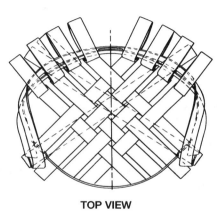

TOP VIEW

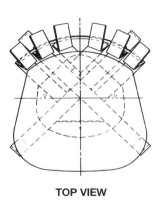

TOP VIEW

Drawings: The Frank Gehry Bentwood Collection
Crosscheck armchair (above)
28" × 33.5" (72.4 × 85.1 cm), Scale: 1"=1'0"
Hat trick armchair (right)
23.4" × 33.5" (59.4 × 85.1 cm), Scale: 1"=1'0"
Medium: Ink on paper
Courtesy of Knoll

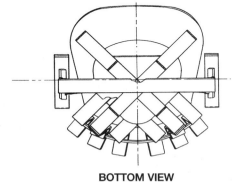

BOTTOM VIEW

With just a front view and a top view, you can visualize the shape of most chairs and other pieces of furniture. With small objects like chairs, two or three views (top, front, and side) are adequate. With buildings, it is normal to use four or more views (see p. 127).

ORTHOGRAPHIC VIEWS

PROJECTION SYSTEMS COMPARED

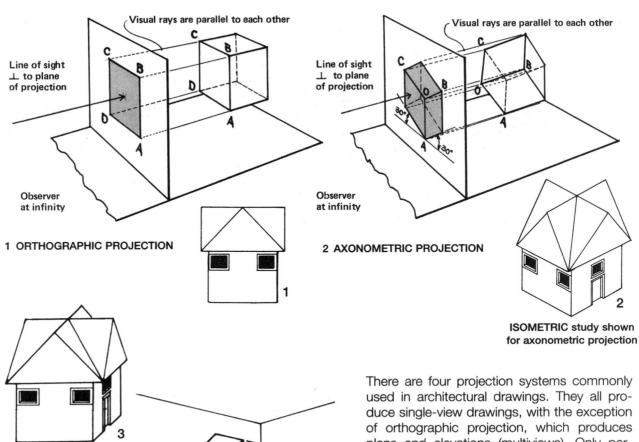

Visual rays are parallel to each other

Line of sight ⊥ to plane of projection

Observer at infinity

1 ORTHOGRAPHIC PROJECTION

Visual rays are parallel to each other

Line of sight ⊥ to plane of projection

Observer at infinity

2 AXONOMETRIC PROJECTION

ISOMETRIC study shown for axonometric projection

3 OBLIQUE PROJECTION

There are four projection systems commonly used in architectural drawings. They all produce single-view drawings, with the exception of orthographic projection, which produces plans and elevations (multiviews). Only perspective projection is characterized by nonparallel lines. All projection systems have four elements: an object, a picture plane, a viewer, and projected visual rays. **Visual rays** are the projection lines from the observer's eyes to various points on the viewed object or scene. For convenience and time savings, slightly foreshortened axonometric projection lengths are drawn true-length in an axonometric drawing. Note that the perpendicular symbol is ⊥.

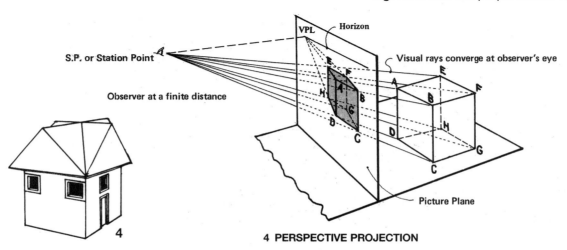

VPL — Horizon

S.P. or Station Point

Visual rays converge at observer's eye

Observer at a finite distance

Picture Plane

4 PERSPECTIVE PROJECTION

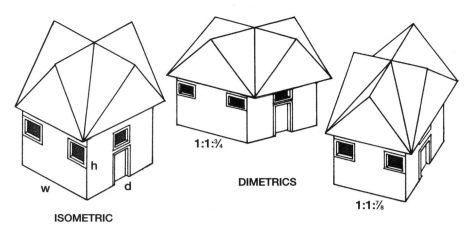

ISOMETRIC

DIMETRICS

Isometric—All three primary axes are set at the same scale: 1:1:1.*

Dimetric—Any two of the three primary axes are set at the same scale.

Trimetric—All three primary axes are set at different scales. Seldom used in professional practice.

*Scale ratios for the width (w), depth (d), and height (h) of the building.

Paraline axonometrics (from Greek) or **axiometrics** (from English) exhibit projectors that are **perpendicular** to the picture plane and **parallel** to each other. They exhibit a vertical front edge and nonconverging side planes.

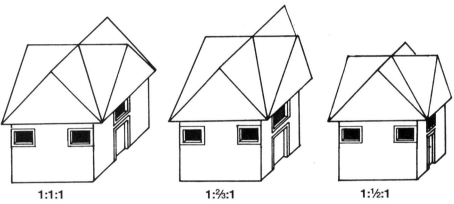

These are **elevation obliques**. In an elevation oblique, one elevation is parallel to the picture plane and seen in true size and true shape. Often the receding planes seem too elongated in their true-length. In practice they are usually shortened by as much as one-third to one-half to give visual comfort.

Paraline obliques (here in the form of elevation obliques) exhibit projectors that are **oblique** to the picture plane and **parallel.** They exhibit a flat, true-size frontal shape and nonconverging side planes. Historically, they derive from drawings of ancient European fortifications.

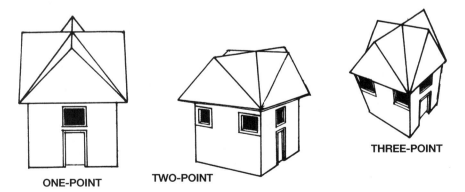

ONE-POINT   **TWO-POINT**   **THREE-POINT**

Perspectives, which will be covered in detail in a following chapter, are single-view drawings that approach a person's optical perception. For two-point and three-point perspectives, the various surfaces are at a variety of angles to the picture plane, whereas one surface is parallel to the picture plane for a one-point perspective.

Perspectives exhibit projections that are at a variety of angles to the picture plane and they display the characteristics of **point convergence.** They show converging side planes. Historically, they derive from drawings of the European Renaissance.

DRAWING TYPES COMPARED

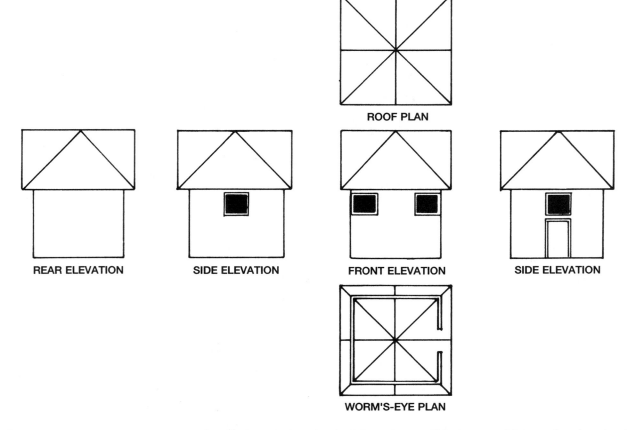

ROOF PLAN

REAR ELEVATION   **SIDE ELEVATION**   **FRONT ELEVATION**   **SIDE ELEVATION**

WORM'S-EYE PLAN

The drawing above shows six orthographic views of a building shape. This is a **multiview** drawing. In the design process, two-dimensional multiviews help us envision and communicate what the composite three-dimensional form will look like. And similarly, knowing the three-dimensional pictorial (see below) makes it easier to visualize how the multiviews will lay out and relate to each other.

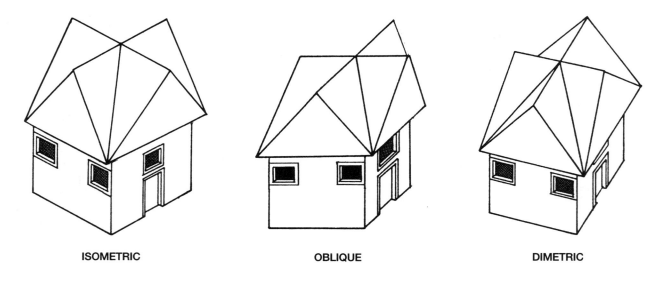

ISOMETRIC   **OBLIQUE**   **DIMETRIC**

Isometric, oblique, and dimetric are three types of **single-view paraline** drawings. A **dimetric** drawing, unlike an isometric drawing, has the flexibility of being able to emphasize one or two of its primary planes. Unusual paralines are the **transparaline** drawings (see pp. 512, 516, and 517). Seen at the bottom on the facing page is a fourth type of single-view drawing identified as a perspective.

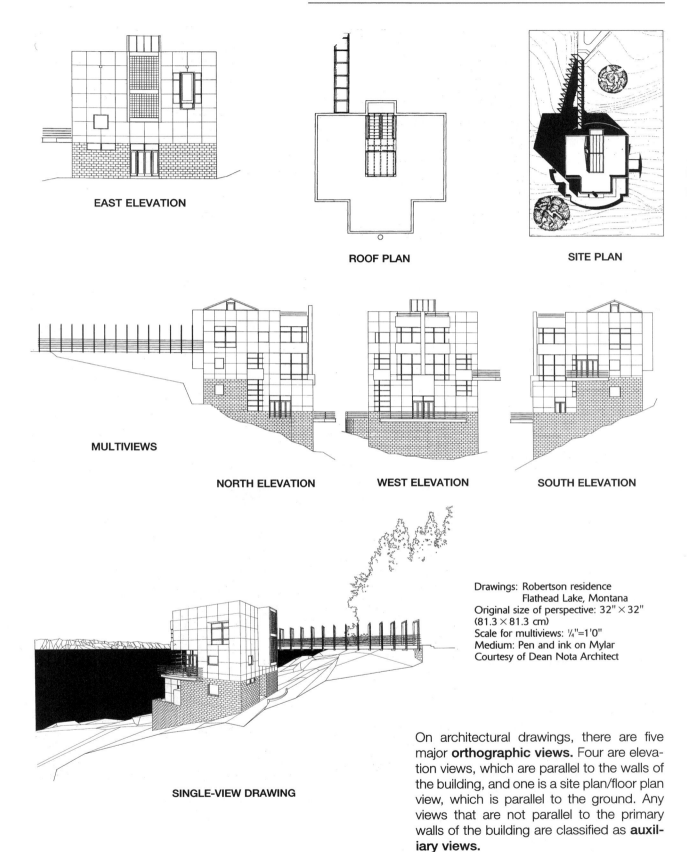

EAST ELEVATION

ROOF PLAN

SITE PLAN

MULTIVIEWS

NORTH ELEVATION

WEST ELEVATION

SOUTH ELEVATION

SINGLE-VIEW DRAWING

Drawings: Robertson residence
Flathead Lake, Montana
Original size of perspective: 32" × 32"
(81.3 × 81.3 cm)
Scale for multiviews: ¼"=1'0"
Medium: Pen and ink on Mylar
Courtesy of Dean Nota Architect

On architectural drawings, there are five major **orthographic views.** Four are elevation views, which are parallel to the walls of the building, and one is a site plan/floor plan view, which is parallel to the ground. Any views that are not parallel to the primary walls of the building are classified as **auxiliary views.**

MULTIVIEW AND SINGLE-VIEW DRAWINGS

CONSTRUCTING ISOMETRIC DRAWINGS

Isometric, when literally translated, means "has equality of measurement." True-lengths parallel to any of the orthographic axes will be the **same** as in the isometric drawing. An isometric projection is not composed of true angles, whereas a plan oblique projection (see p. 133) does have a true angle. A bird's-eye view gives the illusion of parallel lines when in reality the lines are converging.

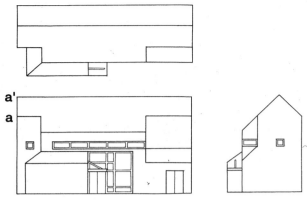

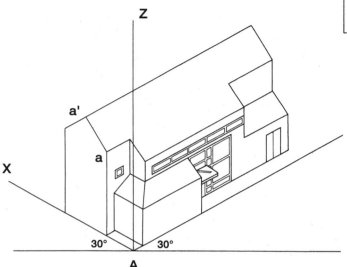

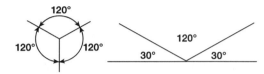

The three axes when projected on the picture plane are always 120° apart. Conventionally and for simplicity, the two non-vertical axes are constructed 30° to a horizontally drawn line.

The **isometric** drawing is one of the most important types of **axonometric drawings.** Principles for its construction are as follows:

- The axes (**AX** and **AY**) on the ground plane are always drawn 30° from the horizontal.
- Measure all orthographic distances along the three axes **AX, AY,** and **AZ,** and only along these axes.
- Any lines that are not along the isometric axes (inclined or nonaxial lines) should be located by locating the end points of the line (see **a'-a** above). These lengths will not be the same in the isometric view and the orthographic views.
- Parallel lines in an orthographic drawing remain parallel in the corresponding isometric drawing.
- Vertical lines in an orthographic drawing remain vertical in an isometric drawing.
- Hidden lines are normally not drawn in an isometric, but they can be used to help visualization.
- Corner points may be labeled in each orthographic view and in the isometric view to help visualize the isometric drawing.
- One disadvantage of the isometric is that it cannot use the orthographic view in the actual orthographic (plan/elevation) layout.

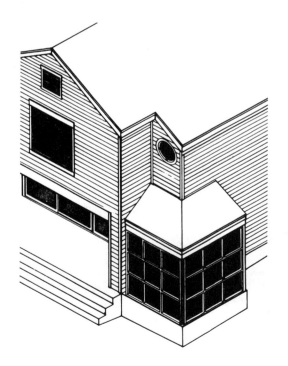

Drawing: Partial isometric
Sprague Lakehouse
Lake Cypress Springs, Texas
24" × 36" (61 × 91.4 cm), Scale: ¼"=1'0"
Medium: Ink on vellum
Courtesy of Todd Hamilton, Architect

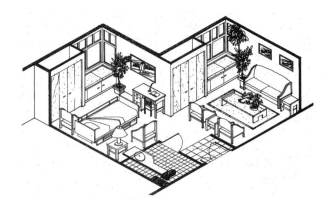

Drawing: Glacier Hills Retirement Health Center,
            Ann Arbor, Michigan
Orig. size: Approx. 20" × 30" (50.8 × 76.2 cm)
Medium: Ink on Mylar
Courtesy of Ellerbe–Becket, Inc.,
designed by Dale Tremain, AIA

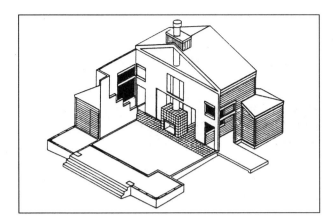

Drawing: Sprague Lakehouse
            Lake Cypress Springs, Texas
24" × 36" (61 × 91.4 cm), Scale ¼"=1'0"
Medium: Ink on vellum
Courtesy of Todd Hamilton, Architect

An **isometric drawing** shows a more mechanistic type of perception. Perspective drawing, which will be studied in a later chapter, is much closer to natural human perception. Nevertheless, isometrics are used because seeing three nonconverging faces of an object is still quite convincing in understanding its form. The observer is limited to viewing only bird's-eye views (above 30') in an isometric. Due to its low angle of view, an isometric drawing does not permit the viewer to see interior spaces unless the roof and side walls are removed. The examples above have all three of these elements absent and also show a partial isometric plan. The examples below show two other ways to reveal the interior configuration. The lower right drawing uses a cutaway partition as well as an isometric section. The lower left drawing requires a transparent isometric (see p. xi).

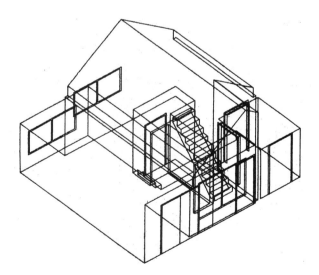

Drawing: Student project by Haden Smith
            Graduate Student Housing
10" × 8" (25.4 × 20.3 cm), Scale: ¼"=1'0"
Medium: CAD
Courtesy of Washington University
School of Architecture, St. Louis, Missouri

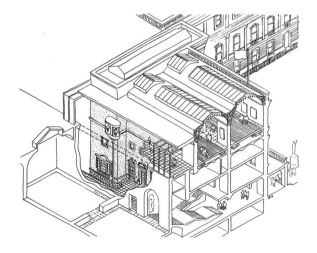

Drawing: Sackler Galleries, Royal Academy, London, England
Medium: Pencil on trace 16.5" × 11.7" (418 × 291 mm)
Courtesy of Foster Associates, Architects and Engineers
Drawn by Lord Foster of Thames Bank

ISOMETRIC DRAWINGS—INTERIOR APPLICATIONS

CONSTRUCTING ISOMETRIC CIRCLES

In paraline drawings all circles appear as ellipses except when they appear in planes parallel to the picture plane (true circles). The four-center ellipse procedure below is the most precise method for approximating true ellipses. See procedures to construct other elliptical forms on pages 282–283.

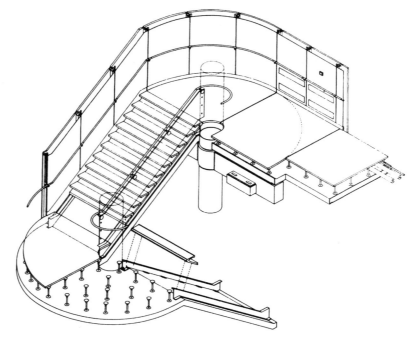

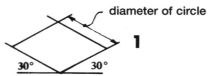

1

diameter of circle

2

midpoints

Drawing: Staircase isometric, Lloyd's of London
London, England
33" × 45.5" (83.8 × 115.6 cm)
Medium: Rottering pen on tracing
Courtesy of the Richard Rogers Partnership, Architects

3

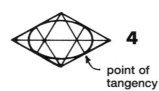

4

point of tangency

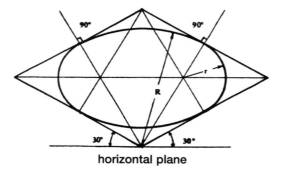

horizontal plane

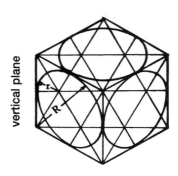

vertical plane

Procedure for the Four-Center Ellipse

1. Draw an isometric square using the desired circle's diameter.
2. Find adjacent side midpoints. Large radius *R* has two centers at the closest corners of the parallelogram. The intersections of the perpendiculars to both opposite sides determines the terminal points of the arc.
3. Construct the arcs.
4. Small radius *r* has two centers at the intersections of the perpendiculars within the parallelogram. These small arcs meet the large arcs to complete the ellipse.

The entire construction can be made with a T-square and 30° × 60° triangle. The same procedure applies for circles in both vertical planes and horizontal planes.

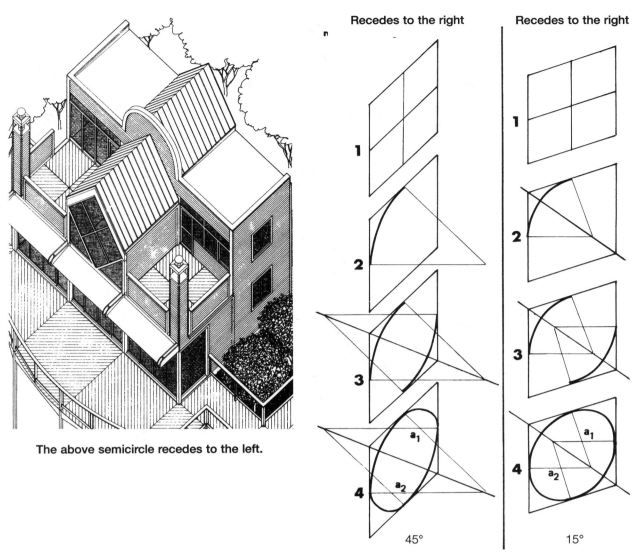

Recedes to the right   **Recedes to the right**

1

2

3

4

45°   15°

The above semicircle recedes to the left.

Drawing: Compact House, Bayview, Lake Pend
                  O'Reille, Idaho
18" × 24" (45.7 × 61 cm), Scale: ¼=1'0"
Medium: Ink on vellum
Courtesy of David A. Harris, DHT² Architects & Planners
Reprinted from *New Compact House Designs*, edited by Don Metz,
with permission of Storey Communications/Garden Way Publishing,
Pownal, Vermont.

CONSTRUCTING PARALINE CIRCLES

The four-center ellipse method shown on the previous page applies for non-30°–30° axonometric circles in left and right receding vertical planes only. Note that in the horizontal plane, circles are seen in true shape.

1. Draw a paraline square.
2. Find adjacent side midpoints and construct intersecting perpendiculars. The intersection becomes an arc-center.
3. Repeat the process for a symmetrical mirror image arc on the opposite side.
4. Using points a_1 and a_2, complete smaller arcs to accomplish the total axonometric circle.

COMPARING AXONOMETRICS AND OBLIQUES

AXONOMETRICS

PLAN OBLIQUES

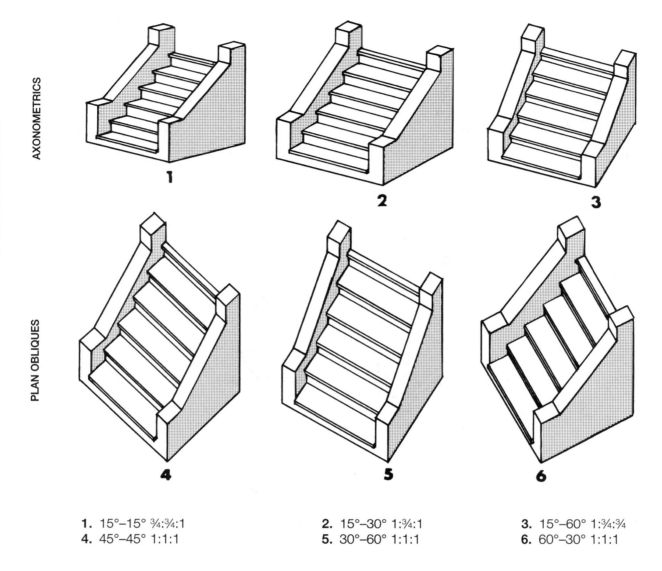

1. 15°–15° ¾:¾:1
4. 45°–45° 1:1:1

2. 15°–30° 1:¾:1
5. 30°–60° 1:1:1

3. 15°–60° 1:¾:¾
6. 60°–30° 1:1:1

Paraline **axonometrics** (axis measure) and paraline **plan obliques** allow for a great variety of choices in deciding which viewpoints are best relative to the type of object being depicted. The six alternatives shown are some of the more common angle and axes scale combinations that are used. In the oblique views of the staircase, all horizontal surfaces, such as the tread (horizontal part of the step) areas, are shown in their **true shape** and **true size** (actual plan dimensions). A small percentage of the actual riser (vertical part of the step) area is visible in the oblique situations. In contrast, note that in all of the axonometric views, the percentage of actual tread area is less and more riser area becomes visible. You must first decide what is most important to show or emphasize before selecting the desired angle and axes scale combinations. This decision process will become more apparent as you study the various examples shown toward the end of this chapter. Note that through many years of professional usage it has become popular to classify "plan obliques" as "axonometrics." Loosely defined, the terms are **interchangeable,** even though they are technically two separate terms with distinct definitions.

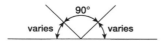

Plan obliques are quite flexible in the sense that the axes angles can have any angular combination that you desire whereas an axonometric like an isometric (30°–30°) has fixed angles (see page 128).

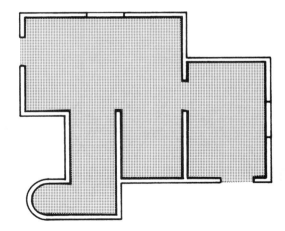

The **plan** view is essential for drawing both **isometric** and **plan oblique** drawings for interior spaces. In professional practice, the plan is always available at common scales such as ¼"=1'0". This same scale would be used for plan obliques. The plan becomes a three-dimensional drawing when the vertical dimension is added. When drawn manually, the easy and quick transfer of the plan view dictates its preferable use for interiors.

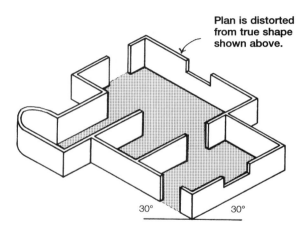

Plan is distorted from true shape shown above.

30° 30°

In a 30°–30° isometric, the interior partitions conceal large parts of the rooms, making it difficult to see the interior furniture, plants, people, etc. **Isometrics** are more commonly used for building **exteriors**, whereas **interiors** are best displayed with **plan obliques,** as shown below. An exception for the use of interior isometric drawings is the use of transparent partitions (see p. 129). Note also that the walls are more visible in the isometric than in the 45°–45° drawing below. In plan obliques, the cut is usually taken in the range of ½ to ⅞ of the full floor-to-ceiling height.

Axes angles such as 45°–45° (see example at right), 60°–30°, and 75°–15° allow the observer to obtain a **higher** vantage point than the 30°–30° isometric. The partitions conceal less of the rooms in the 45° axes and the plan becomes a **true shape.** These drawings can be termed **true-shape plan obliques**; they are simply a variation of the general oblique. As a drawing type, plan obliques give the best simultaneous representation of plan and elevation. They also give an excellent analytical view of the spatial organization of the plan. All paralines are excellent tools for verifying three-dimensional relationships.

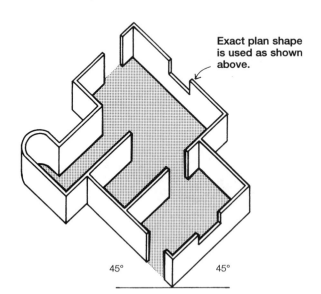

Exact plan shape is used as shown above.

45° 45°

ISOMETRIC AND PLAN OBLIQUE DRAWINGS

PLAN OBLIQUE MEASUREMENTS

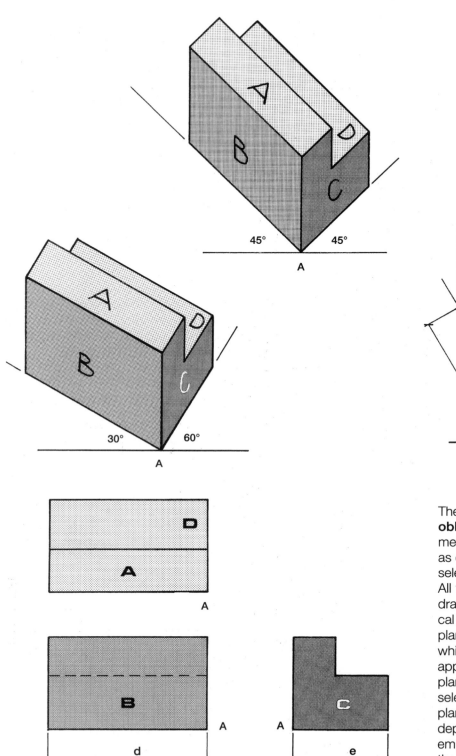

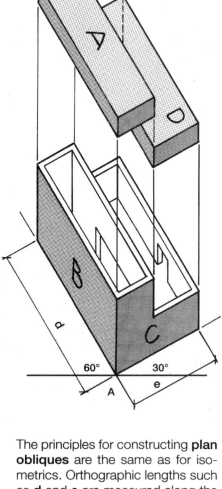

The principles for constructing **plan obliques** are the same as for isometrics. Orthographic lengths such as **d** and **e** are measured along the selected plan oblique axes angles. All vertical lines in the orthographic drawings (elevations) remain vertical and parallel to the Z-axis in the plan oblique. The vertical scale, which can be foreshortened if it appears too elongated, and the plan scale are kept the same. The selection of a set of appropriate plan oblique or axonometric angles depends on how the object will be emphasized. At appropriate angles these drawings become a powerful tool for showing the scale, mass, and bulk of a design.

With a multitude of vertical and horizontal elements, it is most efficient to construct each element separately. No matter how complex the building, follow the basic principle of projecting the plan configuration upward to the exact elevation heights. This will result in a volumetric solid based on the plan view.

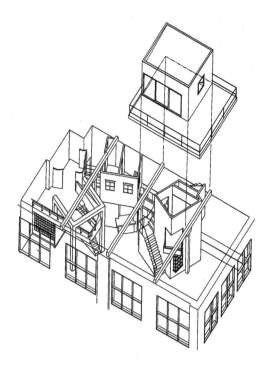

Drawing: Clybourne Lofts
        Chicago, Illinois
30" × 40", (76.2 × 101.6 cm), Scale: ¼"=1'0"
Medium: Ink on Mylar
Courtesy of Pappageorge Haymes Ltd., Chicago, Architects

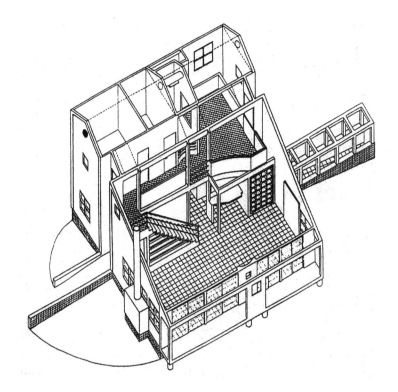

Drawing: Peele residence, North Andover, Massachusetts
24" × 36" (61 × 91.4 cm), Scale: ⅛"=1'0"
Medium: Ink with Pantone film colors
Adam Gross, Project Associate
Courtesy of Perry, Dean, Rogers, and Partners: Architects
Reprinted from *The Compact House Book*, edited by Don Metz with permission of Storey Communications/Garden Way Publishing, Pownal, Vermont.

Removing the roof from a building form helps to reveal the interior spaces drawn at plan oblique axes angles. Plan obliques (either looking down or looking up as on pp. 168–169) provide an unnatural but informative way of looking at architecture. As a procedural rule, always construct the wall or roof outline first (as in the Clybourne Lofts, above left) before adding material wall or floor texture (as in the Peele residence, above right). Spatial definition can be enhanced by the generous use of tonal values. These values produce contrast between the horizontal and vertical planes.

PLAN OBLIQUE CONSTRUCTION/VIEWS

PLAN OBLIQUE CONSTRUCTION

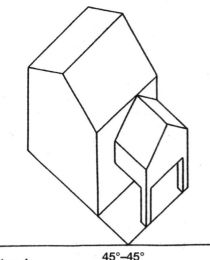

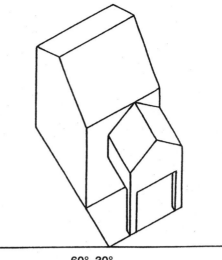

Step 4   45°–45°

Step 4   60°–30°

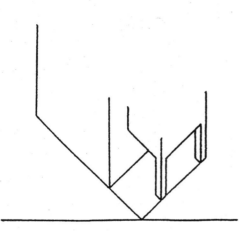

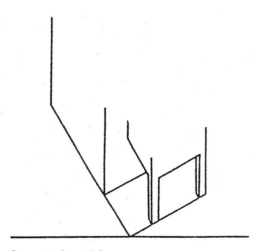

Steps 1, 2, and 3

Steps 1, 2, and 3

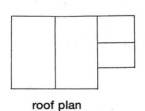

roof plan

elevation

elevation

For exterior forms:

1. Access the plan configuration (roof or floor plan) and one or two elevations, all drawn to the same scale.
2. Place and rotate the plan to any axes angle combination. Construct the true-shape plan view (examples shown are 45°–45° and 60°–30°). For exteriors, some of the sides may not be visible.
3. From the elevations, scale and construct all vertical lines.
4. Complete other true-length horizontal and non-true-length lines.

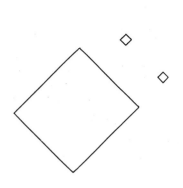

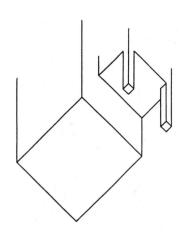

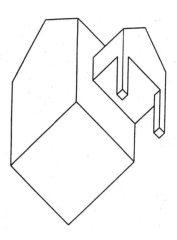

oblique up view

Draw the overall plan configuration of the up view.

Then draw verticals and true-length horizontals.

Then draw other non-true-length lines.

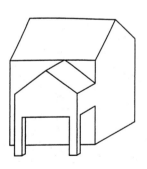

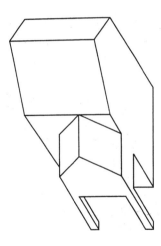

elevation oblique

nonvertical z-axis oblique

Draw the true-shape elevation view.

Then draw all parallel receding lines and other nonparallel lines.

Procedure is the same as other obliques, with the vertical axis swung and drawn left or right of actual vertical.

OTHER OBLIQUE CONSTRUCTIONS

The latter part of this chapter will introduce you to three other types of drawings that are related to the plan oblique. The construction procedure is shown above for these three types, identified as oblique up views (pp. 168–171), elevation obliques (pp. 150–157), and nonvertical z-axis obliques (pp. 148–149).

AXIAL AND NON-AXIAL LINES/ADDING NONLINEAR FORMS

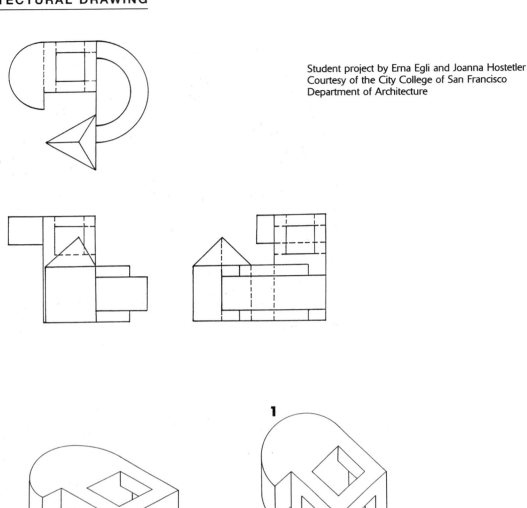

Student project by Erna Egli and Joanna Hostetler
Courtesy of the City College of San Francisco
Department of Architecture

In complex paraline drawings the order of construction can vary, but in general subordinate forms like **1** and **2** are commonly constructed as an addition to the primary form (square-shaped element). Note that the pyramid form **3** shown in this design has three non-axial lines. See if you can identify them. Linear lines in paraline drawings must either be **axial** (parallel to one of the three main axes) or **non-axial** (not parallel to any of the three main axes). When there are nonlinear elements in a design, such as circular and curvilinear shapes, these elements are frequently constructed last. Plan oblique circles, as well as plan oblique curvilinear forms, are always projected upward to their true elevation heights.

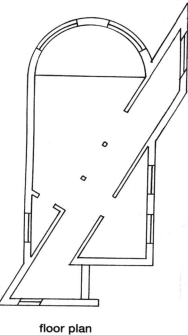

Drawings: House, Austin, Texas
Courtesy of Kwok Gorran Tsui, an architecture graduate
of the University of Texas at Austin

floor plan

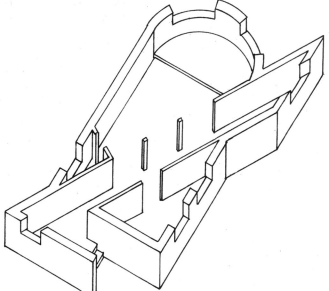

ADDING ADDITIONAL AXES

For interior spaces:

1. Access the scaled plan view.
2. Choose desired axes angles.
3. Construct scaled vertical lines to a desired height that best reveals the interior spaces.
4. Construct the true-length horizontal lines.
5. Construct any nonlinear forms.
6. Complete the same procedure for additional axes angles.

When solid intersecting elements in a building form intersect at other than 90°, this will result in more than one set of plan oblique axes angles. The best procedure is to construct the primary volume with its one set of axes angles first, and then construct secondary volumes.

PLAN OBLIQUE HORIZONTAL CIRCLES

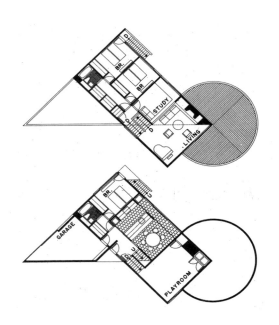

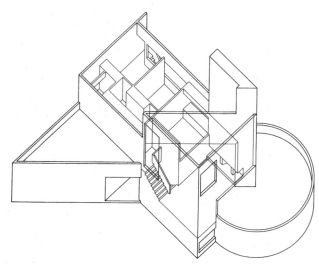

Drawings: House, Oldfield, New York
13.5" × 15.5" (34.3 × 39.4 cm), Scale: ¼"=1'0"
Medium: Ink
Courtesy of Hobart D. Betts, Architect

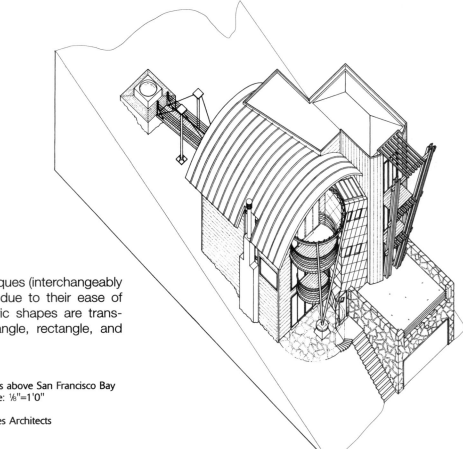

The popularity of plan obliques (interchangeably termed axonometrics) is due to their ease of construction. All geometric shapes are transferred true-size (note triangle, rectangle, and circle above).

Drawing: Schuh Box (unbuilt), hills above San Francisco Bay
11" × 17" (27.9 × 43.2 cm), Scale: ⅛"=1'0"
Medium: Ink on trace
Courtesy of David Baker Associates Architects

Drawings: Meyer residence, Malibu, California
Both 24" × 36" (61 × 91.4 cm), Scale: ¼"=1'0"
Medium: Ink on Mylar
Courtesy of Gwathmey Siegel & Associates, Architects

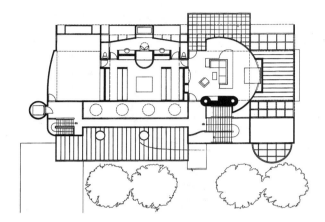

In the plan view and the plan oblique view, some-times geometric solids are shortened by cutting off a part (truncated). The truncated semicylinder in the above design has a circle that will appear true shape in neither the plan view (foreshortened) nor the plan oblique view. The circle must always be in the horizontal plane to be true shape in the plan view.

Regardless of the axes angles combination, **circles** and other curvilinear forms in horizontal planes retain their **true size** and **shape** in the plan oblique because the plan view is a true-shape view.

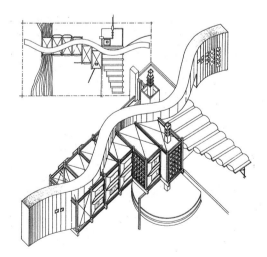

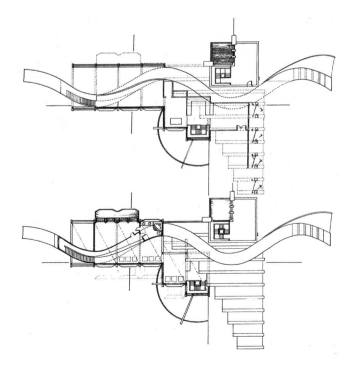

Drawing: Student project by John Crump
              Dwelling with a Bridge
Medium: Ink on Mylar
M. Saleh Uddin, Professor,
Savannah College of Art and Design, Savannah, Georgia;
Southern University, Baton Rouge, Louisiana

PLAN OBLIQUE HORIZONTAL CIRCLES

PLAN OBLIQUES — 45°-45° AXES ANGLES

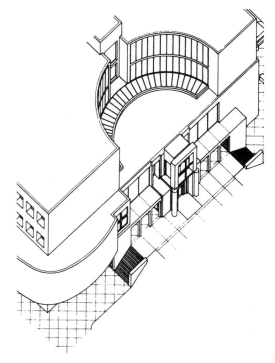

Drawing: Tallahassee City Hall, Tallahassee, Florida
24" × 36" (61 × 91.4 cm), Scale: 1/16"=1'0"
Medium: Ink on tracing paper
Courtesy of Heery International, Inc.

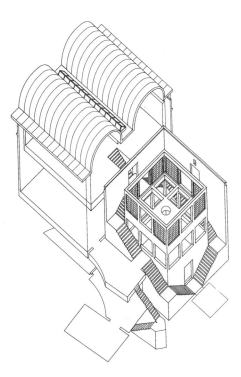

Drawing: Whanki Museum, Seoul, Korea
18" × 24" (45.7 × 61 cm), Scale 1:500
Medium: Ink on vellum
Courtesy of Kyu Sung Woo, Architect

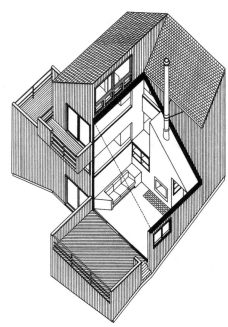

Drawing: Dattelbaum house
 Kezar Lake, Center Lovell, Maine
18" × 23" (45.7 × 58.4 cm), Scale: 1/4"=1'0"
Medium: Ink on Mylar
Courtesy of Solomon & Bauer Architects Inc.

Plan obliques are commonly drawn with axes angles of 30°–60°, 60°–30°, and 45°–45°. The plan in its true shape can be quickly transferred to construct the oblique drawings. The observer's vantage point appears **higher** than in an isometric drawing. These plan obliques use axes angles of 45°–45°. Facade details show equally well on either receding axis. Roof configurations and interior spaces are also clearly seen. Partial roof cutaways help to focus on the interior spaces. Detail on a nonlinear facade will show especially well (upper left). Obliques lack the characteristic of size diminishment (as in a perspective) and thus have the advantage of retaining size, detail, and information.

Also note the use of a dashed line to indicate the volume removed in the Dattelbaum house (left). A line with short dashes or a very thin line (see p. 144, left drawing) is the accepted way of showing the **cutaway** portion that is removed.

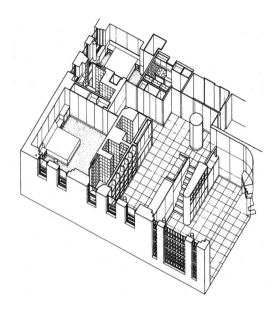

Drawing: Manhattan pied-à-terre, New York City
24" × 36" (61 × 91.4 cm), Scale: ¼"=1'0"
Medium: Ink on Mylar
Courtesy of Gwathmey Siegel & Associates, Architects

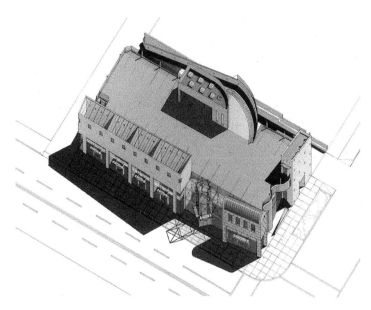

Drawing: Montana Collection, Santa Monica, California
24" × 36" (61 × 91.4 cm), Scale: ¼ = 1'0"
Medium: Ink on Mylar with Zipatone
Courtesy of Kanner Architects

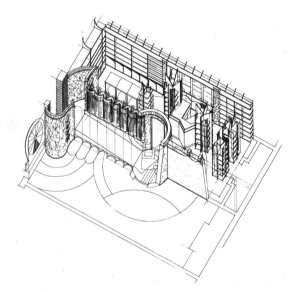

Drawing: Contemporary Arts Center Bookstore and Artware
   Cincinnati, Ohio
24" × 36" (61 × 91.4 cm), Scale: ½"=1'0"
Medium: Pencil on vellum
Courtesy of Terry Brown Architect

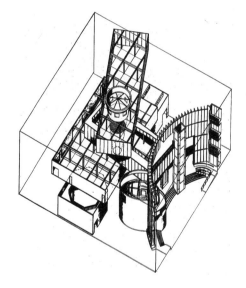

Drawing: Contemporary Arts Center
   New Orleans, Louisiana
30" × 40" (76.2 × 101.6 cm), Scale: ¹⁄₁₆"=1'0"
Medium: Plastic lead on Mylar
Courtesy of Concordia Architects, New Orleans, Louisiana

These plan obliques use axes angles of 30°–60°. This orientation allows the observer to clearly see interior spaces or roof configurations. Usually the 30° receding facade receives the most emphasis. However, if the facade is not linear, as with the New Orleans Arts Center, then a 60° receding axis can be the choice to show the more detailed facade. The Cincinnati Arts center above and the Whanki Museum on the facing page show how the interior anatomy of a building can be further revealed by dissecting it both horizontally and vertically (combining two or more section cuts).

PLAN OBLIQUES — 30°-60° AXES ANGLES

PLAN OBLIQUES—60°–30° AXES ANGLES

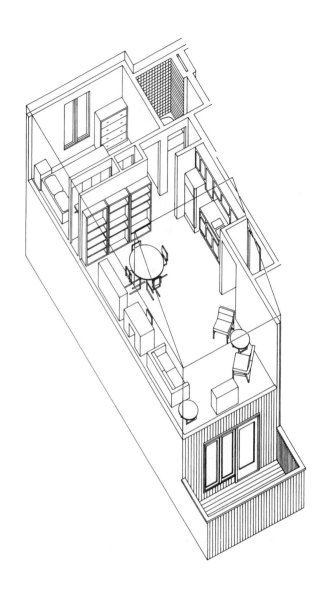

Drawing: Married student housing, University of Alaska
          Fairbanks, Alaska
11" × 17" (27.9 × 43.2 cm), Scale: ¼"=1'0"
Medium: Ink on Mylar
Courtesy of Hellmuth, Obata, and Kassabaum, Architects

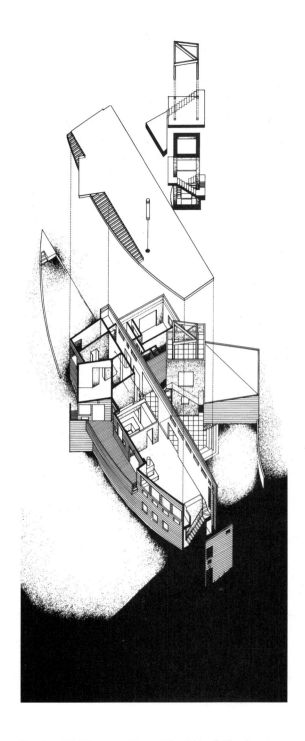

Drawing: Waldhauer residence, Woodside, California
20" × 48" (50.8 × 121.9 cm), Scale: ¼"=1'0"
Medium: India ink and airbrush on Mylar
Courtesy of House + House, Architects
Mark David English, Architectural Illustrator

These plan obliques use axes angles of 60°–30°. Normally the 30° receding facade is emphasized. However, note that much detail can be shown on the 60° receding facade if part of the facade is nonlinear. All built-in and movable furniture pieces retain their verticality and true heights (see p. 404). The 60°–30° axes angles allow the observer to clearly see the interior spaces when the roof and parts of both side elevations are removed.

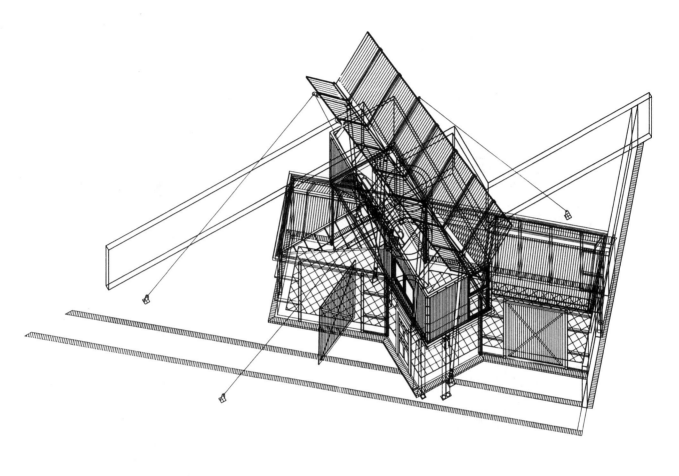

Drawing: Studio, The Ivy Villa, Pretoria, South Africa
400 × 300 mm (15.7" × 11.8"), Scale: 1:100
Medium: Ultimate CAD program
Drawn by Ian Thompson
Courtesy of Ora Joubert, Architect

DUAL-AXES AND TRI-AXES ANGLES

This drawing has one structure with axes angles of 9°–81° and another structure with axes angles of 60°–30°. The intersection of solid elements will always require two (dual) or more sets of plan oblique axes angles. Note that the structure with the 9°–81° orientation shows details on its 9° facade extremely well, whereas its 81° facade is barely visible. Also shown above are structural cables, which are not true-length in the plan oblique. Also in evidence is the relative transparency of all drawn elements. With the design of more high-tech buildings, the drawing of dual-axes and tri-axes plan oblique angles has become commonplace.

PLAN OBLIQUES—INCREMENTAL GROWTH

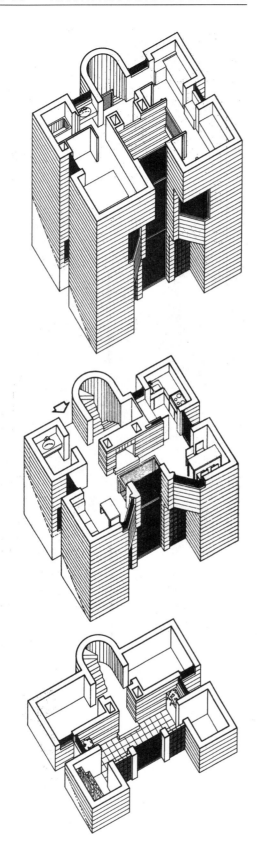

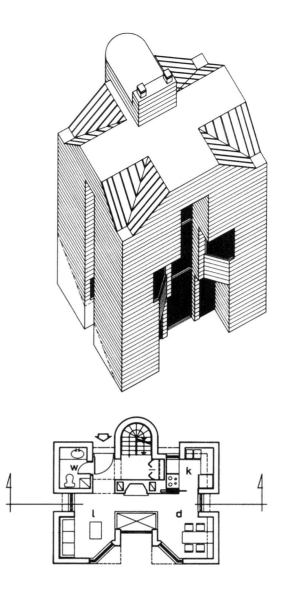

For multistory building types, the plan oblique can be effectively used in showing a **growth** (layering) sequence of floor levels. These drawings become an efficacious visual means of conveying how the entire building shell relates to the interior spaces.

Drawings: One-family prototype house, Toronto, Ontario, Canada
Courtesy of G. Nino Rico and Giancarlo Garofalo
Reprinted from *The Compact House Book*, edited by Don Metz with permission of Storey Communications/Garden Way Publishing, Pownal, Vermont.

Plan obliques illustrating incremental growth can clarify details in plan view cuts taken at different locations. Axes angles of 45°–45° were used in the example to the right, whereas 60°–30° was used in the example on the facing page.

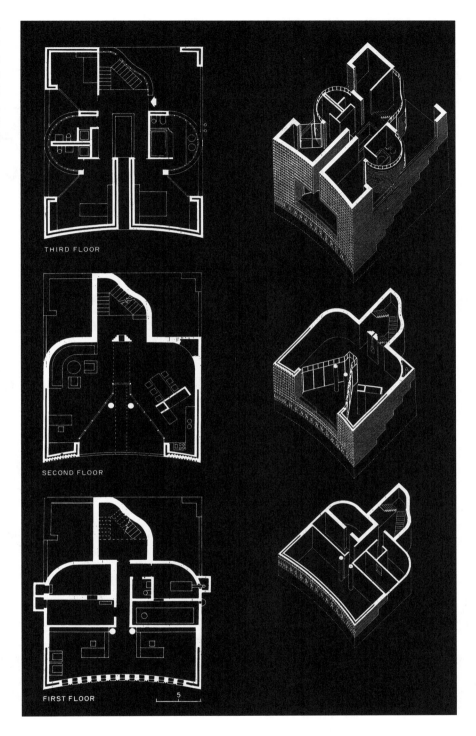

THIRD FLOOR

SECOND FLOOR

FIRST FLOOR   5

Drawings: Posteria residence, Morbio Superiore, Switzerland
Courtesy of Mario Botta, Architect, Lugano, Switzerland

PLAN OBLIQUES—INCREMENTAL GROWTH

PLAN OBLIQUES – NONVERTICAL Z AXIS

A variation to the typical plan oblique is one in which the *Z* axis thrusts the vertical planes upward (most commonly at 45° or 60°) from the horizontal. This gives the observer a vantage point that is almost directly **overhead**. This method has the advantage of revealing more of the important horizontal planes. However, distortion appears greater than in the typical plan oblique.

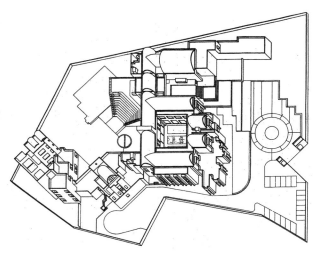

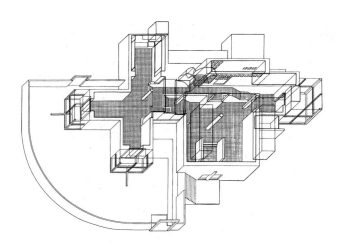

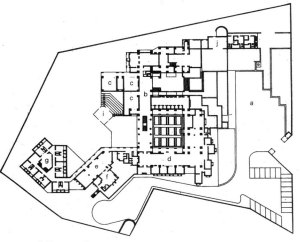

ground floor plan

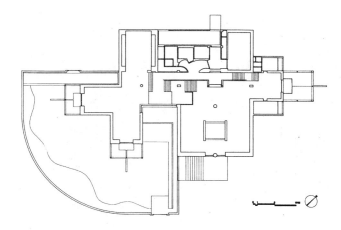

Drawings: Iwasaki Art Museum, Kagoshima Prefecture, Kyushu, Japan
Axon: 23.2" × 16.9" (59 × 43 cm)
Plan: 28.3" × 19.7" (72 × 50 cm), Scale: 1:100
Medium: Ink on vellum
Courtesy of Fumihiko Maki and Associates, Architects

Drawing: Gandhi Labour Institute, Ahmedabad, Gujrat, India
26" × 39" (66 × 99 cm), Scale: 1:200
Medium: Ink on Gateway (tracing paper)
Courtesy of B.V. Doshi, Architect

The plan oblique with a plan sectional cut (left) retains the plan geometric configuration better than does the plan oblique (above), which shows a site plan view of the roof configuration.

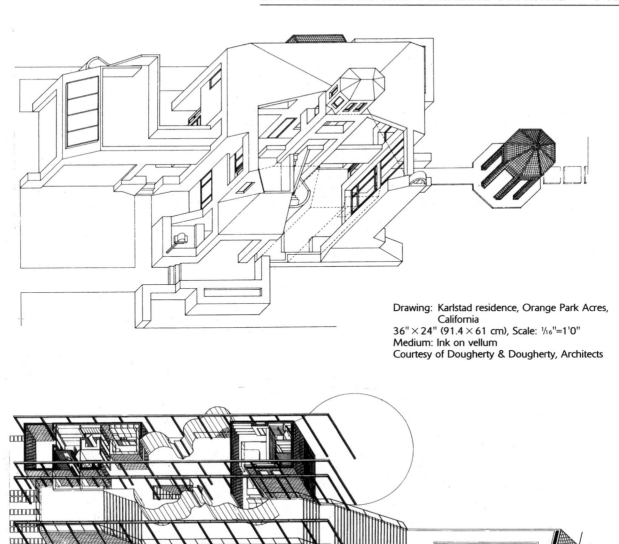

Drawing: Karlstad residence, Orange Park Acres, California
36" × 24" (91.4 × 61 cm), Scale: 1/16"=1'0"
Medium: Ink on vellum
Courtesy of Dougherty & Dougherty, Architects

Drawing: Casa Canovelles, Granollers (Barcelona), Spain
26.4" × 54.3" (67 × 138 cm)
Medium: Ink on vellum paper
Courtesy of MBM Arquitectes
Josep Martorell, Oriol Bohigas, and David MacKay

PLAN OBLIQUES—NONVERTICAL Z AXIS

The nonvertical Z axis can be swung either left or right of the vertical direction. These examples show that vantage points from either direction are equally effective: the choice is based on the viewing information one wishes to convey.

ELEVATION OBLIQUES: A COMPARISON

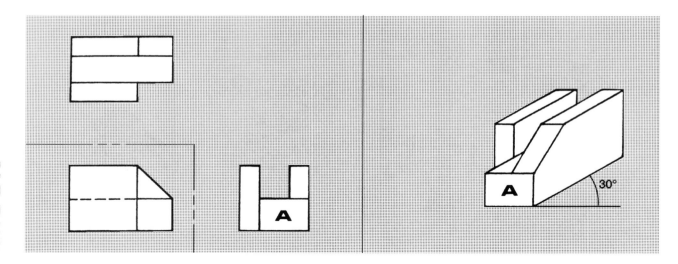

In an **elevation oblique** a chosen elevation view is seen as **true size** and **true shape.** Elevation surface **A** is used in this example. It is easy to draw elements like true-shape circles or curves on true-shape surfaces (**4** is **2** with a surface modification). The receding lines are usually drawn at 30°, 45°, or 60° angles from the horizontal. Measure the "notated" oblique angle from due north. For example **1**, this would be 90° minus 30° = 60°. The next two notations are the elevation scale and the receding line scale. For example **1**, this would be 1:1.

1. 60° — 1:1   **2.** 45° — 1:1   **3.** 30° — 1:1   **4.** 45° — 1:1   **5.** 45° — 1:⅔   **6.** 45° — 1:½

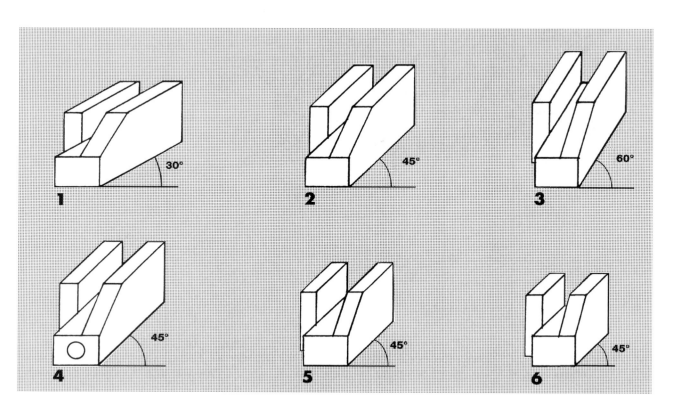

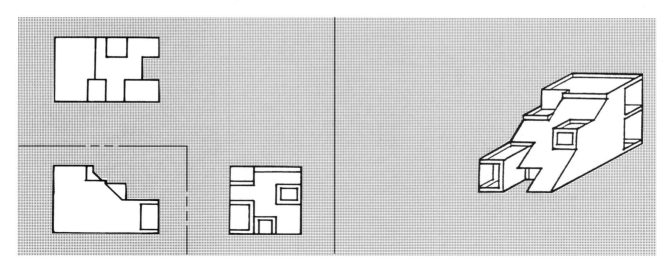

The building form shown in this example has a geometric configuration similar to that of the example shown on the opposite page. Note that all surfaces parallel to the vertical front elevation plane retain their true size and true shape. It is common practice to show the elevation with the most irregular form as the frontal elevation. The direction of the receding lines and the scale ratio of each drawing corresponds to the six drawings on the previous page. Receding lines can be set at any oblique angle.

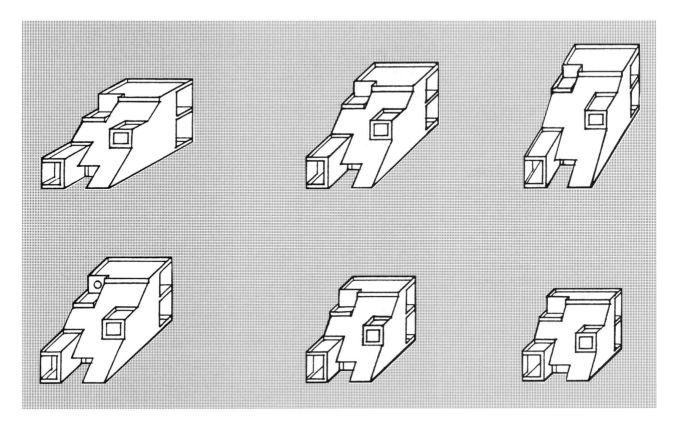

ELEVATION OBLIQUES: A COMPARISON

ELEVATION OBLIQUES: BUILDING EXAMPLES

Drawing: Villa dall'Ava, Paris, France
23.4" × 16.5" (59.5 × 41.8 cm)
Medium: Ink
Courtesy of Office for Metropolitan
Architecture (OMA)

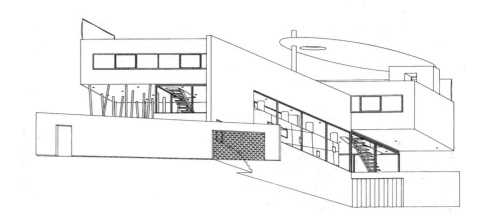

This elevation oblique of a house recedes down to the right. The result is a worm's-eye view looking up. Note that one can easily see interior details through the receding facade.

Drawing: Boathouse, St. Andrew's School
               Middletown, Delaware
18" × 6" (45.7 × 15.2 cm), Scale: ⅛"=1'0"
Medium: Technical pen
Drawing by Kim Haskell
Courtesy of Richard Conway Meyer, Architect

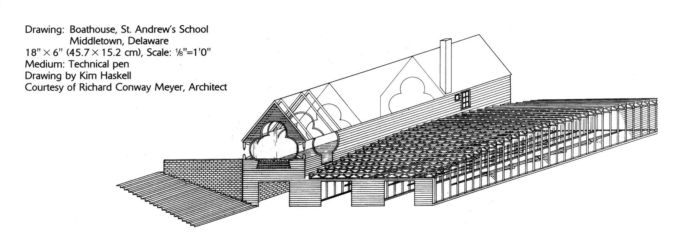

In most cases, elevation obliques recede up to the right or up to the left at a selected angle. Regular or irregular curvilinear forms are commonly seen in the true-size elevation. It is sometimes necessary to use a cutaway wall or a transparent oblique to reveal interior spaces.

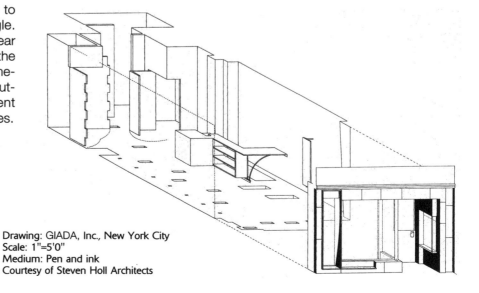

Drawing: GIADA, Inc., New York City
Scale: 1"=5'0"
Medium: Pen and ink
Courtesy of Steven Holl Architects

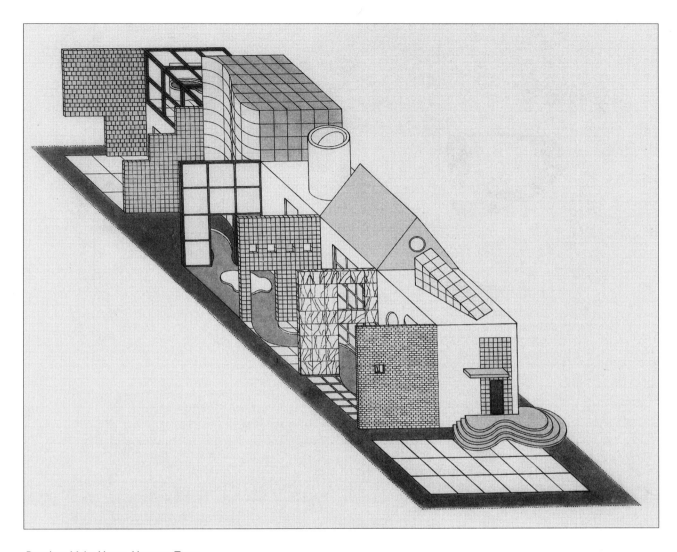

Drawing: Maba House, Houston, Texas
36" × 24" (91.4 × 61 cm)
Medium: Ink on Mylar
Courtesy of Arquitectonica International Corporation

This view was chosen because it best represented the whole house as a series of smaller cubes. The rendering was executed in 1982 on Mylar which was colored on the back. At that time this was typical of Arquitectonica's early visualization techniques. The design of the house was conceived as a series of five little houses, each with its own roof/light feature, court with walls, and different aspects of a continuous pool. The five units provide varied experiences in terms of texture, color and light. The fenestrations vary and entreat light differently within each cubic space. The courtyard of each house is varied and represents a totally unique experience within each. The water element is the only continuous element running through the various cubes.
[Architect's statement]

This elevation oblique has its ground plane receding 45° to the left. It is not difficult to see why a frontal orientation was selected to best describe this house, with its numerous parallel elements of different complexities. An elevation oblique may or may not be foreshortened to avoid distortion, but a plan oblique is never foreshortened.

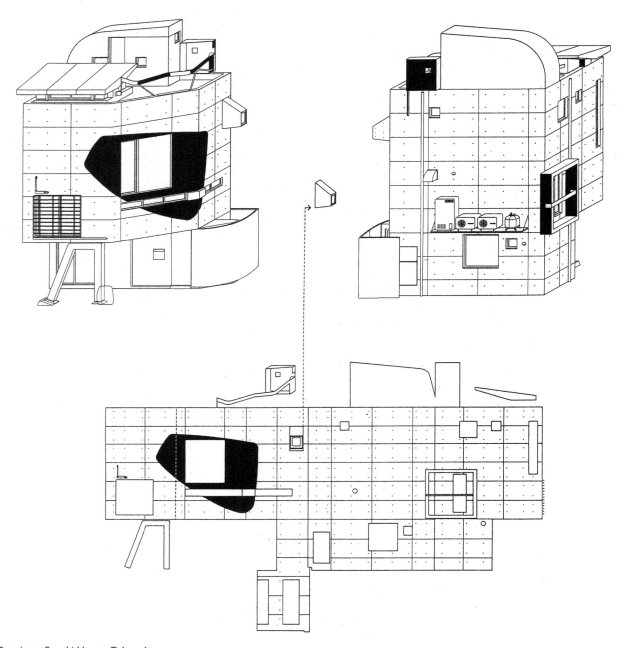

Drawings: Suzuki House, Tokyo, Japan
8.7" × 11" (22 × 28 cm), Scale: 1:30 (Japanese scale)
Medium: Ink on trace
Courtesy of Architekturbüro Bolles–Wilson + Partner

The elevation obliques above are geometrically correct in one elevation, preferable to axonometrics where the plan is true. But elevations do not show the building as experienced. In the foldout, the facade is one continuous pattern of concrete shuttering.
[ARCHITECT'S STATEMENT]

These two elevation obliques show all sides of this building, which also has its skin elevation completely unwrapped and laid out flat.

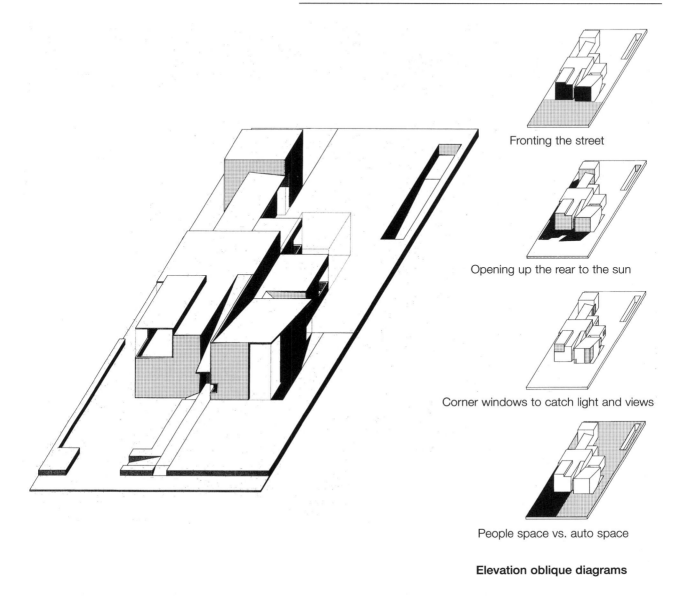

Fronting the street

Opening up the rear to the sun

Corner windows to catch light and views

People space vs. auto space

Elevation oblique diagrams

Drawing: Adelman/Llanos residence, Santa Monica, California
Medium: Ink
Courtesy of Mack Architects; Mark Mack, principal

USING THE ELEVATION OBLIQUE

Elevation obliques can be very effective in showing how the building design responds to various design parameters. This example shows a simple form repeated five times with an upward receding angle of 60° for the purpose of diagramming design concepts. Note the use of gray tone and black to express the parameters. The largest diagram expresses rooms as volume; in this drawing, vertical planes were toned black or gray to accentuate building components. Artificial toning can give the needed planar contrast to help enhance the understanding of a design, especially in cases where material texture is absent or not shown (see pp. 160, 166).

FRONTAL ELEVATION OBLIQUE 0°-1:1

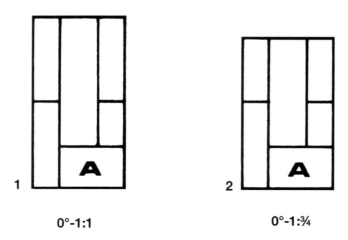

1   **0°-1:1**

2   **0°-1:¾**

In examples **1** and **2**, the front elevation remains true size. Example **2** shows that the plan dimension is sometimes reduced from true length to give a more realistic (foreshortened) view. This reduction can range from very little to as much as 25%. Most architects and designers, however, tend to maintain a true-size plan. Both examples below, as well as the drawings at left, show their elevations and roof plans true-size and true-shape. This unusual variation of an elevation oblique results when either the roof plan or floor plan (see facing page) has one of its sides parallel to the picture plane.

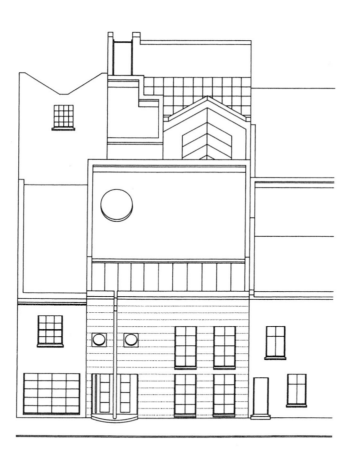

Drawing: Pond Place, London, England
Medium: Ink
Courtesy of Troughton McAslan Architects

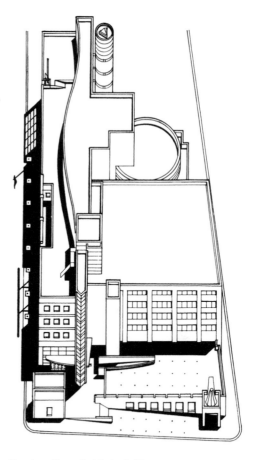

Drawing: Eugenio Maria de Hostos
           Community College, New York City
20" × 30" (50.8 × 76.2 cm), Scale: ⅛"=1'0"
Medium: Ink on Mylar
Courtesy of Bartholomew Voorsanger, FAIA

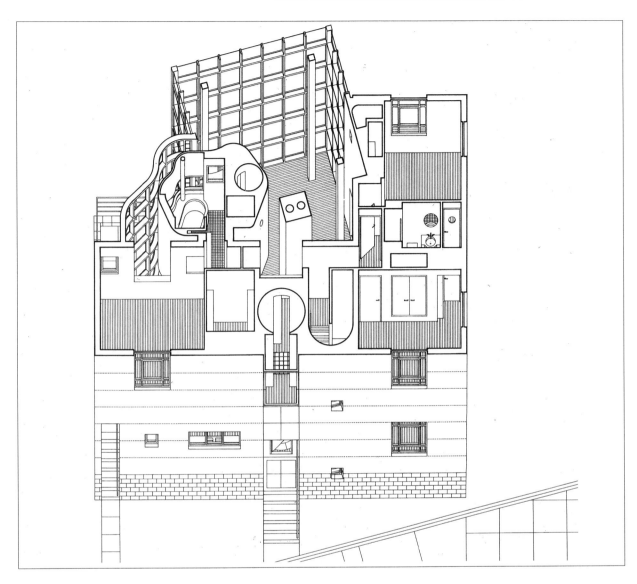

Drawing: Martinelli residence, Roxbury, Connecticut, 1989
22.5" × 22.5" (57.2 × 57.2 cm), Scale: ¼"=1'0"
Medium: Ink
Courtesy of Anthony Ames, Architect

The roof is removed from the building in this frontal axonometric drawing in order to illustrate the room locations on the second floor and their relationship to the double height living and dining space with the cloud like element that encloses the master bathroom.
[ARCHITECT'S STATEMENT]

As with the drawings shown on the previous page, this frontal elevation oblique does not give an illusion of the third dimension. This type of drawing allows us to see vertical dimensions and fenestration patterns simultaneously with the roof structure configuration or plan layout.

MULTIOBLIQUE COMBINATIONS

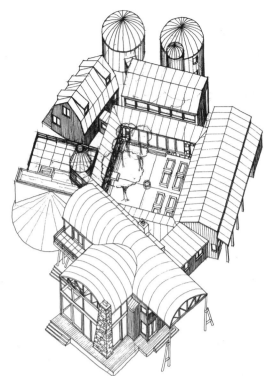

Drawing: Residence, Sun Valley, Idaho
24" × 30" (61 × 76.2 cm), Scale: ⅛"=1'0"
Medium: Pencil on vellum
Courtesy of Frederick Fisher, Architect

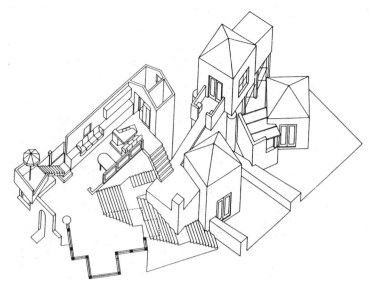

Drawing: Jaeger Beach House, La Jolla, California
24" × 36", Scale: 1"=30'
Medium: Ink on Mylar
Courtesy of Rob Wellington Quigley, Architect

It is quite common to find many building configurations that exhibit **multioblique** combinations. The addition of shades and shadows (see pp. 353 and 356) gives depth to a multioblique drawing.

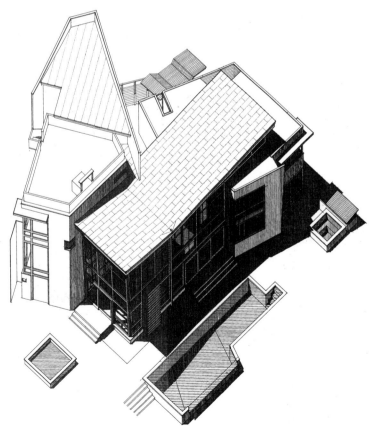

Drawing: Summer compound,
Barnegat Light, New Jersey
42" × 48" (106.7 × 121.9 cm), Scale: ¼"=1'0"
Medium: Ink on Mylar
Courtesy of Brian Healy Architect

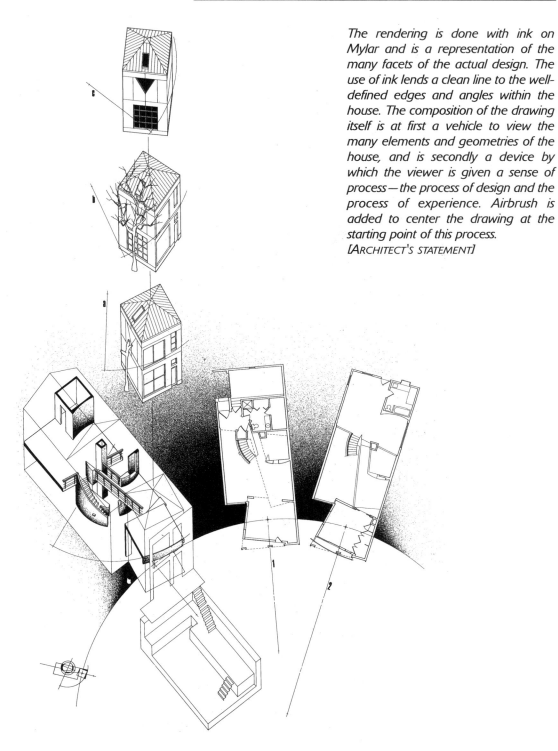

The rendering is done with ink on Mylar and is a representation of the many facets of the actual design. The use of ink lends a clean line to the well-defined edges and angles within the house. The composition of the drawing itself is at first a vehicle to view the many elements and geometries of the house, and is secondly a device by which the viewer is given a sense of process—the process of design and the process of experience. Airbrush is added to center the drawing at the starting point of this process.
[ARCHITECT'S STATEMENT]

MULTIOBLIQUE COMBINATIONS

Drawing: Exploded axonometric and plan composite
Chason residence, San Francisco, California
30" × 52" (76.2 × 132.1 cm), Scale: ³⁄₁₆"=1'0"
Medium: India ink on Mylar
Courtesy of House + House Architects, San Francisco
Michael Baushke, Architectural Illustrator

THE EXPLODED VIEW

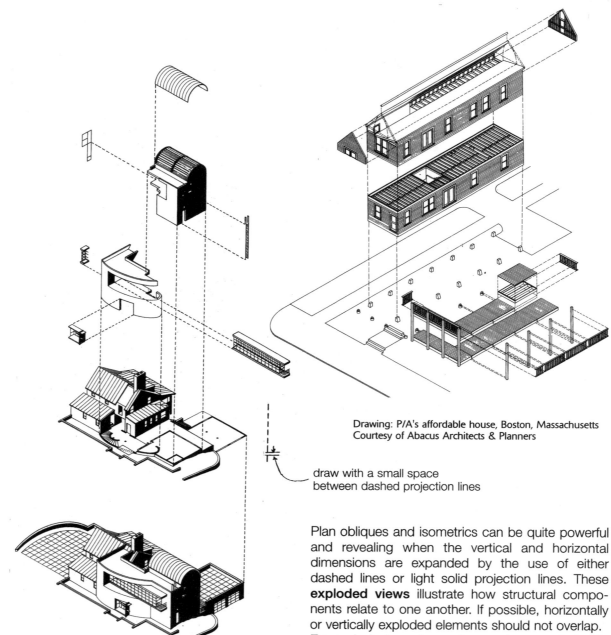

Drawing: P/A's affordable house, Boston, Massachusetts
Courtesy of Abacus Architects & Planners

draw with a small space
between dashed projection lines

Drawing: Gorman residence, New Canaan, Connecticut
24" × 36" (61 × 91.4 cm), Scale: 1/16"=1'0"
Medium: Pen and ink
Courtesy of Hariri & Hariri Design, Architects

Plan obliques and isometrics can be quite powerful and revealing when the vertical and horizontal dimensions are expanded by the use of either dashed lines or light solid projection lines. These **exploded views** illustrate how structural components relate to one another. If possible, horizontally or vertically exploded elements should not overlap. **Expanded views** (opposite page) are exploded in one direction only, as shown with the numerous roof removals on the previous pages.

The amount that the building parts are displaced (movement axes are usually parallel or perpendicular to the building axes) depends on finding the most explanatory positional relationship of the parts to each other and to the whole. Note in the Gorman residence (left) how easily the disparate elements seem to come together to make a coherent whole.

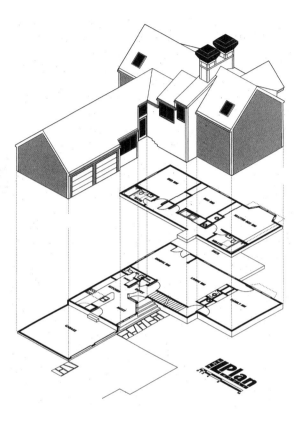

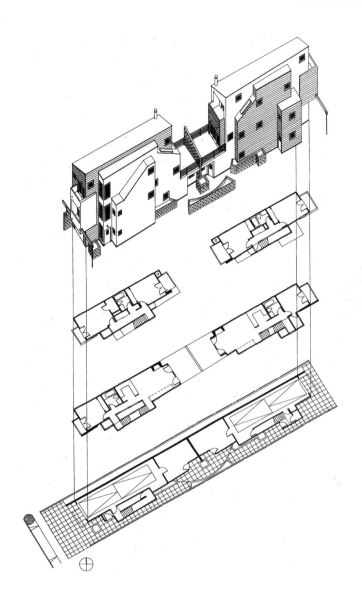

Drawing: Armacost duplex, Los Angeles, California
24" × 36" (61 × 91.4 cm), Scale: ⅛"=1'0"
Medium: pencil
Courtesy of Rebecca L. Binder, FAIA, Architect

Drawing: House, Connecticut
8.5" × 11" (21.6 × 27.9 cm), Scale: ¹⁄₁₆"=1'0"
Originally drawn at ¼"=1'0"
Medium: Macintosh computer in Power Draw
Courtesy of Robert T. Coolidge, AIA, Architect

THE EXPANDED VIEW

The concept of the expanded view in both plan obliques and isometrics is frequently applied to buildings with two or more floors. Stacked floors usually exhibit similar geometric configurations. These examples illustrate how the floor plans can be removed from the building shell to help visualize the vertical relationship of all levels in conjunction with the exterior form. Both expanded and exploded views allow us to see the internal makeup of a building. In this sense, they are quite similar to cutaway views (see pp. 142–144).

EXPLODED ISOMETRIC

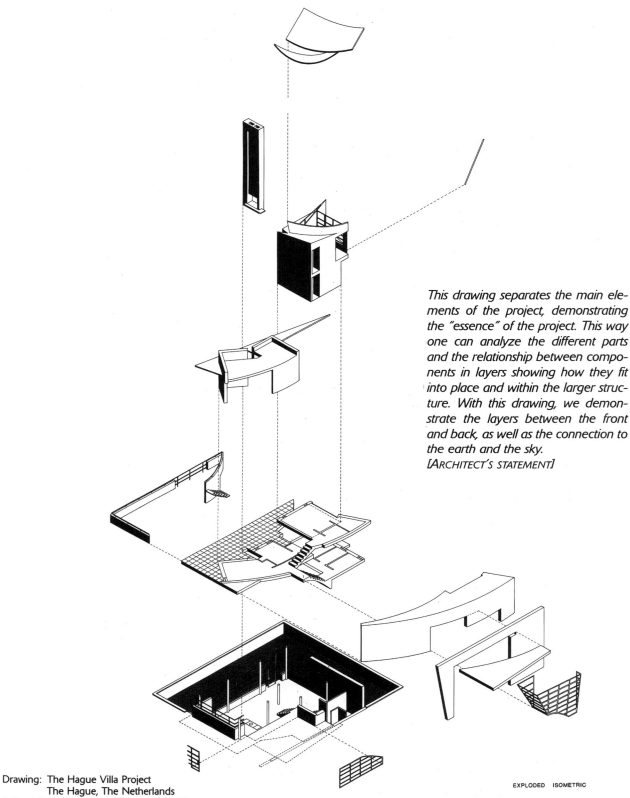

This drawing separates the main elements of the project, demonstrating the "essence" of the project. This way one can analyze the different parts and the relationship between components in layers showing how they fit into place and within the larger structure. With this drawing, we demonstrate the layers between the front and back, as well as the connection to the earth and the sky.
[ARCHITECT'S STATEMENT]

EXPLODED ISOMETRIC

Drawing: The Hague Villa Project
      The Hague, The Netherlands
24" × 36" (61 × 91.4 cm), Scale: ¹⁄₁₆"=1'0"
Medium: Pen and ink
Courtesy of Hariri & Hariri, Architects

The element axonometric drawing is a composition of design elements: public street facade, private courtyard facade, axis, focal point, and circulation elements. The drawing visually analyzes the different design approaches to and the relationship between the public street and the private courtyard, and the sequence of circulation spaces that connect the major street to the inner courtyard, with the linkage of the street entry porch to the rotated courtyard gazebo, the axis, and the focal point. The floor plan anchors the drawing as a basic reference.
[ARCHITECT'S STATEMENT]

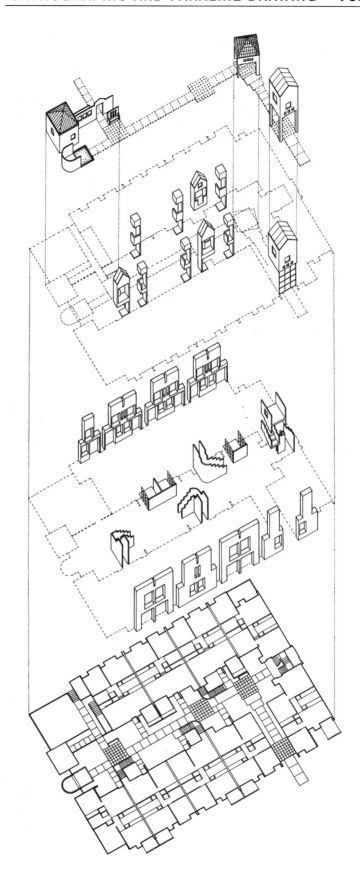

ELEMENT AXONOMETRIC

Drawing: Yorkshire Terrace, Los Angeles, California
34" × 42" (86.4 × 106.7 cm), Scale: ⅛"=1'0"
Medium: Ink
Courtesy of John V. Mutlow, FAIA, Architects

THE EXPANDED VIEW

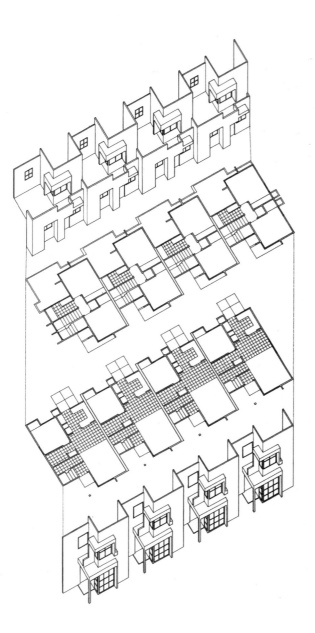

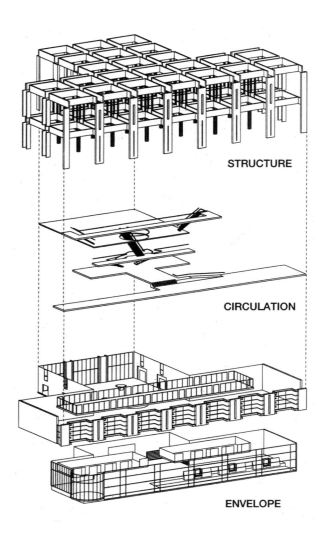

STRUCTURE

CIRCULATION

ENVELOPE

Dimetric of components

Drawing: Cabrillo Village, Saticoy, California
24" × 36" (61 × 91.4 cm), Scale: ⅛"=1'0"
Medium: Ink
Courtesy of John V. Mutlow, FAIA, Architects

Drawing: Library, Toronto, Canada
Medium: Ink
Courtesy of A.J. Diamond, Donald Schmitt, Architects

*The front and rear elevations below and above the floor
plans help to project the three-dimensional richness of the
facade from the two-dimensional floor plans.*
[ARCHITECT'S STATEMENT]

This expanded view uses a paraline axonometric in
the form of a dimetric. The lower angle of view permits one to see the linking circulation elements
between floors. Dimetrics are more flexible than
isometrics because a variety of viewing positions
are possible.

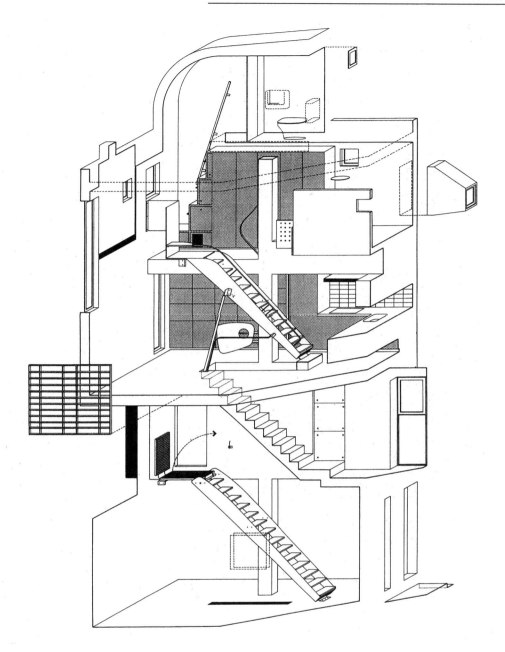

Drawings: Suzuki House, Tokyo, Japan
8.7" × 11" (22 × 28 cm), Scale: 1:30 (Japanese scale)
Medium: Ink on trace
Courtesy of Architekturbüro Bolles–Wilson + Partner

THE EXPLODED VIEW

The space of the house at all levels is visible on one projection. The central stair is understood as the connecting sequence…as in Japanese painting, what is not shown is as important as what is shown.
[ARCHITECT'S STATEMENT]

Both exploded and expanded views are excellent tools for examining the way details are put together, whether they are small structural components or large building elements. This is an interior elevation oblique with exploded parts.

EXPANDED ELEVATION OBLIQUE

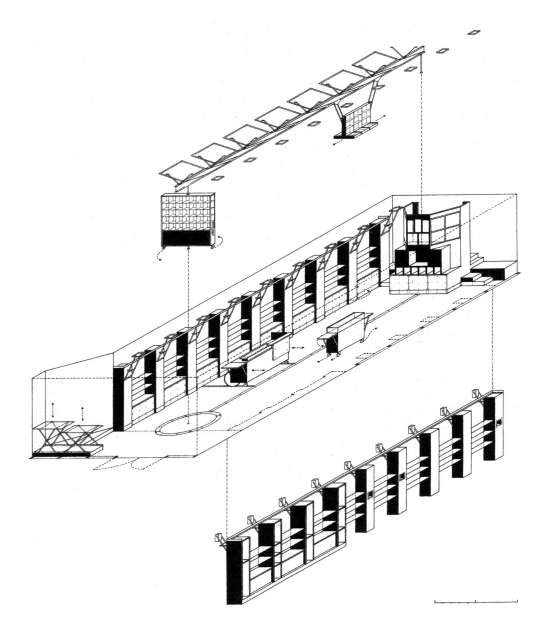

Drawing: Techsis Retail Store, San Francisco, California
17" × 22" (43.2 × 55.9 cm), Scale: ¼"=1'0"
Medium: Ink on Mylar
Courtesy of Jensen + Macy Architects

The elevation oblique was chosen because it gives more emphasis to the vertical planes (the display fixtures) than the plan oblique, which emphasizes plan relationships. This drawing type has an analytical quality allowing one to understand space/object relationships not graspable from the single fixed vantage point of the perspective. The extension above and below of parts of the drawing allows a reading of the separate components of the store in the composition. [ARCHITECT'S STATEMENT]

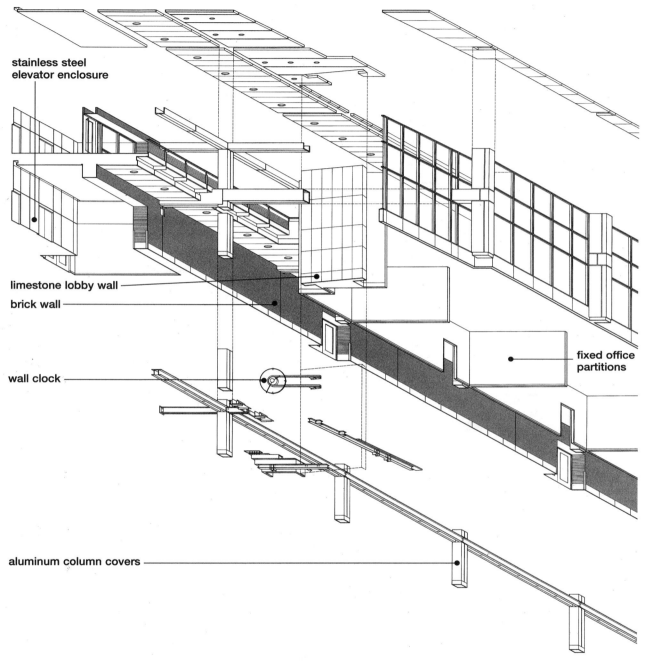

stainless steel
elevator enclosure

limestone lobby wall

brick wall

wall clock

aluminum column covers

fixed office
partitions

EXPANDED ELEVATION OBLIQUE UP VIEW

This is an expanded elevation oblique worm's-eye (up) view of the ground floor.

Drawing: New Office Building and Parking Garage
            for the Pennsylvania Higher Education Assistance Agency
            Harrisburg, Pennsylvania
36" × 48" (91.4 × 121.9 cm)
Medium: Ink on vellum (developed as a CADD drawing)
Courtesy of Bohlin Cywinski Jackson Architects

These dramatic worm's-eye views permit the viewer to peer upward into the buildings. This method was first developed and utilized by August Choisy in the nineteenth century. In design drawings it is sometimes necessary to show the relationship between the ceiling or the soffit and the walls. The disadvantage of this type of drawing is that they are sometimes very difficult to interpret, especially for beginning students and the layperson.

UP VIEWS

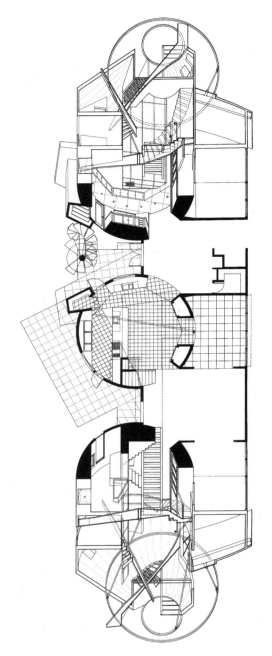

Split worm's-eye axonometric

Drawing: Lawson/Westen House, Los Angeles, California
Medium: Ink on Mylar
Courtesy of Eric Owen Moss, Architects

Drawing: Student project by Colin Alley
         Community center
Medium: Ink on Mylar
Courtesy of Washington University
School of Architecture, St. Louis, Missouri

This drawing simultaneously allows one to understand the building's form and organization while giving clues as to how the designers conceived the building: a modest shell which bends to accommodate and encourage movement and circulation; a pure cylinder at the center of the mass as a primal gathering place; and a peaked conical roof capping the cylinder as a distinguishing image at the center of a four building residential village.
[ARCHITECT'S STATEMENTS]

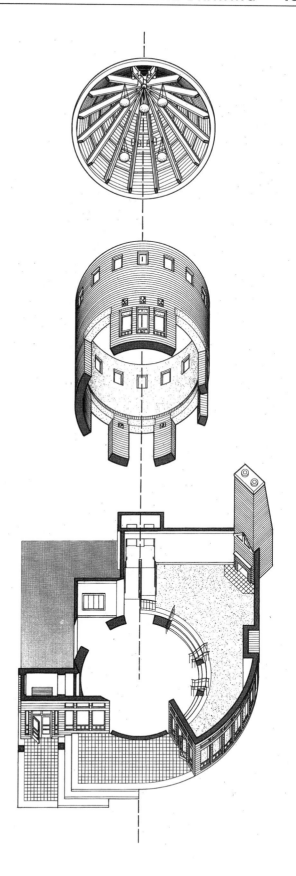

This drawing combines a plan oblique down view with plan oblique up views. Its advantage is that it allows us to simultaneously understand the total geometric configuration of a design.

Drawing: Bates College Social/Study Center
              (Residential Halls project), Lewiston, Maine
12" × 30" (30.5 × 76.2 cm), Scale: ¼"=1'0"
Medium: Ink on Mylar
Courtesy of William Rawn Associates,
Architects, Inc., Boston, Massachusetts

SIMULTANEOUS UP AND DOWN VIEWS

UP VIEWS AS DIMETRICS AND ISOMETRICS

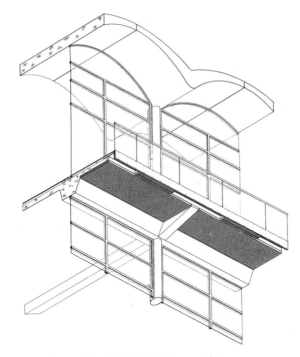

Isometric detail of balcony edge

Drawing: Lycée Polyvalent de Fréjus
        Fréjus School, Fréjus, France
16.5" × 23.4" (418 × 595 mm)
Medium: Ink on film
Drawn by Keith Allen
Courtesy of Lord Foster of Thames Bank

Axonometric up views in the form of isometrics or dimetrics allow one to see
more detail between floor levels than
would be seen in a plan oblique up view.
Note the isometric curvilinear form above
and the horizontal and vertical dimetric
circles shown at right. With the advantage
of more vantage points, **dimetric drawings** looking up or looking down are not
as inflexible and restrictive as isometric
drawings.

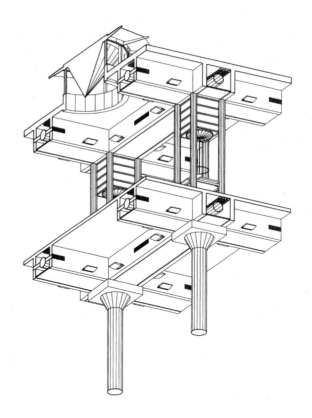

Dimetric of typical bay

Drawing: Richmond Hill Library, Toronto, Canada
Courtesy of A.J Diamond, Donald Schmitt, Architects

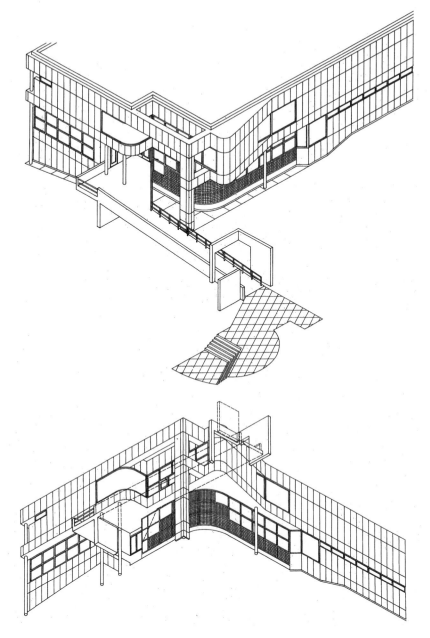

Drawings: Postindustrial factory, Dorval, Quebec, Canada
30" × 48" (76.2 × 121.9 cm), Scale: ⅛"=1'0"
Medium: Ink on Mylar
Courtesy of Michael Fieldman & Partners, Architects

A pair of axonometric views—one aerial, the other worm's-eye—were used to describe a complex 3D corner entrance. Together they convey the spatial quality of the design.
[ARCHITECT'S STATEMENT]

SIMULTANEOUS UP AND DOWN VIEWS

SIMULTANEOUS UP AND DOWN VIEWS

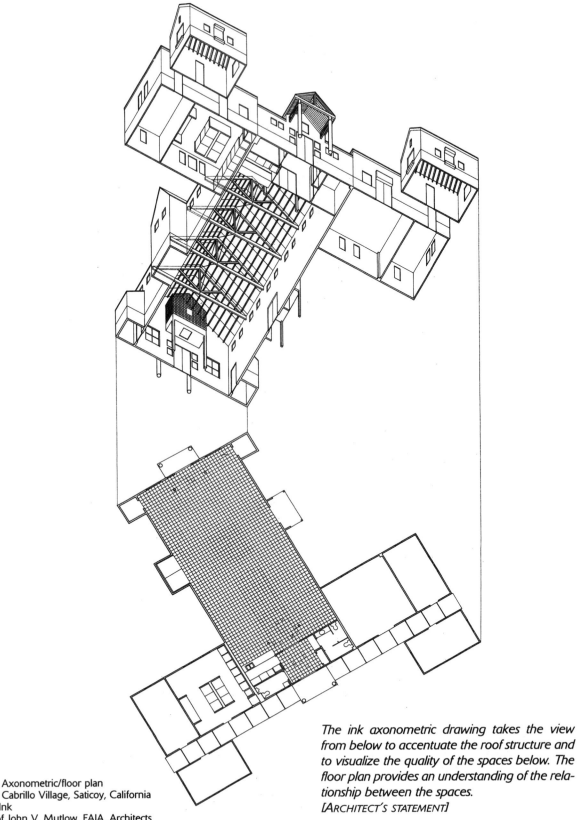

The ink axonometric drawing takes the view from below to accentuate the roof structure and to visualize the quality of the spaces below. The floor plan provides an understanding of the relationship between the spaces.
[ARCHITECT'S STATEMENT]

Drawing: Axonometric/floor plan
          Cabrillo Village, Saticoy, California
Medium: Ink
Courtesy of John V. Mutlow, FAIA, Architects

Relating to and radiating out from the floor plan, these sequentially rotated views allow the observer to simultaneously experience different viewpoints. Sequentially rotated simultaneous views are also frequently seen as plan obliques radiating out from a centrally drawn floor plan. Seeing many views from different vantage points (same altitude) at one time gives a quick comprehensive overview of any structure (see p. 512).

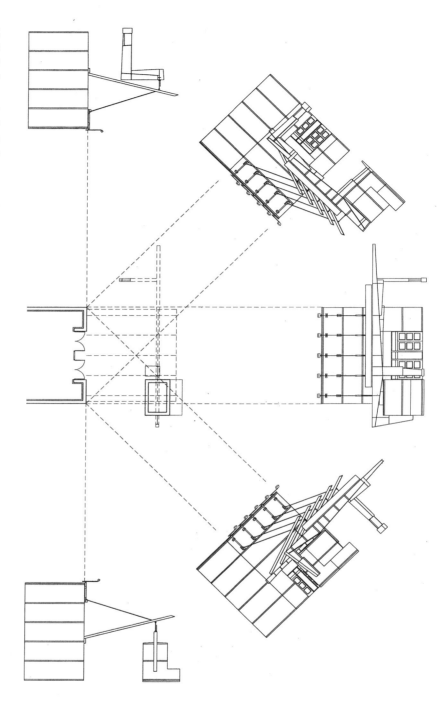

Image: Administration Building, Kennedy Senior High School
         Granada Hills, California
Courtesy of Rebecca L. Binder, FAIA (Architecture & Planning)
Hardware: PC   Software: ACAD 14, 2000   3D Studio

Honing in on a given detail to explain its relationship to the building element.
[ARCHITECT'S STATEMENT]

PLAN WITH SIMULTANEOUS EXPLODED OBLIQUE VIEWS

6

Linear Perspective Drawing

Perspective drawings give the most realistic or lifelike view of the built environment and the urban landscape. On a two-dimensional surface, pictorial views of three-dimensional forms can be represented in a visually believable manner using perspective methods.

Preliminary design drawings must clearly show form, scale, texture, light, shapes, shadows, and spatial order. Presentation design drawings take on a more precise character with these and related components. As a final step, they may be translated into perspective renderings to complement and enhance a presentation.

The intent of this chapter is to introduce the theory and methods of constructed architectural perspectives. It stresses the importance of visualizing in parallel (one-point) or angular (two-point) perspective from the plan and the elevation of an object. This, of course, comes with patience, perseverance, and, most of all, practice.

In summary, following are some of the important skills, terms, and concepts you will learn:

How to use one-, two-, and three-point perspectives
How to change the pictorial effect by changing the perspective variables

Station point	Picture plane	Horizon line	Ground line
Vanishing point	Line of sight	Cone of vision	Distortion
Office method	Oblique lines	Perspective circles	Measurement systems

Linear Perspective Drawing

TOPICS: CONE OF VISION, DEPTH JUDGMENT

Ching 1990, 118–121.

TOPICS: DIAGONALS, X, Y, Z AXIS, STATION POINT, PICTURE PLANE, HORIZON LINE, VANISHING POINTS, CENTER OF VISION, VERTICAL MEASURING LINE, MIDPOINT, PERSPECTIVE FIELD, PERSPECTIVE VIEWPOINT, PERSPECTIVE SETUP.

Ching 1990, 114.
Hanks and Belliston 1980, 16–19; 21–23.
Montague 1998.
Porter and Goodman 1985, 108–115.

TOPIC: ONE-POINT PERSPECTIVE USING 45° DIAGONAL LINES

Ching 2003, 99–102.

TOPICS: VERTICAL VANISHING LINES, DIAGONAL LINES, OBLIQUE LINES, OBLIQUE VANISHING POINTS, DIAGONAL VANISHING POINTS, 45° VANISHING POINTS.

Forseth 1980, 154–158.

Montague 1998.

TOPIC: ONE-POINT OFFICE METHOD, SECTION PERSPECTIVE, PLAN PERSPECTIVE, PERSPECTIVE CHARTS

Ching 1998, 234–236.
Lin 1993, 116–120, 124–134.

TOPIC: THREE-POINT PERSPECTIVE

Gill 1989, chapter 6.

TOPICS: MULTIPLYING AND DIVIDING, CIRCLES, CIRCLES AND ELLIPSES

Ching 2003, 116, 121.
Ching 1990, 52, 122–123.
Forseth 1980, 168–169, 170.
Hanks and Belliston 1980, 122–123.
Helms 1990, 102–105, 109, 179, 182–183, 218–222.
Montague 1993, 69–72, 170.

Chapter Overview

After studying this chapter and doing the related exercises in the book's final section, you will understand important perspective terms, as well as how to construct one- and two-point perspectives. For continued study of the principles discussed in this chapter, refer to Forseth's *Graphics for Architecture* and Ching's *Architectural Graphics*.

Perspective is a method of depicting the manner in which objects appear to the human eye with respect to their relative positions and distance. The optic mechanism of seeing the urban landscape is done simultaneously with both eyes, and as a result we visually experience things three-dimensionally or spatially. The term "perspective" comes from the Latin *perspectare,* which means "to view through." The origin of linear perspective theory comes from the Renaissance. The perceptual schema of western philosophy and civilization values a drawing system that logically duplicates an individual's visual experience. Thus, linear perspective is considered "correct" in the sense that it values representation.

Architects use perspectives in both preliminary and final design stages. They utilize both drafting's traditional construction methods and new computer techniques to generate desired perspective views to aid in the design process. To fully appreciate perspective drawing it is important to understand the time-consuming manual procedures before embarking on quick methods that can be done by the computer.

In the preliminary design stages, rough, freehand perspective drawings are the norm. In the final presentation stages, perspectives are accurately constructed for the purpose of rendering them (see section on delineating and rendering entourage). In 1949, Frank Lloyd Wright did a rendered conceptual drawing (see p. 81) for his famous Guggenheim Museum in New York City. The rendering showed a tower in the background, which at the time was not built, with the original museum. The complete dream in the perspective rendering finally came to fruition with the completion of the tower addition in 1992.

Theories, definitions, and concepts (pp. 179–199) will be discussed before various step-by-step methods are explained.

Frank Lloyd Wright
Solomon R. Guggenheim Museum (night rendering), circa 1950–1951
37" × 26" (94 × 66 cm)
Medium: Tempera and black ink on composition board
Collection Peter Lawson–Johnston
Photograph by David Heald © The Solomon R. Guggenheim Foundation, New York

INTRODUCTION

Photo: Waterfront pier
San Francisco, California

© Albert Lee

Whether we are viewing the environment or attempting to realistically depict what we see on a two-dimensional, flat drawing surface, we experience four major phenomena: (1) diminution, (2) overlapping, (3) convergence, and (4) foreshortening. **Diminution** occurs when equal-sized objects, such as the lampposts above, appear to diminish in size with distance. This can be seen on the opposite page, where a fixed observer notices that columns and arches of equal size appear to diminish with distance. Photographs require the cameraperson to view from a frozen position, much like the single vantage point of any perspective drawing. Thus, perspectives have a photolike quality to their appearance.

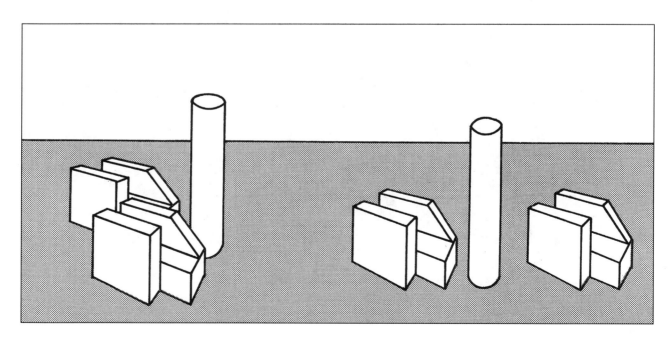

When we see objects **overlapping,** a sense of depth and space is achieved. Isolated objects give no sense of spatial depth.

Stanford University quadrangle, Palo Alto, California
Shepley, Rutan and Coolidge, Architects

These two photographs of a series of arches were taken from two different vantage points. The oblique angle at left is not quite as sharp as the oblique angle shown below and viewed from behind the series of arches. In both cases the **convergence** of parallel lines occurs. That is, the line that is tangent to all the arches vanishes to the same point as the line that touches the bases of all the columns.

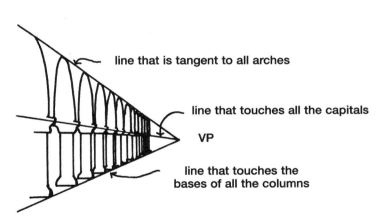

line that is tangent to all arches

line that touches all the capitals

VP

line that touches the
bases of all the columns

FORESHORTENED ARCHES

**The three lines that converge above would be parallel
if drawn in the true-size view below.**

TRUE-SIZE ARCHES

In a head-on view, there would be no illusion of perspective space because no convergence would be evident. The arches would be seen in their maximum or true size. At an oblique angle the arch size becomes **foreshortened** since it is no longer in its true size. The semicircular arch becomes elliptical in all oblique-angle positions.

CONVERGENCE AND FORESHORTENING

At the same time, all of us see objects from a different viewing angle since we cannot occupy the same physical space. However, once we vacate a physical space, another person can experience the same viewpoint. The eye-level line changes as the observer sits down, stands up, or stands on top of an object to view the chair. Notice the foreshortening of the legs of the chair as the observer moves higher and higher. The eye-level line is always at right angles to the observer's line of sight and is theoretically considered to be located at an infinite distance.

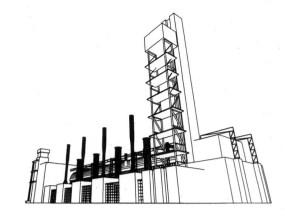

Worm's-eye view at ground level with upward convergence

CAD Drawings (above and below):
Student projects by Bradford Winkeljohn and Jordan Parnass
Excerpted from abstract, Columbia School of Architecture Planning and Preservation (CSAPP)

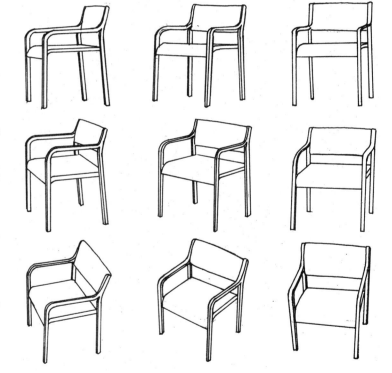

In the design-drawing process, it is important to study a design from every conceivable vantage point. For this reason, examples of other more unique perspective views (above and below vantage points, etc.) are shown on pages 192 to 197.

Bird's-eye view at a high angle

BIRD'S-EYE, EYE LEVEL, AND WORM'S-EYE VIEWS

For the most part, we view the urban environment at eye level in a standing position. The two views not at eye level are commonly termed worm's-eye and bird's-eye. Both are dramatic, although unnatural, views. A worm's-eye view can be at ground level or below the ground plane as shown at right.

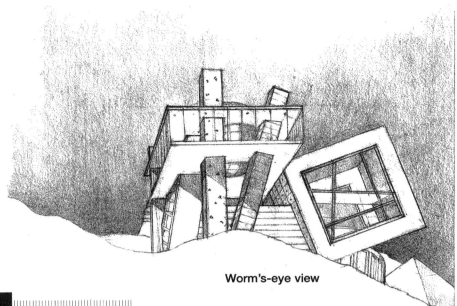

Worm's-eye view

Drawing: House in Hollywood Hills
          Los Angeles, California
8" × 5" (20.3 × 12.7 cm)
Medium: Pencil
Courtesy of Kanner Architects
Drawn by Stephen Kanner

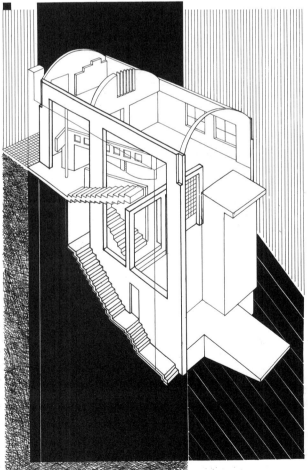

Drawing: Shay House (1985), San Francisco, California
9.5" × 15.5" (24.1 × 39.4 cm), Scale: ⅜"=1'0"
Medium: Pen and ink
Courtesy of James Shay, AIA Architect

By stripping away exterior walls and casting the perspective as a "bird's-eye," the complex interior is communicated. The rendered areas around the building are read in plane rather than perspective, creating interesting ambiguity.
[ARCHITECT'S STATEMENT]

Bird's-eye view

BIRD'S-EYE AND WORM'S-EYE VIEWS

Webster's Dictionary defines *cue* as a hint or intimation. We pick up visual cues all the time. The cues may not always be exactly how we see the physical environment. In general, what we see can be called "perspective" cues. The most fundamental and efficient types of drawing cues are those that employ lines to record the edges of surfaces as we experience them in reality. These are called perspective cues because they represent the relationships between the edges of surfaces at a particular point in time and space—they represent a particular perspective on the world. The perspective cues have been codified into three drawing systems: linear perspective, paraline perspective (used here to include axonometric and oblique systems), and orthographic perspective (multiview drawings). None of these is exactly how we see the world all the time. Each represents certain perceptual and cognitive realities—some combination of what we see and what we know about things.

Linear Perspective Cues

Linear perspective is most acutely experienced in places where long rectangular surfaces begin near the observer and recede into the distance, such as long, straight roads. The essential experience is that the parallel lines seem to come together in the distance. The edges of surfaces are represented by lines that follow the rules of linear perspective and each has a line grammar. One-point perspectives have vertical lines, horizontal lines, and perspective lines (lines that go to vanishing points). Two-point perspectives have vertical lines and perspective lines. Three-point perspectives have only perspective lines.

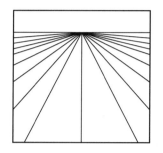 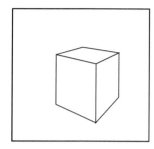

Diagrams and text: Courtesy of
William R. Benedict, Assistant Professor
California Polytechnic State University
College of Architecture & Environmental Design
San Luis Obispo, California

Paraline Perspective Cues

The western perceptual schema is culturally biased toward linear perspective. To other cultures and in other times a paraline drawing looked more "correct" than one using linear perspective. When things are small relative to our visual field their edges and surfaces tend to retain their dimensions. The degree to which the edges vanish is so slight that our knowledge of their equality in length and angle can easily be more important than their adherence to the linear perspective. Paraline systems codify this view of reality. The edges of surfaces are represented by lines that follow the rules of paraline drawing conventions. The edges of parallel surfaces remain parallel and retain direct measured relationships to each other and the thing being represented. Verticals remain vertical and the other axes slope at specified angles.

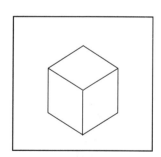

Orthographic Perspective Cues

Orthographic perspective is less acceptable to our eyes and requires experience with its conventions to be able to read it visually. It represents a single object with multiple drawings and requires an ability to assemble the drawings in your mind. We experience things in orthographic perspective when their surfaces are relatively flat and we are standing directly in front of and facing them. As we move away from an object, our experience more closely corresponds to an orthographic drawing. The edges of surfaces are represented by lines that follow the rules of orthoghraphic drawing. Parallel edges remain parallel and retain direct measured relationships to each other and the thing being represented. Verticals remain vertical, horizontals remain horizontal, and the depth axis is represented by a point.

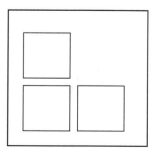

PERSPECTIVE CUES

Two of the most accurate mechanical methods for generating linear perspectives are shown in this chapter. They are the plan elevation (office) method and the measuring point method. **Linear perspective** drawing is a tool for the designer or delineator to make a reasonably accurate representation of a three-dimensional object on a two-dimensional surface (the drawing sheet). A linear perspective drawing is an image of an object projected upon an assumed plane (Picture Plane—PP) that is parallel to the observer's face or eyes. When used as a representational tool for the design–drawing process, it is of utmost importance not to misrepresent the physical appearance of buildings with inaccurate perspective representations. The following are the most commonly used terms in the vocabulary of perspective drawing techniques.

TERM	ABBREVIATION	DEFINITION
Station Point	(SP)	• A vantage point location to view an object or group of objects; the location of the observer's eye.
Picture Plane	(PP)	• A stationary, transparent, two-dimensional, vertical plane or "window." This window receives a true-size image from the projection lines that converge to the station point. Perpendicular to the observer is the line of sight.
Line of Sight	(LS)	• An imaginary line that perpendicularly intersects the vertical picture plane as it is projected from the observer's eye (station point).
Horizon Line or Eye-Level Line	(HL)	• Represents the observer's eye level. The horizon line is recorded on the picture plane. It is the vanishing line for all horizontal lines and planes.
Ground Line	(GL)	• The line where the picture plane and the ground meet. The ground line lies within a ground plane from which vertical measurements are made.
Ground plane	(GP)	• The reference plane where the observer is situated. It can be at any level, depending on the vantage point of the perspective view.
Vanishing Point	(VPL, VPR, and VP_o)	• A point on the horizon line where any group of parallel horizontal lines converge in perspective. Groups of oblique (inclined) parallel lines vanish either above (sloping upward) or below (sloping downward) the horizon line. Parallel lines that are parallel to the picture plane do not converge.
Vertical Measuring Line	(VML)	• A vertical line within the picture plane. Vertical height dimensions are transferred from an elevation to this vertical true-length line in order to be projected into the perspective drawing.
MidPoint	(M)	• A point located on the horizon line that lies halfway between the vanishing points in a two-point perspective.
Horizontal Measuring Line	(HML)	• A horizontal line lying in the picture plane, therefore a true-length line.

PERSPECTIVE GLOSSARY

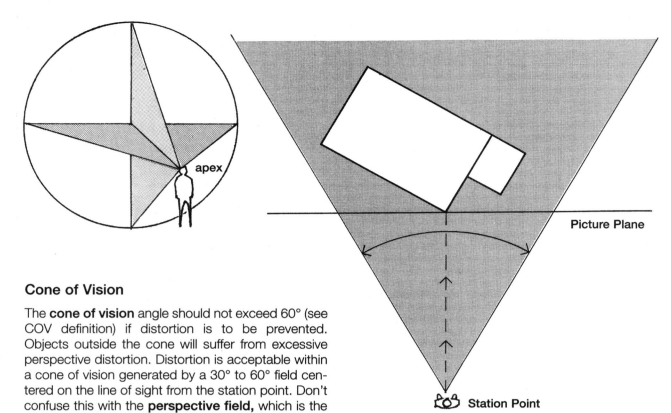

CONE OF VISION

Cone of Vision

The **cone of vision** angle should not exceed 60° (see COV definition) if distortion is to be prevented. Objects outside the cone will suffer from excessive perspective distortion. Distortion is acceptable within a cone of vision generated by a 30° to 60° field centered on the line of sight from the station point. Don't confuse this with the **perspective field,** which is the area defined by a circle whose center is located at the MidPoint (M) and whose circumference intersects the two horizontal vanishing points in a two-point perspective. The office method (see pp. 200–202, 244, 248–249) for drawing perspectives is based on the concept of the cone of vision.

Visualize this as the base of a cone (circle in its true shape) that is perpendicular to the observer's center of vision line of sight. This circular area of the vertical picture plane can be seen in clear focus when the apex angle is less than 60°. The area viewed increases in size as the picture plane moves away from the station point.

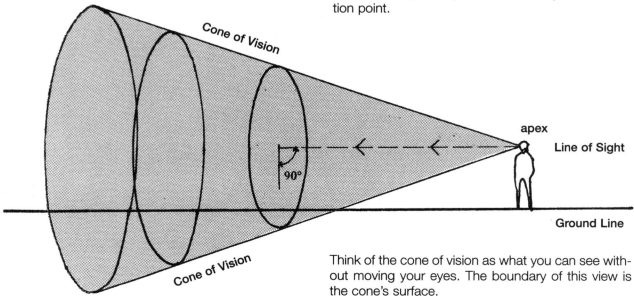

Think of the cone of vision as what you can see without moving your eyes. The boundary of this view is the cone's surface.

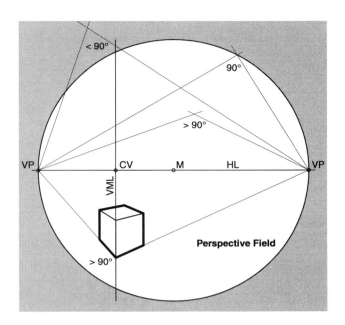

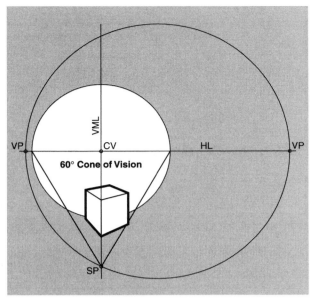

Acceptable Distortion

Linear perspective formalizes through geometry a system that attempts to represent three-dimensional reality on a two-dimensional surface—that is, it attempts to place a portion of the visual field on a page. Because it is a closed system assuming a fixed, one-eyed observer, it has limitations that must be respected if the goal is to accurately represent perceived visual reality—if the goal is for the drawing to "look right." The cube that is drawn with its lead edge coinciding with the vertical measuring line (VML—the line drawn through the center of vision) and centered vertically on the horizon line is the most accurate cube in the perspective. As the cubes move away from this location, they progressively become more distorted. The question, therefore, is how far from this location does a perspective retain sufficient accuracy so as not to be visually disturbing—what are the limits within which the perspective looks right?

Cone of Vision

The cone of vision links the way our eyes work and the control of distortion within the perspective system. A 60° cone is one that extends 30° to either side of our line of sight. A 30° cone is advisable for spheres and circles. The illustration simultaneously shows a 60° cone of vision in both plan and perspective. For any measuring point perspective setup, the cone of vision can be constructed to establish the area within which a perspective will "look most correct."

Diagrams and text: Courtesy of
William R. Benedict, Assistant Professor
California Polytechnic State University
College of Architecture & Environmental Design
San Luis Obispo, California

90° Horizontal Corner

The perspective field can be used to control the near internal angle of horizontal rectangles to 90° or greater. When the angle becomes less than 90°, it does not look right. Any two lines intersecting at the circumference of the perspective field will create a 90° angle. Those intersecting beyond the circumference will create an angle of less than 90°, while those intersecting within the perspective field will create an angle of more than 90°. Therefore, the perspective field provides a guideline for establishing some limits within the linear perspective system.

Measuring point methods for constructing perspectives (See pp. 228–243) are also related to the concept of the cone of vision.

DISTORTION

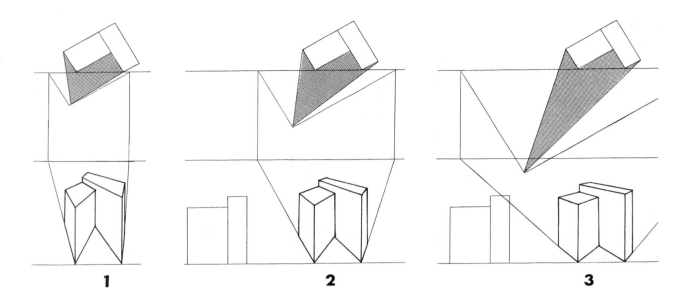

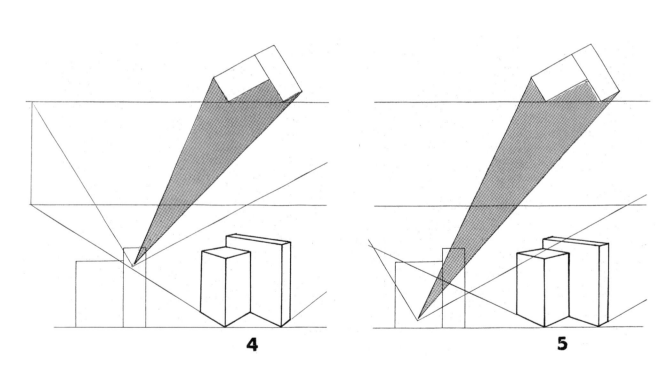

Distortion

Perspective **distortion** is dependent on the spacing of vanishing points. A very close station point location with close vanishing points results in extreme convergence with a great amount of foreshortening (see **1** and **2**). A very distant station point results in minimal convergence with very little foreshortening. In the latter case, the base of the object becomes quite flat. A more natural pictorial view is obtained by spreading the vanishing points apart (see **4** and **5**). However, try not to spread them too far apart so that distorted "flatness" occurs. A good distance is three times the object height.

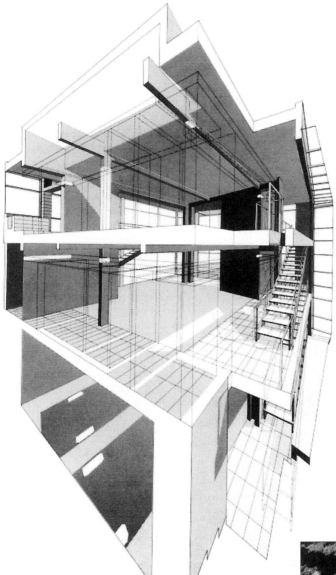

Drawing: Burnett House addition
                   Lake Oswego, Oregon
24" × 36" (61 × 91.4 cm)
Medium: Ink on Mylar with Zipatone
Courtesy of David Rockwood Architects & Associates

Distortion

This interior perspective shows a large amount of foreshortening with conditions similar to example **1** (opposite page). There is a point at which one reaches a state of distortion, with the vanishing points being too close with respect to the height (which relates to the cone of vision).

Example of extreme convergence

This exterior perspective shows a small amount of foreshortening with conditions similar to example **5** on the opposite page.

Example of a natural pictorial view

Drawing: Student project by Steve Gambrel
                   Seafarers' Church Institute
Courtesy of the University of Virginia School of Architecture

DISTORTION

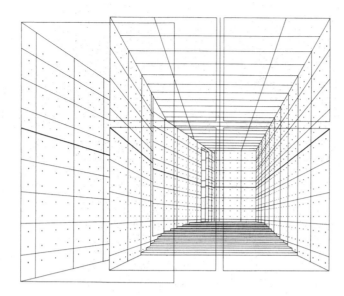

Drawing: Church of the Light, Ibaraki, Japan
23.3" × 16.5" (59.2 × 41.9 cm)
Medium: Ink
Courtesy of Tadao Ando, Architect

The Picture Plane

This transparent interior perspective shows the wall with a cross slit behind the church's altar. The wall simulates a vertical picture plane through which one can capture the perspective view. An exception to the flat, two-dimensional picture plane is the spheroidal (similar to a sphere but not completely round) picture plane used with a fish-eye lens view.

THE PICTURE PLANE

Drawing: Student project by Corvin Matei
Vasari Museum, Florence, Italy
10" × 8" (25.4 × 20.3 cm)
Medium: Ink on Mylar
Courtesy of the University of Texas at Arlington
School of Architecture

A window is a fixed transparent vertical plane. When we look through a window, our eyes receive images of the three-dimensional objects we see. This image is translated onto a two-dimensional plane (the window) at an infinite number of points when our lines of sight intersect the window. Thus, the window becomes **the picture plane.** This drawing shows the viewpoint of an observer looking through a window.

In this example of **parallel** (one-point) **perspective,** the image of the building form is projected on the picture plane. Vertical and horizontal lines retain verticality and horizontality in the image. Lines not parallel to this picture plane will converge to the vanishing point (VP). If the building form is **behind** the picture plane, as illustrated in this drawing, it is projected **smaller** than true size on the picture plane. If **in front,** it is projected **larger** than true size.

The three major perspective types are one-point, two-point, and three-point (referring to the number of vanishing points). A one-point perspective always has a plane parallel to the picture plane. Planes perpendicular to the picture plane vanish to one point.

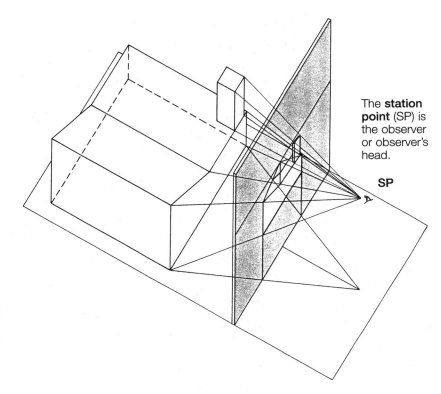

The **station point** (SP) is the observer or observer's head.

SP

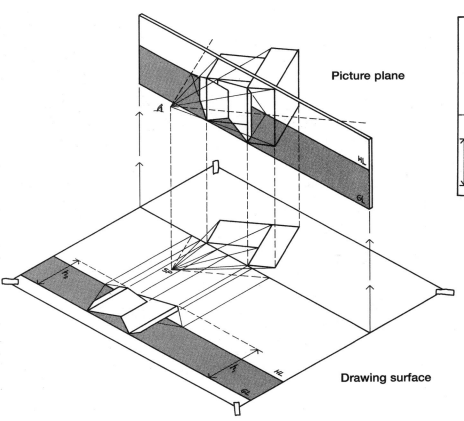

Picture plane

Drawing surface

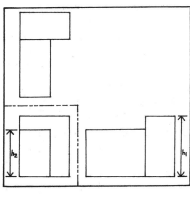

THE PICTURE PLANE

The **picture plane** is always perpendicular to the drawing surface and represented by a **line** on the drawing. Also on the drawing, the observer reduces to a dot and the building form to a two-dimensional plan view. True heights (h_1 and h_2) are always obtained from a set of orthographic drawings (plans and elevations). They are measured vertically from the ground line.

ONE-POINT PERSPECTIVE

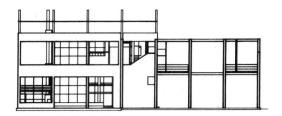

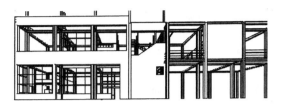

Drawing   Chapel for Rose Hills Memorial Park
           Whittier, California
24" × 36" (61 × 91.4 cm), Scale: ¼"=1'0"
Medium: Pencil and ink
Courtesy of Fay Jones & Maurice Jennings, Architects
Drawn by Barry McNeill/Jones & Jennings

Drawings: Student project by Lois McGinnis and Michael Patrick
          Shelby's Lake House—A project in CAD
Courtesy of the University of Texas at Arlington
School of Architecture

One-Point Perspective

The above one-point perspective seen at ground level is much more descriptive than its flat two-dimensional elevation.

The three main types of perspectives are classified based on the drawing's primary vanishing points. Many drawings have secondary minor vanishing points. These building examples show that all horizontal lines that recede away from the observer's eye converge to **one** vanishing point. Therefore, they can be classified as **one-point** perspectives.

Drawing: Milam residence
          St. John's County, Florida
33" × 30" (83.8 × 76.2 cm)
Medium: Ink on board,
Courtesy of Paul Rudolph, Architect

Two-Point Perspective

These building examples show their dominant facades converging on left and right sides to **two** vanishing points on their respective horizon lines. Therefore, they can be classified as **two-point** perspectives.

Drawing: Student project by Leopoldo Chang
Poet's Hotel, New York
Medium: Ink on Mylar
Excerpted from Abstract, Columbia School of
Architecture Planning and Preservation (CSAAP)

Drawing: Studio Durant (unbuilt), Berkeley, California
Medium: Computer-generated plot (size dependent on size of plot)
Courtesy of David Baker Associates Architects

TWO-POINT PERSPECTIVE

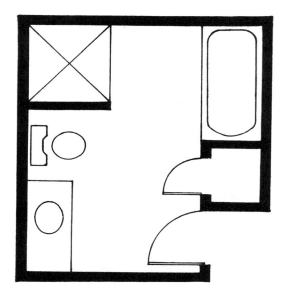

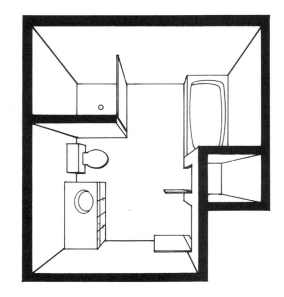

An unusual variation of the **one-point** perspective is a bird's-eye view with the line of sight perpendicular to the ground plane. This variation, which is achieved by transposing the positions of plan and elevation, is commonly used for small interior spaces and interior or exterior courtyard areas.

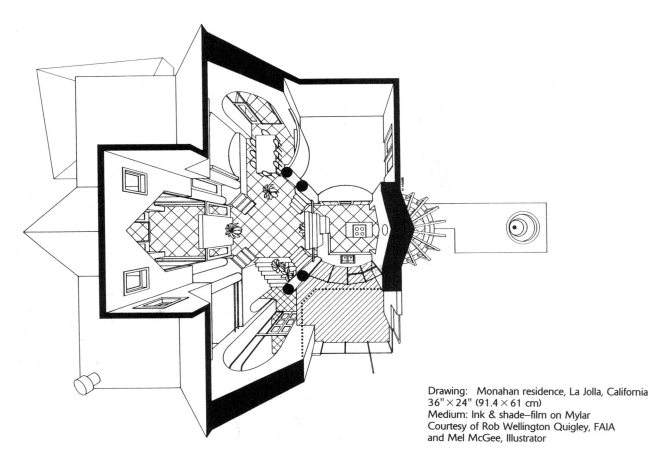

Drawing: Monahan residence, La Jolla, California
36" × 24" (91.4 × 61 cm)
Medium: Ink & shade—film on Mylar
Courtesy of Rob Wellington Quigley, FAIA
and Mel McGee, Illustrator

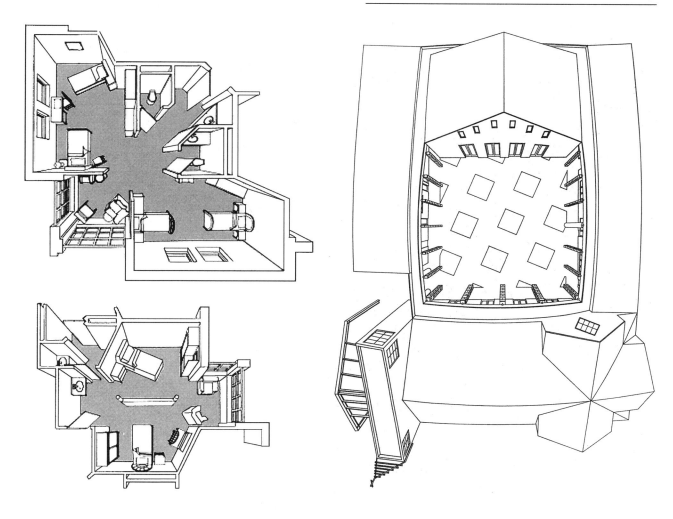

Drawings: Freeport Hospital Health Care Village,
Kitchener, Ontario, Canada
Courtesy of NORR Partnership Ltd./
NORR Health Care Design Group

Drawing: New Hope Church, Duarte, California
24" × 36" (61 × 91.4 cm)
Medium: Ink on vellum
Courtesy of Rebecca L. Binder, FAIA

ONE-POINT FROM ABOVE

Interior views from above are very descriptive and hence quite informative, especially to a person (client) who may not completely understand an architectural plan. In most cases, they simulate a one-point perspective view that one would have if the roof or ceiling of a scale model were removed. Quick construction of the view can be achieved by placing the plan view so that it coincides with the picture plane. Vertical height lines through all corners of the plan are then drawn converging to one vanishing point in a relatively central location. Height lines are terminated where descriptively appropriate (typically where the plan section cut is taken). With the church at right above, there is no plan section cut and the curving of the roof elements gives a "fish-eye" lens effect.

ONE-POINT FROM BELOW

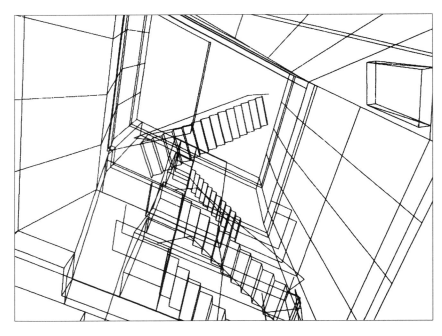

View up through tower

This computer-generated wire frame drawing is essentially a one-point perspective that has the sides of the structure tilted with respect to the edges of the picture plane and converging to other far-distant vanishing points. The stairs also converge to other distant vanishing points.

Drawing: 3ER House, Venice, California
Medium: CAD
Courtesy of COOP HIMMELB(L)AU Architects
Wolf D. Prix, Helmut Swiczinsky & Partner

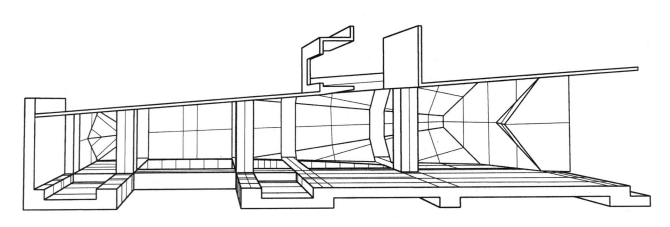

Drawing: Ackerman Student Union, UCLA
Medium: AutoCAD release 12
Courtesy of Rebecca L. Binder, FAIA

The entry elements and circulation in this remodel/addition project are key to the establishment of a "new" whole. The ceilings are integral to the design, articulated in finished plywood. This floor view perspective offers a clear description of this northeast entry element.
[ARCHITECT'S STATMENT]

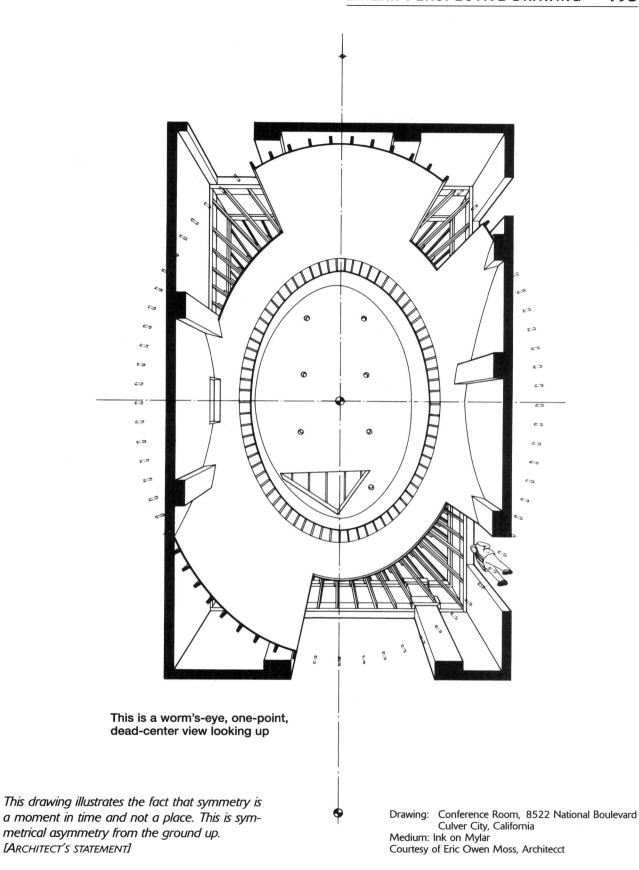

ONE-POINT FROM BELOW

This is a worm's-eye, one-point, dead-center view looking up

This drawing illustrates the fact that symmetry is a moment in time and not a place. This is symmetrical asymmetry from the ground up.
[ARCHITECT'S STATEMENT]

Drawing: Conference Room, 8522 National Boulevard
Culver City, California
Medium: Ink on Mylar
Courtesy of Eric Owen Moss, Architecct

When the lines of sight of our bird's-eye and worm's-eye views are parallel to an inclined plane, we are looking downhill and uphill. We see downhill and uphill perspective views in the natural landscape as well as in street scenes in the cityscape. Downhill and uphill views inside or outside a building's environment are characterized by stairs, escalators, or ramps.

LOOKING DOWNHILL AND UPHILL

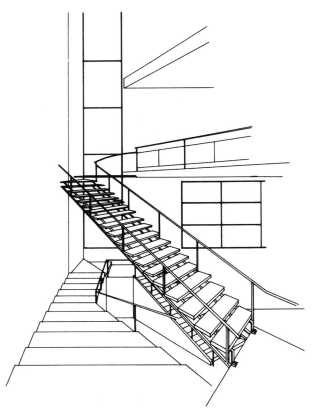

Drawing: Student project by Stacey Wenger
          Barcelona studio, Barcelona, Spain
Medium: Ink on Mylar
Courtesy of Washington University
School of Architecture, St. Louis, Missouri

Drawing: The Sainsbury Wing: An extension to the National Gallery
          London, England
28" × 40" (71.1 × 101.6 cm)
Medium: Pencil on vellum
Courtesy of Venturi, Scott Brown and Associates, Inc., Architects

Drawings: Student project by Thanh Do
              San Francisco downhill and uphill views
4" × 6" (10.2 × 15.2 cm)
Medium: Ink on vellum
Courtesy of the City College of San Francisco
Department of Architecture

Photo: Great Wall of China near Beijing, China

Downhill and uphill views produce false horizon lines and result in oblique vanishing points (see pp. 212–215). The observer's view is parallel to the sloping hills. The true horizon lines are where the vanishing point of all the horizontal lines on the building facade rests. The streetcar in the downhill view vanishes at a point on a false horizon line below the true horizon line. Likewise, the streetcar tracks in the uphill view vanish at a point on a false horizon line above the true horizon line. In both the downhill and the uphill situations, the different vanishing points align themselves vertically above and below each other.

LOOKING DOWNHILL AND UPHILL

TWO-POINT AND ONE-POINT PERSPECTIVES

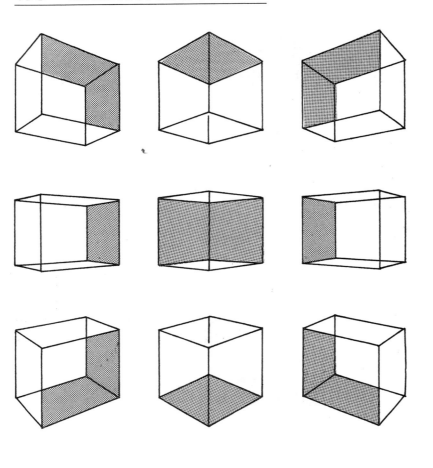

In the **two-point perspective** views shown at left, note how two sets of parallel horizontal lines converge to the left and to the right. In reality, vertical lines remain vertical only in the middle row where the line of sight is horizontal. Looking up or down from the horizon line results in the appearance of upward or downward convergence of the vertical lines.

Look at cardboard cartons (boxes) and try to visualize them moving around in space. From a rectilinear or cubic form, one can draw and derive other geometric forms. The human senses of sight and touch allow us to experientially model all kinds of shapes.

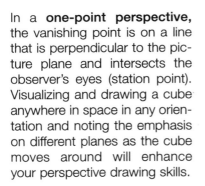

In a **one-point perspective,** the vanishing point is on a line that is perpendicular to the picture plane and intersects the observer's eyes (station point). Visualizing and drawing a cube anywhere in space in any orientation and noting the emphasis on different planes as the cube moves around will enhance your perspective drawing skills.

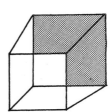
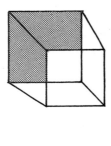
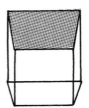
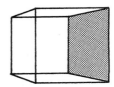
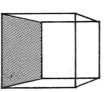

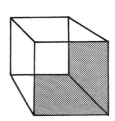
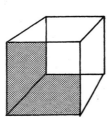

Drawing: Theater lobby, Perry Community
Education Village, Perry, Ohio
36" × 24" (91 × 61.4 cm)
Medium: Ink on Mylar
Courtesy of Perkins & Will, Architects

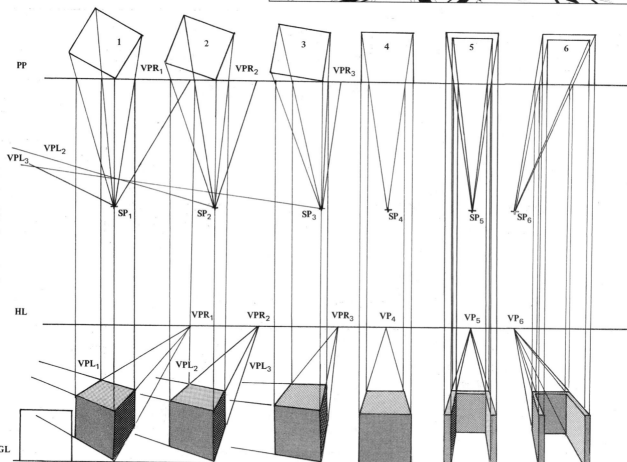

TWO-POINT AND ONE-POINT PERSPECTIVES

It is generally easiest to learn how to construct a two-point perspective before attempting a one-point perspective. A one-point perspective can be termed a special case of a two-point perspective in which the plan view is not rotated and one set of lines are either parallel or coincident with the picture plane. Note how the cube transforms from a two-point perspective image (**1–3**) to a one-point perspective image (**4**). The open cube is also shown in one-point perspective variations (**5** and **6**). In one-point perspective, the plan view must be placed parallel to the picture plane so that the profile and the ground plane can project to the one vanishing point.

The drawing example at the top of this page shows characteristics of both one- and two-point perspectives. Also note the tilted ellipses (see p. 279).

PLAN/ELEVATION OFFICE METHOD

The first method (known as **office** or **common**) that we will examine for constructing an accurate perspective is a traditional one. It is dependent on both the **plan** and the **elevation.**

1. In the top or plan view, place the outline of the object or objects (buildings) with an arbitrary orientation angle θ (based on the view desired).
2. Arbitrarily locate the picture plane and the station point in the plan view to create a distortionless view. It is advantageous to have the corner of the object touch the picture plane; this establishes a convenient vertical measuring line.

In a preliminary design drawing, an overlay of the floor plan, roof plan, and elevation would be made with tracing paper. If possible, never draw on the original drawings (use prints).

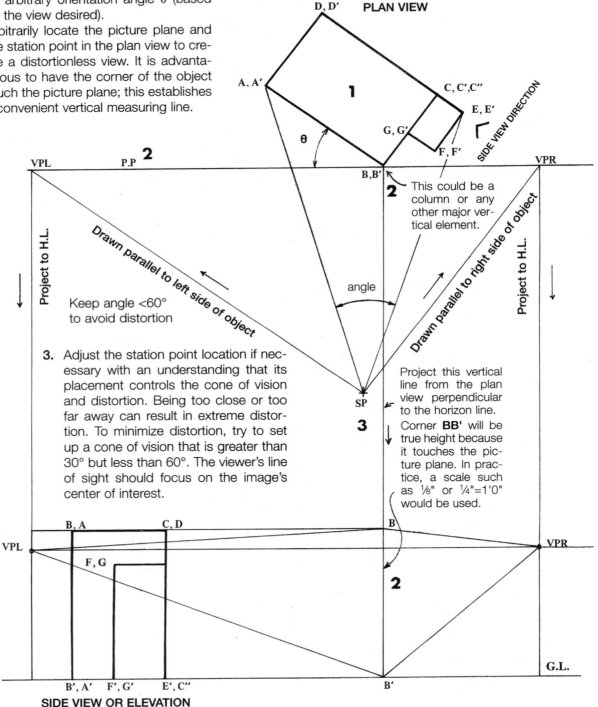

Keep angle <60° to avoid distortion

3. Adjust the station point location if necessary with an understanding that its placement controls the cone of vision and distortion. Being too close or too far away can result in extreme distortion. To minimize distortion, try to set up a cone of vision that is greater than 30° but less than 60°. The viewer's line of sight should focus on the image's center of interest.

This could be a column or any other major vertical element.

Project this vertical line from the plan view perpendicular to the horizon line.

Corner **BB'** will be true height because it touches the picture plane. In practice, a scale such as ⅛" or ¼"=1'0" would be used.

SIDE VIEW OR ELEVATION

4. Draw lines parallel to the sides of the object from the station point until they intersect the picture plane. At these points, drop vertical tracer lines until they inersect the horizon line established for the perspective. The intersection points become the vanishing points for the perspective.

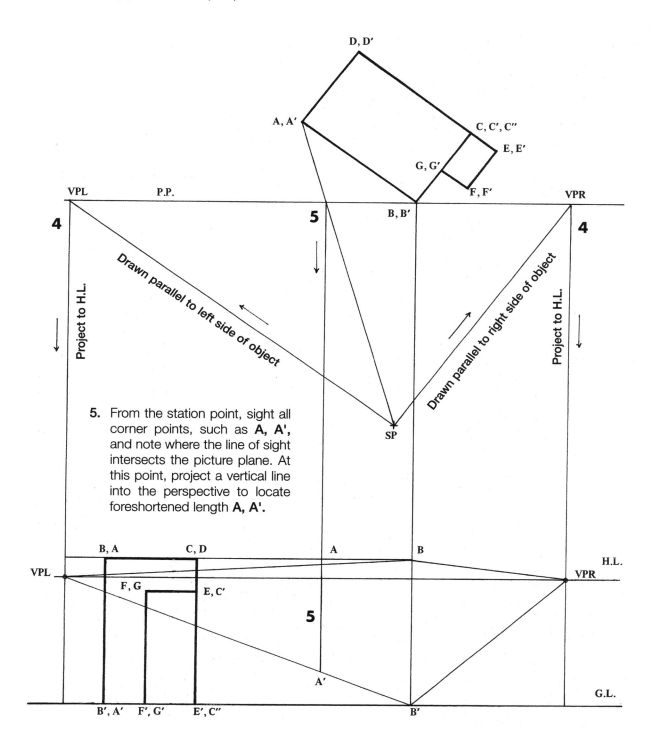

5. From the station point, sight all corner points, such as **A, A'**, and note where the line of sight intersects the picture plane. At this point, project a vertical line into the perspective to locate foreshortened length **A, A'**.

PLAN/ELEVATION OFFICE METHOD

PLAN/ELEVATION OFFICE METHOD

6. Project all sighting intersection points on the picture plane into the perspective in order to complete the perspective of the object. Hidden lines are optional.

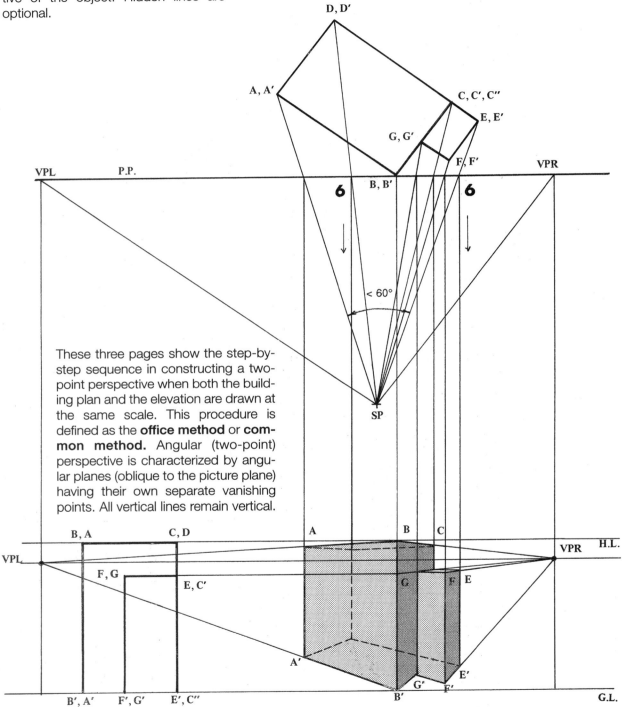

These three pages show the step-by-step sequence in constructing a two-point perspective when both the building plan and the elevation are drawn at the same scale. This procedure is defined as the **office method** or **common method.** Angular (two-point) perspective is characterized by angular planes (oblique to the picture plane) having their own separate vanishing points. All vertical lines remain vertical.

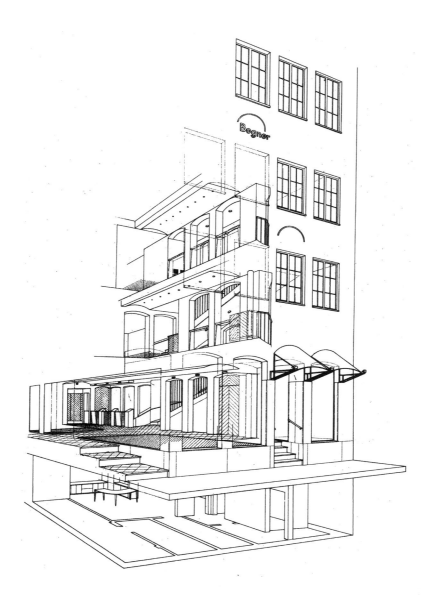

Drawing: Bogner Fashion House, Munich, West Germany
Medium: Ink
Courtesy of MACK—Mark Mack, Architect
Heino Stamm Planungsbüro; Bruckner & Partner, Associated Architects

APPLICATION: TWO-POINT PERSPECTIVE

This unique two-point cutaway sectional perspective (see pp. 254–255) has lines going to two vanishing points on a horizon line. Note that the basement level shows a partial perspective plan view. The two vanishing points on the previous page are more evenly spread apart from the observer's line of sight and the cone of vision than are the vanishing points shown above. This is because the observer's line of sight is almost exactly at the corner of the object. In the above drawing, the vanishing points are quite unevenly spread apart because the front facade is almost parallel to the observer's face and the sectional cut surface is almost perpendicular to the observer's face (foreshortened).

1. Label each block element and find the vanishing points for each. This particular example has six vanishing points.
2. Drop true-height tracer lines (circled points) from where the object touches the picture plane. Transfer corresponding true heights from the elevation.
3. Draw lines from the top and the bottom of the true-height lines to the appropriate vanishing points.
4. From the station point, sight all object corners and follow appropriate procedures to complete the perspective view.

OFFICE METHOD—MULTIPLE VANISHING POINTS

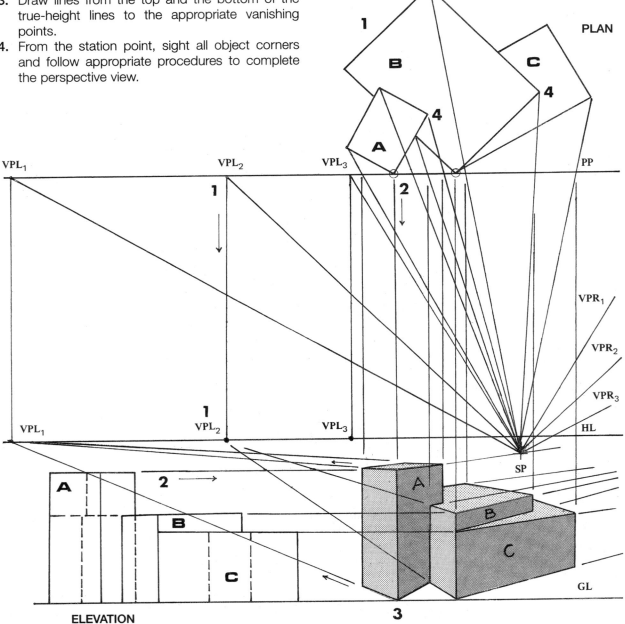

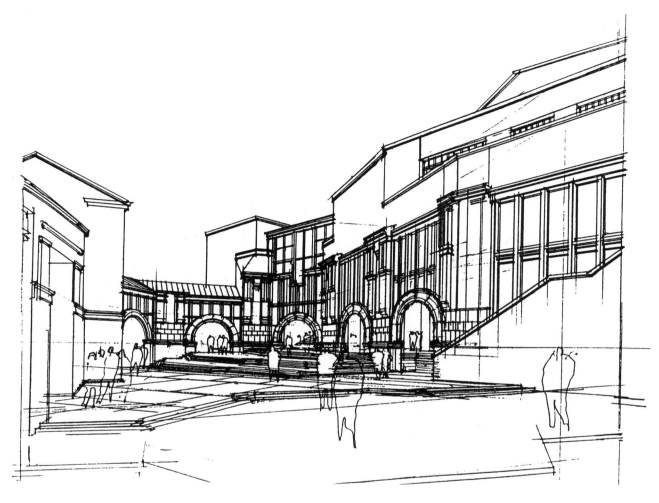

Drawing: California Center for the Arts, Escondido, California
              Moore Ruble Yudell Architects
17" × 14" (43 × 36 cm)
Rough layout before a final line sketch and the use of watercolor as the medium (see pp. 295–301)
Courtesy of Al Forster, Architectural Illustrator

Multiple Vanishing Points

The blockout began as if there was just one ground plane. Plaza levels were added or (as in foreground) subtracted from the ground plane and the figures in the final drawing were placed below or above the horizon line on their proper plaza levels. In a complicated drawing like this one with multiple levels, vanishing points, and detail, it is easier to disguise certain inevitable errors than it is in a very simple drawing.
[ARCHITECTURAL ILLUSTRATOR'S STATEMENT]

This entry plaza is partially enclosed by wall planes that have multiple vanishing points on the horizon line.

1. Project extension lines from the left and right sides of the object to the picture plane and drop vertically to the ground line.

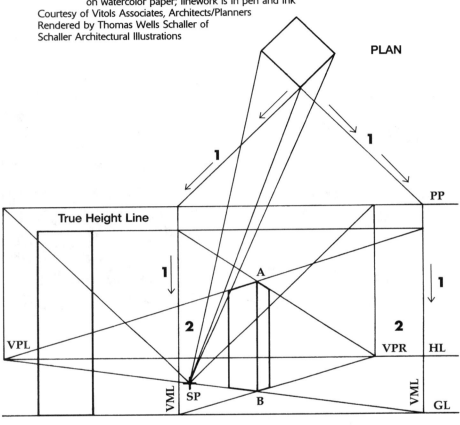

Drawing: Lotus Mansion, Shanghai, China
16.75" × 22" (42.5 × 55.9 cm)
Medium: Watercolor by brush and airbrush
on watercolor paper; linework is in pen and ink
Courtesy of Vitols Associates, Architects/Planners
Rendered by Thomas Wells Schaller of
Schaller Architectural Illustrations

PLAN

True Height Line

ELEVATION

Building corner height AB is defined by
the intersecting perspective planes.

2. Project the perspective planes back to **VPR** and **VPL** for both sides.

Object/PP Relationship

Objects that are behind the picture plane usually fall well within the cone of vision and show no distortion (see p. 210). The high-rise illustration was drawn with a greater degree of convergence to the left vanishing point than the example diagram to the right. Nevertheless, the view is well within the cone of vision. To find all the vanishing points when an object does not touch the picture plane, always construct (or trace) the plan view and note all the planar elements and their angles relative to the picture plane. Draw light construction lines parallel to all these planar elements, regardless of whether they are on the left or right side of the building. Drop these projection lines vertically from the picture plane to the horizon line. Relative to the station point, all left-side planar elements go to left vanishing points and all right-side planar elements go to right vanishing points.

Drawing: Student project by A. Zainie Zainul
Medium: Ink on Mylar
Courtesy of Washington University
School of Architecture, St. Louis, Missouri

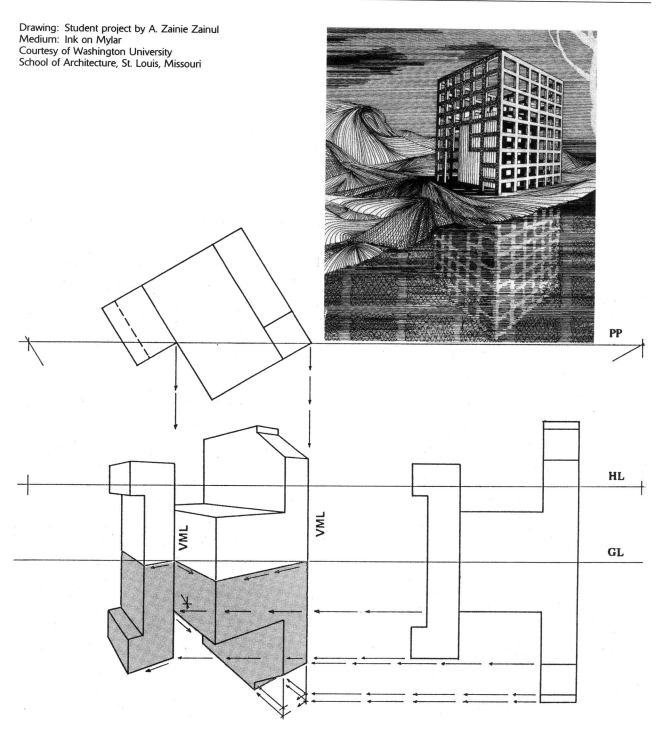

PP

HL

VML

VML

GL

OFFICE METHOD—OBJECT/PP RELATIONSHIP

Objects completely in front of the picture plane will have a distorted perspective image because they begin to fall outside the cone of vision. However, partial penetration of the picture plane by an object is usually visually acceptable, as shown above. Use all **vertical measuring lines (VML)** that touch the picture plane to project construction lines into the volume in front of the picture plane. The schematic example shown has a reflection (see pages on reflections) that also falls partially in front of the picture plane.

You can manipulate a perspective image by changing certain variables. These include moving the picture plane, changing the orientation, changing the station point location with respect to the object, and moving the horizon line up and down.

PICTORIAL EFFECT: VARIABLE SP HT AND HL

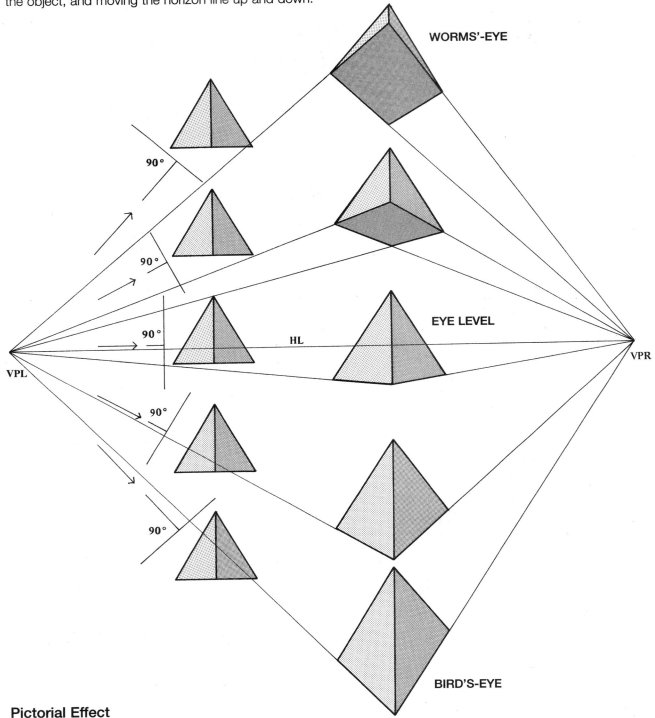

WORMS'-EYE

90°

90°

90°

HL

EYE LEVEL

VPL

VPR

90°

90°

BIRD'S-EYE

Pictorial Effect

In this example, the picture plane, the orientation, and the station point location remain fixed. The horizon line with respect to the ground plane moves up and down.

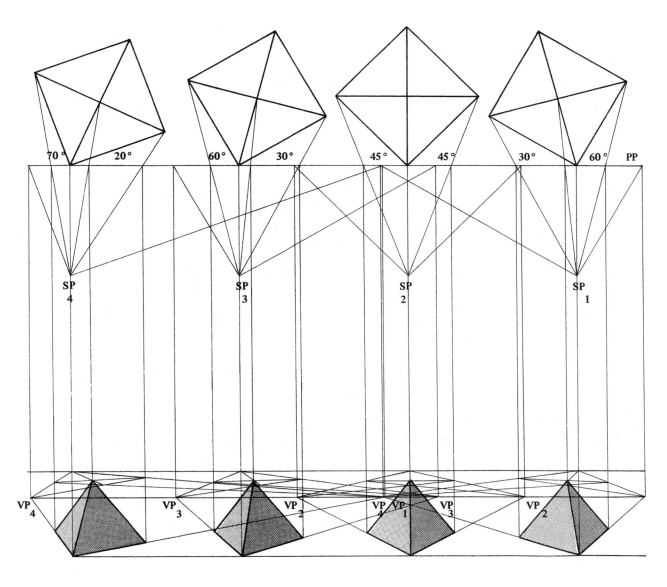

Each **orientation** change produces a new set of angles with respect to the picture plane.

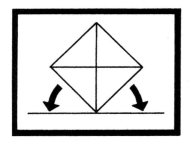

In this example, the picture plane, the station point location, and the horizon line remain fixed. The orientation changes.

PICTORIAL EFFECT: VARIABLE ORIENTATION

Note that increasing the distance from the picture plane to the station point (**PP₄** to **PP₁**) causes a progressive enlargement of the perspective image.

PICTORIAL EFFECT: VARIABLE PICTURE PLANE

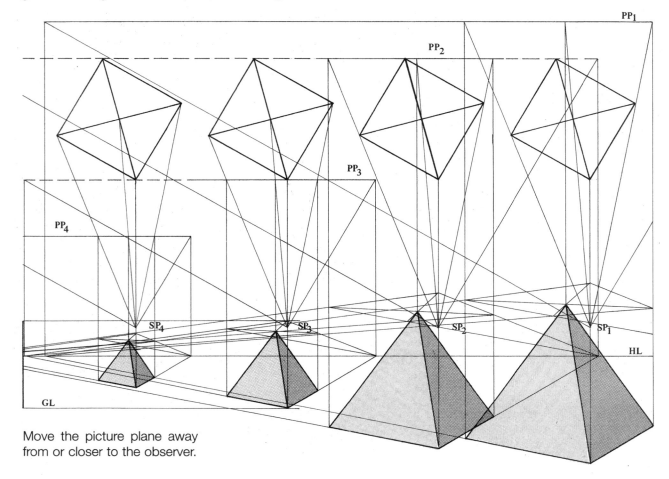

Move the picture plane away from or closer to the observer.

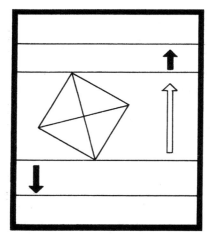

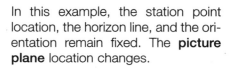

In this example, the station point location, the horizon line, and the orientation remain fixed. The **picture plane** location changes.

Drawing: The Pyramid at Le Grand Louvre, Paris, France
30" × 16" (76 × 41 cm)
Medium: Acrylic
Pei Cobb Freed & Partners / Michel Macary Architects
Courtesy of Lee Dunnette, Architectural Illustrator

Note that increasing the station point distance to the object (**SP₄** to **SP₁**) causes a decrease in foreshortening due to the two vanishing points progressively moving away from each other.

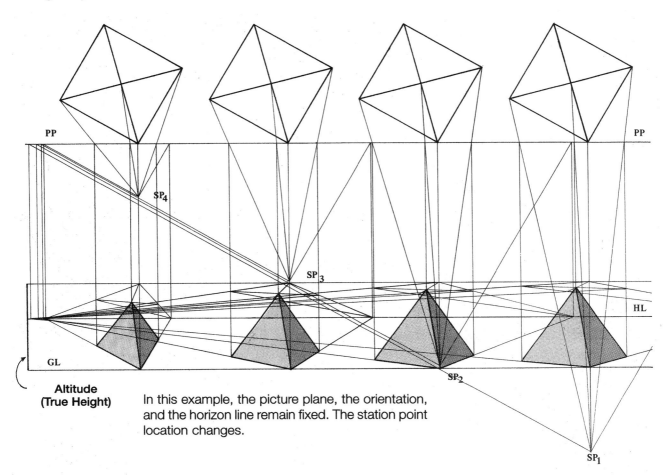

Altitude (True Height)

In this example, the picture plane, the orientation, and the horizon line remain fixed. The station point location changes.

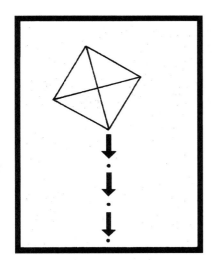

The **observer moves** from near to far away from the viewed object.

© Olallo L. Fernandez

PICTORIAL EFFECT: VARIABLE STATION POINT

OBLIQUE VANISHING POINTS

Drawing: Student project by Jennifer Kinkead
          Bicycle factory, Mexico
Medium: Ink on Mylar
Excerpted from Abstract, Columbia School of
Architecture Planning and Preservation
(CSAPP)

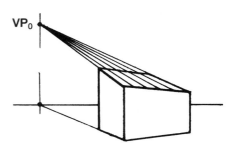

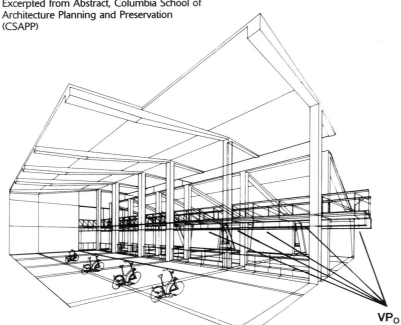

VP_O=oblique vanishing point

Oblique Vanishing Point

It is quite common to find a series of **oblique** (also termed sloping and inclined) edges that are parallel in building forms. In such cases an oblique vanishing point **(VP_O)** expedites perspective construction.

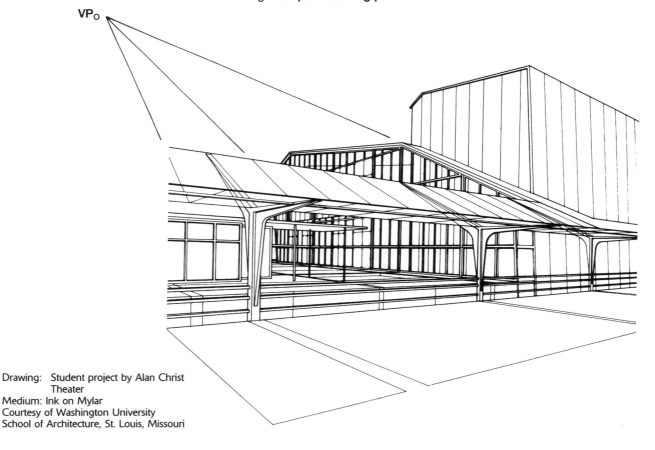

Drawing: Student project by Alan Christ
          Theater
Medium: Ink on Mylar
Courtesy of Washington University
School of Architecture, St. Louis, Missouri

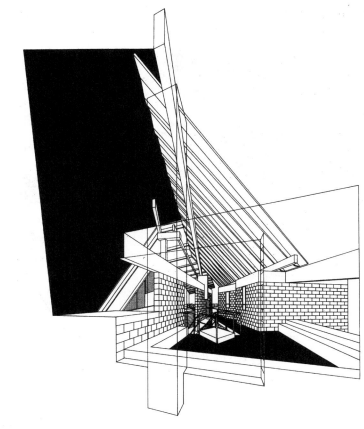

Drawing: Glass–Kline residence
                  New Paltz, New York
14" × 17" (35.6 × 43.2 cm)
Medium: Ink on vellum
Courtesy of Taeg Nishimoto &
allied architects

This interior perspective has structural ceiling elements that have oblique vanishing points both down to the right and down to the left.

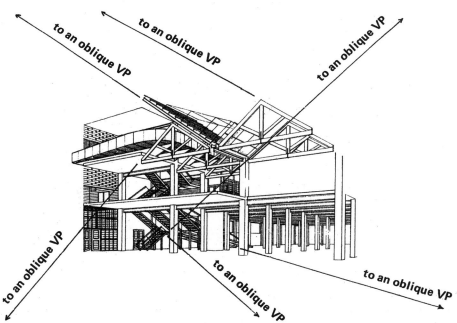

Drawing: La Llauna School, Badalona, Spain
Medium: Ink on Mylar
Courtesy of Enric Miralles & Carme Pinós, Architects

Edges that are **parallel** in an inclined plane converge to a **common** vanishing point. This vanishing point is not on the eye-level line. The vanishing points for a building's **oblique** lines fall either above or below its eye-level vanishing points. The process of determining the proper direction is discussed on the next two pages. The perspective of this building has numerous inclined lines and planes and, consequently, many oblique vanishing points. Sloping lines in perspective are a common occurrence with staircases and ramps.

OBLIQUE VANISHING POINTS

OBLIQUE VANISHING POINTS: LEFT SIDE

If a building has parallel inclined (slanted) edges that are neither horizontal nor vertical, as seen in the plan view to the left, their vanishing traces will converge to an oblique vanishing point above or below the vanishing point for horizontal lines. These trace lines are all located in the same or parallel planes.

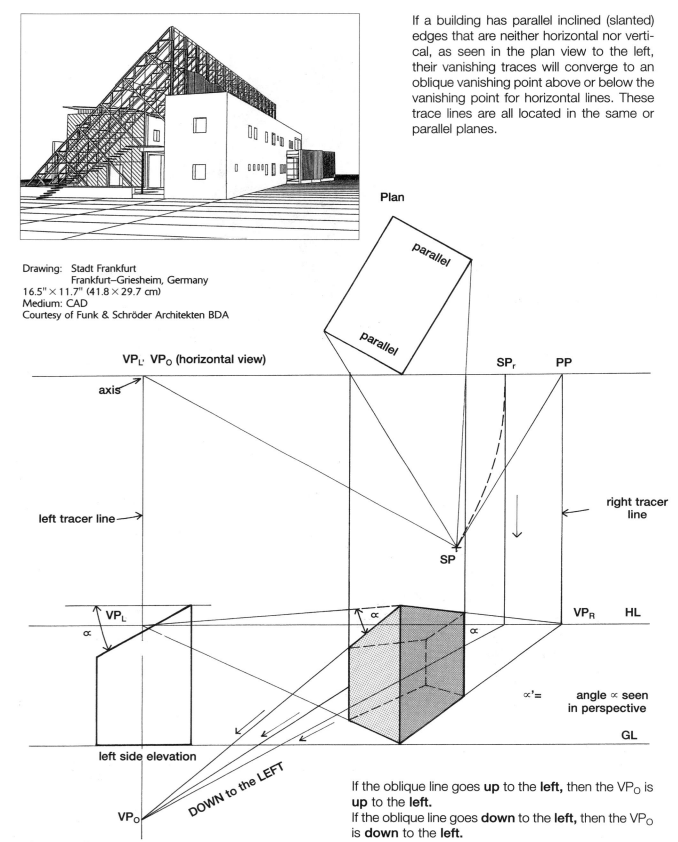

Drawing: Stadt Frankfurt
Frankfurt–Griesheim, Germany
16.5" × 11.7" (41.8 × 29.7 cm)
Medium: CAD
Courtesy of Funk & Schröder Architekten BDA

If the oblique line goes **up** to the **left**, then the VP_O is **up** to the **left**.
If the oblique line goes **down** to the **left**, then the VP_O is **down** to the **left**.

ΔABC is proportional to **ΔSP$_r$, VP$_R$, VP$_O$** where **r** means rotated.

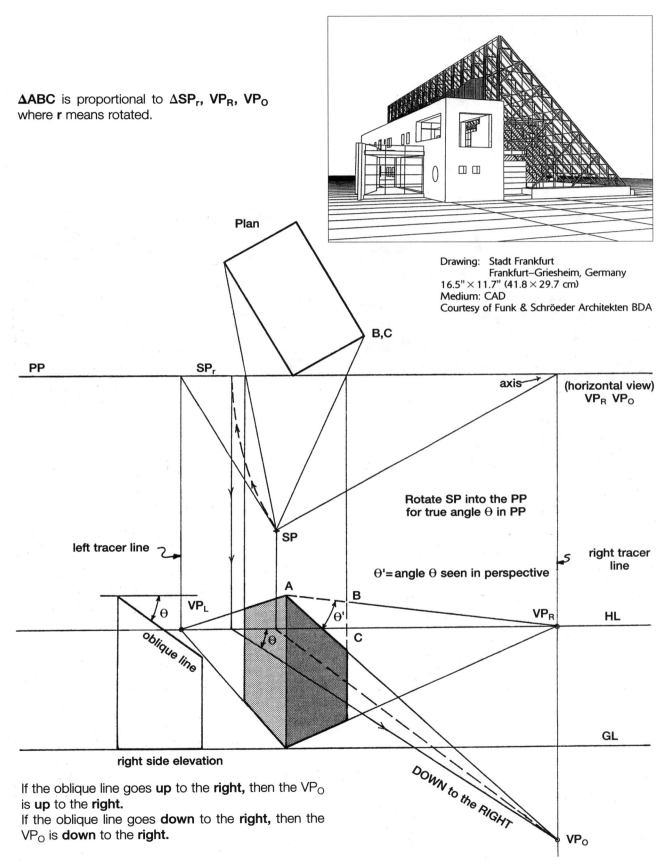

Drawing: Stadt Frankfurt
               Frankfurt–Griesheim, Germany
16.5" × 11.7" (41.8 × 29.7 cm)
Medium: CAD
Courtesy of Funk & Schröeder Architekten BDA

Plan

B,C

PP

SP$_r$

axis

(horizontal view)
VP$_R$ VP$_O$

Rotate SP into the PP
for true angle θ in PP

SP

left tracer line

right tracer
line

θ'= angle θ seen in perspective

A   B

θ   θ'

VP$_L$

VP$_R$ HL

oblique line

θ

C

DOWN to the RIGHT

GL

right side elevation

If the oblique line goes **up** to the **right,** then the VP$_O$ is **up** to the **right.**
If the oblique line goes **down** to the **right,** then the VP$_O$ is **down** to the **right.**

VP$_O$

OBLIQUE VANISHING POINTS: RIGHT SIDE

Drawing: Perry Community Education Village, Perry, Ohio
36" × 24" (91.4 × 61 cm)
Medium: Ink on Mylar
Courtesy of Perkins & Will Architects

The plan/elevation method (for both two- and one-point) is just one of many ways to generate mechanical perspective drawings. In the future, new methods may be emerging, and it is important not to be afraid to experiment with them. The balance of this chapter will, for the most part, discuss other methods.

Once an initial cube has been constructed, concepts and techniques for **multiplying, dividing,** and **transferring** dimensions in perspective space can be employed. These techniques support the development of a perspective without adding to its constructional framework. They build and reinforce an understanding of the perspective structure and the relationships between things within it regardless of the generated perspective method used. They do not require drawing space beyond the perspective itself and they can be applied to any part of any existing perspective. Armed with this set of concepts and strategies for their employment, anything can be accurately drawn in perspective.

The application of the multiplying, dividing, and transferring techniques is of particular importance because it provides the means for linking sketching with the computer. The ability to quickly and accurately sketch within and extend a computer-generated perspective supports the exploration of alternatives and the development of presentation drawings. It allows three-dimensional modeling programs to be used to create simpler and more efficient mass models for generated perspective frameworks that can also be elaborated on by hand.

Diagram (p. 217) and text (pp. 216–217): Courtesy
of William R. Benedict, Assistant Professor
California Polytechnic State University
School of Architecture, San Luis Obispo, California

MULTIPLYING, DIVIDING, AND TRANSFERRING

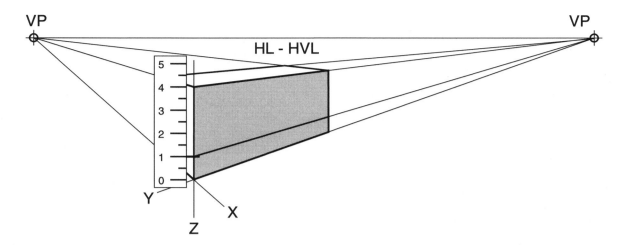

X, Y, and Z Axes

The *X, Y,* and *Z* axes are the axes of the Cartesian coordinate system that are parallel to the three sets of parallel edges of a cube or any rectangular object or rectangular space. Moving through perspective space can be visualized as moving successively along the axes to arrive at the desired location. The *Z* axis is parallel to the picture plane; therefore, all lines parallel to it will retain their true orientation — that is, they will be drawn as vertical lines.

Dividing by Measuring

A common need in drawing is to give a line some scale and establish dimensions along it. You may have a line of some length that you wish to call a specific dimension (give a specific scale), say four feet, and then establish a point on the line that is one foot from one end.

Three techniques can be used: Direct Measurement, Vanished Transfer, and Parallel Transfer. All three techniques are intended to give a line scale and locate specific dimensions. Once this has been done, other techniques must be used to move the dimensions within the drawing. Direct measurement, parallel transfer, and a variation of parallel transfer with vertical and horizontal lines will be discussed.

Direct Measurement

This technique involves directly measuring the line. It is used when establishing dimensions through visual judgment or direct measurement with a scale. Direct measurement with the eye involves making visual judgments that proportionally divide the line. For example, if the line is assumed to be four feet long and a one-foot increment is needed, you can visually divide the line in half and then in half again to locate one foot. This works very well because we can accurately judge the middle of things. With practice you can also divide a line into thirds or fifths. By combining judgments of halves, thirds, and fifths, you can easily and accurately use your eye to establish dimensions in a drawing.

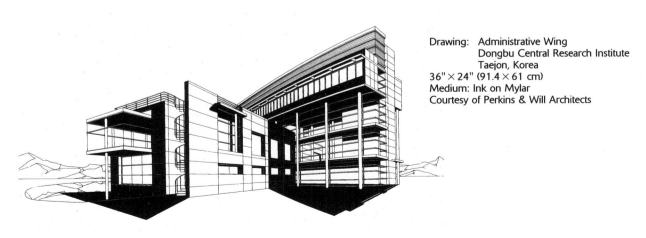

Drawing: Administrative Wing
          Dongbu Central Research Institute
          Taejon, Korea
36" × 24" (91.4 × 61 cm)
Medium: Ink on Mylar
Courtesy of Perkins & Will Architects

DIRECT MEASUREMENT

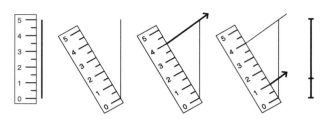

Parallel Transfer

The existing line that you want to make four feet may be of a dimension that is not readily divisible by four. Identify the line that is parallel to the picture plane that you want to make equal to the desired dimension (e.g., four feet).

Choose a scale that is reasonably close to the actual length of the line. Align the zero mark on the scale to one end of the line to be dimensioned. Angle the scale away from the line. Mark the desired dimensions along the edge of the scale, including the one that designates the full length of the line (e.g., four feet).

Draw a line from the full-length dimension along the scale to the end of the line you want to dimension. The angle of this line will be used to transfer all other dimensions from the scale to the line. Draw lines that are parallel to the line created in the preceding step between all dimensions along the scale and the line you are dimensioning (e.g., one foot). You have now proportionally dimensioned the base line and can proceed with the drawing construction using other techniques.

PARALLEL TRANSFER

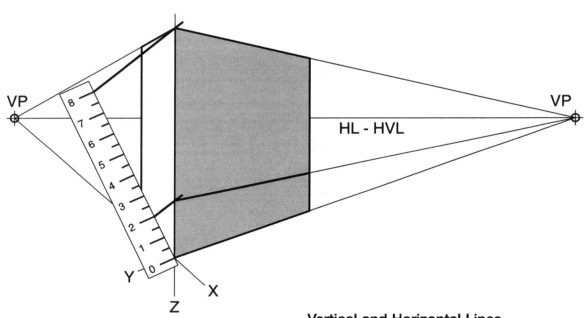

Vertical and Horizontal Lines

The parallel transfer technique translates directly to any line that is parallel to the picture plane, such as those that are vertical and horizontal. The perspective example above shows the technique being used for a vertical edge—a condition that occurs in both one- and two-point perspectives.

Diagrams and text (both pages): Courtesy of William R. Benedict, Assistant Professor California Polytechnic State University School of Architecture, San Luis Obispo, California

Multiplying by Measuring

The assumption is that you have a visually and proportionally correct square and wish to generate additional squares above or below.

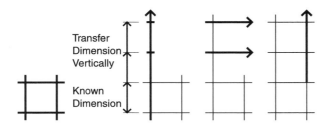

Draw or identify the base square whose vertical edges are parallel to the picture plane. All edges are parallel in orthographic drawings.

Extend a vertical edge of the base square to function as a measuring line. Transfer the height of the base square (the known dimension) along this edge. You can transfer dimensions above and/or below the base square as many times as needed.

Principle: Vertical lines in both one- and two-point perspectives represent edges that are parallel to the picture plane—they do not vanish. This means that a dimension or portion of the dimension (½, ¼, etc.) established on any vertical line within a perspective can be transferred vertically along that line.

Draw horizontal lines through these points (orthographic) or lines that go to the vanishing point for the plane (perspective).

Principle: In both one- and two-point perspectives, sets of parallel horizontal lines not parallel to the picture plane vanish to a common vanishing point on the horizon line. This means that dimensions can be transferred horizontally between vertical lines on the same plane by using the vanishing point for horizontal lines for that plane.

Extend the remaining vertical edge to complete the additional squares.

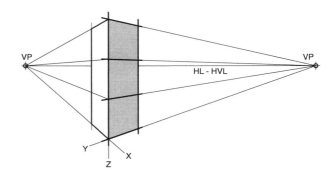

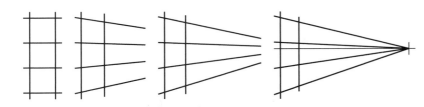

Drawing: Torre de Telecomunicacions de Montjuïc
Barcelona, Spain, 1992
Santiago Calatrava, Architect
4.5" × 7" (11.4 × 17.8 cm)
Medium: Ink on vellum
Drawn by Kwok Gorran Tsui, architecture
graduate, University of Texas at Austin

MULTIPLYING BY MEASURING

DIVIDING/OBLIQUE TWO-POINT GRID

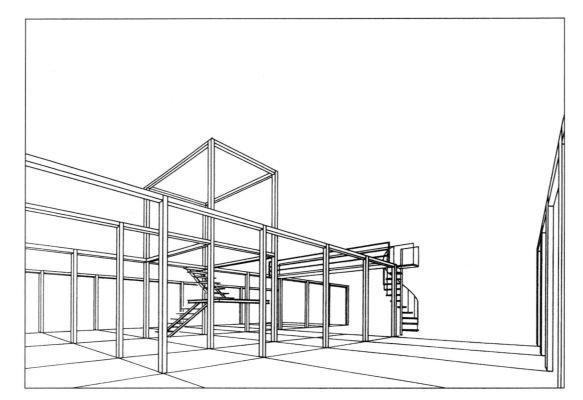

Drawing: T residence, Hayama, Kanagawa, Japan
Courtesy of Iida Archiship Studio

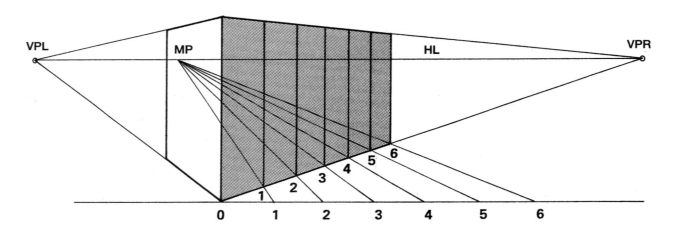

Oblique Grid

The above method shows a diagonal vanishing point (also defined as a measuring point, **MP**) that is generated by a particular station point in the measuring point system (see pages on measuring points). A vertical building facade (exterior face) can be divided with proper projected depths using this concept (see pp. 226–227).

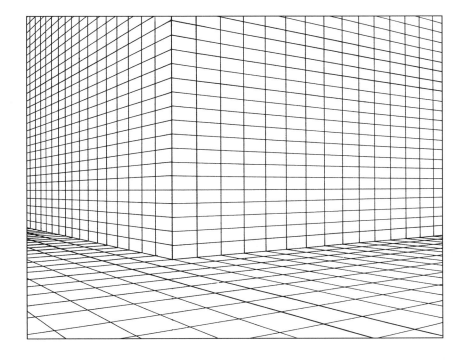

Perspective charts that are available commercially save time and space, especially when a large layout is required (residential layouts may need five feet or more). The time factor is reduced immensely, especially when generating many similar images. Nice features of perspective charts are (1) that the scale of the grid lines is flexible to suit the size of the structure being drawn, and (2) that the observer's relationship to the horizon line (bird's-eye, worm's-eye, eye level, etc.) can always be adjusted. The major undesirable feature is the restricted freedom in selecting the station point position and the picture plane placement. Charts that are made for both one- and two-point perspectives are divided into two categories: those with a relatively high horizon line and those with a relatively low horizon line.

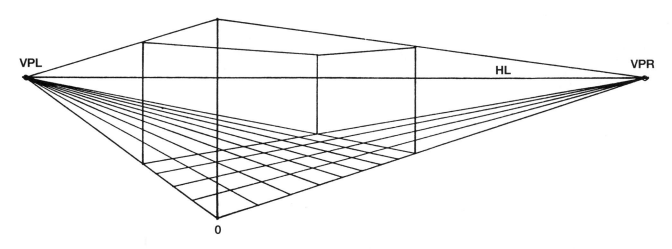

A perspective plan can be divided by using the two vanished lines from corner point **0**. The result is a two-point perspective grid. A two-point perspective grid is useful for drawing either exterior or interior perspectives. The grid can be used to accurately locate elements in the urban landscape. The grid can also position scale elements such as furniture and human figures in their accurate relative positions (see p. 406).

Transferring with the Diagonal

Suppose that you have a visually and proportionally correct square with dimensions located on one side that you want to transfer to an adjacent side.

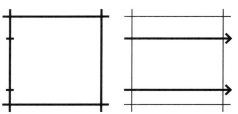

Draw or identify the base square and the dimensions. The vertical edges are parallel to the picture plane. All edges are parallel in orthographic drawings. Extend the dimensions across the square. Draw one of the diagonals of the square. Draw lines that intersect with the sides of the square through the intersections of the diagonal and dimension lines.

Principle: A 45° line drawn through the intersection of two perpendicular lines will transfer dimensions from one line to the other. The diagonal you choose to draw will control the side to which a dimension is transferred. This technique has slightly different results when used in a square, as illustrated, than when used in other rectangles. The diagonal of a square will transfer the exact dimensions (2' to 2'), while the diagonal of a rectangle will transfer only proportions (¼ to ¼) .

Diagrams and text (both pages): Courtesy
of William R. Benedict, Assistant Professor
California Polytechnic State University
College of Architecture & Environmental Design
San Luis Obispo, California

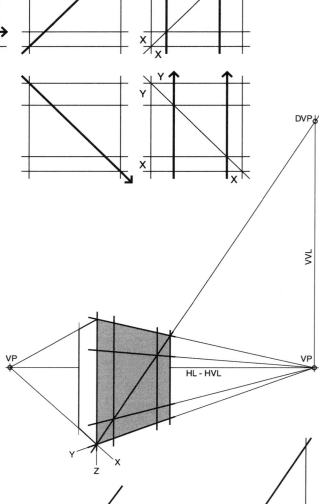

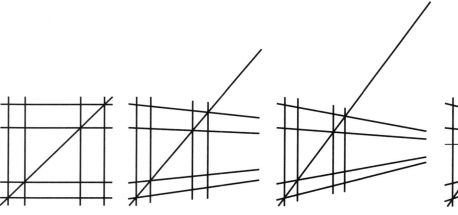

TRANSFERRING WITH THE DIAGONAL

Multiplying by Measuring Plus the Diagonal

Suppose that you have a visually and proportionally correct square and wish to generate additional squares to one or more sides. The strategy combines the vertical transfer of dimensions introduced in Multiplying by Measuring, p. 219, with transferring the diagonal of a square.

As the illustrations show, the diagonal can be further extended to intersect a vertical line **(VVL)** drawn through the vanishing point **(VP)** for the horizontal lines. This creates a diagonal vanishing point **(DVP)** to which all parallel diagonals will converge. You do not need to create the diagonal vanishing point to use this technique. The diagonal vanishing points may be above or below or to either side of a VP.

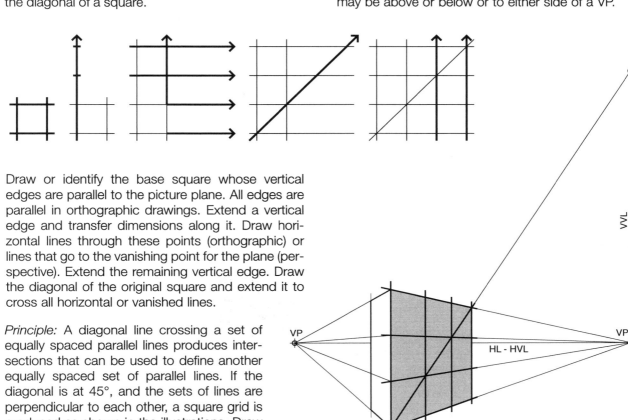

Draw or identify the base square whose vertical edges are parallel to the picture plane. All edges are parallel in orthographic drawings. Extend a vertical edge and transfer dimensions along it. Draw horizontal lines through these points (orthographic) or lines that go to the vanishing point for the plane (perspective). Extend the remaining vertical edge. Draw the diagonal of the original square and extend it to cross all horizontal or vanished lines.

Principle: A diagonal line crossing a set of equally spaced parallel lines produces intersections that can be used to define another equally spaced set of parallel lines. If the diagonal is at 45°, and the sets of lines are perpendicular to each other, a square grid is produced as shown in the illustrations. Draw vertical lines through each intersection of the diagonal with a horizontal or vanished line to complete the additional squares.

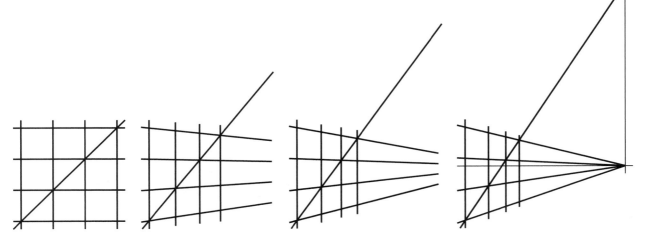

MULTIPLYING BY MEASURING PLUS THE DIAGONAL

Multiplying With the Diagonal

Suppose that you have a visually and proportionally correct square and wish to generate additional squares to either side, above or below.

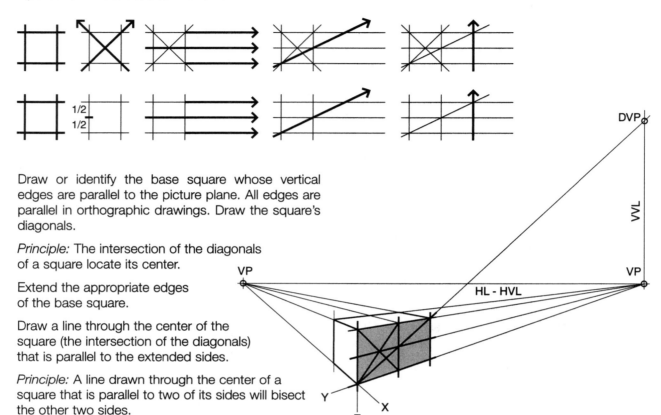

Draw or identify the base square whose vertical edges are parallel to the picture plane. All edges are parallel in orthographic drawings. Draw the square's diagonals.

Principle: The intersection of the diagonals of a square locate its center.

Extend the appropriate edges of the base square.

Draw a line through the center of the square (the intersection of the diagonals) that is parallel to the extended sides.

Principle: A line drawn through the center of a square that is parallel to two of its sides will bisect the other two sides.

Alternative (bottom illustration): Sometimes it is faster to divide a vertical edge with a scale or by visual judgment. In this case, draw a line through the center of the side that is parallel to the extended sides.

Draw a line from one corner of the square through the center of an opposite side. Extend this line until it intersects one of the extended sides. This line is now the diagonal of a rectangle that is twice as wide as the original square.

Draw a line through the intersection of the line just completed and the side of the square to define the new square.

As the illlustrations show, the diagonal of the double-wide rectangle can be further extended to intersect a vertical line **(VVL)** drawn through the vanishing point for the horizontal lines. This creates a diagonal vanishing point **(DVP)** to which all similar diagonals will converge. You do not need to create the diagonal vanishing point to use this technique.

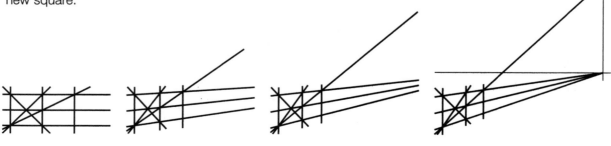

Dividing With the Diagonal

It is a good strategy to draw the largest inclusive form possible as a first step in constructing a perspective and then to subdivide that form to locate smaller elements. This technique assumes that you have a visually and proportionally correct square and wish to divide it into halves, quarters, eighths, etc.

As the illustrations show, the diagonals can be further extended to intersect a vertical line **(VVL)** drawn through the vanishing point **(VP)** for the horizontal lines. This creates a diagonal vanishing point **(DVP)**. You do not need to create the diagonal vanishing point to use this technique. The diagonal vanishing points may be above or below or to either side of a VP.

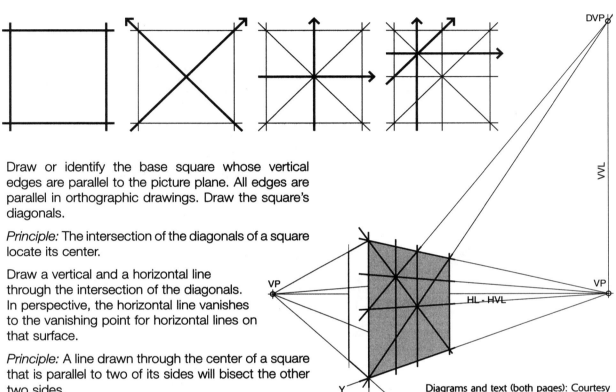

Draw or identify the base square whose vertical edges are parallel to the picture plane. All edges are parallel in orthographic drawings. Draw the square's diagonals.

Principle: The intersection of the diagonals of a square locate its center.

Draw a vertical and a horizontal line through the intersection of the diagonals. In perspective, the horizontal line vanishes to the vanishing point for horizontal lines on that surface.

Principle: A line drawn through the center of a square that is parallel to two of its sides will bisect the other two sides.

The vertical and horizontal lines have defined four smaller squares that have the same proportions as the original but are one-quarter the size. This process can be repeated within each progressively smaller square until the desired subdivision is produced. Each subdivsion halves the square (e.g., a twelve-foot square becomes four six-foot squares.

Diagrams and text (both pages): Courtesy of William R. Benedict, Assistant Professor California Polytechnic State University College of Architecture & Environmental Design San Luis Obispo, California

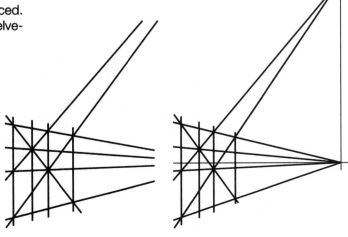

DIVIDING WITH THE DIAGONAL

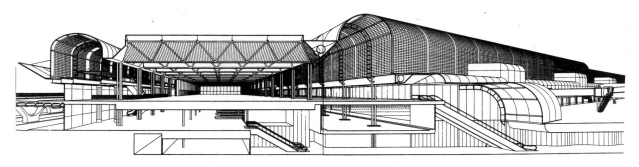

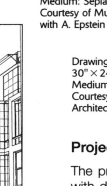

Drawing (above): United Airlines Terminal
Chicago, Illinois
30" × 24" (86.4 × 55.9 cm)
Medium: Sepia ink on 1000H paper
Courtesy of Murphy/Jahn, Architects
with A. Epstein & Sons, Architects

Drawing (left): Storrow Drive, Boston, Massachusetts
30" × 24" (76.2 × 61 cm)
Medium: Ink on Mylar
Courtesy of Koetter Kim & Associates, Inc.
Architects and Urban Designers

Projected Depths

The principles for multiplying and dividing with diagonals are frequently used on the fenestration of buildings in terms of distributing elements along a plane.

In building structures of great lengths (institutional, commercial, etc.), it is common to have **equally** spaced repetitious elements. Perspective construction can be expedited by the use of **diagonals;** this is possible because all diagonals of squares and rectangles intersect in the exact center of the figure (see pp. 224–225).

Drawing: Crown Hall, Illinois Institute of Technology, Chicago, Illinois
Ludwig Mies Van der Rohe, Architect

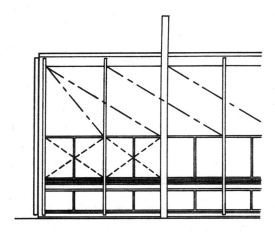

TYPICAL PARTIAL ELEVATION

PROJECTED DEPTHS USING DIAGONALS

1. Decide on the spacing between two primary window mullions, **a** and **b**.
2. Draw diagonals between *a* and *b* to determine the mullion midline bisector.
3. Locate mullion **c'c** by drawing a line from **a'** through the midpoint of **b'b**.

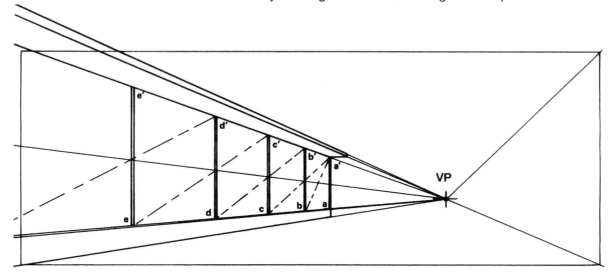

4. Repeat the procedure in step 3 to locate **d'd** starting from **b'**, **e'e** starting from **c'**, etc.
5. Locate secondary window mullions **1'1**, **2'2**, **3'3**, etc., by drawing diagonals between the primary window mullions.

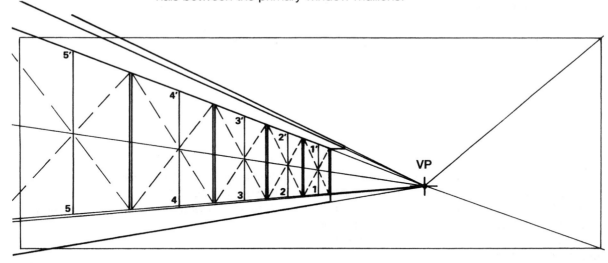

NOTATION ── – ── – ── – ── **Diagonal lines locating primary window mullions.**
── – ── – ── – ── – **Diagonal lines locating secondary window mullions.**

Follow steps 1 through 5 to accurately locate equally spaced lines in perspective. In both one-point (above example) and two-point perspectives, it is frequently necessary to repeat lines that are equally spaced. For example, window mullions seen in both exterior or interior perspective views are often equally spaced. Many other elements that are seen in our urban landscape are equally spaced, such as lampposts, parking meters, telephone poles, building types with repetitious units, columns in a colonnade, and sidewalk units. **Diagonals** provide the best method of determining projected depths in perspective.

PROJECTED DEPTHS USING DIAGONALS

Diagrams and text (both pages): Courtesy
of William R. Benedict, Assistant Professor
California Polytechnic State University
College of Architecture & Environmental Design
San Luis Obispo, California

DIAGONAL VANISHING POINTS

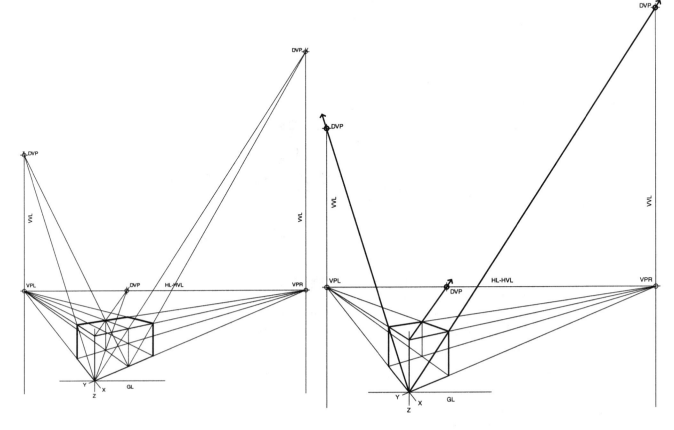

The techniques of multiplying, dividing, and transferring discussed on pp. 222 to 225 become especially applicable as methods for constructing two-point perspectives. These techniques have the advantage of requiring fewer construction lines than the plan-elevation cone of vision method.

Diagonal Vanishing Points

Draw and extend the diagonals of the visible faces of the cube until they intersect with their respective vanishing lines. Label the diagonal vanishing points **(DVP)**. There are two possible diagonal vanishing points for each square face. One will be above and one below the horizon line on the vertical vanishing lines. The illustrations show only one set to save

space, and we usually draw only one for the same reason. The decision to draw one or the other or both depends on what is useful in constructing a specific perspective.

The illustration at left above shows that the diagonals of the opposite faces of the cube go to the same vanishing point because they are parallel; therefore, their diagonals are parallel. All parallel lines go to the same vanishing point. The use of the diagonal to generate (multiply) a new cube is also illustrated.

If you become confused as to which diagonal vanishing point to use, first find the vanishing point for horizontal lines on the same plane. The vanishing line for the diagonals will pass through the vanishing point for the horizontal lines on the plane.

Drawing (partial): D.O.M. Headquarters
Cologne, Germany
Medium: Ink on Mylar
Courtesy of Machado & Silvetti Associates
Rodolfo Machado and Jorge Silvetti

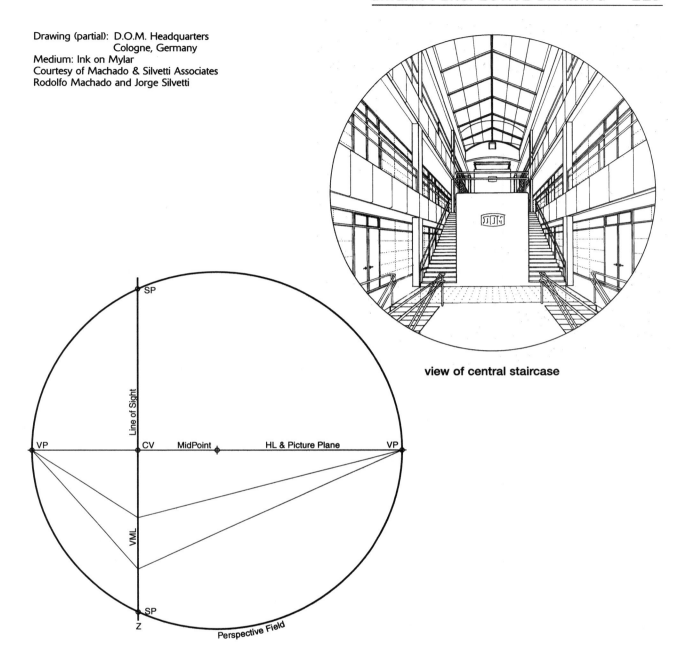

view of central staircase

MidPoint and Perspective Field of View

Locate the MidPoint between the two vanishing points, and use it to draw a circle that passes through the two vanishing points — to construct the perspective field of view. The intersection of the perspective field and the vertical line through the center of vision (the line of sight) locates the station point **(SP)**.

The perspective field of view is the interface between our visual experience of the world and the geometry of the linear perspective. The vanishing points for the horizontal edges of an object within our visual field can fall anywhere along the perceived horizon line from directly in front of us to the limits of our peripheral vision. The perspective field of view encompasses the two vanishing points for a specific rectilinear object within our visual field, or the one vanishing point in a one-point perspective, as shown above.

Center of Vision (CV): The point created by the orthogonal (90°) intersection of the line of sight and the horizon line on the picture plane. The **CV** in the example above is near the circle's center.

Diagrams and text (both pages): Courtesy
of William R. Benedict, Assistant Professor
California Polytechnic State University
College of Architecture & Environmental Design
San Luis Obispo, California

VERTICAL VANISHING LINES

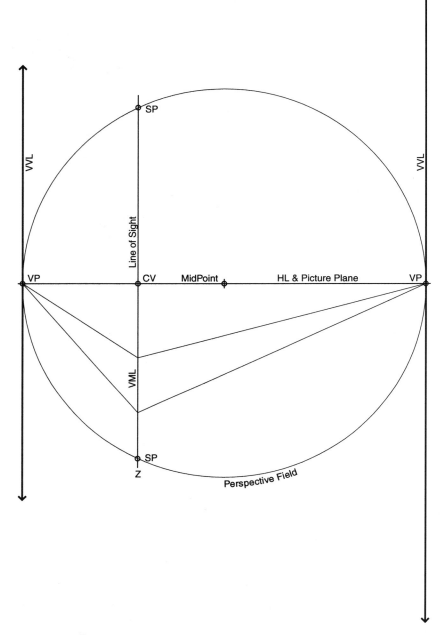

Vertical Vanishing Lines

Vertical vanishing lines **(VVL)** must be drawn through both vanishing points **(VP)**. These are the vanishing lines for all planes and lines parallel to the vertical faces of the cube. We now have the information necessary to locate the 45° diagonal vanishing points for the two vertical surfaces of the cube or any surfaces parallel to them. The 45° diagonal vanishing points are the points to which the two sets of 45° lines lying on a particular plane will vanish. They are located on the vanishing line for the plane.

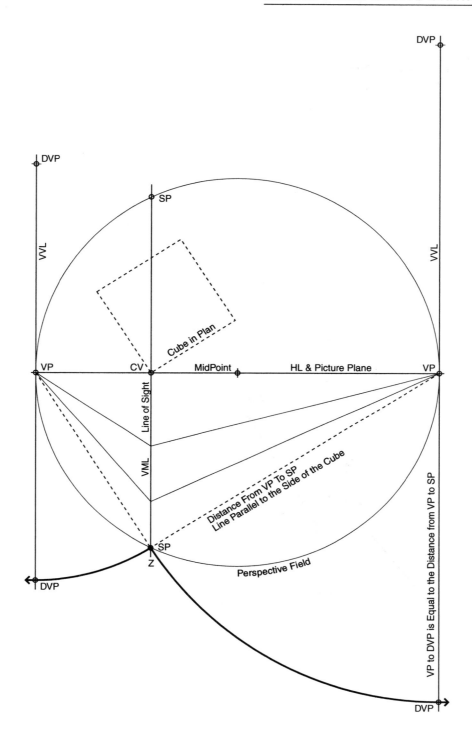

The following labels appear in the illustration:

DVP

DVP

VVL

SP

Cube in Plan

VVL

VP CV MidPoint HL & Picture Plane VP

Line of Sight

VML

Distance From VP To SP
Line Parallel to the Side of the Cube

VP to DVP is Equal to the Distance from VP to SP

SP
Z

DVP

Perspective Field

DVP

CONSTRUCTING DIAGONAL VANISHING POINTS

Constructing Diagonal Vanishing Points

Transfer the distance from each **VP** to the **SP** to the vertical vanishing line passing through the respective VP. This can be done with a compass, as shown in the illustration, or with a scale. The 45° diagonal vanishing points can be generated for each plane—one will be above and one below their respective vanishing points. One diagonal vanishing point for each plane is often all that is necessary for construction, as indicated in the illustration.

Diagrams and text (both pages): Courtesy
of William R. Benedict, Assistant Professor
California Polytechnic State University
College of Architecture & Environmental Design
San Luis Obispo, California

CONSTRUCTING CUBE FACES

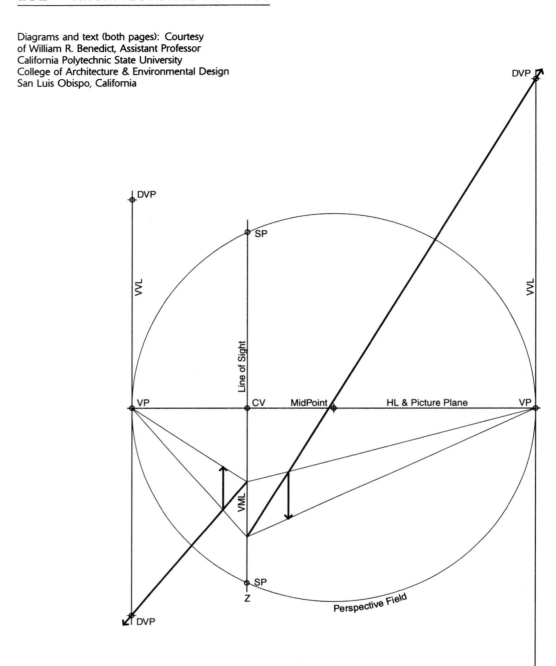

Constructing Cube Faces

Draw lines from the **DVPs** to one end of the known vertical edge of the cube. Use the DVP that is above or below the **VP** for horizontal lines on the same plane. The diagonal lines are 45° lines; therefore, their intersection with a vanishing edge transfers the length of the vertical edge to the horizontal—that is, it defines a square on each surface. Draw vertical lines through the intersections to establish the vertical faces of the cube.

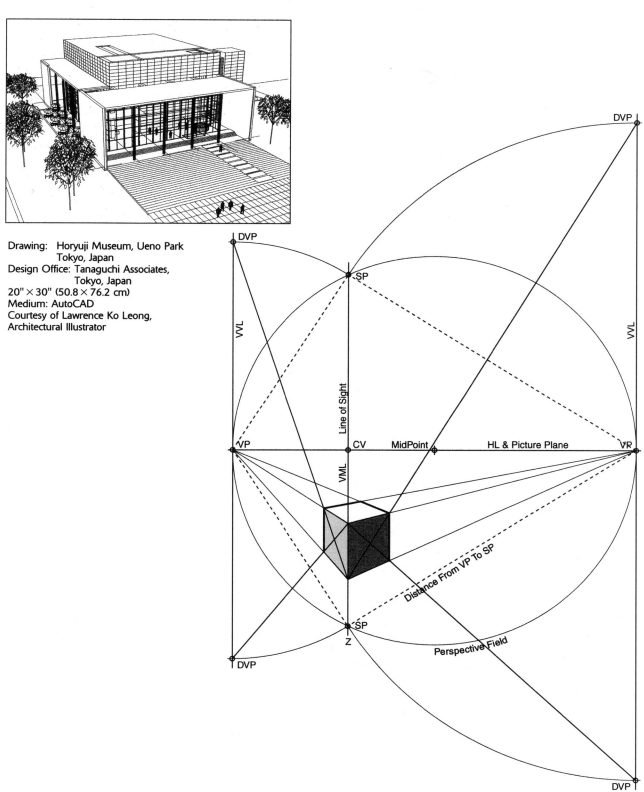

Drawing: Horyuji Museum, Ueno Park
            Tokyo, Japan
Design Office: Tanaguchi Associates,
            Tokyo, Japan
20" × 30" (50.8 × 76.2 cm)
Medium: AutoCAD
Courtesy of Lawrence Ko Leong,
Architectural Illustrator

CUBE COMPLETION

Cube Completion

Vanish lines to define the top face of the cube, and add line weight and value to complete the cube. Additional cubes can be generated using the diagonal.

MEASURING POINTS

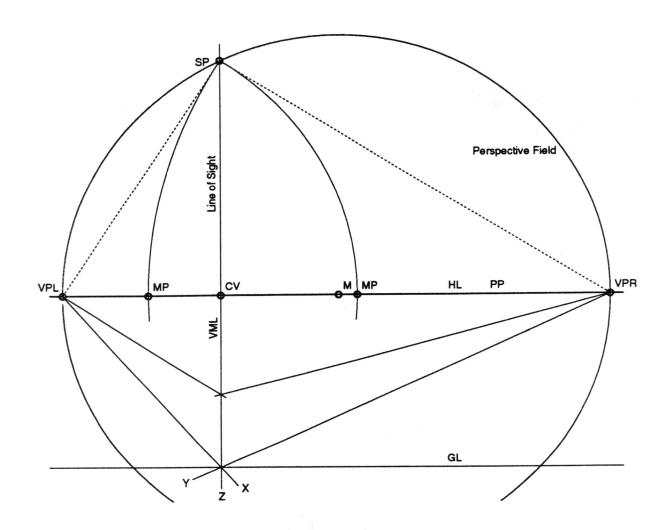

Determining Measuring Points

Cubes as well as other geometric forms can be constructed simply by using **measuring points (MP)**. Measuring points are the points used to transfer scaled dimensions from the horizontal measuring line to lines vanishing through the intersection of the horizontal and vertical measuring lines. Proportional sizes can be transferred with the measuring points from any horizontal line to vanished lines passing through the intersection of that horizontal line and a vertical line. Measuring points offer an additional way of introducing dimensions into a perspective. The process begins with the construction of the horizon line, ground line, vanishing points, midpoint, the perspective field of view, and so forth. Transfer the distances from **VPR** to **SP** and **VPL** to **SP** down to the horizon line. This can be done with a compass, as shown in the illustration, or with a scale. The points on the horizon line resulting from this transfer are the measuring points for the perspective setup.

In two-point perspective, as shown above, there are **two** measuring points; whereas in one-point perspective, there is only **one** measuring point, which is also called a **diagonal vanishing point** (see pp. 251, 252, 260, and 261).

Diagrams and text (both pages): Courtesy of William R. Benedict, Assistant Professor
California Polytechnic State University College of Architecture & Environmental Design
San Luis Obispo, California

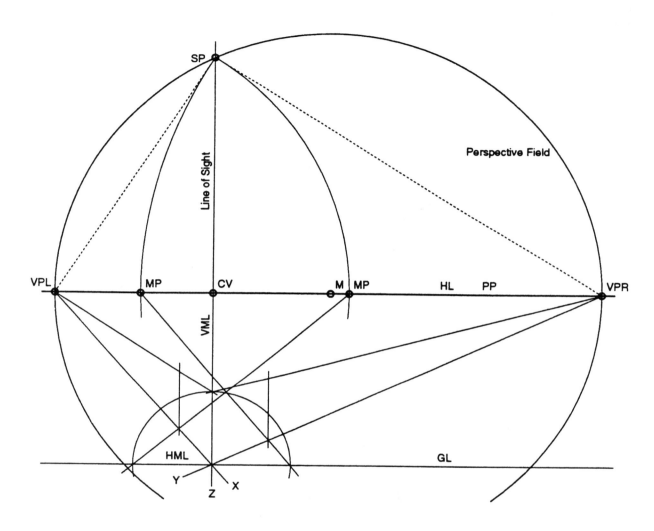

MEASURING POINTS

Entering Dimensions

Enter the horizontal dimensions that you want to transfer into the perspective. The dimensions are entered on a horizontal measuring line **(HML)**. In the example, an arc is used to transfer the height of the cube to either side of its existing lead edge and vertical measuring line.

A horizontal measuring line **(HML)** may be located anywhere along any vertical line within the perspective. The only requirements are (1) that the vertical line can be used to establish the measurement scale or is a vertical measuring line **(VML)**, and (2) that a pair of lines parallel to the X and Y axes be drawn through the intersection of the vertical line and the horizontal measuring line.

Constructing Cube Faces

The measuring points are now used to transfer the dimensions from the horizontal measuring line to the X and Y axes or lines parallel to them. The intersection of the line drawn from the dimension on the **HML** to the appropriate **MP** with the axis transfers the dimension into the perspective. Draw a vertical line through the intersections to define the two faces.

Note: When transferring a dimension back into the perspective—when making it smaller—you use the MP on the opposite side of the vertical line. When transferring it forward—making it bigger—you use the MP on the same side.

Diagrams and text (both pages): Courtesy
of William R. Benedict, Assistant Professor
California Polytechnic State University
College of Architecture & Environmental Design
San Luis Obispo, California

MEASURING POINT SYSTEM

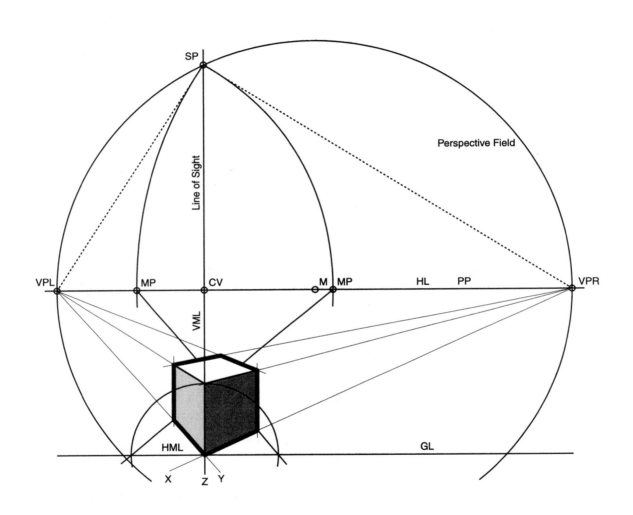

Cube Completion

Vanish lines to define the top surface of the cube, and add line weight and value to complete the cube. This approach brings together the two halves of the measuring point system—the diagonal vanishing points and the measuring points. Once the initial volume is established, any combination of vanishing points and dividing, multiplying, and transferring techniques can be employed along with the measuring points to develop the perspective. The goal is to make choices that complete the drawing as efficiently as possible.

This illustration brings together the basic elements of the measuring point system. Notice, as stated earlier, that the arc defining the diagonal vanishing points is the same one that defines the measuring points. The complexity of the drawing makes a good case for introducing the concepts in a systematic and gradual manner to avoid being caught in the web of lines and concepts.

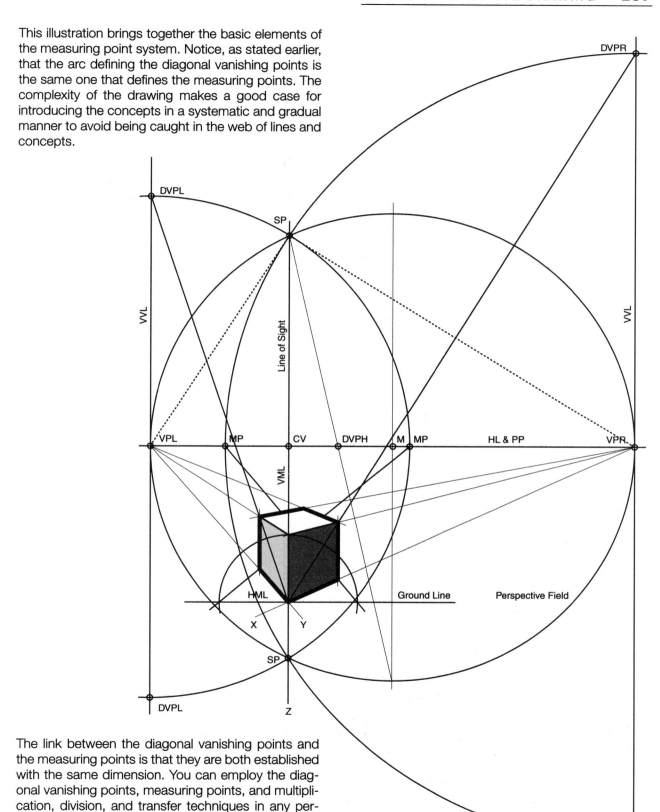

MEASURING POINT SYSTEM

The link between the diagonal vanishing points and the measuring points is that they are both established with the same dimension. You can employ the diagonal vanishing points, measuring points, and multiplication, division, and transfer techniques in any perspective construction. The choice as to which to use should depend on the strategy that will produce the desired results with the greatest efficiency.

MEASURING POINTS AND OBLIQUE LINES

The vertical lines in the diagram below are parallel. In reality, these lines would begin to converge to a third vanishing point far below the horizon line, as seen in the illustration at right (see also pp. 270–273).

Drawing: National Audubon Society's National Headquarters, New York City
9" × 13" (22.9 × 33 cm)
Medium: Wax-based pencil
Courtesy of Paul Stevenson Oles, Architectural Illustrator
Croxton Collaborative Architects

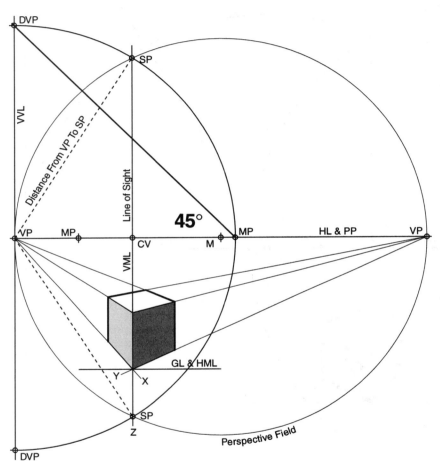

Measuring Points and Oblique Lines

If you combine and examine the construction process for determining the location of the diagonal vanishing points for the faces of the cube and its measuring points, you will realize that a 45° line will connect the corresponding MPs and DVPs. This means that if the location of the measuring points is known, you can construct the 45° diagonal vanishing point by drawing the vertical vanishing lines and then extending 45° lines through the measuring points until they intersect their respective vertical vanishing lines (the one farther away).

It is necessary to construct the measuring points before this technique can be employed. The concept works for sloped planes whose edges are parallel to the X or Y axis. The vanishing point for the inclined edges or lines can be found by drawing a line at the corresponding slope through the appropriate measuring point until it intersects with the corresponding vertical vanishing line.

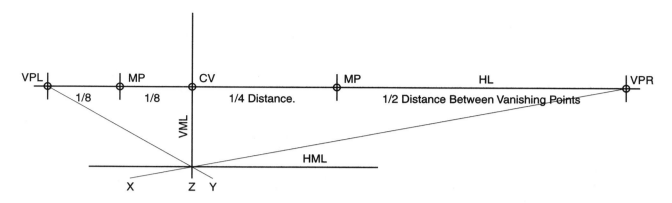

Measuring Points—30°/60° Shortcut

One of the liabilities of the measuring point system is the space and scale of instruments required to construct the framework—especially the diagonal vanishing points. This can be overcome by making a small drawing of the setup to establish the relative dimensions within the framework and then enlarging it proportionally to support the actual construction of the perspective.

The 30°/60° setup provides another way around the problem. Perspectives in which the plan is oriented in a 30°/60° relationship to the picture plane are common and produce a simple set of geometric relationships between the vanishing points, measuring points, and center of the drawing above. By drawing the horizon line, establishing the vanishing points, and subdividing the distance between them accordingly, you can quickly generate the full component of information necessary to construct an accurate perspective framework at any scale. The process simply divides the distance between the vanishing points into successively smaller halves.

Remember that the distance from a vanishing point to the farther measuring point is equal to the distance from that vanishing point to the diagonal vanishing points above and below it on the vertical vanishing line.

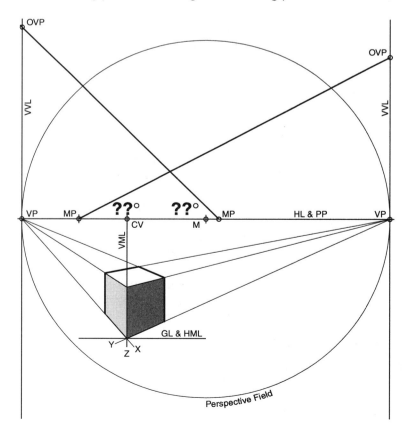

Diagrams and text: Courtesy of
William R. Benedict, Assistant Professor
California Polytechnic State University
College of Architecture & Environmental Design
San Luis Obispo, California

MEASURING POINTS—30°/60° SHORTCUT

ESTABLISHING SCALE IN TWO-POINT PERSPECTIVES

Diagrams and text (both pages): Courtesy of William R. Benedict, Assistant Professor California Polytechnic State University College of Architecture & Environmental Design San Luis Obispo, California

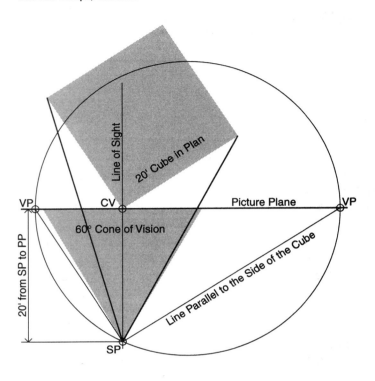

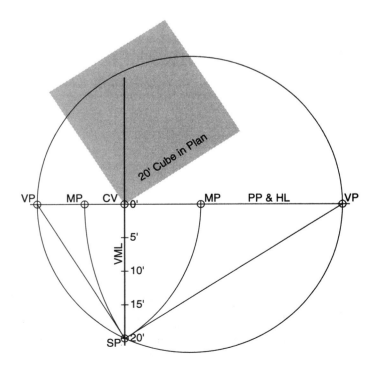

Establishing Scale in Two-Point Perspectives

When the measuring point method is used to construct a perspective using a plan drawing, the scale of the perspective is established by the scale used to construct the drawing (plan, picture plane **[PP]**, center of vision **[CV]**, station point **[SP]**, etc.). The goal is to make the perspective as large as possible while keeping the image projected on the picture plane within a 60° cone of vision. The problem comes when we want to draw a perspective without a plan or before a plan exists. The question is: What rule of thumb can be used to develop a two-point perspective framework for sketching, given only the general dimensions of the form or space?

The rule of thumb can be found in the illustration at left. Notice that when the distance from the station point to the picture plane is equal to the horizontal dimension of the subject, the projected image just fits within the 60° cone of vision. This 1:1 relationship means that to draw a perspective of a 20' wide object, the station point is located 20' back from the picture plane, assuming that the object also touches the picture plane as shown. More generally, the greatest horizontal dimension of the subject establishes the distance from the station point to the picture plane and produces a perspective that will fall within a zone of acceptable distortion.

Basic Setup

Draw a horizon line **(HL)** and vanishing points **(VP)** and locate the center of vision **(CV)**, station point **(SP)**, and measuring points **(MP)**. The location of the vanishing points is arbitrarily established to fit on the sheet of paper being used—the layout has no inherent scale. Given the 1:1 ratio as a guide, scale can be introduced by making the distance from the station point to the picture plane equal to the greatest horizontal dimension of the object being drawn (20' in the example). The distance between the **SP** and the **PP** is proportionally divided along the **VML** to create a scale for the drawing.

Ground Line and Dimensions

The proportional scale created along the VML is used to locate the ground line **(GL)**, which is also a horizontal measuring line **(HML)**. In the example, the ground line is located 5 feet below the horizon line to create an eye-level perspective. The scale created on the VML is then transferred along the VML and HML to locate the needed dimensions.

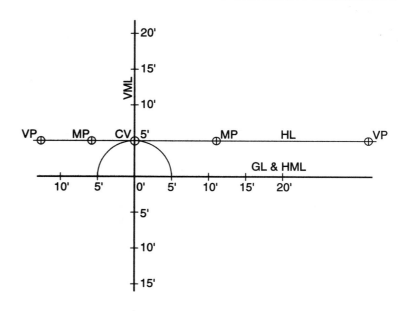

Perspective Construction

Once the dimensions have been established, the perspective can be developed using the measuring point and other construction techniques previously discussed. The resultant drawing will fall within an acceptable zone of distortion. Note that the cube extends vertically beyond the 60° cone of vision for an eye-level perspective and, therefore, if the subject is significantly taller than it is wide, its height should be used to establish the scale. The 1:1 rule of thumb must be adjusted in response to the subject and the desired communication.

Note: The passing of the vertical edges of the cube through the measuring points is coincidental.

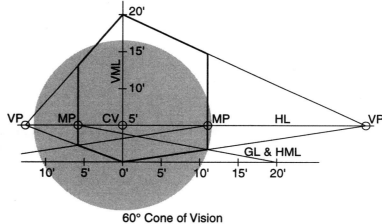

60° Cone of Vision

The Hypotenuse

The points identified as **SP, CV,** and **VP** define two right triangles whose hypotenuse is **VP-SP** (see gray triangle). The hypotenuse establishes a proportional relationship between the two other sides of a triangle. Therefore, if a line parallel to the hypotenuse is drawn through the center point of one side, it will pass through the center of the other side, as illustrated. This is important because it will allow the establishment of scale in some two-point perspectives without requiring us to locate the station point.

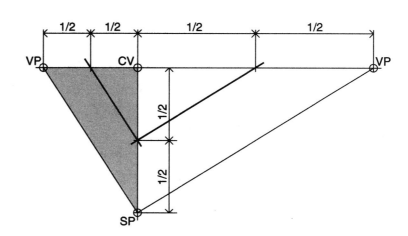

ESTABLISHING SCALE IN TWO-POINT PERSPECTIVES

ESTABLISHING SCALE IN TWO-POINT PERSPECTIVES

Drawing: Boston Ballet School and Studios
          Boston, Massachusetts
30" × 28" (76.2 × 71.1 cm)
Medium: Watercolor on rendering paper
Architect: Graham Gund Architects, Inc.

30°/60° Shortcut Perspective

Draw a horizon line and locate the vanishing points to fit on the sheet of paper being used. Locate the measuring points and center of vision for a 30/60° perspective using the proportions as illustrated and described in the section on the 30/60° shortcut method (see p. 239).

Establishing and Transferring the Scale

Given this approach, there is no station point or line that connects it to the picture plane. In its place, the distance from a vanishing point to the center of vision will be used. Given the 1:1 ratio, scale can be introduced by making the distance from a vanishing point to the center of vision equal to the greatest horizontal dimension of the object being drawn (20' in the example). The distance is then proportionally divided to produce useful dimensions (e.g., the distance from the horizon line to the ground line). Next, the dimension must be transferred to the vertical measuring line that passes through the center of vision. This is accomplished by drawing a line parallel to the hypotenuse of the corresponding **SP, CV, VP** triangle through the known dimension so that it intersects the vertical measuring line. For a 30/60° perspective, the hypotenuse will be at either 30° or 60° (the 60° triangle is being used in the example). In the illustration, a five-foot distance is being transferred to locate the ground line and establish an eye-level perspective.

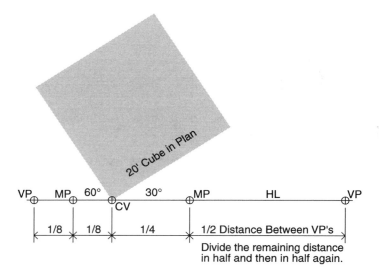

Divide the remaining distance in half and then in half again.

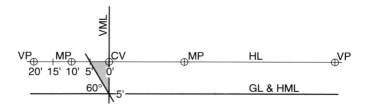

Diagrams and text (both pages): Courtesy
of William R. Benedict, Assistant Professor
California Polytechnic State University
College of Architecture & Environmental Design
San Luis Obispo, California

Drawing: Scripps Memorial Hospital
View of entrance
Chula Vista, California
23" × 24" (58.2 × 61 cm)
Medium: Ink on Mylar
Courtesy of Perkins & Will Architects
Associate Architect James A. Leary
Architecture & Planning

Dimensions

The dimensions transferred to the vertical measuring line establish a scale for the drawing. These dimensions can then be transferred along the vertical and horizontal measuring lines to locate the needed dimensions.

Perspective Construction

Once the dimensions have been established, the perspective can be developed using the measuring point and other construction techniques previously discussed. If it is desirable to have the perspective fall more completely within the cone of vision, then the controlling dimension is set to something greater than the width of the subject (e.g., 30').

A standard 6' figure is excellent for sizing objects in a perspective. In the subsequent chapter on perspective view development, note that all the views start with a horizon line and a scale figure that seems appropriate to begin the blockout of the drawing. There is no "scale" other than the assumed 6' figure.

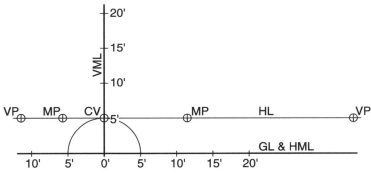

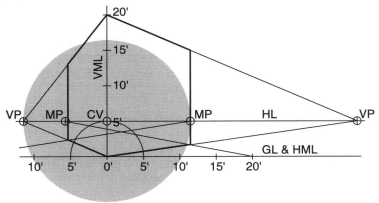

60° Cone of Vision

ESTABLISHING SCALE IN TWO-POINT PERSPECTIVES

TWO-POINT INTERIOR – OFFICE METHOD

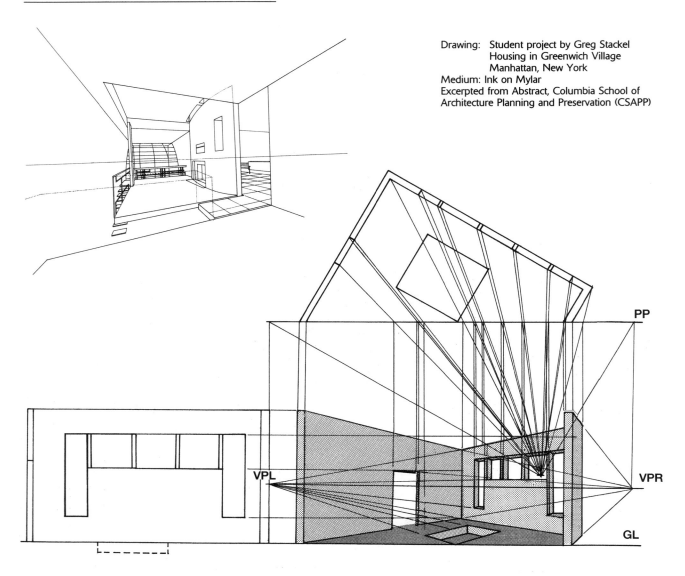

Drawing: Student project by Greg Stackel
Housing in Greenwich Village
Manhattan, New York
Medium: Ink on Mylar
Excerpted from Abstract, Columbia School of
Architecture Planning and Preservation (CSAPP)

Interior Two-point

Let's examine the two-point **plan-elevation** office method (pp. 200–202) again. These perspectives are commonly constructed for both exterior and interior two-point perspectives. The method is basically the same in both cases. This method can also be applied to exterior and interior one-point perspectives. Choose a station point that best describes the important interior elements and the feeling you would like to convey. Frank Lloyd Wright favored the two-point interior view, which is essentially a one-point made slightly oblique to the picture plane, resulting in a very long second vanishing point (see p. 407). Also avoid placing the eye-level horizon line in a position where it coincides with any horizontal structural element (e.g., the window sill shown above).

1. Select locations of SP, HL, and PP based on the perspective desired.
2. Select a PP that will cut both walls of an interior space and will intersect corners of important or major interior elements.
3. Construct the appropriate parallel lines to find vanishing points.
4. Transfer true heights from the elevation view to vertical tracers from the interior wall intersections.
5. Converge the wall planes to their appropriate vanishing points and subsequently construct the details of the interior space.

Compare this method to the one-point office procedure (pp. 248–249, 258–259).

Image: A new COACH store, 342 Madison Avenue
         New York City
Medium: Ink on Mylar
Courtesy of Kennethpark Architecture • Planning • Interiors

This interior two-point was created during the design development phase using AutoCAD Release 14 and Photoshop for rendering color. It was extremely useful in communicating and showing the design ideas discussed in meetings. It helped to catch desirable and undesirable aspects of the design; the client was able to see what they liked or didn't like. Ultimately, this helped to speed the design process along and gave the client a workable model to refine and shape.
[ARCHITECT'S STATEMENT]

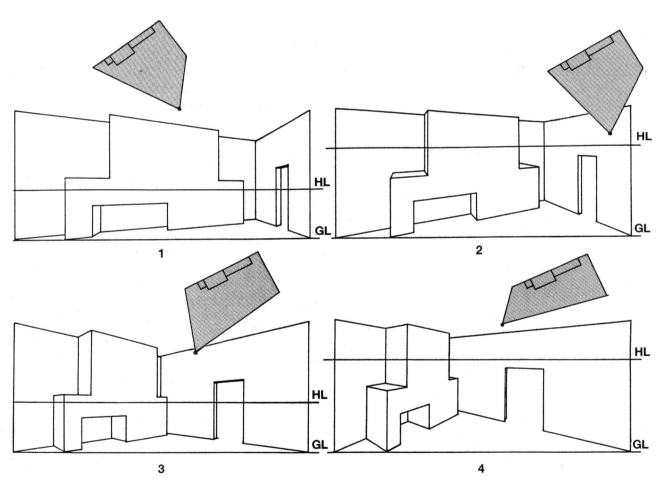

TWO-POINT INTERIOR – PICTORIAL EFFECT

In any interior perspective, visual emphasis on the left or right wall is governed by the **variable station point.** The station point also dictates whether the wall vanishing points fall within or out of the drawing. Note how the images of the fireplace and the door change as one moves from being close to the wall with the door (**1**) to being close to the fireplace wall (**4**). Also note that the higher horizon line in **2** and **4** allows the viewer to see more floor and less ceiling (above normal eye level).

TWO-POINT INTERIOR — EXAMPLES

These interior two-point perspectives have a greater **sense of enclosure** than the interior on the previous page simply because a third wall or third side is included. This third element has its own vanishing point.

Drawing: Master bath
　　　　Westview Grande Condominium
　　　　Indian Shores, Florida
5" × 4" (12.7 × 10.2 cm)
Medium: Computer imaging; Macintosh system using Strata Studio Pro and Adobe Photoshop. Completely computer-generated.
Courtesy of Robert L. Montry,
Media IV Design & Marketing Services, Inc., Largo, Florida

Drawing: Seagram Museum, Waterloo, Ontario, Canada
33" × 23.5" (83.8 × 59.7 cm)
Medium: Ink on paper
Courtesy of Barton Myers Associates Architects/Planner

Drawing: Carnegie Mellon Research Institute
                 Pittsburgh, Pennsylvania
11" × 8.5" (27.5 × 21.5 cm)
Medium: Pantone on Photostat
Courtesy of Peter D. Eisenman, FAIA,
of Eisenman Architects

The interior at left is primarily a one-point perspective. It is modified by an additional wall element that has its own vanishing point. The lobby below has essentially only one vanishing point, but the interior corridor in the background is curvilinear and has multiple vanishing points. These drawings can be called **modified one-points** in the sense that they have one vanishing point in the picture area, even though the total drawing is a multipoint perspective.

Drawing: GSA-IRS Competition project
Original size: approx. 18" × 17" (45.7 × 43.2 cm)
Scale used: ⅛" and ¼"=1'0"
Medium: Pen and ink with colored pencil on vellum paper
Perkins & Will Architects
Courtesy of Manuel Avila, Architectural Illustrator

INTERIOR EXAMPLES

In a one-point persective, a group of lines will vanish to one point and this group will not be parallel to the picture plane. All vertical lines remain vertical and all horizontal lines remain horizontal in the constructed perspective. The plan and the elevation of the room should always be traced to obtain exact dimensions.

ONE-POINT INTERIOR—OFFICE METHOD

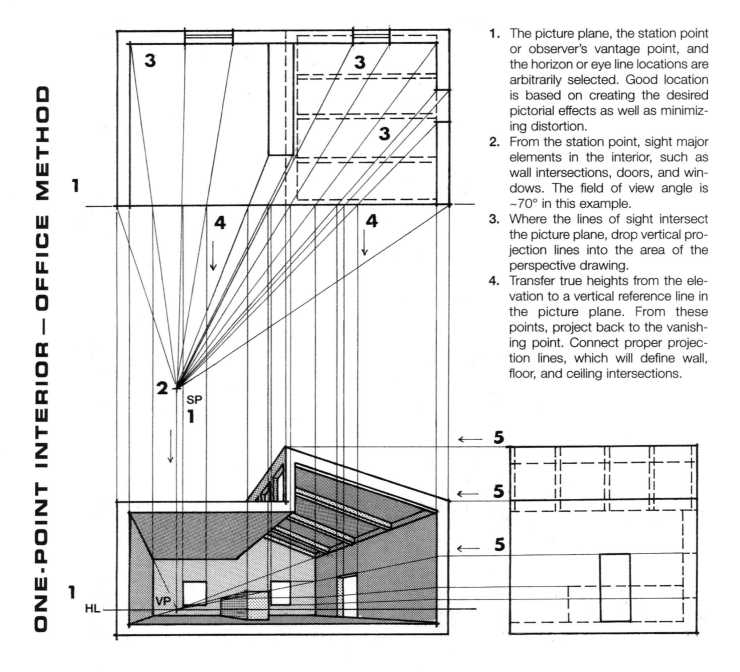

1. The picture plane, the station point or observer's vantage point, and the horizon or eye line locations are arbitrarily selected. Good location is based on creating the desired pictorial effects as well as minimizing distortion.
2. From the station point, sight major elements in the interior, such as wall intersections, doors, and windows. The field of view angle is ~70° in this example.
3. Where the lines of sight intersect the picture plane, drop vertical projection lines into the area of the perspective drawing.
4. Transfer true heights from the elevation to a vertical reference line in the picture plane. From these points, project back to the vanishing point. Connect proper projection lines, which will define wall, floor, and ceiling intersections.

Interior One-point

As with two-point perspectives, the **office** or **common method** is frequently used for one-point perspectives. A one-point is always characterized by at least one plane within the object being parallel to the picture plane. This plane or these planes are always perpendicular to the line of sight of the observer. The picture plane makes a sectional cut through the building or object. See discussion on pages 252–255.

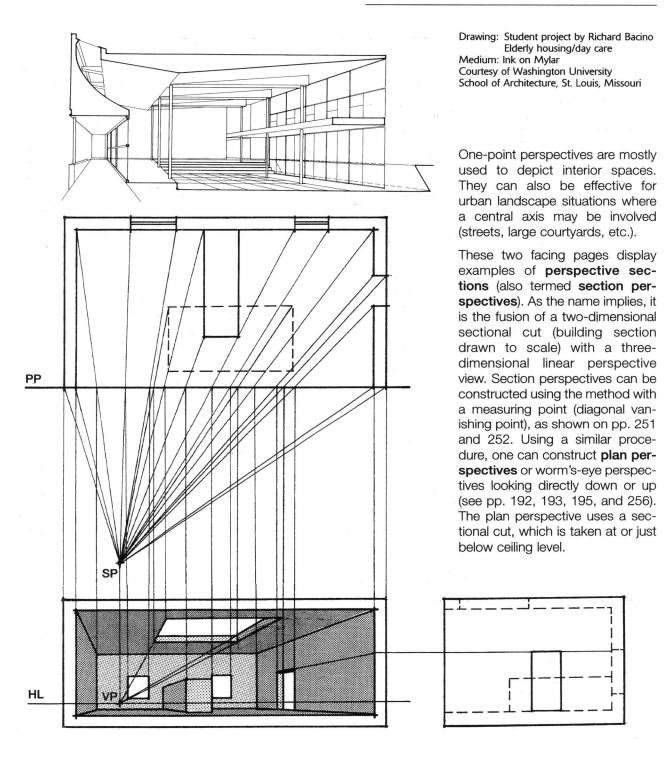

Drawing: Student project by Richard Bacino
Elderly housing/day care
Medium: Ink on Mylar
Courtesy of Washington University
School of Architecture, St. Louis, Missouri

One-point perspectives are mostly used to depict interior spaces. They can also be effective for urban landscape situations where a central axis may be involved (streets, large courtyards, etc.).

These two facing pages display examples of **perspective sections** (also termed **section perspectives**). As the name implies, it is the fusion of a two-dimensional sectional cut (building section drawn to scale) with a three-dimensional linear perspective view. Section perspectives can be constructed using the method with a measuring point (diagonal vanishing point), as shown on pp. 251 and 252. Using a similar procedure, one can construct **plan perspectives** or worm's-eye perspectives looking directly down or up (see pp. 192, 193, 195, and 256). The plan perspective uses a sectional cut, which is taken at or just below ceiling level.

ONE-POINT INTERIOR — OFFICE METHOD

The placement of the vanishing point will govern what one sees in the interior space. If the vanishing point is high, very little ceiling will show but much of the floor will show. If the vanishing point is near the center, an equal amount of ceiling and floor will show. If the vanishing point is low, much of the ceiling and very little of the floor will show. Moving the vanishing point to the right or to the left on the back wall has a similar effect on the side walls—that is, if near the left, more of the right wall will show; and if near the right, more of the left wall will show.

GRID IN ONE-POINT PERSPECTIVE

Drawing: Kiahuna Resort, Kauai, Hawaii
14" × 11" (35.6 × 27.9 cm)
Medium: Ink on Mylar
Bull Stockwell & Allen Architects
Courtesy of Chun/Ishimaru & Assoc., Architectural Illustrators

Interior One-point Grid

Design professionals frequently study interior space usage. An efficient method for locating interior furniture within a plan grid setting is the **measuring line and point method.** This method has the advantage of not needing a plan and elevation as in the office method; it also has the advantage of allowing one to start with the approximate size of perspective one desires. The primary goal of this method is to divide a line in perspective into equal or unequal parts. True heights are measured in the picture plane and projected back along the walls. True widths are similarly projected back on the floor. Chairs, tables, and lighting elements can be positioned quickly (see opposite page), and the drawing susequently rendered as shown above.

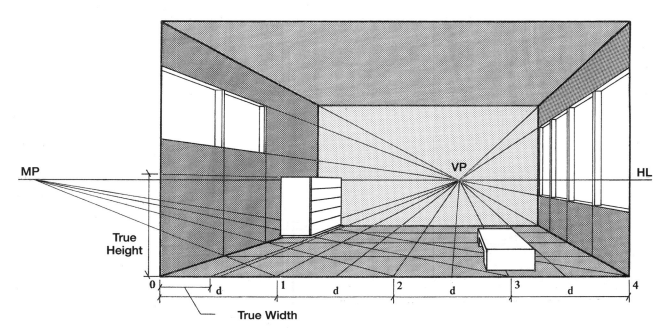

Measuring (Diagonal Vanishing) Point Method

These steps explain how to generate a grid in parallel perspective using a logically well-placed **measuring point (diagonal vanishing point)**. Acute perspective foreshortening will occur if one moves the measuring point too close to the vanishing point along the horizon line. A general rule is to keep the width of the drawing smaller than the distance between the measuring point and the vanishing points. The drawing above slightly violates this rule but is still within the limits of a correctly foreshortened perspective.

1. A horizontal line is drawn through point **0**, which in this case is a part of the room interior.
2. Decide on the relative depth locations of elements (mullions) in the perspective. Select a measuring point **(MP)** on the horizon line and connect to outside point **4**.
3. The measuring line at the ground line where the section cut is taken is divided into *n* equal increments **(d)**, the number *n* being based on how many mullions or other interior elements must be spaced in perspective (in this case, four).
4. Horizontal lines can be located in perspective at the intersection of the measuring-point diagonals and the line from **0** to the vanishing point.
5. Complete the grid by generating vanishing parallels from points **1, 2, 3**, and **4** to the vanishing point.
6. The diagonal line from **0** can also be divided unequally using the same principles in order to locate furniture or other interior elements.

GRID FOR ONE-POINT USING A MEASURING POINT

The addition of wall, floor, and ceiling thicknesses to the plan grid measuring point drawing on page 251 would create a section cut. The cut coincides with the picture plane, and this plane frames a three-dimensional view of pictorial space that communicates an interior design. Construction of the **section perspective** is time- and space-saving because as with measuring point methods, no projection from a plan veiw is needed and thus excess drawing space is not needed.

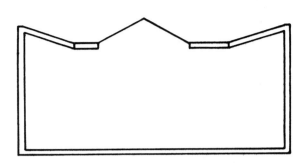

1. Determine where the section will be taken.

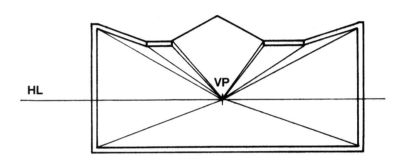

2. Establish the locations of the horizon line and the vanishing point. Project vanishing corner lines from the sectional corners.

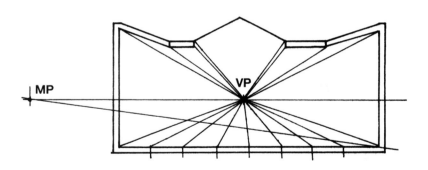

3. Mark equal increments along the sectional floor line. Select an arbitrary measuring point **(MP).** The farther away the measuring point is placed from the vanishing point on the horizon line, the less the distortion. Draw a diagonal line from the measuring point to the farthest lower corner.

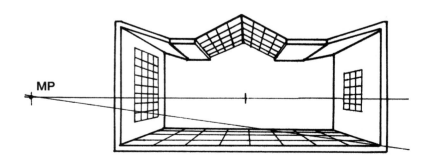

4. At the intersections of the diagonal line and the receding floor plane lines, construct horizontal lines that divide the floor, wall, and ceiling in perspective.

Generating a perspective from a building section sometimes has the drawback of exaggerating the apparent length of spaces (see p. 254).

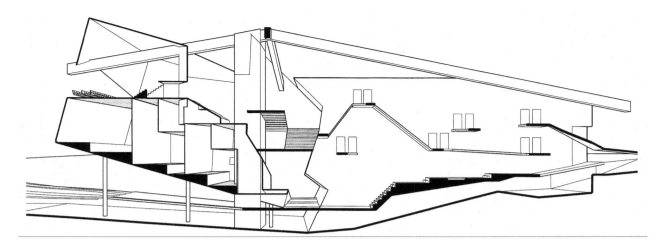

Drawing: Wagrammer Strasse, Vienna, Austria
Medium: Computer-generated
Courtesy of Eric Owen Moss Architects

Section Perspective Views

The perspective view above has a shallow depth of field. The perspective view (right) creates its own frame with a profile line that defines the section plane. Perspective sections are useful in making the often difficult-to-read section more communicative. Note that the vanishing point is placed within the major space. Avoid placing the vanishing point in smaller secondary spaces like the basement level shown at right.

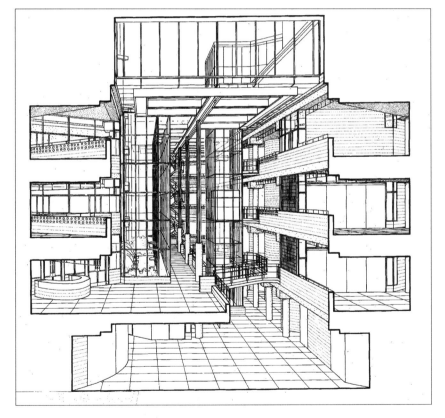

Drawing: Ministry of Social Welfare and Employment
           The Hague, The Netherlands
31.5" × 31.9" (80 × 81 cm)
Medium: Ink on calque
Drawn by R. Rietveld
Courtesy of Herman Hertzberger, Architect

SECTION PERSPECTIVE VIEWS

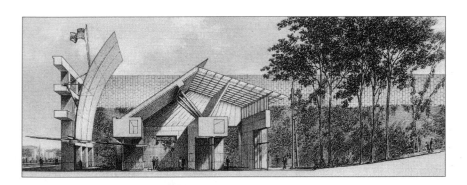

Competition drawing: U.S. Embassy, Berlin, Germany, Garden area
21" × 8⅜" (53.3 × 21.3 cm)
Mixed media: Colored pencil/pastel/other
Courtesy of Bohlin Cywinski Jackson
Joint venture with Sverdrup Facilities

SECTION PERSPECTIVE VIEWS

Drawing: J. B. Speed Art Museum addition
                  Louisville, Kentucky
Courtesy of GBQC Architects

Drawing: Class of 1927/Clapp Hall
                  Princeton University, Princeton, New Jersey
24" × 24" (61 × 61 cm)
Medium: Ink on Mylar
Courtesy of Koetter, Kim & Associates, Inc.
Architects and Urban Designers

A perspective section adds a dramatic effect to the two-dimensional section. The receding third dimension reveals the pictorial quality of the interior spaces. The sectional perspective is more commonly seen as a one-point perspective. A two-point sectional perspective, as shown at left, is also possible but not frequently used. Emphasis should always be placed on the interior details of the cut spaces, as opposed to the structural details within the sectional cuts.

The pictorial or "real" view quality is a perspective section's strength; its weakness is that it does not convey the overall organization of spaces as well as does a plan oblique (axonometric).

Drawing: Residential/commercial building,
          Seaside, Florida
30" × 24" (76.2 × 61 cm)
Medium: Prismacolor on blueprint paper
Courtesy of Machado and Silvetti Associates
Rodolfo Machado and Jorge Silvetti

SECTION PERSPECTIVE VIEWS

As with shadows cast within the section view (p. 345), shadows cast in perspective sections as shown above and in the Berlin U.S. Embassy drawing (facing page) add depth and a three-dimensional quality. Perspective sections delineate the structural profile of a building. If the purpose of the section is to show spatial relationships, then keep accessories (people, furniture, etc.) to a minimum.

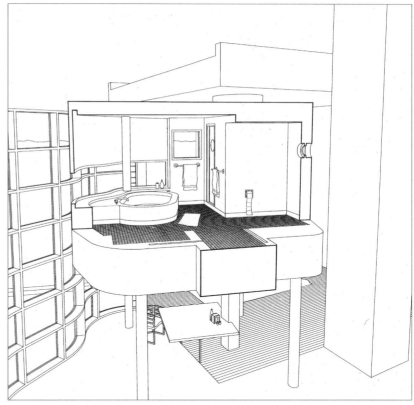

Drawing: Martinelli residence
          Roxbury, Connecticut, 1989
24" × 24" (61 × 61 cm)
Medium: Ink
Courtesy of Anthony Ames, Architect

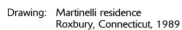

Horizontal and vertical cuts are made in the master bathroom in this perspective drawing, showing its location in a cloudlike form on columns, hovering above the dining area.

[ARCHITECT'S STATEMENT]

ONE-POINT PLAN PERSPECTIVE VIEWS

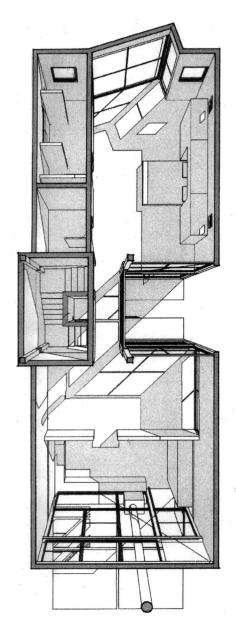

Second Story Plan

Images: Bernal Heights residence
San Francisco, California
Principal in charge: Mark English
Architectural illustrations: Star Jennings
Courtesy of Inglese Architecture

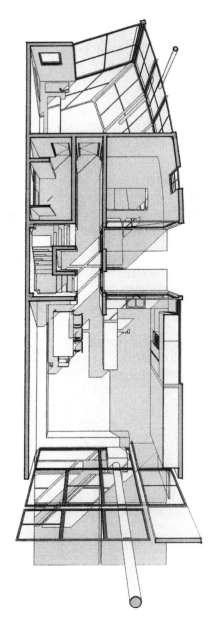

Ground Level Plan

Plan Perspective Views

One-point perspective plan views are used to show the floor layout with additional volumetric information. In this case, the observer is close enough to see some window and facade details.

[ARCHITECT'S STATEMENT]

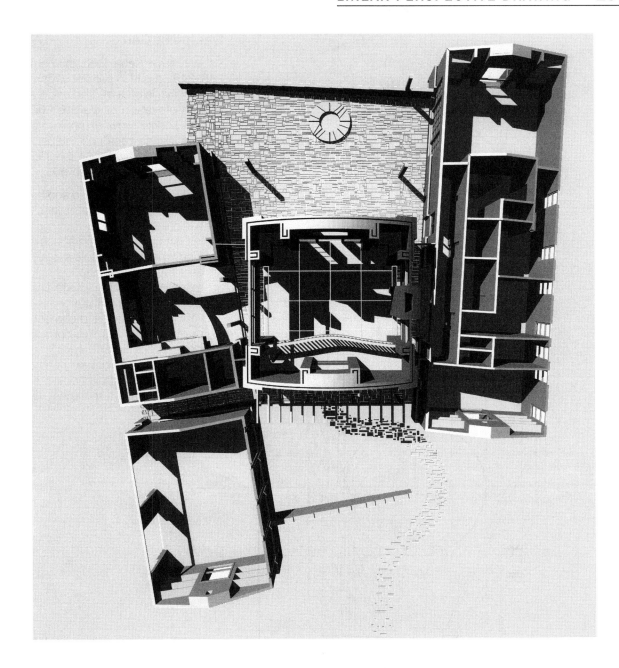

Image: The Devitt residence, Austin, Texas
Medium: Computer-generated
Principal in charge: Mark English
Architectural illustrations: Star Jennings
Courtesy of Inglese Architecture

Plan Perspective Views

In keeping with the vernacular architectural traditions, the two wings of this residence are simple rectangles with gable roofs. The arrangement of building elements is anchored by a paved north-facing patio. This image is a one-point perspective showing the building and some adjacent landscape features. Our intent is to describe the floor layout as well as capture volumetric characteristics. Indications of floor pattern and material are given where clarity is required.

[ARCHITECT'S STATEMENT]

EXTERIOR ONE-POINT GRID EXAMPLE

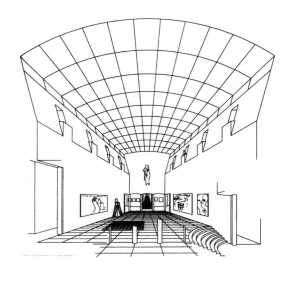

One-point Grid

As we have seen with interiors (pp. 248–249), a grid in parallel or one-point perpsective is constructed using a **plan** with an **elevation** or elevation heights. In this exterior view example, you are given standing rectilinear slabs and a circular pond drawn to a specific scale (scale and heights not shown).

1. Draw both the plan grid and the perspective grid. Construct lines to the vanishing point to see how grid lines in plan converge in perspective.
2. Find where the objects in plan intersect the picture plane.
3. Establish a section image and project through the critical points to the vanishing points. Find corner points of objects by sighting corresponding plan points **(a)**.
4. Draw the completed perspective image of the first plan object selected (in this case a rectilinear slab).

PP

a'
a

Do for each grid line.

aₚ

Section image

GL

Drawing: Museum of Modern Art, Frankfurt, Germany
31.5" × 31.5" (80 × 80 cm)
Medium: Ink
Courtesy of Hans Hollein, Architekt

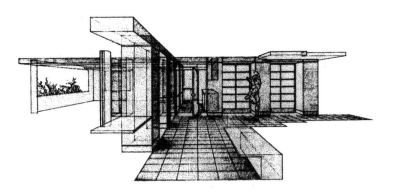

Drawing: The Rittenhouse square apartment
                Philadelphia, Pennsylvania
Medium: Ink
Courtesy of Wesley Wei, AIA, Wesley Wei Architects

5. Follow the same procedure to complete the other rectilinear objects in the perspective.

6. For the pond, enclose the circle within a square. Divide the circle into quarter-circles. Sight critical points **k, l, m,** and **n,** and project picture plane intersections into the perspective image of these same points. Use a french curve and construct the pond (takes the form of an ellipse).

Hand-drafted grids are useful for constructing both one- and two-point perspectives. The hand-drawn grid can be blown up or reduced to a suitable scale and design sketches can be done on trace overlays. With the development of perspective charts and especially computer-aided drafting, grids can be ready or made ready for immediate use.

EXTERIOR ONE-POINT GRID EXAMPLE

Drawing: Student project by Howard Fineman
Augusta City Hall
Medium: Ink on Mylar
Courtesy of Washington University School of Architecture,
St. Louis, Missouri

SP PLACEMENT AND 45° DIAGONAL LINES

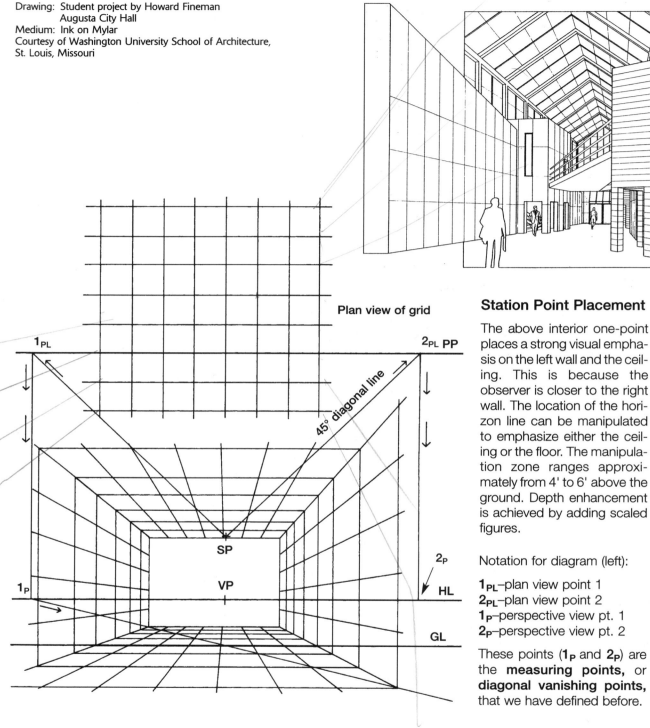

Plan view of grid

45° diagonal line

1_{PL}   2_{PL} PP

SP

VP

1_P   2_P   HL

GL

Station Point Placement

The above interior one-point places a strong visual emphasis on the left wall and the ceiling. This is because the observer is closer to the right wall. The location of the horizon line can be manipulated to emphasize either the ceiling or the floor. The manipulation zone ranges approximately from 4' to 6' above the ground. Depth enhancement is achieved by adding scaled figures.

Notation for diagram (left):

1_{PL}–plan view point 1
2_{PL}–plan view point 2
1_P–perspective view pt. 1
2_P–perspective view pt. 2

These points (**1_P** and **2_P**) are the **measuring points,** or **diagonal vanishing points,** that we have defined before.

45° Diagonal Plan Lines

This quick procedure simply utilizes 45° diagonal plan lines from the station point. This results in an equilateral (45°) triangle. The length of the bisector from the station point will always be equal to the distance from points **1** or **2** to the picture plane intersection point. The diagonal line in perspective passes through the lower left or right corners of the picture plane. Its intersection with converging vanishing lines on the ground plane produces all the needed horizontal grid lines in perspective.

Drawing: Triton Museum of Art, Santa Clara,
          California
14.5" × 9" (36.8 × 22.9 cm)
Medium: Pencil on vellum
Courtesy of Rosekrans and Broder Inc., Architects

This one-point has an excellent field of view. Don't be afraid to step back when attempting to depict an interior space; most problems in distortion come from being too close to the picture plane. With interior one-points it is essential to give the feeling that you are part of the viewed space. This requires good judgment in cropping interior features on the ground plane (see pp. 406 and 415).

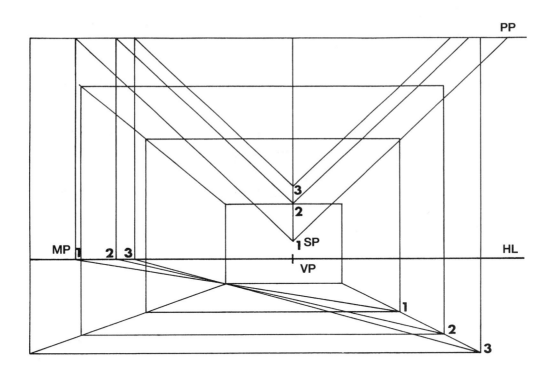

Station Point Movement

Using 45° diagonal plan lines, what will happen when the station point **(SP)** is moved along the line of sight? The station point location will affect the corresponding point location on the horizon line (and thus the picture plane). The placement of the points **1, 2**, and **3** along the horizon line controls perspective distortion of the grid. The farther the point is moved away from the vanishing point (and thus, the picture plane), the less the distortion will be. The field of view also changes as one moves farther away. The observer's view is a much larger area and thus the cone of vision is much greater. Even though the 45° **VP** is a direct function of the station point distance from the picture plane, within limits it is nevertheless variable, even arbitrary, in a one-point perspective.

VARIABLE SP IN ONE-POINT PERSPCTIVES

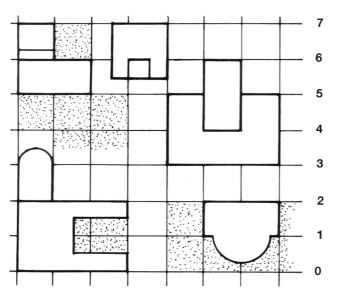

BIRD'S-EYE PERSPECTIVES

Bird's-Eye View

Technically, the terms **bird's-eye** and **aerial** are synonymous.

A grid procedure for bird's-eye perspectives is advantageous when the building complex or urban landscape is in a predominantly regular arrangement. After transposing the elements from plan grid to perspective grid, structural forms can be "eyeballed" and sketched using appropriate heights. The plan grid and perspective grid can be at different scales, but the total number of grid lines must correspond. Relate the plan shown at the left to the selected aerial perspective view shown below. Note that the eight (**0** to **7**) grid lines correspond.

Foreground building details show better with a low angle of view. A higher angle of view shows orientation and traffic patterns better. The goals and purpose of your illustration will determine the proper station point location.

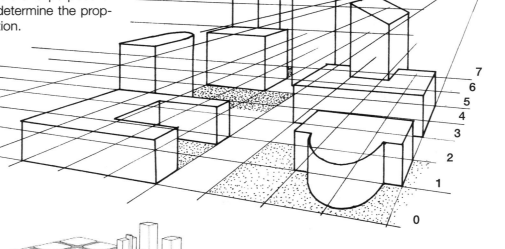

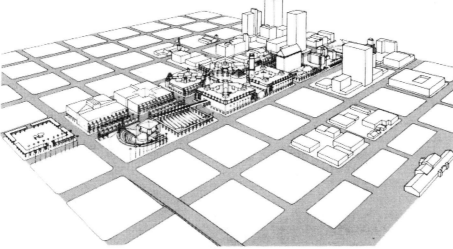

Drawing: Masterplan concept
Phoenix Municipal
Government Center
Phoenix, Arizona
Courtesy of John Schreier,
Barton Myers Associates, Architects

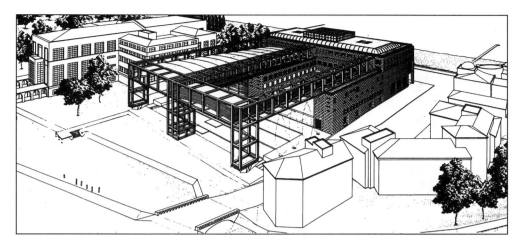

Drawing: A Film Palace
Venice, Italy
Courtesy of Oswald Mathias
Ungers, Architect

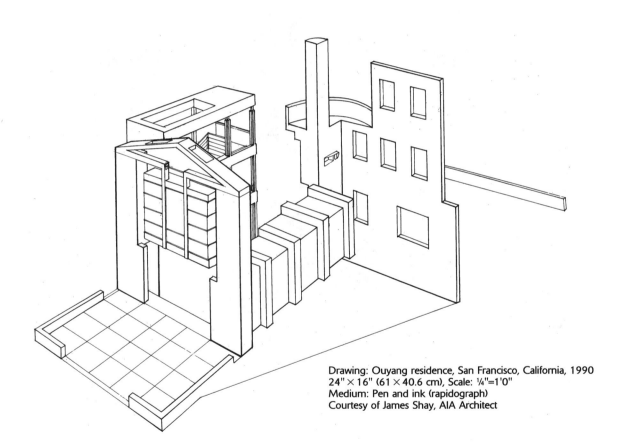

Drawing: Ouyang residence, San Francisco, California, 1990
24" × 16" (61 × 40.6 cm), Scale: ¼"=1'0"
Medium: Pen and ink (rapidograph)
Courtesy of James Shay, AIA Architect

BIRD'S-EYE EXAMPLES

This is drawn to show important parts of the house without showing the entire building. This enables the architect to clearly communicate what he or she regards as most important.
[ARCHITECT'S STATEMENT]

Most bird's-eye view perspectives that are slightly above roof level are characterized by a horizon line that is in the range of 40' to 80' above the ground plane. It has the advantage over an eye-level view perspective of revealing the surrounding landscape (trees, group of buildings, townscape, etc.) as well as unexpected roof line details.

CITYSCAPE BIRD'S-EYE VIEW PERSPECTIVE

Drawing: First Street Plaza, Los Angeles, California
Courtesy of First Street Plaza Partners
and TAC, The Architects Collaborative
Renderer: Jim Arp

Bird's-Eye Perspective

Large-scale bird's-eye views are used frequently, not only by architects but also by landscape architects, city planners, urban designers, environmental analysts, and site engineers. In comparing the above bird's-eye perspective to the bird's-eye plan oblique (axonometric) on the facing page, note that the perspective has the advantage of revealing more building facade, whereas the plan oblique has the advantage of showing more of the pedestrian streetscape and the open spaces between buildings.

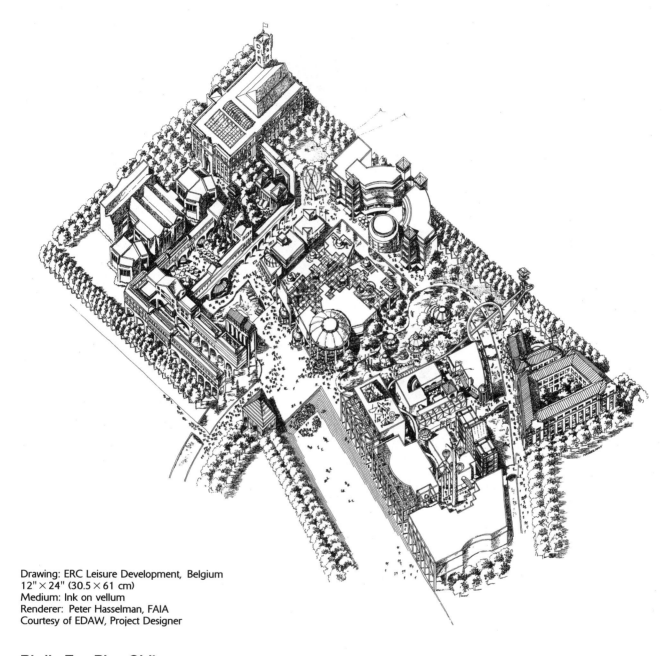

Drawing: ERC Leisure Development, Belgium
12" × 24" (30.5 × 61 cm)
Medium: Ink on vellum
Renderer: Peter Hasselman, FAIA
Courtesy of EDAW, Project Designer

Bird's-Eye Plan Oblique

Bird's-eye plan obliques are similar to steep angled perspectives. Landscaping patterns, as well as vehicular and pedestrian circulation patterns, are usually more easily visible with an oblique view.

LOOKING UP AND LOOKING DOWN

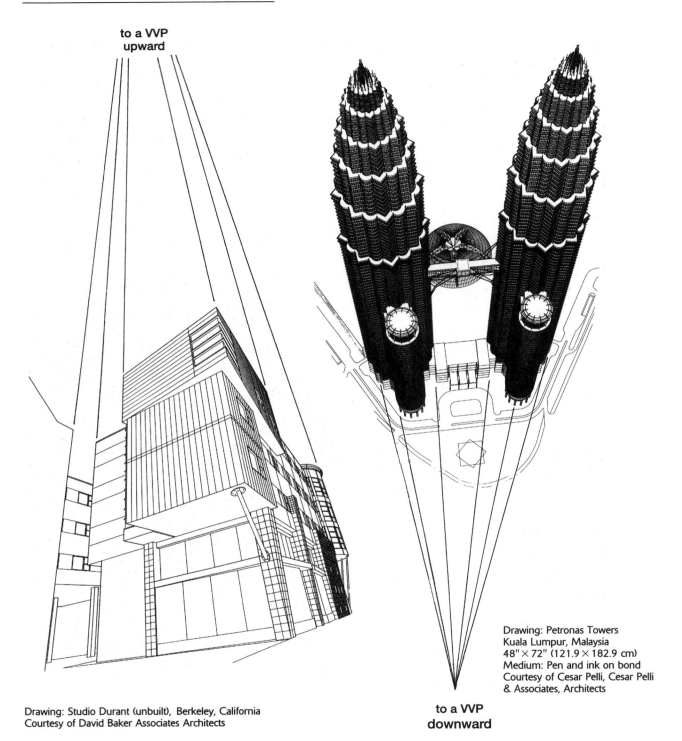

to a VVP
upward

Drawing: Petronas Towers
Kuala Lumpur, Malaysia
48" × 72" (121.9 × 182.9 cm)
Medium: Pen and ink on bond
Courtesy of Cesar Pelli, Cesar Pelli
& Associates, Architects

to a VVP
downward

Drawing: Studio Durant (unbuilt), Berkeley, California
Courtesy of David Baker Associates Architects

Looking up results in an upward convergence of vertical lines; looking down results in a downward convergence of vertical lines. A view with upward or downward convergence has the characteristic of a tipped picture plane. The picture plane is inclined at an angle to the ground plane, not perpendicular as with one- and two-point perspectives. The vertical vanishing points above and below are usually placed closer to the ground plane than they normally would be, in order to exaggerate the soaring (see p. 80) or plunging (see p. 49) feeling. See the discussion on three-point perspectives on the following pages.

In comparison with the images on the opposite page, these images show a less exaggerated and more natural view of downward and upward convergence.

Images: Merrill Lynch headquarters, Jersey City, New Jersey
                Client: Merrill Lynch
Courtesy of Fox & Fowle Architects

LOOKING UP AND LOOKING DOWN

A strong commitment to the integration of computer-aided design (CAD) technology into the firm's design and production processes has allowed this system to grow into more than 65 advanced CAD workstations, all part of the firm's local area network of more than 80 computers. CAD technology is applied through every phase of architectural design and construction document production. Digital zoning studies and area analyses become 3D massing models and spatial studies, which in turn are developed into computer-rendered presentations. These renderings can be either highly stylistic or photorealistic.
[ARCHITECT'S STATEMENT]

Upward Convergence

Any object seen in a three-point perspective is characterized by projection
lines, which are extensions of vertical
lines in the object converging to a vertical vanishing point **(VVP)**. Note that
the ski resort is actually a more than
three-point (multipoint) perspective
due to other horizontal lines vanshing
left or right (see below).

Drawing: Ski resort
Avoriaz, France
Courtesy of Jacques LABRO et
Jean-Jacques ORZONI, Architectes

LOOKING UP

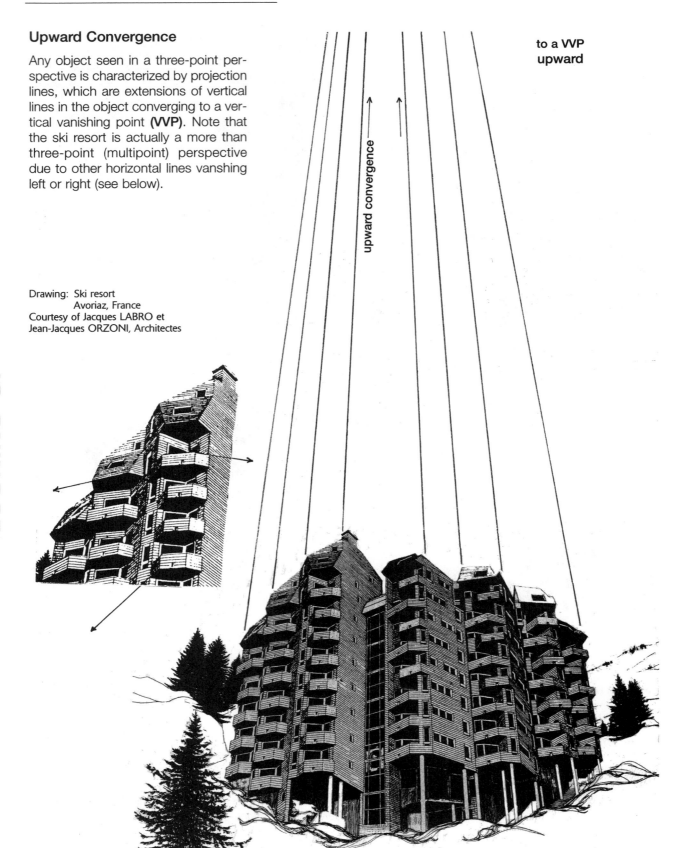

to a VVP
upward

upward convergence

Drawing: Hong Kong aerial, Hong Kong, China
A3-size tracing paper (16.5" × 11.5")
Medium: Color pencil with black marker and overlaid paint highlights (spirit-based)
Courtesy of Peter Edgeley, Architectural Illustrator

LOOKING DOWN

This drawing was used as a planning document to explain preliminary design studies of the Hilton Hotel and to explain softening landscape elements to the surrounding streetscape (the Hilton Hotel is the bronze-clad building).
1. An impressionistic technique was chosen to match the preliminary nature of the submission as part of a "discussion paper." A hard-edge photographic effect was avoided.
2. The hills in the background were treated by broad soft strokes of crayon, whilst closer buildings and rows of street trees were given finer details and more contrast. This helped focus the attention where the main decisions of master planning and landscape architecture were being made.
[ARCHITECTURAL ILLUSTRATOR'S STATEMENT]

Downward Convergence

This is an example of a very high vantage point view looking down with a lot of downward convergence. Architectural illustrators use such vantage points to increase the dramatic effect of a rendering.

THREE-POINT PERSPECTIVE

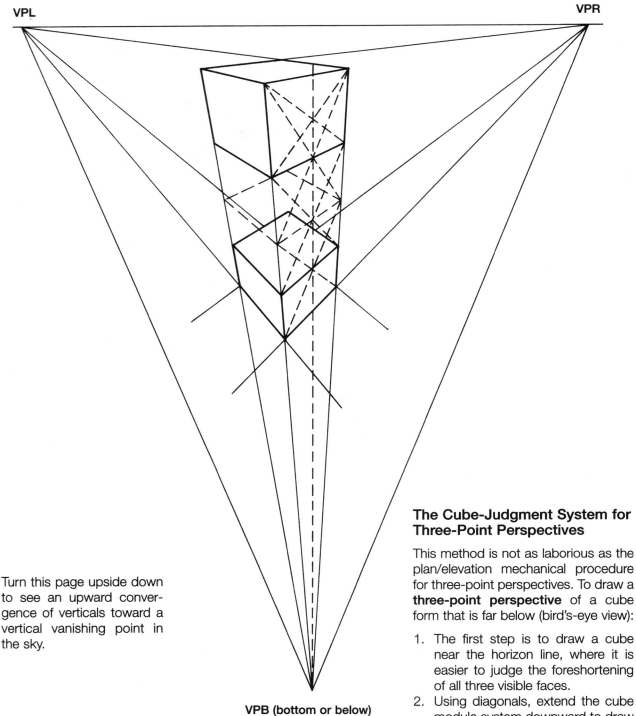

VPL

VPR

VPB (bottom or below)
This is arbitrarily placed.

Turn this page upside down to see an upward convergence of verticals toward a vertical vanishing point in the sky.

Diagram and text: Courtesy of Dik Vrooman, Professor
Texas A&M University
Department of Architecture

The Cube-Judgment System for Three-Point Perspectives

This method is not as laborious as the plan/elevation mechanical procedure for three-point perspectives. To draw a **three-point perspective** of a cube form that is far below (bird's-eye view):

1. The first step is to draw a cube near the horizon line, where it is easier to judge the foreshortening of all three visible faces.
2. Using diagonals, extend the cube module system downward to draw the correct perspective of the cube on the ground.
3. Also using diagonals, you can extend this system laterally.
4. Building design shapes other than cubes are measured from these cubes.

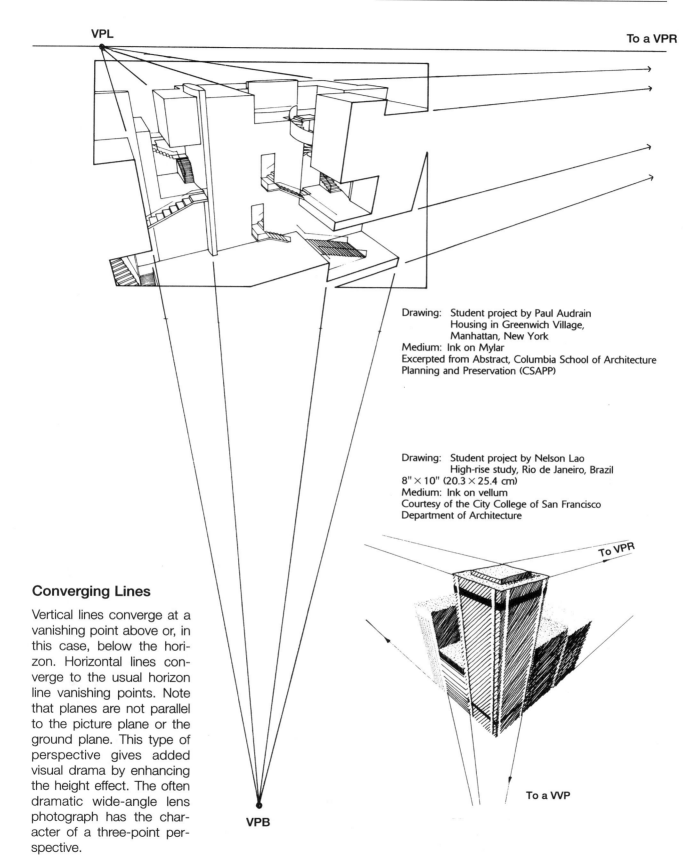

VPL

To a VPR

Drawing: Student project by Paul Audrain
　　　　　Housing in Greenwich Village,
　　　　　Manhattan, New York
Medium: Ink on Mylar
Excerpted from Abstract, Columbia School of Architecture
Planning and Preservation (CSAPP)

Drawing: Student project by Nelson Lao
　　　　　High-rise study, Rio de Janeiro, Brazil
8" × 10" (20.3 × 25.4 cm)
Medium: Ink on vellum
Courtesy of the City College of San Francisco
Department of Architecture

To VPR

To a VVP

Converging Lines

Vertical lines converge at a vanishing point above or, in this case, below the horizon. Horizontal lines converge to the usual horizon line vanishing points. Note that planes are not parallel to the picture plane or the ground plane. This type of perspective gives added visual drama by enhancing the height effect. The often dramatic wide-angle lens photograph has the character of a three-point perspective.

VPB

THREE-POINT PERSPECTIVE

THREE-POINT PERSPECTIVE

This method of construction produces an accurately measured **three-point perspective** drawing. The principle is based on the measured two-point perspective method: The image is generated on a picture plane by projecting lines from the object to a single eye point. In three-point perspective, in addition, the picture plane will be tilted at an angle, as one would tilt a camera to photograph a tall object. When the picture plane (and the camera) are tilted, the lines in the vertical direction will converge as well. The principle is illustrated in the diagram below. Using a scale for the perspective layout allows control of the image. In the example, 1"=50' scale was used.

1. Determine the distance of the observer (the eyepoint E) from the picture plane. A larger distance will produce a smaller but less distorted image. This distance is the radius of the circle drawn.

2. To generate the vanishing point for the vertical lines **(VVP)**, the eye point (E) must be rotated around the centerline **(CL)** from the center of the circle **(c)** into the surface of the picture plane. The point received **(EV)** will be used for generating measurements in the vertical direction.

3. Determine the tilting of the picture plane. A larger angle produces a closer vanishing point. In the example, the angle is 20°. Draw a line **(h)** with the angle from EV. The intersection with the center line (CL) gives the location of the horizon line. Perpendicular to the line (h), draw a line (v). The intersection with the center line (CL) will give the vanishing point **(VVP)** for the vertical lines. Note that the tilted picture plane is the surface of the paper; thus, the horizontal and vertical lines (h and v) must be drawn tilted instead.

4. Rotate the EV eyepoint around point H into the center line (CL) to generate the eyepoint **(EH)**. This point will be used to construct the perspective in the horizontal direction.

5. Determine the distance of the base plane from the horizontal plane. In the example it is 60'. In this perspective, the base plane was selected at the top of the object to reduce the drawing size. The **baseline** (BL), the intersection of the base plane and the picture plane, is drawn in scale 60' below the **horizon line** (HL).

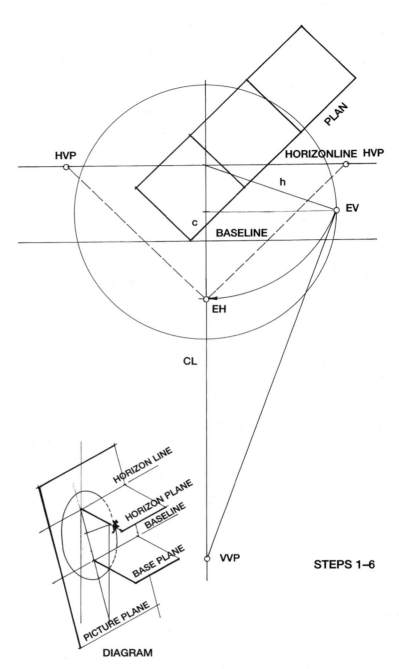

STEPS 1–6

DIAGRAM

Text and diagram: Courtesy of Arpad Daniel Ronaszegi, Assistant Professor Andrews University Division of Architecture

6. Position the plan on the base plane. Here, the object was placed behind the picture plane with one corner touching it. From EH we can construct the vanishing point **(HVP)** by drawing parallel lines with corresponding sides and intersecting with the horizon line (HL).

7. Construct the perpsective image of the plan by connecting lines to the appropriate horizontal vanishing points **(HVP)**. The lengths of the lines will be measured by connecting points to the eyepoint **(EH)** and intersecting them with the corresponding lines.

8. The image of vertical lines can be constructed by connecting points from the plan image to the vertical vanishing point **(VVP)**.

9. The heights in the vertical direction will be generated from the vertical measuring line (VML). Draw a parallel line with the line **v**, starting from the point where the plan touches the picture plane (**BL** on the drawing). On the line generated **(vml)**, the actual heights can be measured out. In this example, the elevation is drawn orthogonal to the VML and then projected onto it.

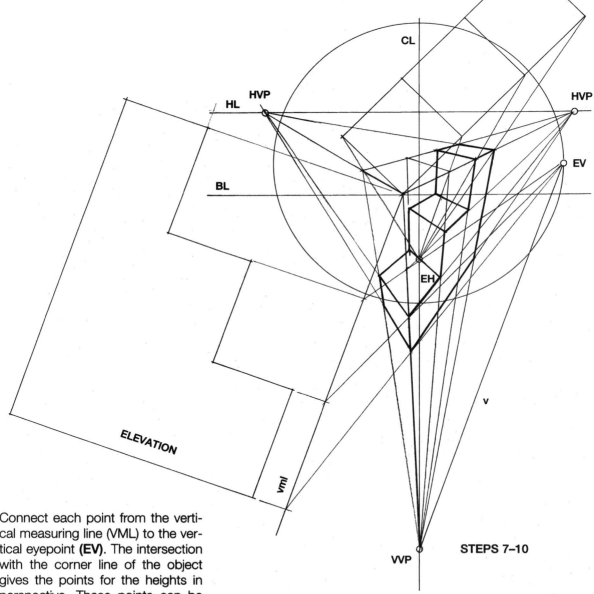

10. Connect each point from the vertical measuring line (VML) to the vertical eyepoint **(EV)**. The intersection with the corner line of the object gives the points for the heights in perspective. These points can be connected to the appropriate HVP points to finish the construction of the image.

STEPS 7–10

Text and diagram: Courtesy of Arpad Daniel Ronaszegi, Assistant Professor Andrews University Division of Architecture

THREE-POINT PERSPECTIVE

EXPLODED PERSPECTIVE

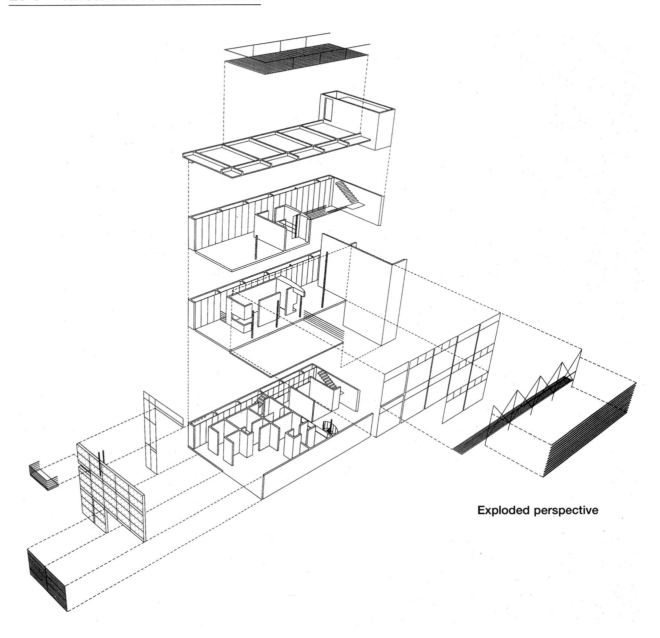

Exploded perspective

Drawing: HOUSE LE, Colonia Condesa, Mexico City, Mexico
Courtesy of TEN Arquitectos-Enrique Norten
Bernardo Gomez-Pimienta, Carlos Ordoñez, project coordinators

Exploded Perspective

Each layer in this exploded perspective gives an unimpeded view of the interior and exterior details of the house. The individual layers must be far enough apart to distinguish each layer (horizontal and vertical), yet be close enough so that they "read" as a coherent whole.

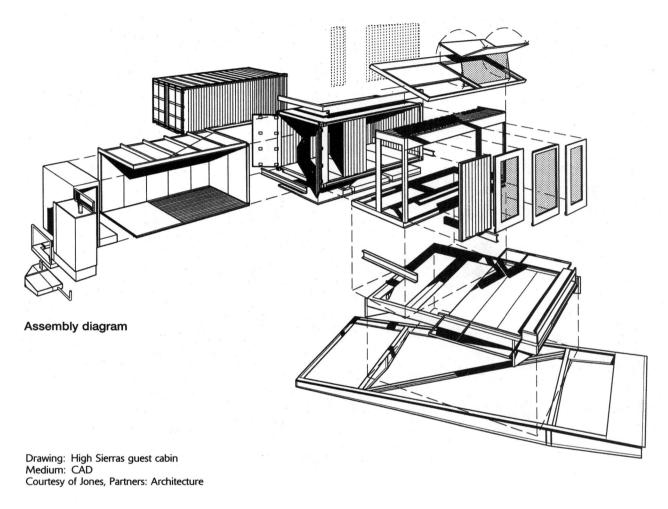

Assembly diagram

Drawing: High Sierras guest cabin
Medium: CAD
Courtesy of Jones, Partners: Architecture

ASSEMBLY DRAWING

Exploded Assembly Drawing

The use of the exploded view highlights the nature of this structure as an assemblage of standardized parts and shows the genesis of the primary building module in the standard 20' shipping container. The primary modular assembly occupies the horizontal plane established by the existing container in the background, while accessory elements are, where possible, exploded along the vertical axis. Corrugated steel removed from the existing container is shown dotted in.
[ARCHITECT'S STATEMENT]

HYBRID DRAWINGS

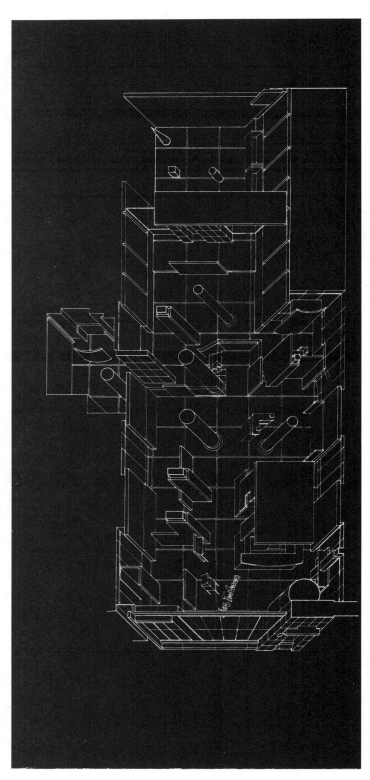

Drawing: Les Tuileries Restaurant, New York City
20" × 30" (50.8 × 76.2 cm), Scale: ¼"=1'0"
Medium: Ink and Mylar
Courtesy of Diane Lewis, Peter Mickle,
and Christopher Compton, R.A., Designers

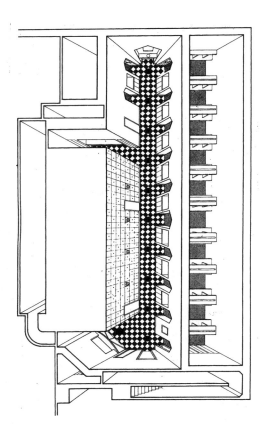

Drawing: The WEB (Work Stations in Evans Basement)
University of California, Berkeley
12" × 18" (30.5 × 45.7 cm), Scale: ⅛"=1'0"
Medium: Ink on Mylar
Courtesy of Sam Davis, FAIA, of Davis & Joyce Architects

*An aerial one-point perspective shows the orga-
nization of the various rooms as would a simple
plan, while also showing the volumetric relationships of the spaces. Certain liberties are necessary in the construction of such a drawing, but
revealing so much conceptual information at a
single glance is often valuable.*
[ARCHITECT'S STATEMENT]

Hybrid Drawings

When drawing types are superimposed, the
result is a **hybrid** drawing. These two hybrid
drawings with unusual overhead views combine the principles of paraline and perspective drawing. At first glance, they appear to
be overhead one-point perspectives. On
closer examination, however, one notices
many internal structural elements having infinitely parallel lines.

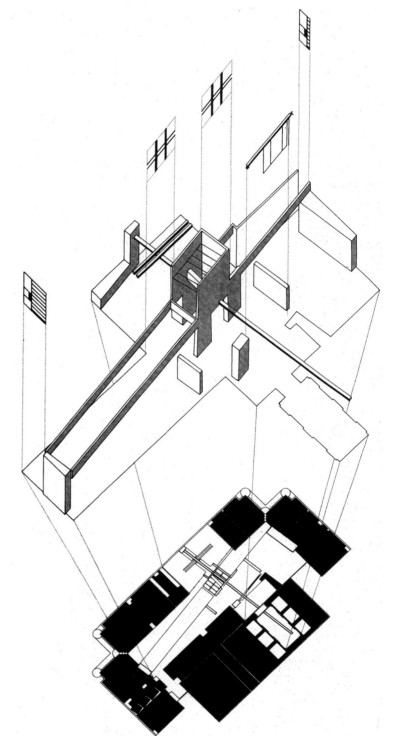

ENLARGED AND EXPANDED VIEW

Hybrid Drawing

This hybrid drawing combines a one-point persective with a vertically expanded plan oblique. Note that the perspective convergence results in the plan being enlarged, allowing for a clearer view of many details.

This drawing was made in order to illustrate a relation between a plan (in this case a floor plan) and certain three-dimensional elements contained within that plan. The plan is made as a figure/ground drawing in which the central void space of the office is highlighted. It is out of that void space that the three-dimensional parts are drawn as an axonometric projection.
[ARCHITECT'S STATEMENT]

Drawing: World Savings Center Executive Suite, Oakland, California
14" × 26" (35.6 × 66 cm), Scale: ⅛"=1'0"
Medium: Ink on vellum
Courtesy of Jim Jennings, Architect, of Jennings + Stout, Architects
Drawn by Jim Jennings

Drawing: Residence, Palm Springs,
California
8" × 5" (20.3 × 12.7 cm)
Medium: Prismacolor
Courtesy of Kanner Architects
Drawing by Stephen Kanner

Perspective Circles

Circles in perspective take the form of an **ellipse.** We see this form not only in architectural subjects but also in everyday things such as bottles, dishware, pots, waste containers, coins, and wheels for transportation. Architecturally, **vertical circles** are commonly part of arches, semicircular windows, and circular vertical cylindrical forms.

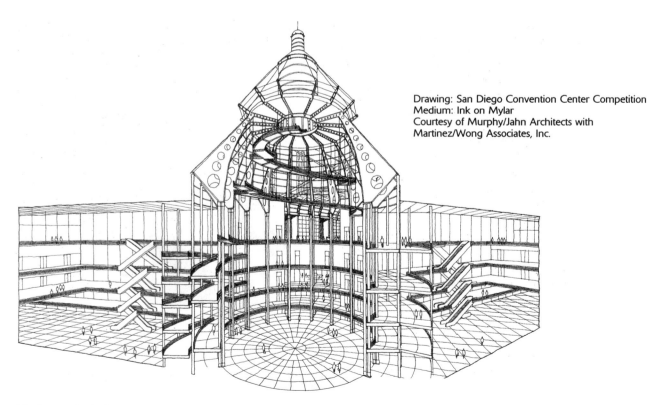

Drawing: San Diego Convention Center Competition
Medium: Ink on Mylar
Courtesy of Murphy/Jahn Architects with
Martinez/Wong Associates, Inc.

Horizontal circles are commonly part of semicircular or circular skylights and semicircular or circular horizontal cylindrical forms (e.g., rotundas).

Visualize a circle, such as a bicycle wheel. The wheel below can take the form of a **horizontal** circle as it rotates about its horizontal diameter. This diameter can be described as major (longest true length). The minor diameter (axis) is perpendicular and foreshortened and becomes progressively smaller. Or, the wheel can take the form of a **vertical** circle as it rotates about its vertical diameter. The minor diameter (axis) is perpendicular and becomes progressively smaller, as in the first case.

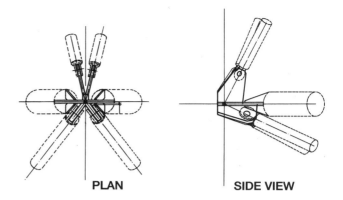

PLAN   SIDE VIEW

Drawing: Structural connection details
           Sydney Football Stadium, Sydney, Australia
Medium: CADD, Scale: 1:10
Courtesy of Cox Richardson
Architects and Planners
Ove Arup, Structural Engineer

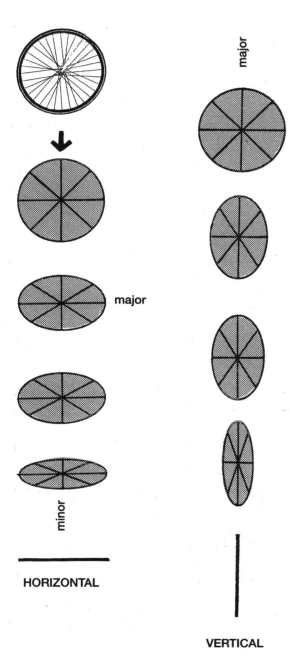

HORIZONTAL

VERTICAL

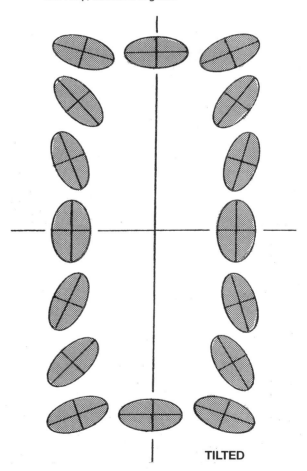

TILTED

The above diagram illustrates how a circle seen in perspective as an ellipse will change in orientation from a horizontal to a vertical condition for the major axis. The intermediate conditions result in **tilted ellipses,** the degree of which depends on the inclination of the axes relative to the observer's position.

CIRCLES IN PERSPECTVE

VERTICAL CIRCLE IN PERSPECTIVE

Drawing Perspective Circles

To draw a circle or a portion of a circle accurately in perspective requires that you first draw its circumscribing square. With experience and practice, you will be able to derive from the square all the reference that is needed for quick sketches. However, as accuracy requirements and circle size increase, so does the need to construct additional points of reference to assist in constructing the circle. The following sections describe the four-, eight-, and twelve-point techniques for constructing circles.

The Four-Point Perspective Circle

The four-point technique locates the points of tangency between the circle and square.

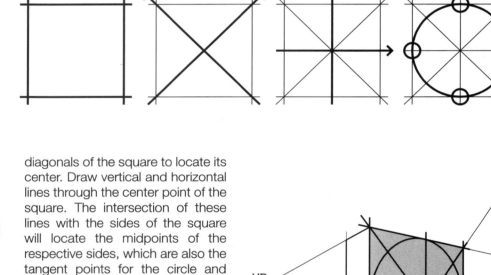

diagonals of the square to locate its center. Draw vertical and horizontal lines through the center point of the square. The intersection of these lines with the sides of the square will locate the midpoints of the respective sides, which are also the tangent points for the circle and square. Draw a smooth curve that connects the four points to create a circle in perspective. Visually adjust the circle until it looks correct.

Note that the highest and lowest points of the circle are to the near side of their respective tangent points.

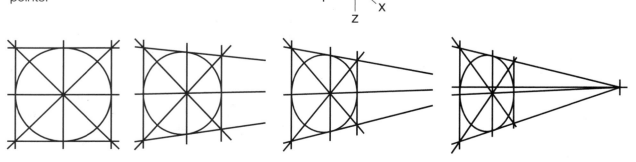

The Eight-Point Perspective Circle

The eight-point technique builds directly on the four-point system with a visual approximation that provides four more points.

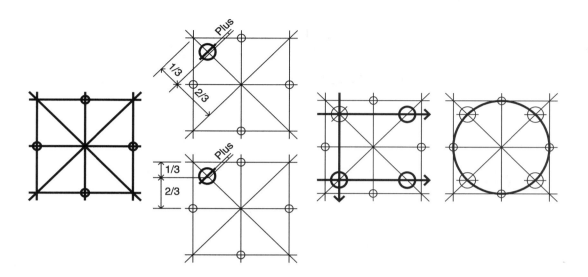

Follow the four-point procedure to locate the first four points. The diagonals used in this process are now divided to locate the additional points.

Divide the near half of one of the diagonals into thirds to locate the two-thirds point as shown. This can be done either directly along the diagonal or along the corresponding half of the square's side. If you use the square's side, you must transfer the two-thirds mark to the diagonal.

Mark a point just beyond the two-thirds point of the diagonal. This locates the point at which the circle will intersect the diagonal.

Transfer this point to the other diagonals with lines that are parallel to the respective sides. This locates the other three points, giving you eight points to guide your circle construction.

Draw a smooth curve that connects the eight points to create a circle. Visually adjust the circle until it looks correct.

Drawing (partial): The Peninsula Regent, San Mateo, California
16" × 24" (40.6 × 61 cm)
Medium: Ink on Mylar
Courtesy of Backen Arrigoni & Ross, Inc.
Architecture, Planning & Interior Design
Peter Szasz, Architectural Illustrator

VERTICAL CIRCLE IN PERSPECTIVE

VERTICAL CIRCLE IN PERSPECTIVE

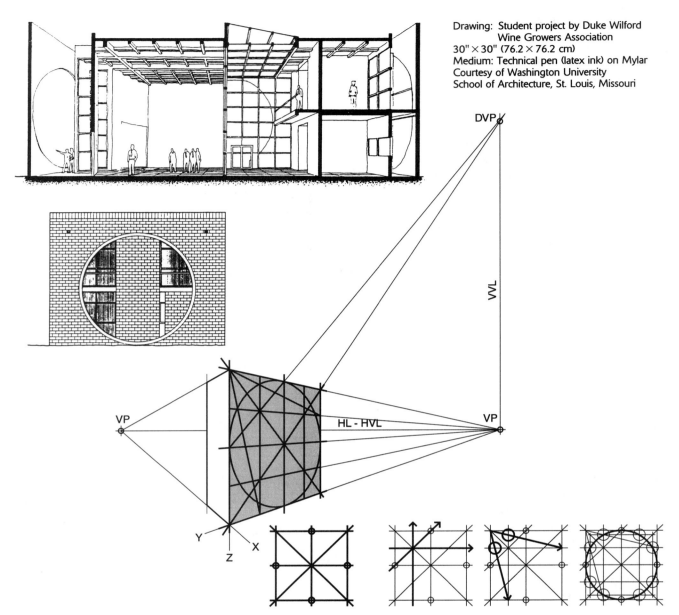

Drawing: Student project by Duke Wilford
              Wine Growers Association
30" × 30" (76.2 × 76.2 cm)
Medium: Technical pen (latex ink) on Mylar
Courtesy of Washington University
School of Architecture, St. Louis, Missouri

The Twelve-Point Perspective Circle

Follow the four-point procedure to locate the first four points.
Draw a diagonal through a near quarter of the original square to find its center. Draw vertical and horizontal lines through this point.

Draw lines from the corner of the original square to the one-quarter points on the opposite sides as shown. The intersection of these lines with the nearest horizontal or vertical one-quarter line defines two new points on the circle.

Use transfer techniques to create the other vertical and horizontal lines and then transfer the location of the two new points on the circle to the appropriate lines. This locates the other six new points and provides twelve to guide circle construction. Draw a smooth curve that connects the twelve points to create a circle. Visually adjust the circle until it looks correct.

Diagrams and text (pp. 280–282): Courtesy of William R. Benedict, Assistant Professor
California Polytechnic State University School of Architecture
San Luis Obispo, California

The **twelve-point** procedure is equally effective in constructing a horizontal perspective circle. It can also be used to construct an isometric circle. (See construction of isometric circles on p. 130).

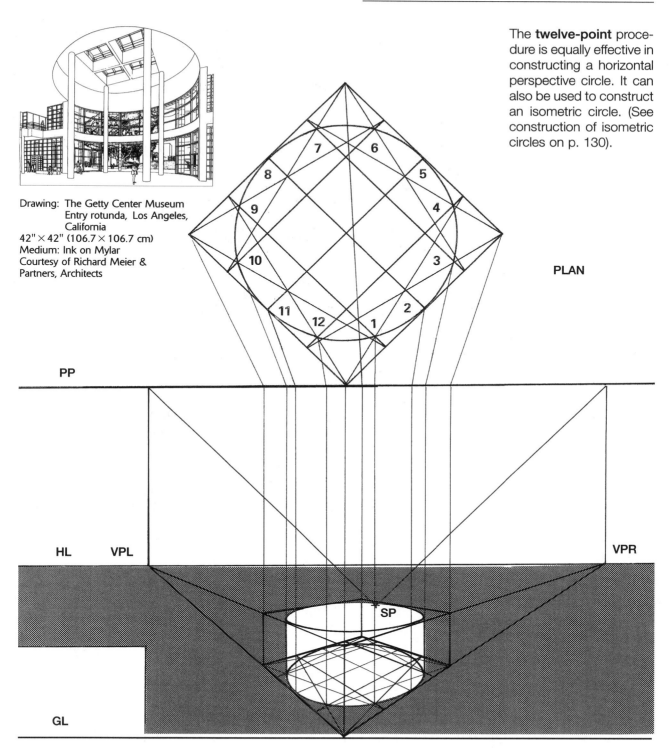

Drawing: The Getty Center Museum
Entry rotunda, Los Angeles,
California
42" × 42" (106.7 × 106.7 cm)
Medium: Ink on Mylar
Courtesy of Richard Meier &
Partners, Architects

PLAN

PP

HL   VPL

VPR

SP

GL

ELEVATION

HORIZONTAL CIRCLE IN PERSPECTIVE

The Twelve-Point Perspective Circle

1. Divide the encompassing square into sixteen squares of equal size.
2. Project lines from the four major corners to the farthest corner of the smaller squares.
3. Intersection points (8) for the circle occur at the first intersection of the two lines.
4. The other four points are the tangent points. Carefully draw the elliptical curve connecting the twelve points.

NONCIRCULAR CURVES IN PERSPECTIVE

Noncircular curvilinear forms in architecture can be elliptical in nature or even undulating (wavelike continuum), as seen in the work of Alvar Aalto.

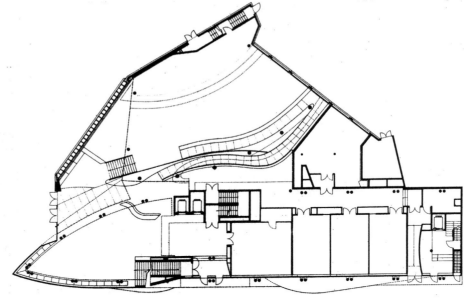

Ground floor plan

Interior perspective: Entrance Hall

Noncircular curvilinear horizontal or vertical forms can be plotted by using a similar point-by-point technique, as shown with perspective circles. Contemporary graphic strategies dictate that its expeditious accurate plotting be computer-generated or approximated by "eye" using freehand techniques. These curves in the horizontal plane are much easier to draw in plan obliques because they are seen in true shape and true size.

Drawings: Maison du Sport Français
Paris, France
Courtesy of Atelier Henri Gaudin,
Architect

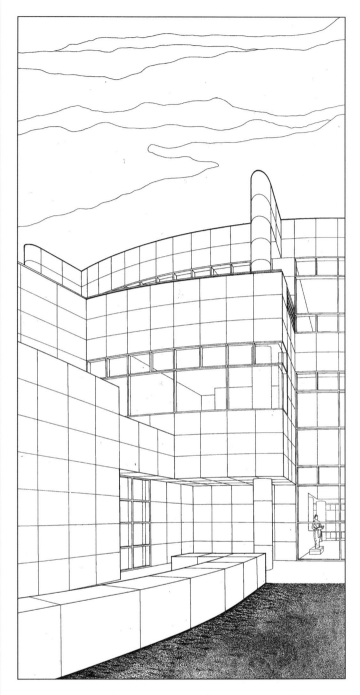

Drawing (partial): The Getty Center for the History of Art and the
                   Humanities, Los Angeles, California
Medium: Ink on Mylar
Courtesy of Richard Meier & Partners, Architects
Reprinted from The Getty Center Design Process
with permission of The J. Paul Getty Trust

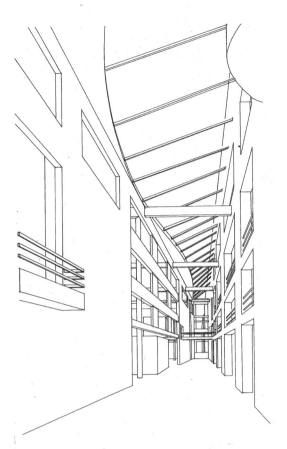

Drawing: Student project by Cort Morgan
         Film Institute in Vicenza, Italy
Medium: Ink on Mylar
Courtesy of the University of Texas at Arlington
School of Architecture

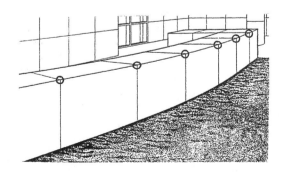

NONCIRCULAR CURVES IN PERSPECTIVE

Plot a series of points using a plan grid to determine the proper curvature.

THE PHYSICS OF REFLECTIONS

Oakland Museum pool structure, Oakland, California
Oakland Museum
Kevin Roche, John Dinkeloo, and Associates, Architects

© Rendow Yee

Reflections

In most cases, a reflecting surface causes a visually interesting and appealing phenomenon. One associates reflections in architecture with the more predominant reflecting surfaces. These could be water, glass window panes, glass mirrors, wet pavement, and materials with a shiny surface, such as polished granite. Light causes the phenomenon of reflections. A **reflecting surface** results in an **extension** of any viewed perspective. The rendering of reflections (pp. 420–427) helps one understand a building within its contextual setting. The analytical drawing of the sculpture and its reflection is the idealistic case of the reflected inverted object being identical to the size of the object itself. In reality, when one observes a horizontally reflected object, the perspective seen of the object does not give an exact mirror image of the reflected perspective of the object. This is due to the fact that the observer's eye level is always above the ground (reflecting surface) line. This results in different distances between the eye and any point, and its corresponding reflected point on the inverted image.

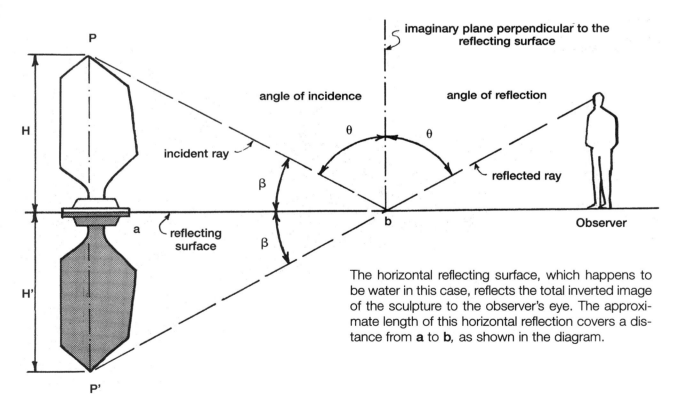

The horizontal reflecting surface, which happens to be water in this case, reflects the total inverted image of the sculpture to the observer's eye. The approximate length of this horizontal reflection covers a distance from **a** to **b**, as shown in the diagram.

Building Touching the Reflective Surface

1. Construct the perspective of the building.
2. Extend all vertical lines into the reflection. The reflected lengths will be equal to the existing building verticals **(aa'= aa")**.
3. Horizontal lines in the reflection vanish to the same vanishing points as their corresponding horizontal lines in the existing building.

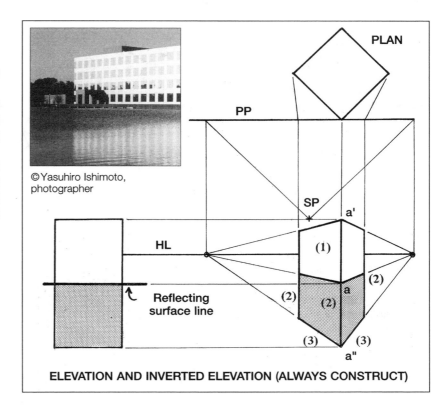

©Yasuhiro Ishimoto, photographer

Photo: Team Disney Building
Lake Buena Vista, Florida
Courtesy of Arata Isozaki &
Associates, Architects

ELEVATION AND INVERTED ELEVATION (ALWAYS CONSTRUCT)

Building Not Touching the Reflective Surface

1. Construct the perspective of the building.
2. The reflecting surface does not extend under the building; therefore, parts of the reflection will be concealed. Construct the projection of the building onto the plane of the reflecting surface. The verticals are measured to the plane of the reflecting surface.
3. These vertical distances are duplicated to construct the reflection.

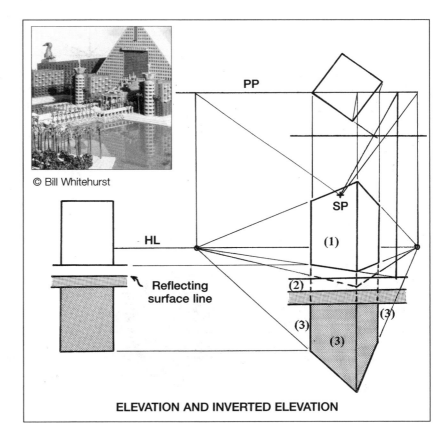

© Bill Whitehurst

Photo: Dolphin and Swan Convention Hotels
Orlando, Florida
Photo by Bill Whitehurst
Courtesy of Michael Graves, Architect, and
Courtesy of Tishman Realty & Construction
Company

ELEVATION AND INVERTED ELEVATION

REFLECTIONS IN PERSPECTIVE

REFLECTIONS IN PERSPECTIVE

If a building has **parallel inclined** edges, as seen in the plan view at right, the vanishing trace lines will converge to an oblique vanishing point above or below the vanishing point for horizontal lines. These trace lines are all located in the same or parallel planes.

Line **AB** is part of an inclined surface that has its own vanishing point oblique. Its reflected image **(A'B')** vanishes at an oblique vanishing point that is an equal distance above the **HL** as its nonreflected counterpart **VP$_O$** is below.

Horizontal reflections in perspective are always seen with the horizon line **higher** than the reflecting surface line, resulting in the reflected lines always sloping at a **sharper angle** than those of the building itself.

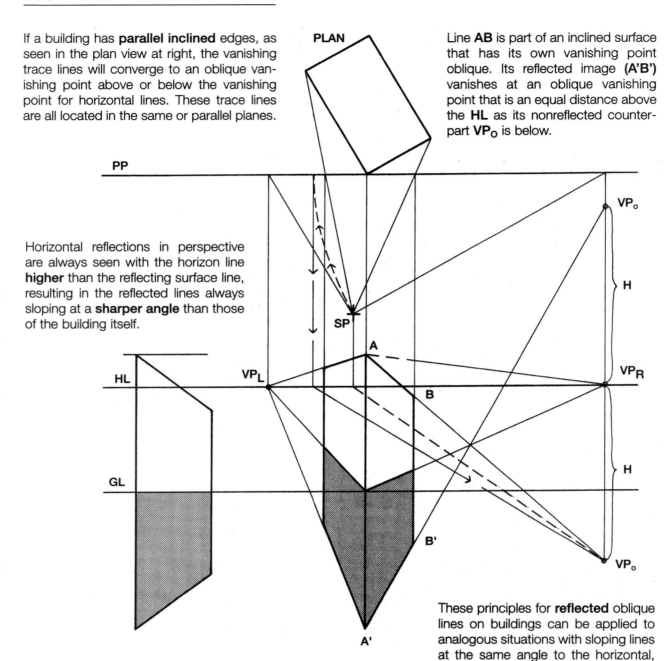

These principles for **reflected** oblique lines on buildings can be applied to analogous situations with sloping lines at the same angle to the horizontal, such as stair railings.

Drawing: Kitakyushu International Conference
Center
Kitakyushu, Fukuoka, Japan
23.4" × 18.9" (59.4 × 48.1 cm)
Medium: Crayon paint
Courtesy of Arata Isozaki & Associates, Architects
Drawn by Arata Isozaki

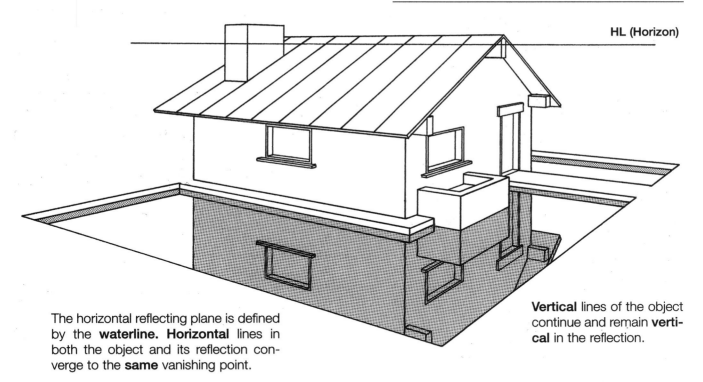

HL (Horizon)

The horizontal reflecting plane is defined by the **waterline. Horizontal** lines in both the object and its reflection converge to the **same** vanishing point.

Vertical lines of the object continue and remain **vertical** in the reflection.

Artificial reflecting pools commonly display **partial** reflections because of the pool's enclosing elements. Natural bodies of water display almost total reflections. The bottom of the reflected image above is concealed by the area around the pool's edge, whereas the top of the reflected image is hidden by the pool's deck in the photo below.

© Norman McGrath, Photographer

Photo: Sklar House
   Westchester County, New York
Courtesy of Christohper H.L. Owen, Architect
and Norman McGrath, Photographer

The soft light of a late fall day established the mood of this photograph. The selection of a low viewpoint captures an almost complete reflection of the house and emphasizes the strong geometry of the design. A strong conscious effort was made to establish the sympathetic relationship of the house setting with freshly fallen leaves around and on the pool's surface. Some photographers might have "cleaned up," producing a stiffer more formal result. Recognizing and taking advantage of unpredictable circumstances such as those shown here can produce images that are both aesthetic and informative. A 4 × 5 view camera with a wide-angle lens was used to produce this photograph.
[ARCHITECTURAL PHOTOGRAPHER'S STATEMENT]

REFLECTIONS IN WATER

REFLECTIONS IN PERSPECTIVE

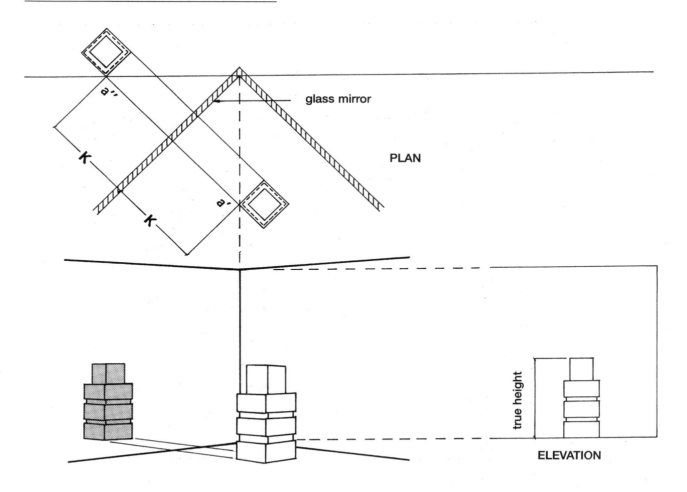

glass mirror

PLAN

true height

ELEVATION

Drawing: Pico Partners, San Clemente, California
Courtesy of Architect: ARC-ID CORPORATION
Renderer: Robert J. Reynolds

It is common to have either interior perspective views or urban landscape perspective views where vertical reflecting surfaces (such as a mirror in this case and a building facade in the case study on the opposite page) give an added dimension to the perspective. The added dimension for a mirror is the optic expansion of a small interior space. This enlargement seen in the mirror usually shows parts of the room not seen from the perspective vantage point. For vertical reflections, the most important principles to remember are:

- A point such as **a'** in front of a reflecting surface is reflected back an **equal distance (K)** to its reflected image **a"**.
- A point **a'** and its corresponding reflected image **a"** always lie on a line **perpendicular** to the reflecting surface.
- The object and its reflected image follow the same rules for perspective construction.

This aerial shows buildings being reflected into other buildings in a three-point perspective.

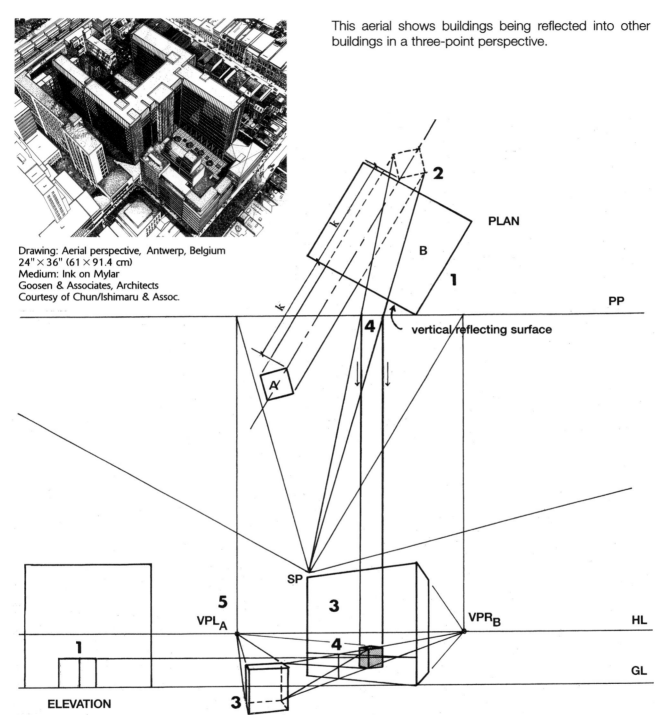

Drawing: Aerial perspective, Antwerp, Belgium
24" × 36" (61 × 91.4 cm)
Medium: Ink on Mylar
Goosen & Associates, Architects
Courtesy of Chun/Ishimaru & Assoc.

VERTICAL REFLECTING SURFACE

1. Construct plan and elevation views of the buildings (**A** and **B**) involved.
2. Construct the plan view of the building (**A**) reflected in a reverse image, an equal distance (k) beyond the reflecting surface.
3. Construct a two-point perspective of the reflecting surface and the building (**B**) being reflected.
4. Construct the reflected reverse image by first finding an image height on the reflecting surface and then projecting rays from the **SP** through the **PP** and down into the perspective view.
5. The reflected reverse image of the building uses the same set of vanishing points as the building itself.

7

Perspective View Development

Once one understands the theory of linear perspective drawing, one can learn how to develop perspective views, from the rough to the finished form. In the profession of architectural illustration this requires an understanding of the design of the project being illustrated as well as skills in managing the balance, composition, and arrangement of all the many elements in the drawing.

The intent of this chapter is to show the process of view development by using actual examples of sketches and drawings from working architectural illustrators.

In summary, following are some of the important terms and concepts you will learn.

Rough blockout	Tracing paper overlay	Line transfer
Preliminary layout	Line and tone rendering	Finished rendering

Perspective View Development

Topic: Developing Line and Tone Drawings

Lockard 1994b.

Topic: Perspective Transfer Alternative Methods and Nontraditional Perspective Techniques

Koplar 1993, 111–133.

Reid 1987, 192–197.

Chapter Overview

This chapter provides an introduction to how professional architectural illustrators balance and compose the many elements in a drawing. For continued study, refer to Lin's *Designing and Drawing with Confidence.*

Step 1

Drawing: Peek & Cloppenburg Department Store competition winner,
Leipzig, Germany
14" × 17" (35.6 × 43.2 cm)
Medium: Full watercolor over pencil line transfer
Moore, Ruble, Yudell, Architects
Courtesy of Al Forster, Architectural Illustrator

The process of doing a rough layout to a line tranfer rendering is shown on this and the following two pages. The architectural illustrator must decide how best to view the project so that the architect's client will accept the design concept.

INTRODUCTION

VIEW DEVELOPMENT—ROUGH LAYOUT

Step 2

Drawing: Peek & Cloppenburg Department Store competition winner, Leipzig, Germany
14" × 17" (35.6 × 43.2 cm)
Medium: Full watercolor over pencil line transfer
Moore, Ruble, Yudell, Architects
Courtesy of Al Forster, Architectural Illustrator

The project site was a narrow street/mall. The rough layout was done to determine the view and the relationship to the background building. The view of the final line transfer was done from a photograph supplied by the client to each competitor so that each scheme could be compared from the same fixed station point. Note the actual amount of background building that shows versus the perceived amount of the building that shows in the rough layout.
[ARCHITECTURAL ILLUSTRATOR'S STATEMENT]

VIEW DEVELOPMENT — LINE TRANSFER

Step 3   Drawing: Peek & Cloppenburg Department Store competition winner, Leipzig, Germany
14" × 17" (35.6 × 43.2 cm)
Medium: Full watercolor over pencil line transfer
Moore, Ruble, Yudell, Architects
Courtesy of Al Forster, Architectural Illustrator

VIEW DEVELOPMENT—ROUGH LAYOUT

Step 1

Step 2

Step 3

Drawing: Sybase Hollis Street Campus, San Francisco, California
18" × 12" (45.7 × 30.5 cm)
Medium: Sketch watercolor on mounted presentation blackline
print of pencil drawing
Robinson Mills & Williams, Architects
Courtesy of Al Forster, Architectural Illustrator

VIEW DEVELOPMENT—LINE TRANSFER

Step 1: At the time of a rough blockout, human figures, cars, and tree forms are sketched in for scale, depth, and possible (or actual) placement (see facing page).
Step 2: An entourage tracing paper overlay is used for clean figures, cars, etc. . . . can be done directly onto rough blockout (step 1).
Step 3: A final line sketch or pencil transfer incorporates building and entourage together. More tree detail is now added, as well as (small) distant, hand-drawn figures not necessarily on the entourage overlay. (See pp. 240–243 for a discussion of scale.)
[Architectural Illustrator's statement]

The advantage of a constructed perspective layout is that before the renderer finalizes tone and values, he or she can experiment with additions, deletions, and corrections to apparent distortions. Also, tonal values and color can be applied to varying degrees with overlays to help determine how to finalize the rendering.

VIEW DEVELOPMENT—ROUGH LAYOUT

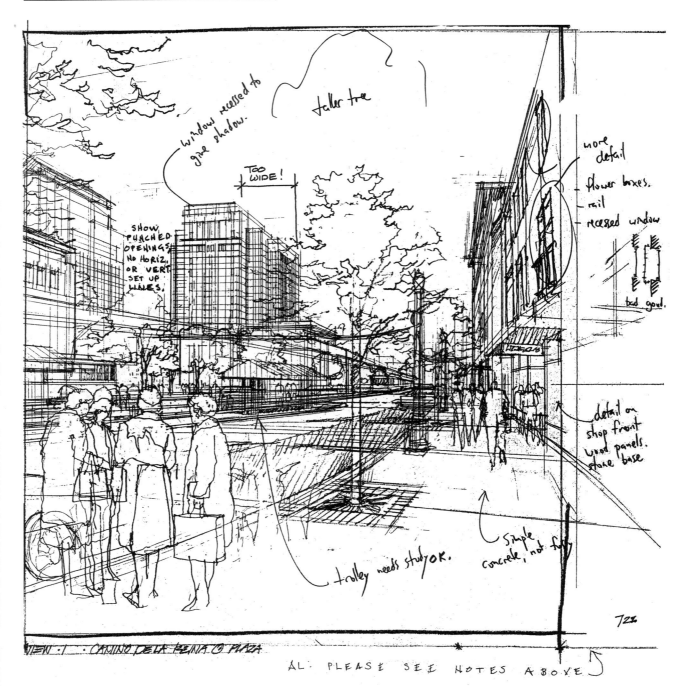

Drawing: Concept study, Riverwalk, Mixed-use project, San Diego, California
14" × 17" (35.6 × 43.2 cm)
Medium: Full watercolor over pencil line transfer
Robert A. M. Stern with Fehlman LaBarre Architects
Courtesy of Al Forster, Architectural Illustrator

Written comments on the rough layout allow on-the-spot corrections, refinements, and adjustments and provide a record that can become a legal document for disputes that might arise later.
[ARCHITECTURAL ILLUSTRATOR'S STATEMENT]

Drawing: Concept study, Riverwalk, Mixed-use project, San Diego, California
14" × 17" (35.6 × 43.2 cm)
Medium: Full watercolor over pencil line transfer
Robert A.M. Stern with Fehlman LaBarre Architects
Courtesy of Al Forster, Architectural Illustrator

Compare the development of individual parts and pieces of the drawing in the before and after examples, as well as the illustrator's response to actual comments.
[ARCHITECTURAL ILLUSTRATOR'S STATEMENT]

Within a perspective layout the architect/designer/renderer can experiment by adding accessories such as cars, trees, and human figures (see Chapter 9, Delineating and Rendering Entourage, for a more detailed coverage of perspective accessories). Even with the most recent computer-generated drawing techniques, accessories such as trees and people can still be time-consuming to generate. Therefore, it is of utmost importance that students and design professionals develop good freehand techniques to draw accessories.

VIEW DEVELOPMENT—LINE TRANSFER

REFLECTION SETUP

Drawing layout: Edoff Memorial Bandstand
          Proposed reconstruction and seismic retrofitting
          Oakland, California
Courtesy of Stephan Hoffpauir, AIA

When there is very little air movement, reflections on a body of water become very sharp. In such instances a building at the water's edge will look almost as though it is being reflected in a mirror. The mood created under these conditions is one of placid tranquility.

To recreate this effect in an illustration, one simply draws the building upside down. The reflection of the building should be rendered slightly darker than the building itself, and the vertical lines made somewhat wavy. This technique is particularly successful in elevations and has the advantage of being both easy and dramatic. [ARCHITECTURAL ILLUSTRATOR'S STATEMENT]

The circle that was constructed in the water (facing page) was to be a reflection of the moon. As the renderer was completing the watercolor composition, he decided to omit it.

FINISHED RENDERING

Drawing: Edoff Memorial Bandstand
Proposed reconstruction and seismic retrofitting
Oakland, California
12" × 21" (30.5 × 53.3 cm)
Medium: Watercolor
Courtesy of Stephan Hoffpauir, AIA

VIEW DEVELOPMENT—LINE TRANSFER

This layout was developed thanks to the use of computer-generated images, which helped us get the best angle. The collaboration with architects was very important in finding and deciding the view to develop. Our intention was to create a very attractive and slender building that sits next to the harbor. By extending down the bottom of the drawing to include water reflections and doing the illustration at nighttime to get more contrast, the overall view of the project is presented in a more dramatic way.
[ARCHITECTURAL ILLUSTRATOR'S STATEMENT]

This view in the preliminary studies did not include the extension of water, because we wanted to emphasize the brightness of the building at dusk. However, to achieve a more vertical feeling, reflections in the water were added to expand the lightness of the tower. The water was done in colored pencil to create the dark reflections and in pastels to bring the light reflections up.
[*ARCHITECTURAL ILLUSTRATOR'S STATEMENT*]

Drawing: Shekou Harbor Building, China
Medium: Ink, colored pencil, pastel, and airbrush
Loebl, Scholossman and Hackl, Architects; in conjunction with the
Shenzen University Institute of Architectural Design
Courtesy of Manuel Avila Associates, Architectural Illustrator

FINISHED RENDERING

VIEW DEVELOPMENT—LINE TRANSFER

Drawing: Sears Tower Renovation Project, Chicago, Illinois
DeStefano & Partners, Architects
Courtesy of Manuel Avila Associates, Architectural Illustrator

To establish the proportions and the size of the new enlarged interior space (original space consisted of only two floors instead of three), we set ourselves as close to the entrance wall as we could to show the full extension of the room with all the new floor materials, new clad columns, and glass walls. We always try to show three sides of the room to feel enclosement (see p. 246). Although we only partially see the entrance wall, we will emphasize its presence with the sunlight coming in.
[Architectural Illustrator's statement]

Drawing: Sears Tower Renovation Project, Chicago, Illinois
DeStefano & Partners, Architects
Courtesy of Manuel Avila Associates, Architectural Illustrator

In this interior, the technique of shadows flooding the space was used to establish different levels of contrast, because the materials used were basically light. The different levels of contrast in shadows and reflections were achieved first by the use of pen and ink followed by the use of colored pencil to saturate and emphasize forms. To make the illustration more complete, people were done very carefully and detailed to bring more reality to the floor activity.
[ARCHITECTURAL ILLUSTRATOR'S STATEMENT]

FINISHED RENDERING

VIEW DEVELOPMENT—LINE TRANSFER

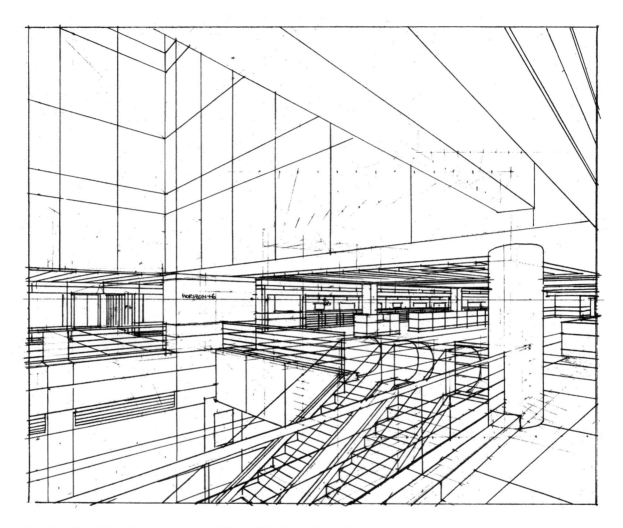

Drawing: Sears Tower Renovation Project, Chicago Main Post Office, Chicago, Illinois
Medium: Pen and ink
Courtesy of Knight Architects Engineers Planners, Inc., and
Manuel Avila Associates, Architectural Illustrator

After providing a series of different preliminary layouts to find out which was the most compelling and descriptive space view, this one was chosen to be developed. All the details and design elements were then drawn in collaboration with the architects, so all the correct information is included. The completion of the layout was done technically by hand. By the time the illustrator was ready to draw the final black and white illustration, the layout was completed and ready to be rendered.
[ARCHITECTURAL ILLUSTRATOR'S STATEMENT]

FINISHED RENDERING

Drawing: Sears Tower Renovation Project, Chicago Main Post Office,
Chicago, Illinois
Original size: (approx.) 24" × 20½" (61 × 52.1 cm), Scale used: ¼"=1'0"
Medium: Pen and ink
Courtesy of Knight Architects Engineers Planners, Inc., and
Manuel Avila Associates, Architectural Illustrator

After the layout is completed, the rendering is done in pen and black ink. The focus of the drawing is, first of all, to show the main floor amenities; second, to show how busy the space is: people moving, buying stamps, using mail boxes, etc.; and finally, to pay attention to the multistoried lobby that precedes the main floor.
[Architectural Illustrator's statement]

VIEWS FROM A COMPUTER-GENERATED WIRE FRAME

Top rendering: Belize Resort Hotel
Belize, Honduras
24" × 13" (61 × 33 cm)
Media: Acrylic and gouache
D.E. Miller Architect
Courtesy of Charlie Manus, Architectural Illustrator

Bottom rendering: Proposed hotel
Palm Springs, California
24" × 16" (61 × 40.6 cm)
Media: Acrylic and gouache
D.E. Miller Architect
Courtesy of Charlie Manus, Architectural Illustrator

My process for rendering is to start with a computer-generated wire frame to establish the desired view. After the view is selected, I complete the layout by hand or computer. I send the final layout to the client for their approval. I then transfer the image to illustration board by means of a graphite sheet and begin to paint. I believe a high-contrast rendering works best, so I try to get as much contrast as possible. For example, the right color values and color intensities help define shade and shadows against a sunlit side. I also try to make the illustration as dramatic as possible and avoid covering the corners of the building. I believe all illustrators should consider how the illustration will appear reduced in a brochure or newspaper or enlarged to appear on a billboard.
[ARCHITECTURAL ILLUSTRATOR'S STATEMENT]

Top rendering: Renaissance Center
Memphis, Tennessee
22" × 14" (56 × 36 cm)
Media: Acrylic and gouache
Architect: Weston Design
Courtesy of Charlie Manus, Architectural Illustrator

Bottom rendering: Speculative office building
Memphis, Tennessee
25" × 14" (63.5 × 35.6 cm)
Media: Acrylic and gouache
Looney, Ricks, Kiss Architects
Courtesy of Charlie Manus, Architectural Illustrator

The majority of my illustrations are "finished" or "formal" simply because I believe most architectural firms have some-one in-house to provide quick sketch styles.
[ARCHITECTURAL ILLUSTRATOR'S STATEMENT]

VIEWS FROM A COMPUTER-GENERATED WIRE FRAME

8

Light, Shade, and Shadow

Light allows us to have vision. With light we can structure and put order into the environment. It enhances our senses for experiencing architecture as we move through space over a period of time. A thorough knowledge and understanding of light and the application of shades and shadows to presentations of the built environment helps to further client/architect understanding during the design process. Shadows accent orthographic (particularly elevations and site plans), paraline, and perspective drawings, adding a sense of clarity and substance to the represented forms.

The intent of this chapter is to develop your ability to draw and construct shades and shadows in plan, elevation, paraline, and perspective drawings.

In summary, following are some of the important terms and concepts you will learn:

How to construct shades and shadows in plans, elevations, axonometrics, obliques, and perspectives

| Light | Shade | Shadow | Casting edge |
| Altitude | Azimuth | Sun's bearing | Vanishing point of sun's rays |

Light, Shade, and Shadow

TOPICS: CASTING EDGE, VERTICAL CASTING EDGE, ALTITUDE AND AZIMUTH, SUN'S BEARING, SUN BEARING VANISHING POINT, SUN'S RAY, SUN RAY VANISHING POINT, SUN RAY TRIANGLE, HORIZONTAL CASTING EDGE, SHADOWS IN PLAN

Ching 2003, 144–156.

Ching 1990, 130–133.

Hanks and Belliston 1980, 66–67.

Helms 1990, 240–296.

Leach 1990, 85–107.

Montague 1998.

Pérez-Gomez and Pelletier 1997, 111–124.

Porter and Goodman 1985, 22–27.

Chapter Overview

This chapter and the related exercises in the book's final section will teach you how to cast shadows in plan, in elevation, in paralines, and in perspectives. For continued study, refer to Forseth's *Graphics for Architecture* and Lockard's *Design Drawing*.

Photo: Stylus in sundial courtyard
       Team Disney Building, Lake Buena Vista, Florida
Courtesy of Arata Isozaki and Associates, Architects

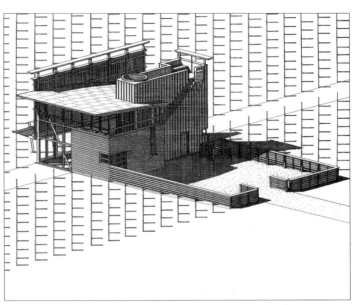

Drawing: A small lodge, Saint Helena, California
24" × 24" (61 × 61 cm), Scale: ¼"=1'0"
Medium: Ink on Mylar
Courtesy of Brian Healy Architects

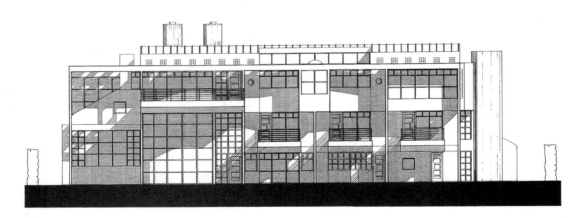

Drawing: Meyer residence, Malibu, California
Medium: Ink on Mylar
Courtesy of Gwathmey Siegel & Associates, Architects

During the daytime hours, our constant companion, whether we are aware of it or not, is our shadow (see p. 197). Shade on that part of our body not receiving direct light is also constantly with us. We perceive shades and shadows on both animate and inanimate objects. Empirically, most of us can generally sense why an object's shadow takes on a certain geometric configuration. However, that shadow sense is inadequate for architectural students, architectural illustrators, and architects. To properly convey a design concept, it is imperative that we learn how to construct precise shadow drawings.

Four terms can appropriately describe our timeless response to and interpretation of shadows: (1) mysterious, (2) vague, (3) dramatic, and (4) dimensional. Dimensional refers to a shadow's unique property of delineating form and scale in the urban landscape. Shades and shadows were of utmost importance in providing depth to the facades for front elevations during the early periods of architecture. The added illusion of depth was aesthetically pleasing. It clarified overlapping elements on the facade to the layperson. Knowing how to delineate and draw shades and shadows helps us to better understand spatial concepts in our designs. **Sciagraphy** is the science of shade and shadow graphics and is an indispensable tool for architects, designers, and delineators. Sciagraphy provides a tool for obtaining a finished and realistic appearance to any drawing.

The illustration below left emulates the work of the late professional renderer Hugh Ferriss. It is rendered to give form to a lighting quality that has mystery and drama. The other illustration typifies the meticulous delineation techniques that were instilled by the 19th-century École des Beaux Arts. Light, shade, and shadow are purposely articulated to create artificial lighting effects for compositions of classical details. Shadows play an important role in conceptual design stages of contemporary graphic strategies. Fenestration patterns on conceptual elevations are visually articulated and enhanced by the use of shadows. These studies of the interplay of solids, voids, and inclined planes give a surface modulation to make interrelated parts understandable.

Drawing: Student project by Ed Yeomans
          Rudder Tower
18" × 24" (45.7 × 61 cm)
Medium: Charcoal
Courtesy of Texas A&M University
Department of Architecture

Drawing: Student project by Eberhard Lenz
          Classical details
18.5" × 25.5" (47 × 64.8 cm)
Medium: Ink wash
Courtesy of Washington University
School of Architecture, St. Louis, Missouri

The application of sciagraphy is of great importance to the design professional. Light, shade, and shadow define form and space. A **shadow** indicates the shape of the object casting the shadow and can in many ways indicate the texture of the surface receiving the shadow. When **light** rays are intercepted by an object, the portion of the object on the light side will be illuminated, while the portion opposite the light side will be protected from the light rays. This shielded portion can be defined as **shade.** The boundary line that separates light from shade determines the **shadow line** on a receiving surface. The boundary of the shadow line determines the dark area "cast" onto the surface on which the object rests and which receives the cast **shadow.** To produce a shadow, three conditions are required:

1. A **light source**
2. An **object** to cast the shadow line, or to intercept the light ray
3. A **surface** to receive the shadow line and shadow

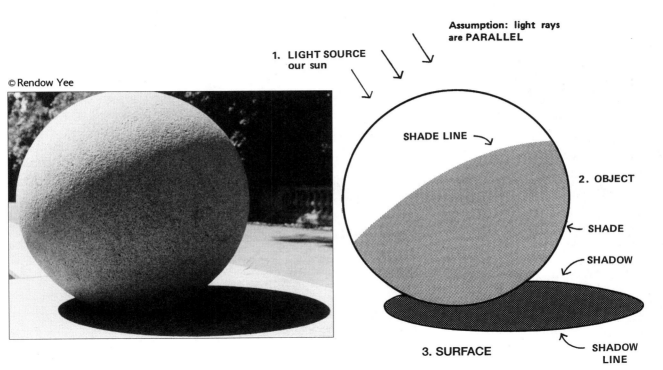

© Rendow Yee

BASIC CONCEPTS

Basic Shadow concepts

Due to the enormous distance of the earth from the sun, the light rays from the sun are considered to be parallel (In reality, the rays are diverging). This condition can be contrasted with artificial light, which gives radiating rays of light because of the proximity of the light source. The photograph of the spherical solid above shows that human perception sees shade and shadow to be approximately the same value intensity or darkness. When sketching, the gradual transition in tone from shade to light seen in the photo is described as a "soft-edge" area. A sharply defined border such as the edge of the shade area is described as "hard-edge." In architectural drawings, shadow is always shown darker than shade regardless of the sketching or rendering medium.

SOLAR ANGLE DIAGRAMS/DEFINITIONS

The direction of solar rays is identifed by two angles described as **bearing** and **azimuth**. Both bearing and azimuth are measured only in the plan view. The bearing acute angle of an inclined line is always measured in degrees.

Altitude is the angle between the sun's position in the sky vault and the earth's horizontal plane for a given latitude.

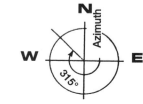

Example
N 45°W is a bearing
or
315° azimuth

Light rays are notated by their **bearing** relative to due north or south, and their **azimuth** is measured clockwise from due north.

Azimuth is the angle between the sun's bearing and a horizontal line that is in a plane perpendicular to the horizonal plane of the earth's surface.

Latitude is the angular distance north or south from the equator measured in degrees on the meridian of a point. **Longitude** is the angular distance east or west between the meridian of a particular place and that of Greenwich, England, expressed in degrees.

WINTER SUNSET

W

SUMMER SUNSET

S

N

WINTER SUNRISE   SUMMER SUNRISE

E

**SAN FRANCISCO BAY AREA
38° LATITUDE
122° LONGITUDE**

Sun path diagram: Courtesy of Thomas L. Turman, Professor
11"×8½" (27.9 × 21.6 cm)
Medium: Ink (freehand)
Laney College Department of Architecture

Solar Angle Diagrams/Definitions

One of the most important factors in architectural design is natural sunlight. How the sun moves across the sky for different locations affects how architects design. Architects are concerned about radiant heat energy as well as the design of shading devices for buildings.

Solstice is defined as either of the two times a year when the sun is at its greatest distance from the celestial equator. The summer solstice occurs about 21 June and the winter solstice occurs about 21 December. In North America, which is in the northern hemisphere, 21 June marks the sun's highest point in the sky and thus the longest solar day, whereas 21 December marks the sun's lowest point in the sky and thus the shortest solar day. A solar day is from 12 o'clock noon to 12 o'clock noon. The simple diagram above is for the San Francisco Bay Area in the United States.

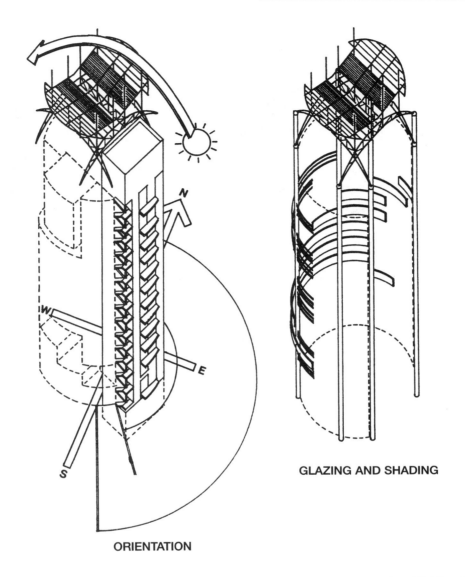

ORIENTATION

GLAZING AND SHADING

Drawing: Menara Mesiniaga (IBM Tower)
Selangor, Malaysia
T. R. Hamzah & Yeang, Architect

SOLAR ANGLE DIAGRAMS

Solar Angle Diagrams

Tall buildings are more exposed to the full impact of the sun and heat than low-rise structures. Office towers throughout the world do not adapt to their local climates. Rather they fight it using the twentieth century's arsenal of mechanical systems such as air conditioning, artificial light, and heating.
[ARCHITECT'S STATEMENT]

Perspective solar angle diagrams are the most difficult and most complex of all shadow diagrams for the beginner. For this reason, this chapter progressively examines shadow constructions, starting with prismatic forms in orthographic views. It then focuses on common construction situations in elevations such as overhangs, canopies, colonnades, arcades, stairs, niches, dormers, and inclines. This is followed by a study of paraline shadow constructions, and, finally, perspective shadow constructions. Techniques for using shades and shadows to accentuate architectural form and space are explored in Chapter 9, Delineating and Rendering Entourage.

Drawing: West Adams Place, Los Angeles, California
36" × 24" (91.4 × 61 cm)
Medium: Ink
Courtesy of John V. Mutlow FAIA, Architects, and
Iraj Yamin Esfandiary, Illustrator

These building solids cast shadows and show shade with a line hatching technique (shadow darker than shade). The foreground road has the heaviest hatching.

SHADOW PRINCIPLES

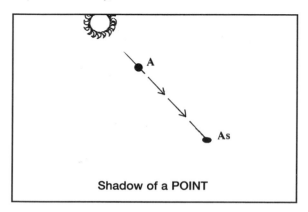

Shadow of a POINT

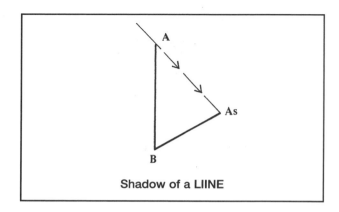

Shadow of a LIINE

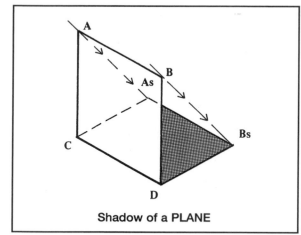

Shadow of a PLANE

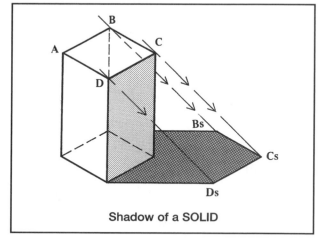

Shadow of a SOLID

Shadow development can be analyzed by studying shadow progressions from points to lines to planes and finally to solids. Begin by studying point shadows, since a finite series of points will ultimately

1. Determine shadows of **lines** (lines being composed of points)
2. Determine shadows of **planes** (planes being composed of lines)
3. Determine shadows of **solids** (solids being composed of planes)

The shadow of a line, a plane, or a solid is most efficiently determined by locating the shadows of the **critical** points of the line, plane, or solid.

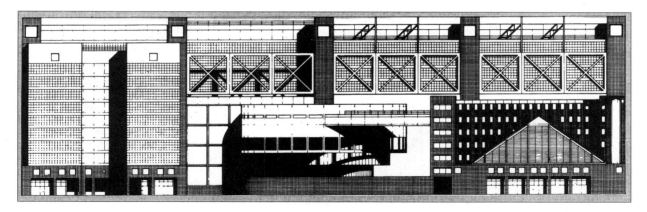

Drawing: City Hall, Missisauga, Ontario, Canada
48" × 30" (121.9 × 76.2 cm), Scale: ⅛"=1'0"
Medium: Ink on Mylar
Courtesy of Michael Fieldman and Partners

Shadow Principles

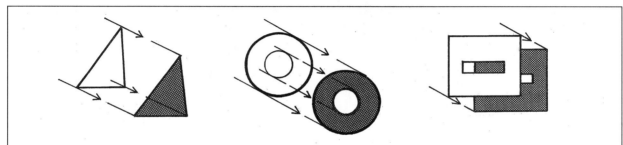

The shadow of a plane figure on a parallel plane is identical in size, shape, and orientation with the figure. The more distant the parallel plane (triangle and donut), the more shadow will show.

For architectural graphics a 45° angle light ray direction from the left in plan and in elevation is conventionally used. In cubic form this can be represented by the diagonal of a cube with a slope of 35°15'52" (θ). Also commonly used is a 45° angle light ray direction from the right. Note that the **slope** angle of the light ray is the inclination relative to the horizontal plane.

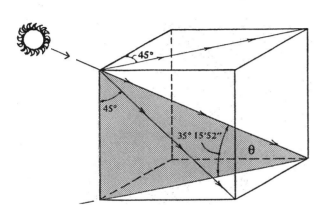

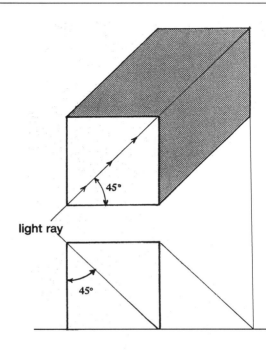

light ray

SHADOW PRINCIPLES

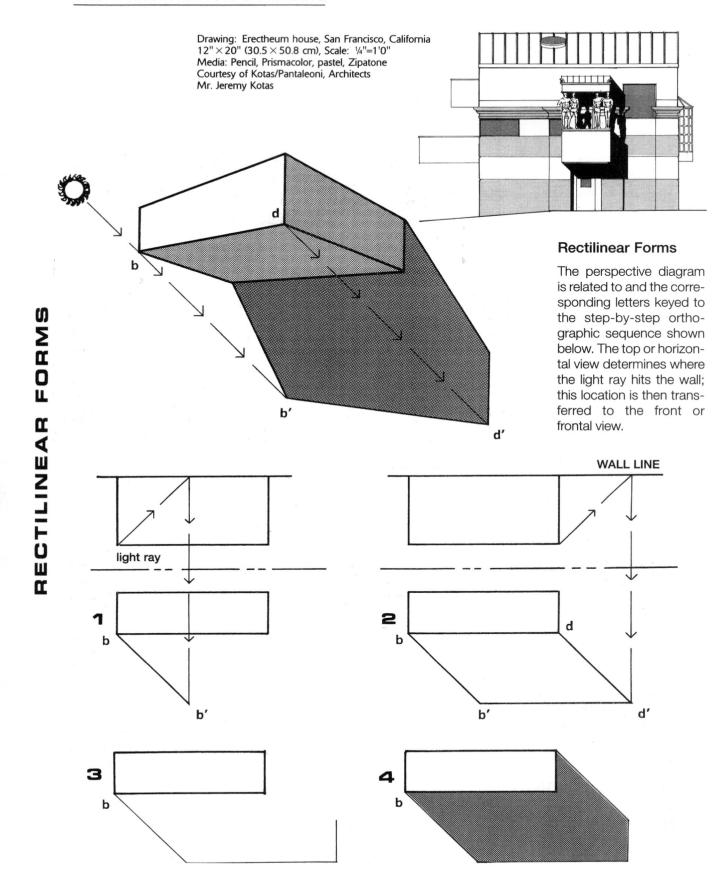

Drawing: Erectheum house, San Francisco, California
12" × 20" (30.5 × 50.8 cm), Scale: ¼"=1'0"
Media: Pencil, Prismacolor, pastel, Zipatone
Courtesy of Kotas/Pantaleoni, Architects
Mr. Jeremy Kotas

RECTILINEAR FORMS

Rectilinear Forms

The perspective diagram is related to and the corresponding letters keyed to the step-by-step orthographic sequence shown below. The top or horizontal view determines where the light ray hits the wall; this location is then transferred to the front or frontal view.

WALL LINE

light ray

1

2

3

4

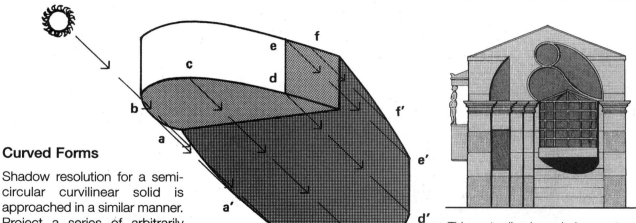

Curved Forms

Shadow resolution for a semi-circular curvilinear solid is approached in a similar manner. Project a series of arbitrarily located shadow points to determine the shadow curvature on the wall. Remember that every point on the line that separates light from shade **(shade line)** will cast a shadow point on the **shadow line.**

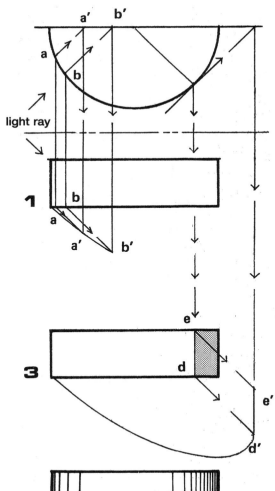

This protruding bay window casts a **curvilinear** shadow on a flat surface.

Drawing: Erectheum house, San Francisco, California
12" × 20" (30.5 × 50.8 cm), Scale: ¼"=1'0"
Media: Pencil, Prismacolor, pastel, Zipatone
Courtesy of Kotas/Pantaleoni, Architects
Mr. Jeremy Kotas

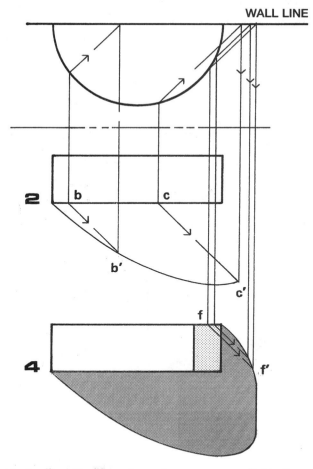

CURVILINEAR FORMS

A cylindrical or curvilinear surface always appears flat in the front elevation. To create a feeling of depth, alternatives to a uniform shade value are to use a series of unequally spaced fine lines or increasing dot density (see pp. 101–102).

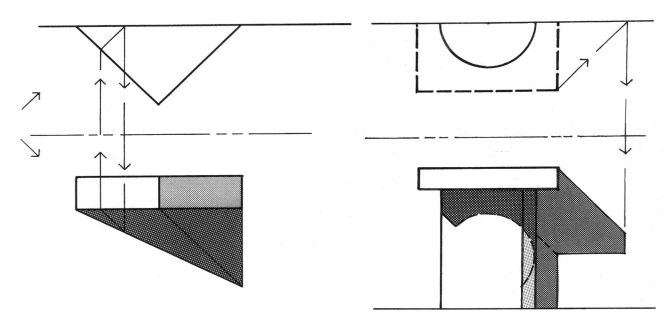

Elevation View Shadows

The study of wall condition shadows for various geometric forms, such as the previously described rectilinear and curvilinear forms and the variety shown on this page, provides the necesary framework for the analogous situations encountered in site plan and roof plan shadows. This analogy becomes apparent by turning any wall condition drawing upside down and realizing that the "wall line" is now the "ground line" and the "wall object" is now the object seen in the plan view.

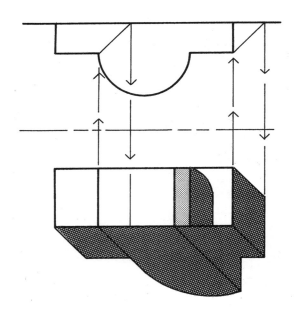

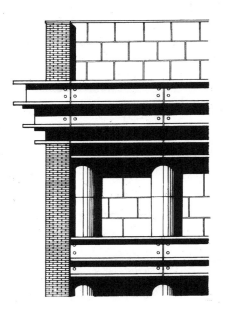

Partial elevation: Hotel Il Palazzo
Fukuoka, Japan
18" × 24" (45.7 × 61 cm), Scale: 1:50 m
Medium: Black ink on Mylar
Courtesy of Aldo Rossi, Studio di Architettura
New York, Architect

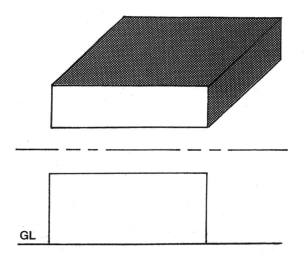

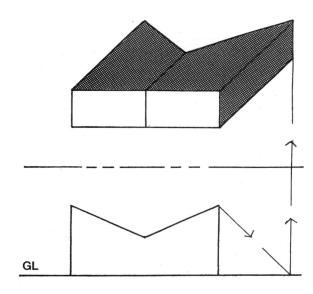

Plan View Shadows

These drawings illustrate the analogy between wall elevation shadows and site/roof plan shadows. The height of the solid forms above the "ground line" determines the length of the shadow cast in the plan view. Note that by simply turning the drawing upside down and switching the plan and elevation views, wall elevation conditions result.

Drawing: Town Square, four houses and chapel
                Port Ludlow, Washington
Scale: 1"=40'0"
Medium: Pen and ink
Courtesy of Steven Holl Architects

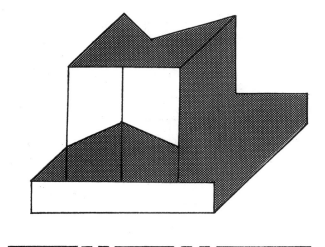

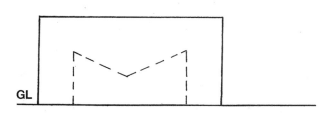

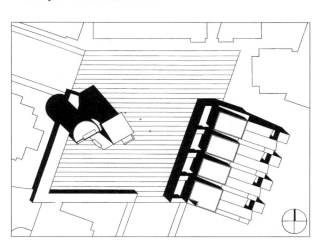

Singular Forms Combined

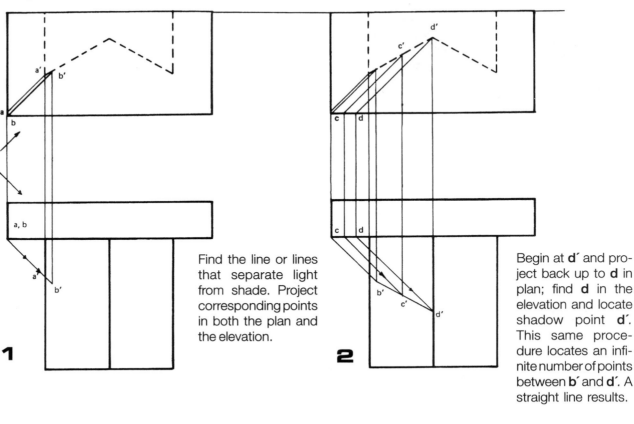

1 Find the line or lines that separate light from shade. Project corresponding points in both the plan and the elevation.

2 Begin at **d′** and project back up to **d** in plan; find **d** in the elevation and locate shadow point **d′**. This same procedure locates an infinite number of points between **b′** and **d′**. A straight line results.

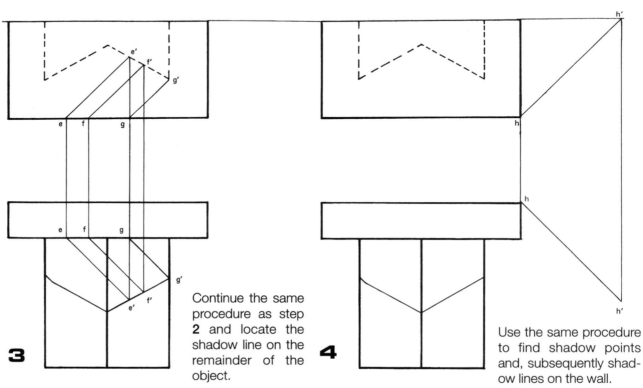

3 Continue the same procedure as step **2** and locate the shadow line on the remainder of the object.

4 Use the same procedure to find shadow points and, subsequently, shadow lines on the wall.

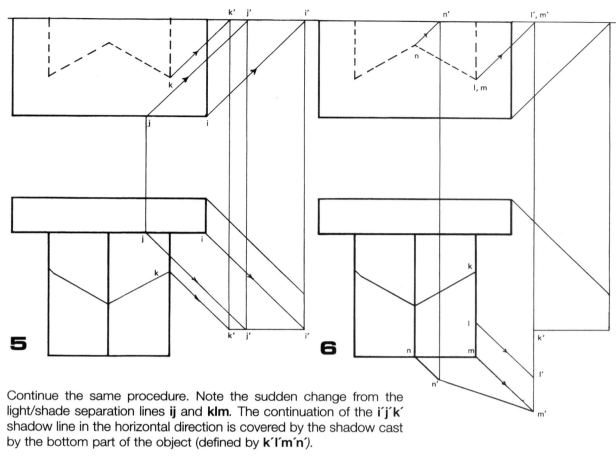

Continue the same procedure. Note the sudden change from the light/shade separation lines **ij** and **klm**. The continuation of the **i′j′k′** shadow line in the horizontal direction is covered by the shadow cast by the bottom part of the object (defined by **k′l′m′n′**).

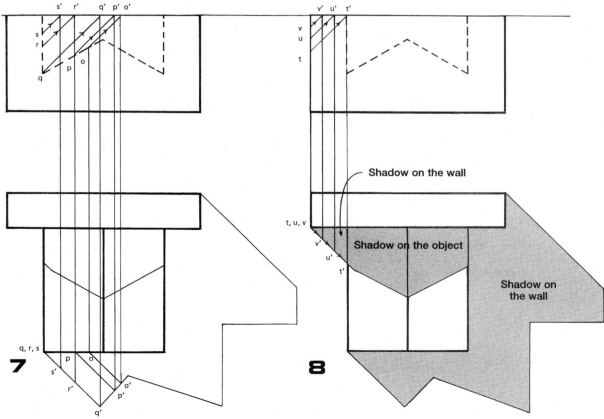

SINGULAR FORMS COMBINED

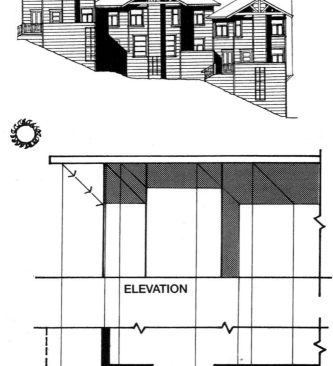

Drawing: Parkview Commons, San Francisco, California
36" × 24" (91.4 × 61 cm), Scale: ⅛"=1'0"
Medium: Ink on Canson paper
Courtesy of David Baker Architects

SOLID OVERHANG SHADOWS

ELEVATION

PLAN

Flat overhang parallel to wall

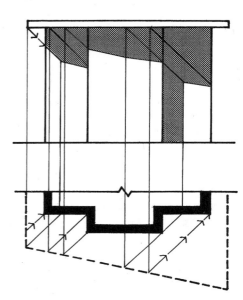

Flat overhang oblique to wall

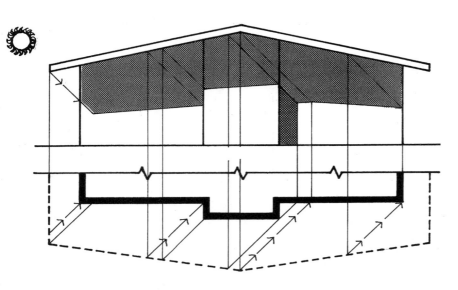

Inclined overhang oblique to wall

Solid Overhang Shadows

It is common to encounter buildings that have either flat or inclined solid overhangs. The edge casting the shadow line on the vertical wall can be either parallel or oblique to the wall. The previously explained shadow casting principles for objects on a vertical wall also apply for overhangs. Use the plan view to transfer critical points into the elevation. Notice that if the angle of the light ray with respect to the ground line becomes steeper, the length of the resulting shadow will become longer.

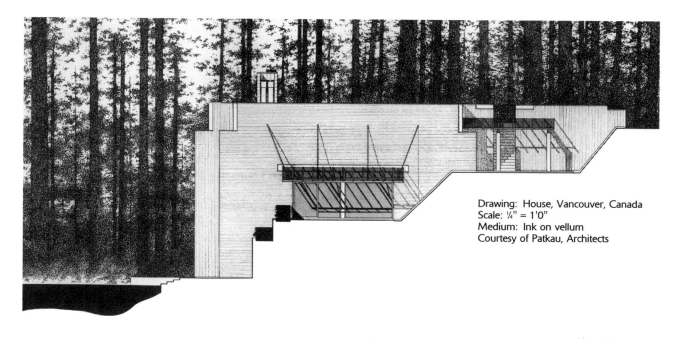

Drawing: House, Vancouver, Canada
Scale: ¼" = 1'0"
Medium: Ink on vellum
Courtesy of Patkau, Architects

Perforated Overhang Shadows

This overhang condition is characterized by openings or perforations. To cast the shadow in elevation, construct the plan, the elevation, and a sectional elevation in profile. Critical shadow points are located by transferring corresponding points between views.

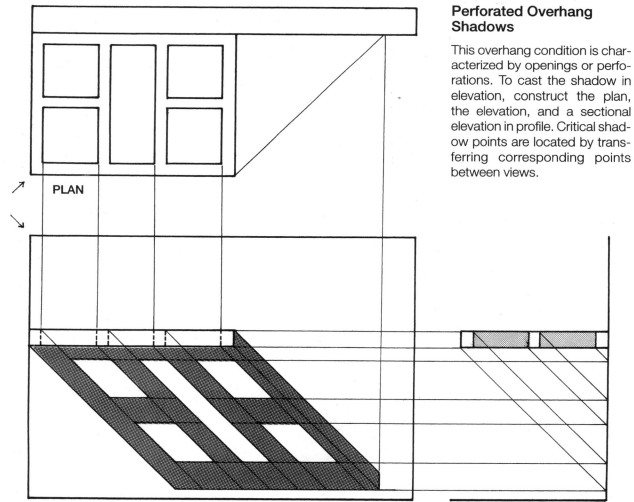

PLAN

ELEVATION

PERFORATED OVERHANG SHADOWS

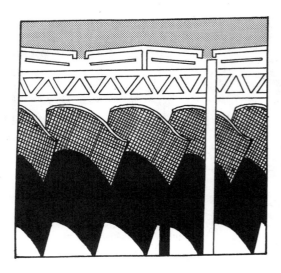

Drawing: Student project by Kwok Gorran Tsui
2.5" × 2.5" (6.4 × 6.4 cm)
Medium: Ink and Zipatone on vellum
The Menil Collection Museum, Houston, Texas
Courtesy of Renzo Piano Architect, Piano & Fitzgerald, Houston
and the City College of San Francisco Department of Architecture
Structural Consultant: Ove Arup

CANOPY SHADOWS

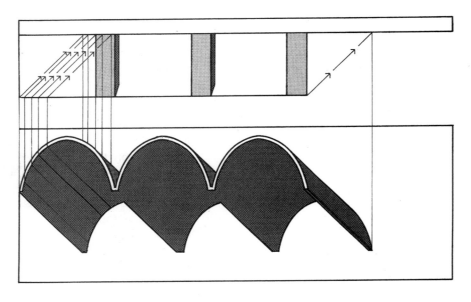

Canopy, Colonnade, and Arcade Shadows

The principle of the shadow of a plane figure casting on a parallel plane is demonstrated on these two facing pages. The bottom edges of the canopies cause a wall shadow line that has the same orientation and configuration as the canopy forms. Likewise, the same geometric shapes of the arcade and the colonnade are cast and seen on the recessed wall shadows. The repetition of geometric forms in all cases gives a shadow rhythm on the receiving surfaces. Note the shade on the underside of the sinuously curved roof canopy (upper left).

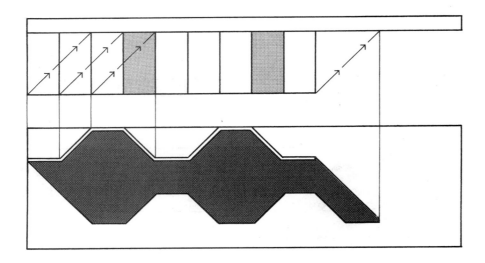

Drawing: San Francisco
              Waldorf School
36" × 24" (91.4 × 61 cm)
Scale: ¼"=1'0"
Medium: Ink on Mylar
Courtesy of Tanner Leddy
Maytum Stacy, Architects

Drawing: Texas Rangers Ballpark, Arlington, Texas
24" × 18" (61 × 45.7 cm), Scale: ¼"=1'0"
Medium: Watercolor and pencil on mounted Bristol paper
Courtesy of David M. Schwarz/Architectural Services

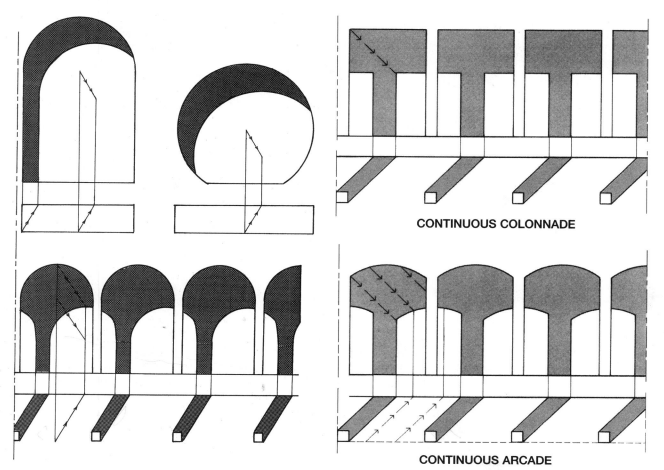

CONTINUOUS COLONNADE

CONTINUOUS ARCADE

COLONNADE AND ARCADE SHADOWS

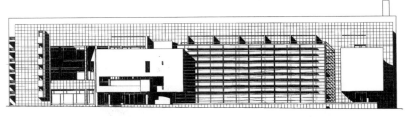

Drawing: Museum of Contemporary Art
Barcelona, Spain
36" × 48" (91.4 × 121.9 cm)
Medium: Ink on Mylar
Courtesy of Richard Meier
& Partners, Architects

NONOVERLAPPING SHADOWS

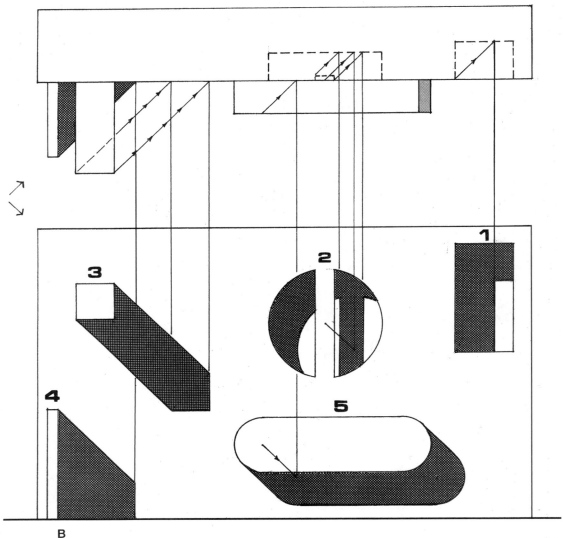

Nonoverlapping Shadows

In the wall of shadows shown above, the light source is coming from the left at 45° (see direction arrows in the elevation and the plan views). When we apply the general rule that shadows of plane figures on parallel planes cause shadows of the same size, shape, and orientation, the shadow configurations seen in conditions **1** and **2** become readily apparent and are easily understood. When edges are perpendicular to a vertical wall as in condition **3** and the top edge of condition **4**, the shadow line produced is in the sunlight-bearing direction. Likewise, edge AB is perpendicular to the horizontal ground surface, and the shadow line produced on the ground is in the sunlight-bearing direction (plan view) as well as parallel to edge AB when it is intercepted by the vertical wall (elevation view). Condition **5** follows the aforementioned rules.

© Markova Nadine, photographer

Photo: Renault Factory (partial elevation), northern Mexico
Gómez Palacio, Durango, Mexico
Courtesy of Legorreta Arquitectos—Ricardo Legorreta,
Victor Legorreta, Noé Castro

This photograph was taken early in the morning in order to obtain hard shadows. Facade details were taken with a 200 mm telefoto lens. I used a Minolta camera with a polarizing filter.
[ARCHITECTURAL PHOTOGRAPHER'S STATEMENT]

OVERLAPPING SHADOWS

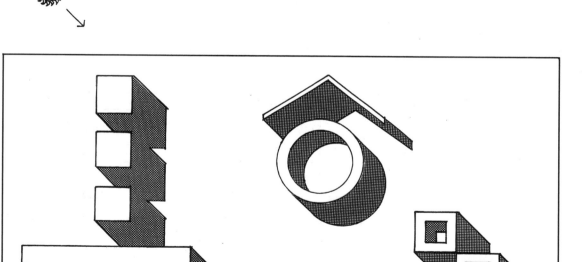

Drawing: Student project by William Xie and Daniel Orona
Design of a sculptural wall of shadows
Studio professor: Pershing C. Lin
Courtesy of the City College of San Francisco
Department of Architecture

Overlapping Shadows

When casting shadows of protruding elements that are in close proximity to each other, it is common to find shadows that are interrupted before they hit the major receiving surface. The shadow lines that we do not see sneak across the lighted surface closest to their neighbor.

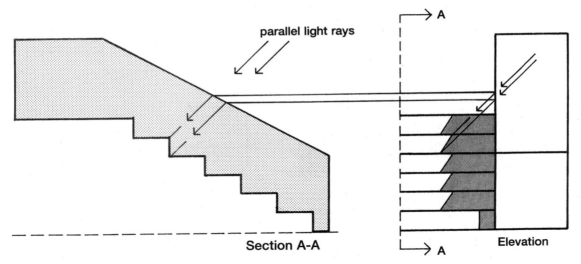

parallel light rays

Section A-A

Elevation

STAIRWAY SHADOWS

Stairway Shadows

Project corresponding points to find the shadow line of an oblique line on the steps above. Light rays maintain a parallel condition regardless of the geometric configuration of the receiving surface. See condition **A** in both elevation and plan below. A horizontal edge is seen as a point in the elevation **1**. It causes shadow line **A** seen in elevation.

Section B-B

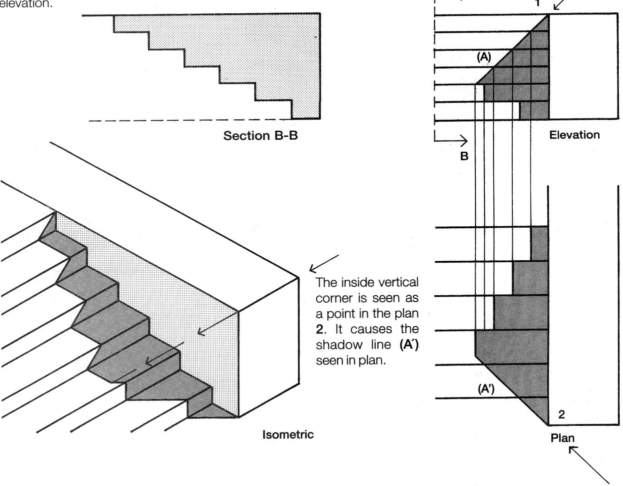

The inside vertical corner is seen as a point in the plan **2**. It causes the shadow line **(A′)** seen in plan.

Isometric

Plan

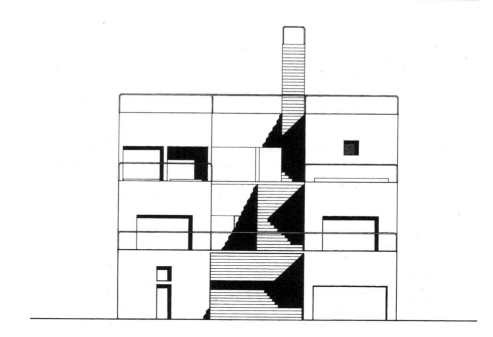

Drawing: Les Echelles
          House for a musician
          Mallorca, Spain
12" × 12" (30.5 × 30.5 cm)
Medium: Ink on Mylar
Courtesy of Diana Agrest, Architect

There are three parallel angled shadow lines cast on the building elements above. The three horizontal edges casting these lines all appear as points (see **1** on the facing page). This fact helps us understand that each floor level must step back and that we are not seeing a continuous vertical facade. Shadows model a building form and give us clues to its shape and disposition. Note that the elevation shadows on the stairway take the same configuration (see facing page) regardless of the direction of the sun's rays. Sometimes stairway configurations protrude from a vertical surface (see below left).

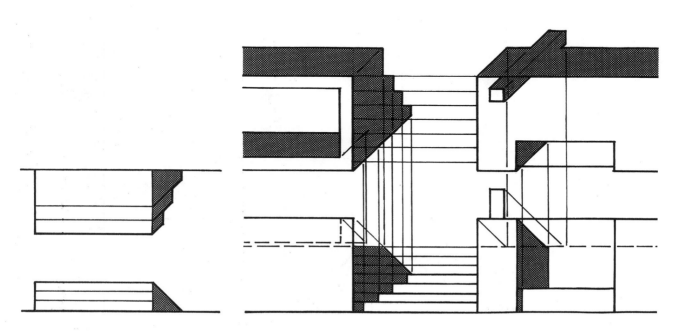

STAIRWAY SHADOWS

Drawing: Kunibiki Messe, Matsue, Shimane, Japan
48.6" × 33.1" (118.9 × 84.1 cm)
Medium: Airbrush
Courtesy of Shin Takamatsu Architect & Associates, Kyoto

Shadows on Cylindrical Forms and Niches

Triangular and trapezoidal niches and cylindrical forms produce interesting shadows. The protruding element on this facade is slightly larger than a semicylinder, producing a shadow that begins in a hidden position, as seen in the frontal elevation.

CYLINDRICAL FORMS AND NICHES

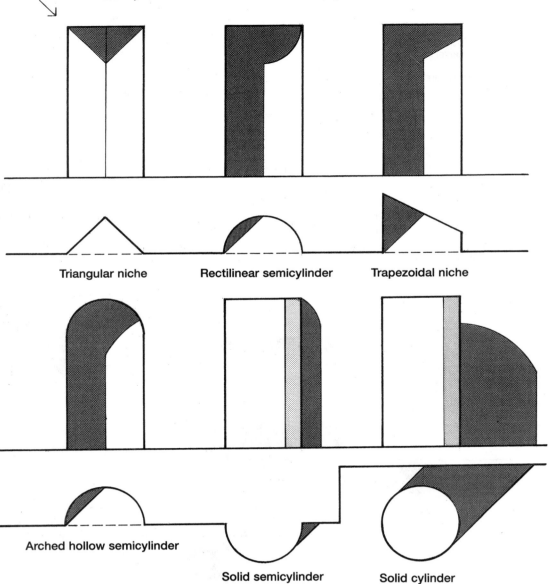

Triangular niche

Rectilinear semicylinder

Trapezoidal niche

Arched hollow semicylinder

Solid semicylinder

Solid cylinder

Shadow designs (two facing pages): Courtesy of Ann Cederna, Associate Professor
8½" × 11" (21.6 × 27.9 cm)
Original medium: Pencil
The Catholic University of America School of Architecture & Planning

Shadows on Niches, Recessions, and Protrusions

We see overhangs and niches (see following two pages) primarily as elevation views. The shadows they cast give us hints as to the depth of overhangs and the amount of recessions.

Rectilinear niches and overhangs also produce interesting shadows. Overhangs in this example cast shadows on both flat and curvilinear surfaces. The curvilinear shape beneath the flat facade results in a curvilinear shadow line.

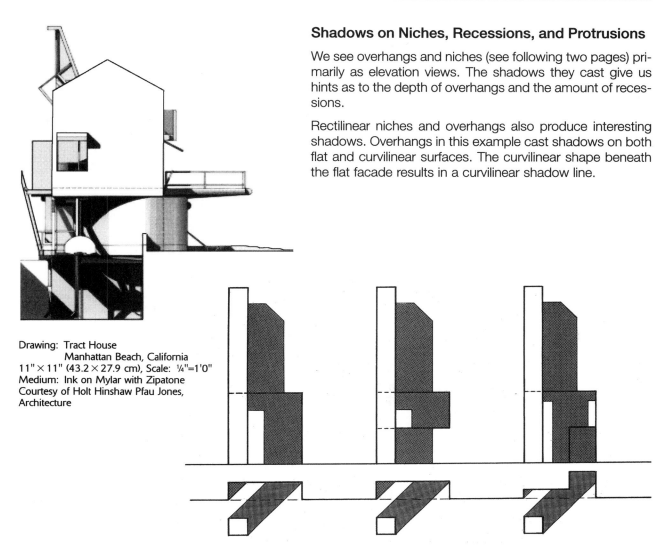

Drawing: Tract House
           Manhattan Beach, California
11" × 11" (43.2 × 27.9 cm), Scale: ¼"=1'0"
Medium: Ink on Mylar with Zipatone
Courtesy of Holt Hinshaw Pfau Jones,
Architecture

Rectilinear columns casting shadows on rectilinear niches

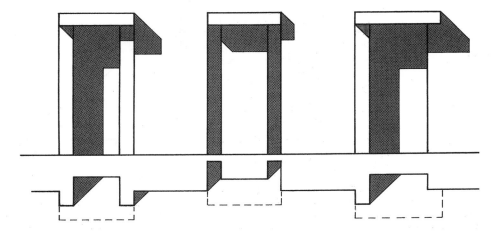

Overhangs casting shadows on rectilinear wall recessions and protrusions

NICHES, RECESSIONS, AND PROTRUSIONS

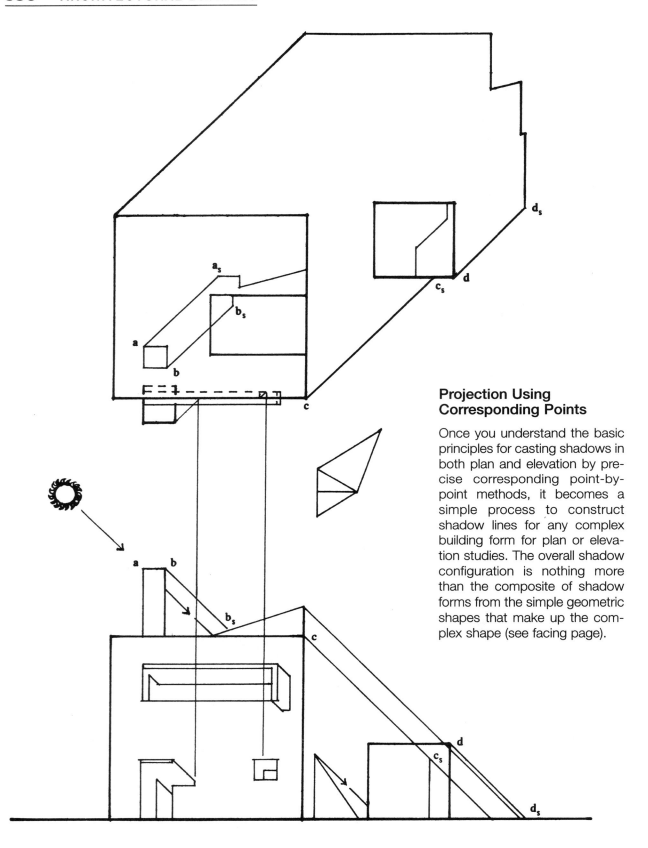

PROJECTION USING CORRESPONDING POINTS

Projection Using Corresponding Points

Once you understand the basic principles for casting shadows in both plan and elevation by precise corresponding point-by-point methods, it becomes a simple process to construct shadow lines for any complex building form for plan or elevation studies. The overall shadow configuration is nothing more than the composite of shadow forms from the simple geometric shapes that make up the complex shape (see facing page).

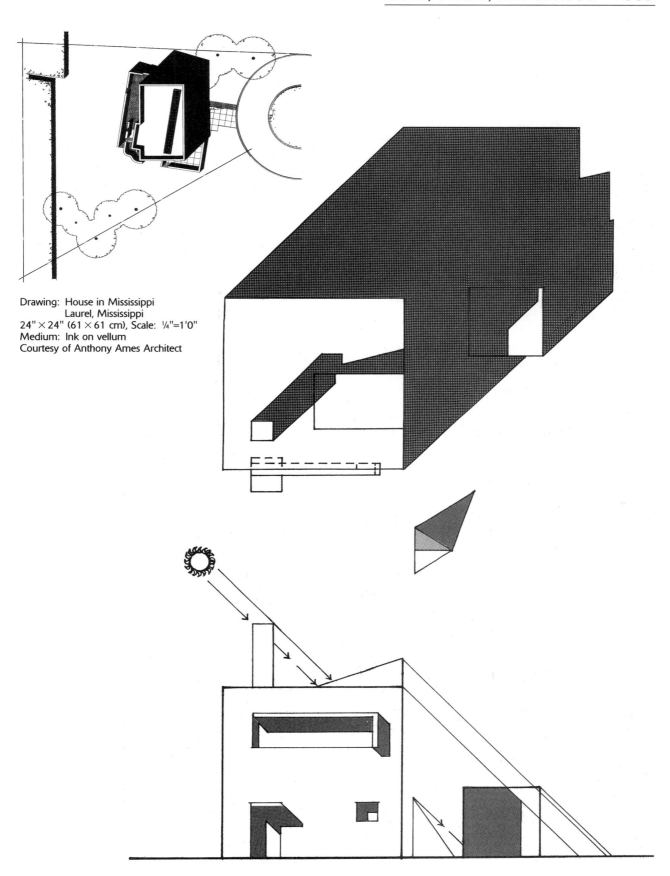

Drawing: House in Mississippi
          Laurel, Mississippi
24" × 24" (61 × 61 cm), Scale: ¼"=1'0"
Medium: Ink on vellum
Courtesy of Anthony Ames Architect

SHADOWS IN PLAN AND IN ELEVATION

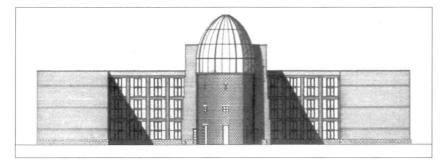

Drawing: Bonnefanten Museum
        Maastrich, Holland
33.25" × 23.5" (84.1 × 59.4 cm), Scale: 1:200
Medium: Black and red ink on vellum
Courtesy of Aldo Rossi, Architect
with Etienne Van Sloun & Gregor Ramaekers

Shadows in Elevation

The form displacement and composition of the fenestration on building facades cannot be rendered without shadows. Intersecting 90° exterior walls (above) produce a continuous shadow line. Intersecting exterior walls at uneven heights produce a broken shadow line. If a cylindrical form has a shaded side as shown above, the shaded area cannot have any shadow fall on it.

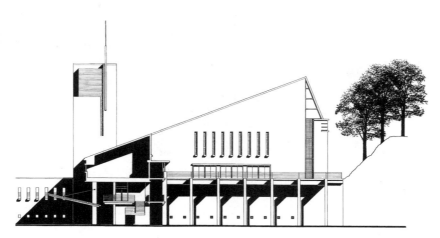

Drawing: Singapore American School, Singapore
36" × 24" (91 × 61.4 cm)
Medium: Ink on Mylar
Courtesy of Perkins & Will Architects

Shadows give us clues as to how a facade articulates. For example, the wider the shadow on its receiving surface, the more the protruding element that casts the shadow on the surface will extend outward. Shadows on elevations are an effective means of showing the massing and character of protruding and recessed elements. All of these examples with deeply cast shadows illustrate how two-dimensional elevations can be given a three-dimensional feeling and quality.

The purpose of elevation shadows in presentation drawings is to provide contrast in order to suggest a third dimension. In practice, the designer or delineator has the liberty to choose the sunlight direction and is not required to keep the standard 45° light ray from the top behind the left shoulder convention. One should select the sun's position in a manner that would accentuate the architectural design.

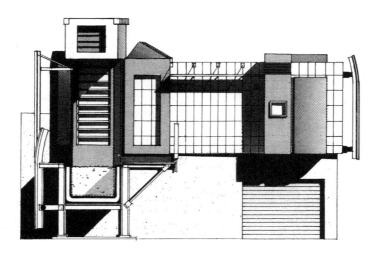

Drawing: Private studio, Venice, California
10" × 8" (25.4 × 20.3 cm), Scale: ⅛"=1'0"
Medium: Vellum, ink, and Zipatone
Courtesy of William Adams Architect

Drawing: Central Chiller Plant and Cogeneration Facility, UCLA
        North elevation detail
24" × 30" (61 × 76.2 cm), Scale: ½"=1'0"
Medium: Ink on Mylar and Zipatone
Courtesy of Holt Hinshaw Pfau Jones Architecture

This north elevation has no true solar orientation. Therefore, in order to create a convincing portrayal of the complex building planes, the shade and shadow were constructed intuitively to best illuminate the juxtaposition of the orthogonal and nonorthogonal geometries.
[ARCHITECT'S STATEMENT BY PAUL C. HOLT]

The tight composition of this drawing allows it to be read both as a representation of three-dimensional space and as an abstract two-dimensional composition. Due to the fact that the corrugated receiving surface slopes away from the viewer, the cast shadows rake across it, introducing a secondary geometry to this otherwise orthogonal composition. Moreover, they afford a greater sense of depth to a drawing format which traditionally tends to compress space.
[ARCHITECT'S STATEMENT BY WES JONES]

SHADOWS IN ELEVATION – BUILDING EXAMPLE

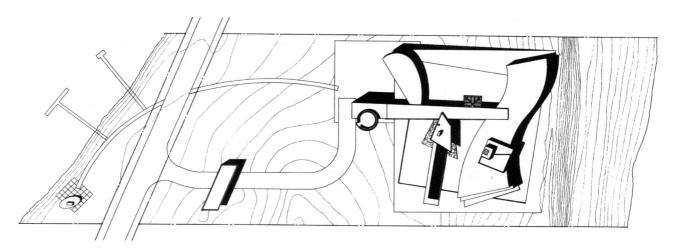

Drawing: Worrel residence, Hillsborough, Florida
36" × 24" (91.4 × 61 cm)
Medium: Ink on vellum
Courtesy of Arquitectonica International Corporation

SHADOWS ON ROOF AND SITE PLANS

Shadows on Roof and Site Plans

When there are many elements in a site plan, as shown in these examples, the resolution of their proper shadow lengths will require both the plan and the elevation (height) of each element. Note that the procedure is analogous to resolving shadow lengths for wall elements seen in elevation. Note that the shadows cast by the structures above mimic the size, shape, and orientation of the structures' roof lines. We can infer that the structures are all about the same height above the ground plane, which for the most part has a flat topography.

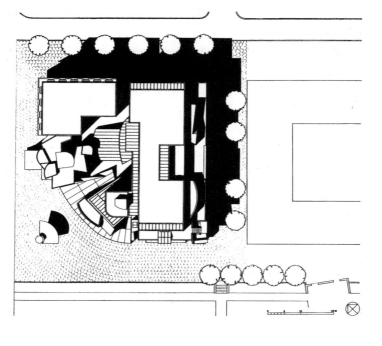

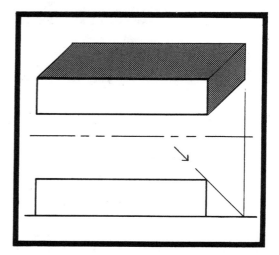

Drawing: American Center, Bercy Park, Paris, France
30" × 40" (76.2 × 101.6 cm)
Medium: Ink on Mylar
Courtesy of Frank O. Gehry & Associates, Architects

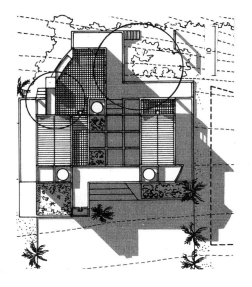

Drawing: Lohmann House
Akumal, Yucatan, Mexico
16" × 24" (40.6 × 61 cm), Scale: 1:100
Medium: Ink and Zipatone
Courtesy of George C. T. Woo, Architect, FAIA

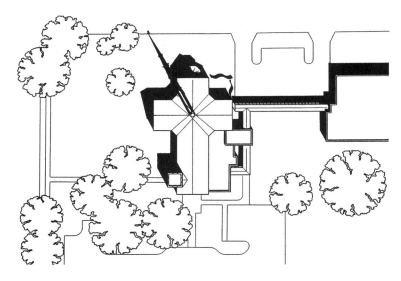

Drawing: The Church of St. Therese
Wilson, North Carolina
9.5" × 7" (24.1 × 17.8 cm), Scale: 1"=20'0"
Medium: Ink on Mylar
Courtesy of Allen, Harbinson & Associates, Architect

Circled situations in the above left site plan adhere to the following principles: In the plan view, light rays and shadow lines cast by vertical light/shade lines maintain **parallelity** regardless of the geometric configuration of the receiving surfaces. The shadow line retains continuity in a straight line when it strikes the receiving geometric forms. The shadows of all the posts in the drawing at right are parallel to each other as well as parallel to the shadows of the other structural elements, following the parallelity principle.

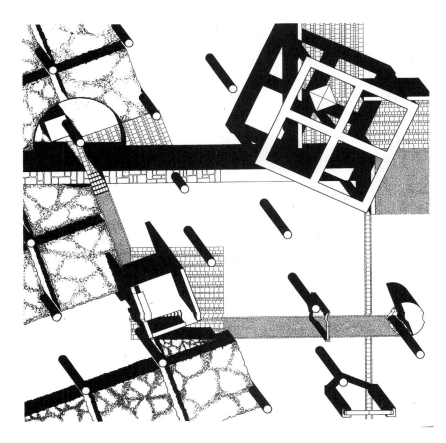

Drawing: Student project by Stephen Roberts
and Doug Lincer
Garden Intervention
Medium: Ink on Mylar
Courtesy of the University of Texas at
Arlington School of Architecture

SHADOWS ON ROOF AND SITE PLANS

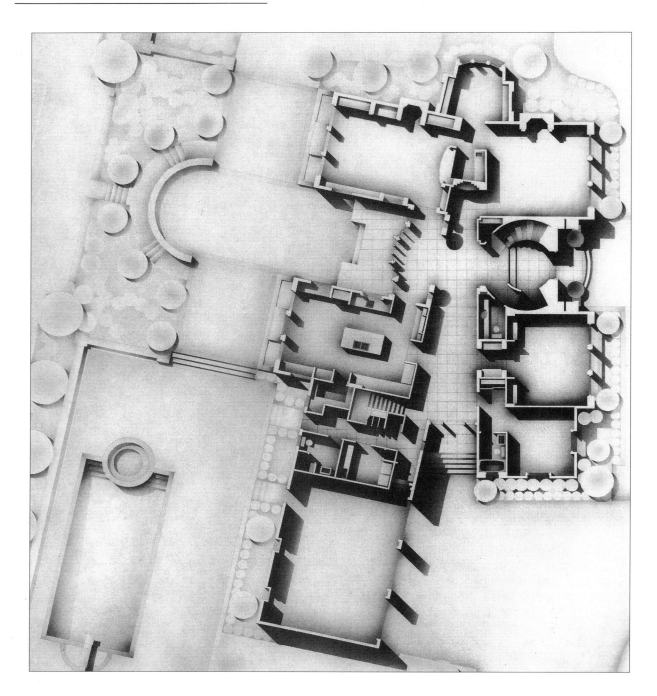

Drawing: Kahn residence, Hillsborough, California
24" × 30" (61 × 76.2 cm), Scale: ¼"=1'0"
Medium: Airbrush using acrylic inks over latex paint on masonite board
Courtesy of House + House, Architects, San Francisco
Mark David English, Architectural Illustrator

Shadows within the Plan

This drawing shows shadows cast in the plan view by vertical elements cut in plan. The purpose is to make the drawing "read" better by accentuating the heights of the elements (walls, columns, etc.) to give a greater feeling of depth and to eliminate the flatness of the plan view.

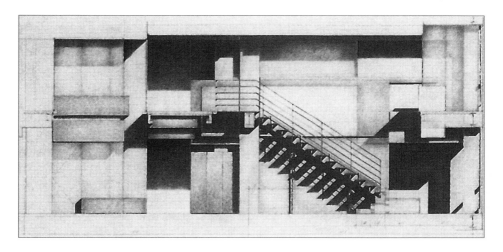

Drawing: The Stainless Steel Apartment, Chicago, Illinois
36" × 24" (91.4 × 61 cm), Scale: ½"=1'0"
Medium: Colored pencil
Courtesy of Krueck & Sexton, Architects, and
Ludwig Mies Van der Rohe, Building Architect

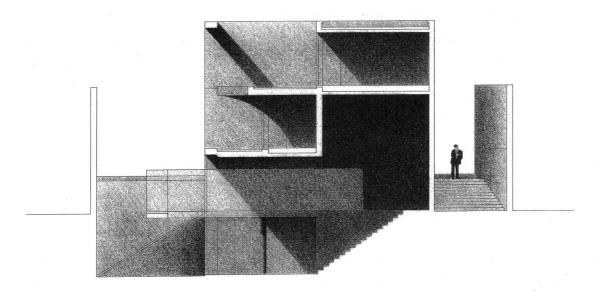

Drawing: I Gallery, Tokyo, Japan
429 × 297 mm (16.9" × 11.7"), Scale: 1:100
Medium: Colored pencil on the copy of the inked drawing
Courtesy of Tadao Ando, Architect

Shadows within the Section

These drawings show shadows cast in a cut section. All elements that protrude (e.g., wall, floor, roof, stairs, built-in furniture, etc.) will cast a shadow. This allows a normally flat two-dimensional section to "punch out." In the Gallery drawing, note the nice gradual change in the tonal value of the shadows cast. This rendering technique helps to more clearly define the interior spaces. Architects and designers use shadows to help accentuate and articulate their design ideas and goals.

Drawing: Villa Gables
            Meersbusch near Dusseldorf, Germany
Southwest facade 15" × 9" (381. × 22.9 cm), Scale: 1:50
Medium: Colored pencil on yellow tracing paper
Courtesy of Michael Graves, Architect
Photo credit: Marek Bulaj

The representational style that architect Michael Graves uses in his soft colored pencil conceptual sketches is characterized by predominantly frontal views such as elevations, plans, and projections (see Bibliography).

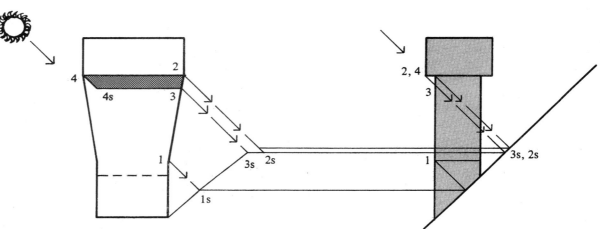

Shadows on Inclined Surfaces

Chimneys are commonly seen casting shadows on a roof plane that is inclined. Most chimney shapes are rectilinear; this example shows a slight variation. With two or more elevations, you can project shadow construction lines from one to the other to determine the proper shadow configuration. Always label the critical points in all views and be systematic in your convention.

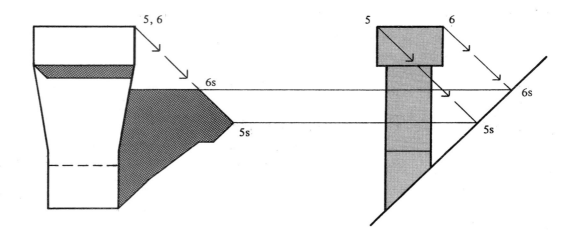

SHADOWS ON INCLINED SURFACES

Drawing: Villa Gables
           Meerbusch near Dusseldorf, Germany
Northwest facade 14" × 9" (35.6 × 22.9 cm), Scale: 1:50
Medium: Colored pencil on yellow tracing paper
Courtesy of Michael Graves, Architect
Photo credit: Marek Bulaj

A dormer is characterized by a projection that extends above a wall and intersects a sloping roof. Windows on its front vertical face provide light, ventilation, and attic space. These two examples show typical shade and shadow conditions.

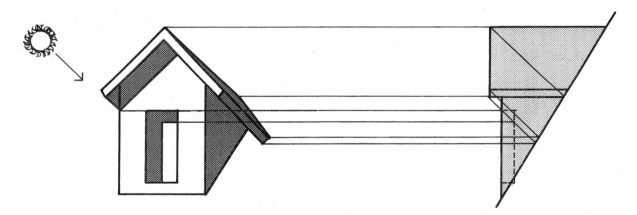

Dormers exhibit a combination of shadows on vertical and inclined surfaces seen in elevation. The profile of the side elevation of the dormer that is seen in shade will cast critical points on the sloping roof. These points are horizontally projected back into the front elevation in order to locate the same critical points seen in the front elevation view.

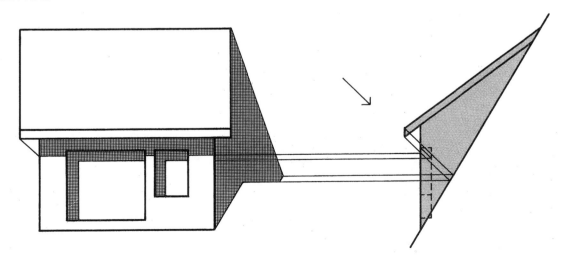

SHADOWS ON INCLINED SURFACES

SHADOWS ON INCLINED SURFACES

Since the sun's light rays are assumed to be **parallel,** they cause vertical (parallel) object lines to cast **parallel shadow lines** on flat or inclined surfaces. This is always true for shadow lines seen either in the plan view or in the elevation view (see the example at right).

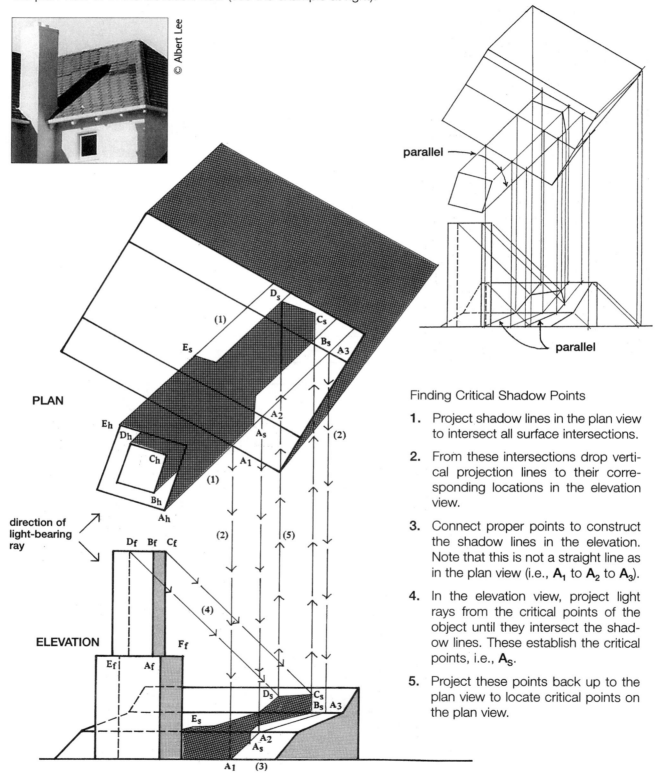

© Albert Lee

parallel

parallel

Finding Critical Shadow Points

1. Project shadow lines in the plan view to intersect all surface intersections.

2. From these intersections drop vertical projection lines to their corresponding locations in the elevation view.

3. Connect proper points to construct the shadow lines in the elevation. Note that this is not a straight line as in the plan view (i.e., A_1 to A_2 to A_3).

4. In the elevation view, project light rays from the critical points of the object until they intersect the shadow lines. These establish the critical points, i.e., A_s.

5. Project these points back up to the plan view to locate critical points on the plan view.

PLAN

ELEVATION

direction of light-bearing ray

This curvilinear roof fenestration casts a strong shadow in the sectional elevation. This is another nice example of shadows cast within the section.

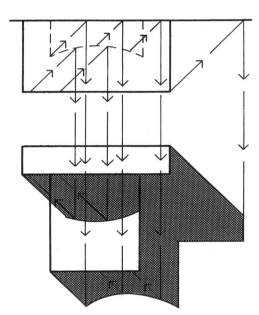

Shadows on Curvilinear Surfaces

Curvilinear surfaces differ from inclined surfaces in the sense that a series of points, rather than just end points, are needed. Shadow lines on a curvilinear surface cast by a horizontal line can be determined by plotting arbitrary points. Likewise, the same procedure applies for a curvilinear line casting a shadow line on a horizontal surface.

Drawings: Sugita House, Katsushika-ku, Tokyo, Japan
9.88" × 13.88" (25.1 × 35.3 cm), Scale: ⅟₃₀"=1'0"
Medium: Charcoal
Courtesy of Riken Yamamoto & Field Shop, Architects
Drawing by Monica Shanley

SHADOWS ON CURVILINEAR SURFACES

45° Light ray condition:
Paraline conditions exhibit light rays parallel to the picture plane.

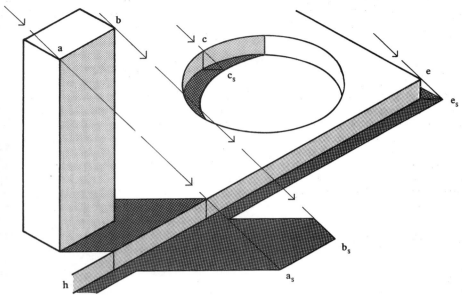

Drawing: Faculty Housing
        The Rockefeller University
        Pocantico Hills, New York
Partial drawing is shown
30" × 48" (76.2 × 121.9 cm)
Scale: ⅛"=1'0"
Medium: Oil paint and colored
pencil on black line diazo print
Courtesy of Michael Fieldman
& Partners, Architects

Isometric Paraline shadows

Critical paraline shadow points are determined by constructing triangular planes parallel to the picture plane.
A vertical drop or rise **(h)** in the horizontal surface connects paraline shadows on different horizontal surfaces.
A drop in a horizontal receiving surface always results in a longer shadow. A rise in a horizontal receiving surface always results in a shorter shadow.

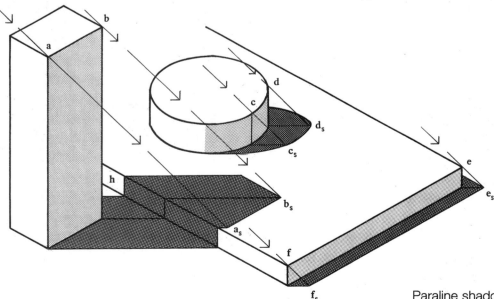

Paraline shadows of cylindrical forms can be determined by finding and plotting a series of arbitrary points (**c** and **d**) on the light/shade boundary.

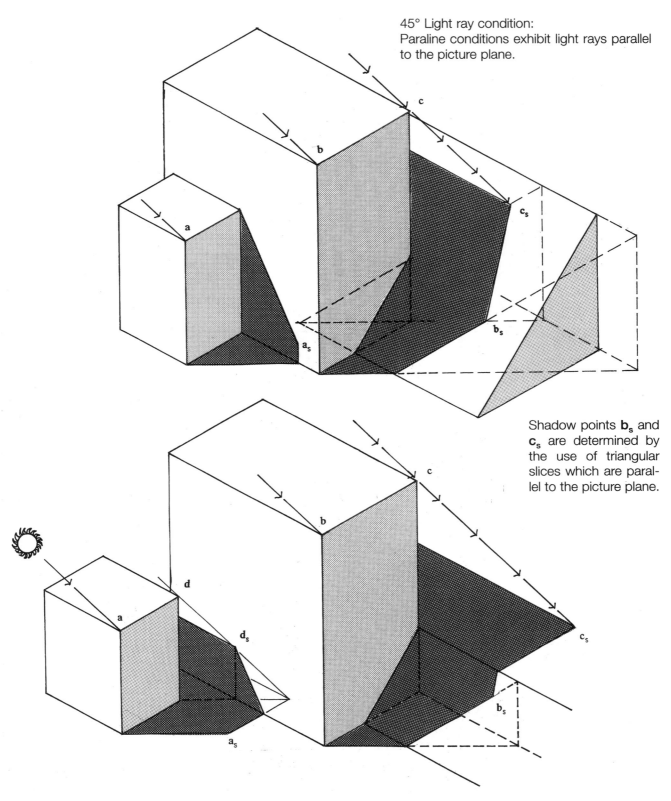

45° Light ray condition:
Paraline conditions exhibit light rays parallel to the picture plane.

Shadow points **b_s** and **c_s** are determined by the use of triangular slices which are parallel to the picture plane.

ISOMETRIC PARALINE SHADOWS

For separate blocks, to determine the shadow on the vertical wall, it is best to cast a shadow on the ground assuming there is no wall. Then project horizontal and vertical trace lines until they intersect the light-bearing rays.

PLAN OBLIQUE PARALINE SHADOWS

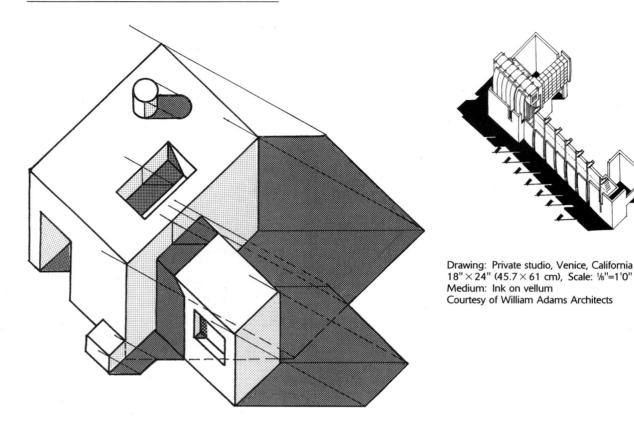

Drawing: Private studio, Venice, California
18" × 24" (45.7 × 61 cm), Scale: ⅛"=1'0"
Medium: Ink on vellum
Courtesy of William Adams Architects

Plan Oblique Paraline Shadows

These plan oblique (45-45°) drawings exhibit shadows cast from light rays that are parallel to the picture plane. Critical shadow points on the ground are determined by the intersection of sloping light rays from a casting edge (height or altitude) and the bearing line on the ground. In the above example, the small building elements intercept the light rays cast by vertical and horizontal casting edges of the large building element. This results in a shadow line that climbs across the small element.

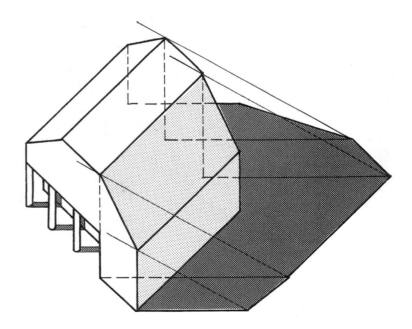

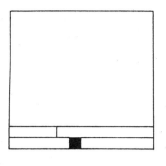

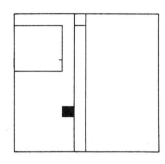

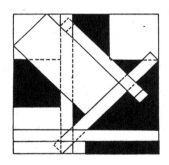

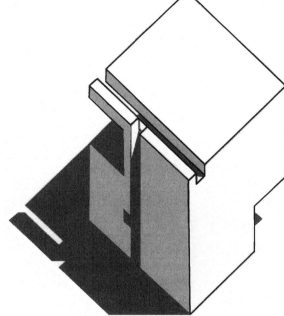

Drawing: Student project by Andrew Von Mauer, Solid void relationship investigation
17" × 11" (43.2 × 27.9 cm), Scale: Full-size after model
Medium: Ink on Mylar
Courtesy of Andrews University, Division of Architecture, 1st year Graphics Studio
Studio Professor: Arpad Daniel Ronaszegi, Assistant: Tom Lowing

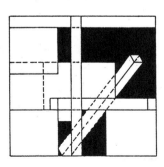

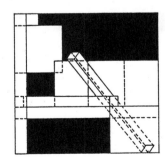

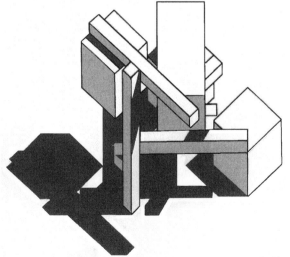

Drawing: Student project by Andrew Von Mauer, Solid void relationship investigation
17" × 11" (43.2 × 27.9 cm), Scale: Full-size after model
Medium: Ink on Mylar
Courtesy of Andrews University, Division of Architecture, 1st year Graphics Studio
Studio Professor: Arpad Daniel Ronaszegi, Assistant: Tom Lowing

PLAN OBLIQUE PARALINE SHADOWS

MANUALLY CAST AND COMPUTER-GENERATED SHADOWS

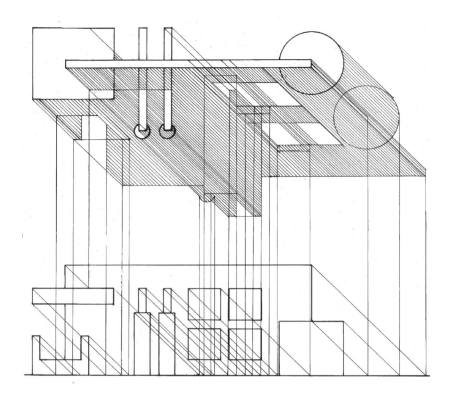

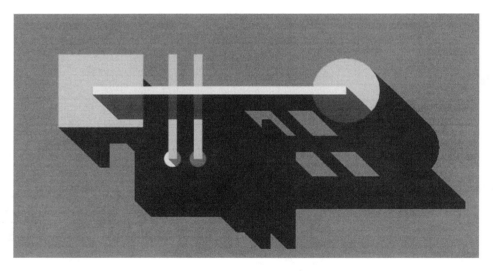

Student: Mark Stegeman
Professor: M. Saleh Uddin
Course: Design Communication-I
Courtesy of University of Missouri–Columbia
Department of Environmental Design

Comparing Manually Casted and Computer-Generated Shadows

Hand constructed shadows can be verified by casting the same shadow in a 3D computer environment. The drawings above shows the manually constructed shadow using the principle of corresponding points. The drawing below shows the computer-generated shadow. A sun altitude and bearing angle of 45° was used for both the plan and elevation.
[PROFESSOR'S STATEMENT]

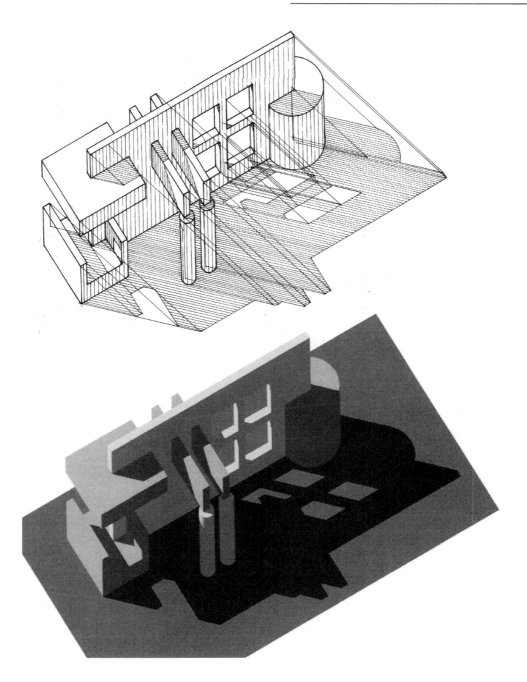

Student: Mark Stegeman
Professor: M. Saleh Uddin
Course: Design Communication-I
Courtesy of University of Missouri–Columbia
Department of Environmental Design

As on the facing page, the manual projection above was compared with the computer projection below for this plan oblique drawing. The sun altitude and bearing angles in these examples were also at 45°. Note in the casting of shadows by a vertical plane with thickness that a casting edge is hidden. With wall openings, it is necessary to cast shadows by all of the horizontal and vertical edges to resolve the correct shadow configuration.
[PROFESSOR'S STATEMENT]

MANUALLY CAST AND COMPUTER-GENERATED SHADOWS

PARALINE SHADOWS

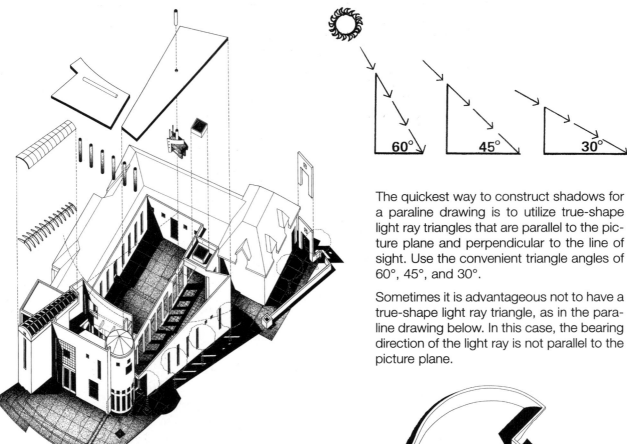

Drawing: Shamash residence, Hillsborough, California
20" × 28" (50.8 × 71.1 cm), Scale: ⅛"=1'0"
Medium: Pen and ink and airbrush on Mylar
Courtesy of Steven House, Architect

The quickest way to construct shadows for a paraline drawing is to utilize true-shape light ray triangles that are parallel to the picture plane and perpendicular to the line of sight. Use the convenient triangle angles of 60°, 45°, and 30°.

Sometimes it is advantageous not to have a true-shape light ray triangle, as in the paraline drawing below. In this case, the bearing direction of the light ray is not parallel to the picture plane.

Shadows Cast in Paraline Drawings

Shadows on buildings in paraline drawings create a strong three-dimensional feeling, as shown in these examples. A paraline drawing without shadows is relatively flat. Absent or just lightly rendered shade on planes is permissible when fenestration detail must be clear (see above). Always choose a convenient angle (45° or 60°) and direction for the slope of the light rays. Complex configurations can best be resolved by a series of shadow point casting triangles.

Drawing: Kress residence, Albuquerque, New Mexico
20" × 30" (50.8 × 76.2 cm), Scale: ¼"=1'0"
Medium: Ink on vellum
Courtesy of Robert W. Peters FAIA,
Alianza Arquitectos/An Architect's Alliance

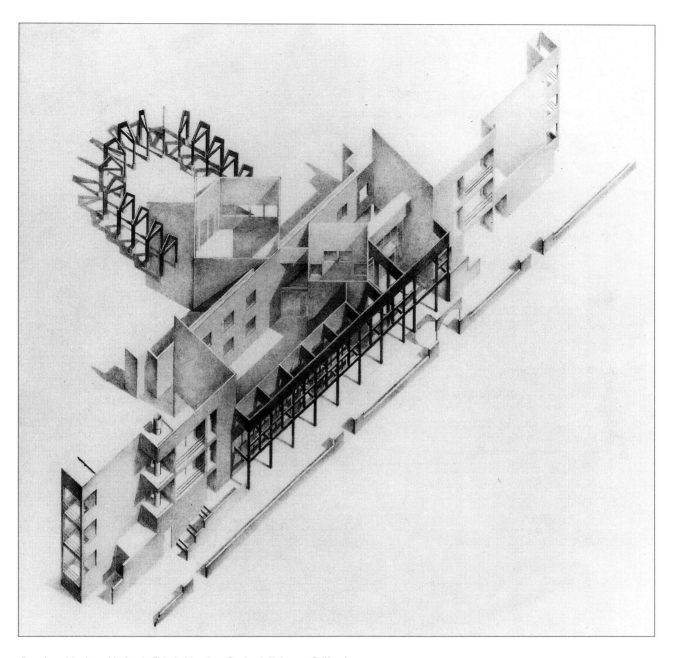

Drawing: Verdugo Hacienda Elderly Housing, Sunland, Tujunga, California
24" × 24" (61 × 61 cm), Scale: ⅛"=1'0"
Medium: Ink and colored pencil
Courtesy of John V. Mutlow FAIA, Architects

To articulate the basic premise of this courtyard building, only the important public spaces and enclosure planes were selected for delineation. The brise-soleil shades the south-facing front elevation, and the rotating volumes connect the off-center enclosure to the axial courtyard and lanai. The shadows were then cast in order to best articulate the building form and movement sequence.
[Architect's statement]

This drawing also does not use a true-shape light ray triangle. Note the use of nice soft shadows.

SHADOW AND SUN'S RAYS VANISHING POINTS

Select the location of the vanishing point of the sun's rays on the vertical tracer line. The vanishing point of the shadow will also fall on this line. Note that the small triangle (**ABC**) and the large triangle are similar.

VP$_S$ or **VPS** is the vanishing point of the shadow.

VP$_{SR}$ or **VPSR** is the vanishing point of the sun's rays.

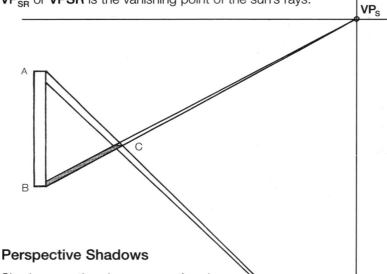

Drawing: Skid Row Development Corporation
        Los Angeles, Caifornia
Medium: Ink
Courtesy of Ron Silveira, AIA, Architect;
James Bonar, FAIA; and the
Los Angeles Community Design Center

Perspective Shadows

Shadow casting in **perspective** is similar to paraline shadow casting. The difference is that the sun's rays and the shadow lines (outlines) converge to vanishing points. The light rays can either be parallel or oblique to the picture plane (see pp. 360–365).

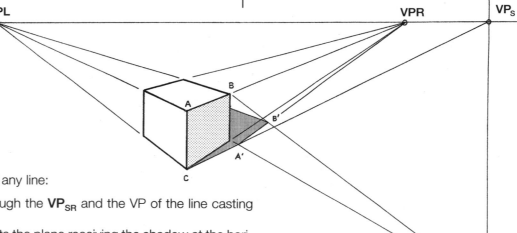

Locating the **VP$_S$** of any line:

1. Draw a line through the **VP$_{SR}$** and the VP of the line casting the shadow.
2. The line intersects the plane receiving the shadow at the horizon line.
3. This intersection is the VP of the required shadow line.

NOTE: **A′B′** is parallel to **AB** in the plan view; therefore, they vanish at **VPR** in perspective. Vertical line **AC** casts shadow line **A′C**. **A′C** will vanish on the horizon at **VP$_S$**; therefore, all vertical lines will cast shadows that vanish at **VP$_S$**.

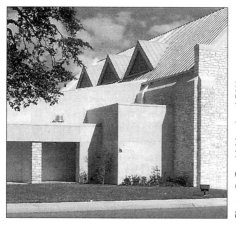

Photo: Notre Dame Catholic Church, Kerrville, Texas
Courtesy of Tapley/Lunow Architects,
Gerald Moorhead FAIA

Photo © Gerald Moorhead FAIA

Shadows Cast on a Combination of Horizontal and Vertical Surfaces

1. Vertical light/shade line **ab** casts shadow line **ab$_s$** on the ground and this line vanishes at the **VPS**.

2. Vertical light/shade line **bc** casts shadow line **b$_s$c$_s$**. This is a case of a vertical line casting a shadow line on a vertical surface.

3. Horizontal light/shade line **cd** casts shadow line **c$_s$d$_s$**, which vanishes at the intersection of the line through the **VPSR** and the **VPR** and the vertical traces through the **VPL**.

4. Vertical light/shade line **de** casts shadow line **d$_s$e$_s$** following the principle stated in step 2.

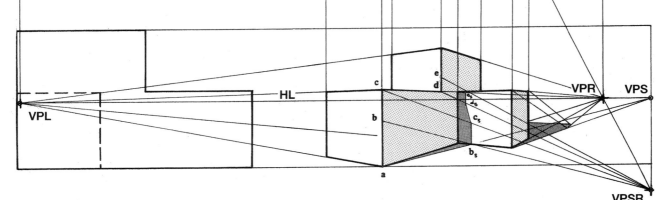

PERSPECTIVE SHADOWS ON INTERSECTING SURFACES

PERSPECTIVE SHADES AND SHADOWS

Photo (right): Newport Center/Fashion Island
Newport Beach, California
Courtesy of the SWA Group

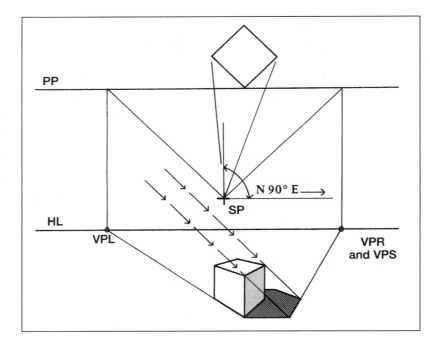

Light rays parallel to the picture plane

Light rays **parallel** to the picture plane can be cast at any convenient angle, such as 45°, depending on the effect desired. A **vertical line** casts a shadow line that is **parallel** to the **HL** and the **PP** in the direction of the bearing of the light rays. Lines **parallel** to the ground plane cast shadow lines that are **parallel** to the line casting the shadow line.

Light rays oblique to the picture plane

Given conditions:
Bearing of light rays = S 60° W
Slope = 22°

Note that the **VPSR** is **above** the **HL**.

The vanishing point of the sun's rays **(VPSR)** is located by **rotating** the bearing line into the **PP** and dropping a vertical to locate the corresponding point on the **HL**. From this point the slope of the light ray is drawn until it intercepts the vertical tracer line drawn from the penetration point on the **PP** by the bearing of the light rays. The vanishing point of the shadow **(VPS)** lies at the intersection of this vertical tracer and the **HL**.

BEARING — the direction of the line (in this case a light ray) relative to due north or south. It is always measured in the plan view and expressed in degrees.

SLOPE — the slope angle of a line measured in the elevation view relative to the horizon line and expressed in degrees.

View from west

Perspective Shades and Shadows

View from northwest

Drawing: High Sierra Meadow's Edge Cabin
Medium: CAD
Courtesy of Jones, Partners: Architecture

PERSPECTIVE SHADES AND SHADOWS

PERSPECTIVE SHADES AND SHADOWS

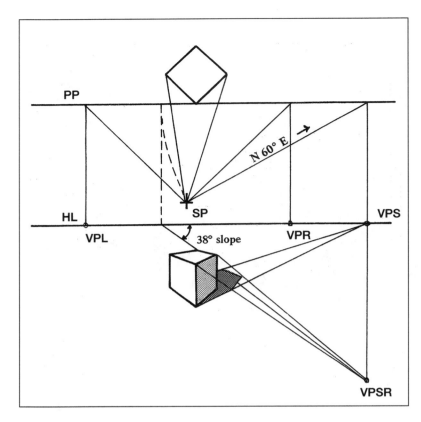

Light rays oblique to the picture plane

Given conditions:

Bearing of light rays = N 60° E
Slope = 38°

Note that the **VPSR** is **below** the **HL.**

Photo: Bollard, Alcoa Building Plaza
(Maritime Plaza)
San Francisco, California
Courtesy of the SWA Group

Light rays oblique to the picture plane

Given conditions:

Bearing of light rays = S 45° E
Slope = 30°

Note that the **VPSR** is **above** the **HL.**

Photo: Garden area of Pitney Bowes
World Headquarters
Stamford, Connecticut
Courtesy of I. M. Pei & Partners, Architects
© 1987 Steve Rosenthal

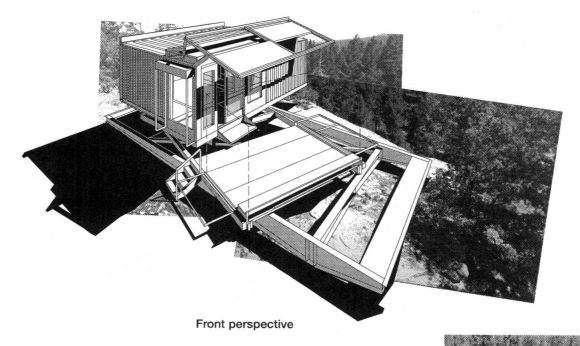

Front perspective

Perspective Shades and Shadows

Rear perspective

Drawings: High Sierras Guest Cabin
Medium: CAD
Courtesy of Jones, Partners: Architecture

Integral to this project is the contrasting nature of human-generated systems [as represented by the modular container element] and naturally generated systems [the site environs]. The juxtaposition of hardline, shadowed rendering with scanned photographic information underscores this dichotomy. The representation of shade and shadow provides a link between these two graphic modes.
[ARCHITECT'S STATEMENT]

PERSPECTIVE SHADES AND SHADOWS

PERSPECTIVE SHADOWS ON SURFACES

Perspective Shades and Shadows

The separation of the two block forms causes shadows to be cast on both horizontal and vertical surfaces in a manner similar to the two building elements of the Swan House. Light rays are parallel to the picture plane for these two perspective conditions. Triangular slice **rst** is in a plane that is parallel to the picture plane. Its location is determned by horizontal line **qrt**. Line **rs** determines the locus for piercing points for a variety of light ray angles.

Drawing: Swan House, North Fork
Long Island, New York
36" × 24" (91.4 × 61 cm)
Medium: Ink
Courtesy of Charles W. Moore, FAIA,
and Mark Simon, FAIA, of Centerbrook

45° Light ray condition

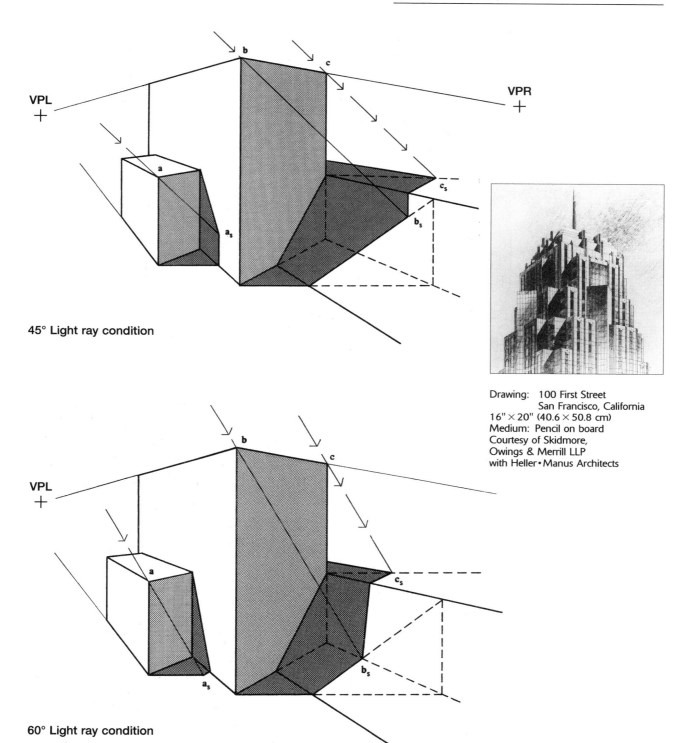

VPL
+

VPR
+

45° Light ray condition

VPL
+

60° Light ray condition

Drawing: 100 First Street
San Francisco, California
16" × 20" (40.6 × 50.8 cm)
Medium: Pencil on board
Courtesy of Skidmore,
Owings & Merrill LLP
with Heller•Manus Architects

PERSPECTIVE SHADOWS ON SURFACES

Perspective Shades and Shadows

As on the previous page, light rays for these two perspective conditions are parallel to the picture plane, and they are also parallel to each other. To determine the critical shadow piercing point on the sloping surface (**b_s**), set up a triangular slice (dashed lines) parallel to the picture plane. Critical point **c_s** also lies in a plane that is parallel to the picture plane.

Perspective Shadows of Dormers and Overhangs

As the sun moves during the daytime, the solar angle changes, causing the perspective shadow of a dormer on an inclined roof to have an infinite number of positions as it moves across the sloping roof. Two conditions on opposite uphill sides of a dormer are shown on this and the facing page.

Dormer shadows sloping uphill are always shorter than they would be on a horizontal surface, regardless of the light ray direction. When sloping downhill, they are always longer than on a horizontal plane.

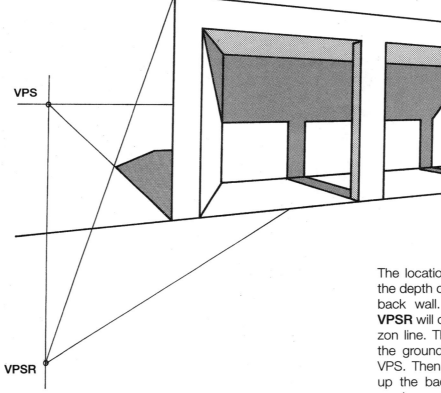

VPS

VPSR

The location of the VPSR will determine the depth of the overhang shadow on the back wall. A vertical line through the **VPSR** will determine the **VPS** on the horizon line. The columns cast shadows on the ground whose edges vanish at the VPS. Then the shadow creeps vertically up the back wall and connects to the overhang shadow.

Drawing: Private house, Wilmington, North Carolina
24" × 36" (61 × 91.4 cm), Scale (site plan): 1"=20'0"
Medium: Ink on Mylar
Courtesy of Gerald Allen & Jeffrey Harbinson, Architects, P.C.

Three-dimensional objects can be understood, for the most part, by the result of how they mold shadow and light. The house in the drawing above uses no lines to define its form. Instead, its image is entirely a result of the shadows that it casts.
[ARCHITECT'S STATEMENT]

Because of reflected light, when surfaces are rendered to indicate shade and cast shadows, they are rarely shown with one uniform value as has been seen with all of the technical drawings in this chapter. The underneath area of the porch overhang exhibits a lot of reflected light, which lightens the shaded surface (see more examples on pp. 344, 388, and 389).

PERSPECTIVE SHADOWS OF DORMER AND OVERHANG

PERSPECTIVE SHADOWS/COMPUTER IMAGING

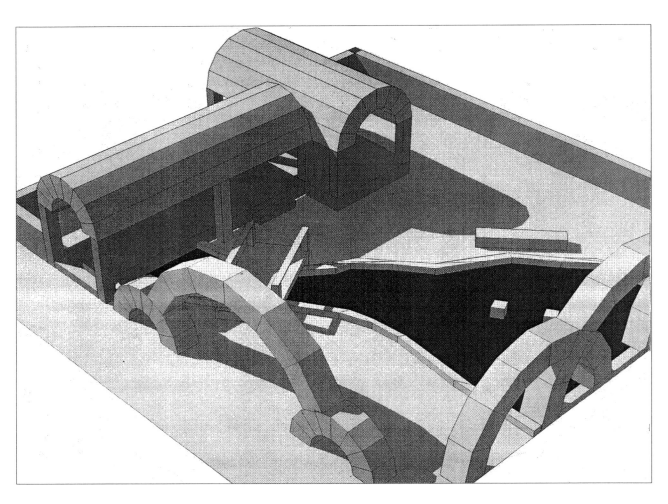

Drawings: Student project by Jeremy McFarland
  Bird's-eye and pedestrian views (opposite) of a building complex
Medium: Drawings done on Silicon Graphics Indigo computers using Alias Upfront software
Studio Professor: Dick Davison
Courtesy of Texas A&M University College of Architecture

Computer Imaged Perspective Shadows

An understanding of shadow constructions is important for anyone involved in creating two-dimensional images that are meant to be realistic or believable as three-dimensional concepts. After the manual methods of perspective and shadow construction are understood, the time-saving computer-generated image can be fully appreciated. Most computer programs that offer perspective can create shadows for any possible shadow-casting scenario.

This and the facing page represent a project that involved the design of a pavilion within a 100' square space. The modeling capability of the computer software makes it possible to create quick views within the space (as in the above perspective through the arch). The shadow configuration is, of course, also in perspective. Computer-generated shadow constructions will generally give the same added sense of realness that hand-drawn shadows offer. However, a truly practiced eye will be able to render nuances of light and shadow that will not be found in the more "automatic" CADD renditions. [STUDIO PROFESSOR'S STATEMENT]

In reality, solar reflected light and the material texture of surfaces can affect the perceived tonal value within and on the edges of cast shadows as well as on surfaces in shade. Shaded surfaces can be quite distinct in value from surfaces with shadow (see above) or they can be quite similar in value (see facing page). "Nuances of light and shadow" as they are applied in order to articulate form and express depth will be examined in the next chapter.

PERSPECTIVE SHADOWS/COMPUTER IMAGING

PERSPECTIVE SHADOWS/COMPUTER IMAGING

Image: Family house, Reykjavik, Iceland
Software: ArchiCad
Courtesy of Gudmundur Jonsson, Architect

Image: The Millenium House, Reykjavik, Iceland
Software: ArchiCad
Courtesy of Gudmundur Jonsson, Architect

Computer-generated drawings can produce nice clear shadows as shown on the exterior church rendering on the facing page and the shades and shadows on the house exterior above. Also note the nice interior shadows and window reflections in the above interior.

Drawings: Student project by Tami Nguyen and Daniel Yang
               San Juan Capistrano Mission
               San Juan Capistrano, California
Software: form Z with RenderZone
Courtesy of Professors Karen Kensek and Douglas Noble
University of Southern California School of Architecture

Computer Imaged Perspective Shadows

*In 1812, after a disastrous earthquake during Sunday services, the stone church
of the San Juan Capistrano Mission lay in ruins. About 185 years later, this mas-
terpiece of the California missions was digitally reconstructed. Most of the buildings at the mission were not difficult to reconstruct on the computer; the Historic
American Building Survey (HABS) has an excellent set of drawings to use as reference, and many of the structures still exist. The church itself was more chal-
lenging. Daniel Yang modeled and rendered the ruins of the stone church (without the scaffolding currently holding it in place). Tami Nguyen, after visiting local
Mission-style churches and researching the project, constructed her interpretation
of what the church might have looked like before that fateful Sunday in 1812.
[Studio Professors' statement]*

PERSPECTIVE SHADOWS/COMPUTER IMAGING

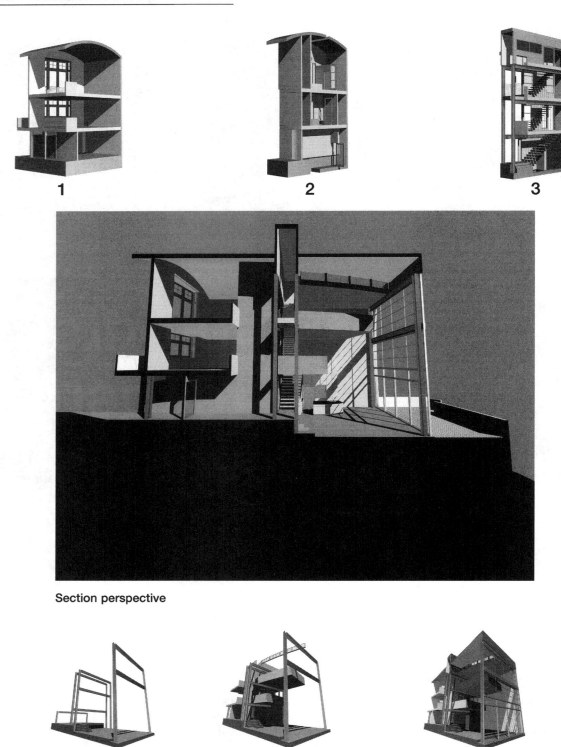

1

2

3

Section perspective

1

2

3

The top row on these two facing pages shows a nice use of the two-point perspective section in sequence (**1** to **6**) to reveal a dissected model of the residence and important details of the interior spaces. The bottom row on this page shows a three-point perspective used in the sequence (**1** to **3**) of analytical perspectives. Also note the beautiful use of computer-generated shadows in the one-point perspective section (with slight upward convergence).

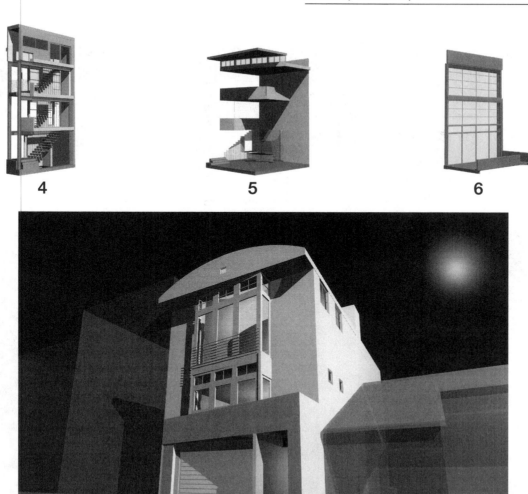

4   5   6

Night perspective

Images: Buena Vista residence, San Francisco, California
Principal in Charge: Mark English
Architectural Illustrations: Star Jennings
Courtesy of Inglese Architecture

PERSPECTIVE SHADOWS/COMPUTER IMAGING

All design and construction documents produced in the office are digitally created or manipulated. The CAD program used for the creation of 3-dimensional drawings is ArchiCad 6.0, in conjunction with Artlantis Renderer and Photoshop. Hardware used is the Macintosh G4, Umax 1200s scanner, and Epson Stylus Photo 1200 printer.

Inglese is a young design firm located in San Francisco's Jackson Square District. The firm is dedicated to fine residential, commercial, and civic architecture and interior design. Mark English and associates Star Jennings, Alessandro Miramare, and Ani Balarezo follow a team approach to design wherein talented builders and artisans are involved as collaborators from the beginning of the design process through construction.

[ARCHITECT'S STATEMENT]

SHADOWS IN SKETCHES AND RENDERINGS

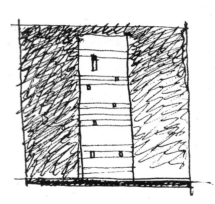

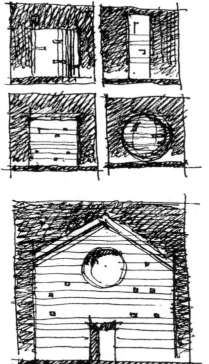

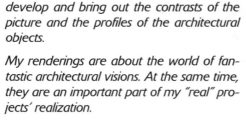

One says that a colored picture is harmonious only if its black and white illustration is correct as well. Therefore, I use shadows in my preliminary black and white sketches to develop and bring out the contrasts of the picture and the profiles of the architectural objects.

My renderings are about the world of fantastic architectural visions. At the same time, they are an important part of my "real" projects' realization.

The layers of the city skyline—old or new—and of watercolor and brushstrokes—transparent or opaque—traverse and create an ever-changing intersection between the old and the new.

[ARCHITECTURAL ILLUSTRATOR'S STATEMENT]

Shadow studies and rendering: The simple forms, 1999
16" × 24" (41 × 61 cm)
Medium: Watercolor, pen, and sepia ink
Courtesy of Sergei Tchoban, Architectural Illustrator

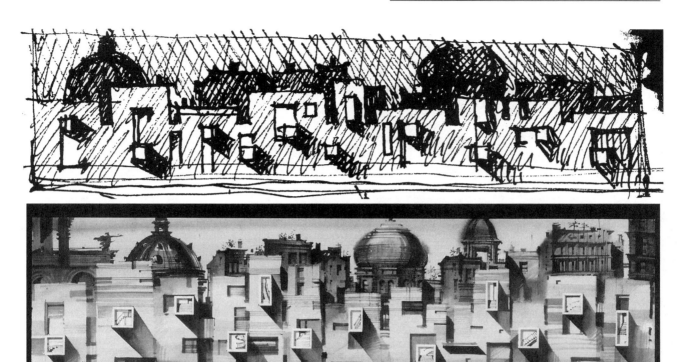

Shadow study and rendering: Bridges, 1/2000
8.5" × 40" (30 × 100 cm)
Medium: Watercolor, pen, and sepia ink
Courtesy of Sergei Tchoban, Architectural Illustrator

Shadow studies and rendering: The life on the back side, 1993
24" × 24" (60 × 60 cm)
Medium: Watercolor, pen, and sepia ink
Courtesy of Sergei Tchoban, Architectural Illustrator

Shades and shadows are often used to embellish conceptual elevations and paraline/perspective massing studies. The introduction of shadows makes these images less diagrammatic.

9

Delineating and Rendering Entourage

The major communicative drawings (plan, elevation, section, paralines, and perspectives) are part of a presentation package. It is of utmost importance to accentuate these drawings with the use of contrast so that they "read" for the prospective client. This process of delineating and rendering is critical in the presentation phase of a design project. Contrast must be properly balanced for a presentation to be clear; thus, different shades of dark values must be played against various degrees of light values. The amount of rendered contrast is based on the contextual relationship of the adjacent forms.

The intent of this chapter is to introduce techniques of delineation and rendering as applied to contextual elements—or, to use the Beaux Arts term, "entourage"—such as landscaping, human figures, furniture, cars, and building materials.

In summary, following are some of the important terms, skills, and concepts you will learn:

Rendering	Value	Contrast	Entourage
Ground textures	Scribbling	Spatial profiling	Stippling
Hatching	Foliage textures	Delineating figures	Delineating cars

Delineating and Rendering Entourage

TOPIC: CONTOUR & FORM LANGUAGE

Ching 2003, 134.

Ching 1990, 44–45.

TOPIC: BASIC VALUE LANGUAGES

Ching 2003, 125–143.

Ching 1990, 48, 78–83.

TOPIC: RENDERING HUMAN FIGURES

Burden 1981, 12–137.

Ching 2003, 158–161.

Ching 1990, 174–175.

TOPIC: RENDERING ENTOURAGE (OTHER THAN PEOPLE)

Lorenz and Lizak 1988, 23–40.

Porter 1990, 58–87.

Reid 1987, 93, 95, 100, 101.

Wang 1997.

White E. A., 1972.

Chapter Overview

After studying this chapter and practicing the techniques discussed, you will be able to delineate and render various types of drawings. For continued study, refer to Lockard's *Design Drawing Experiences,* Porter and Goodman's *Manual of Graphic Techniques 4,* and Lin's *Designing and Drawing with Confidence.*

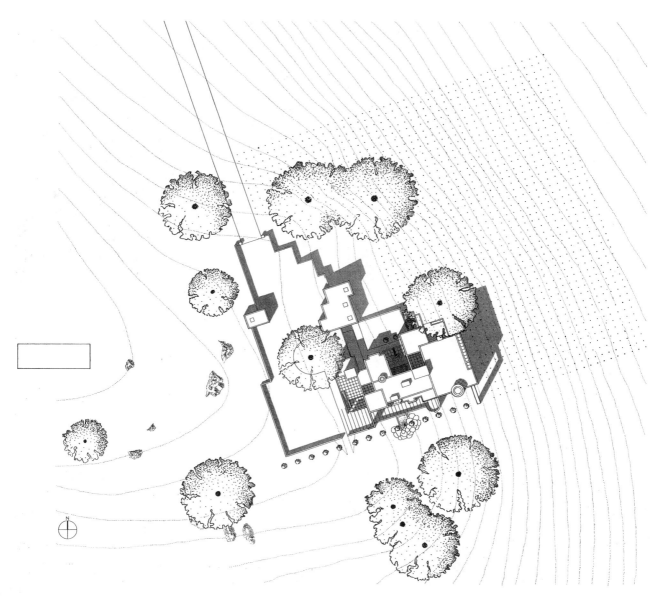

Drawing: Private residence, Healdsburg, California
24" × 36" (61 × 91.4 cm), Scale: ⅛"=1'0"
Medium: Ink on Mylar
Courtesy of Sandy & Babcock, Inc.
Architecture & Planning

SITE PLAN

When there is a dark field caused by tonal values in the surrounding contextual environment, a site plan's figure–ground/light–dark/positive–negative areas give better depth because of **contrast.** We see this strong contrast in the drawing of architect William Kessler's house on p. 392. The rendering above lacks this contrast, but instead shows soft shadows cast by the building that cause the plan to "punch out." Contrast in architectural drawings is achieved by **rendering.** Rendering is the application of artistic delineation to site plans, elevations, paralines, perspectives, and other architectural drawings. The objective of rendering drawings is either to further client understanding of the proposed design or for publicity and promotion. This chapter and web site Chapter 12 (Color Techniques) give only a brief introduction to this complex topic. Refer to the Bibliography for many excellent resources in this subject area. This chapter does not cover color techniques in rendering.

VALUE TYPES

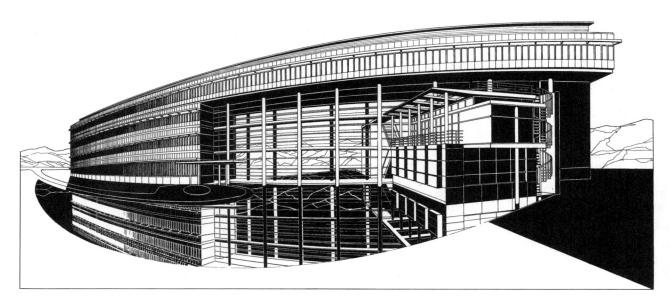

Drawing: Dongbu Central Research Institute, Taejon, Korea, view from south
36" × 24" (91.4 × 61 cm)
Medium: Ink on Mylar
Courtesy of Perkins & Will Architects

Diagrams and text: Courtesy of William R. Benedict, Assistant Professor
California Polytechnic State University College of Architecture and
Environmental Design, San Luis Obispo, California

Basic Value Types

A value is any technique that directly describes a surface rather than its edges. The edges are made visible by the limits of and/or a sharp change in value. A value (sometimes called a tonal value or tone in drawing) can be a continuous value or created by lines. A **continuous** value is even, small in scale, and fine in implied texture. A **value of lines** has texture that is significant in scale and composed of individual marks that retain their identity within the value. These marks include stippling, lines, cross-hatching, scrubbing, scrubbing over texture, and scribbling. The classification of a value as continuous or created by lines depends on the media and application technique employed.

The role of value in a drawing includes describing the area of a surface, the gradations produced by the surface's texture, the orientation of the surface to the light source, and the surfaces's attributes—materiality, texture, uniformity, reflectance, transparency, color, etc. In representing these qualities, the scale, coarseness, form, and hue of the value can be manipulated. Gradations are value changes on a surface or form.

2H, H, HB, and 4B pencils (left to right)

Ink pen on all four scales

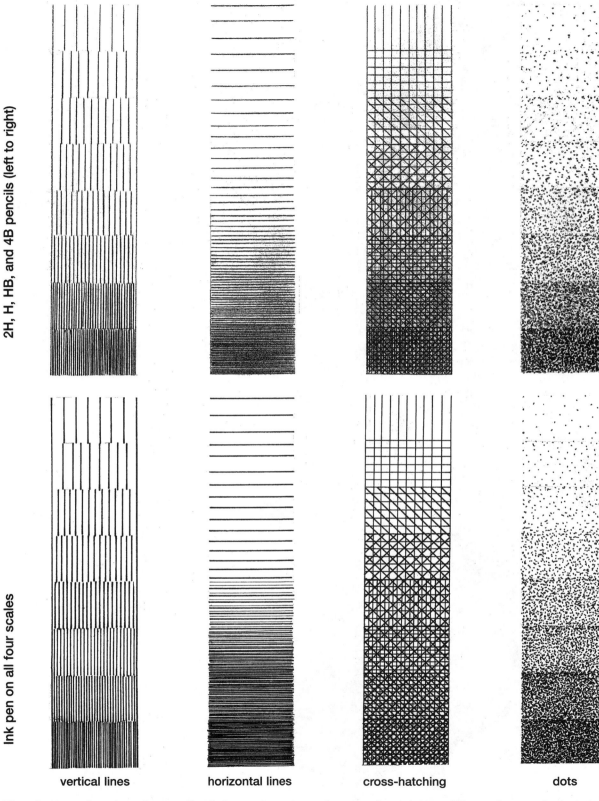

vertical lines   horizontal lines   cross-hatching   dots

The use of dots is also termed "stippling" (see pointillism, p. 388)

VALUE SCALES USING VALUE GRADING TECHNIQUES

The above scales show four methods to render value using pencil or ink pen. Other value-producing media are ink wash, watercolor wash, markers, and dry-transfer Zipatone.

CONTOUR LANGUAGE

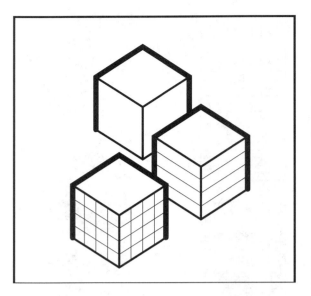

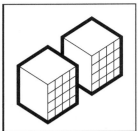

Primary Contours

Primary contours define the outermost extremities of a form —they record the outline or profile of an object. They are edges formed by the meeting of two surfaces when only one surface can be seen. They respond to and record all edge textures and irregularities. Drawing only the profile of an object tends to flatten the object.

Contour and Form

The language of contour and form relates line weight choices to the aspect of the form that they are representing. The language identifies primary, secondary, and tertiary edge conditions using a vocabulary of three different line weights, with the grammar defining primary contours as heavy, secondary contours as medium, and tertiary contours as light.

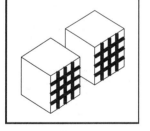

Secondary Contours

Secondary contours describe the edges of surfaces when both surfaces are visible. They respond to and record all edge textures and irregularities.

Tertiary Contours

Tertiary contours describe changes in the uniformity of a surface or plane. They respond to and record linear markings on a surface and the edges of values, shadows, textures, and colors. Tertiary contours disclose the volume of an object. They are plastic and emphasize the three-dimensionality of the object.

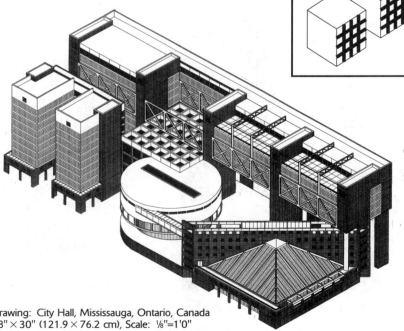

Drawing: City Hall, Mississauga, Ontario, Canada
48" × 30" (121.9 × 76.2 cm), Scale: ⅛"=1'0"
Medium: Ink on Mylar
Courtesy of Michael Fieldman & Partners, Architects

Diagrams and text (both pages): Courtesy of William R. Benedict, Assistant Professor California Polytechnic State University College of Architecture & Environmental Design San Luis Obispo, California
Software: Aldus Freehand

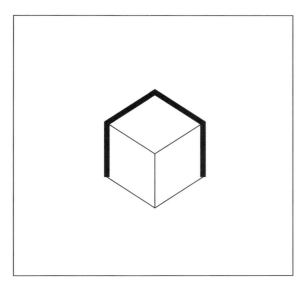

Spatial Profiling

Edges are perceived under two conditions: when both surfaces defining the edge are visible and when only one surface is visible. Lighter lines indicate an edge between two planes when both can be seen. Heavier lines — profile lines — indicate an edge between two planes where only one plane can be seen. To one side of a profile edge you are looking through space to some distant surface. The greatest spatial differential — the heaviest profile line — occurs at the edge between the object and the sky and earth (the object's environment or background). Lines become heavier as the distance between the edge they represent and the surface against which the edge is seen increases.

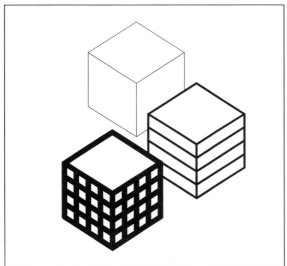

Contours and Distance

A heavy black line on a white sheet of paper reads as closer than a light line due to its size and our experience with the effect of aerial perspective on contrast. A thin black line appears as lighter in value than a thick black line because it has less surface area with which to communicate its value. From these cues we can establish a language that says that the closest contours are the heaviest and weight decreases with distance. Lines of varying distance can taper. The illustration at left categorizes all the lines of a cube as the same, but the language can become much subtler by further varying the line weights within each cube.

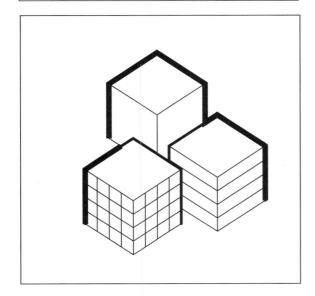

Contours and Depth

Primary contours record edges where one of their defining surfaces can be seen. Therefore, to one side of the contour is the surface that the contour is defining, and to the other there is some distance or depth of space until another surface is encountered. The greater the depth, the heavier the contour line. This language is a development of the spatial profiling cues.

CONTOUR LANGUAGE

VALUE LANGUAGE

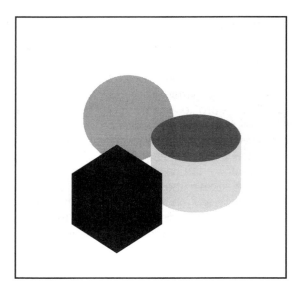

Value and Color

Value directly represents the color of the surface. Whatever color (value, hue, chroma) that a surface possesses is represented in the drawing. If the surface is dark red, the surface is drawn dark red. Issues of relative illumination and orientation of the surface are not considered. The liability of this language is that it tends to flatten and disguise form, as indicated in the illustration at left.

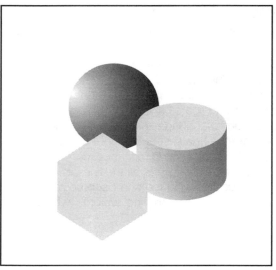

Value and Form

Value can delineate form by defining and differentiating surfaces. The simplest value and form language represents flat surfaces with uniform values and curved surfaces with tonal gradations. As in the value and color language, issues of relative illumination and orientation of the surface are not considered; here too the liability of the language is that it can flatten and disguise form, as indicated in the illustration at left.

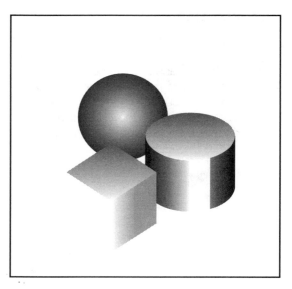

Value and Texture

If a surface has some perceivable textural qualities, then value can represent the surface's textural gradients. A surface that is directly facing the observer has a uniform textural gradient and is represented by a uniform value. A surface that is oblique to the observer has a varying textural gradient and is represented by a gradation that goes from light to dark as it moves away from the observer. A textured surface will also appear darker as it turns away from the observer—as it moves from perpendicular to parallel to the observer's line of sight.

Diagrams and text: Courtesy of William R. Benedict, Assistant Professor California Polytechnic State University College of Architecture & Environmental Design, San Luis Obispo, California

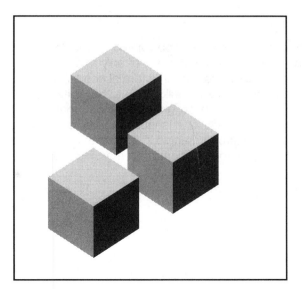

Value and Orientation

Using value to represent orientation requires the assumption of a light source. A surface's value corresponds to its orientation to the light source. In this example, flat surfaces are represented by uniform values. The values are then adjusted to represent the surface's orientation to the assumed light source. The surfaces most directly facing the source are the lightest, and the surfaces facing most directly away from the source are darkest. Surfaces with the same orientation receive the same value no matter where they are within the drawing.

Value and Shadow

This language builds on the orientation language. The orientation of the surfaces to the light source must be established before shadows can be cast. Once the orientation is established, shadows are cast and values are adjusted for reflected light. The example at left shows all values as flat or even. In reality, bounced light modifies the values.

Value and Distance

Value is also affected by the aerial cues of contrast and blueness. The closest cubes will have the greatest contrast within themselves and with the environment, while those farther away will have less. Furthermore, as the cubes get farther away, they move toward a middle gray because of the intervening atmosphere.

VALUE LANGUAGE

SUN/SHADE/SHADOW/VALUE LANGUAGE

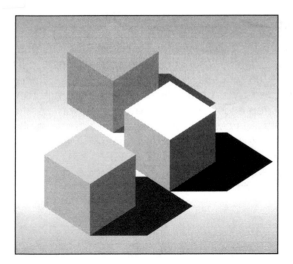

Sun, Shade, and Shadow

This language employs an abbreviated vocabulary and grammar. The vocabulary consists of only three continuous values and responds to three formal conditions. The surfaces that are in direct sunlight are to be white, those that are in shade are to be gray, and those that are in shadow are to be black. This language tends to abstract reality and create strong graphic images with sharp contrast. It is useful in compositional and massing studies.

Orientation, Shadow, and Texture

In this combination the orientation and shadow languages have been enriched to include gradations created by the surface's textures. The textural gradations cause the surfaces to get darker as they move away from the viewer. This is true for all surfaces not parallel to the face of the viewer. The greater the angle, the more dramatic the gradation.

Created in Fractal Design Painter

Value and Expression

The technique used, media, key (value or tonal range), and distribution of values within a drawing can support different moods—freehand is different from drafted, pen is different from pencil, high key is different from low key, and variegated is different from uniform. Each combination will create a different mood.

A high-key drawing is one in which all the values are at the light end of the value scale, while a low-key drawing is the opposite.

The scale and shape of the marks—the style or technique used to create the values—also influence the expression of the drawing and communicate additional meaning. The example at left feels very different from the previous drawings.

Diagrams and text: Courtesy of William R. Benedict, Assistant Professor California Polytechnic State University College of Architecture & Environmental Design, San Luis Obispo, California

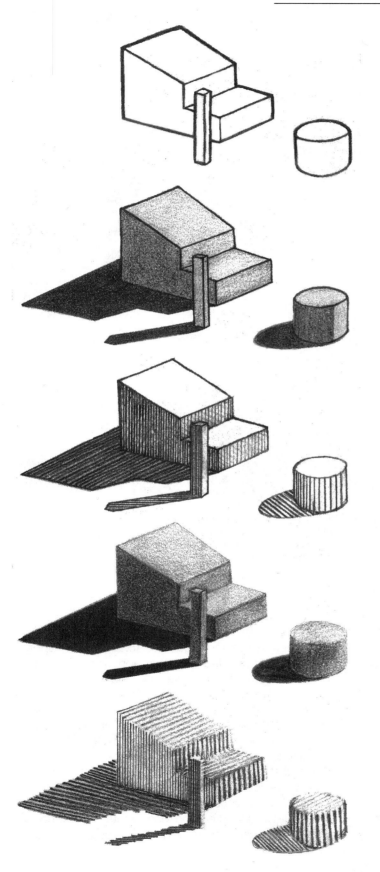

Line with space-defining edges accented (profiled)

Profiling or silhouetting gives a needed contour to help define any form against negative space.

Line with **value**

Shadow is rendered darker than shade. Silhouetting against negative space is normally not done.

Line with **value** of **lines**

Planar edges are defined by both line and value of lines. Silhouetting against negative space is normally not done. For directional reinforcement, use vertical lines for vertical planes and horizontal or near horizontal lines for horizontal planes.

Value

Planes rendered with different pure values define planar edges. Shadow is rendered darker than shade.

Value of **lines**

Planar edges are defined when two planes, each with a value of lines, meet. A flat plane uses evenly spaced lines. A curvilinear form uses unevenly spaced lines (see p. 323).

SUN/SHADE/SHADOW/VALUE LANGUAGE

Stippling is used to build up shade and value. Its objective of modeling form is the same as that of the linear technique of cross-hatching (see p. 381). By varying the size and spacing of dots, one can create tone values and model form. This dot technique is called "pointillism" and originated with the French artists (Georges Seurat, etc.) who made experiments with light and vision (see p. 389). Although quite time-consuming, this method gives excellent control over gradations and produces a copylike quality. Note the stippling for the sky area in the villa rendering and on the building exterior on the facing page.

Hatching is the use of approximately parallel (short or long) lines in a tonal arrangement in order to portray surface or form. It can describe light, space, and material as an abstraction of reality (see sky and glass on p. 425).

Rendering: Philothei Villa, Greece
24" × 36" (61 × 91.4 cm), Scale: ⅛"=1'0"
Courtesy of Hugh Newell Jacobsen, FAIA, Architect,
and Stephen S. Evanusa, Architect

Drawing: Van Kirk House, San Francisco, California, 1991
7.5" × 7.5" (19.1 × 19.1 cm), Scale: ¼"=1'0"
Medium: Pen and ink
Courtesy of James Shay, AIA Architect

This style of rendering communicates visual tonal values very effectively. The high contrast achieved creates a lot of visual "snap."
[ARCHITECT'S STATEMENT]

Scribbling is used to produce a tonal value by applying randomly directed lines that appear haphazard in their arrangement (see foreground above). Pen and ink is an excellent medium for producing a variety of stroke patterns. These illustrations show the use of straight and curved lines, cross-hatched lines, and dots to give excellent tonal values. Regardless of the technique, the density of tone produced gives the needed contrast. Different stroke techniques are often used in combination to depict shape clusters. The number of techniques that should be employed is dependent on how much detail and precision one wants. Spontaneous loose, imprecise strokes are more suggestive and symbolic.

Drawing: Student project by Richard Tsai
          Interior study
Medium: Ink on Mylar
Courtesy of Washington University
School of Architecture, St. Louis, Missouri

The rendering at right is an exercise using dots or very short strokes with the objective of creating a line drawing. Only dots of varying intensity and dimension were used. The effect of lines is created with dots only. The student begins this exercise by carefully studying shade and shadow conditions on the building.

When rendering shades or cast shadows on surfaces, there should be a transparent quality. We should be able to see through the applied value and recognize the detailed aspects of the surfaces' form and texture.

Drawing: Student project by Roosevelt Sanders
Medium: Ink on Mylar
M. Saleh Uddin, Professor, Savannah College of Art and Design,
Savannah, GA; Southern University, Baton Rouge, Louisiana

APPLICATION OF VALUE SCALES AND TONING TECHNIQUES

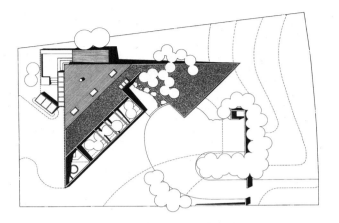

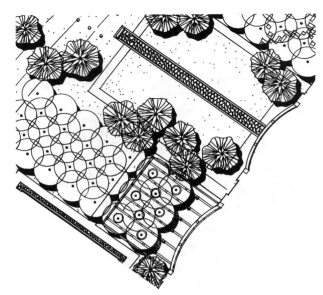

Drawing: Brugler residence, The Sea Ranch, California
20" × 15" (50.8 × 38.1 cm), Scale: ⅛"=1'0"
Medium: Rapidograph ink pen
Courtesy of Obie G. Bowman, Architect AIA

TREES IN PLAN

There are numerous ways to depict an abstract rendered tree in plan. The nature and quantity of abstract detail is dependent on the scale and objective of the drawing. Different types of plan trees can be interchanged. Deciduous and coniferous trees are commonly rendered. Coniferous trees (below middle) are delineated with radiating bicycle-spokelike lines. Sometimes smaller trees and shrubs are clustered as a group with one continuous outline.

Drawing (partial): Takamiya
Country Club
Hiroshima, Japan
Medium: Pencil
ED2 International Architects
Courtesy of the SWA Group

Note the range of the plan tree types above, from a simple circle to more elaborate forms. Ground textures can give a value contrast that causes the trees to have distinct edges. Trees, ground textures, and other plan entourage should always complement and be secondary to the architectural building elements to which they are adjacent. Site plan entourage provides vital field–background (dark–light) tonal contrast to give added drawing depth.

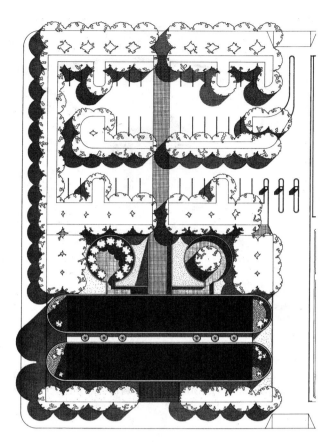

Drawing: Savings Association Headquarters
Denver, Colorado
24" × 32" (61 × 81.3 cm), Scale: ¹⁄₁₀"=1'0"
Medium: Ink on vellum with pressure-applied screens (Zipatone)
Courtesy of James Ream FAIA, San Francisco, California

Note at left the use of both tree plan and much smaller shrub plan symbols. These symbols, along with ground cover texture symbols, constitute the three most important landscape vegetation symbols. The trees shown in both of these rendered site plans nicely complement the building forms that they are near. Added depth is given to both site plans by the use of cast shadows. Circular trees cast circular shadows. Draw with a circle template. A sense of depth can be achieved by a slight displacement of one circle forming two intersecting circles. When circular shadows are cast as a whole group (left), the sense of depth achieved can be very effective.

Trees in plan fall into two categories: (1) sectional trees, as shown on the facing page, in which a horizontal cut reveals branching, trunk size, and foliage (or no foliage); and (2) nonsectional trees (overhead view), in which shade on the foliage gives a three-dimensional effect. When plan tree symbols overlap, as in the Takamiya Country Club drawing on the facing page, care must be taken not to obscure or completely block any plan symbol.

Drawing: Amancio Ergina Village
San Francisco, California
24" × 36" (61 × 91.4 cm), Scale: ¹⁄₁₆"=1'0"
Medium: Ink on vellum
Courtesy of Daniel Solomon FAIA

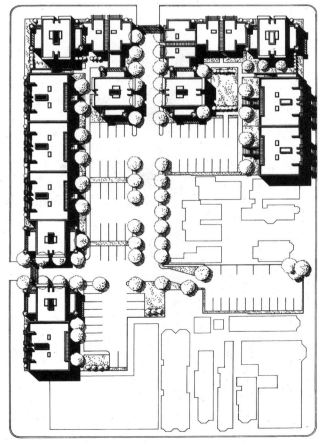

TREES IN PLAN

GROUND TEXTURES FOR SOFT SURFACES

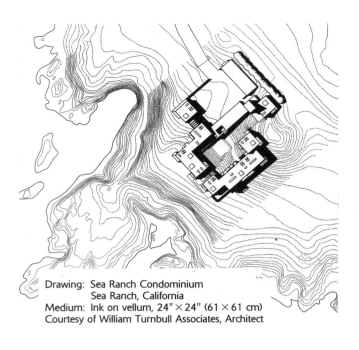

Drawing: Sea Ranch Condominium
 Sea Ranch, California
Medium: Ink on vellum, 24" × 24" (61 × 61 cm)
Courtesy of William Turnbull Associates, Architect

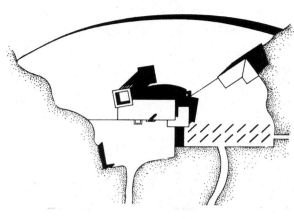

Drawing: Bargonetti, Kent, Connecticut
11" × 14" (27.9 × 35.6 cm), Scale: 1"=32'0"
Medium: Ink on Mylar
Courtesy of Steven Harris & Associates, Architect

There are many ways to indicate groundcover for soft surfaces such as grass. Clockwise from upper left: (1) contour lines; (2) dot clusters; and (3) short lines ordered into layers defining contours. When rendering ground line textures, it is less confusing when the lines are even and consistent in line width.

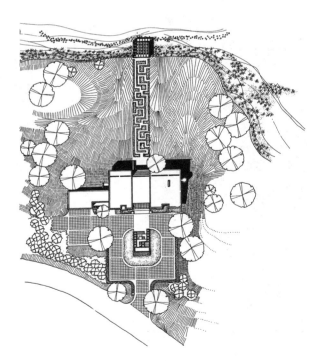

Drawing: Private house, southeastern Michigan
20" × 30" (50.8 × 76.2 cm), Scale: 1"=30'0"
Medium: Ink on vellum
Courtesy of William Kessler and Associates Architects

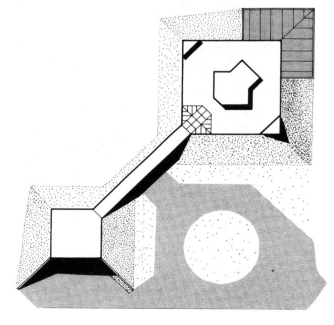

Drawing: Private residence, Gainsville, Florida
24" × 24" (61 × 61 cm), Scale: ⅛"=1'0"
Medium: Ink on Mylar film with Zipatone shading
Courtesy of William Morgan FAIA,
William Morgan Architects, P.A.

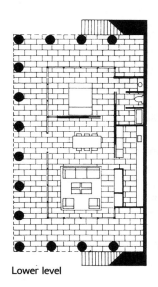 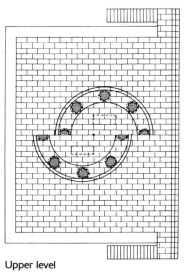

Lower level　　　　Upper level

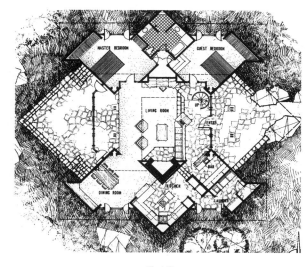

First floor

Drawing: Two crypts near Athens, Greece
24" × 36" (61 × 91.4 cm), Scale ⅛"=1'0"
Courtesy of Hugh Newell Jacobsen FAIA

Drawing: Davenport house, Evergreen, Colorado
18" × 24" (45.7 × 61 cm), Scale: ¼"=1'0"
Medium: Ink on vellum
Courtesy of Fay Jones + Maurice Jennings, Architects

Landscaping indication symbols for hard surfaces should be consistent with the interior floor material of the building they surround. These symbols provide a clue as to how the interior relates to its adjacent transitional spaces as well as to its external landscape/environment.

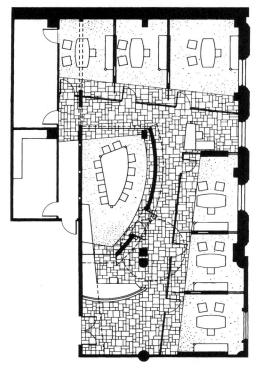

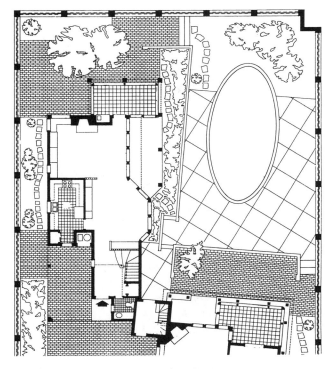

Drawing: Shinko Management, Beverly Hills, California
24" × 36" (61 × 91.4 cm), Scale: ¼"=1'0"
Medium: Ink on Mylar
Courtesy of David Kellen, Architect

Drawing: Salasky/Sedel house, Virginia Beach, Virginia
30" × 40" (76.2 × 101.6 cm), Scale: ⅛"=1'0"
Medium: Ink on Mylar
Courtesy of B FIVE STUDIO

GROUND TEXTURES FOR HARD SURFACES

RENDERING FLOORSCAPE

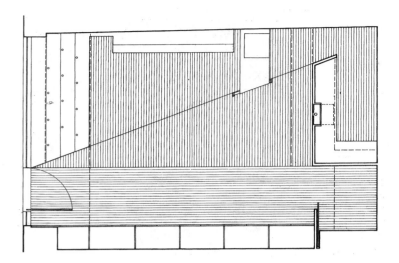

Drawing: Kinder Kind Shop I
Repulse Bay, Hong Kong, China
14" × 10" (35.6 × 25.4 cm)
Medium: Ink on Mylar, Scale: 1:20
Courtesy of Tsao & McKown Architects

As with ground textures, the rendition of materials within the plan view helps to give depth through contrast with an otherwise flat two-dimensional plan. Major circulation areas can be quickly identified when defined with a uniform tone value (see below). Floorscape is normally the material symbol of the actual material seen presented in a simplified technique.

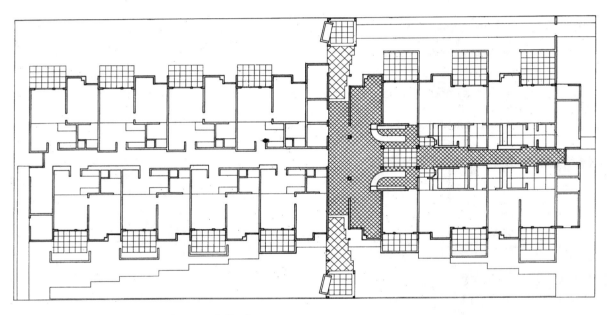

Drawing: Plymouth Place Housing, Stockton, California
31" × 36" (78.7 × 91.4 cm), Scale: ⅛"=1'0"
Medium: Ink
Courtesy of John V. Mutlow, FAIA, Architects

The rendition of floor patterns in a two-dimensional plan assists in the understanding of the design intention of the project. The floorscape identifies the areas of public circulation space, the sequence of the public spaces and accentuates the principle elements, the major axis and the circulation. The variation in floor pattern intensity differentiates the inside space from the outside; and the diagonal to the square pattern, the public to the private.
[ARCHITECT'S STATEMENT]

Most ground floor plans show the relationship of the interior floorscape to the immediate exterior landscape. Thus, the surrounding area not occupied by the building plan should be rendered with a ground texture (see the Salasky/Sedel house on the previous page).

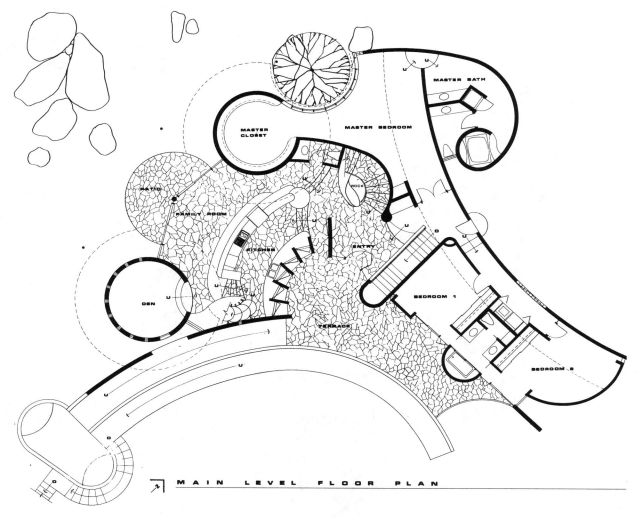

MAIN LEVEL FLOOR PLAN

Drawing: Prince house, Albuquerque, New Mexico
24" × 36" (61 × 91.4 cm), Scale: ¼"=1'0"
Courtesy of Bart Prince, Architect

*This drawing done in pencil on Mylar indicates the floor areas, which are to be finished in random slate stone.
Note that the stone paving continues uninterrupted from the inside to the outside and over floor level changes,
thus integrating several areas and increasing the sense of space.*
[ARCHITECT'S STATEMENT]

A better understanding of how to represent floorscape and the surrounding groundscape can be achieved by observing how artificial light and sunlight affects these materials: Make a careful study of interior floor materials as well as exterior masonry and cobblestone walks, concrete paving, rock/gravel beds, wooden decks, and patios. Practice rendering abstract graphic representations for all of these using both pen and pencil.

FLOOR SURFACE MATERIAL INDICATIONS

GROUND SURFACE INDICATIONS

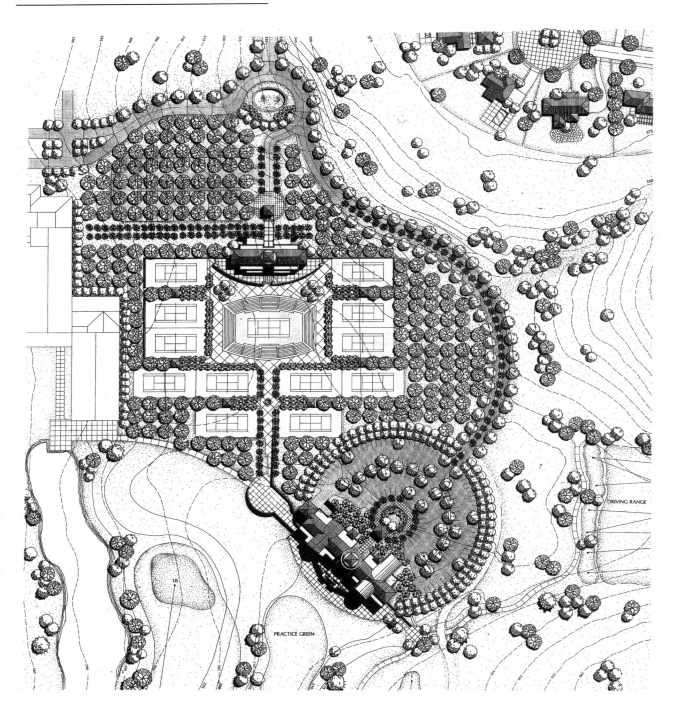

Drawing: ATP Tennis Center/ TPC Clubhouse, Black Mountain Ranch
        San Diego County, California
30" × 42" (76.2 × 106.7 cm), Scale: 1"=40'
Medium: Ink on Mylar
Courtesy of Sandy & Babcock Inc., Architecture & Planning

As the size of a site plan becomes larger and larger, less and less detail is needed to indicate a tree in plan. Regardless of the scale, a value differentiation between the trees and the ground cover must be maintained.

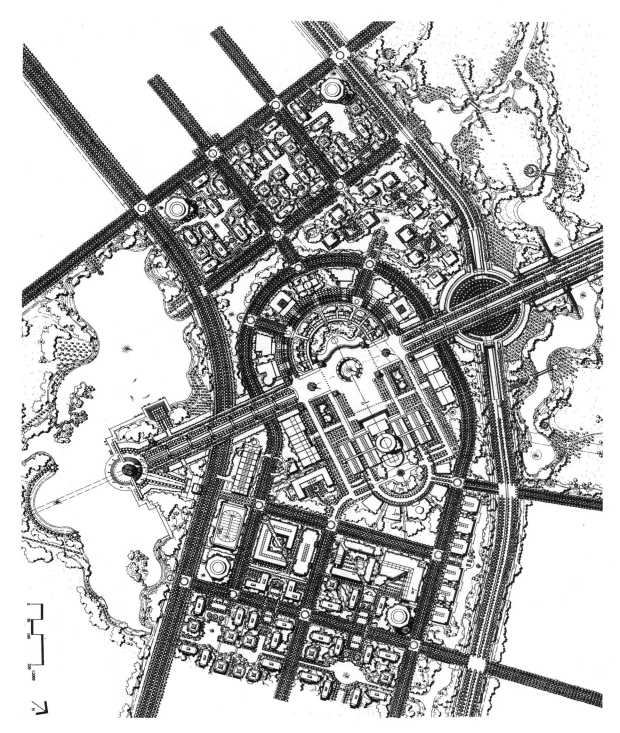

GROUND SURFACE INDICATIONS

Drawing: Shanghai Civic Center District, Shanghai, China
36" × 48" (91.4 × 121.9 cm), Scale: 1:2000
Medium: Pencil
Drawn by John L. Wong, Landscape Architect
Courtesy of The SWA Group

In this site plan, the trees no longer "read" as individual trees, but rather as a clustered group that produces a dense value and a circulation pattern.

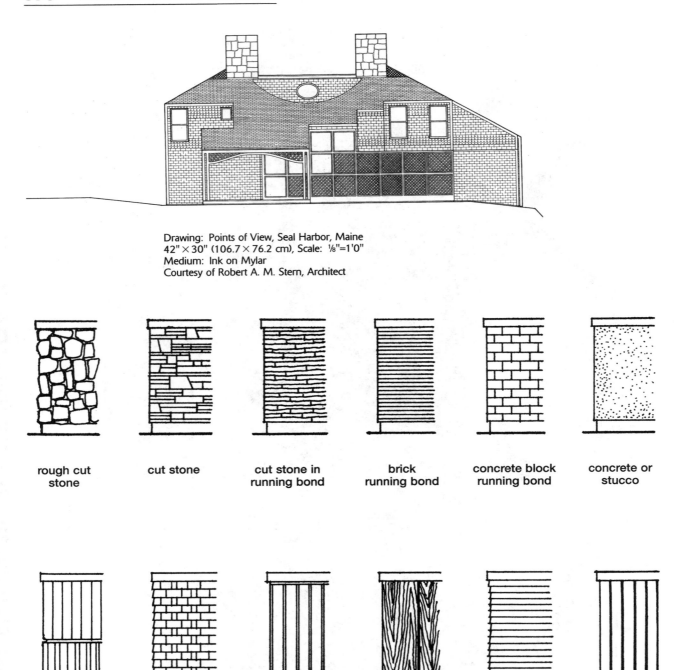

Drawing: Points of View, Seal Harbor, Maine
42" × 30" (106.7 × 76.2 cm), Scale: ⅛"=1'0"
Medium: Ink on Mylar
Courtesy of Robert A. M. Stern, Architect

ELEVATION MATERIAL SYMBOLS

rough cut
stone

cut stone

cut stone in
running bond

brick
running bond

concrete block
running bond

concrete or
stucco

concrete with
board forms

shingle siding

board and batten—
normal or reverse
siding

plywood

lap siding

vertical siding

As with floorscape, building elevations are commonly rendered with material symbols in order to accentuate their typical flatness and communicate building material choices. Generally, the materials are drawn simplified because of the small scales used. The material texture indication symbols above are selected examples. Material textures rendered on plan obliques and perspectives are, for the most part, similar to their corresponding elevation textures (see the many examples in this chapter).

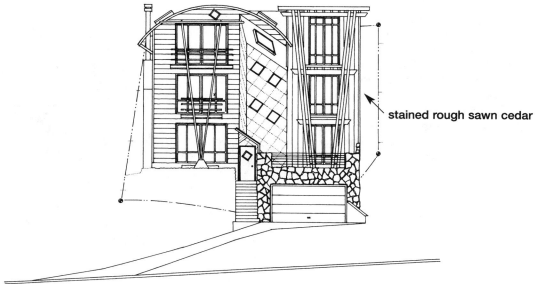

stained rough sawn cedar

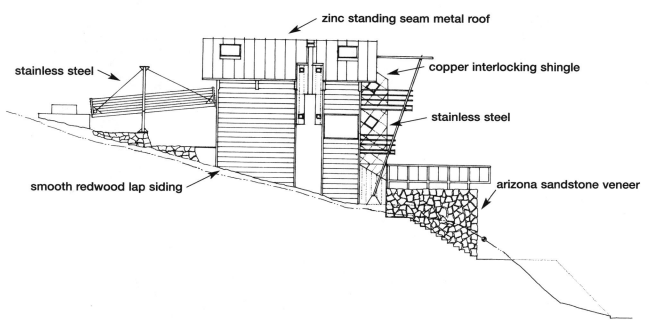

zinc standing seam metal roof

stainless steel

copper interlocking shingle

stainless steel

smooth redwood lap siding

arizona sandstone veneer

ELEVATION MATERIAL SYMBOLS

Drawing: Schuh Box (unbuilt), hills above San Francisco Bay
Medium: Ink on trace
Courtesy of David Baker Associates Architects

Distinct natural-finish materials, such as copper, zinc, stainless steel, transparent stain on rough sawn cedar, smooth red-wood, and Arizona sandstone, are used to code the distinct volumetric elements that compose this design.
[ARCHITECT'S STATEMENT]

Floor and elevation material symbols are commonly shown in pictorial drawings such as obliques, axonometrics, and perspectives. In this example, wall and floor material textures help enhance the powerful spatial quality that is created. In these two drawings, note the extensive use of material texture (porcelain enamel panels, concrete blocks, etc.) on both horizontal and vertical planes.

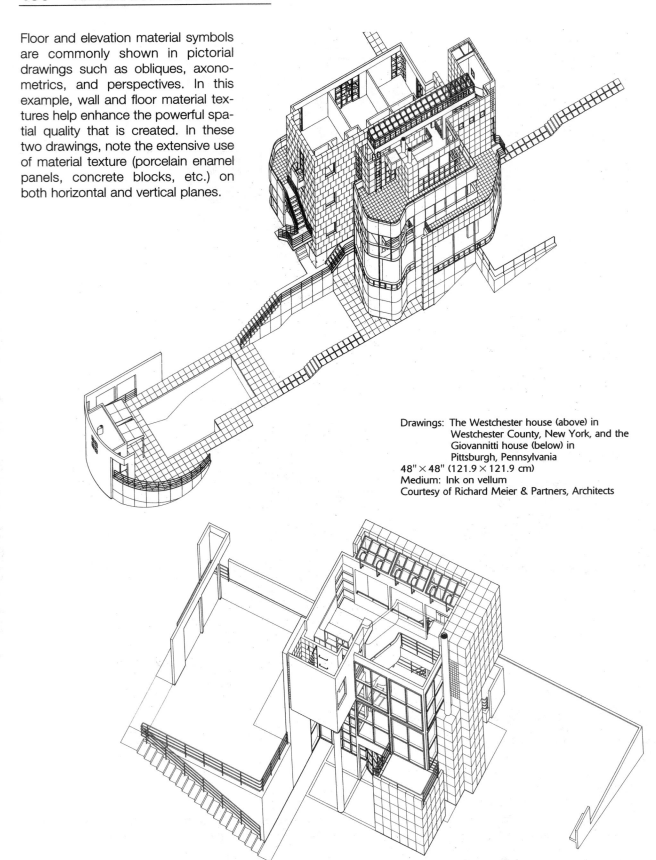

Drawings: The Westchester house (above) in Westchester County, New York, and the Giovannitti house (below) in Pittsburgh, Pennsylvania
48" × 48" (121.9 × 121.9 cm)
Medium: Ink on vellum
Courtesy of Richard Meier & Partners, Architects

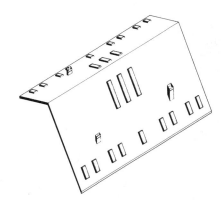

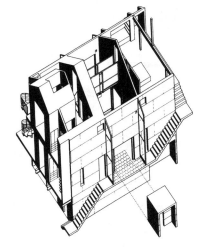

The exploded axonometric view was selected to express the conceptual basis of this design: the creation of a tectonic dialogue between past and present. A contemporary dwelling, articulated as a new wooden "box," is inserted within the old stone shell of a Pennsylvania barn. A family of other new elements, clad in metal and abstracted from nearby agrarian forms, engage the exterior of the stone shell at various places.
[ARCHITECT'S STATEMENT]

MATERIAL SYMBOLS

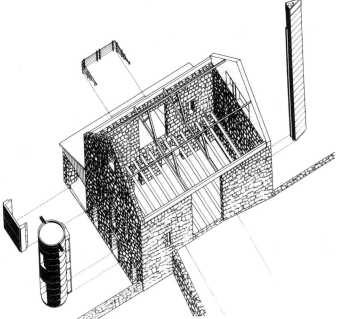

Drawing: Martin residence
Kennett Square, Pennsylvania
20" × 48" (50.8 × 121.9 cm), Scale: ¼"=1'0"
Medium: Ink on Mylar
Courtesy of Tanner Leddy Maytum Stacy Architects

This exploded drawing of a design scheme of a "box inside a box" shows a small box faced with cherrywood inside a large rough stone shell. The material symbols on the walls are easily identifiable.

DELINEATING TREES

Drawing: The Moir Building
San Jose, California
36" × 42" (91.4 × 106.7 cm)
Medium: Pentel on vellum
Courtesy of Jerome King, AIA
Renderer: Barney Davidge Associates

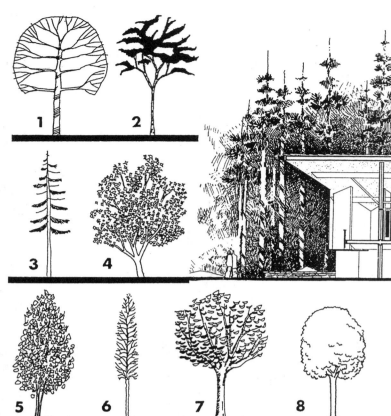

Drawing: Rendered trees, Davenport house,
Evergreen, Colorado
18" × 24" (45.7 × 61 cm), Scale: ¼"=1'0"
Medium: Ink on vellum
Courtesy of Fay Jones + Maurice Jennings, Architects

Rendered trees can show branching (**3** and **6**), branching with outline (**1**), partial texture with outline (**8**), full texture (**2**, **4**, and **5**), or full texture with shade (**7**). Texture with shade is based on directional sunlight. Trees form a parachute shape as they react to gravity.

Drawing: Foliage texture for foreground trees
Medium: Ink on vellum
Herbert Cuevas, AIA Architect
Courtesy of Brigette Nalley

Symbolic trees can be abstract or representational. They should always complement rather than compete with or overpower the human-built environment they are surrounding. Trees can be made darker (top right) or lighter than the building they are behind to give more contrast. Tracing excellent existing delineated tree examples will build up your graphic vocabulary for these symbols.

TREES IN PERSPECTIVE

Drawing: The Peninsula Regent, San Mateo, California
24" × 24" (61 × 61 cm)
Medium: Ink
Courtesy of Backen Arrigoni & Ross, Inc. Architecture, Planning & Interior Design
Peter Szasz, Architectural Illustrator

Trees and other vegetation, human figures, furniture, moving vehicles, and ground textures are defined as **entourage** (French for "surroundings") in an architectural rendering. These supporting elements should always complement the human-built environment, not compete with it. Accurately drawn entourage also helps to give scale to the drawing.

The trees in this illustration and on the following page are quite detailed and realistic in appearance. When delineating abstract or realistic trees in perspective, you can create more visual interest to the composition by changing the height of the trees; and you can add more depth to the rendering by casting ground shadows (see p. 404).

FOREGROUND TREES

Drawing: Burnett residence, 17 Mile Drive, Pebble Beach, California
36" × 24" (91.4 × 61 cm)
Medium: Pen and ink on Mylar
Simpson Gumpertz & Heger, Inc., Architects
Courtesy of Markus Lui & Associates, Architectural Illustrators

Foliage texture for foreground trees should exhibit more detail. The more highly detailed a symbolic tree, the more time-consuming it will be to draw. These foreground trees frame the building in the background. The sun is behind the observer causing ground shadows that are cast away from the observer. This location for the light source permits both sides of the building to be in sunlight. The foreground tree trunk bark texture and the foreground grass are both rendered darker than the background tree trunks and background grass.

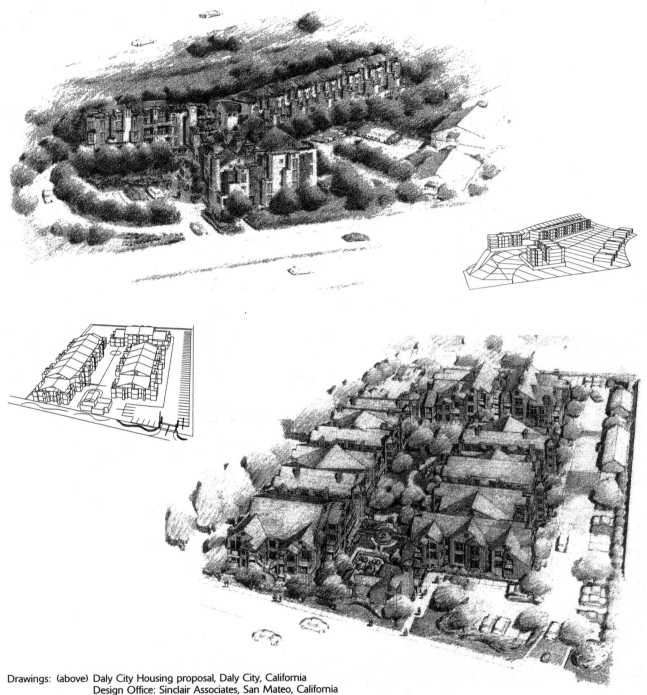

TREES IN BIRD'S-EYE VIEW

Drawings: (above) Daly City Housing proposal, Daly City, California
Design Office: Sinclair Associates, San Mateo, California
(below) Santa Clara Housing Project, Santa Clara, California
Client: Santa Clara development
Both 20" × 30" (50.8 × 76.2 cm)
Courtesy of Lawrence Ko Leong, Architectural Illustrator

Drawing method: First, an AutoCAD wire-frame massing model was done to select a viewpoint and as a base for a black and white Prismacolor pencil hand drawing. A baseline print is made with intense colored pencil colors. The black and white version was done so the client could use it for monochrome copies. For both landscaping and building, "soft," short, even strokes were used to give a smooth, consistent look and feel.
[ARCHITECTURAL ILLUSTRATOR'S STATEMENT]

DELINEATING INTERIOR VEGETATION

Drawing: 1333 Broadway, Oakland, California
36" × 24" (91.4 × 61 cm)
Medium: Pen and ink on Mylar
ED2 International, Richard Hom, Architects
Courtesy of Markus Lui & Associates, Architectural Illustrators

Interior vegetation should complement and not overpower interior architecture. The plant in the right foreground above increases the feeling of perspective depth in the interior space. The lower perspective on the facing page is a good example of a "fudged one-point," also called a "soft two-point." A soft two-point is essentially a one-point view with a very long second vanishing point. The effect is basically of a one-point, but is less "static." This very natural drawing type was a favorite of Frank Lloyd Wright (see Bibliography).

Drawing: 12-plex motion picture theater, Gateway Center, Arizona
36" × 24" (91.4 × 61 cm)
Medium: Pen and ink on Mylar
Vincent Raney, AIA, Architect
Courtesy of Markus Lui & Associates, Architectural Illustrators

Like trees, plant and shrub vegetation can be simplistically symbolic or realistically detailed.

Drawing: Cheeca Lodge Resort, Islamadora, Florida
24" × 13" (61 × 33 cm)
Medium: Pencil on vellum
Courtesy of Simon Martin–Vegue Winkelstein Moris
Interior design and illustration by G. Lawrence Saber

DELINEATING EXTERIOR AND INTERIOR VEGETATION

DELINEATING EXTERIOR VEGETATION

Drawings: AQIS (Australian Quarantine Inspection Service)
Brisbane, Australia
23.6" × 11.8" (60 × 30 cm)
Medium: Ink, pencil, and pastel
Architect: Donovan Hill
Client: Brisbane Airport Corporation
Courtesy of Jane Grealy, Architectural Illustrator, 2000

DELINEATING EXTERIOR VEGETATION

This is a recent project for which I used a different approach. I had been studying the illustrations of urban theorist and designer Gordon Cullen (1914–1994). His work was always beautifully composed and I was particularly attracted to the textural qualities of the Biot series (1967). I resolved to concentrate on the composition of my drawing, completing four or five studies of four different views. Small-scale studies were done quickly by overlaying the computer-generated line drawing with detail paper and by adding tone using a black drawing pencil. I used two (right-angled) cardboard mats to frame the drawing and experimented until I found a composition that had some potential for further development. Two views were chosen and they were enlarged so that they could be placed on the full-sized sheet layout.

Attention was paid to the landscaping detail and the black and white part of the perspective was hand drawn using black felt pen and pencil. This was printed onto acetate and placed over a sheet of gray Stonehenge paper onto which the background color of pastel and pencil was applied. When choosing the color palette, I wanted a restrained, almost monochromatic effect to reflect the colors of the building materials used. I experimented with color combinations, often referring to landscape photographs where such palettes might occur naturally. The drawing was intended to be viewed with the black line and tone as dominant and the color muted and subtle. It is interesting to see the line drawing and color drawing as separate and supplementary images. It has been told that this drawing has a "sixties" feel, so perhaps Gordon Cullen's influence is showing through!

[ARCHITECTURAL ILLUSTRATOR'S STATEMENT]

DELINEATING HUMAN FIGURES

¹⁄₁₆"=1'0"

⅛"=1'0"

¼"=1'0"

⅜"=1'0"

Grouped figures (2nd row left)
Medium: Ink
Courtesy of Martin Liefhebbe,
Barton Myers Associates, Architects

Grouped figures (5th row left)
Medium: Ink
Courtesy of Chun/Ishimaru,
Architectural Illustrators

Keep in mind the following when using human figures:

- Figures show the scale of a drawing.
- Figures are secondary to the architecture.
- Figures should not cover space defining intersections.
- Figures should imply activity yet not be shown to be over-active.
- Figures should have simple details for clothes.
- Grouped figures should show overlap (see pp. 412–413).

Drawing (partial): Walking figures
Medium: Ink
Courtesy of Chun/Ishimaru & Assoc.,
Architectural Illustrators

Keep a reference clipping file of photographs and drawings of people in different poses singly as well as in groups. Use a Polaroid camera or a digital camera (with a computer and printer) to freeze figure images for future referrals. These photos can be reduced or enlarged on a copier to suit the size of your drawing.

½"=1'0"

The people in the drawing at right are abstract, with little or no clothing detail. Abstract figures (either with contour outline or with gray shades) are usually adequate for most drawings. Clothing detail for figures is dependent on the scales, style, and intent of the drawing.

Drawing (partial): East Wing of the National Gallery of Art
                    Washington, D.C.
Entire original: 21" × 14" (53.3 × 35.6 cm)
Medium: Black Prismacolor on vellum
Pei, Cobb, Freed, and Partners, Architects
Courtesy of Paul Stevenson Oles FAIA, Renderer

Drawing (partial): Waterfront Development Plan
                    Asbury Park, New Jersey
Medium: Ink
Courtesy of Koetter, Kim & Associates, Inc.
Architects and Urban Designers

As the scale of the human figure increases in size, a simple form without clothing detail is no longer adequate. When adding clothing detail, keep it to a minimum so as not to distract from the architectural subject. The drawing at right successfully keeps clothing detail minimal, as it adds important human scale for the background building. Avoid drawing extremes in clothing fashion, which often tend to be "eye-catching."

Drawing: Renovation Santa Fe Depot, San Diego, California
          Hanna/Olin Ltd. Landscape Architecture
16" × 24" (40.6 × 61 cm)
Medium: Full watercolor over pencil line transfer
Courtesy of Al Forster, Architectural Illustrator

DELINEATING HUMAN FIGURES

HUMAN FIGURES AND THE HORIZON LINE

Drawing: University of Maryland Center for the Performing Arts competition winner
          Moore Ruble Yudell Architects
18" × 12" (45.7 × 30.5 cm)
Medium: Sketch watercolor on mounted presentation
blackline print of ink line drawing
Courtesy of Al Forster, Architectural Illustrator

In the perspective above, note that almost all of the human heads are on the observer's horizon line. It does not matter whether the figure is closer to or farther away from the observer. If the human figure is taller than the observer, his or her eyes will be above the horizon line. Likewise, the same relationship is valid for a shorter human figure. On the facing page, the children standing have their heads below the horizon line. Figures on higher elevations (see staircase above) are far above the observer's eye level.

Drawing: Proposed NTC Navy housing playground area, San
        Diego, California
Fehlman Labarre Architecture & Planning
18" × 12" (45.7 × 30.5 cm)
Medium: Full watercolor over pencil line transfer
People overlay courtesy of Al Forster, Architectural Illustrator

Human figures should be well distributed in a perspective drawing in order to give a proper sense of depth. This distribution should be in three zones: the foreground, or the area nearest to the observer; the middleground, or the area that has the observer's attention (building on facing page and playground structure above); and the background, or the area behind that which has the observer's attention (smallest figures). When possible, carefully insert figures in the distinct areas of the foreground, the middleground, and the background, whether they be single or in a group.

HUMAN FIGURES AND THE HORIZON LINE

DELINEATING FURNITURE

Drawing: Villa Sheraton Senggigi
Indonesia
17" × 11" (43.2 × 27.9 cm)
Medium: Felt pen, markers, and
pencil crayons on white
tracing paper
Courtesy of the Timothy Seow
Group Architects

Furniture must suit the style of the interior space. Sofas and chairs are commonly seen in groups of two or more.

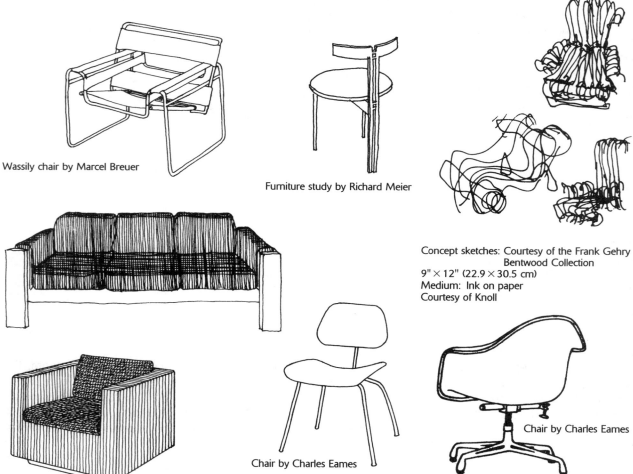

Wassily chair by Marcel Breuer

Furniture study by Richard Meier

Concept sketches: Courtesy of the Frank Gehry
Bentwood Collection
9" × 12" (22.9 × 30.5 cm)
Medium: Ink on paper
Courtesy of Knoll

Chair by Charles Eames

Chair by Charles Eames

Become familiar with good furniture design. Outstanding furniture has been designed by many noted architects, including Alvar Aalto, Charles Eames, Frank Lloyd Wright, Eero Saarinen, Marcel Breuer, Richard Meier, Frank Gehry, and Michael Graves. As for people and cars, keep a reference photo file.

Drawing: The Peninsula Regent, San Mateo, California
20" × 24" (50.8 × 61 cm)
Medium: Pencil on vellum
Courtesy of Backen Arrigoni & Ross, Inc.,
Architecture, Planning and Interior Design
Jim Gillam, Architectural Illustrator

DELINEATING FURNITURE

Furniture accessories, such as lighting elements, chairs, sofas, and tables, should complement the interior architecture and show how interior space is used. The size and scale of an interior space can be indicated when human figures are added with the furniture. Drawing properly scaled people in the interior space will help in drawing properly scaled furniture. It is easier to start with the scaled person first and then draw the piece of furniture on which he or she is sitting (see p. 407).

PLAN OBLIQUE ACCESSORIES: FURNITURE AND FIGURES

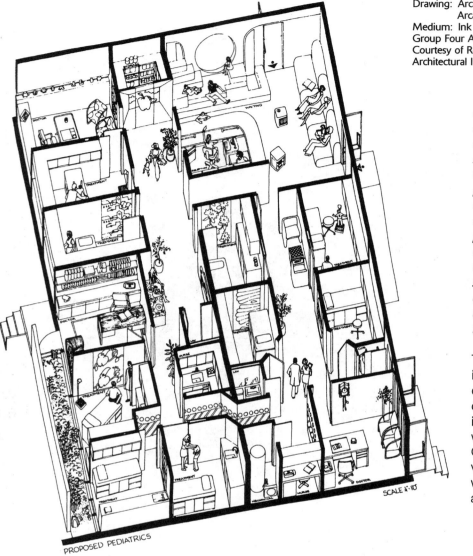

PROPOSED PEDIATRICS

75°–15°

Drawing: Arcadia Clinic
Arcadia, California
Medium: Ink
Group Four Architecture, Research, and Planning
Courtesy of Robin Chiang, Architect and
Architectural Illustrator

The projected drawing shown here depicts actual (to scale) room dimensions...including heights of walls and counters. As a preliminary sketch, this was an efficient method of presentation...giving an idea of the sorts of activities while allowing users to measure proposed scales. With one drawing, it was possible to convey information on a single sheet that was copied and distributed to fourteen users.
[ARCHITECT'S STATEMENT]

The plan oblique down view is the appropriate view when communicating interior accessories such as furnishings and examining how the walls meet the floor plane. Compare this with the up view on p. 172, where the walls meet the ceiling plane and ceiling structure.

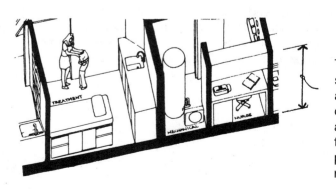

The height of the horizontal section (plan view) cut is usually taken slightly below the ceiling height (7' to 8'). This allows a clear view of important interior elements. People, plants, furniture, and columns retain verticality.

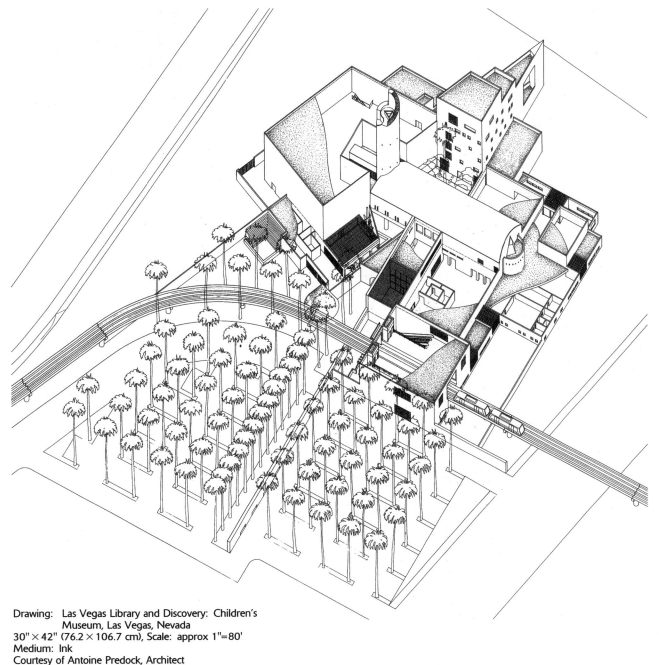

Drawing: Las Vegas Library and Discovery: Children's
          Museum, Las Vegas, Nevada
30" × 42" (76.2 × 106.7 cm), Scale: approx 1"=80'
Medium: Ink
Courtesy of Antoine Predock, Architect

The fragility of both the desert and the communities that colonize it is apparent when one views Las Vegas, Nevada, from the air. This confluence of nature, fantasy, urbanization, and science underscores the complexities of the desert environment and the task of making architecture responsive to its many faces.
[ARCHITECT'S STATEMENT]

Trees retain their verticality in plan obliques. In this drawing, a group of trees complements the building complex. Moving vehicles (trains, cars, etc.) also retain their verticality. The nice "partial roof removal" revealing technique allows the building to retain the feeling of a complete enclosure while at the same time permitting glimpses of the interior spaces.

PLAN OBLIQUE ACCESSORIES: TREES

DELINEATING CARS IN PLAN AND IN ELEVATION

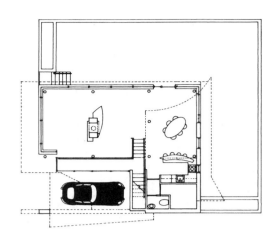

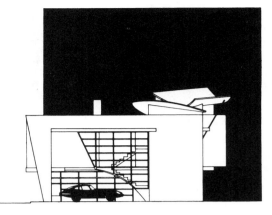

Drawings above: The Hague Villa Project
The Hague, The Netherlands
10" × 8" (25.4 × 20.3 cm), Scale: ¼"=1'0"
Medium: Pen and ink
Courtesy of Hariri & Hariri, Architects

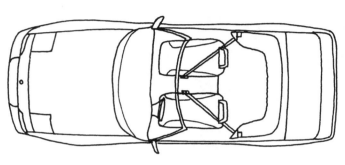

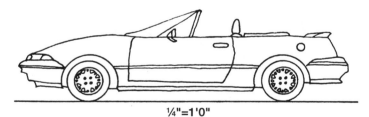

¼"=1'0"

Cars seen in the plan view are good scale indicators when placed on driveways and roadways in site plans. Likewise, cars seen in elevation, as with human figures, are good scale indicators for buildings. They can be symbolic as shown above or delineated with more detail.

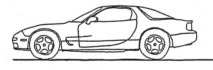

⅛"=1'0"

¼"=1'0"

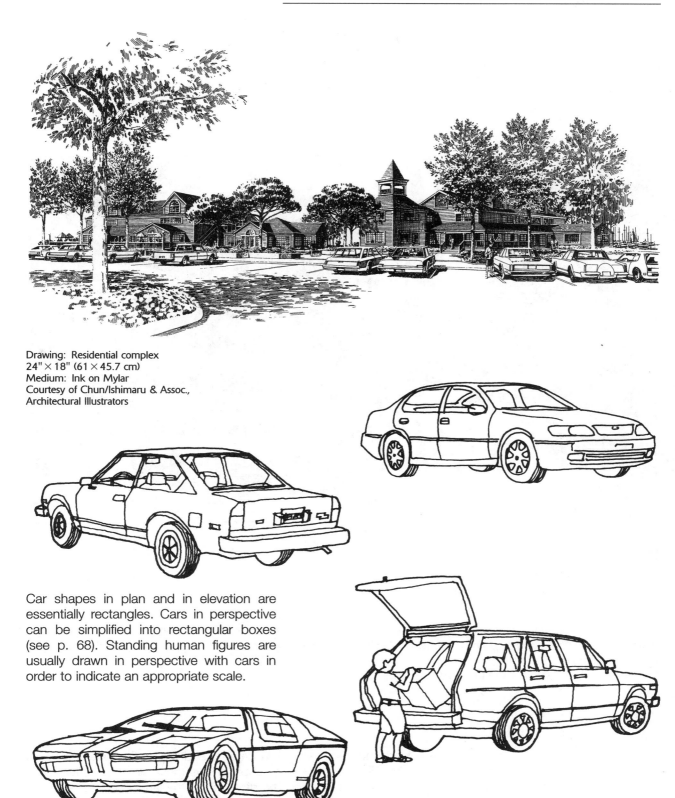

Drawing: Residential complex
24" × 18" (61 × 45.7 cm)
Medium: Ink on Mylar
Courtesy of Chun/Ishimaru & Assoc.,
Architectural Illustrators

Car shapes in plan and in elevation are essentially rectangles. Cars in perspective can be simplified into rectangular boxes (see p. 68). Standing human figures are usually drawn in perspective with cars in order to indicate an appropriate scale.

As with people and landscaping entourage, cars should complement the architecture. Keep a reference file of photos and drawings for cars. Periodically update this file with the latest car designs.

DELINEATING CARS IN PERSPECTIVE

RENDERING WATER REFLECTIONS

Drawing: Project, Japan
Courtesy of Projects International, Palo Alto
and Christopher Grubbs, Illustrator

Both water reflection drawings measure 8"×5" and were drawn with a Uniball Micro pen on Clearprint. These images represent the first of a two-step process in which the drawings were copied and Prismacolor was applied to the copies for a color version.
[ARCHITECTURAL ILLUSTRATOR'S STATEMENT]

Buildings or small structures in the urban landscape appear light in daylight and their reflections should be shown lighter than the value of the body of the water. The above example shows these elements reflected as pure white with minimal horizontal strokes within the white area. The dark part of the landscape (background trees) is reflected in the water with closely spaced short horizontal marks. The water reflections on both of these pages show slight agitation, with a general feeling of calmness and serenity. A horizontal reflection actually begins where the object reflected meets the reflecting surface. Part of the reflection may be concealed by a non-reflecting surface (see steps at lower left in the drawing above).

Water can be rendered either as **still** or with **ripples.** Still water is best illustrated with precise parallel **horizontal** lines. These can be equally spaced or unequally spaced at increasing intervals, depending on the nature of the body of water. Wave ripples have a convex and concave form that reflects objects at different angles. The resulting visual phenomenon is that of irregular stripes. Small **wavy** freehand lines produce the best results for depicting agitated water. In this river scene, the darker value of the boats reflects darker than the background foliage. Also note the multiple directions for the wavy lines to represent agitated water.

Drawing: Saigon City, Vietnam
Courtesy of Skidmore, Owings, and Merrill, San Francisco
and Christopher Grubbs, Illustrator

Shifting reflective water surfaces tend to intimidate the artist. But water is just as tangible a material as brick. The first rule is not to overdraw the surface. This is best achieved by planning ahead. In the preliminary drawing, flip upside-down those elements that will best express reflections. Anticipate the scale change of big strokes (foreground waves) versus tiny strokes (distant waves). Since water surfaces are so varied and quick to change, it's very important to establish a specific instant of time or condition for your scene and to anticipate the graphic implications: Is there a breeze rippling the surface or is it glassy? Is this a pond or an ocean?
[ARCHITECTURAL ILLUSTRATOR'S STATEMENT]

RENDERING WATER REFLECTIONS

RENDERING GLASS REFLECTIONS

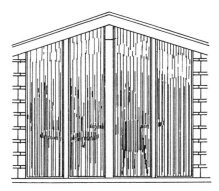

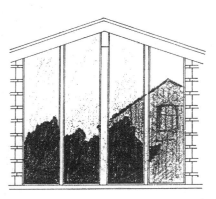

Most glass situations are reflective. A **nonreflective** situation results in a see-through transparency. Show human figures, vegetation, and furniture seen in the interior space to give a realistic effect. A **reflective** situation will show objects behind the observer, such as trees, buildings, vehicles, and the sky condition. A **partial reflective/partial transparent** situation shows objects (e.g., clouds) behind the observer as well as human figures and furniture within the space.

Drawing: New England Sunbox
　　　　　Methuen, Massachusetts
9" × 11" (22.9 × 27.9 cm)
Medium: Black Prismacolor on
　　　　　vellum with watercolor
　　　　　paper underlay
Courtesy of Interface Architects
Illustration: Paul Stevenson Oles, FAIA

This drawing is a straightforward example of wax-based pencil on vellum with a watercolor paper underlay. The reflections in the glazing were carefully plotted, using a folded-tracing device. To do this, plan elements were traced which will be seen as reflected, then the tracing was folded 180° about the axis (in plan) of the reflecting surface (glass, in this case), and the perspective image was constructed beyond the glass in exactly the usual way. Deciding on tonal values for superimposed images (real and virtual) is a little tricky and requires some analysis; but intuitive judgments allow a reasonably convincing depiction of transparent and reflective glazing. [ARCHITECTURAL ILLUSTRATOR'S STATEMENT]

Drawing: Student project by Corvin Matei
          D.A.R.T. (Dallas Rapid Transit Systems)
18" × 18" (45.7 × 45.7 cm)
Medium: 2B pencil on Strathmore paper
Courtesy of the University of Texas at Arlington
School of Architecture

This drawing is an investigative study rather than a straightforward representation of a space. It tries to convey the differences and similarities between "virtual" and "real." This is done by assigning different textures only to the surfaces important to the study. The glass, which is the focus of this drawing, is assigned the darkest tone, while other, unimportant areas are left blank. The sketches at the lower right are section and plan studies done simultaneously with the perspective; they become part of the study and help to better understand and develop the design of the piece.
[ARCHITECTURE STUDENT'S STATEMENT]

This reflection is typical of a night scene (dark exterior) and is caused by the artifical illumination inside the train. This is analogous to observed reflections on windows separating a dark interior from a sunlit exterior. In the daytime, a train traveller would experience completely transparent glass.

RENDERING GLASS REFLECTIONS

RENDERING GLASS REFLECTIONS

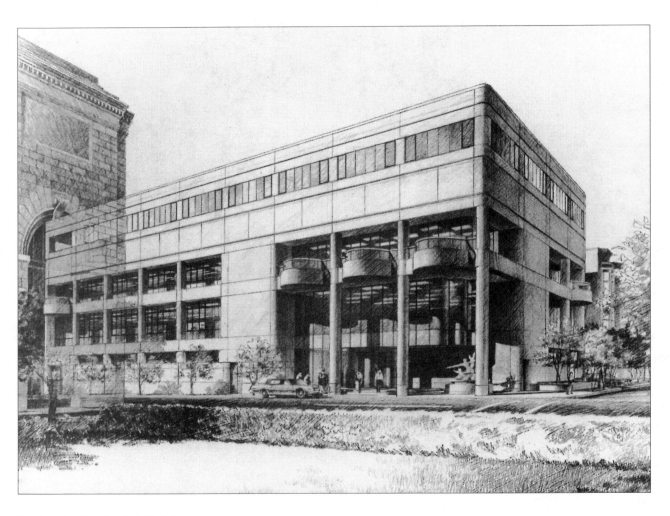

Drawing: San Francisco Ballet building
40" ×30" (101.6 × 76.2 cm)
Medium: Pencil
Rendered by J. Poey
Courtesy of Beverly Willis, FAIA

This nicely rendered two-point perspective shows a combination of reflective glass on the windows at the top and see-through, transparent glass on the windows below. One sees the interior ceiling lighting fixtures predominating over the balcony shadows. The Opera House building (left) is seen visible and "ghosted" over the part of the building that the Ballet building would obscure. This shows reflective glass seen from an interior space. Ghosting is a technique that allows us to see the complete exterior shape of a building as well as building forms hidden behind or within the major building. Successful ghosting depends on subtle color shading changes that do not affect the building exterior in preference to the building interior or the hidden building beyond.

Drawings: Bank of Tokyo of California
Headquarters building
San Francisco, California
Rendered by Carlos Diniz Associates
Visual Communication

For high-rise buildings with a predominantly glass facade, the sky and clouds generally will give reflections to the windows up high and the surrounding urban landscape will give reflections to the windows down below.

Hatching techniques can effectively indicate reflections in glass. A series of approximately parallel thin marks or lines are hand-drawn to simulate tone. Lines closely spaced give a dark tone or value; lines spaced farther apart give a light tone or value. **Hatching** or **cross-hatching** (crisscrossing hatched lines) makes a rendered surface seem more animated than if it were toned a solid shade. Here, the renderer has given the feeling of an overcast sky by using a cross-hatching technique to create tone density.

RENDERING GLASS REFLECTIONS

RENDERING POLISHED SURFACES

Drawing: New England Sunbox
Methuen, Massachusetts
Medium: Black Prismacolor on vellum
Courtesy of Interface Architects
Illustration: Paul Stevenson Oles, FAIA

The three horizontal shiny surfaces (floor, table, counter) are indicated as partially reflective by repeating the high-contrast patterns of the bright openings with their vertical edges and mullions. The nearer reflections become less precise and contrasty because the angle of incident view is greater. The vertical smooth surface (picture glazing on the left) is shown very brightly and precisely reflective because of the extremely raking angle of incident view.
[ARCHITECTURAL ILLUSTRATOR'S STATEMENT]

Drawing: Dolby Building, San Francisco, California
18" × 24" (45.7 × 61 cm)
Medium: Ink on Mylar
Courtesy of Chun/Ishimaru & Assoc., Architectural Illustrators

The most important purpose of any rendering to us is the readability of the space. We will purposely manipulate shadows and reflections to further this end. In the final analysis, it is a matter of simple composition and the use of darks against lights and lights against darks…this is true for any medium. Interiors are more difficult to illustrate because there are so many options and choices of light sources. Exteriors are rather simple because once the light source direction is determined, it is just a matter of putting in lighted surfaces, shaded surfaces, and shadows.
[ARCHITECTURAL ILLUSTRATOR'S STATEMENT]

RENDERING POLISHED SURFACES

RENDERING ARTIFICIAL LIGHTING IN INTERIORS

Drawing: Ahmanson Theatre
renovation
Los Angeles,
California
24" × 24" (61 × 61 cm)
Medium: Pen and ink with
oil and acrylics
Ellerbe Becket, Architects
Courtesy of Art Zendarski,
Architectural Illustrator

The intent of the rendering was to meet two requirements. First, the drawing was needed to communicate the design renovation to the Music Center administrators. Second, the rendering, in conjunction with the new Music Center being designed by Frank Gehry, would be incorporated into a marketing package used for fund raisers seeking private and public donations to cover the cost of construction.

Expressing the architect's complex, unconventional design to first-time viewers posed quite a challenge. Numbers of study views were analyzed to capture just the right vantage point. The study views and initial perspective blockout were created by computer. To clearly and accurately depict the complexity of the ceiling acoustic forms and lighting design elements and also the additional balcony and box seating, I used the technique of pen and ink on vellum. The ink-line drawing was then transferred photographically onto photomural paper. Oils and acrylics were used to complete the rendering. Working in pen and ink also helped in meeting the marketing specifications that called for the rendering to provide both black and white and color reproduction capabilities.

The rendering was meticulously detailed to give a true and accurate portrayal. Also, the drawing needed to depict a level of excitement that would get potential investors enthusiastic about the project. The artificial lighting is a strong visual element used to build this excitement. The diagonal thrust of light from the ceiling onto the stage is a composition device that creates a sense of drama and focal point for the drawing while prominently featuring the new lighting design elements. The careful composition of the viewpoint that draws the viewer into the interior space, lighting, texture, the on-stage scene from the popular play Les Misérables, *and the animation of the people in the audience, were all added to give the drawing a sense of reality.*
[ARCHITECTURAL ILLUSTRATOR'S STATEMENT]

The purpose of this illustration was to portray the drama and monumental scale of the elliptical entrance rotunda. An exaggerated shaft of light emanating from the dome's oculus was chosen to achieve a dramatic quality, while the low station point emphasizes the monumental scale of the space.
[ARCHITECTURAL ILLUSTRATOR'S STATEMENT]

The rendering of both artificial lighting and natural lighting helps to create an ambiance and a mood in interior spaces. Artificial exterior lighting (spotlights, etc.) can produce dramatic sky patterns and enliven a rendering (see Shekou Harbour Building, p. 305). The artificial interior lighting on the facing page helps to highlight the architectural design of the interior space. Natural solar lighting shown on this page functions in a similar manner.

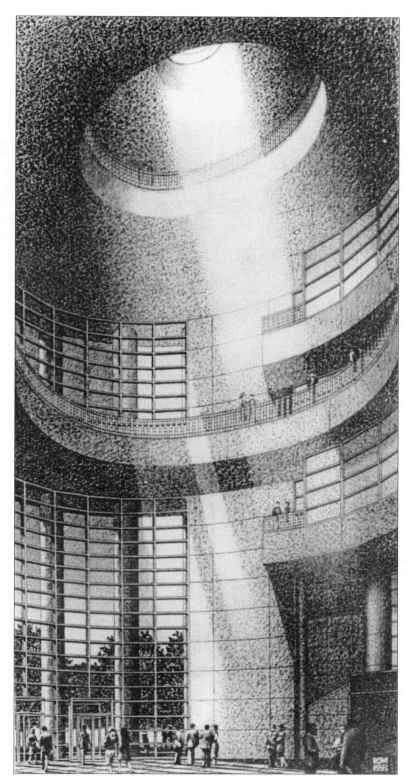

Drawing: Federal Courthouse, St. Louis, Missouri
9½" × 20" (24.1 × 50.8 cm)
Medium: Pencil on vellum
Architect: Hellmuth, Obata & Kassabaum, Inc.
Courtesy of Kenneth E. Miller, Architect, Architectural Illustrator

RENDERING NATURAL LIGHTING IN INTERIORS

PEN AND INK RENDERING

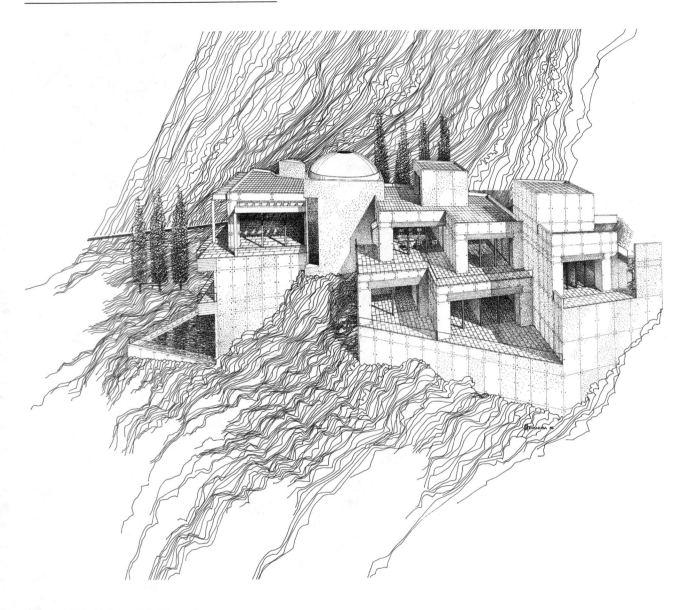

Drawing: Villa Syrigos, near Athens, Greece
36" × 24" (91.4 × 61 cm), Scale: ⅛"=1'0"
Medium: Ink on Mylar, Rapidograph pen
Courtesy of Hugh Newell Jacobsen, FAIA, Architect
Rendered by Stephen S. Evanusa, Architect

The careful study of shadows and reflections is an essential element in this rendering.
[DELINEATOR'S STATEMENT]

Design drawings, which are examined in detail in the following chapter, are more "developmental" and take less time to produce than rendered drawings that are made for a final presentation to a client. Finalized rendered delineations can be (and often are) manipulated to obscure design flaws in order to increase the design's acceptability and marketability. Architects frequently contract out renderings for their designs to specialists called "delineators" or "architectural illustrators." Their primary goal is to generate a drawing that will "sell" a design to a potential client.

Drawing: Villa Andropoulos, near Athens, Greece
36" × 24" (91.4 × 61 cm), Scale: ⅛"=1'0"
Medium: Ink on Mylar, Rapidograph pen
Courtesy of Hugh Newell Jacobsen, FAIA, Architect
Rendered by Stephen S. Evanusa, Architect

PEN AND INK RENDERING

The character of this drawing is derived by the interplay of two ink drawing line techniques: line and tone. The house is described by shade and shadow, drawn with a "stippled" texture; the surrounding rocky mountain by freehand contour. [DELINEATOR'S STATEMENT]

Note the long continuous contour lines on the hillsides in these two renderings. Regardless of whether they are linear or curvilinear, they tend to have a deliberate feeling because of their length. When closely spaced, these lines can be very effective in describing the shape and overall form of a landscape.

CONCEPTUAL RENDERING USING MIXED MEDIA

Images: Asian Studies Building
        University of California at Berkeley
Tod Williams Billie Tsien Architects
Courtesy of Lawrence Ko Leong, Architectural Illustrator

A familiar assignment, the task was to create an image for funding purposes of a project without much design development information. In this case, the approach was appropriate because we wanted to suggest the proposal's potential without committing too much detail design in light of the compressed timeframe. Throughout the short two-week timeframe, the preliminary layouts were transferred to the design architects, who used them as study overlays for their conceptual design input. At the same time, review with the university facilities management, development offices, and the Asian studies departments took place.

I chose to use a computer overlay technique of compositing. First a hand drawn image based on a highly abstract massing CAD model that the architects had produced was scanned and placed onto a site photograph showing adjacent context that people familiar with the site could relate scale and space to. I felt this was appropriate to show the proposal in context while providing artistic control and an ethereal quality. From a practical standpoint, by creating the image via a digital process, there is a great deal of flexibility in the reproduction process and ease in distributing "in-progress" images and final digital output, either inserted in a desktop publishing format or on a presentation enlargement board.

[ARCHITECTURAL ILLUSTRATOR'S STATEMENT]

Images: Asian Studies Building
        University of California at Berkeley
Tod Williams Billie Tsien Architects
Courtesy of Lawrence Ko Leong, Architectural Illustrator
To see these images in color, go to www.lkldraw.com

To take the hard edge off the context photo, the hand drawn overlay with Prismacolor pencil was softly delineated and composited over the background photo, which was "filtered" in a digital photoediting program. The various layers: the filtered background photo, the sketched background overlay, the hand drawn new proposal, and, finally, the color and final touchups using the digital editing tools.
[ARCHITECTURAL ILLUSTRATOR'S STATEMENT]

CONCEPTUAL RENDERING USING MIXED MEDIA

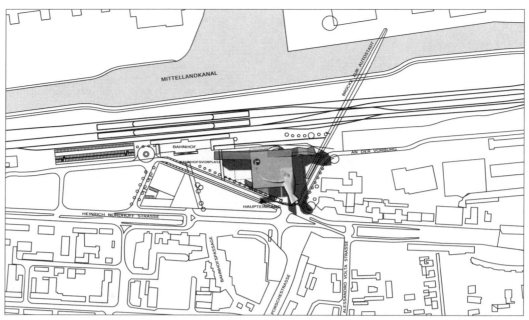

Site plan

© by Armin Hess, A-1060 Vienna, Morizgane 8/21 fon + fax: 0043 1 9610363

Bird's-eye perspective

© by Armin Hess, A-1060 Vienna, Morizgane 8/21 fon + fax: 0043 1 9610363

Computer renderings: Above—Site plan   Below—Aerial perspective
Science Center, Wolfsburg, Germany
Medium: Software—AutoCad and Form-Z
Courtesy of COOP HIMMELB(L)AU

This office does perspective renderings rather than elevations as part of any of their competition drawings. Their competition drawings are always computer-generated.

DIGITAL RENDERINGS

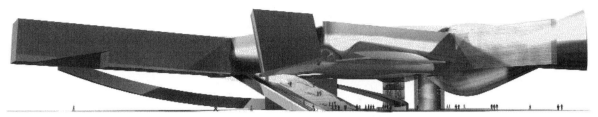

Eye-level perspective

© by Armin Hess, A-1060 Vienna, Morizgane 8/21 fon + fax: 0043 1 9610363

Eye-level perspective

© by Armin Hess, A-1060 Vienna, Morizgane 8/21 fon + fax: 0043 1 9610363

© by Armin Hess, A-1060 Vienna, Morizgane 8/21 fon + fax: 0043 1 9610363

Close-up of large entrance staircase

Computer-rendered perspectives: Science Center, Wolfsburg, Germany
Medium: Software—AutoCad and Form-Z
Courtesy of COOP HIMMELB(L)AU

The mutation of the form from rigid solids into malleable, fluid forms is a metaphor for the infinite scientific process of gaining knowledge that is the center's program. Research is understood as a cyclical process between basic scientific knowledge and discovery through the introduction of hypothetical solutions. Through the dramatic combination of completely different bodies and their hybridization, the building represents in architecture what recent theories in the sciences do: It rejects the idea of boundaries as being hard and definite; rather, they are seen as soft and transient, like osmotic membranes. [ARCHITECT'S STATEMENT]

Diagramming and Conceptual Sketching

Diagrams and conceptual sketches are integral parts of the design-drawing process. They are the means by which the designer ideates, generates, and organizes his or her ideas.

Conceptual diagrams constitute an abstract language that must be understood and communicated properly among the design community. It is through graphic diagramming that one develops a design vocabulary and can convey an understanding. Elements like arrows, nodes, lines, and other symbols help the beginner use graphic techniques to explore ideas.

Conceptual (or design) sketches are quickly drawn syntheses that represent a range of alternative design ideas for an imagined conception. Such visualizations may be crude initial images or somewhat more refined, developed drawings. Although speculative and abstract in nature, conceptual sketches are attempts to depict the reality of the design in its idealized and essential state.

This chapter introduces the vocabulary of diagramming and shows a wide range of professional examples of both diagrammatic models and conceptual sketches.

In summary, following are some of the important terms and concepts you will learn:

Graphic diagram	Circulation	Node	Visualization
Bubble diagram	Thumbnail sketch	Arrowed line	Ideational drawing
Conceptual thinking	Partí diagram	Line	Symbolic language

Diagramming and Conceptual Sketching

TOPIC: DIAGRAMMING

Brooks 1997.

Ching 2003, 200–205.

Clark and Pause, 1996.

Grimaldi 1990.

Guiton and Guiton 1981.

Kasprisin and Pettinari 1990.

White 1983.

TOPIC: DESIGN SKETCHING EXAMPLES

Miguel Angel Roca. 1994, Architectural Monographs no. 36.

Tomas Taveira. 1994, Architectural Monographs no. 37.

Herbert 1993.

Kammer 1996.

Lin 2000.

LeCorbusier's Sketchbooks.

Paulo dos Santos 1993.

Pfeiffer 1990, 7–8, 99, 141.

Portoghesi 2000.

Robbins 1997.

Roca 1994.

Soleri 1971.

Taveira 1994.

Vonmoos 1996.

Zardini 1996.

Chapter Overview

After studying this chapter, you will have a better understanding of how diagramming and conceptual sketching are important in design communications. For continued study, refer to Laseau's *Graphic Thinking for Architects and Designers.*

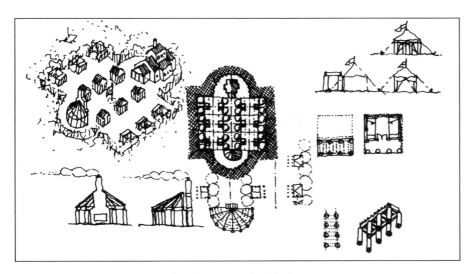

Preliminary schematic diagrams are frequently the seeds for the final design and, ultimately, the built project. They can take a two-dimensional or three-dimensional configuration, as shown in the Hoover Center. The diagrams below use a combination of point, line, and two-dimensional zone to explain the design concept.

Diagrams: Hoover Outdoor Education Center, Yorkville, Illinois
Medium: Felt-tipped pen on trace
Courtesy of Tigerman McCurry Architects

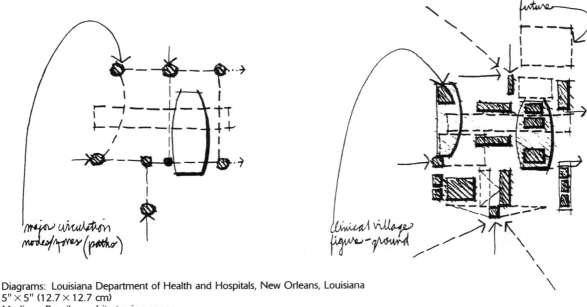

Diagrams: Louisiana Department of Health and Hospitals, New Orleans, Louisiana
5" × 5" (12.7 × 12.7 cm)
Medium: Pencil on white tracing paper
Courtesy of R-2 ARCH Designers/Researchers
Ben J. Refuerzo and Stephen F. Verderber

Once an architecture student's freehand graphics skills are honed, he or she will begin to appreciate the potential of these skills not only in drawing contextual elements (people, vegetation, cars, etc.) but also in drawing **conceptual diagrams.** The students are immediately confronted with developing sketches on tracing paper (termed yellow trace, flimsy, or bumwad [British]) as part of the design process in a design studio project. Beginning with the first course in architectural design, students will be faced throughout their academic careers and professional lives with the task of developing numerous alternative ideas or schemes for each design problem. The ability to do quick freehand graphics in the form of scribbles and doodles is imperative. These **graphic diagrams** help us to explore alternative solutions and encourage **visualization, visual thinking,** and **transformative understanding.**

INTRODUCTION

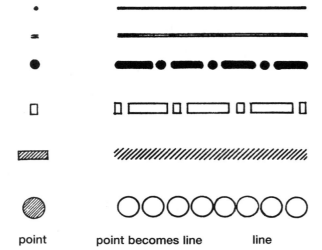

point point becomes line line

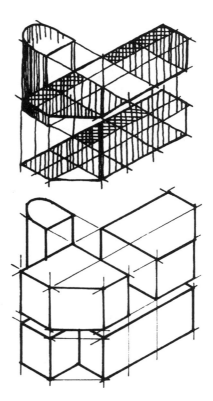

Diagram: Waterfront Development Plan
Asbury Park, New Jersey
6" × 3" (15.2 × 7.6 cm)
Medium: Ink on trace
Courtesy of Koetter, Kim & Associates, Inc.
Architects and Urban Designers

Every drawing type can be used as a conceptual analytical diagram. **Graphic diagrams** can be two-dimensional or three-dimensional in their abstract communication of a design scheme. Through point, line, symbol, and zone diagrams, a building's organization can be represented in terms of user movement (**circulation**), space usage (**zoning**), site plan and site section analysis, structural analysis, and volumetric enclosure (geometric configuration). The use of diagrams early in the design process allows for creative exploration of an array of alternatives unfettered by rigid programmatic constraints.

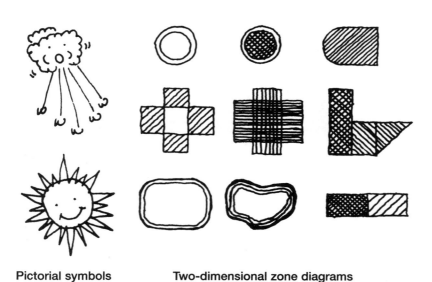

Pictorial symbols Two-dimensional zone diagrams

Three-dimensional zone and
volume diagrams

Students hear a new vocabulary in the design studio. Terms like bubble diagram, schematics, flow, circulation, zoning, hierarchy, and metaphor become commonplace. The many new terms of this studio language, coupled with incessant demands for an abundance of ideas, sometimes overwhelms beginning students. An understanding of the language comes with reading architectural literature.

DIAGRAM SYMBOLS AND TYPES

Diagram: Scheme C
        Gleneagles Hospital and M.O.B.
        Jalan Ampang–Kuala Lumpur, Malaysia
17" × 11" (43.2 × 27.9 cm)
Medium: Ink on bond paper
Courtesy of KMD/PD Architects
Joint venture with the Architectural Network

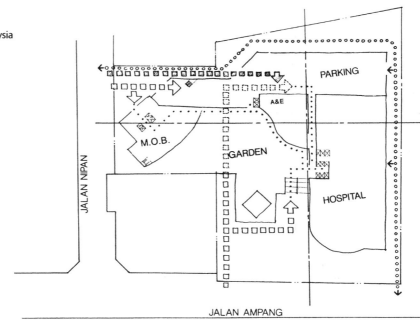

This is a good example of circulation analysis in an early schematic stage of the design process. Note that each type of movement has a different symbol. A clear **symbolic language** is essential in communicating graphically important collected data to others as well as to yourself.

KEY

□ □ □ □ PUBLIC ACCESS

▨ ▨ ▨ ▨ EMERGENCY ONLY

o o o o o o SERVICE/FIRE/STAFF

• • • • • PEDESTRIAN

DIAGRAM SYMBOLS

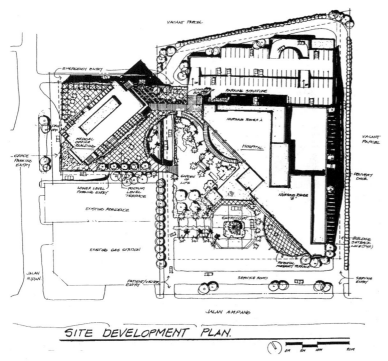

Site development plan for scheme C
24" × 36" (61 × 91.4 cm), Scale: 1:300
Medium: Ink on vellum

Circulation traces the path and flow of user movement two-dimensionally in plan and in section or three-dimensionally in pictorial diagrams (see p. 164). The movement can be horizontal or vertical. Points where movement begins, are called **nodes.** A node is a point of focus for other diagrammitic symbols. On diagrams one frequently sees nodes (central points or points of concentration) being connected by lines of movement.

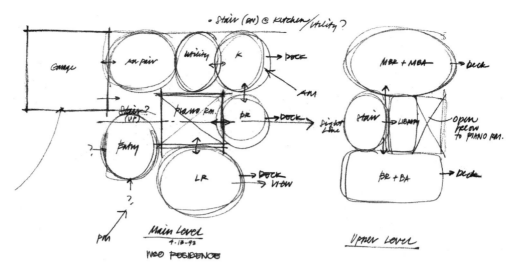

Sketch: Woo residence, Oakland, California
Medium: HB pencil
Courtesy of Kenzo Handa, Architect

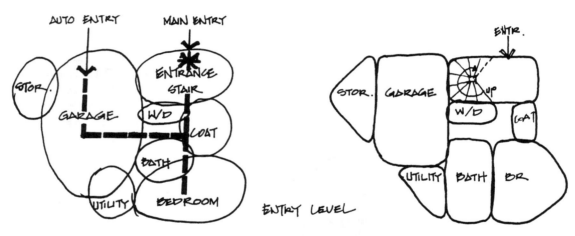

Bubble diagrams relate the functions and relative sizes of spaces to each other as well as to external site determinants. Circulation linkages can quickly be analyzed and evaluated.

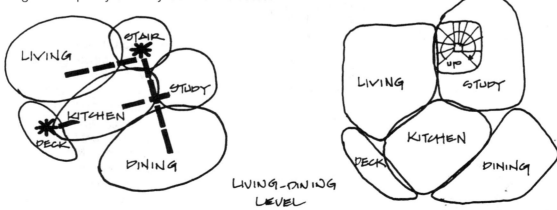

With an area (square footage or square meters) program, it is important to set up functional zone adjacencies. These diagrams hint at the proximity relationships and the possible arrangements for a final solution.

RELATIONSHIP DIAGRAMS

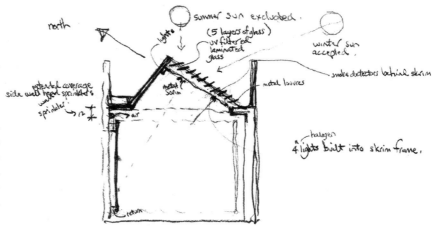

The use of light, both natural and artificial, is central to the conception of the Getty Museum and is therefore the focus of these sketches. These drawings explore the uses of light and its ability to mediate between the building's exterior and interior.
[Architect's statement]

Arrow symbols are frequently used in diagrams, especially in plan and section diagrams. The vertical section diagram at the top of this page uses sun symbols to show the effect of winter and summer solar angles. Light direction is represented by a directional arrow that enhances the viewer's understanding of how light enters the museum's space. Note also the integration of architectural design with structural and mechanical concepts.

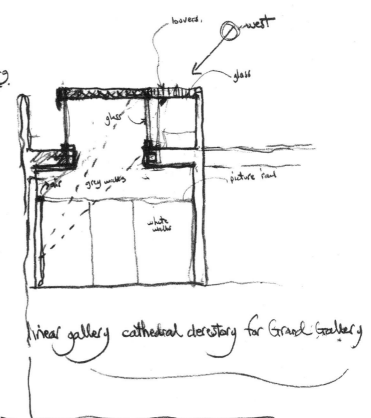

Drawings: Conceptual sketch studies of museum sections
The Getty Center Museum
Los Angeles, California
Both 18" × 18" (45.7 × 45.7 cm)
Medium: Graphite pencil on yellow trace
Courtesy of Richard Meier & Partners, Architects
Reprinted from The Getty Center Design Process
with permission of The J. Paul Getty Trust

VERTICAL SECTION DIAGRAMS

DIAGRAM SYMBOL USAGE

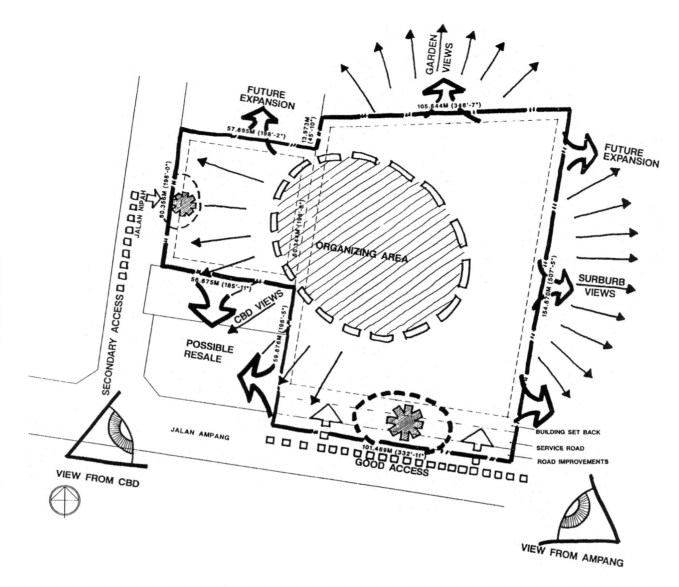

Diagram: Site analysis, Gleneagles Hospital and M.O.B., Jalan Ampang–Kuala Lumpur, Malaysia
36" × 24" (91.4 × 61 cm)
Medium: Ink on vellum with Kroy type
Courtesy of KMD/PD Architects
Joint venture with the Architectural Network

Diagrams are generated in the earliest stages of the design process. Diagrammatic models are some of the most important types of drawing for the designer, yet paradoxically they are rarely if ever seen by the client. **Diagrams** are a visual means for collecting and sorting information, for testing ideas and exploring alternative solutions—for looking into the very heart of a design problem. They represent that crucial intimate conversation with oneself, a conversation conducted in a very specific language that has its own current vocabulary, grammar, and syntax. They also communicate your ideas to your classmates or professional peers so that their soundness can be tested.

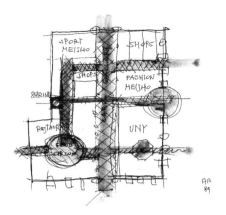

Plan sketch diagram: Shimizu Corporation
Nagoya, Aichi, Japan
Courtesy of Aldo Rossi, SDA, Architect

The drawing at left is a diagrammatic schematic plan sketch showing pedestrian pathways. Note the use of node symbols. The four different schemes sketched below were evaluated with respect to vehicular and pedestrian movement (circulation). Graphic symbols for flow and bubbles are scaleless and are thus ideal for both small- and large-scale projects.

Straight or curved **lines** on diagrams are commonly used as boundaries (see pp. 444 and 450), or as axial elements, as seen below, or as organizing elements for conceptual ideas on site, relationship, and circulation diagrams (see p. 448 and 478–479).

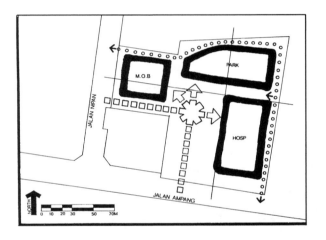

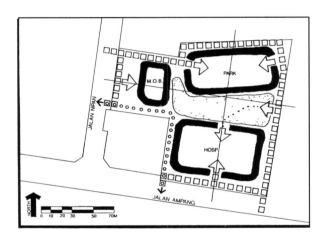

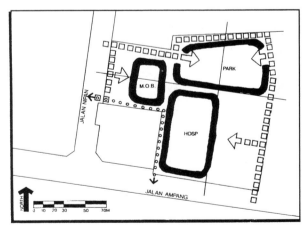

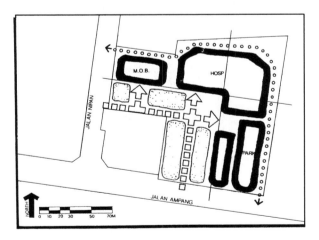

Diagrams: Four alternative schemes
Gleneagles Hospital and M.O.B., Jalan Ampang–Kuala Lumpur, Malaysia
Each drawing 17" × 11" (43.2 × 27.9 cm), reduced and composed on 36" × 24" (91.4 × 61 cm)
Medium: Ink on bond paper
Courtesy of KMD/PD Architects
Joint Venture with the Architectural Network

SYMBOLS IN TWO-DIMENSIONAL DIAGRAMS

SYMBOLS IN TWO-DIMENSIONAL DIAGRAMS

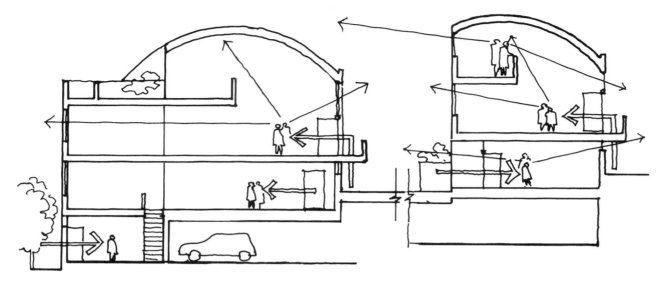

Diagram sketch: Franklin/La Brea Family Housing, Los Angeles, California
6" × 6" (15.2 × 15.2 cm), Scale: ¹⁄₁₆"=1'0"
Medium: Technical pen on Mylar
Courtesy of Adèle Naudé Santos and Associates, Architects

This section diagram clearly shows user view (thin arrowed line) and user movement (thick arrowed line). The arrow can symbolize the direction of an action or a movement (can be one- or two-way).

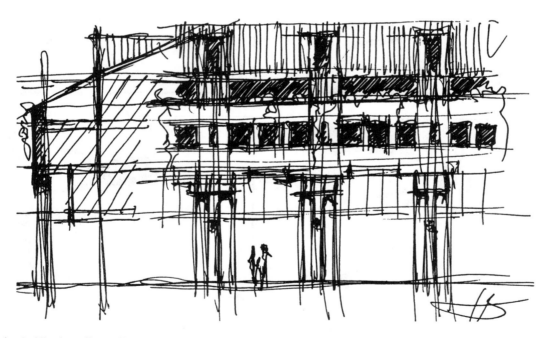

Diagram sketch: Mixed-use Center, Turin, Italy
8" × 6.5" (20.3 × 16.5 cm)
Medium: Black marker pen on smooth paper
Courtesy of Gunnar Birkerts and Associates, Inc., Architects

Graphic diagrams should be drawn with fluid and loose line strokes. The looser the line quality, the more evocative the image is to the viewer. Sectional diagrams should include human figures to give scale to the sketches.

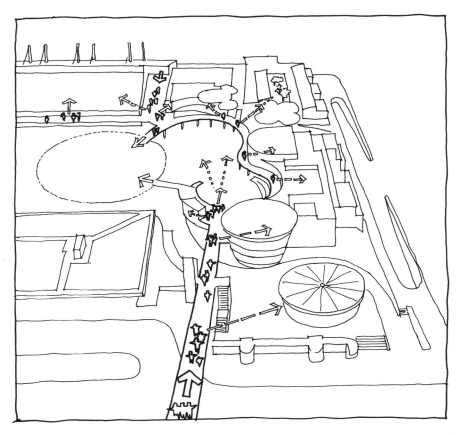

These diagrams are part of a series that was used to engage the users of the site and facilities in a public design process. Specifically, the diagrams describe routes through the site and a sequence of visual experiences. They were keyed to vignettes depicting views of the buildings and the activities observed within.
[ARCHITECT'S STATEMENT]

Arrowed lines can vary in thickness (see p. 444) and tone intensity (see p. 450) depending on the importance and type of relationship.

Movement diagrams: Yerba Buena Gardens Children Center San Francisco, California
6" × 6" (15.2 × 15.2 cm)
Medium: Technical pen on vellum
Courtesy of Adèle Naudé Santos and Associates, Architects

These diagrams make extensive use of a point and a line symbol to depict pedestrian movement. The bird's-eye view is more descriptive than a site plan in showing user circulation. Three-dimensional diagrams such as perspectives and plan obliques are as depictive as two-dimensional diagrams. Some-times the same diagram can be used to explain different information factors. These diagrams can be presented individually or as a set in which transparent overlays are used. A composite set should have a clear hierarchy of the informational aspects being considered to avoid information overload.

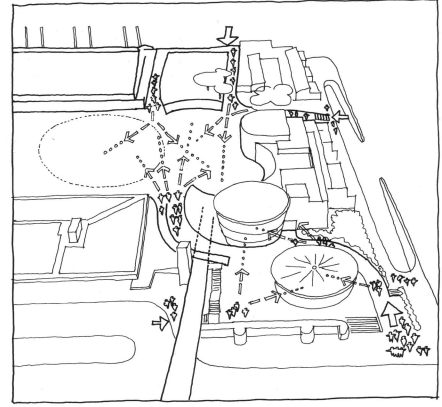

SYMBOLS IN THREE-DIMENSIONAL DIAGRAMS

DIAGRAMMING ALTERNATIVES

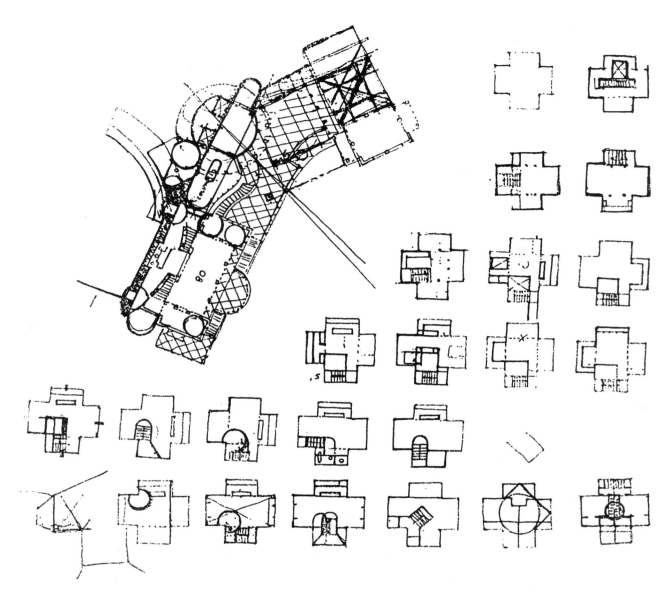

Conceptual diagrams: Villa Linda Flora (unbuilt), Bel Air, California
8½" × 11" (21.6 × 27.9 cm)
Medium: Ink on sketch paper
Courtesy of Hodgetts + Fung, Design Associates

In any design project, there are numerous alternative solutions to be analyzed. Seen above is a juxtaposition of diagrams showing potential alternatives. During the design process, **design drawings** (diagrams, design sketches, etc.) are crucial in testing alternative schemes and themes. This project shows the wide range of possible stairway types and stairway locations within the same geometric plan configuration. Diagrams are frequently drawn with a consistent graphic format, as shown above. This allows one to analyze a particular problem or focus on one specific issue (in this case, stairway location) by comparing one alternative with another.

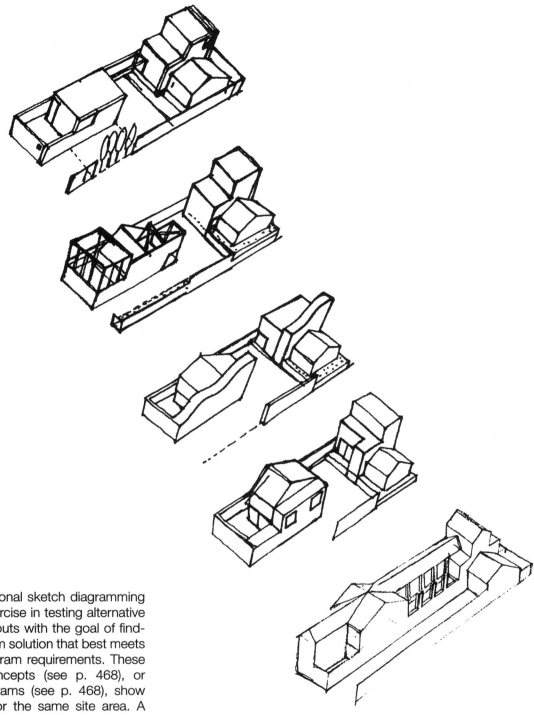

DIAGRAMMING ALTERNATIVES

Three-dimensional sketch diagramming can be an exercise in testing alternative geometric layouts with the goal of finding an optimum solution that best meets all of the program requirements. These thumbnail concepts (see p. 468), or "napkin" diagrams (see p. 468), show five options for the same site area. A conceptual massing sketch should show fairly accurate proportions, but it should not be overly detailed.

Alternative diagrams: Click Agency, West Hollywood, California
Medium: Ink on sketch paper
Courtesy of Hodgetts + Fung, Design Associates

SITE DIAGRAMS

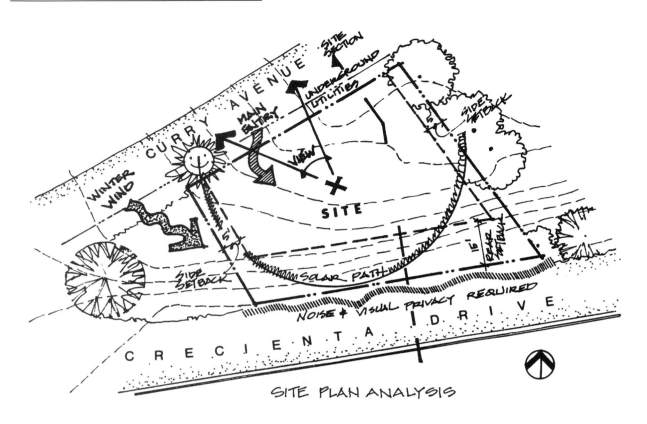

SITE PLAN ANALYSIS

Schematic analytical diagrams for site plans and site sections are frequently sketched in the design process. Site diagrams commonly have pictorial symbols like those of the sun and the plan trees shown above, which represent an abstract simplification of physical reality. By using diagramming **symbols**, influential factors on the site such as contours, traffic circulation, view, solar and wind conditions, noise, zoning regulations, property lines, land use, and adjacent landscaping can quickly be graphically recorded and analyzed.

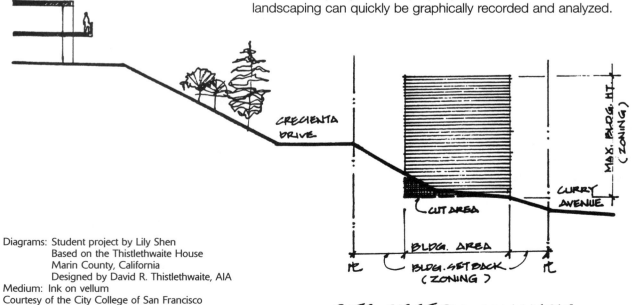

Diagrams: Student project by Lily Shen
          Based on the Thistlethwaite House
          Marin County, California
          Designed by David R. Thistlethwaite, AIA
Medium: Ink on vellum
Courtesy of the City College of San Francisco
Department of Architecture

SITE SECTION ANALYSIS

Drawings: House in
Northern California
Medium: Pencil on trace
Courtesy of Legorreta Arquitectos,
Ricardo Legorreta, Victor Legorreta,
Noe Castro

Design drawings document the design process. The initial stages are frequently sketched in black and white with the goal of describing only the architectural form and its relation to the surrounding conditions. Later stages incorporate the use of color.

Diagrams simplify information so that one can clearly examine specific aspects. As one simplifies, one abstracts reality. These graphic diagrams of a location plan, a site plan, a site section, and an elevation are precursors for the more three-dimensional diagrams of paraline and perspective sketches. It is important that designers acquire the ability to relate the size and proportion of various architectural elements to buildings and their site conditions. Note the use of various scales in this study.

Site plan, location plan, and site section diagrams

SITE DIAGRAMS

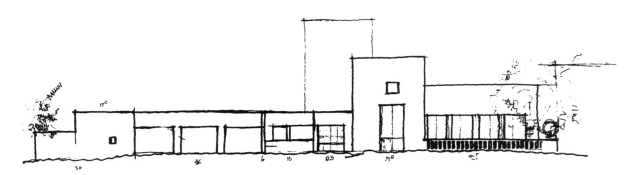

Elevation study, Scale: ⅛"=1'0"

PLAN DIAGRAM

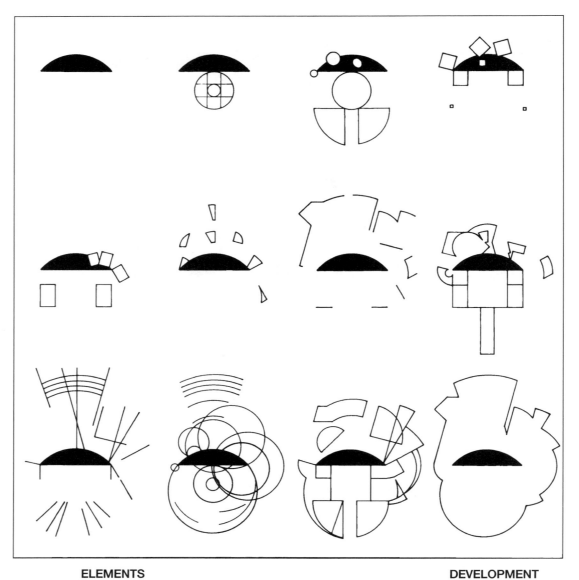

ELEMENTS   DEVELOPMENT

Diagrams: Private residence, Illinois (1988–1990)
Medium: Ink
Courtesy of Stanley Tigerman, Architect

Storyboard showing the evolution of elements. The house begins with a wedge, generating other forms that tumble off of it.
[ARCHITECT'S STATEMENT]

In addition to site analysis and site synthesis diagrams shown on the preceding pages, plan diagrams, along with section and elevation diagrams shown on the following pages, are most often used during the initial phase of the design process. As the process continues, layers of tracing paper are used to refine the development of design ideas.

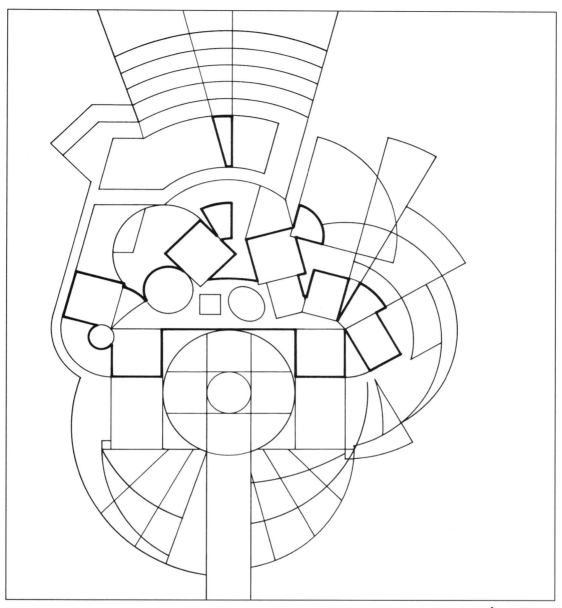

PLAN DIAGRAM

PARTÍ DIAGRAM

Diagrams: Private residence, Illinois (1988–1990)
Medium: Ink
Courtesy of Stanley Tigerman, Architect

In the partí diagram, the house expands into the site, and geometric repetitions radiating from the home into the landscape are indicated.
[ARCHITECT'S STATEMENT]

A **partí diagram** shows the basic schematic assumption of a plan. It is the fundamental overarching or big idea (scheme) of a plan.

The ongoing refinement process allows for the evolution of a mature solution that satisfies the restrictions and requirements of the program.

PLAN, SECTION, AND ELEVATION DIAGRAMS

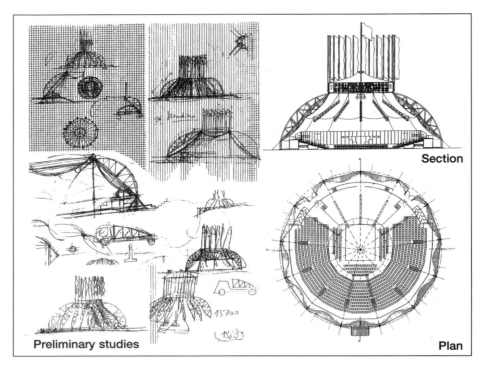

Section

Plan

Preliminary studies

Design sketches: Tent for the 700th Anniversary of Switzerland
Medium: Pencil
Courtesy of Mario Botta, Architect, Lugano, Switzerland

Envisioning and exploring a design concept in the conceptual design stages is a time-consuming, gradual process. Quick freehand doodles and thumbnail speculative sketches are the vital images that make this process work. The preliminary sketch studies in this example typify an analysis stage, whereas the hard-line drawings typify and represent a synthesis stage.

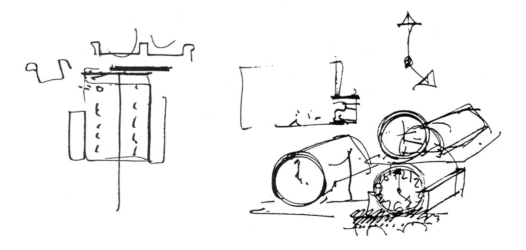

Conceptual sketches: Whitehall Ferry Terminal, New York City
Medium: Felt-tipped pen on yellow trace
Courtesy of Venturi, Scott Brown and Associates, Inc.
Sketches by Robert Venturi

...early studies for the Whitehall Ferry Terminal, featuring the big clock whose scale relates to and accommodates to its setting—including Manhattan's skyline, harbor, and the Statue of Liberty—and establishes its civic presence, and whose form symbolizes its transportation function and generates its barrel vault, which monumentally shelters its interior activities. [ARCHITECT'S STATEMENT]

When the human mind has an image, it's very hard to change; so in thinking of the form for a building, it's important to prevent having the image as long as possible, and only after all the information has been gathered.
[ARCHITECT'S STATEMENT]

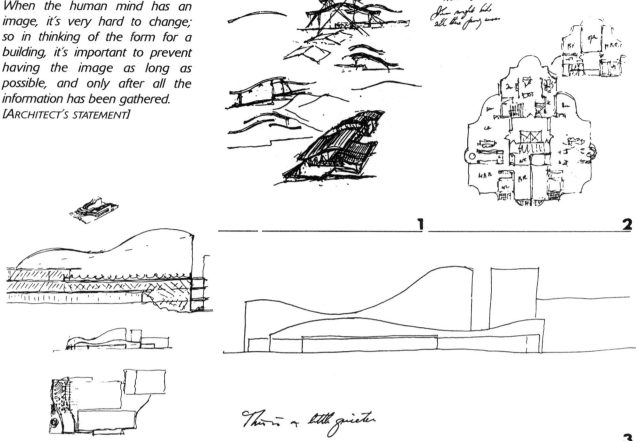

Medium: Black fine-point felt-tipped pen on white trace
Courtesy of Arthur Erickson, FAIA, FRAIC

Sketches: 1. Piney Valley Ranch
Magnus Lindholm
Eagle, Colorado
11" × 14" (27.9 × 35.6 cm)

2. "Nick & Diane, John might like all these fancy curves."
1300 West Pender
Noel Developments
Vancouver, B.C., Canada
11" × 14" (27.9 × 35.6 cm)

3. "This is a little quieter."
Performing Arts Centre
California Polytechnic State University
San Luis Obispo, California
48" × 16" (121.9 × 40.6 cm)

In classic examples of diagramming and design sketching, such as Mendelsohn's drawings for the Einstein Tower at Potsdam (circa 1920) or Ludwig Mies Van der Rohe's sketches for the Barcelona Pavilion (circa 1929), we again see how initial impressions are often precursors to, or contain the essence of, the subsequent, more developed design.

PLAN AND ELEVATION DIAGRAMS

SKETCHED ELEVATION AND SECTION DIAGRAMS

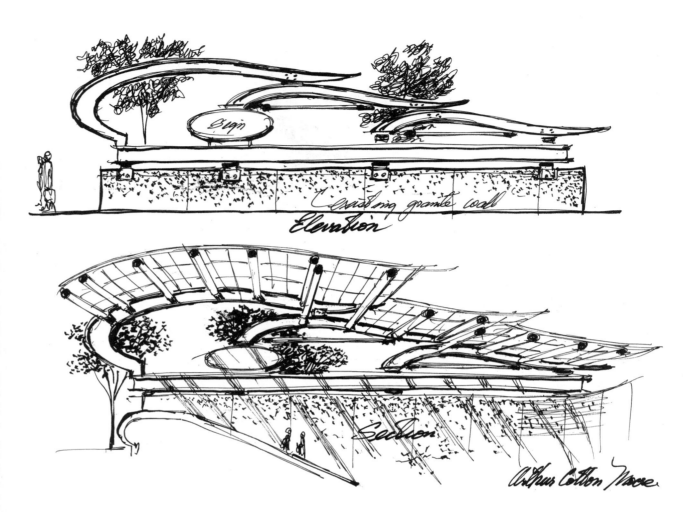

Sketch: Canopies over Metro entrances
        Washington, D.C.
8.5" × 11" (21.6 × 27.9 cm)
Medium: Ink on vellum
Courtesy of Arthur Cotton Moore/Associates,
Architects • Planners, Washington, DC • Royal Oak, MD
Drawn by Arthur Cotton Moore FAIA

Sketch of proposed canopies over the existing Metro entrances for metropolitan Washington, D.C., transit system. The curved beams are bent or cut out of stainless steel sheets and are designed to expand or contract laterally in order to adapt to the wide variety of existing entrances. The curved beams support pipe purline and glass roofs. The canopies are shaped to have natural ventilation and to be evocative of a rapid transit system. The intent is to provide a light, airy, signature structure that will quickly become identified with the system.
[ARCHITECT'S STATEMENT]

Diagrammatic exploration is a way of design sketching that can be evocative. Hand-generated diagrams and computer-modeled diagrams (pp. 458–465) are both forms of conceptual sketching. Likewise, conceptual modeling by fabricating "hands-on" models (study models) using any kind of found material is also a form of conceptual "sketching" in three dimensions.

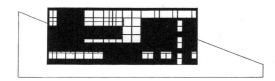

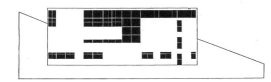

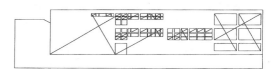

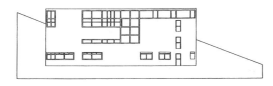

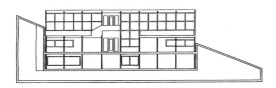

Diagrams: Student projects by Darlene Lawrence (above)
          and Karla Armas (right)
          Facade studies
Medium: Ink on Mylar
Courtesy of the University of Texas at Arlington
School of Architecture

HARDLINE ELEVATION DIAGRAMS

These facade studies of elevation diagrams show the strong use of **figure and ground** in the representation of solid (wall) and void (window). In a reductive manner, these diagrams allow one to concentrate on the geometric treatment of the fenestration. This simplification of the facade prevents one from being distracted by other aspects that may appear in an elevation, such as material texture or construction detail.

New forms of graphical expression for analysis can be achieved in a computer environment by exploiting various options of 3D modeling features. A whole new generation of 3D diagrams (unlike hand drawn diagrams with only lines) can be accomplished with the use of surface color, variations of shades, levels of transparency, various options of color wireframe, combination of wireframe and non-wireframe, and surface texture. This is similar to a designer's creation of an architectural expression motif. Using computer modeling features, it is possible to express the designer's representation trademark in all of these diagrammatic representations of analysis.
[PROFESSOR'S STATEMENT]

COMPUTER-MODELED DIAGRAMS

Form Organization

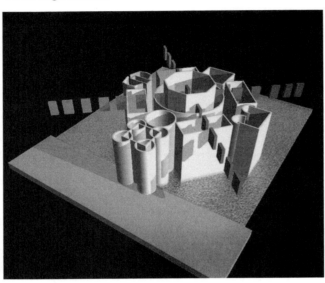

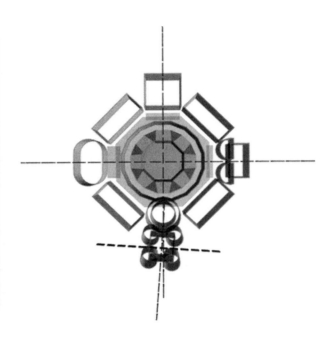

The Assembly building is a composite structure comprising eight independent blocks linked together to serve as a unified building. The inner zone, an octagonal form, is the main assembly chamber; the middle zone is internal circulation; and the outer zone contains spaces for various offices and their related activities. The mosque is integrated with the building and nestled between four hollow cylindrical columns. The building is placed in the middle of a lake; its entry is under the mosque, from a public plaza linked to the building.

Notable mid-twentieth-century architect and architecture educator Louis I. Kahn designed the National Assembly building in Dhaka, Bangladesh. As shown here and on the following four pages, Professor M. Saleh Uddin developed a comprehensive set of computer-modeled diagrams with accompanying notes in order to graphically analyze this building.

Text and diagrams: Courtesy of M. Saleh Uddin, Ph.D.
Professor, Department of Environmental Design
University of Missouri–Columbia

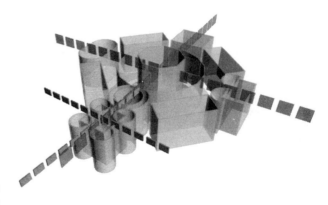

Axis and Balance
Spatial direction or axes of the mosque are intentionally shifted a few degrees in relation to the main building to reinforce direction to Mecca, thereby resulting in two axes systems.

These implied sets of axes also illustrate the symmetric nature of the spaces relative to their axes.

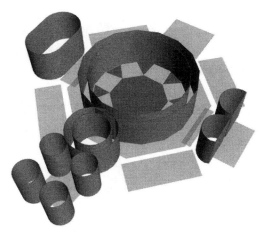

Repetitive to Unique Forms

Two contrasting platonic form-volumes, a cylinder and a cube, and variations on these forms, combine to construct the total composition of the building. Forms and their variations are used in a repetitive manner to create the other volumes as unique elements.

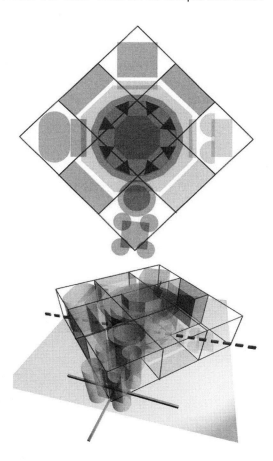

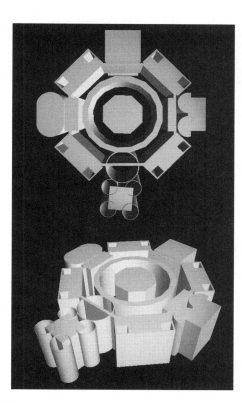

Grid Organization

Repetitive primary modular volumes of the Assembly building fall into a grid pattern transformed from nine equal implied volumes of spaces.

Solid to Void

The relationship of solids to voids represents enclosed occupiable spaces (served spaces) and supporting service spaces. Void spaces, representative of circulation and light wells, are total-height hollow volumes pierced through solid volumes.

Text and diagrams: Courtesy of M. Saleh Uddin, Ph.D.
Professor, Department of Environmental Design
University of Missouri–Columbia

COMPUTER-MODELED DIAGRAMS

COMPUTER-MODELED DIAGRAMS

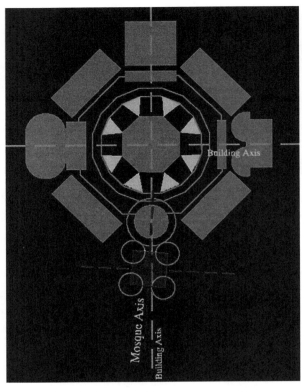

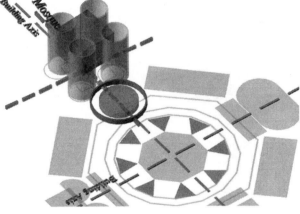

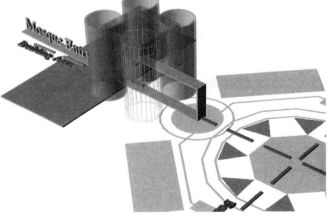

Mosque and Building Axes

Instead of being separate, the mosque is joined with the Assembly, placed off-axis and oriented to the holy city of Mecca.

Circular geometry is used as a transitional form to allow the shift of axis.

Ablution court and stairwell in a circular form works as a transition of form between the mosque and the main Assembly.

Entry

The main entry route to the Assembly leads under the elevated mosque, and is then directed to form a circular path.

The main entry route under the elevated mosque turns upward and pierces the cube to create entry to the mosque.

Text and diagrams (this and facing page): Courtesy of M. Saleh Uddin, Ph.D.
Professor, Department of Environmental Design
University of Missouri–Columbia

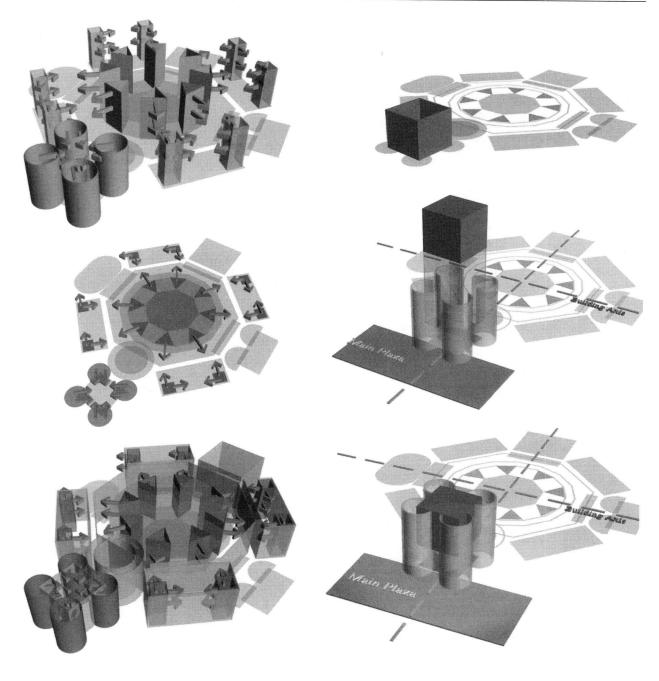

Natural Light

Vertical light wells bring light to interior spaces through their openings, or by means of surface reflections. Eight identical triangular light wells bring natural light to various floors through openings on wall surfaces. Four larger peripheral square light wells bring light through windows. Four cylindrical light wells bring light inside the mosque by using their concave surfaces for reflection and dispersion.

Form Organization of Mosque

The central cubic volume of the mosque is interlinked with four cylindrical forms at its four corners. The mosque is strategically elevated to express its religious importance.

Religious sense of the Assembly is achieved by combining Assembly and prayer hall. The joining of the Assembly building and the prayer hall came from the powerful realization of the spiritual dimension of the Assembly.

COMPUTER-MODELED DIAGRAMS

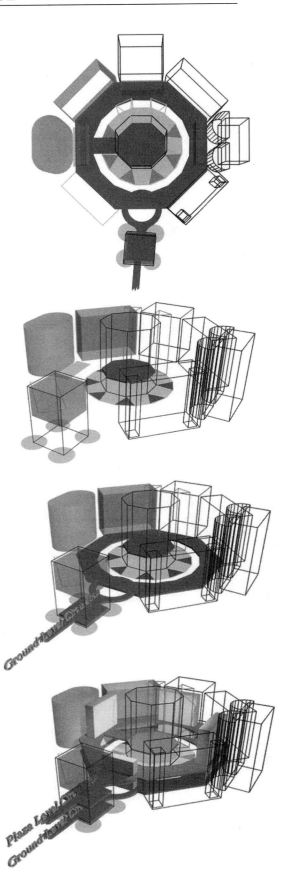

Circulation

The primary circulation path is directed to a middle loop that gives access to all peripheral blocks.

Four vertical circulation shafts are connected to the middle loop to access various floor levels.

Both plaza and ground level horizontal circulation paths are linked to the vertical shafts. Plaza-level circulation gives access to the main octagonal Assembly chamber in the middle.

The diagrams of Kahn's building speak to the notion that one diagram alone cannot convey a full understanding of a building. A true analysis of a building project requires **comprehensive diagramming.**

Text and diagrams: Courtesy of M. Saleh Uddin, Ph.D.
Professor, Department of Environmental Design
University of Missouri–Columbia

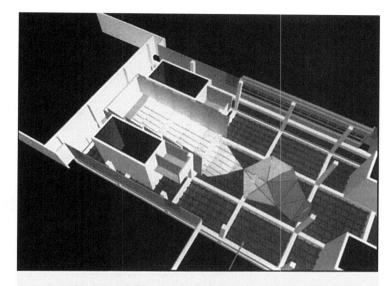

High-contrast computer models help to define form with precise shades and shadows. **Computer modeling** allows for the generation of an infinite number of orientations as well as easy adjustment of shape and size.

Digital modeling programs like form Z and 3DViz offer three-dimensional features for diagramming that hand drawing alone cannot. For example, variable colorations and transparencies done digitally can add to an image aspects that a hand drawn diagram cannot match. Also, eye-level simulation diagrams offer human-scale aspects.

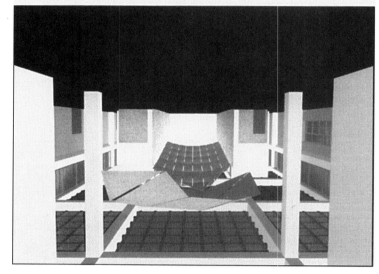

Through modeling in various views, we explain the massing and the impact of sculptural elements proposed within an existing volume.
[ARCHITECT'S STATEMENT]

Images: Visitor's Pavilion—UC Irvine
              Irvine, California
Courtesy of Rebecca L. Binder FAIA Architecture & Planning
Hardware: PC
Software: ACAD 14, 2000; 3D Studio

COMPUTER-MODELED DIAGRAMS

COMPUTER-MODELED DIAGRAMS

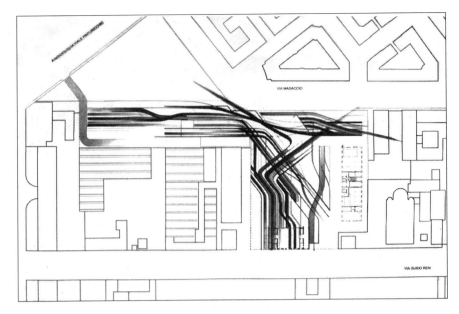

Computer drawing: Contemporary Arts Center, Rome, Italy
Courtesy of Zaha Hadid Architect

This drawing has been drawn and modified using Minicad 7 and Vectorworks. In this document a Pict file was imported, which was created through scanning a sketch, which was then edited in Photoshop.
[ARCHITECT'S STATEMENT]

Computer drawing: Contemporary Arts Center, Rome, Italy
Courtesy of Zaha Hadid Architect

This is a rendering from a computer model which has been enhanced in Photoshop.
[ARCHITECT'S STATEMENT]

Hand sketches are done by Zaha Hadid at the start of most projects. Computer modeling—rendering and drawings are done simultaneously by the office in each project.
[STATEMENT BY BARBARA KUIT IN THE OFFICE OF ZAHA HADID]

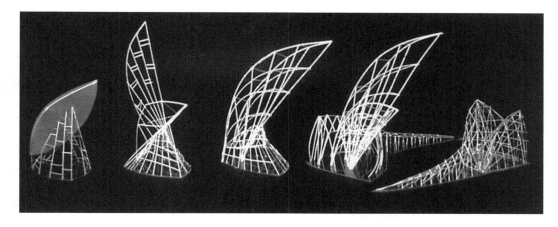

Computer-generated wireframes, like manually executed contour and cross-contour drawings, describe the form of an object. Cross-contour drawings are drawings in which typically parallel lines are used to traverse the surface of an object. With the wireframe drawing, it is possible to visualize the overall shape of a building in a pure sense; that is, without the "distractions" of nonarchitectural features.

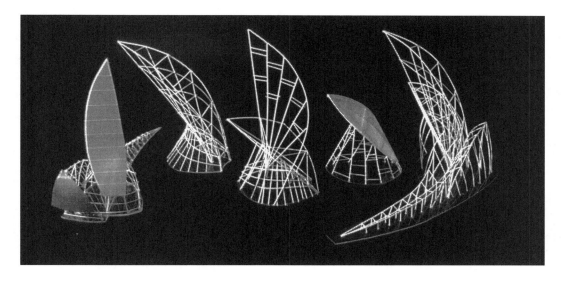

Computer wireframe studies: National Museum of Contemporary Art
Osaka, Japan
Courtesy of Cesar Pelli & Associates Architects
Photo credit: M. LaFoe with Cesar Pelli and Associates

Digital photo rendering of aerial view
The National Museum is in the central foreground.
Courtesy of Jun Mitsui Associates

COMPUTER-MODELED DIAGRAMS

SKETCHING IDEAS

very abstract initial doodle

less abstract

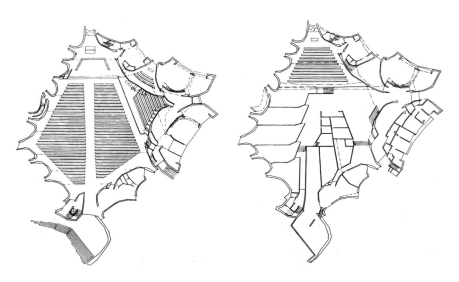

refinement from the abstract

Sketches and drawings: Kaleva Church, Tampere, Finland
Scales: upper left and bottom 1:50, upper right 1:100
Medium: Charcoal
Courtesy of Raili and Reima Pietilä, Architects

Images in the mind are first visualized (a mental act) and then sketched (a physical act). Sketching ideas on paper helps to evolve other ideas; these concepts are constantly evaluated and reevaluated. The examples here show a progression from creative abstract sketches to more refined drawings.

The ability to formulate mental images comes with practice. Visualizing everyday objects will form the basis for sharpening the conceptual imagination. As ideas occur, they are put on paper. This is an **ideational** drawing. An idea on paper is a visual representation of what something may conceptually look like. Some ideas will be discarded; some ideas will be changed, modified, refined, and expanded.

Diagrams are abstract in the sense that they use symbols to simplify pictorial reality. This abstraction aids in the analysis and development stage of the design process. Since it is a crucial part of the process, it develops and changes as a concept transforms.

Reima Peitilä (1923–1993), a world-renowned Finnish architect in the period after Alvar Aalto, stated the following:

Creating architecture is a multimedia process. It involves verbal programming and directing; visualization by sketching floor plans, sections, elevations; spatialization with the help of a scale model; materialization by building. Both words and pictures are used to explain architectural form. Neither one nor the other alone is enough to make architecture as a phenomenon sufficiently comprehensible.

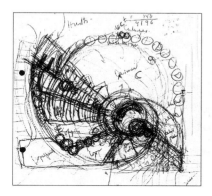 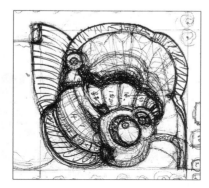 

Conceptual sketches and model photo: Tampere Main Library ("Metso"), Tampere City, Finland
Sketches 4" × 4" (10.2 × 10.2 cm), Model scale: 1:200
Courtesy of Raili and Reima Pietilä, Architects

This transparent "silk" (tracing paper) is my miraculous design medium. Almost a nonmaterial, it is cheap and of little value in the artist's permanent works. As my own design tool, this transparent or, more exactly, semitranslucent membrane functions as a catalyst, enabling visions to be fixed. The sketch has no further value after it has delivered its graphic message to the copy machine. Upon construction of the building, perhaps the production drawings go to the archives; but these sketches, though having helped mediate the path towards the form, usually get thrown in the wastepaper basket before too long.

I have thought, however, that these process sketches could be of use in allowing us an insight into how architecture emerges from "scrap" or how architecture emerges almost from that indefinite "anything" that can be behind or beneath the architectural concepts. The pictorial material of this processing design often has very little final form or character: Instead, it possesses more an artistic multiple message load. Though the sketch is beyond the limited categories of logic and such consequent thinking, the sketch itself is not irrelevant or irrational. The good sketch is a multi-interpretive idea; it can give suitable impulses for feasible alternatives. We must then train ourselves to learn to read them, patiently, allowing much time.

Usually I lay sketch upon sketch, perhaps up to ten times, carefully holding the previous one as a basis for the following sketch until I feel "it is there." Usually then it is. My professional visualization opens up its possible routes through such sketch paper procedure. Architectural characteristics, features, traits, etc., are transported, transformed, and transfigured via the sketches. At the end of the process, there are, of course, the final plans, sections, elevations, and details. Architectural graphics is an art where the expressive form follows the implicit function. Its latent message value is much higher than we usually assume and it is the sketch graphics that generate the spatial vision, which will, in turn, become actual architecture.

These sketches here are merely a sample from hundreds; but it is still possible to note how, through these sketches, the building grows on the drafting table. It should be emphasized that these sketches are "conceptual tools" on the way to becoming objects and not in themselves detached objects like an artist's graphics. I would advise everyone not to break this vital growth link between these sketches and the actual building they become.
[REIMA PIETILÄ]

Notes on sketches and the architectural process
Courtesy of Raili and Reima Pietilä, Architects
Reprinted from: *PIETILÄ Intermediate Zones in Modern Architecture* with permission of Raili Pietilä
and the Museum of Finnish Architecture and the Alvar Aalto Museum

SKETCHING IDEAS

THUMBNAIL SKETCHES

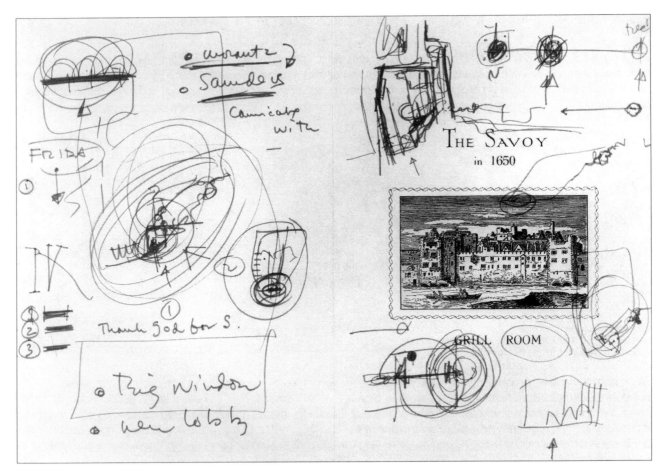

Diagrammatical sketches (both pages): National Gallery, Sainsbury Wing
London, England
Medium: Red felt-tipped pen
Courtesy of Venturi, Scott Brown and Associates, Inc., Architects

The ideal sketches are those that evolve from intuition indirectly guiding the hand more than from the mind directly guiding the hand. Also, combinations of images and words enrich the process.
[ARCHITECT'S STATEMENT]

These two-dimensional "napkin sketches" (in this case a dinner menu) were done by architect Robert Venturi. Designers and architects usually sketch at a minute size, thus giving us the term **"thumbnail sketches,"** shown above, which are the size of Venturi's small doodles. Sketching at a small scale allows one to explore more ideas and thus consider more possibilities and choices for a design problem. Activities such as working, playing, eating, or answering nature's call can all be times when the mind can generate creative thoughts. In other words, creative thinking is not altogether controllable and it is important for the designer to be "on alert" for the creative insight.

Colored or black **ink** is usually a better medium than color or toned pencil values for thumbnail sketches, especially if you plan to do a percentage reduction of the thumbnails to accomodate a certain page or panel size in a presentation.

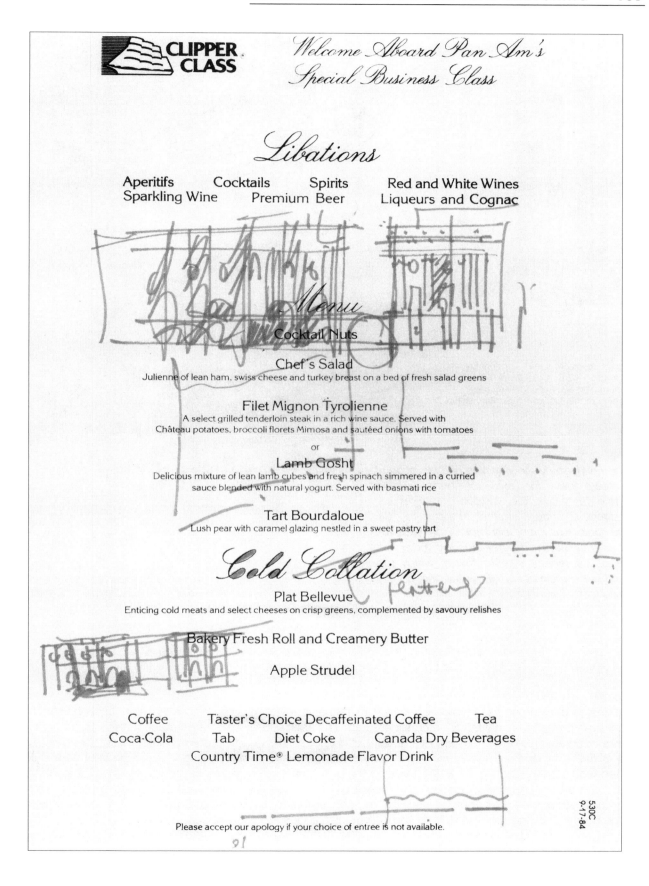

CLIPPER CLASS

Welcome Aboard Pan Am's Special Business Class

Libations

Aperitifs   Cocktails   Spirits   Red and White Wines
Sparkling Wine   Premium Beer   Liqueurs and Cognac

Menu

Cocktail Nuts

Chef's Salad
Julienne of lean ham, swiss cheese and turkey breast on a bed of fresh salad greens

Filet Mignon Tyrolienne
A select grilled tenderloin steak in a rich wine sauce. Served with
Château potatoes, broccoli florets Mimosa and sautéed onions with tomatoes

or

Lamb Gosht
Delicious mixture of lean lamb cubes and fresh spinach simmered in a curried
sauce blended with natural yogurt. Served with basmati rice

Tart Bourdaloue
Lush pear with caramel glazing nestled in a sweet pastry tart

Cold Collation

Plat Bellevue
Enticing cold meats and select cheeses on crisp greens, complemented by savoury relishes

Bakery Fresh Roll and Creamery Butter

Apple Strudel

Coffee   Taster's Choice Decaffeinated Coffee   Tea
Coca-Cola   Tab   Diet Coke   Canada Dry Beverages
Country Time® Lemonade Flavor Drink

Please accept our apology if your choice of entree is not available.

530C
9-17-84

THUMBNAIL SKETCHES

CONCEPTUAL SKETCHING

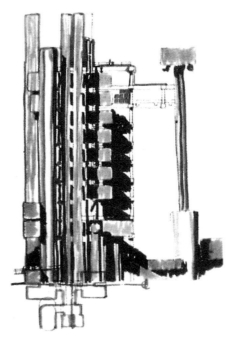

Sketch: Lloyds of London, London, England
33" × 45.5" (83.8 × 115.6 cm)
Medium: Pen and ink on tracing paper
Courtesy of the Richard Rogers Partnership, Architects

A very early study showing plan and elevation of a satellite tower for Lloyd's of London. At this stage of the project the provision of services was considerably underestimated. In particular, the plant room was eventually more than twice the size of that shown. This free-standing tower was one of six servant satellite towers which surrounded the main atrium of the building.
[ARCHITECT'S STATEMENT]

Sketch: University of Toledo's Center for the Visual Arts
          Toledo, Ohio
12" × 9" (30.5 × 22.9 cm)
Medium: Ink on paper
Courtesy of Frank O. Gehry, Architect

Sketch: Pocono Pines House
          Mount Pocono, Pennsylvania
17" × 11" (43.2 × 27.9 cm)
Medium: Pen and ink
Courtesy of Aldo Rossi, Studio di Architettura
New York, Architect

The design-drawing process typically begins with freehand sketches. The sketched design drawings should be artful even though they will rarely be considered art. The artist usually creates permanent artifacts, whereas the designer creates sketches that are referential, but do not exist as ends in themselves. These documents give rise to built form and are afterwards largely forgotten. The sketches on this page resulted in outstanding completed works by the architects noted. Develop the good habit of carrying a **sketchpad** with you as you travel within the urban landscape; observe and record what you see with quick sketches. Fostering this habit will eventually strengthen your ability to visualize and conceptualize. **Conceptual thinking** is the crucial initial step in the design-drawing process to help you communicate ideas to yourself and to others.

Himmelsgärten

Eckstruktur wird betont, um ein "feste" wand zur strasse zu schalten

Stadtbäume

Kirchnerstrasse

Ein Wasserwand

Läden

Bänke

Offentlicher Innenraum.

Kaiserplatz

Conceptual sketch: Commerzbank, Frankfurt, Germany
11.7" × 8.23" (297 × 209 mm)
Medium: Pencil on paper
Courtesy of Foster Associates, Architects & Engineers
Sketch by Lord Foster of Thames Bank

The sketch explores the three-dimensional geometrics that meet at this critical junction—the entrance to the public spaces. It is also mindful of the role that it can play to communicate ideas to others.
[ARCHITECT'S STATEMENT]

Freehand conceptual sketching is the most potent means of generating ideas for any type of design. It is unlikely that any medium will fully supplant the immediacy and directness of freehand drawing. In the architectural design discipline, to be able to record and evolve ideas as they occur is of utmost importance; and this oldest and most primal method of recording ideas is still essential to the designer. The designer should always record exploratory ideas with any accompanying notes (the notes on the sketch above are in German) on a sketchpad or in a **sketchbook** (logbook) with bond paper that takes any kind of media. Many architects keep sketchpads or sketchbooks on hand at all times for the express purpose of recording their design ideas. A "sketch journal" or visual diary can be an invaluable reference source during the design process.

CONCEPTUAL SKETCHING

CONCEPTUAL SKETCHING

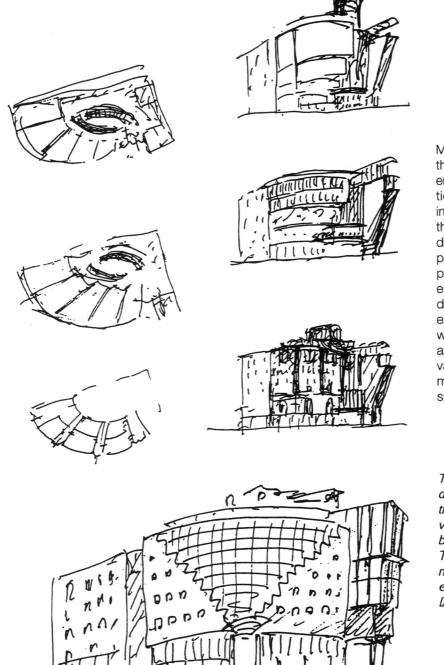

Much like nondirected research in the sciences, sketches can be generated for the purposes of speculation and reflection without any immediate goal in mind. Sometimes these highly imaginative doodles are developed without regard for the pragmatic constraints found in the physical world (e.g., gravity, climate, etc.). Every design professional develops his or her own language in expressing concepts graphically as a way of seeing. Concepts can be approached by thinking in plan, in elevation, in section, in paraline axonometric/oblique images, or in perspective images.

These sketches show two different approaches investigated. The upper three sketches show stone facades as a veneer and a cantilevering part of the building to separate two urban spaces. The lower sketch investigates a symmetrical approach with a central entrance, which was not followed up. [ARCHITECT'S STATEMENT]

Early conceptual sketches: Haas–Haus Stephansplatz, Vienna, Austria
Medium: Ink
Courtesy of Hans Hollein, Architekt

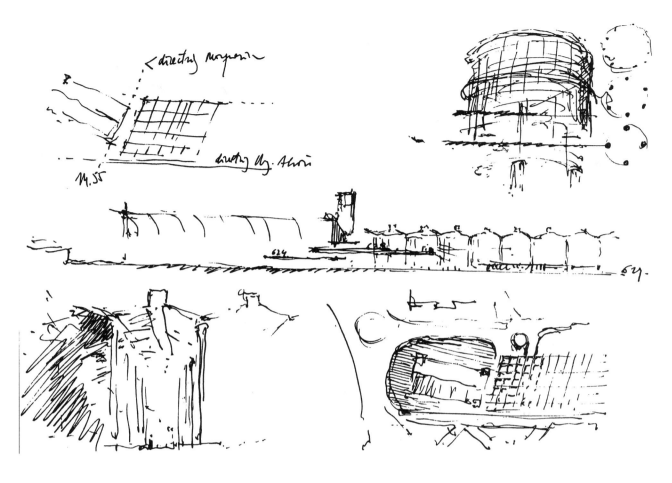

Conceptual sketches: Atocha Station
                                    Madrid, Spain
31.5 × 21.5 cm (12.4" × 8.5")
Medium: Ink
Courtesy of Jose Rafael Moneo, Architect

Several sketches of the Atocha Railway Station. Two of them speak about the plan and show the importance of the existing axes in defining the project. Another two are more related to the description of what a space atmosphere should be: One is related to the lantern, the other to the big hall. The sketch in the middle shows a section.
Sketches help to fix the floating ideas in the architect's mind. They often record this early moment when architects foresee the space to come.
[ARCHITECT'S STATEMENT]

As you examine the design sketches in this chapter, be aware that different types of media directly affect the feeling of space that is perceived. Architects and design professionals have adopted many traditional artistic media (graphite, ink wash, watercolor, pastel, gouache, etc.) to express their ideas; now they are beginning to exploit the medium of digital technology (see interactive web site Chapter 12).

CONCEPTUAL SKETCHING

CONCEPTUAL SKETCHING

The axonometric below, although an unrealistic view, is utilized to help my client understand the massing, proportions, and relationships of the building components, whereas the perspective at right portrays a humanistic view and expresses the impact of the receding facade. Soft pencil allows a varied expression of line and tone weight within a single stroke, giving an informal quality to the sketches.

This is a conceptual massing study of a hillside residence in the area of Oakland, California. Blended within a hillside setting, it utilizes the advantages of light and view while borrowing the massing style of Tuscany.
[ARCHITECT'S STATEMENT]

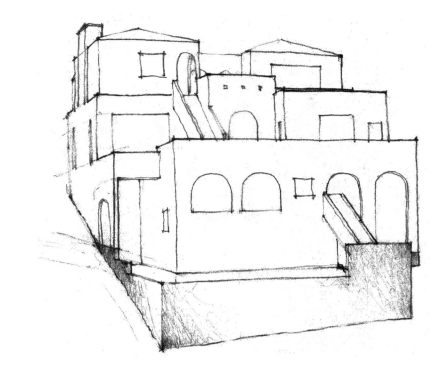

Sketches: Woo residence, Oakland, California
Perspective: 12" × 12" (30.5 × 30.5 cm)
Axonometric: 18" × 18" (45.7 × 45.7 cm)
Scale: ⅛"=1'0"
Medium: HB pencil
Courtesy of Kenzo Handa, Architect

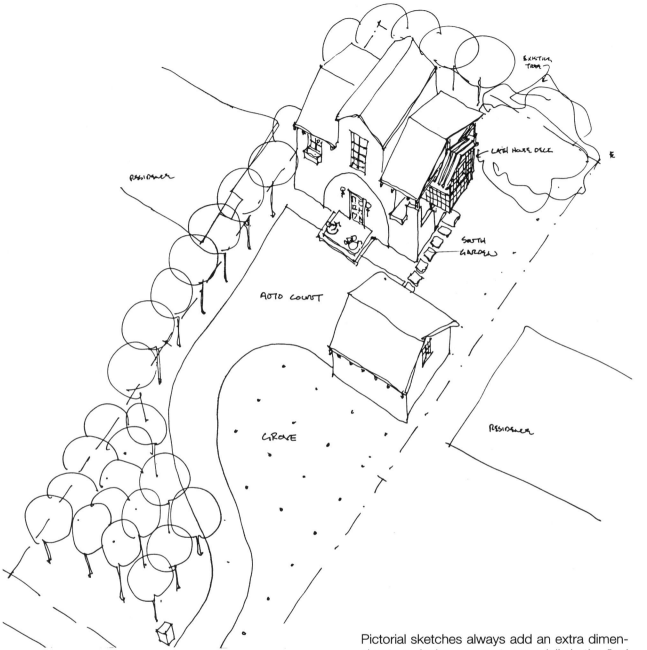

Drawing: Concept sketch for the Oxley residence, La Jolla, California
11" × 17" (27.9 × 43.2 cm)
Medium: Y & C stylist (black fine-tipped pen) on trace
Courtesy of Rob Wellington Quigley, FAIA

Pictorial sketches always add an extra dimension to a design concept, especially in the final schematic phases of any project. Spatial concepts (not seen in orthographic sketches) are more clearly revealed. This sketch aided in the development of conceiving and confirming ideas prior to the building process.

CONCEPTUAL SKETCHING

CONCEPTUAL SKETCHING

Sketches: Khalsa Heritage Memorial Complex
           Anandpur Sahib, Punjab, India
Medium: Orthello pastel pencils and ink
Courtesy of Moshe Safdie Architect
Sketch done in the office of Moshe Safdie by Moshe Safdie

The Khalsa Heritage Memorial is a new museum of the Sikh people located in the holy town of Anandpur Sahib near Chandigarh in the Punjab state. The museum celebrates 500 years of Sikh history and the 300th anniversary of the Khalsa, the scriptures written by the tenth and last Guru, Gobind Singh, founder of the modern Sikh faith. It is located on a 75-acre site overlooking the town. The memorial is divided into two complexes that straddle a ravine and are linked by a bridge. The western complex is connected to the town; it is organized around an entrance piazza and contains a 400-seat auditorium, a two-story library, and exhibition galleries. The eastern complex contains permanent interpretive exhibit space. This space is housed in two clusters of undulating galleries that evoke the fortress architecture of the region with a dramatic skyline image against the sand cliff terrain. The clustering of the galleries in groups of five reflects the Five Virtues, a central tenet of the Sikh faith. A series of dams in the ravine creates pools that reflect the complex at night.
[ARCHITECT'S STATEMENT]

Thumbnail sketches are often put together as a package comprising a storyboard of conceptual ideas. The storyboard can be sifted through and simplified and the remaining sketches amplified to target the more salient issues.

Sketch: Hibiscus House, Coconut Grove
Florida
4" × 6" (10.2 × 15.2 cm)
Medium: Graphite on vellum
Courtesy of DPZ & Company
Drawn by Architect Elizabeth Plater-Zyberk

This house recalls that period when local classically trained architects first encountered European Modernism. In the style that developed, traditional compositional devices, freed from ornament, appear with unusual clarity. This design consists of three buildings: a loggia, a living room, and a block of utilitarian rooms. Although each building has its own particular and appropriate system of openings, they share several important axes.
[ARCHITECT'S STATEMENT]

Sketch: Greenpeace, Alameda, California
12" × 18" (30.5 × 45.7 cm)
Medium: Pencil and technical pens
Courtesy of William P. Bruder, Architect

...pen and ink sketch developed over photo prints of existing buildings and context to show reuse potentials. This technique is a quick way to present concept ideas three-dimensionally.
[ARCHITECT'S STATEMENT]

CONCEPTUAL SKETCHING

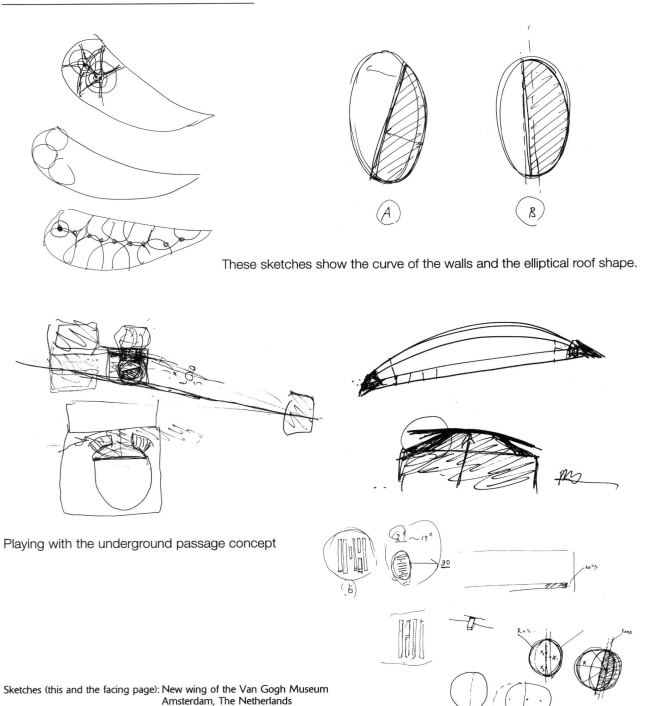

These sketches show the curve of the walls and the elliptical roof shape.

Playing with the underground passage concept

Sketches (this and the facing page): New wing of the Van Gogh Museum
Amsterdam, The Netherlands
Medium: Ink on paper
Courtesy of Kisho Kurokawa Architect

Design concept—The new wing was built in the open space adjacent to the main building of the museum, which was the last work of the Dutch Modernist architect Rietveld. Considering the whole of the landscape, 75 percent of the building's area (excluding the main exhibition hall) was constructed underground in an effort to minimize the space it would have taken above the ground. The new wing connects to the main building through an underground passage.
[ARCHITECT'S STATEMENT]

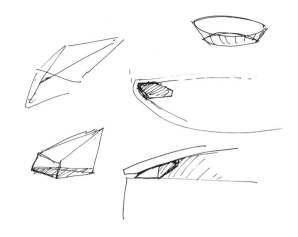

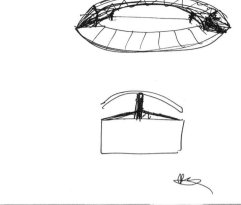

Working on the sunken pool idea

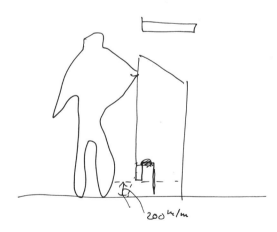

200 h/m

Experimenting with the tilt of the roof

Although Rietveld and Kurokawa share the Modernist idea of geometric abstraction, Kurokawa's new wing departs from Rietveld's linear style with curvilinear shapes and lines, employing a traditional Japanese idea of abstraction. One characteristic expressing this idea is the sunken pool, situated between the new wing and the main building. Symbiosis between the new wing and the main building is attained through the open intermediate space created by the pool. The tilt of the elliptical roof and curve of the walls dislocate the center, underscoring the Japanese aesthetic of asymmetry. Through highly abstract simple geometric shapes made complex and, further, through careful manipulation, the abstract symbolism of the new wing strikes a balance between the international and the local.
[ARCHITECT'S STATEMENT]

CONCEPTUAL SKETCHING

CONCEPTUAL SKETCHING

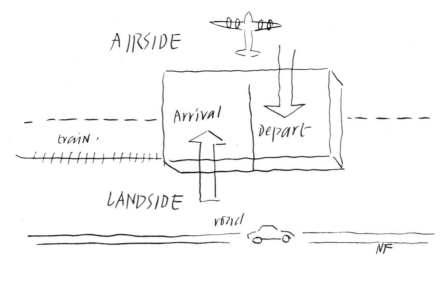

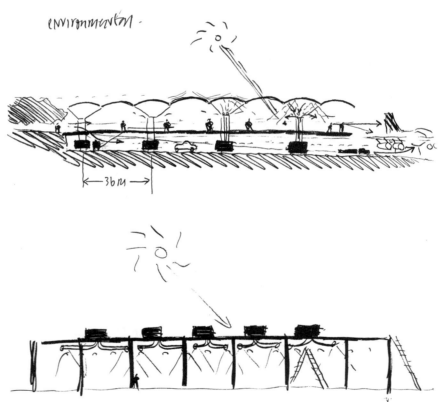

Sketches: London Airport
Stansted, England
8.3" × 11.7" (21 × 29 cm)
Medium: Pencil (graphite) on paper, size A-4
Courtesy of Foster Associates, Architects & Engineers
Drawn by Lord Foster of Thames Bank

Lord Foster usually does all of his sketches in an A-4 sketchbook. His conceptual sketches are done by hand, but sometimes computer drawings are used as a guide for the sketches.

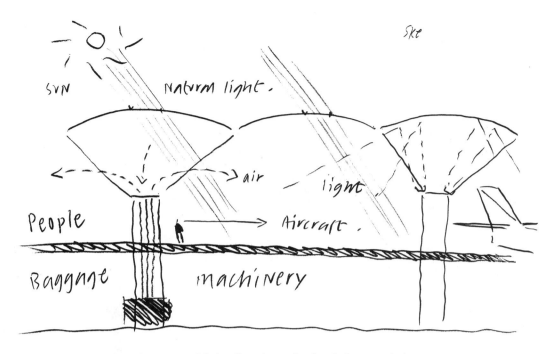

Sketch diagram showing natural light direction, air circulation, and view

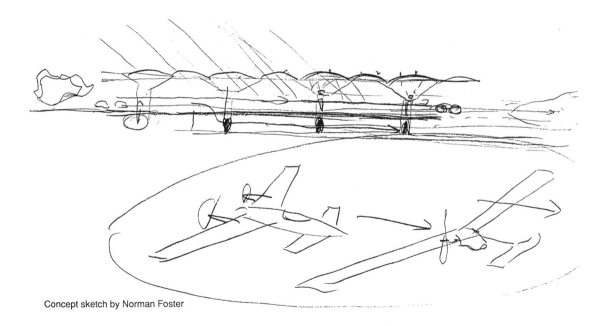

Concept sketch by Norman Foster

With many of the sketches here, I was trying to explain our proposals for the International Terminal at Stansted, London's new third airport. We had drawn inspiration from the early days of flying when airfields were very simple affairs. There was always a clear airside and landside, so you were never in any doubt about where you were. To depart you walked towards the aircraft, which was an enjoyable part of the travel experience—there was no need for signs or complex level changes. The arrival sequence was the same straightforward process in reverse.
[ARCHITECT'S STATEMENT]

CONCEPTUAL SKETCHING

CONCEPTUAL SKETCHING

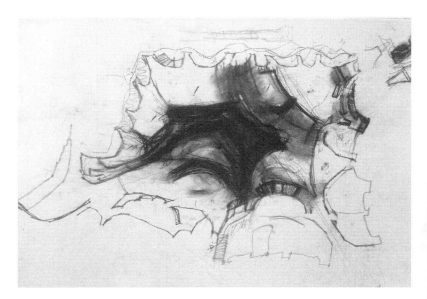

Sketches: Kaleva Church, ground floor
Tampere, Finland
45" × 29" (114.3 × 73.7 cm)
Media: Charcoal and crayon on sketch paper
Sketches by Reima Pietila
Courtesy of the Pietila Archive, Helsinki

Photo: Kaleva Church interior, 1966
Courtesy of Raili Pietila

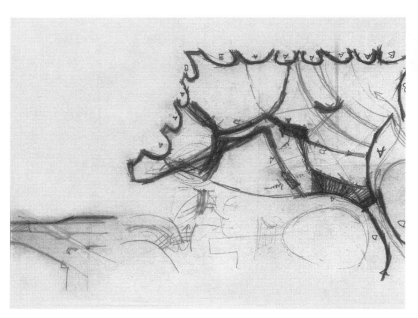

A diagram or diagrams with a photograph is very telling, because it shows how the character of the sketch is evident in the actual building (see pp. 478–479).

Perhaps many modernistic designs should be grateful for this thin unqualified sketch paper. The aesthetic expression of architectural integrity or totality can also be seen to derive from the skillful techniques of transparent designing. These sketches here are merely a sample from hundreds, but it is still possible to note how through these sketches the building grows on the drafting table. It should be emphasized that these sketches are "conceptual tools" on the way to becoming objects, and not in themselves detached objects like an artist's graphics. I would advise everyone not to break this vital growth link between these sketches and the actual building they become.
[Architect's statement]

Sketches: Bharat Diamond
           Bourse Mumbai
           (near Bombay), India
Size: A-5
Media: Ink and pastel
Courtesy of Balkrishna Doshi,
Architect

Bharat Diamond Bourse is composed of many textures, surfaces, and volumes. These counterpoised elements conjure constrasts to construct illusionary images, reality encountered usually as part of our dreams. Moving through the crystal-shaped forms of shops, offices, and trading halls, etc., one rediscovers the immense sense of freedom offered by the skies as all the glass surfaces integrate the outer universe and fuse the waterfall and the landscape around. This place, because of the ancient rock that has been made a part of our design, has now become the most sacred place in India. [ARCHITECT'S STATEMENT]

CONCEPTUAL SKETCHING

COMPOSITE CONCEPTUAL SKETCHING

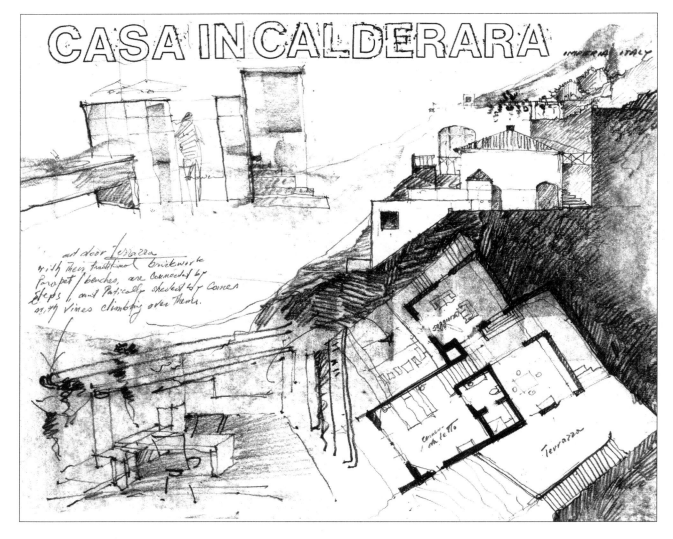

Drawing: House in Calderara
           Imperia, Italy
Medium: Pencil
Courtesy of Professor George S. Loli
Department of Architecture
University of Louisiana–Lafayette

*This **composite design sketch** shows a house in disrepair undergoing a renovation where views and consequently terraces become important design considerations. This drawing documents the client/designer dialogue, which discusses the initial design opportunity.*
[PROFESSOR'S STATEMENT]

Compare the composite conceptual sketches on this and the facing pages with the hardline integrated composite presentations in Chapter 11, Presentation Formats, and in the drawing exercise on p. 608.

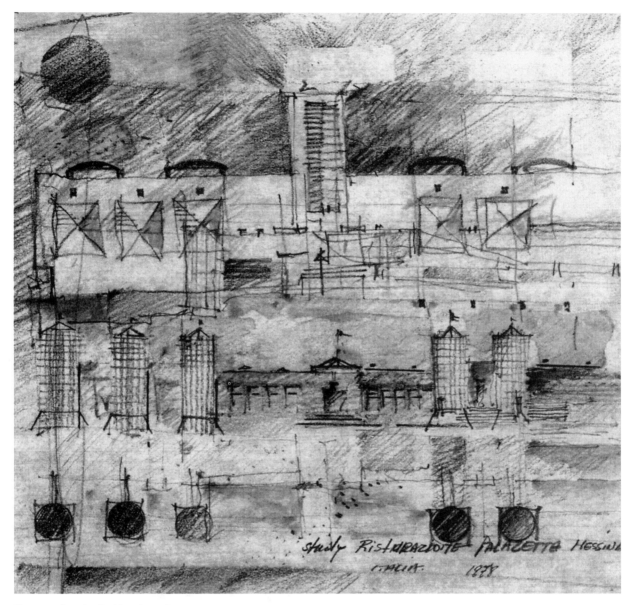

Conceptual study of a Venetian palazzo
Medium: Pencil and colored pencils on yellow tracing paper
Courtesy of Professor George S. Loli
Department of Architecture, University of Louisiana–Lafayette

This is a conceptual study utilizing the superimposition of various drawing conventions to render and reveal the idea of transforming a dilapidated Venetian palazzo.
[PROFESSOR'S STATEMENT]

Study the strengths and limitations of the materials you can utilize for conceptual studies, whether they be pencil, pen, colored pencils, or other media. In this way, you can select the appropriate medium or combination of media to express the feeling and mood you want to create.

COMPOSITE CONCEPTUAL SKETCHING

CONCEPTUAL MODELING AND SKETCHING

Schematic design study using freehand sketches and computer 3D models. Design for a dwelling within a bridge. Freehand pen and ink and felt-tipped marker drawings. Computer 3D models with form-Z application.

Freehand sketch provides fluidity of design at the very early stages of idea generation. Computer 3D model helps to test and develop the schematic idea into more concrete parameters.

[PROFESSOR'S STATEMENT]

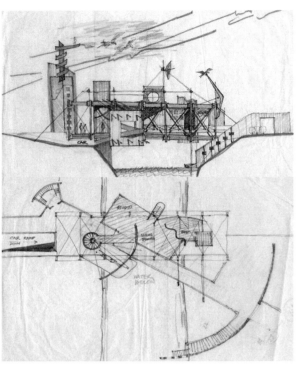

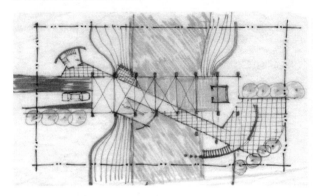

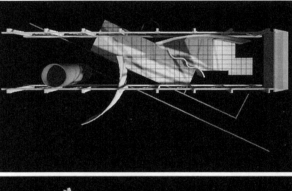

Sketches and conceptual models: Dwelling Within a Bridge
Courtesy of Mohammed Saleh Uddin, Ph.D.
Professor, Environmental Design
University of Missouri–Columbia

A photograph of a model can provide a diagrammatic understanding.

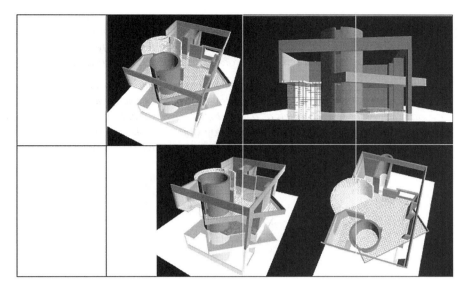

Computer 3d study models and photographs of the completed front facade and interior stair details.

One-family residence with the option of vertical expansion, accommodating privacy of the current design. Restricted site boundaries forced the design to be sculpted from a cubic massvolume. Subtracted mass in the front protects the glazed wall and sucks air inside the building that counterbalances the double-height void in the dining area, facilitating natural air flow year-round. All openings were carefully designed (most openings pushed inward to avoid direct exposure to climatic extremes) to respond to the environmental conditions of the region's hot-humid climate. [PROFESSOR'S STATEMENT]

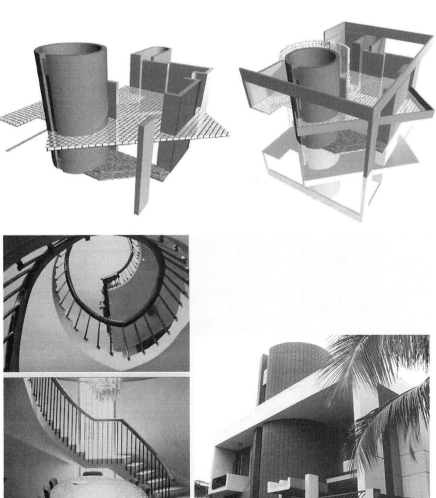

CONCEPTUAL MODELING

Conceptual models: Rahman residence, Dhaka, Bangladesh
Courtesy of Mohammed Saleh Uddin, Ph.D.
Professor, Environmental Design
University of Missouri–Columbia

The general program requirements were evolved in plan and section initially and continually developed during the course of massing/**partí** study. The sketches below are just a small part of a series done for daily brainstorming sessions to develop the appropriate **partí** to accommodate the technology theme and reconcile the site geometry; in this case, twin curves engaging each other in a high-tech "yin–yang" composition.

A quick 3D AutoCAD model was developed for the variations and was used as a base for the spontaneous black Prismacolor pencil sketches. Both scaled elevational views and aerial perspectives were used as tools in conjunction with myriad quick foam study models as a basis for discussion and review. The design team was certainly not shy about generating as many options as possible for study and evaluation. Note the series of vignette sketches of how we might engage the sky plane with an appropriate communications/technology gesture.

[DESIGN ILLUSTRATOR'S STATEMENT]

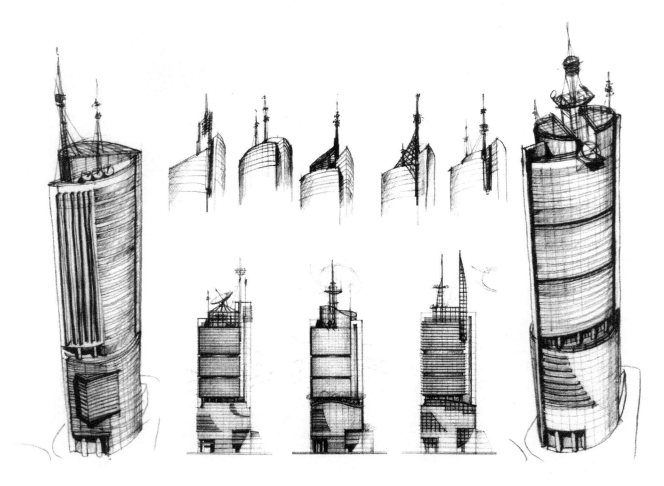

Images: Communications Center Office Tower Competition,
        Shanghai, China
Courtesy of KMD, San Francisco: Design Office
Herbert McLaughlin, Design Principal
Lawrence K. Leong, Design Illustrator
Architectural Concept Imaging, San Francisco

CONCEPTUAL SKETCHING WITH AUTOCAD

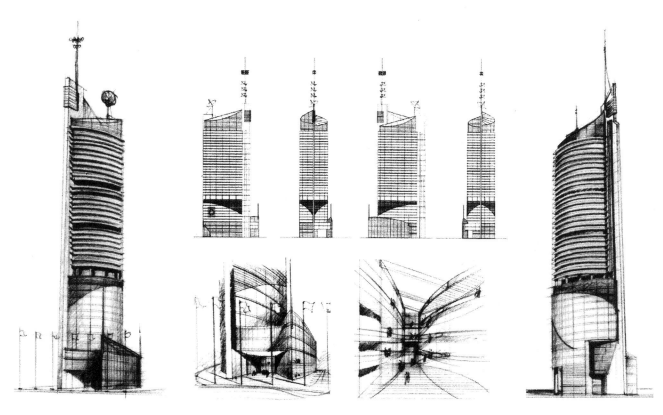

Images: Communications Center Office Tower Competition,
Shanghai, China
Courtesy of KMD, San Francisco: Design Office
Herbert McLaughlin, Design Principal
Lawrence K. Leong, Design Illustrator
Architectural Concept Imaging, San Francisco

Once a partí direction was decided upon, we refined the black Prismacolor 3D sketch study vignettes with a concentration on the eye-level experience and viewpoints of key locations. I used AutoCAD elevations to formalize the design conclusions and passed them on to the design team as a base for further refinement and final presentation.
[DESIGN ILLUSTRATOR'S STATEMENT]

Through the end of the twentieth century and into the beginning of the twenty-first, it has been thought by some that conventional software impedes the creative aspect of visualization in the very early stages of the schematic design process. The inability to replicate the ease and immediacy in conceptual hand drawn sketches that architects and designers have done for countless design projects has been one of the major barriers in the development of computer technology in architecture. New software applications like @Last Software—Sketchup, which can mimic hand sketched drawings, are now emerging to make design thinking with a computer comparable in its fluidity and spontaneity to freehand conceptual sketching.

CONCEPTUAL SKETCHING WITH AUTOCAD

11

Presentation Formats

A fine set of presentation drawings is invaluable in architect/client or designer/client relationships for the purpose of graphic communication. An architectural drawing presentation usually includes conceptual diagrams/sketches, a site plan, floor plans, exterior elevations, site sections, building sections, axonometrics, obliques, and perspectives. The initial stage of the design-drawing process is involved with conceptual diagrams and conceptual drawings. As the design concept evolves, more formal methods of presentation are needed. These presentation formats, whether conventional or avant-garde in approach, must effectively communicate to the targeted audience.

The intent of this chapter is to illustrate various presentation formats with respect to traditional wall presentations. The excellent books listed in the Bibliography should be explored for their coverage of other presentation modes (slides, reports, models, etc.).

In summary, following are some of the important terms and concepts you will learn:

Presentation formats   Transparaline   Transoblique
Transmetric   Composite drawings   Competition panels

By viewing a large number of professional competition drawings, you will develop new and fresh ideas on how to handle your own presentations.

Presentation Formats

TOPIC: ARCHITECTURAL PRESENTATIONS

Hart 1987.

TOPIC: ARCHITECTURAL COMPETITION PRESENTATIONS (EXAMPLES)

Competitions magazine

Miralles 1996.

TOPIC: PORTFOLIOS

Burden 1992.

Marquand 1994, 37–39.

Mitton 1999.

Linton 1996.

Porter 2000.

Foote 1996.

Metzdorf 1991.

Chapter Overview

After studying this chapter, you will understand how wall presentations are laid out. You will learn about composite integrated presentations. You will be able to glean ideas for organizing your own single-panel or multipanel presentations. For continued study, refer to Ching's *Architectural Graphics.*

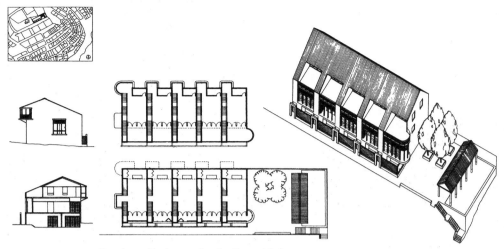

Drawings: Student project by Susan M. Stern
Row housing, Barcelona, Spain
Courtesy of Washington University School of Architecture, St. Louis, Missouri

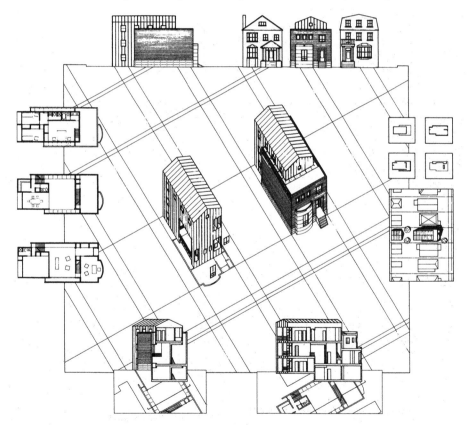

Drawing: Student project by Doug Dolezal
Central West End townhouse
Courtesy of Washington University School of Architecure, St. Louis, Missouri

The primary goal of an architectural presentation is to effectively present design concepts. Implemented design concepts should be drawn and organized in an orderly, structured **format.** Over the years, architects and designers have used many different formats, with the ultimate goal always being the same. This page shows both traditional and more conceptual presentation methods for graphic communications.

INTRODUCTION

GRAPHIC COMMUNICATIONS—PRESENTATION FORMATS

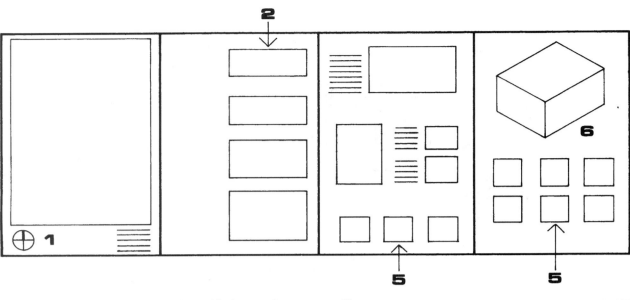

- If possible, orient the site plan with the north arrow up (**1**).
- With adequate vertical space, orient floor plans and elevations to fit in an aligned vertical order (**2**).
- Similarly, floor plans and elevations can relate horizontally if there is adequate horizontal space (**3**).
- Building sections should relate vertically or horizontally to floor plans and elevations in an aligned sequence (**4**).
- Details and notes should be grouped in a visually organized manner (**5**).
- Paralines/perspectives are the cohesive and integrative drawings that help to unify the presentation (**6**).
- The generally accepted order for exhibited drawings is left to right and top to bottom.

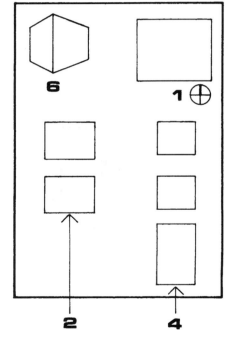

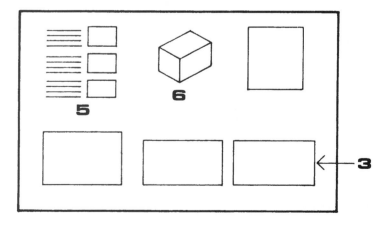

In the section on conventional orthogonal terminology, the primary architectural drawings were introduced. By themselves as an isolated entity, these drawings have little importance. However, when combined as a totality in a **presentation format,** these drawings become a strong **communicative** tool. Architectural presentations are commonly done on sequential sheets or boards. The organization and composition of drawing elements is flexible as long as there is a thread of continuity and unity as well as a conceptual focus.

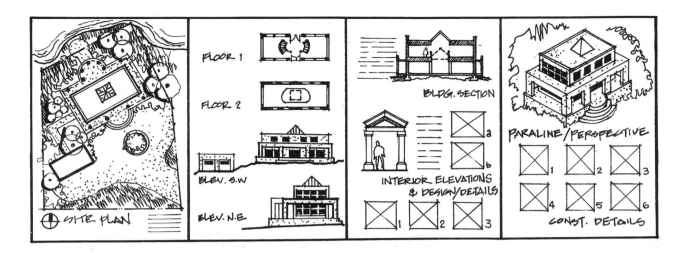

Wall presentations have the advantage of allowing a large audience to view all the drawings in context with each other. The primary components in an architectural presentation are the site plan, floor plans, elevations, sections, and paralines/perspectives. An effective presentation unifying these elements will generally require consistency in scale, orientation, and presentation technique/medium. The size of the audience and the viewing distance are normally the determinants for the choice of scale and the type of medium used.

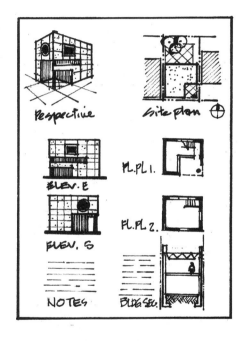

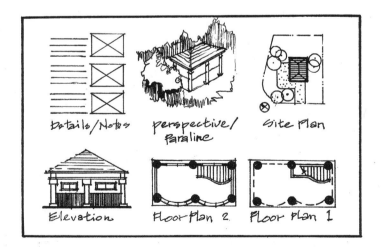

Architectural wall presentation formats are most effective when organized vertically or horizontally. The examples shown are (1) vertically oriented boards or sheets that flow and read horizontally (top row); (2) a horizontally oriented one-board or one-sheet presentation that reads as a total composition (left); and (3) a vertically oriented one-board or one-sheet presentation that reads as a total composition (right). It is often helpful to orient the site plan and floor plans in the same direction. The wall presentation is commonly supplemented with scale models, slides, reports, and the Internet (with other schools, private offices, and the lay public).

PRESENTATION FORMATS

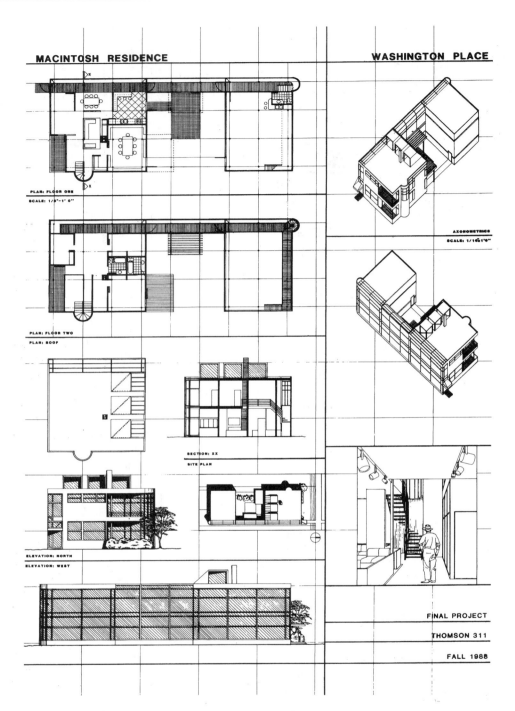

GRID FORMAT

Drawing: Student project by Vaughn Dierks
Macintosh House, St. Louis, Missouri
Courtesy of Washington University School of Architecture, St. Louis, Missouri

This presentation was effectively laid out using a **grid** format. The grid is extremely effective in helping to organize all the drawings and bits of information that go into a comprehensive presentation. The grid should be lightly drawn. The amount of negative space between the drawings is extremely important. Too much space results in drawings that "float"; too little results in a congested layout. As with any artistic composition, the proper figure–background balancing is crucial for all drawings to exist in harmony.

GRID FORMAT

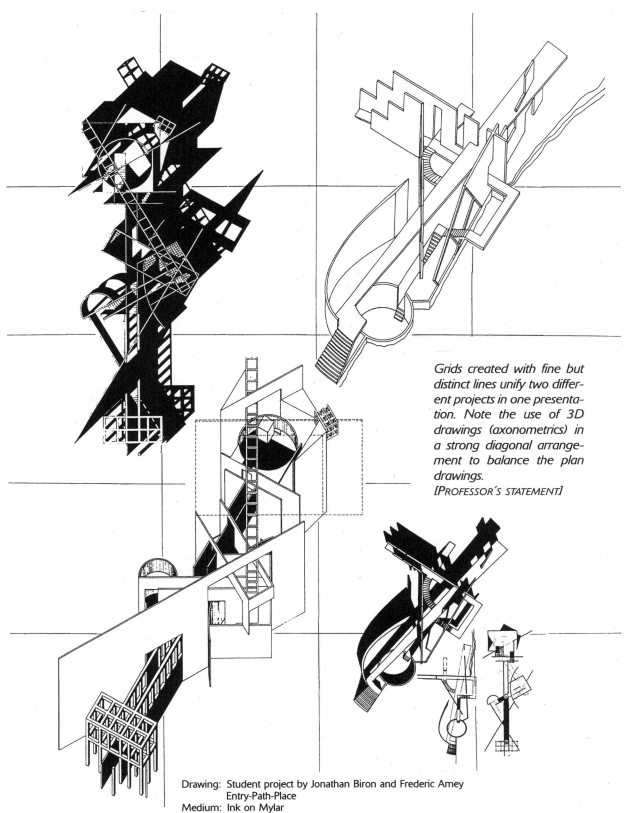

Grids created with fine but distinct lines unify two different projects in one presentation. Note the use of 3D drawings (axonometrics) in a strong diagonal arrangement to balance the plan drawings.
[PROFESSOR'S STATEMENT]

Drawing: Student project by Jonathan Biron and Frederic Amey
              Entry-Path-Place
Medium: Ink on Mylar
M. Saleh Uddin, Professor, Savannah College of Art and Design,
Savannah, Georgia; Southern University, Baton Rouge, Louisiana

COMPOSITE DRAWINGS

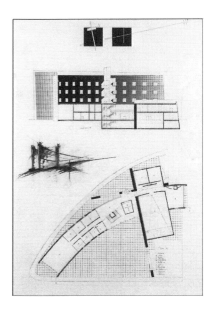
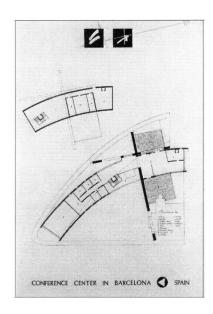
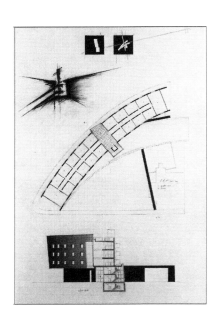

Competition drawings: Student project by Mohd Fadzir Mohd Suhaimi
Barcelona Tile Competition, Barcelona, Spain
Courtesy of Washington University School of Architecture, St. Louis, Missouri

Before the 1980s, a typical set of presentation drawings would have each drawing (plan, elevation, section, etc.) on a separate panel (also termed sheet or board). The eighties showed a movement toward combining several drawing types into one presentation. Since the eighties and into the twenty-first century, design competitions have become more restrictive in their size requirements. This has led many competitors to experiment with and design innovative new formats. When various drawing types are combined on one panel, it is termed a **composite drawing.**

Letter size for titles or labels and any text for architectural presentations depends on how the drawings will be viewed and used. A design jury (a group of teachers, students, or peers that passes judgment on the material being presented) or client responds to the text at different viewing distances, depending on the purpose of the information. A hierarchy of size is clearly shown on the panel on p. 525. The largest letters are in the title: "The Center for Innovative Technology." Second largest are the labels for the drawing: "Ground Floor Plan, Principal Floor Plan, Regional Site Plan," etc. Third largest are the room labels. And the smallest in size is the text for the Concept Statement. Ideally, drawings should "speak for themselves"; the inclusion of text should be minimized as much as possible. In general, use the smallest lettering size and the simplest style that is legible from the desired distance. In multipanel presentations, try to keep consistency in format, size, shape, orientation, and style of the drawing images. Panel continuity in terms of the medium used can also help unify your presentation. The illustration above shows a student presentation composed of three panels. The latter part of this chapter will show you many professional multipanel competition drawings.

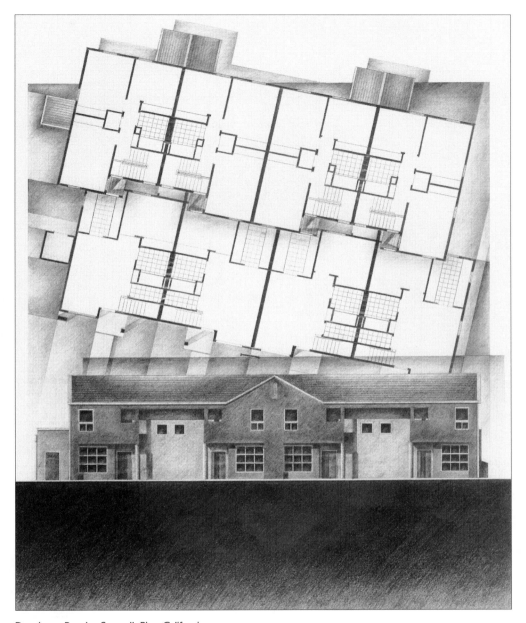

Drawings: Rancho Sespe II, Piru, California
Medium: Pencil
Courtesy of John V. Mutlow, FAIA, Architects

In this composite drawing, the plan and the elevation are composed as one presentation. Care must be taken so that each drawing can be read without losing its clarity. New types of composite drawings using a combination of see-through or transparent drawings, superimposed drawings, and hybrid drawings are becoming commonplace in competitions.

The 6B pencil rendition of a two-dimensional elevation with the combination of the dwelling unit floor plans assists in an understanding of the three-dimensional quality of the facade. The design intention is to generate eight different building designs by assembling three unit types to create building identity from unit repetition (the set urban piece). The shade and shadow on the elevation quickly distinguish individual building identity.
[ARCHITECT'S STATEMENT]

COMPOSITE DRAWINGS

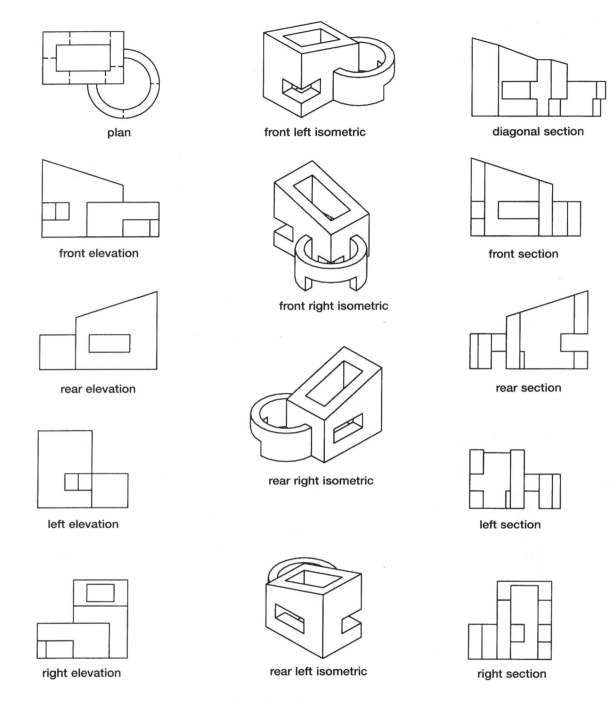

plan

front left isometric

diagonal section

front elevation

front right isometric

front section

rear elevation

rear right isometric

rear section

left elevation

left section

right elevation

rear left isometric

right section

Drawings and subsequent composites designed by Kwok Gorran Tsui,
an architecture graduate of the University of Texas at Austin
Scale: $\frac{3}{32}$"=1'0"

Three organizational methods for setting up a composite drawing are shown on the following three pages using the geometric elements on this page. Before designing schematic layouts for a composite drawing, be sure you have accumulated all of the drawing elements and text for the composition. Also determine whether there will be a primary center of focus drawing and whether all other drawings will play an equally subordinate role. Examine whether there will be any variation in the scale of the drawings. Think about how to utilize the negative space or background area as well as how to use framing elements to establish boundaries (real or implied).

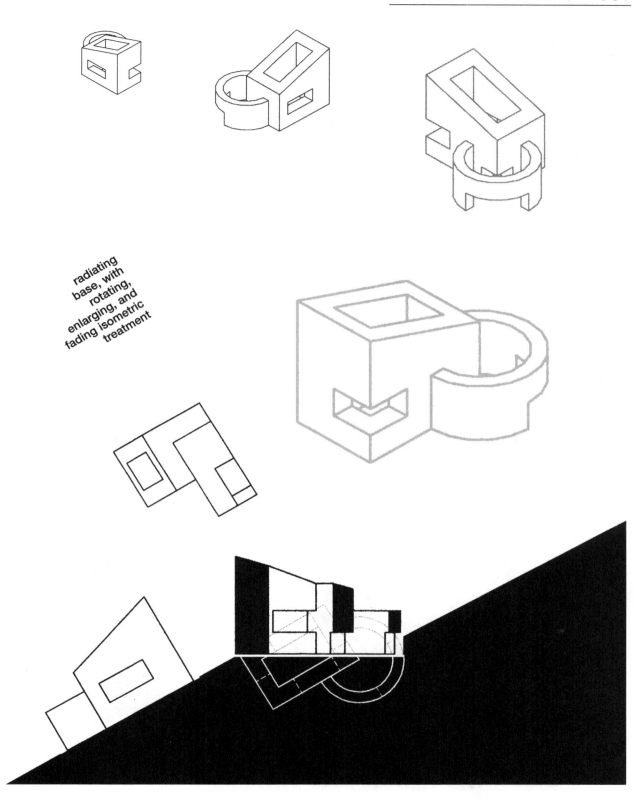

radiating base, with rotating, enlarging, and fading isometric treatment

COMPOSITE DRAWINGS

Paraline drawings like the isometrics shown here, are extemely effective in composite integrated presentations. They refer easily to and relate well with orthographic multiview drawings. Perspective drawings can also relate well to multiview drawings, but tend to be more independent (see pp. 532–535).

COMPOSITE DRAWINGS

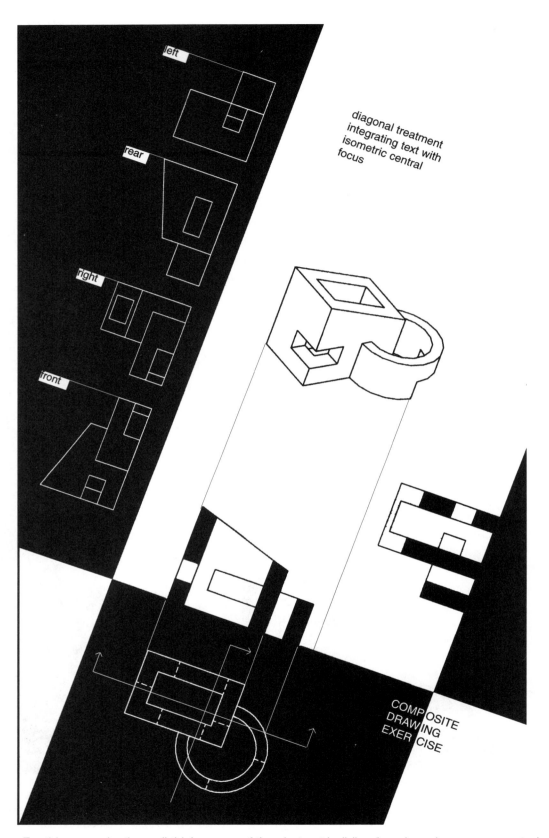

diagonal treatment
integrating text with
isometric central
focus

COMPOSITE
DRAWING
EXERCISE

For this example, the wall thicknesses of the abstract building form have been exaggerated.

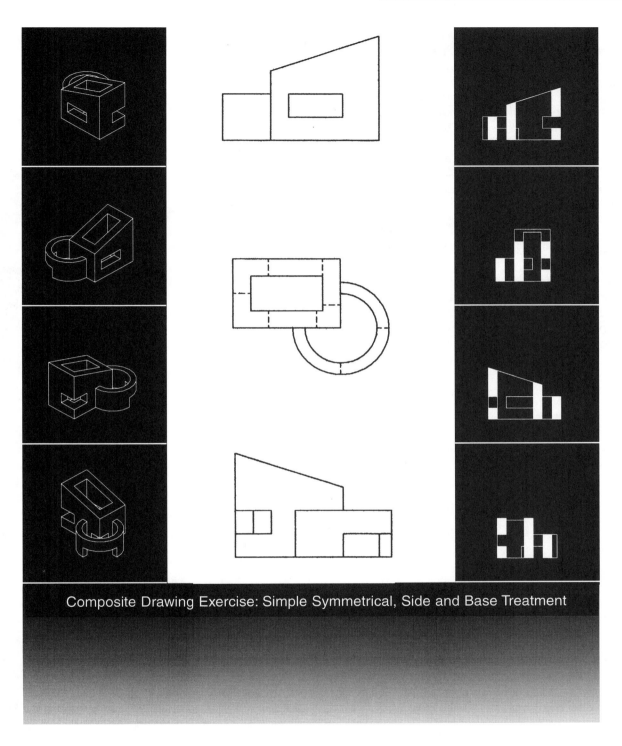

Composite Drawing Exercise: Simple Symmetrical, Side and Base Treatment

COMPOSITE DRAWINGS

In formulating a composition for a composite drawing layout for any design project, try to be creative in balancing and arranging the elements in the drawing field. The examples on pp. 501–506 all use a contrasting (in this case dark) field to help organize and unify the seemingly disparate fragments in all of the presentations. A dark or contrasting field with or without a value change can represent the base or ground area where a building sits as an elevation, a section, a perspective, etc. A dark field can also function as a negative space for a drawing field of white lines for text material, or it can act as a border to help organize specific drawings in their relationship to one another.

This presentation uses a diagonal format, which is achieved by rotating a rectilinear grid format so that it makes an angle with the horizontal and vertical axes. This presentation format refers to the relationship between the new site and the present site of the existing facilities in the historic downtown district of Savannah, Georgia (grid pattern). The presentation is composed of the schematic diagrams on its form-evolution, the site plan, floor plans, elevations, sections, plan obliques, and descriptive text.
[PROFESSOR'S STATEMENT]

This presentation utilizes reversed printing, in which white lines are drawn on a black background. White on black usually appears more intense than black on white.

COMPOSITE DRAWINGS

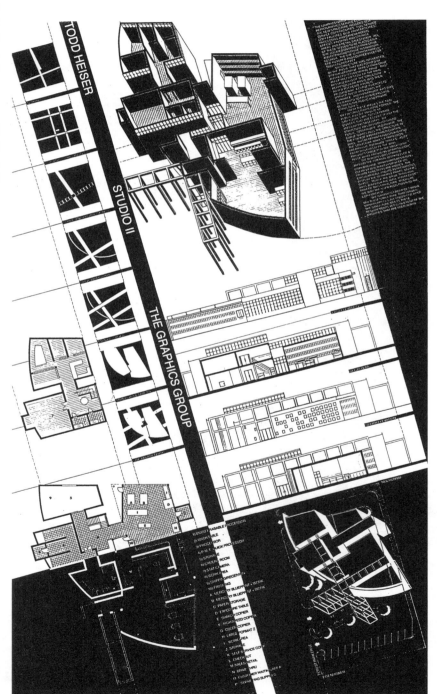

Drawing: Student project by Todd Heiser
          Savannah Blue Print and
          Reprographics
Medium: Ink on Mylar
M. Saleh Uddin, Professor, Savannah College of Art and Design, Savannah, Georgia; Southern University, Baton Rouge, Louisiana

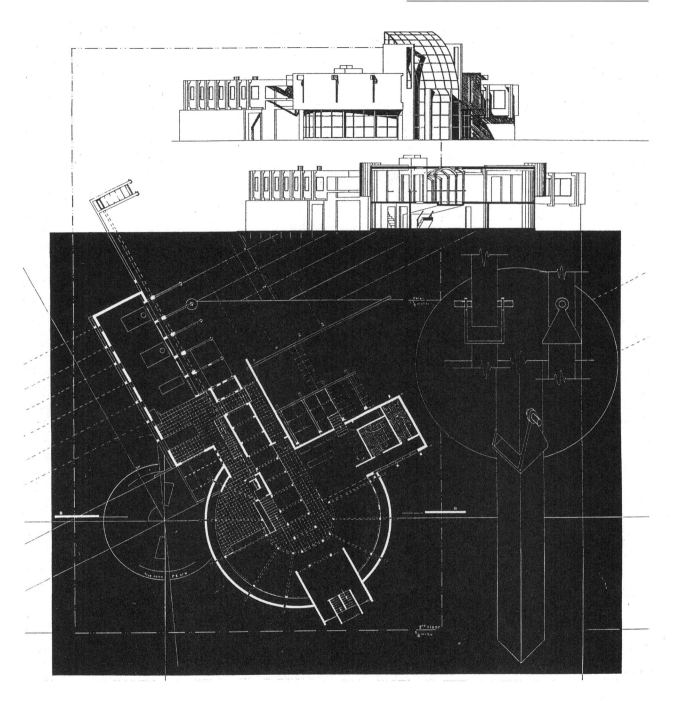

COMPOSITE DRAWING

Drawing: Student project by Kevin Schellenbach
Savannah Blue Print and Reprographics
Medium: Ink on vellum
M. Saleh Uddin, Professor, Savannah College of Art and Design,
Savannah, GA; Southern University, Baton Rouge, Louisiana

This presentation is one sheet of a three-sheet presentation. The composition engages positive and negative images of orthographic drawings. The reverse images of the floor plan and the detail create a baseline for the section drawing. This particular technique effectively separates and highlights section-elevation drawings from floor plans and detail drawings.
[PROFESSOR'S STATEMENT]

COMPOSITE DRAWING

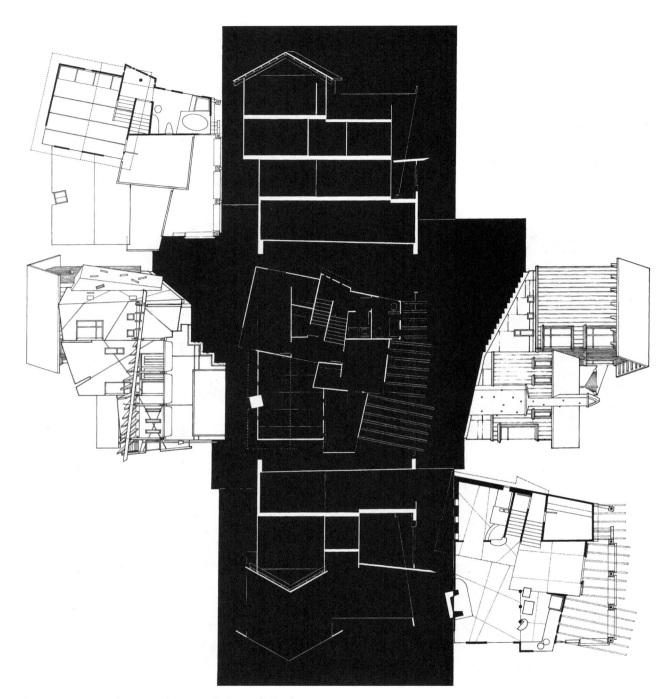

Drawing: Revenge of the stuccoids house, Berkeley, California
24" × 36" (61 × 91.4 cm), Scale: ¼"=1'0"
Medium: Ink on canson paper
Courtesy of David Baker Associates Architects and Nancy Whitcombe

The house represented by this drawing is complex, a collage of discrete ideas and architectural strategies. The complexity of the drawing is compatible with that of the project: simple plans, elevations, and sections alone would not relate the underlying emotional content of the design. The subliminal design intent described intuitively in this composite drawing is greater than the sum of the linear information contained in the separate technical drawings that are its components.
[ARCHITECT'S STATEMENT]

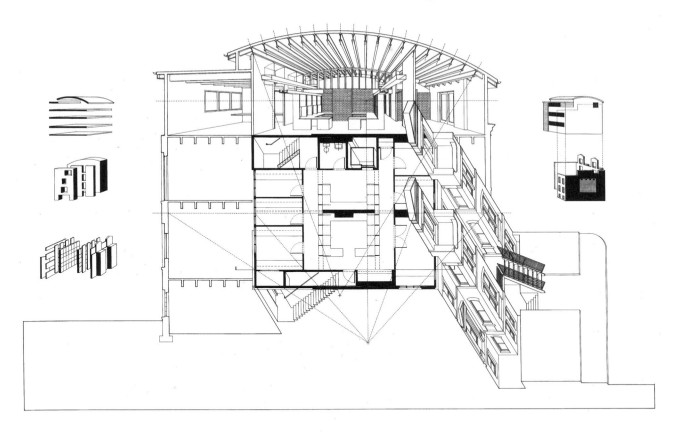

Drawing: National Minority AIDS Council, Washington, D.C.
30" × 42" (76.2 × 106.7 cm), Scale: ¼"=1'0"
Medium: Ink on Mylar
Courtesy of Vyt Gureckas/CORE

The inadequacy of representing a three-dimensional artifact in two dimensions has traditionally been overcome by generating a number of different drawings. However, the act of reconnecting the various drawings or views is left to the mind. Cubism has offered an alternative to this process by presenting simultaneous views on one surface. This drawing is an attempt to take advantage of such a strategy, but whereas cubism relies on transparency and incidental juxtaposition, this drawing employs a more precise set of tangent lines or shared edges to graft one drawing to another. Construction lines are left in place to underscore this process of delineative reconstruction.
[ARCHITECT'S STATEMENT]

The ultimate goal of a composite presentation is to effectively combine the different types of drawing conventions and explanatory text that are being utilized. This will be dependent to a large degree on the restrictions to the size and shape of the presentation panel(s) and on the organizational method chosen to combine the drawings (grid, toned background, radiation and rotation, central focus, etc.). This **hybrid** presentation combines a perspective section with a plan and a nonvertical Z-axis plan oblique. Scan the ingenious and well-thought-out single- and multipanel presentations in the rest of this chapter for hints on how to approach your own presentation format problems.

COMPOSITE DRAWING

SUPERIMPOSED COMPOSITE DRAWING

Drawing: Blades residence, Goleta, California
Medium: Graphite on Mylar
Courtesy of Morphosis and Thom Mayne with Sarah Allan, Architects

Superimposed composite drawings can have the look of a beautiful artistic composition. Their drawback is that they can become confusing in the myriad array of lines and shapes used to compose them. Sometimes only the originator can understand them.

PRESENTATION FORMATS **509**

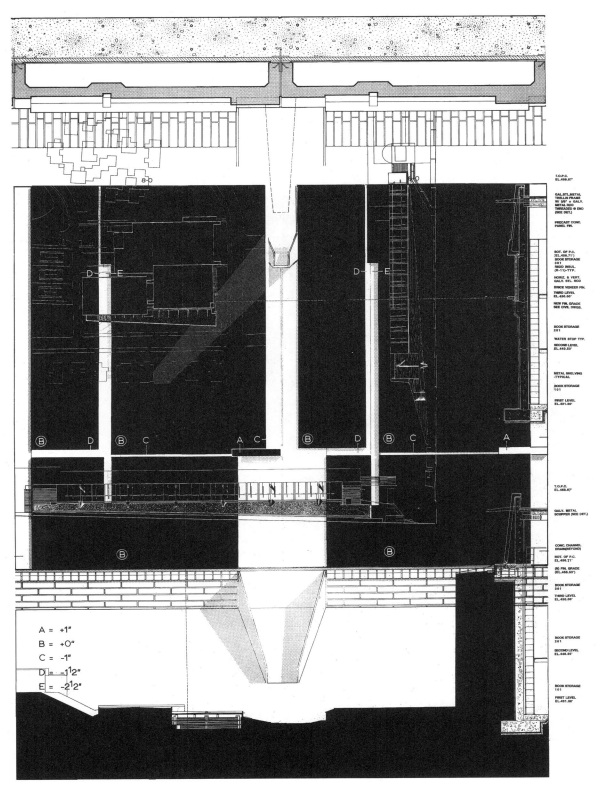

A = +1"
B = +0"
C = -1"
D = -1½"
E = -2½"

SUPERIMPOSED COMPOSITE DRAWING

Drawing: UCLA southern regional library
30" × 40" (76.2 × 101.6 cm), Scale: ⅛"=1'0"
Medium: Ink and reversed printing
Courtesy of Franklin D. Israel Design Associates, Inc., Architects

PLAN/ELEVATION/DETAILS COMPOSITE

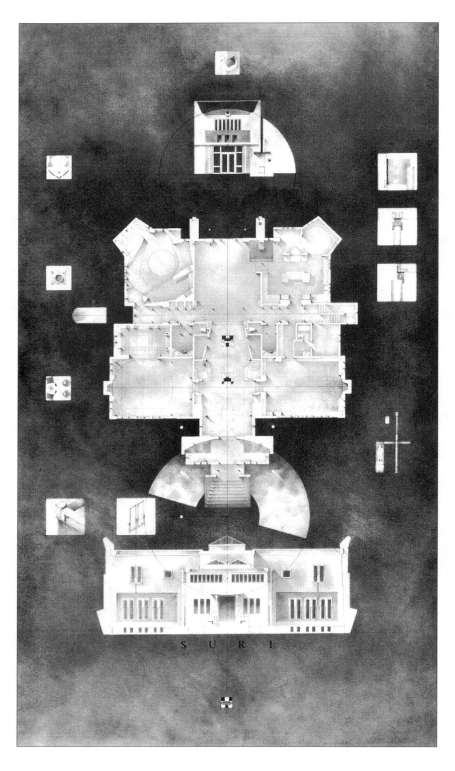

The rendering showcases the character of the building through the representation of several of its defining elements. The plan and front elevation dominate the drawing to express the overall formality of the design. Interior elevations and smaller details ring the edge of the drawing to provide a texture of scale and show off the attention to detail within the actual house. The technique of pencil on vellum, both hardline and graphite shadowing, is meant to lend a classical and stately air to the overall composition.
[ARCHITECT'S STATEMENT]

Drawing: Suri residence, Los Angeles, California
Plans, elevations, and details composite.
32" × 54" (81.3 × 137 cm), Scale: 3⁄16"=1'0"
Medium: Pencil and graphite on vellum
Courtesy of House + House Architects, San Francisco
Michael Baushke, Architectural Illustrator

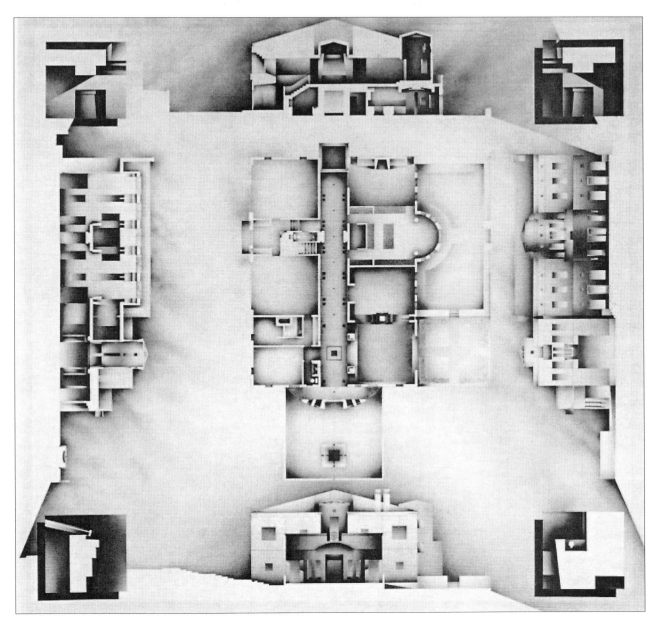

Drawing: Liu residence, Hillsborough, California
         Fold-out plan, section and elevation composite
40" × 40" (101.6 × 101.6 cm), Scale: ³/₁₆"=1'0"
Medium: Airbrush using acrylic inks on cold-press illustration board
Courtesy of House + House Architects, San Francisco
Mark David English, Architectural Illustrator

The overall composition of the drawing emphasizes the importance of each of the four cardinal directions in the design concept and is statically balanced to reflect harmony. The plan, with white walls and lack of shadowing, illustrates its hieroglyphic nature, which is literally intended to be "read." Elevations, sections, and details are carefully rendered to express the massive quality of the actual building. The four floating detail squares again emphasize the cardinal directions and pictorially bring the details closest to the viewer.
[ARCHITECT'S STATEMENT]

COMPOSITE WITH TRANSMETRIC DRAWINGS

Drawing: Edwards residence, Belize, Central America
        Fold-out sections, oblique elevations and enlarged detail frame composition
40" × 40" (101.6 × 101.6 cm), Scale: ³⁄₁₆"=1'0"
Medium: Ebony pencil on 1000H vellum
Courtesy of House + House Architects, San Francisco
Mark David English, Architectural Illustrator

The overriding theme of the drawing emphasizes the importance of "stage-set design" inherent in the building itself. Framing the main image of the drawing with an overscaled arch and column detail enhances the theatrical nature of the drawing while solidly anchoring the dynamic elements within. The drawing is oriented to the cardinal directions where north is the top of the page. The plan reflects its difference from north. As a result two oblique elevations can show all facades and create a dynamic presentation.
[ARCHITECTURAL ILLUSTRATOR'S STATEMENT]

Transparaline drawings can be either **transmetric** (showing two sides foreshortened) or **transoblique** (showing one side true size and the other either foreshortened or true size). The Edwards residence is transmetric in its elevation views. The Hammonds residence (p. 516) is transoblique (section/elevation is true size) in its elevation view. Also, the Ka Hale Kakuna residence (p. 517) shows both of its elevations in transoblique.

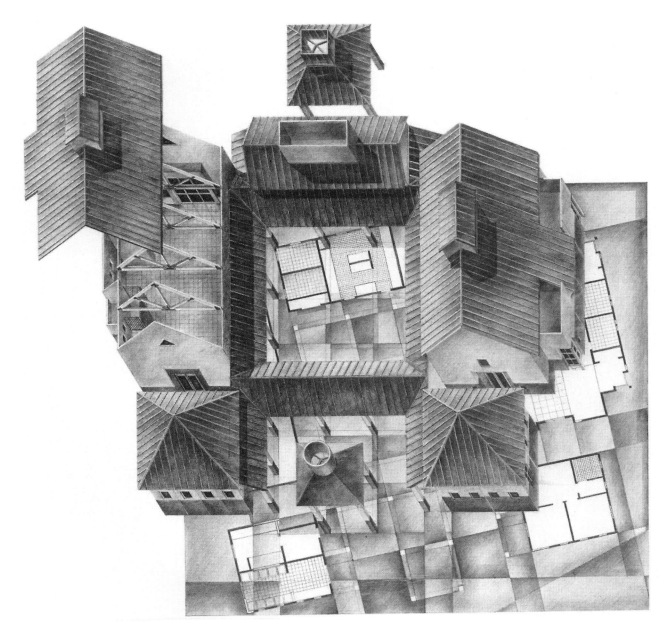

Drawing: Rancho Sespe II, Piru, California
30" × 33" (76.2 × 83.8 cm), Scale: ³⁄₃₂"=1'0"
Medium: Pencil
Courtesy of John V. Mutlow, FAIA, Architects

The 6B draughtsman pencil rendering of the community building axonometric drawing with shade and shadow provides an understanding of the three-dimensional form. The axonometric drawing illustrates the roofscape and accentuates the courtyard and its enclosure. The exploded roof axon and the rendered floor plan as background imply and demonstrate the richness of the spaces and activities.
[ARCHITECT'S STATEMENT]

COMPOSITE WITH A NONVERTICAL Z AXIS DRAWING

COMPOSITE BASED ON A BUILDING THEME

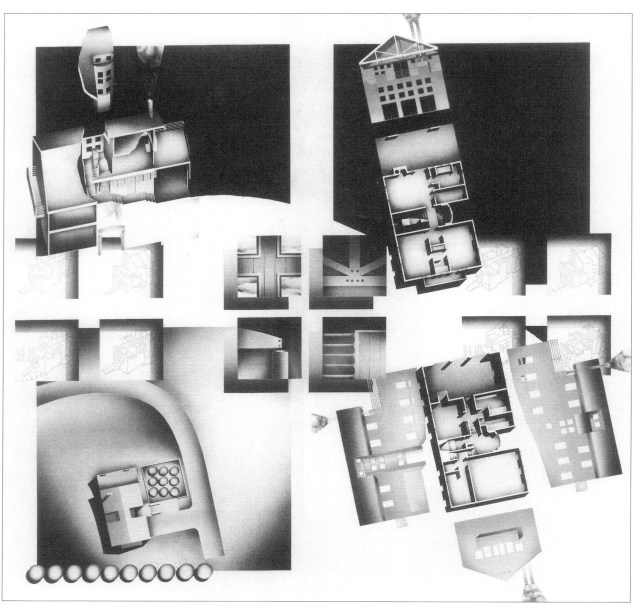

Drawing: Kerby residence, San Anselmo, California
                 Exploded axonometric with details
30" × 30" (76.2 × 76.2 cm), Scale: ⅛"=1'0"
Medium: Airbrush using acrylic inks on cold-press illustration board; line sketch copier image transfer using
mineral spirits
Courtesy of House + House Architects
Mark David English, Architectural Illustrator

The drawing is conceived of as a collage of geometries, scales, and media arranged to represent the interaction between the very graphic building form and the natural setting. The partially exploded axonometric is small in scale to emphasize the overall prototypic "house" form, while the deviation in orientation to the drawing boundary emphasizes the natural setting. The four detail blocks contain the most important architectural "words" and lift off of the picture plane with dropped shadows in an arrangement mirroring a window pattern found as a theme in the house. The concept drawing sketches exhibit their primacy by seemingly receding into the picture plane.
[ARCHITECT'S STATEMENT]

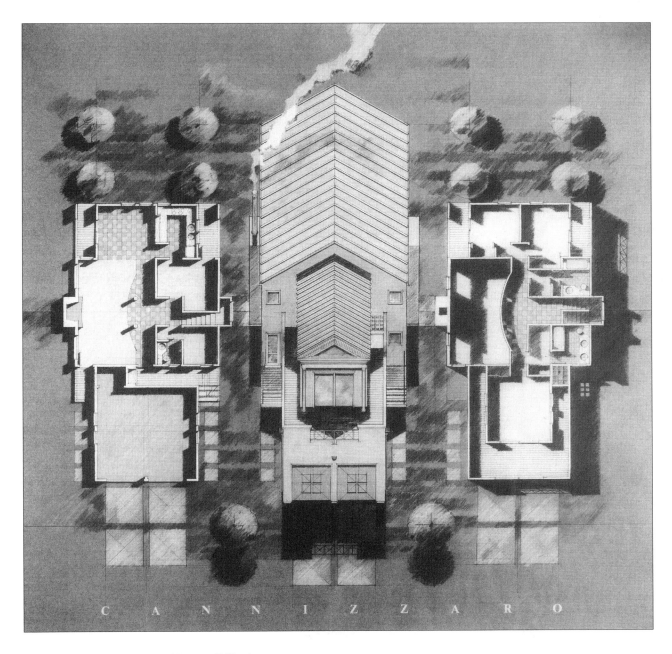

Drawing: Cannizzaro residence, Montara, California
Plan and elevation-oblique composite.
36" × 36" (91.4 × 91.4 cm), Scale: ¼"=1'0"
Medium: Pencil, Prismacolor, and spray paint on vellum
Courtesy of House + House Architects
James Cathcart, Architectural Illustrator

This rendering technique was selected to emphasize the formal layout of the plan and the symmetrical nature of the front elevation. After the basic pencil work was completed, the back of the vellum was spray painted black to provide a gray background. Prismacolor was used on the back and front to create a desired soft pastel effect on the house and on the front to also highlight the landscape elements.
[ARCHITECT'S STATEMENT]

PLAN AND ELEVATION OBLIQUE COMPOSITE

COMPOSITE WITH TRANSOBLIQUE DRAWINGS

This house was designed to replace one that was destroyed in Oakland's tragic firestorm. As in all of our projects, we began the design process by carefully analyzing the site—which in this case was a steep, narrow, downhill lot. We produced a series of relationship diagrams that studied circulation and spaces in relation to the site. We also built simple three-dimensional study models to investigate the impact of various massing alternatives. This series of axonometric sketch studies was done concurrently during the early schematic design process to analyze the building's roof shapes, open spaces, massing, fenestration, and scale. These studies were presented to our client along with our plans and models to convey our design process. We found this method of axonometric sketches a most valuable design tool.

At the conclusion of the project we decided to produce a formal rendering of the project. The final drawing consisted of three parts: an axonometric view of the house, a cross-section through the house, and a series of details. Various angles were studied for the axonometric in order to best convey the building's form. When the overall layout was finalized, the final rendering was drawn with ink on Mylar. Airbursh was later applied to provide background tones and building shadows. We feel that this rendering successfully conveys the building's relationship to the land and its use of form and materials.

[ARCHITECT'S STATEMENT]

Drawing: Hammonds residence, Berkeley, California
30" × 64" (76.2 × 162.6 cm)
Medium: India ink and airbrush on Mylar
Courtesy of House + House Architects, San Francisco

The rendering is a composite of drawings graphically laid out around the geometrics of the plan and interrelated through a system of regulating lines. By using multiple images it is possible to understand the building plan and spatial characteristics within the framework of a single drawing. The precision of pen and ink was needed to allow for the finer features to read clearly.

Design: A massive curving wall anchored in lava cliffs encircles and protects a tropical retreat on the island of Maui. By turning its back on the intense south and west sun, the house caters to clients who desired a site-specific home that utilizes the tropical island's unique character and lifestyle. Indoor and outdoor spaces are inseparably linked with disappearing walls that open each room onto outdoor lanais. Intricate screens cast glittering patterns of light and shadow as they trace the sun's path, while tropical vegetation cascades down the lava cliffs and spills inside, tying the feeling in this house to the lush, garden nature of the site. A linking tower offers distant views to the volcano of Haleakala and the Pacific Ocean beyond.

[ARCHITECT'S STATEMENT]

Both elevations shown are **transoblique** drawings. Note that in each elevation view, one side is shown true size and the other side is foreshortened (see p. 512).

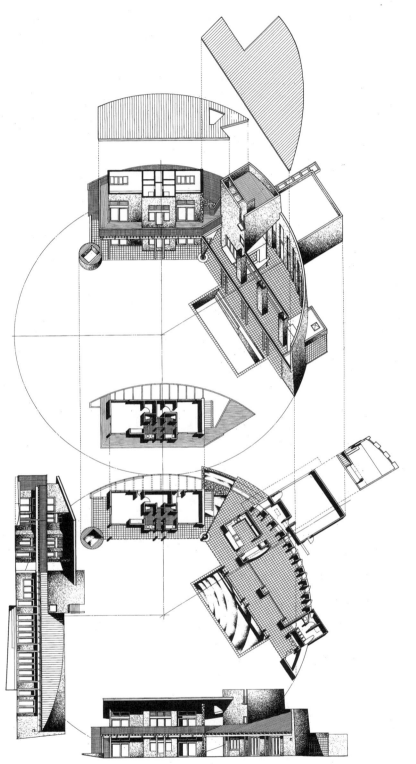

Drawing: Ka Hale Kakuna residence, Maui, Hawaii
Axonometric, plan, and elevation composite
26" × 48" (66 × 121.9 cm)
Medium: India ink and airbrush on Mylar
Courtesy of House + House Architects, San Francisco; David Haun, Architectural Illustrator

COMPOSITE WITH TRANSOBLIQUE DRAWINGS

ONE-PANEL PRESENTATION

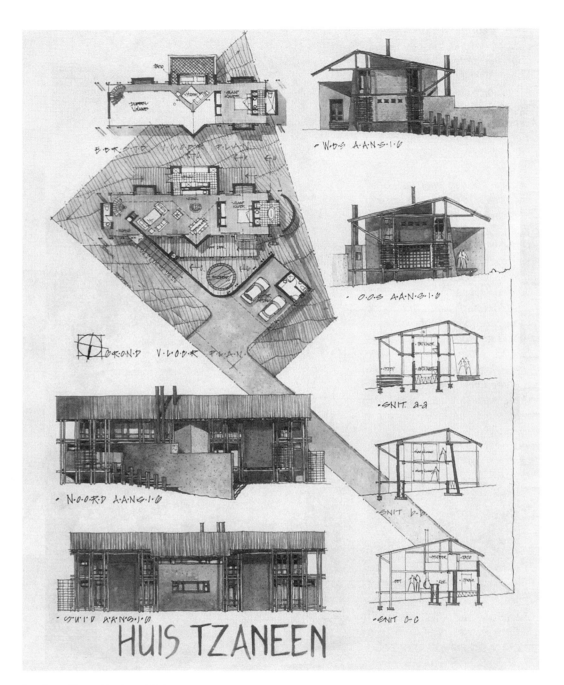

HUIS TZANEEN

Drawings: House Notnhagel-Deiner
Tzaneen, South Africa
Medium: Watercolor and ink
Design team: 'Ora Joubert and Thomas Gouws
Courtesy of 'Ora Joubert Architects, Pretoria, South Africa

Drawings (facing page): House Bergh
Cape Town, South Africa
Medium: Watercolor and ink
Design team: 'Ora Joubert

In brief, House Notnhagel-Deiner (Tzaneen) is part of a genealogy of projects that attempt a synthesis between Eurocentric theoretical premises and socioeconomic and environmental particularities of southern Africa. To that effect, a concerted effort has been made to appropriate local circumstances through the use of readily available materials, local craft techniques, and sound climatic performance, though respecting the spatial integrity and abstract formalism of orthodox Modernism.
[ARCHITECT'S STATEMENT]

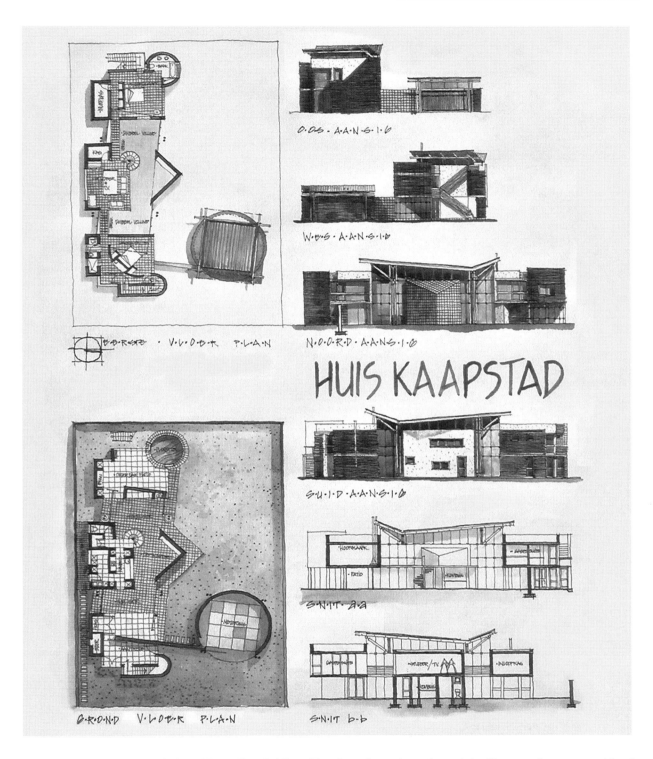

HUIS KAAPSTAD

From a conceptual point of view, House Bergh (Cape Town) explores the universal significance of space, combined with a sustained interest in the dynamics generated by colliding geometries. Since the house is situated close to the coast and on a flat sandy terrain, the slightly lifted floor surface aims at a delicate imprint on the sand. The choice of materials—aluminum roof and ceiling, white bagged walls alternated with flushly jointed plaster brick and black slate floor and wall tiles—accentuates the integrity of the different formal components within the compositional ensemble. [ARCHITECT'S STATEMENT]

ONE-PANEL PRESENTATION

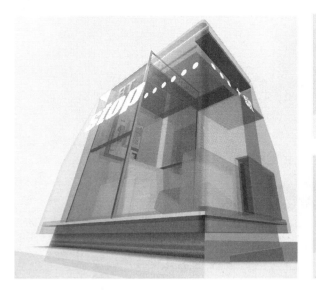

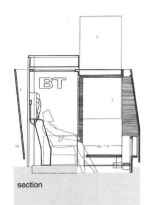

section

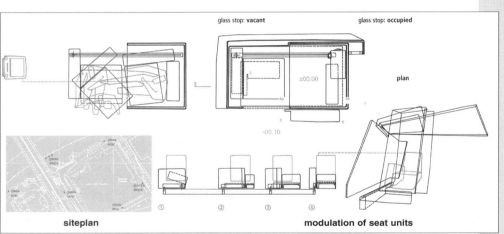

glass stop: **vacant**   glass stop: **occupied**

±00.00

plan

−00.10

siteplan   **modulation of seat units**

1 **Existing telephone booth**
2 **Vari-focus glazed screen:** creates a boundary of changeable privacy. As the door [3] rotates shut, the electric circuit is closed, completing the lines of liquid crystal running around the perimeter of the booth. The movements of the individual within are now obscured to bystanders and any passers-by.
3 **Closer panel**
4 **Armchair**, consisting of parts **a** + **b**. The two separable units form a complete seat, only when money is inserted and the booth occupied.
5 **Meter:** A unit on the exterior of the booth indicates the amount of time purchased. When the session ends, the door automatically opens out and the armchair disassembles to its default position.
6 **Plasma screen TV** with optional Infra-red headphones

The public telephone has become obsolete with the advent of the mobile telephone. Conversely, the rest area within the city hustle and bustle has almost completely vanished, with street furniture specifically designed to deter loitering.

The **GLASS STOP™** is the solution to these two problems. Making use of the phone power points, a temporary living room is created within the city by wrapping a vari-focus glazed screen around the existing units. Fitted with an armchair and a television, it provides a place for people to rest between shopping, or before an evening rendezvous, without having to purchase a coffee or beer.

Panel image: Central Glass Co. Japan: Public Space:
              Glass Booth Competition
Courtesy of Studio 8 Architects: cj Lim with Ed Liu and Michael Kong

The composition attempts to illustrate the social and cultural significance of the telephone booth, now and then into the future. It shows the design in a variety of inhabited and empty conditions, suggesting possibilities of social inhabitation and choreography. The drawings were hand drawn, allowing degrees of imperfection, while the computer rendering shows the contrasting nature between the existing booth and its new shell.
[ARCHITECT'S STATEMENT]

glass stop

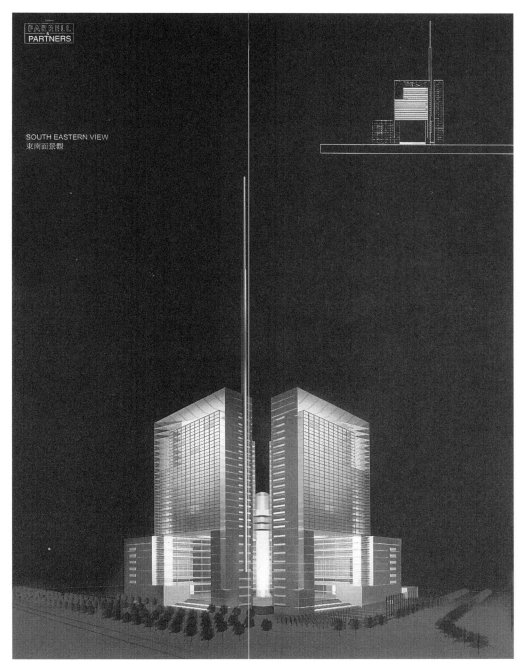

Single-panel image: Competition-winning entry for the Guangzhou Daily Cultural Plaza, Guangzhou, China
Original size: A0
Medium: AutoCad model rendered in form Z
Courtesy of Terry Farrell & Partners Ltd. Architects Planners Designers

ONE-PANEL PRESENTATION

The Guagzhou Daily Cultural Plaza is based around a huge 230,000-square-meter public arts complex that integrates the headquarters of China's largest newspaper publisher, the Guangzhou Daily News, with a 1-hectare public plaza, library, exhibition hall, arts center, hotel, and retail space, including the world's largest bookshop. The overriding intention is to define a cultural quarter for the city that is imbued with a unique sense of place. This will be achieved through the design of a lower-rise, 33-story structure that embraces its location and is permeable to its surroundings.
[ARCHITECT'S STATEMENT]

TWO-PANEL PRESENTATION

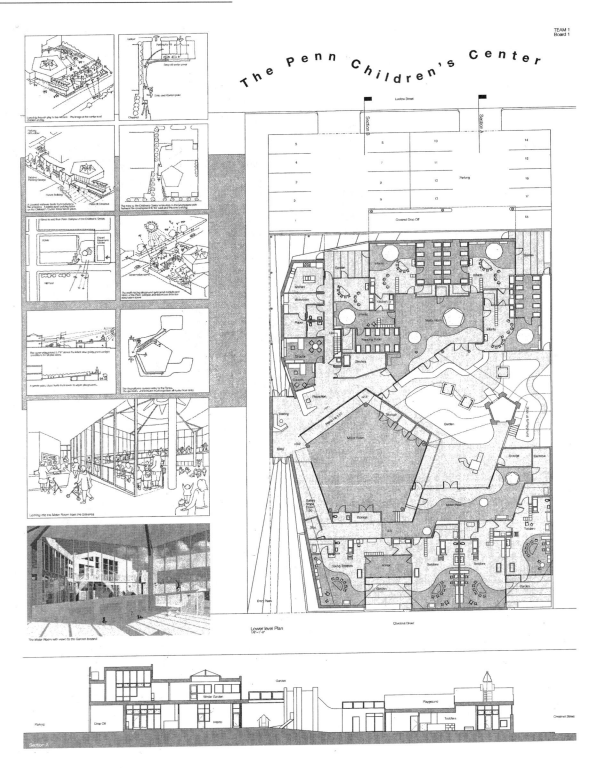

Two panels: Penn Children's Center
Courtesy of Adèle Naudé Santos and Associates

The sections form a base for the layout, while diagrams and vignettes are arranged to tell a story about the scheme.
A large number of required drawings were to be accommodated on two boards.
[ARCHITECT'S STATEMENT]

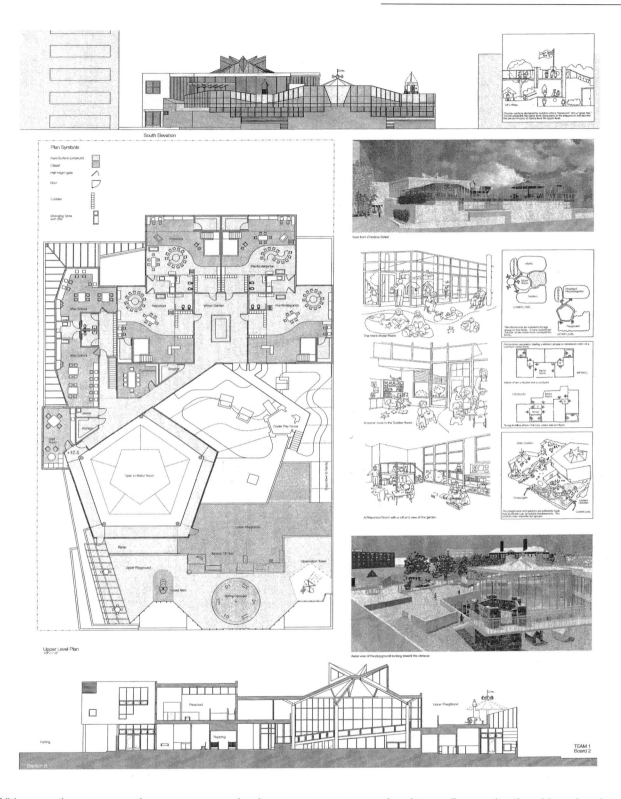

TWO-PANEL PRESENTATION

With more than one panel, one must examine how two or more panels relate well to each other. Here the visually balanced presentation uses building sections on a heavy ground line to tie the two panels together horizontally. See this same method employed using elevations and sections in the four-panel presentation on p. 532.

THREE-PANEL PRESENTATION

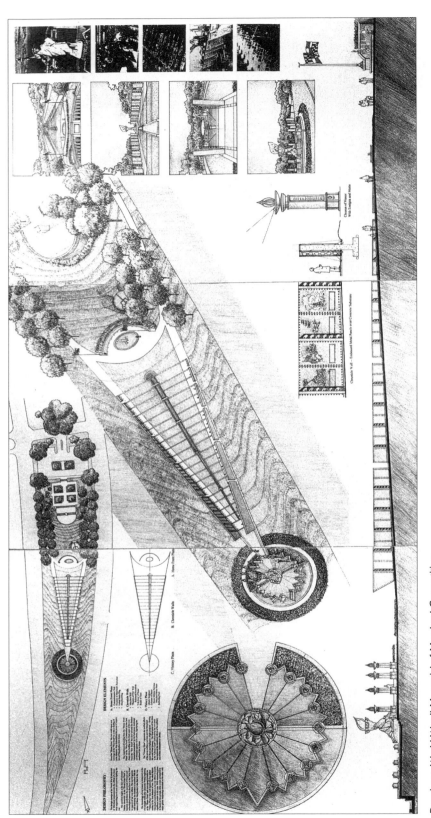

Drawings: World War II Memorial of Maryland Competition
3 Boards, 20" × 30" (50.8 × 76.2 cm) each, various scales
Medium: Felt pen and colored pencil on wheat-colored yellow tracing
drymounted on Styrofoam board

Courtesy of William W. P. Chan, Don Duncan, Nicholas Linehan, and
Chris Rice, competition team architects and designers

While there is no specific requirement for the presentation other than the size of the boards, the designers felt strongly that an axonometric drawing should be the primary focus of the presentation. The remaining elements of the composition, such as the site plan diagram, sections, details, and 3D sketches, should be positioned to visually explain the philosophy of the design. Therefore, adjacency of shapes is the key to the graphic composition.
[COMPETITION TEAM MEMBER'S STATEMENT]

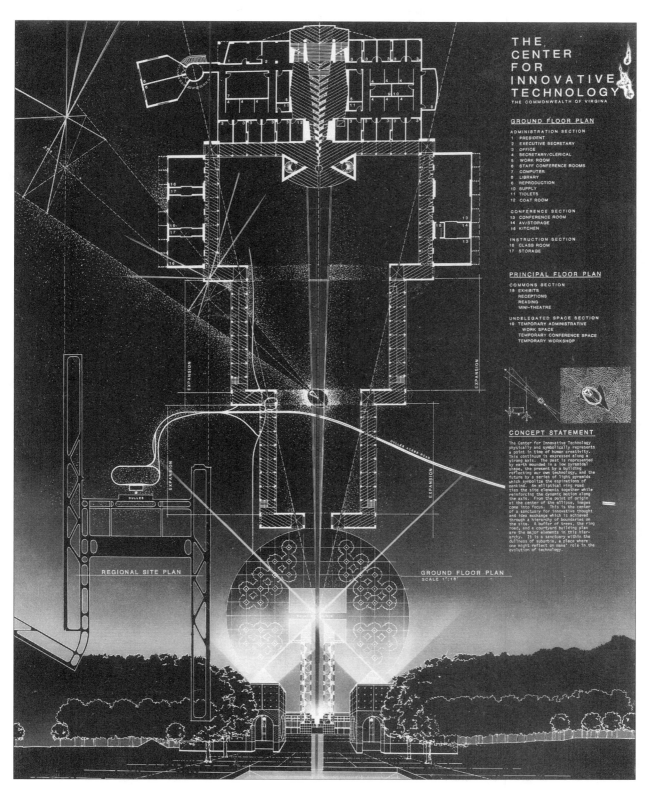

Three panels: The Center for Innovative Technology Competition, Reston, Virginia, first place
All three competition drawings: 24" × 30" (61 × 76.2 cm)
Competition team architects: William W.P. Chan, Peter Fillat, Rod Henderer, Tim Pellowski, and Mark Tuttle
Courtesy of William W.P. Chan, Architect

THREE-PANEL PRESENTATION

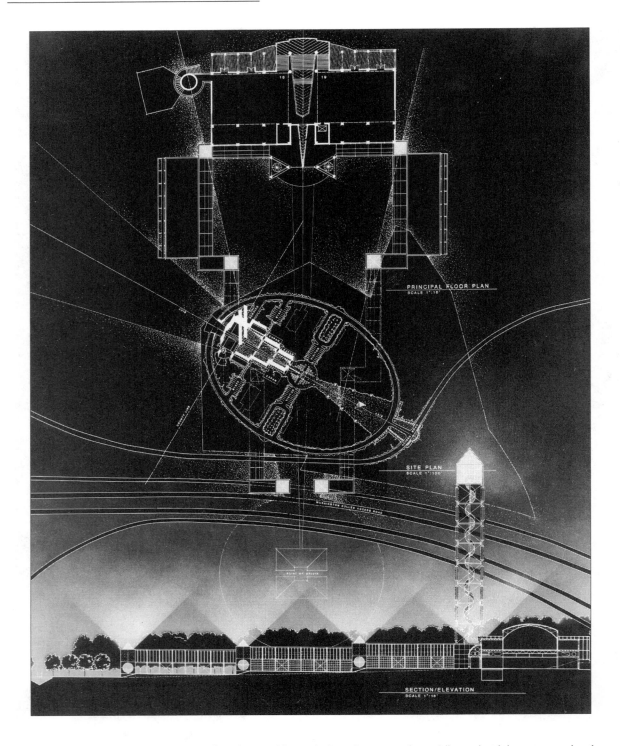

An objective of competition drawings is to achieve clarity of presentation while maintaining strong visual interest and complexity. Since the site plan, elevations, sections, plan obliques (axonometrics), and perspectives depict a specific aspect of the designed environment, we wanted to fuse them together into a graphic whole. Hence, we decided on a black background to unify these disparate elements. White lines on a pure black background appear too cold and lack a three-dimensional quality. A warm glow of airbrush yellow and orange was selectively sprayed onto the print to enhance the effect.
[ARCHITECT'S STATEMENT]

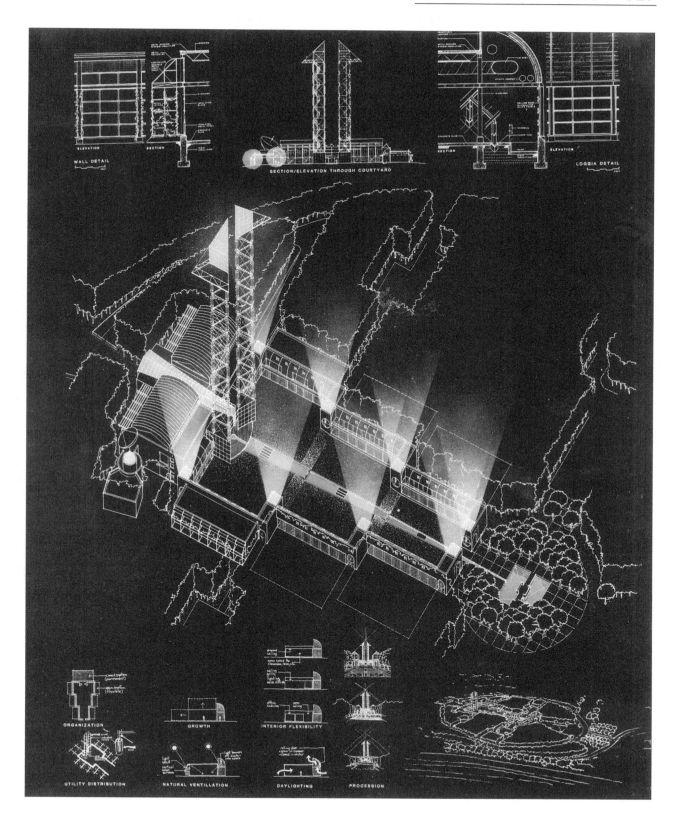

FOUR-PANEL PRESENTATION

In "Production"

Drawing: Four-board presentation for a student competition
        Student project by Theresia Kurnadi, with help from Melissa Hsu
Media: hand sketches; Software: form Z, Photoshop, Pagemaker
Courtesy of Professors Douglas Noble and Karen Kensek
University of Southern California, School of Architecture

In addition to the use of a strong ground line to unify panels (see p. 524), the use of a horizontal band (see also pp. 550–555) with many drawn or photographed elements is also visually unifying for the same purpose.

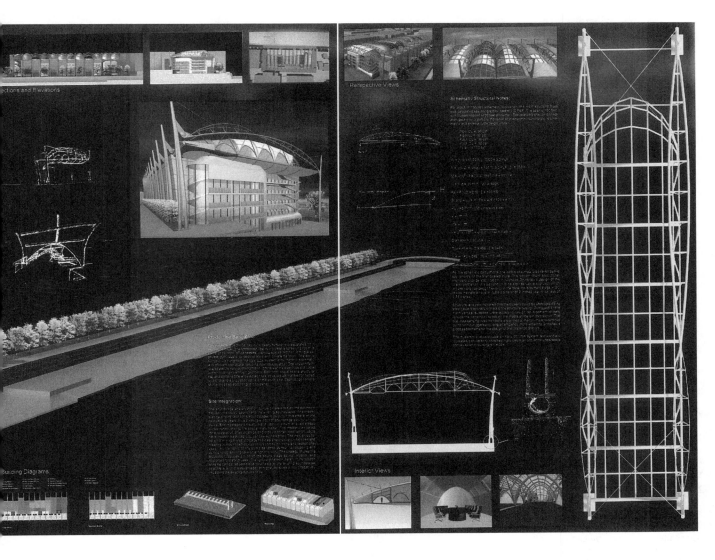

FOUR-PANEL PRESENTATION

This project for an undergraduate design studio competition includes a large film and TV sound stage with a penthouse production facility. After initial sketches, the project was developed entirely on the computer in three dimensions by Theresia Kurnadi. Melissa Hsu assisted in the creation of the four presentation boards.

The presentation boards include hand sketches, site analysis photographs, narrative programmatic and philosophy statements, three-dimensional diagrams, structural analysis, and details. Many of the images were manipulated and composited in Photoshop and then assembled in Pagemaker for the final board layout.

[*PROFESSORS' STATEMENT*]

FOUR-PANEL PRESENTATION

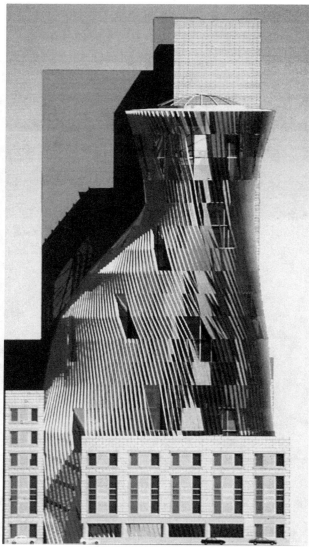

Four panels: New York Public Library, New York City
Computer renderings by Lee Dunnette
Courtesy of Hardy Holzman Pfeiffer Associates

In 1999, the New York Public Library held a design competition for the expansion and renovation of their Mid-Manhattan Branch, seeking to increase technological services and access to new channels of information while accommodating flexibility for the future. HHPA drew on its 33-year experience in library design in its submission for this competition. HHPA's design weaves together a variety of influences, paying homage to the fine legacy of Fifth Avenue architecture and the traditions of great urban libraries, while celebrating the progressive spirit of the New York Public Library and its civic mission. Rather than the formal repetition of a single aesthetic, it appears as a sculptural object set among the rectangular masses of midtown office buildings.

[ARCHITECT'S STATEMENT]

This four-panel presentation utilizes only elevations and perspectives, but the panels are unified by the designed elements of the building.

FOUR-PANEL PRESENTATION

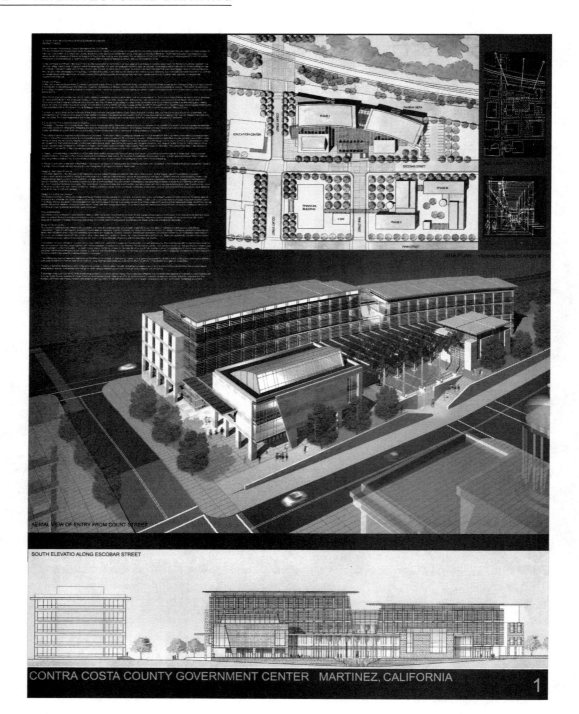

Four panels: Contra Costa Government Competition, Martinez, California
Courtesy of design architect: Moore Ruble Yudell
Principal-in-charge, principal architect: John Ruble
Principal architect: Buzz Yudell
Associate-in-charge/project architect: James Mary O'Connor
Project team: Lisa Belian, Tony Tran, Ed Diamante, Kaoru Orime, Roger Lopez, Ross Morishige, Janet Sager
Digital rendering: Craig Shimahara
Models: Mark Grand, Donald Hornbeck, Joshua Lunn
Associate architect: Fisher-Friedman Associates: Rodney Freidman, Dan Howard, Robert J. Geering
Interior design: Marcy Li Wong Architects
Owner: Contra Costa County
Project management: O'Brien Kreitzberg
Principal: Mark Tortorich

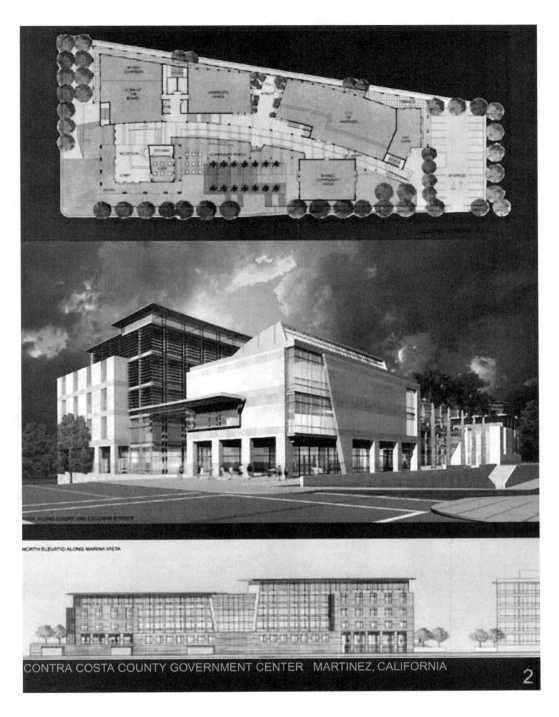

CONTRA COSTA COUNTY GOVERNMENT CENTER   MARTINEZ, CALIFORNIA

FOUR-PANEL PRESENTATION

The four competition boards were presented using a clear organizing principle—a tripartite composition that would read as three horizontal bands when the four boards are put together side by side. The size of each board is 30" wide by 40" high.

The central and largest band contains the digital three-dimensional renderings of the exterior of the building, one rendering on each board. Maximized in proportion, this band is intended to effectively draw the viewer's attention into the deisgn of the architecture. The band at the bottom is composed of elevations and sections, providing a linear base for the boards. The band at the top contains floor plans and a site plan, with the ground-floor plan and second-floor plan at a larger scale than the others.

FOUR-PANEL PRESENTATION

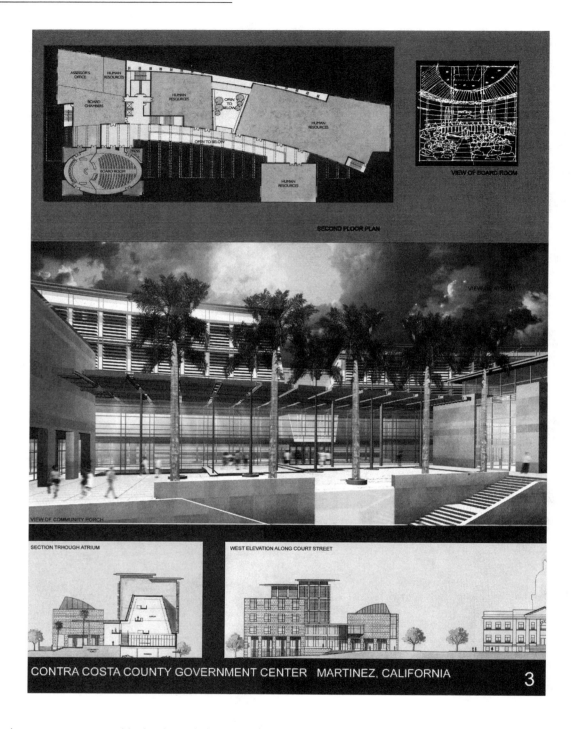

It was important to create this simple and clear composition because in a competition forum there is little time to present your design idea to the jury. The simple and uncluttered organization of images helps the jury visualize and understand the design idea in the quickest and easiest way possible.

[ARCHITECT'S STATEMENT]

LOWER LEVEL FLOOR PLAN

THIRD FLOOR PLAN

GROUND FLOOR PLAN

FOURTH FLOOR PLAN

SECOND FLOOR PLAN

FITH FLOOR PLAN

WALL SECTION THROUGH SOUTH ELEVATION

VIEW ALONG MARINA PARK

LONGITUDINAL SECTION THROUGH BOARD ROOM AND COMMUNITY SPACE

CONTRA COSTA COUNTY GOVERNMENT CENTER MARTINEZ, CALIFORNIA

4

FOUR-PANEL PRESENTATION

FOUR-PANEL PRESENTATION

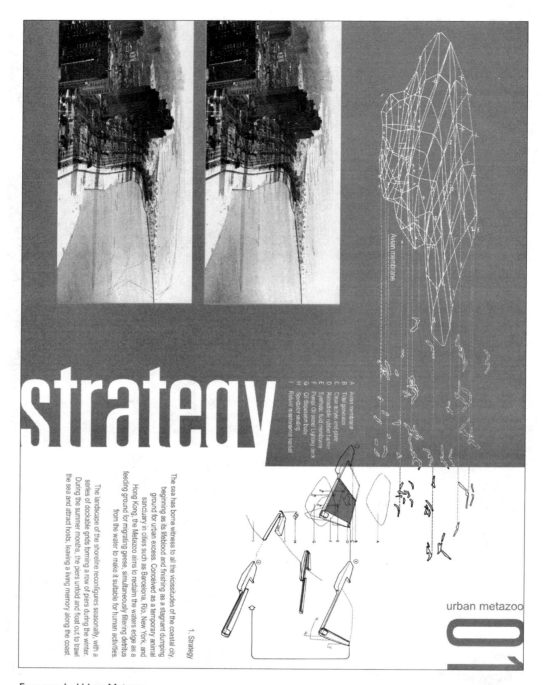

Four panels: Urban Metazoo
Venice Biennale: The City: Third Millennium International Competition of Ideas
Courtesy of Studio 8 Architects: cj Lim with Ed Liu and Michael Kong

The competition The City: Less Aesthetics, More Ethics is part of the on-line forum set up for the Biennale 2000. This will provide real-time exhibition of material, reflecting international participation in the debate and exchange of ideas and images. Participants are invited to express their vision of the City—not necessarily seen as one specific location but rather as a system of relations and structures that define contemporary life. The submissions will contain suggestions, ideas, hypotheses, and outlines that express a personal interpretation of the city of the third millennium.

To take part, one must register by email, accompanied by four digital images of 800 × 600 pixels in 72dpi and JPG or GIF format. These may be produced using any technique or media available.
[ARCHITECTS' STATEMENT]

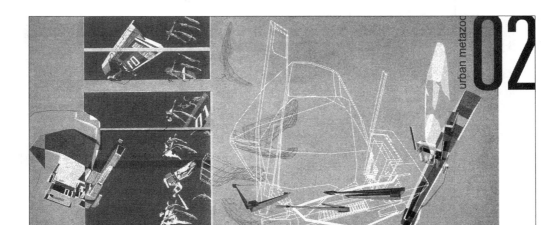

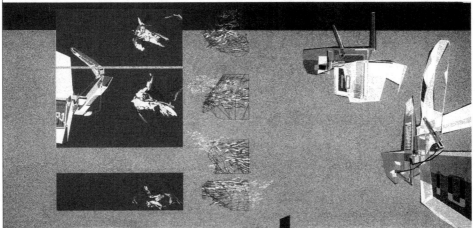

urban metazoo **02**

concept

During migration, the common goose, Branta canadensis, descends upon the shore to feed on the vast shoals of anchovies beneath the water. The flight formation of the geese creates a blanket that constantly changes shape (Avian membrane), periodically scattering as they dive into the ocean. Movement of the birds is dependent on the strata of fish below the water's surface, which effects the illusion of a mirror. Manipulation of the birds for human spectatorship is achieved though the use of a third synthetic membrane composed of a viscous oil-based fluid that floats above the water by virtue of its lower physical density, and magnifies the fish through its increased optical density. These elements combine to suggest a new type of zoo for the third millennium that is both environmentally conscious and ethically-sound - a zoo that is free of inhumane cages and celebrates the soaring dynamics of life in the wild.

FOUR-PANEL PRESENTATION

FOUR-PANEL PRESENTATION

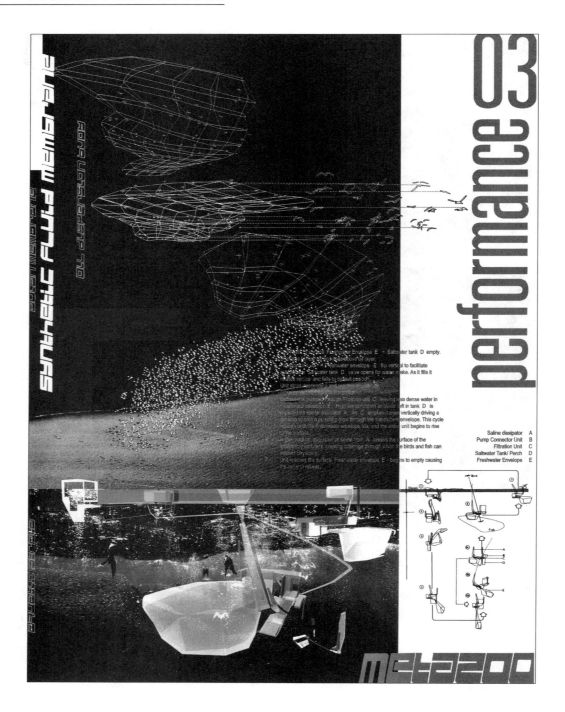

Working with the entry requirements specified, the images were divided into Strategy, Concept, Performance, and Detail. This idea, with the aid of large-size text, created a direct and simple strategy for reading, especially when all the images were read from a computer monitor individually, rather than collectively on a wall. Each image focused on one issue only, starting from the overall picture and finishing with the working detail parts. The common design element of the images was the numbering system on the top right-hand corner. The number is nearly always associated with the title of the project, except on image 3. In this case, the word "Metazoo" was placed at the bottom right to emphasize

FOUR-PANEL PRESENTATION

the verticality of the section drawing. Idiosyncrasy makes the whole process of design exciting and surprising! The individual composition generally consisted of a bold main image, complemented with fine line drawings. This creates a clear
hierarchy in the reading of information. The colors were in the region of orange to red, to complement the existing colors of the individual images. The two successful images were 1 and 4, while the others had too much information on
them or the little detail information was completely lost, e.g., the little fish on the bottom half of image 3.
[ARCHICTECT'S STATEMENT]

FIVE-PANEL PRESENTATION

Five panels: New Integrated Complex, Concordia University, Montreal, Quebec, Canada
Courtesy of Kuwabara Payne McKenna Blumberg Architects and Fichten Soiferman Architects, in joint venture

This series of five panels, each 33"×47", illustrates the winning entry prepared by Kuwabara Payne McKenna Blumberg, Architects, for an invited competition for the new $160-million complex of buildings for the downtown campus of Concordia University in Montreal, Quebec. The architects chose to use bilingual captions on all the panels in order to acknowledge the dual role of both the English and French language on the Concordia campus in this densely built-up area of downtown Montreal. To unify all five panels, the architects employed a horizontal red band running through the middle of each panel. The red color was derived from the University crest and coat-of-arms.

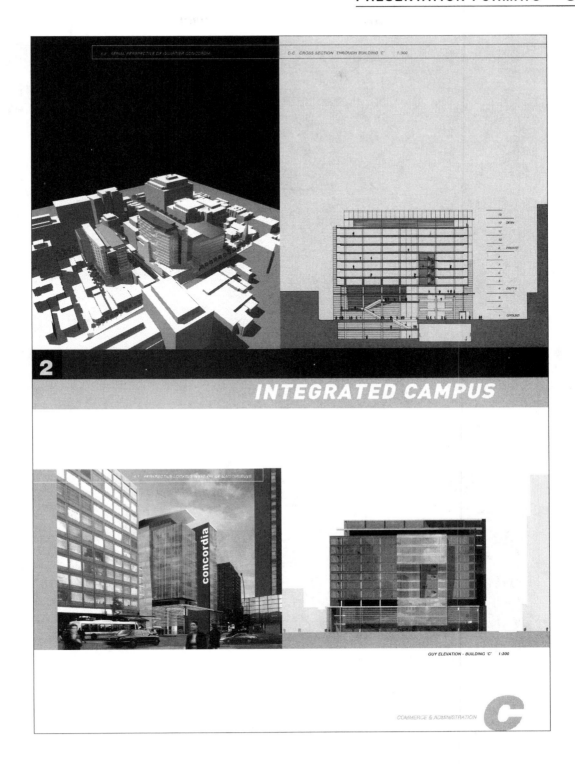

FIVE-PANEL PRESENTATION

The exterior perspectives on panels 2, 3, and 4 were a mandatory requirement, and are drawn from fixed vantage points on the streets adjacent, as specified in the competition conditions. This enabled the jury members to compare each competitor's presentation, showing their respective designs all viewed from the same position of the pedestrian. To convey the idea of the importance of student life and culture in the three new buildings, we chose to show the buildings in both daytime and nighttime perspectives. This idea of "studio culture," of open and accessible buildings used twenty-four hours a day, is further expressed in the "24-7" logo on panel 1.

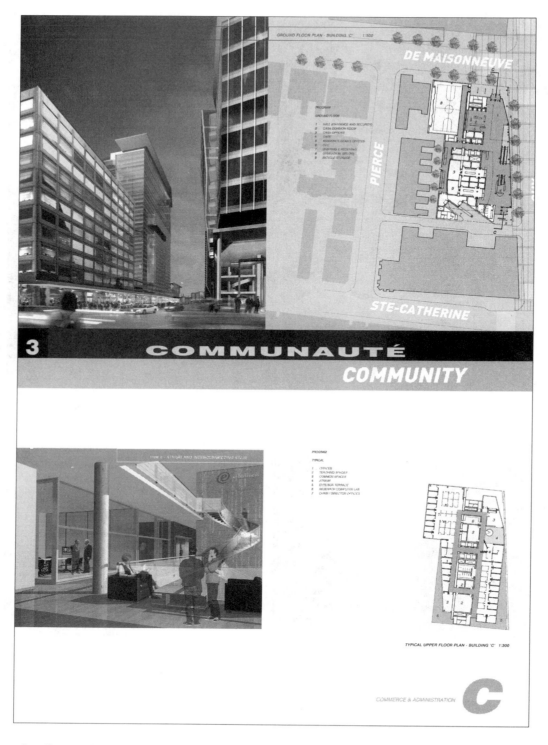

The perspective diagram in panel 1 and the axonometric drawing in panel 4 were also mandatory. We chose to render them as transparent volumes to allow the jury to comprehend the complex layering of streets, sidewalks, subways, vertical core circulation, and circulation at grade throughout the buildings. Green was used on ground-floor plans to denote public space and how it can extend the public realm from sidewalks into and through the new buildings. Gray, another pervasive color found throughout Montreal in the graystone buildings, was used on plans and in one monochromatic perspective on panel 3.

[ARCHITECTS' STATEMENT]

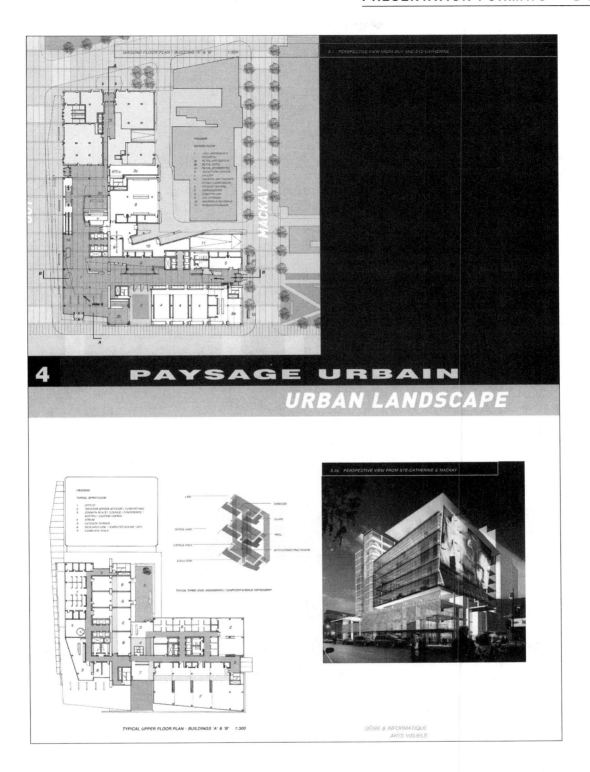

FIVE-PANEL PRESENTATION

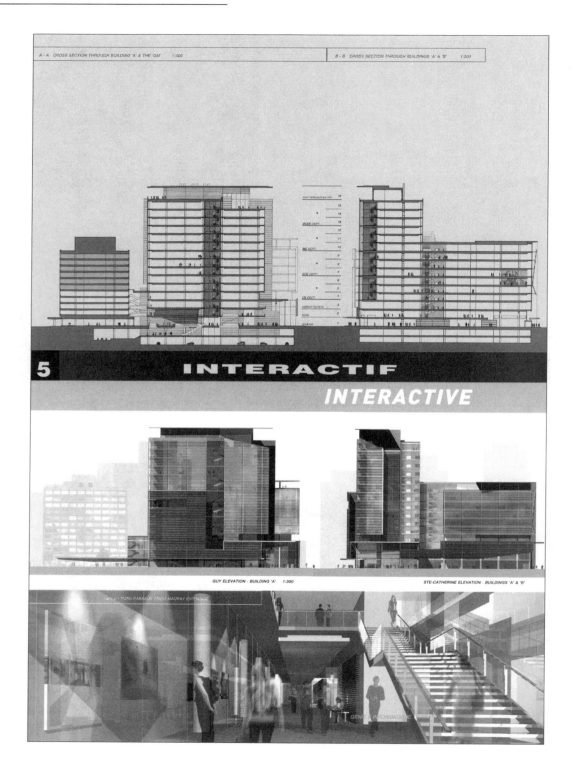

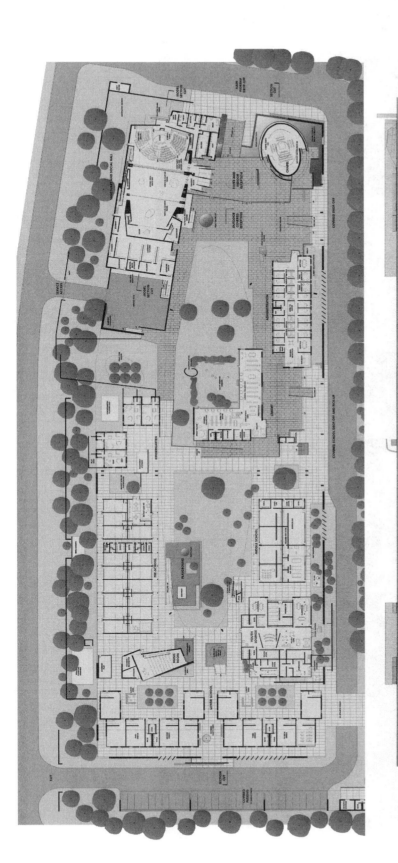

Competition panels and model photographs: Temple Beth Am, Miami, Florida
Courtesy of Tod Williams Billie Tsien & Associates Architects

Our goal in the presentation for the Temple Beth Am Competition was to be as clear as possible. We had three main boards and kept them simple, with only one plan and one site section per sheet. The overall site plan incorporated a series of construction phasing diagrams.

We developed the drawings in AutoCad, and then imported them into CorelDraw for color, shading, and texture. In addition to the line drawings at ¹/₁₆", we presented hand drawn exterior and interior perspective views toned with soft watercolor. The boards were 66"×30", and folded in half for ease of shipping.

Our models were the focus of the competition presentation. The project incorporates twelve buildings, connected by a large roof canopy that stretches over the site. We built an overall site model in basswood, with a removable canopy and spare detail at ¹/₃₂" scale. As a counterpoint, we built a much larger-scale sectional model of the main sacred space—the Temple's sanctuary. The goal was to enable the Temple members to understand the interior space of the scheme and sense the materiality of the project.

[ARCHITECT'S STATEMENT]

FIVE-PANEL PRESENTATION

FIVE-PANEL PRESENTATION

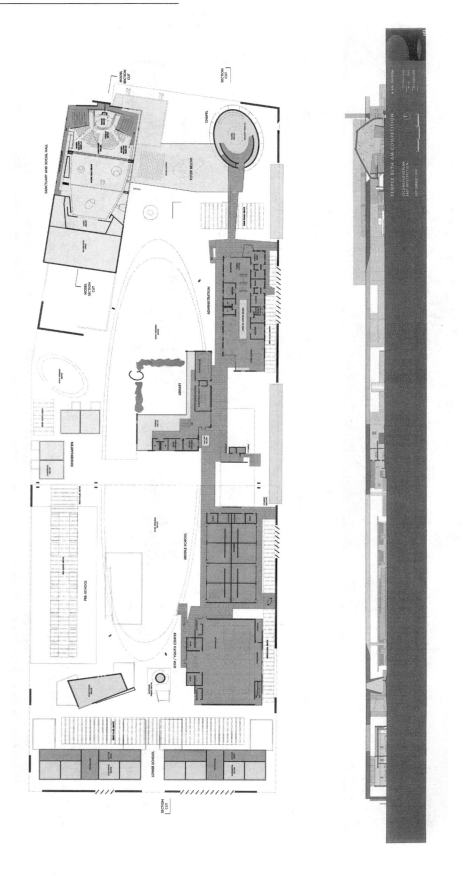

FIVE-PANEL PRESENTATION

FIVE-PANEL PRESENTATION

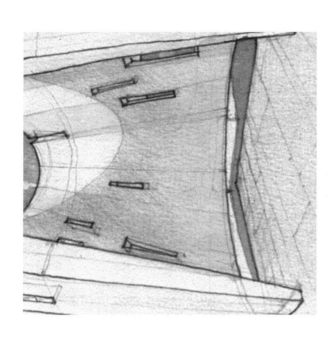

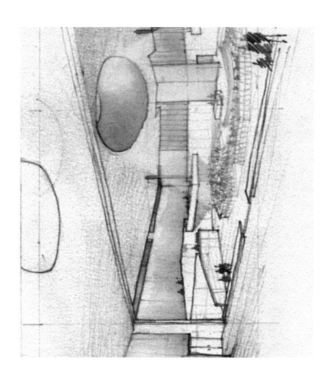

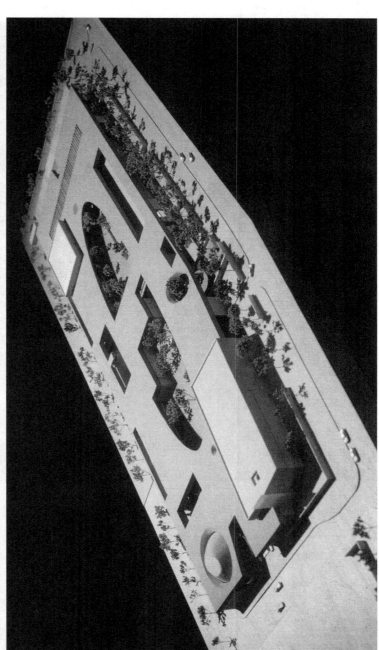

FIVE-PANEL PRESENTATION

SIX-PANEL PRESENTATION

To present the design process of the Sunlaw Project, we created the overall idea of layers of information appearing across each board. The inspiration comes from Hollywood and the metaphor of the movie strip. We used a diverse combination of media, from hand drawn sketches and construction documents to digital images. These are scanned and then assembled to convey the metaphor of the movies.

The movie metaphor is most obviously employed in a continuous running band, similar to a film strip, at the bottom of each page. This band contains images that display various aspects of the project, such as its site, context, and the historical precedents of tower design.

We used a dark blue background on each board as a framing device for the images. This background also contains screened construction drawings of the existing power plant machinery to evoke the context. Superimposed on this background are hand drawn sketches or computer renderings of the new canopy and enclosure. The layering of the existing machine imagery and the dynamic renderings of the new canopy design create a rich and striking contrast.

We used two formats for this presentation: 20" × 20" boards, and a booklet of 11" × 17" heavy sheets.

[ARCHITECT'S STATEMENT]

Six panels: Sunlaw Power Plant Canopy & Enclosure,
　　Los Angeles, California
Courtesy of design architect: Moore Ruble Yudell
Principal-in-charge, principal architect: John Ruble
Principal architect: Buzz Yudell
Associate-in-charge/project architect: James Mary O'Connor
Project team: Ross Morishige, Lisa Belian
Digital renderings: Ross Morishige
Graphic design: Janet Sager
Owner: Sunlaw Energy Corporation
Chairman: Robert N. Danziger
President: Michael A. Levin
Project manager: Timothy G. Smith

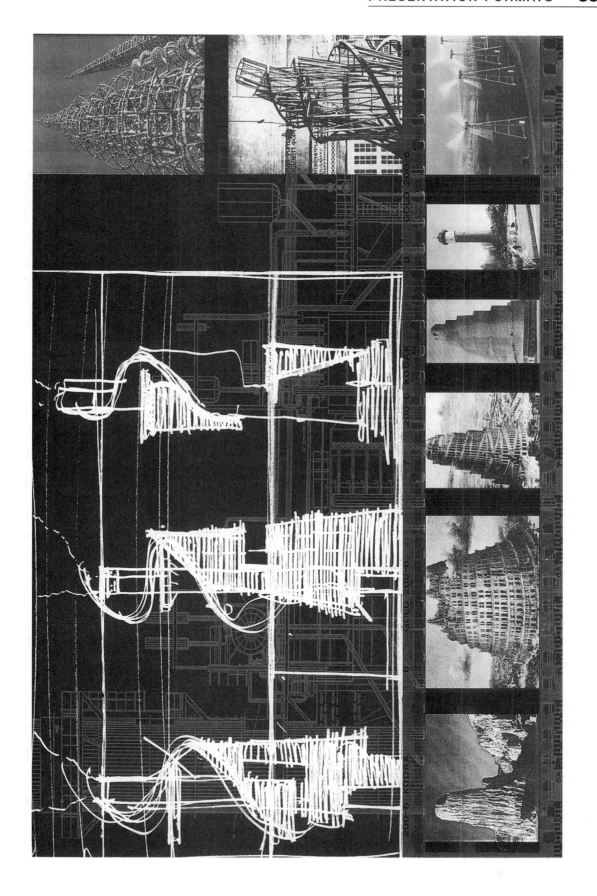

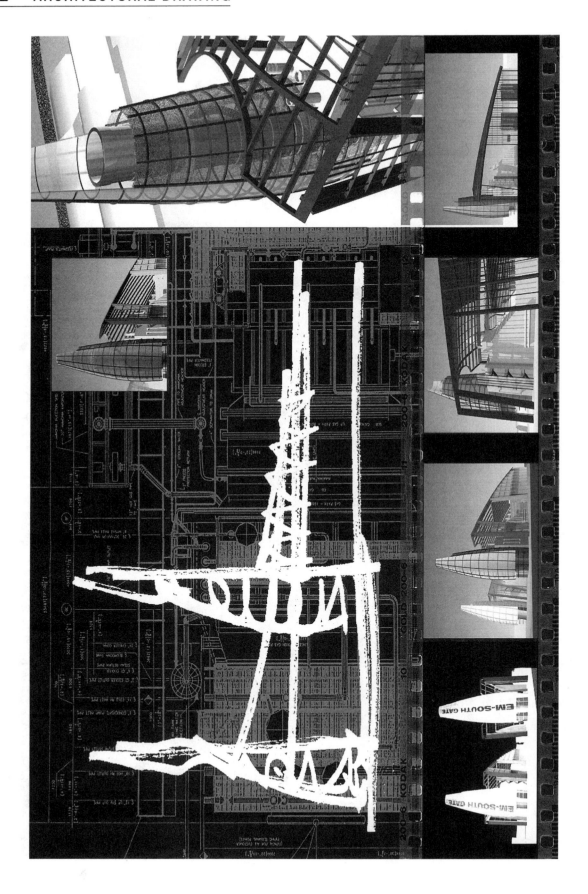

SIX-PANEL PRESENTATION

SIX-PANEL PRESENTATION

SIX-PANEL PRESENTATION

EXPLODED/ERODED AXONOMETRIC COMPOSITE

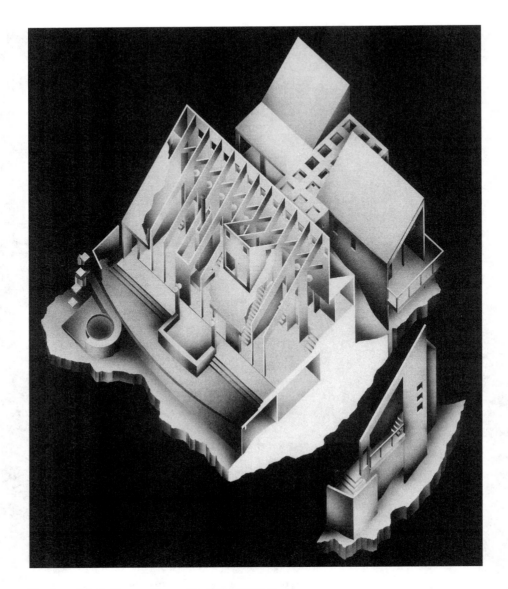

Drawing: Abbott–Elpers residence, Woodside, California
           Composite: Exploded/eroded axonometric
30" × 30" (76.2 × 76.2 cm), Scale: ¼"=1'0"
Medium: Airbrush using india ink and acrylic inks on cold-press illustration board
Courtesy of House + House Architects
Mark David English, Architectural Illustrator

The drawing composite dramatically presents the main spatial ordering system of the shed-roofed volumes of the building by presenting the roof as a see-through membrane. The slope of the land is shown on the spatial section of part of the main image. The color palette is metaphorical: green for natural surfaces, pink for artificial interior surfaces, gray for artificial exterior surfaces and black as the universal background.
[ARCHITECT'S STATEMENT]

Epilogue

The primary intent of this book is to provide students and design professionals with graphic tools essential to visual communication. Architectural graphics skills are a powerful tool for conceptualizing, documenting, and expressing architectural ideas. The variety of drawing types and methods demonstrates that a wide range of graphic tools and techniques are available for conveying architectural ideas in the design process. This primer introduces the various media currently being used, so that the reader may have a sense of the range of visualizing possibilities in the field.

With time and experience, every designer—student and professional alike—eventually settles in with the tools and techniques most suitable for him or her to express, develop, and communicate architectural ideas, whether these are freehand conceptual sketches or hardline representational drawings. Some architects/designers enjoy the feeling of a soft lead pencil on heavy white tracing paper. The softness of graphite can give a suggestive atmospheric character, especially to perspective images. Others become prolific in their expression of ideas when they use a felt-tipped pen or colored pencil on yellow tracing paper. Prismacolor pencils give a soft impressionistic feeling to architectural sketches. And still others prefer the precise feeling of ink on Mylar, especially with paraline drawings. It should be noted that every medium affects the quality of not only spatial perception but also design ideas, especially at the "design-drawing" stage. For example, charcoal causes one to think almost automatically in terms of light and shadow, whereas a fine-point pen may cause one to delineate more and to think in terms of contours, connections, and details.

As the computer and computer-generated drawings become commonplace in design education and practice, it is all the more important to maintain a strong relationship with traditional drawing media and methods, such as freehand sketching. Because of the intimate and immediate reciprocity between the human imagination and drawing, this most ancient form of expression will always remain a powerful and effective way to generate and communicate ideas.

The reader should explore the many books listed in the Bibliography that elaborate on architectural drawing as technique and/or process. Such exploration, along with a careful study of this volume and its related web site, should enrich his or her knowledge of architectural drawing.

Drawing Exercises

A textbook/reference book on architectural drawing would not be complete without suggestions for applications of some of the more important techniques covered. The goal of this section on drawing exercises is to show a variety of problem/project approaches as well as a diversity of applications. The intent is to allow architecture educators to glean information from these exercises so that they can formulate their own creative problems to suit their own classes and educational objectives.

Organization of the Drawing Exercises

The problems/projects in this section have been divided into two levels. Level One consists of very basic problems that are abstract in design and simple in geometric configuration. To pass a beginning course in architectural drawing/graphics, students should demonstrate an overall understanding and skill in solving these exercises. Students should also be encouraged to do freehand sketches to explore possible solutions for each problem.

Level Two problems are more complex than those in Level One and, in some cases, are more purely architectural in character. They usually involve design as well as drawing and are suitable for more experienced beginners or for classes in which students work at their own pace. Students with a strong background in high school mechanical drawing or college engineering drawing, or those with experience in the design professions other than architecture (e.g., graphic design, industrial and product design, and so forth) should concentrate on Level Two problems. As in Level One, the resolution of Level Two problem solutions should stress the incorporation of freehand sketching skills.

Sketches Demonstrating Light and Shade

To work on the following exercise, you may need to bring to class a small item suitable for a still life painting. I suggest a simple shape—a piece of fruit, vegetable, etc. You may also wish to bring a plate or cloth on which to put the item.

In this exercise you may experiment with a variety of mixed media techniques, such as pencil sketch with watercolor, felt pen or ink line with watercolor, pencil, etc.

The intent of this exercise is to demonstrate how the use of light and shade can give an object form—a three-dimensional quality. Choose a simple object and sketch and/or paint in color four postcard-size sketches. You may use an object more than once by changing the light source (i.e., by changing the direction or strength of the light source). Alternatively, you may wish to go outside and sketch (or paint) a simple architectural or landscape subject.

Hint: Choose objects that have a simple basic form—a cube, cylinder sphere, cone, etc.—and have one strong, directional light source. Tonal studies in pencil or monochromatic watercolor may help define light, shade, and composition.

Please include any preliminary studies with your assignment.

You will be assessed on the following criteria:

- use of light and shade
- technique (watercolor, mixed media, etc.)
- use of color
- composition

Courtesy of Professor Jane Grealy
Department of Architecture
Queensland University of Technology
Australia

REFER TO CHAPTER 3

LEVEL ONE

Drawing Positive and Negative

Perceiving forms and shapes is a major step in learning to draw. Everyday objects (such as forks, spoons, chairs, and lamps) make good subjects for learning to draw negative space. Beginning to understand the difference in drawing negative space (that area which is around the object) over positive space (object being drawn) can perceptually alter your approach in drawing.

Drawing negative space is drawing the object of our focus by defining the space around the object. The tendency for beginning students is to want to draw the object. In this case, students must overcome preconceived notions of what they are seeing and are compelled to recognize that the negative space is just as informative about the object being drawn. Issues of foreshortening and perspective become less of a perceptual hindrance to the student because the focus is on shape, not depth.

Charcoal is the best medium to use for this project; it makes the student focus on the importance of negative space. Observe the object from different viewpoints, looking for negative shapes. Capture the shapes of the object first as contours, being careful to capture all the nuances of the object. Once they are delineated, fill these areas with the charcoal.

This assignment makes the complex object simple. It simplifies all the intricate relationships of the object so the student can understand and draw it. Once the basic understanding of positive and negative has been achieved, students may proceed to more complex objects like landscape or architecture. The examples presented with this exercise demonstrate drawing positive and negative with motorcycles. Notice handlebars, mirrors, wheels, spokes, and fenders defined by the delineation of the dark negative shapes. One can even read the reclining nature of the handlebars of the motorcycle.

Project: Courtesy of Professor Fernando Magallanes
Design Fundamentals Studio—Fall 2000
College of Design
North Carolina State University

The student example below is from the Design Fundamentals Studio—Fall 2000
North Carolina State University
Medium: Charcoal on 8½" × 11" sketchpaper

REFER TO CHAPTER 3

LEVEL ONE

Freehand Drawing — Multiple Sketches

Break into groups and, using ink pens of varying thickness, sketch the visual images that you see displayed around the studio. We will begin with 30-second, 60-second, 1.5-minute, and 3-minute sketches. A final sketch of 5 minutes in duration will complete the exercise. The sketches will range in complexity and graphic expression. Pay close attention to the proportion of the image on the page and the style of sketch being used in the examples. Relax…sketch freely and quickly. Place a 5-minute sketch, a 3-minute sketch, a 1.5-minute sketch, a 1-minute sketch, and a 30-second sketch on the page, as shown below.

Problem: Courtesy of Assistant Professor Daniel K. Mullin, AIA, NCARB
Graphic Communication course
Department of Architecture
University of Idaho–Moscow

REFER TO CHAPTER 3

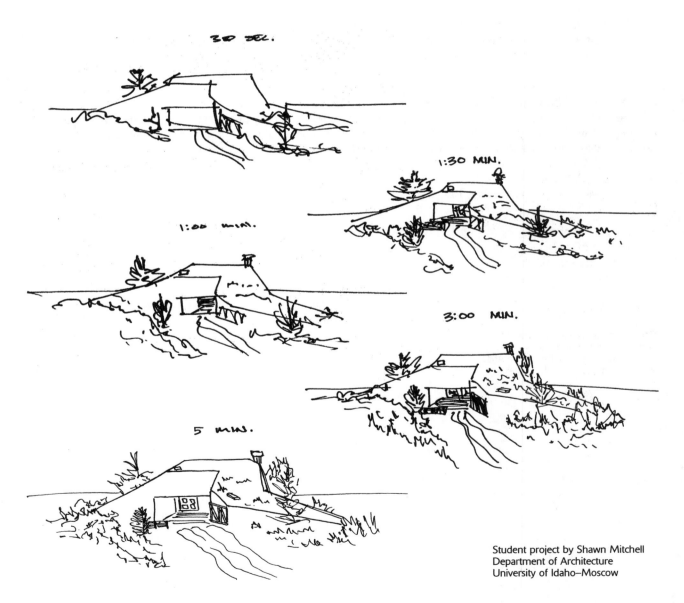

LEVEL ONE

Student project by Shawn Mitchell
Department of Architecture
University of Idaho–Moscow

Freehand Sketching

Drawing a building is a way of remembering it properly. To draw you have to look very hard and I think it is in the looking itself that the building is impressed on the mind.
[CAROLINE MAUDITT, AN ARCHITECT IN ITALY]

THE TASK
This is an exercise in freehand sketching which will be conducted in the Botanic Gardens. The theme of the exercise is *journey.* You are required to complete three frames on one A3 sheet, provided during the tutorial, sketching a subject to convey visually the experience of *journeying.* This can be done by representing one of the following:

- A change in viewpoint (moving viewer, different standpoints)
- A change in scenery (moving object, stationary viewer)
- A change in focus (zooming in or out on a particular element)

THE LOGO
You are also required to create a logo, which should include your name and the title of the exercise, *journey.* Manipulate these to convey your chosen theme; that is, change in viewpoint, scenery, or focus. This logo must be placed in the bottom right-hand corner of the A3 sheet.

REQUIREMENTS
An A3 sheet will be provided with the required layout. The sketching can be done in any dry medium—pencil (2B–6B), ink, charcoal, crayon, conté, etc.—or in watercolor. You may need to apply a fixative, which is available from any art supply shop, to prevent smudging. Make sure that you bring something to lean on, such as an A3 drawing board, a foam board, thick cardboard, or the like.

ASSESSMENT CRITERIA
Students will be assessed on the following:

- Clarity of representation
- Character of drawing
- Selection of viewpoint
- Effective use of medium
- Neatness of presentation

Courtesy of Dr. Samer Akkach
Drawing Architecture & Landscape 1
School of Architecture, Landscape Architecture and Urban Design
Adelaide University, South Australia

REFER TO CHAPTER 3

LEVEL ONE

Still Life: Tone and Texture Exercise

TASK
Assemble and arrange a still life composed of various objects on a surface (such as household objects, food, office supplies, tools, kitchen implements, fabric, etc.). Cast a strong light source from a single lamp in a darkened room.

ASSIGNMENT
Render the forms of the composition with black pen on white paper. You may use light pencil to construct lines. Study the composition to determine which values of the observed shapes receive little or no tone, representing light surfaces, and which receive medium or dark tones, for deep shade or shadows. Pay attention to surface quality and texture (shiny, dull, patterned, etc.), and be conscious of line weight and stroke direction in rendering various textures.

OBJECTIVES
This exercise encourages observation of light source, rendering technique (hatching, stippling, solid tone), and making decisions on defining shape and contrast within the visual field.

MEDIA
Heavy white paper
Black permanent marking pens (assorted weights)

OPTIONS
Try the study without light pencil for bolder decision-making.
Try different shading techniques and hatches.
Use an architectural model of a neighborhood.

SOURCES
1. The work of Giorgio Morandi
2. Guptill, Arthur L. 1976. *Rendering in Pen and Ink.* New York: Watson-Guptill.

Still Life: Value Exercise

TASK
Assemble and arrange a still life composed of various objects on a surface (such as household objects, food, office supplies, tools, kitchen implements, fabric, etc.) on a horizontal surface. Cast a strong light source from a single lamp in a darkened room.

ASSIGNMENT
Render the forms of the composition on a medium-value gray paper using a white and dark rendering media. Study the composition to determine which values of the given shapes receive darker saturation for deep shade or shadows, little or no treatment for medium values, and white saturation for surfaces reflecting light.

OBJECTIVES
This exercise encourages observation of light source, treating light as "material object" through media rendering, and revising typical thinking about drawing with a dark medium on a light surface.

MEDIA
Gray charcoal or pastel paper (40–60%)
Charcoal, or black conté crayon, pastel, or Prismacolor
White chalk, conté, pastel, or Prismacolor pencil

OPTIONS
Use black paper and only white rendering media.
Experiment with various combinations of media on gray paper.
Try a black ink wash with a white medium on gray paper.
Use an architectural model of a neighborhood.

Courtesy of Jonathan Brandt,
Visiting Professor
College of Architecture
Texas A&M University

REFER TO CHAPTER 3

LEVEL ONE

Panoramic Fantasy

TASK
Select several of your favorite sketches and photocopy them to various sizes and dimensions.

ASSIGNMENT
Assemble your sketches into a collage and tape them together. Try to establish interesting or ambiguous relationships between objects in terms of perspective, juxtaposition of scale, and illusion of depth. Trace off a contour drawing.

OBJECTIVE
Expand imagination by recognizing new relationships between juxtaposed images.

MEDIA
Photocopies of sketches
Pen and pencil
Tracing paper

OPTIONS
Try rendering your fantastic contour image in the media of your choice. You may want to make a transfer onto heavier paper.

LEVEL ONE

Field Study: Panorama

TASK
Select a high or commanding vantage point over a city or distinctive site.

ASSIGNMENT
Study a wide-open panoramic view (180° or more) and record selected objects concisely and abstractly in a contour drawing. Record notable buildings, landmarks, natural features, etc. Take notes by labeling or naming them. By doing this, you are enlarging your awareness of the visual field despite recording it in a fixed position. You will also develop keener observation skills.

OBJECTIVE
Develop observation and abstraction skills while learning names and places.

MEDIA
Horizontal format sketchbook or long sketch paper
Pen and pencil
Map of what you see

OPTIONS
Try selectively rendering what you see as time permits.

Courtesy of Jonathan Brandt, Visiting Professor
College of Architecture
Texas A&M University

REFER TO CHAPTER 3

Field Study: Building Context

TASK
Select a building or ensemble of buildings forming a distinctive space.

ASSIGNMENT
Render the forms of the composition on a medium-value paper using ink wash and white rendering media. Record from observation by setting up a freehand pencil line perspective. Study the composition to determine which values of the architectural or natural shapes and voids receive dark saturation for deep shade or shadows, little or no treatment for medium values, and white saturation for the surfaces reflecting light.

OBJECTIVES
Encourage observation of light source, treatment of light as material object through media rendering, and revision of typical thinking about drawing with a dark medium on a light surface.

MEDIA
Medium-value charcoal or pastel paper (30–50%)
Ink and painted wash
White Prismacolor pencil
No. 2 pencil

OPTIONS
Try various medium-value colored papers with colored inks.

Field Study: Plan, Perspective, Detail

TASK
Select a distinctive space bounded by architectural walls.

ASSIGNMENT
Record the plan in space. Select several salient details and record them also, doing quick, analytical contour drawings. Then find two or three views that you feel best describe the space visually, and record them on the plan. Select at least one approach view to give a sense of time in a series of contour drawings with framed views. Arrange your sketches on the page. Also, jot down any verbal notes that make what you see remarkable.

OBJECTIVES
Study an architectural space from observation by recording a range of scales in drawing vignettes, including close-up details as well as more general sketches from a distance. By doing this, you will develop keener observation skills in terms of proportion and scale, while learning names and places.

MEDIA
Sketchbook or sketchpad
Pen and pencil
Guidebook and/or plan of what you see

OPTIONS
Try selectively rendering what you see as time permits.

LEVEL ONE

Courtesy of Jonathan Brandt, Visiting Professor
Texas A&M University
College of Architecture

REFER TO CHAPTER 3

Film/Memory/Drawing

This project will be an exercise in pulling a vision of a place out of your head and putting it on paper. In this case, the place will not be one of your creation but rather one which struck you in a film. The designer always draws from what he or she has seen and experienced—always searching for an innovative interpretation of that experience. You must look for inspiration in every thing you see and do, including films. The following is a suggested list of films for you to see for this project; please choose one. Consult your instructor for approval to choose a film not listed here.

Blade Runner	*Judge Dread*	*The Talented Mr. Ripley*
What Dreams May Come	*Mulan*	*any Batman film*
Gladiator	*Summertime*	*The Phantom Menace*
Cleopatra	*Prince of Egypt*	*The Fifth Element*
Edward Scissorhands	*Memoirs of an Invisible Man*	*Metropolis (1926 film on DVD)*

During the film, think about which places you might like to draw. After the film and before the next class session, pick three places in the film and draw them in your sketchbook. Draw the place just as it struck you in your mind. Don't worry too much about producing a faithful reproduction of the place. Concentrate on transferring the image you see in your mind's eye onto paper.

During the next class session, we will pick one of your sketches to develop into a larger drawing. This drawing will be done in pencil on Bristol. You will use tone, shade, and shadow to convey your image of the place.

This problem was adapted, with slight modifications, from a problem given at the California College of Arts and Crafts.

Problem: Courtesy of the California College of Arts and Crafts
School of Architectural Studies
Studio Professors: Hank Dunlop and Mark Jensen

REFER TO CHAPTER 3

Conceptual Hand Sketching

Sketch a virtual building suspended in airspace above an urban or suburban context. Use your imagination to dream of unthinkable shapes for this building. Do the sketch with a 2B pencil on Strathmore paper. A 2B pencil is almost in the middle of the "soft" range for soft lead pencils. Grades like HB, B, and 2B can give nice dense, dark, soft tones. Textured Strathmore paper of medium weight is very receptive to soft graphite pencils.

REFER TO CHAPTERS 3 AND 10

LEVEL ONE

Drawing Eggs

It is essential for the beginning student to develop sensitivity to light falling on an object and an ability to draw the light qualities on a 2-D surface. The observation of light and the creation of shadows and tones are what the student must capture on paper. The students are asked to bring half a dozen eggs (preferably white eggs) to drawing class. The media for this exercise can be pencil, ink, charcoal, or gray marker. The student will make three drawings using three of the media recommended. Do not allow students to mix various media in their drawings. Each drawing will be made using one medium to allow students to learn the individual strengths and weaknesses of each medium used. One hour is spent on each drawing on 14" × 17" sketchbook paper. Various ways of creating value may be explored: line, smudging, layering, stippling, or random marks.

Set the eggs in different types of light. Draw first in filtered light with minor light variation. Later move the eggs to a place of intense light using full sun or a strong lamp. Place the eggs on a clean white surface, like a sheet of white sketchpaper.

This exercise will introduce the student to various types of light (highlight, shadow, reflective light, and shade) that become apparent in studying the light falling on the eggs. In a one hour-period the light will change, so it is important that the students make an overall still life sketch of the eggs to work on later outside of class.

Project: Courtesy of Professor Fernando Magallanes
Design Fundamental Studio—Fall 2000
College of Design
North Carolina State University

REFER TO CHAPTERS 3 and 9

Student project by Rebecca Pezdek
Medium: Pencil on 81/2" × 11" sketchpaper
Design Fundamentals Studio—Fall 2000
North Carolina State University

LEVEL ONE

LEVEL ONE

Teknoman/Teknowoman

Time frame: A three-week project.

This project has a series of time-related intentions:

1. Learning to draw via the classical method of copying master drawings.
2. Translating your master drawing into a visual idiom truly characteristic of the late twentieth century.
3. "Teasing" the twenty-first century by going beyond conventional materials (optional).

PART 1: RESOURCE GATHERING
Select three master drawings of nude figures (probably pre-twentieth-century) whose style and technique you somehow admire. Each should contain at least one complete human figure. If any drawing contains more than one figure, consider editing out all but one. Bring in black and white photocopies of your selections.

PART 2: OLD MASTER ITERATION
In conjunction with your instructor, select one drawing as source material for further development. A second, high-quality photocopy should be made of this drawing. If color is an issue, this should be a color photocopy or laser print. Also make note of the artist and title of the drawing, plus such notations of size and media of the original as available data allow.

Reproduce the drawing. Effort should be made to: 1) match media (or media appearance); 2) match paper, either in actuality or in appearance; and 3) match size (unless it becomes so large as to be unwieldy; in any event, the drawing must be larger than the photocopy). If you wish, grids may be used to enlarge the reproduction, but grids may not appear in the final drawing (unless the grid used is actually in the original drawing, which is sometimes the case). No other mechanical devices may be used for enlarging the drawing.

Evaluation criterion: accuracy of reproduction, to the stroke.

PART 3: OLD MASTER INTERPRETIVE REITERATION
The "old master" figure is to be translated into an image reflecting the technological nature of the twentieth and twenty-first centuries. This is *not* a robot, but rather an exploration of the dynamics of the human figure metaphorically—and perhaps metaphysically—expressed in a mechanical manner. Every effort should be made to capture the gesture and character of the original figure. Media may vary, but must be a thoughtful response to the essence of the original, and are limited primarily to drawing media (that is, little or no collage, paint, models, etc.).

Computer Option: Students who are conversant with an appropriate software application may, on a voluntary basis, complete Part 3 on the computer. Programs to consider include Imigit or Lumena on the IBM platform, or Photoshop, Oasis, Aldus Freehand, and others on the Macintosh. If this option is exercised, you may start from "scratch" in a manner similar to those who are using conventional materials, or you may "capture" your reproduction (RGB video scanner for IBM, flatbed or Barneyscan slide scanner for Macintosh) and work over it.

Evaluation criteria: elegance of translation, eloquence of drawing, inventiveness and imagination.

Courtesy of Owen Cappleman, Associate Professor
School of Architecture
University of Texas at Austin

REFER TO CHAPTER 3

The Architect's Scale

Using the architect's scale indicated on the left, measure and draw the stipulated lengths indicated above each group. Proper order of sequence corresponds left to right with top to bottom.
3" means 3" = 1'-0".

REFER TO CHAPTER 1

4″, 3¾″, 5½″

Full
Scale
——
——
——

40′-0″, 28′-6″, 64′-0″

3/32″   ——

——

36′-0″, 25′-0″, 41′-6″

1/8″   ——

——

6′-0″, 27′-6″, 18′-6″

3/16″   ——

——

10′-0″, 5′-6″, 22′-0″

1/4″   ——

——

7′-0″, 4′-6″, 13′-8″

3/8″   ——

——

9′-9″, 7′-6″, 4′-3″

1/2″   ——

——

4′-3″, 6′-6″, 7′-0″

3/4″   ——

——

3′-6″, 5′-0″, 5′-9″

1″   ——

——

2′-0″, 3′-4″, 4′-0″

1½″   ——

——

1′-0″, 1′-6″, 2′-1″

3″   ——

——

LEVEL ONE

The Engineer's Scale and the Metric Scale

Using the engineer's scale indicated on the left, measure and draw the stipulated lengths indicated above each group. Proper order of sequence corresponds left to right with top to bottom.
4 means 1"=4'-0"; 30 means 1" = 30'-0".

For the bottom two groups: Using the metric scale, measure either millimeters (mm) or centimeters (cm) to the stipulated lengths indicated above each group.

REFER TO CHAPTER 1

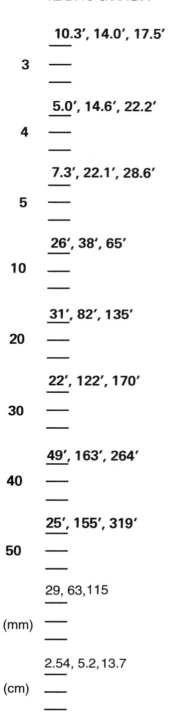

10.3', 14.0', 17.5'

3

5.0', 14.6', 22.2'

4

7.3', 22.1', 28.6'

5

26', 38', 65'

10

31', 82', 135'

20

22', 122', 170'

30

49', 163', 264'

40

25', 155', 319'

50

29, 63, 115

(mm)

2.54, 5.2, 13.7

(cm)

LEVEL ONE

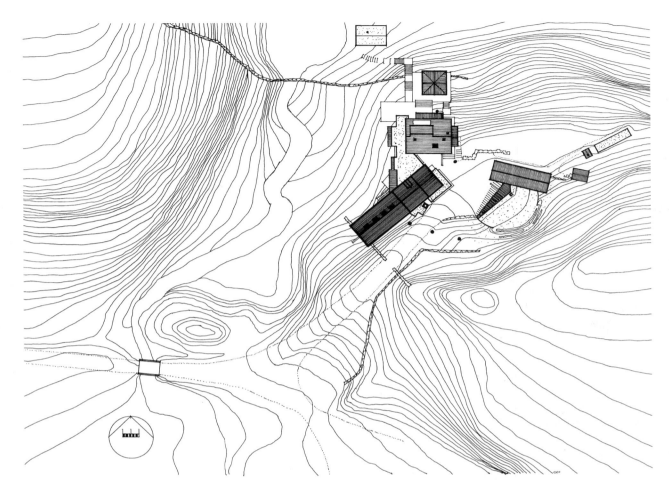

Drawing: Brandenburg's Ravenwood Studio, Ely, Minnesota
22" × 34" (55.9 × 86.4 cm)
Medium: Ink on Mylar
Courtesy of Salmela Architect

Contour Drawing

Answer the following questions about the above contour drawing (as an optional exercise, do the same for the site plans on pp. 379 and 396).

1. Do any of the contour lines cross each other?
2. Circle and label areas where you think there is for the most part a constant slope.
3. Circle and label areas where you think there is for the most part a steep slope.
4. Circle and label areas where you think there is for the most part a gentle slope.
5. Circle and identify the tops of hills.

REFER TO CHAPTER 1

LEVEL ONE

LEVEL ONE

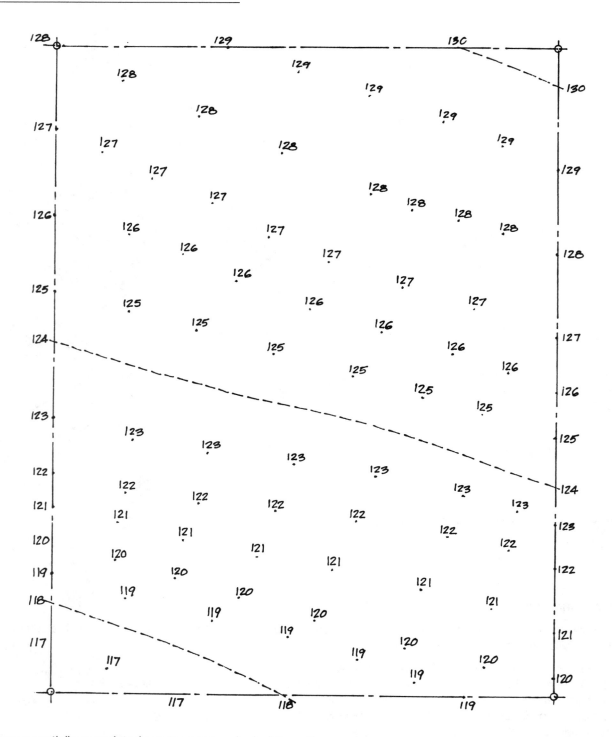

Given: a partially completed **contour** map of a building site

Required: Using a french curve or your own freehand technique, carefully connect contour lines of constant elevation. You can draw the contour lines either as a continuous solid line or as a series of small dashed lines (see p. 396) or as a series of small dots (see p. 379). Cut a small line segment through the contour lines and try to interpolate the correct profile. Do the same for p. 396.

REFER TO CHAPTER 1

Hand Lettering—Freehand, Using Capitals

Tell me something about yourself (with a sharpened soft pencil) and why you are pursuing the path of an architect or interior designer. What do you hope to get out of this class? Tell me a story, anything—just fill this page with writing.

Draw *lightly* ⅛" wide guidelines with a 2H lead. Allow for ¹⁄₁₆" space between the guidelines. Start one inch in from the sides of this typewritten text and one inch down from the bottom of this text and end up one inch up from the bottom of this page. Relax and write using all capitals.

Problem: Courtesy of Assistant Professor Daniel K. Mullin, AIA, NCARB
Graphic Communication course
Department of Architecture
University of Idaho–Moscow

REFER TO CHAPTER 2

LEVEL ONE

Hand Lettering—Freehand, Using Capitals

Using a lettering height and layout as stipulated by your instructor and simple vertical block capitals, carefully letter the following statement by Architect James Wines of SITE.

The range of drawing techniques—from Beaux-Arts watercolors to digital simulation—has become the basis of lively debate and, sometimes, a philosophical battleground. There is still a classically based group that regards all computerization as anathema and clings to the sanctity of eye and hand as the only means of describing the spirit of flux and change in nature. At the opposite pole, there are CAD cadets who have never touched paper with pencil and look on manual rendering as hopelessly out of touch with a cybernetic future. I find myself in the middle zone and look at the ultimate value of any drawing in terms of the quality of the idea it is describing. Thus the computer printout is no different than the pencil sketch, since both can function as evidence of either processed garbage or harvested creativity. [ARCHITECT'S STATEMENT]

REFER TO CHAPTER 2

Drawing Skills/Line Weights

With this project you will continue to learn how to use the drafting tools in which you have made a significant investment. You will be required to draw with your parallel bar or T-square, 30/60 triangle, 45/45 triangle, and compass.

Draw the figures shown on below (enlarge 60% to use) using a graphite lead and a lead holder. Construct the figures and shapes from the data given. Three different line weights are shown in the reference drawing but are exaggerated for clarity. All information that is necessary to complete these drawings is shown. (Remember that squares, circles, and triangles have inherent relational geometries.) Special attention should be given to line quality and the accuracy and consistency of the scaled drawing. All lines are to be done with the aid of drafting tools. *Use no freehand lines.*

Format: On a 12" × 18" sheet of vellum oriented horizontally, begin by drawing a borderline ½" from the edge of the sheet on all sides. Construct the drawing fields as large as possible, 2" from the top and side border lines. Lay out the overall information first, then draw in the figures as indicated by the specific dimensional instructions. Scale is full-size.

Draw a line ¾" from the bottom border line for a title block. Lettering a title block is required. Letters should be ½" high on one line of guidelines within the center of the title block. Center the lettering. Give your name, the date, and the assignment number.

Remember — Some points about drafting to keep in mind:

1. Good line quality requires sharpness, blackness, and proper line weight.
2. You are working with scaled drawings. Scaled drawings are reductions in which all dimensions remain proportional. Construction of drawings is always preferable to measuring and scaling the graphic images. *Never scale the drawings,* unless no other means exists.
3. Construct object outlines lightly at first, then "heavy" them up to achieve proper line weight.
4. Practice before beginning the final drawing. Do not expect to draw this only once.

Grading criteria will include line quality, line weight, accuracy, and graphic presentation.

Project: Courtesy of Professor Steve Temple
School of Architecture
University of Texas San Antonio

REFER TO CHAPTER 2

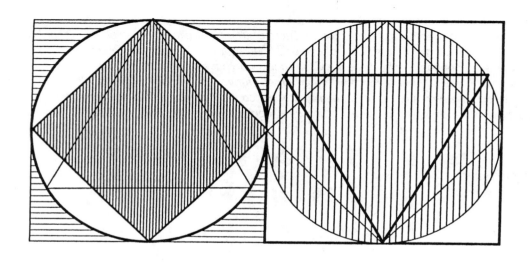

Longitudinal and Transverse Sections

The objective of this assignment is to place an emphasis on the relationship between a found object and drawings developed from that object. The drawings in this exercise will be based on a drawing type termed a *section.*

Begin this exercise by doing experimental research on objects. For example, go to the grocery store and obtain different fruits and vegetables. Slice them in different directions and notice how the sectional configuration changes or remains similar. Compare cross-sectional cuts on a string bean, a watermelon, and a green bell pepper. The string bean and even the watermelon have similar geometric shapes at different sliced locations, but the bell pepper changes dramatically.

Examine biology and botany books showing sections through the human body and tree trunks or tree branches. In medicine, radiologists can cut through an infinite number of locations on the human body when they x-ray. As you vary the x-ray slice through the human body, each image will differ in varying degrees from the previous image.

The section drawing is a way of understanding the contour, volume, edges, and insides of an object in space. It reveals the inner workings of an object and its inner space.

Required.: Obtain three objects that possess interesting sectional characteristics. The objects cannot be transparent. It is best if the sections are not similar or identical as you cut different locations. Your objective is to explain through drawing the inner details of the object. For this assignment, you will develop an elevation and one longitudinal section. You will also be required to develop four transverse sections based on observation, deduction, and scaled measurement. Do on tracing paper first. Do numerous freehand sections to see what explains the object best. The final drawing will be pencil on 18" × 24" smooth white Bristol board. All areas of concern such as placement, composition, and sequence of drawings should be addressed during class and before you begin the final drawings. For one of the section drawings, you will be required to depict the object as it casts shadows on a background.

This problem was adapted, with slight modifications, from a problem given at the school of Architectural Studies/California College of Arts and Crafts.

Problem: Courtesy of the California College of Art and Crafts
School of Architectural Studies
Studio Professors: Hank Dunlop and Mark Jensen

REFER TO CHAPTERS 4 AND 8

LEVEL ONE

LEVEL ONE

Orthographic Projection — Hardline

Time Frame: A one-week project

OBJECTIVES

This assignment is a test of your abilities to resolve a complex abstract object into the three-view orthographic format, as well as to accurately measure and draw to scale. It also provides continued practice in layout and drawing technique.

PROJECT

Draw in **hardline** (not freehand) and in graphite, the *top, front, and side views* in orthographic projection of your choice of objects from those listed below.

1. Draw one **auto part** in full scale (actual size), or
2. Draw two different pieces of **styrofoam** in half scale.

FORMAT

Use a sheet of vellum measuring 18" × 24" oriented horizontally. Draw a borderline ½" from the edge of the sheet. Provide ¾" high guidelines at the bottom of the sheet located ½" from the bottom borderline. Letter your name, project number, and the date.

Lay out the three-view format of each object side-by-side (three views for the auto parts; two separate three-view sets for the styrofoam objects). Spacing between views must be equal. Spacing between sets of views is up to you.

RULES

Large curves in the objects must be drawn on your elevation views. Small radii (less than ¼") can be shown as a corner.

Elements of each view must *project* and *align* from view to view. *No freehand drawing.* Your drawings must be *constructed.* All lines must be drawn with instruments. Construction guidelines, if drawn *lightly,* are acceptable on the finished drawing.

DRAWING TIPS

Prior to beginning your final drawing, make a series of sketches of the objects to explore the relationships of the parts of the objects. Also in sketches, explore the actual size of the drawings that will need to be laid out on your sheet prior to attempting your final drawing.

Project: Courtesy of Professor Steve Temple
School of Architecture
University of Texas San Antonio

REFER TO CHAPTER 4

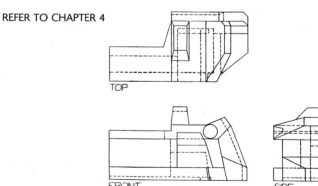

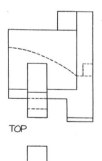

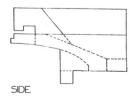

Drawing: Student project by Bethany Biddle
Department of Interior Design
University of North Carolina Greensboro

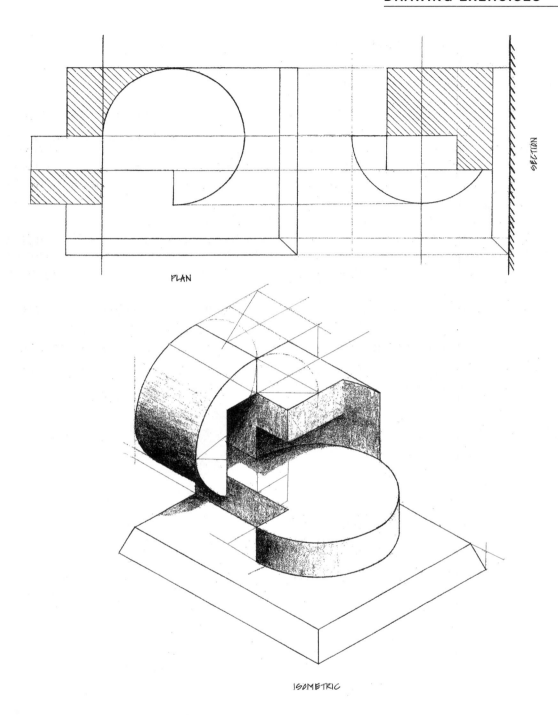

PLAN

SECTION

ISOMETRIC

Plan, Section, and Isometric Drawing Problem

Using rectilinear and cylindrical forms, design a solid abstract object from which plan, section, and isometric drawings will be done. Also make a model of this object using any type of material. Where the cut is made for both the plan and the section, use the proper indication for section lining (see p. 32). Also apply value to both flat and curvilinear surfaces in the isometric drawing to enhance the three-dimensional quality of the object.

Courtesy of Kwok Gorran Tsui, an architecture graduate of the University of Texas at Austin

REFER TO CHAPTERS 4, 5, 8, AND 9

Plan and Elevation Graphic Conventions

Time frame: A one-week project
Required materials: You will need a 25' measuring tape

1. Assemble into groups of three (sign-up sheet). Measure together—draw your final drawing separately.

2. Locate a classroom (seating at least 20 and containing windows) somewhere on campus. Measure the room. On a rough sketch of the floor plan and interior elevations, add the measurements. This will be used as a reference to draw an accurate, scaled drawing of the *floor plan* and *interior elevations.* Assume a horizontal section is cut at 4'0" above the floor. Include all furniture in both the plan and elevations.

3. Individually, each student will then draw the plan and interior elevations from the measurements in $\frac{3}{8}$" = 1'0" scale on a single sheet of 24" × 36" vellum in graphite according to the following format:

    The plan should be located in the center of the sheet with the compass direction NORTH facing to the top of the sheet. The respective interior elevations should then be drawn as projections around the plan: the elevation you see when facing north to the top; the elevation you see when facing east to the right side; and so on.

4. *Draw all furniture and built-in cabinets. Draw all wall elements.* Show three-dimensional ceiling elements on the plan by use of the dashed line convention. Use of templates is permitted.

5. Title block at bottom of sheet: Letter on two lines at $\frac{1}{2}$" high with a $\frac{1}{4}$" space between lines, as follows:

    top line (containing the title): As-Built Drawings, name of campus building, room number
    bottom line: your name, the date, the scale used

Project: Courtesy of Professor Steve Temple
School of Architecture
University of Texas San Antonio

REFER TO CHAPTER 4

LEVEL ONE

Section—Graphic Conventions

Time frame: a two-week or 10-day project

This assignment will introduce you to the graphics of *building section* through the drawing of a building section by projecting it from a plan and another cross-section.

- Choose one of the buildings presented in class.
- Each building is limited to three students.
- A sign-up sheet will be posted for each.

In graphite on a sheet of 24 x 36 vellum, lay out and draw (trace) the floor plan and one section in a projected format, with the plan in correct orientation projected below the section. It will be necessary to enlarge the drawings on a photocopier to fit on the sheet in as large a scale as possible, preferably in a common scale found on an architect's or engineer's scale. Draw a graphic scale on the finished drawing.

Then, **construct** the opposing cross-section that is not given, using **projection lines** as an aid to complete any missing data. *Elements of the two building sections must be consistent with each other and must be drawn using a method of projecting construction lines.*

In order to complete the missing cross-section, it may be necessary to develop a strategy for completing missing information using your knowledge of design and/or research on the particular building.

Provide a lettered title block at least ½" high at the top of the sheet, including your name, assignment number, the name of the building, and the date of the building.

This is a drawing exercise—you are expected to produce a sophisticated drawing using various line weights, good line quality, well-composed layout, and quality lettering.

Project: Courtesy of Professor Steve Temple
School of Architecture
University of Texas San Antonio

REFER TO CHAPTER 4

LEVEL ONE

Identifying Surfaces / Isometric Views / Missing Views

In the first group of three, identify the surfaces in the orthographic views. Note the example at left. In the next group of three, sketch the isometric of each below in the spaces provided. In the final two boxes, sketch the three missing orthographic views from the given isometric drawing.

Evaluation of similar problems will be based on: drawing accuracy and comprehension, composed sheet layout-borders, lettering, etc. (if applicable), and line quality.

REFER TO CHAPTER 5

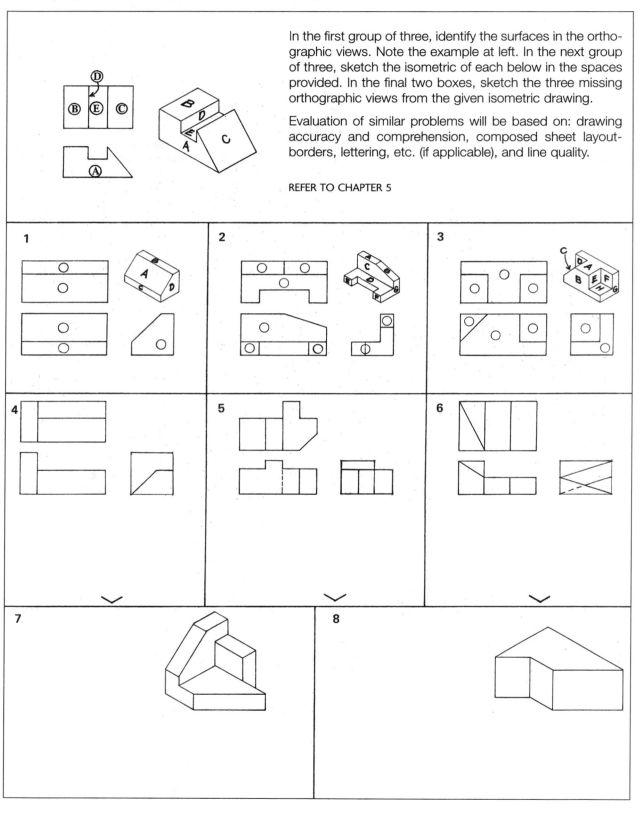

LEVEL ONE

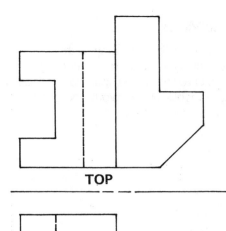

TOP

FRONT   **RIGHT SIDE**

Missing Views

From the given views of the object, construct the left side, back, and bottom views.

Scale: ⅛"=1'0"

Note: Folding plane lines in these two exercises are mainly for instructional purposes. Please feel free to delete in photocopies if your instructor so desires.

Missing Views

From the given views of the object, construct the right side, bottom, and back views.

Scale: ⅜"=1'0"

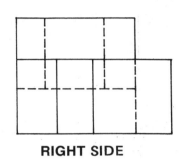

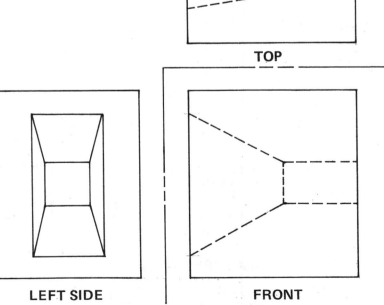

TOP

LEFT SIDE   **FRONT**

LEVEL ONE

In resolving multiview problems, always try to visualize with sketches the three-dimensional construct.

REFER TO CHAPTER 5

LEVEL ONE

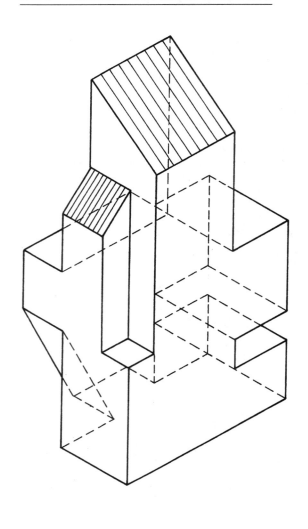

Six Orthographic Views

Shown at left is an isometric drawing with hidden lines to help you visualize the form. Construct six orthographic views. Draw them first with hidden lines and then without hidden lines, as would be seen in architectural plans and elevations.

Student project by Ellen W. Ng
Courtesy of the Department of Architecture
City College of San Francisco

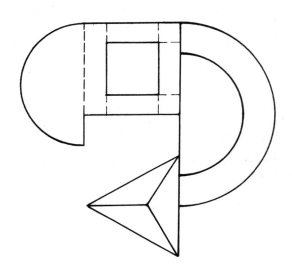

Student project by Erna Egli and Joanna Hostetler
Courtesy of the Department of Architecture
City College of San Francisco

Missing View/Isometric/Plan Oblique

Construct the missing right side elevation from the given plan and elevation views. Then construct an isometric drawing and a plan oblique drawing at 45°–45°.

REFER TO CHAPTER 5

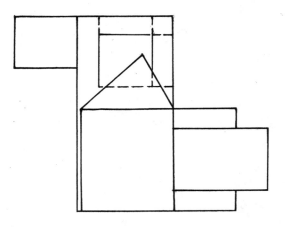

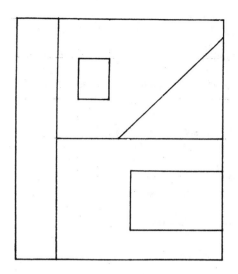

Isometric Views/Dimetric View

From the plan and two elevations of a simple block form, visualize and sketch what you think the four isometric views from the four different corners will look like. Then accurately construct the four isometric drawings. As an optional additional exercise, construct a dimetric view from a vantage point of your choice, emphasizing one or two of the principal planes.

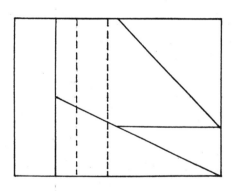

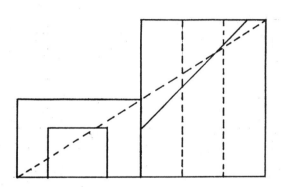

Student project by Linda Gigli
Courtesy of the Department of Architecture
City College of San Francisco

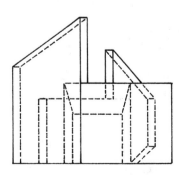

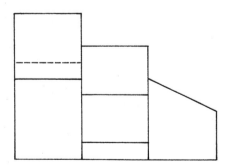

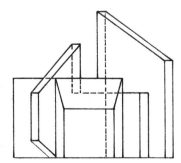

Missing Views

From the three elevation views of this fairly complex form, visualize and sketch what you think the plan view and rear elevation will look like. Then accurately construct these views. Show hidden lines.

REFER TO CHAPTER 5

LEVEL ONE

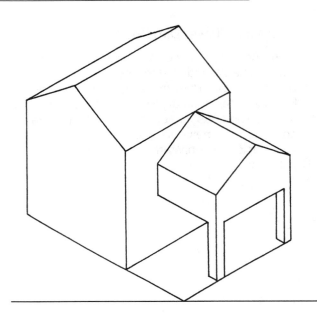

Comprehensive Paraline Problem

1. Construct the roof plan, the front elevation, and the side elevation views.
2. Construct two plan obliques: one at 45°–45° and one at 60°30°.
3. Using the plan configuration, construct a plan oblique with a nonvertical z axis that is 60° from the horizontal.
4. Using the side elevation, construct an elevation oblique, using 45°–1:½:1.
5. Using the side elevation, construct a frontal elevation oblique 0°–1:1.
6. Construct a worm's-eye plan oblique.

Scale: ⅟₁₆"=1'0"

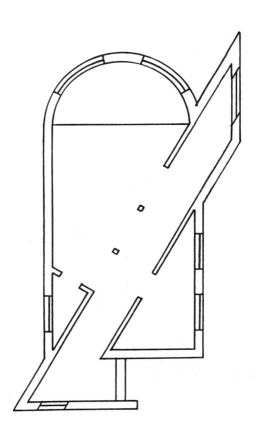

Plan Oblique

Rotate this plan view of a small building 30° from the horizontal so that you can construct a 30°–60° plan oblique view. Make the elevation of the plan cut four feet above the exterior ground level.

Scale: ³⁄₃₂"=1'0"

Courtesy of Kwok Gorran Tsui, an architecture graduate of the University of Texas at Austin

REFER TO CHAPTER 5

Plan Oblique

Time frame: a one-week project

Instructors should develop their own plan and interior elevations and give them to their students. Construct an axonometric view in ½"=1'0" scale in graphite on an 18" × 24" vellum oriented horizontally. Use corner A for the front corner of the axonometric. Remove walls A-B and A-D for a better view of the space.

Format: Draw a borderline ½" from the edge and include a 1" high title block at the bottom. In the center of the title block, in ¾" high lettering guidelines, letter your name, project number, and the date. The orthographic drawings should be in ¼" scale.

Turn in a blueprint for evaluation.

Give thought to the layout on your sheet so as to produce an aesthetically pleasing overall drawing effect. Line weights should be varied to aid in the perception of depth.

Additional

1. Draw the grid on the FLOOR ONLY. (The grid may remain on the walls as light guidelines which will not show on a blueprint).
2. Design and draw a different lamp with a round lamp shade on each of the two side tables.
3. Draw four Platonic objects sitting on the fireplace mantle.
4. Draw two 18"x28" paintings in frames on two of the walls.
5. Draw a six panel door in the doorway of wall C-D.
6. Draw a 24"x42" casement window in wall C-D above the plant. The case molding frame should be rectangular shapes.

Plan Oblique (According to Name)

Last name A through E—45° plan projection
Last name F through J—30° left–60° right plan oblique
Last name K through Q—30° isometric
Last name R through Z—30° right–60° left plan oblique

Project: Courtesy of Professor Steve Temple
School of Architecture
University of Texas San Antonio

LEVEL ONE

LEVEL ONE

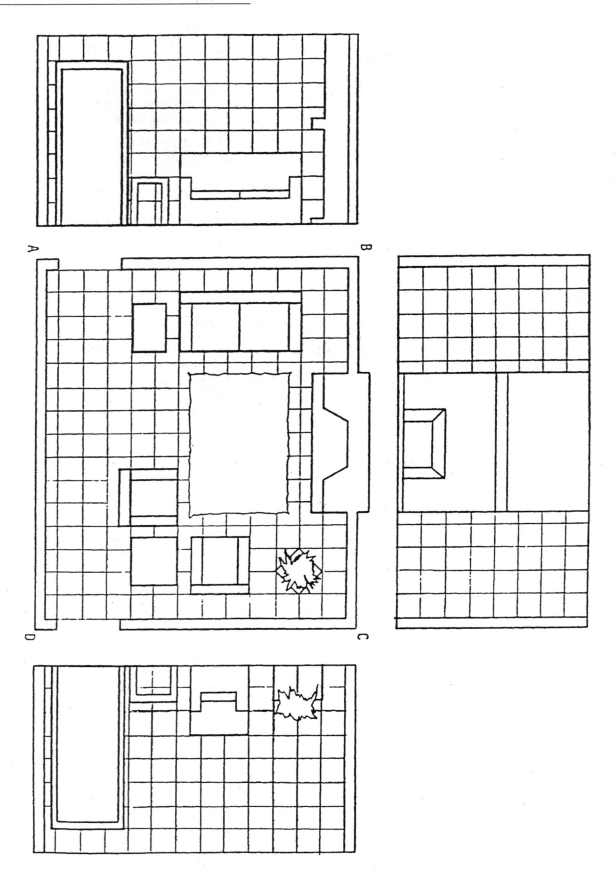

Given: A plan view and one elevation of an L-shaped seating area.

Required: Select a horizon line and station point and construct a **two-point perspective.** Also draw to scale two **human figures** in conversation, one sitting and one standing.

Scale: ¼"=1'0"

Student project by Amy Man
Courtesy of the Department of Architecture
City College of San Francisco

REFER TO CHAPTERS 6 and 9

PLAN

PP

ELEVATION

Given: A plan view and one elevation of a building form.

Required: Construct a **two-point perspective.** The elevation view is looking directly perpendicular to the picture plane. For these two problems, choose a station point which has an angle of about 30° from the station point to the viewed extremes of the object. As an optional additional exercise, add exterior **vegetation** and landscaping.

Scale: ¹⁄₁₆"=1'0"

REFER TO CHAPTERS 6 and 9

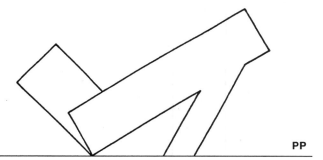

PP

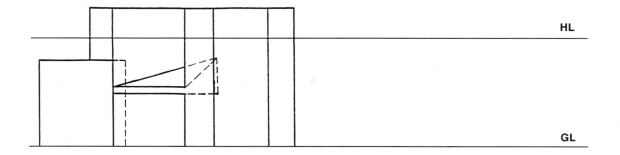

HL

GL

LEVEL ONE

LEVEL ONE

Two-Point Perspective

THE AIM
An exercise in three-dimensional representation utilizing the method of constructing two-point architectural perspective to create a realistic or lifelike image of form and space.

THE TASK
Present a two-point perspective of the Family House at Riva San Vitale by Mario Botta. Select a viewpoint showing the main terrace (e.g., looking at the building from the SE corner). Position the station point and picture plane appropriately to achieve a realistic view. You may show the setup grid and construction lines in the final presentation, using a fine pen (0.1 or 0.2) with red or blue ink. Drawings must be done in black ink, drafted either with technical or felt-tipped pens (uni pin fine-line pens are good).

Re-present the elevations of the building with shadows, using shading techniques described in the lectures. Note that the elevations to be shaded are separate drawings from the perspective drawing. You can cut and paste the elevations (then photocopy the whole sheet) or redraw them (for better line quality) onto your final presentation sheet. When placing the drawings, think about the layout of the sheet for readability and coherence. Attention should be given to the techniques introduced in the previous lectures, including line quality and use of drafting equipment.

REQUIREMENTS
1. In class you will be required to practice setting up two-point perspectives. Bring your drawing tools.
2. For the final hand-in, present a perspective view and three elevations on one A3 sheet of paper, in vertical (portrait) format, with the logo in the bottom right-hand corner. The drawing must be in ink.

ASSESSMENT CRITERIA
Students will be assessed on the following criteria:

- Accuracy and coherence of perspective
- Selection of viewpoint
- Line quality and rendering
- Sheet layout and perspective setup
- Neatness of presentation

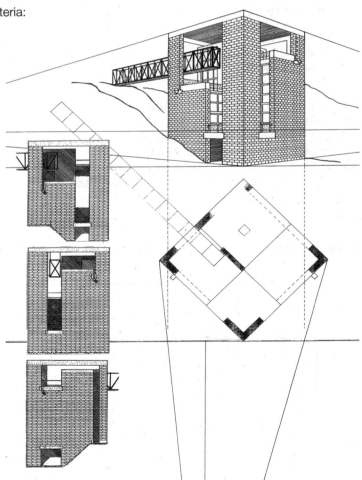

Courtesy of Dr. Samer Akkach
Drawing Architecture & Landscape 1
School of Architecture, Landscape Architecture and
Urban Design
Adelaide University, South Australia

REFER TO CHAPTERS 6, 7, AND 8

Drawing: Student project by Sue Fletcher
Courtesy of the School of Architecture, Landscape
Architecture and Urban Design
Adelaide University, South Australia

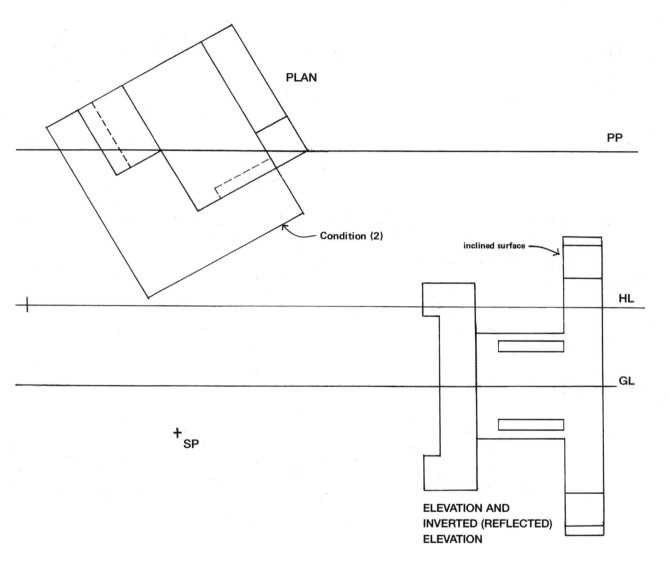

PLAN

PP

Condition (2)

inclined surface

HL

GL

SP

ELEVATION AND
INVERTED (REFLECTED)
ELEVATION

LEVEL ONE

Perspective Reflections

Given: The plan, elevation, and inverted elevation of a building touching a **reflecting surface.**

Required: Draw a two-point perspective of the building and show its exact reflection. Scale: $\frac{1}{16}$" = 1'0"

Condition (2): Draw this edge of a reflecting pool. Notice how this results in a partial reflected image. As an optional additional exercise, render the reflection in the pool.

REFER TO CHAPTERS 6 and 9

Perspective Cutaways and Section Perspectives

Perspective cutaway views and two-point perspective sections are excellent ways of showing the interior of a design concept. This exercise is stated just to encourage the use of these methods for viewing the inside of any building project.

One-Point Perspective

THE AIM
An exercise in three-dimensional representation utilizing the method of construction of one-point architectural perspective to create a realistic or lifelike image of form and space.

THE TASK
You are required to present a one-point perspective of your kitchen (or a friend's kitchen if you do not have one). Try not to use a photograph. Select a viewpoint that gives a representation close to the visual perception of the space. Pay attention to the techniques introduced in the previous lectures, such as line quality, use of drafting equipment, etc. Also, use this exercise to communicate a spatial experience, exploring form, order, texture, shape, and proportion.

REQUIREMENTS
1. Bring in an accurate, scaled sketch plan and sketch elevation(s) of your kitchen.
2. Bring in an appropriate grid and a draft setup of the one-point perspective of your kitchen.
3. For the final hand-in, present the perspective view on one A3 sheet of paper, in vertical (portrait) format, with the logo in the bottom right-hand corner. The drawing may be in pencil or ink.

ASSESSMENT CRITERIA
Students will be assessed on the following criteria:
• Accuracy and coherence of perspective
• Selection of viewpoint and perspective setup
• Line quality and rendering
• Sheet layout and neatness of presentation

Courtesy of Dr. Samer Akkach
Drawing Architecture & Landscape 1
School of Architecture, Landscape Architecture and Urban Design
Adelaide University, South Australia

REFER TO CHAPTERS 6 AND 9

LEVEL ONE

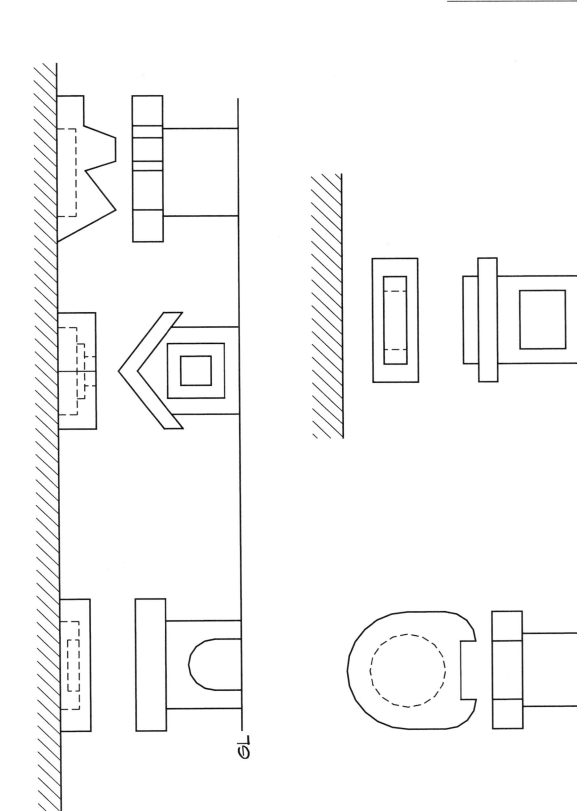

Problem: Courtesy of Professor Rich Correa, Yuba College

LEVEL ONE

Cast wall and ground shadows

REFER TO CHAPTER 8

LEVEL ONE

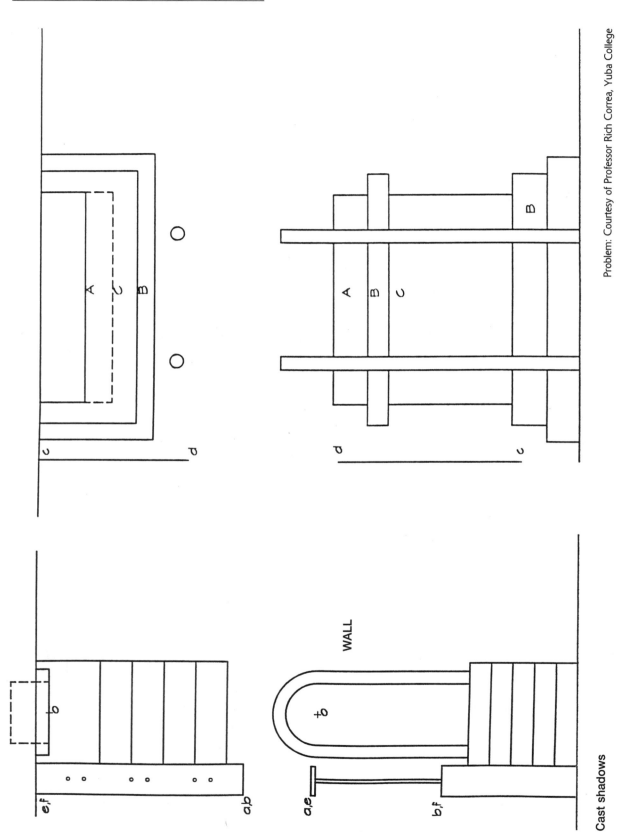

Cast shadows

REFER TO CHAPTER 8

WALL

Problem: Courtesy of Professor Rich Correa, Yuba College

Comprehensive Problem: Paralines, Perspectives, Shadows, and Rendering

1. Draw both isometric and plan oblique sketches of how you think the stair element should appear.
2. Draw two different accurate isometric drawings.
3. Choose perspective variables and draw two two-point perspectives ($\frac{1}{4}$"=1'0").
4. Add shadows and shades to each of the above.
5. Add two human figures, one each at two different levels, drawn to scale.

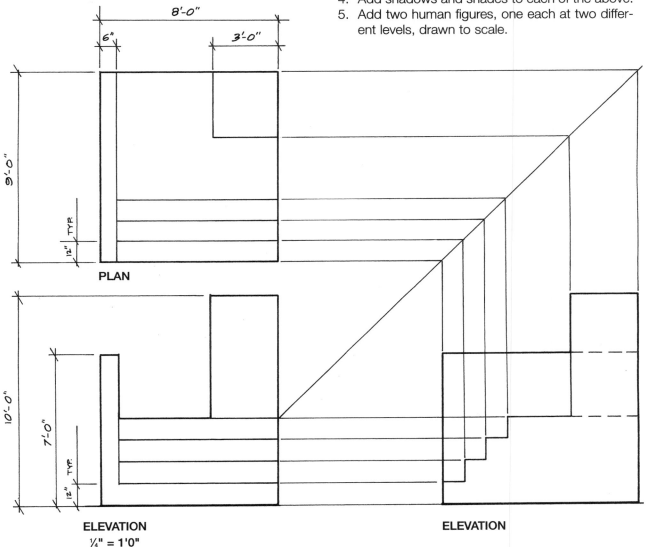

8'-0"

6"

3'-0"

9'-0"

12" TYP.

PLAN

10'-0"

7'-0"

12" TYP.

ELEVATION
$\frac{1}{4}$" = 1'0"

ELEVATION

LEVEL ONE

Problem: Courtesy of Professor Thomas L. Turman,
Department of Architecture
Laney College

REFER TO CHAPTERS 5,6,8, and 9

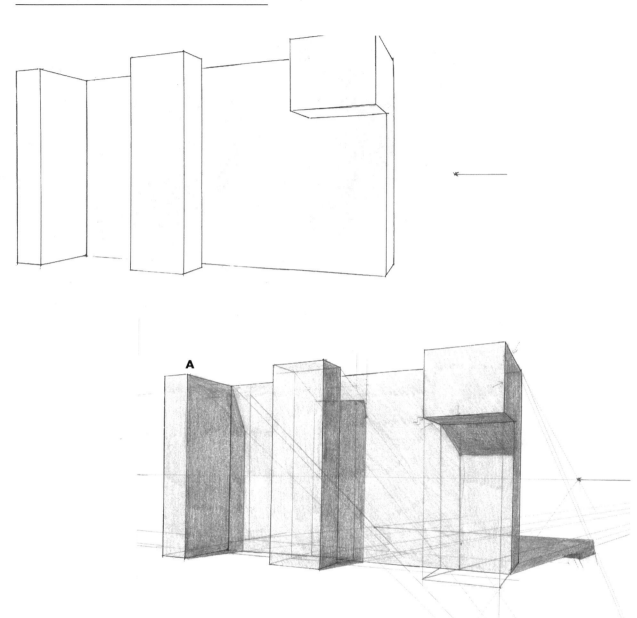

Shadow Construction (Two Vanishing Point Method)

In this exercise, the students are given a handout upon which is a "shadow casting model." The models are designed to create specific shadow shapes that can be constructed using the two vanishing point method. The advantage of this method is that shadows can be constructed in perspective (orthographics not necessary). The first shadow point is given (i.e., casting point A projects a shadow to shadow point A). From there, the shadow VP can be extended, then the Sun's VP and the shadow can be constructed (see example).

Problem: Courtesy of Professor Dick Davison
College of Architecture
Texas A&M University

REFER TO CHAPTER 8

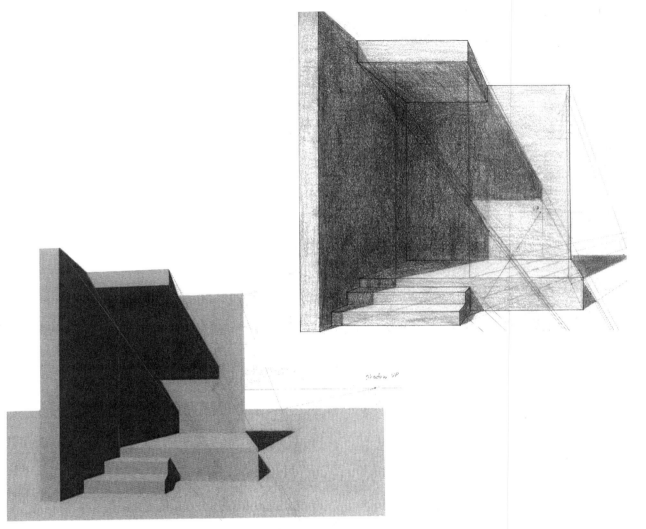

Shadow Construction (2VP Method)

Shadow Model Design (Using 3D Studio Viz)

The students are asked to design and draw a model and then construct shadows using the 2VP method. Requirements for the models are as follows:

- The model should have two vertical walls.
- The model should have a flat "roof."
- There should be a level change with at least one step between levels.

After the model is designed, drawn in perspective, and shadows constructed, the students use 3D Studio Viz to reproduce the model with the same light direction as a check for the hand drawing. Two drawings are turned in: The first is designed and drawn by hand; the second is a computer-generated "copy" of the first.

Drawing: Student project by Rebecca Flannery
Problem: Courtesy of Professor Dick Davison
College of Architecture
Texas A&M University

REFER TO CHAPTER 8

Rendition/Value — Ink Pens — Site Plan

Create a site plan for the Cutler residence and apply rendition/value techniques to trees, topography, roof structure, paths, etc. Use measurements off the plan drawing constructed earlier in the semester with roof plan at $\frac{1}{16}$"=1'0". Establish a free-flowing set of contours, paths, and tree locations, and apply texture to each component. The building may be set into the topography at the student's discretion. Apply shadows from late afternoon or morning sun...approximate for effect. Use 11" × 17" (minimum) vellum and ink pen (either good sketch pens or technical pens) for graphic work. Hard-line the roof plan and deck/step surfaces; freehand the trees, topography, etc. Set the drawing up on trace prior to beginning the final vellum drawing. Strive for various line weights and textural contrast between graphic components of the site plan.

Problem: Courtesy of Assistant Professor Daniel K. Mullin, AIA, NCARB
Graphic Communication course
Department of Architecture
University of Idaho–Moscow

REFER TO CHAPTERS 8 AND 9

Drawing: Student project by Amanda Hallberg
Department of Architecture
University of Idaho–Moscow

LEVEL ONE

Rendering Techniques

Design an abstract composition of geometric forms and draw it in axonometric or plan oblique. Render the composition with the following six techniques: (1) dots, (2) parallel lines, (3) multidirectional lines, (4) scribbles, (5) contrast black and white, and (6) tonal value in lead pencil.

REFER TO CHAPTERS 5 AND 9

Student project by Christopher Wilson
Studio Professor: M. Saleh Uddin
Courtesy of the Department of Environmental Design
University of Missouri–Columbia

Rendering an Interior Space

From a conceptual sketch of an interior space, do a line drawing of this imagined image using a soft lead pencil. Transfer this pencil-drawn image on the adhesive side of a medium-tack airbrush frisket film. Hand render this transferred line drawing on a white Strathmore board using only airbrush and acrylic paint. Show tonal values of shades and shadows.

Student: Mohammad Khasawinah
Professor: M. Saleh Uddin
Course: Design Communication I
Department of Environmental Design
University of Missouri–Columbia

REFER TO CHAPTERS 3,8, and 9

Hand rendering with airbrush and acrylic paint. Black and white rendering techniques using variation of tonal values. Rendering was done by spraying hierarchically from darker shades to lighter shades. Badger 150 airbrush, black acrylic paint, low tack masking film, and Strathmore cold press medium weight board. Rendering of an interior staircase.
[STUDENT'S STATEMENT]

"Plan Oblique" A Mixed Media Drawing
Media: Pastel/graphite/color pencil
Courtesy of Professor Dick Davison
College of Architecture
Texas A&M University

In this drawing, several media are used simultaneously.

1. *I begin with an underlayment of pastel, several colors, but predominantly yellow in this case. Into this base the original plan is drawn in graphite. I do not yet fix the pastel because it is possible to create tonal variations and light effects by erasing into one area or another.*
2. *As the verticals are brought up I develop tones and textures with a mix of color pencil (usually Derwent) and graphite. The pastel acts as a ground to respond to, not unlike the way a marker ground can be drawn over with finer instruments to create sharpness and detail.*
3. *Portions of the building are emphasized and refined more than others. This creates a kind of "optical" quality that contrasts with the uniform scale of the oblique view.*

[PROFESSOR'S STATEMENT]

Project for a mixed media drawing

Study the tips on handling mixed media on the book's web site. Then study the techniques in the example above which has the theme of "Plan Oblique." Using the theme of a "Utopian Building," develop an image using mixed media. Experiment with the following media to create your solution: a graphite drawing, a laser copy of this drawing, colored pencil, and acrylic paint (see professor's creation using this theme on the web site).

Courtesy of Professor Dick Davison
College of Architecture
Texas A&M University

REFER TO CHAPTERS 3, 10, and the bonus chapter "Conventional and Computerized Representation in Color" found at www.wiley.com/go/yee.

The Hourglass

This exercise is so named because the students, using drawing to parallel the design process, gather (draw) large amounts of often random information (the top of the hourglass), come to understand it well enough to reduce it to its core (the center of the hourglass), and then reorganize and re-present it as coherent architectural ideas and forms (the bottom of the hourglass).

The general goals of this drawing exercise (and the five weeks that were devoted to this same issue) were (1) to gain an ability to use drawing to develop ideas rather than merely illustrate them, and (2) to understand how various forms of drawing can look at different aspects of an idea, from the most essential and gestural to more "embellished" drawing, and how the different forms of drawing build on and influence one another and the overall idea.

The students looked at early conceptual drawings by Maya Lin, Corbu, and Ando, making particular connection between Ando's drawing and written language—drawings that isolate or carry the seeds for the entire idea. This type of drawing looks at the whole by, essentially, leaving out the parts. The students also looked at Picasso's one-liners as another model of how to resolve disparate pieces into a fluid whole; in this case, however, the parts are included but are conceived of as a part of a single, fluid whole.

The students used these various forms of drawing (1) to look at existing buildings and "reverse" this process, cooking them down to their essentials, and then (2) to begin to conceive of their own not-yet-existing projects "going in the other direction," from essential summaries to more fully detailed ideas. Those students who were in a concurrent studio were required to use these ideas in their studio projects and to illustrate, in a single image and without words, the connection of these ideas to their studio process. A number of the students were in studios that dealt with a degree of metaphor in the early stages, hence the images that occur in some of their pieces. They initially had to present their ideas on a 2' × 3' board; then they had to reduce the content and the scale down to an 8½" × 11" image.

Project: Courtesy of Professor Bob Hansman
School of Architecture
Washington University, St. Louis, Missouri

Student project by Megan O'Neill
Media: Pen and ink, charcoal
School of Architecture
Washington University, St. Louis, Missouri

REFER TO CHAPTER 10

LEVEL ONE

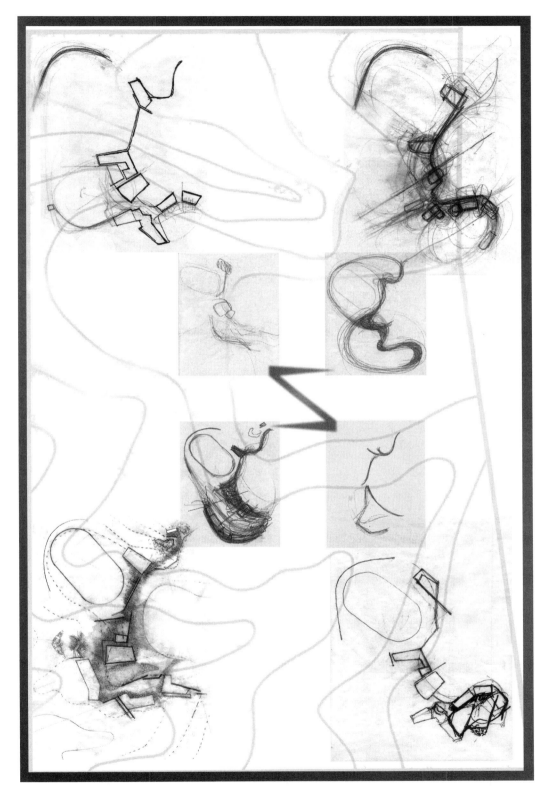

Student project by Jonah Chiarenza
Medium: Pencil and computer touch-up
School of Architecture
Washington University, St. Louis, Missouri

Vocabulary and Diagramming

Developing an architectural vocabulary is an important part of architectural communication and design. On the following page is a vocabulary list used in communicating architectural design principles. It is important that you understand these terms and are able to apply them. You will be expected to use these terms in the review of your own work and that of others. Be prepared to verbally and graphically define these terms at a moment's notice.

Objectives
- Develop a graphic and verbal language for describing concepts, form, and organization principles of design.
- Develop a methodology for diagramming.
- Enhance spatial understanding.
- Develop representation skills for the communication of ideas.

Process
- Define each term on the following page in written *(architectural lettering)* and graphic form *(freehand with black felt-tip pen)*.
- Use your own words for the written definition based on the supporting examples throughout the chapters.
- Create your own diagrams based on the supporting examples throughout the chapters.
- Make a photocopy of the assignment to turn in.

Reading
- *Architecture: Form, Space, and Order,* Ching. CH 2, pp. 33–89.
- Ibid. CH 4, pp. 177–225.
- Ibid. CH 7, pp. 317–373.

Notes
Bring the following materials to class:

- Chipboard—three thicknesses
- Adhesives
- Cutting tools
- Various other modeling supplies, such as Plexiglas, wire, aluminum tubing, basswood, metal screen/mesh, etc.

Project: Courtesy of Professor Steve Temple
School of Architecture
University of Texas San Antonio, and
Professor Edward K. Fabian
Hammons School of Architecture
Drury University

REFER TO CHAPTER 10

LEVEL ONE

Axis:

Symmetry:

Asymmetry:

LEVEL ONE

Continue to lay out rectangles of approximate size 2" × 1½" for the following terms to be illustrated:

Hierarchy	Rhythm	Datum	Linear form
Radial form	Clustered form	Grid form	Centralized organization
Linear organization	Radial organization	Clustered organization	Grid organization
Spatial tension	Edge-to-edge contact	Face-to-face contact	Interlocking volumes
Transformation	Dimensional transformation	Subtractive transformation	Additive transformation

Two-Dimensional Diagramming: Interpretation of Composition

Diagrams are drawings and models that quickly communicate the essence of design ideas by reducing them to their essential parts and ideas. They are typically used at the beginning of the design process to facilitate development and communicate the most critical elements of the design. They are also useful in analyzing existing designs, allowing one to clarify the designer's intentions.

Objectives
- Develop a graphic and verbal language for describing concepts, form and organization principles of design.
- Develop a methodology for diagramming.
- Enhance spatial understanding.
- Develop representation skills for the communication of ideas.

PART A

Process
Create two-dimensional diagrams of the compositional forms and organization of the images of paintings and photographs from the handout.

1. Choose two paintings and two photographs.
2. Use 8½" × 11" paper.
3. Draw three different black and white diagrams of the same painting in 10 minutes.
4. Focus on different aspects of the composition for each of the three diagrams. You should have 12 diagrams of four compositions done after 40 minutes (four pages, three diagrams per page).
5. Discuss the diagrams in studio.

PART B

Process
- Do 12 more diagrams of four additional paintings using the same process described in Part A.
- Produce a final diagram in your sketchbook for each of the additional four paintings you selected.

   1. Draw three diagrams per page in the *front* of your sketchbook. Draw in *freehand with a black felt-tip pen.*
   2. If you do not have your sketchbook yet, do the drawings on sheets of bond paper, which should be inserted into your sketchbook later.
   3. Make photocopies of the four pages (12 diagrams).

- "Bug Models"—Create a three-dimensional model of each of the four *best* diagrams chosen in Part B using a variety of materials (listed below). Models may be no larger than 8" in any one dimension.
- Exhibit the original image, the two-dimensional diagram, and the three-dimensional model.

Notes
Use the terms and diagrams from the preceding exercise, Vocabulary and Diagramming, and from your readings to help you communicate the design.

You will need the following materials to accomplish this assignment:

- Chipboard—three thicknesses
- Adhesives
- Cutting tools
- Various other modeling supplies, such as Plexiglas, wire, aluminum tubing, basswood, metal screen/mesh, etc.

Project: Courtesy of Professor Steve Temple
School of Architecture
University of Texas San Antonio

REFER TO CHAPTER 10

Diagramming Synthesis

Objectives
- Develop a graphic and verbal language for describing concepts, form and organization principles of design.
- Develop a methodology for diagramming.
- Enhance spatial understanding.
- Develop representation skills for the communication of ideas.
- Develop skills in transformation from idea to diagram to space/materials.

Process
Choose **one set** of diagrams and "bug model" from the previous assignment and improve it based on the critique of the previous class. Using these diagrams and model, transform the diagrammatic concepts of the chosen set by designing it to fit into a particular site.

Use the conditions of the site as a factor in causing the diagram/model to transform. Allow materials to develop a dialogue between themselves, the site, and the condition of their respective placement.

- The site is the location where the floor and wall intersect.
- **Scale** of the new design should be four times the size of the original "bug model."
- Do *not* attach to the floor or wall in any way except with push pins.
- You are required to use three different materials. You may use variations of each single material (e.g., wood may be in the form of sticks or boards or flat sheets; paper may be in sheets or rolled into tubes, etc.)
- Use raw materials with no color or printing. Do not add color or printing to the surfaces of materials.

Project: Courtesy of Professor Steve Temple
School of Architecture
University of Texas San Antonio

REFER TO CHAPTER 10

LEVEL ONE

LEVEL ONE

Composite Presentation Boards

Design and create a presentation board communicating the concept and architectural intent of your proposal for your final design studio project, "A Place for Rejuvenation."

Hang your work on the wall outside your studio space.

The board shall consist of eight 10" × 16" boards (to fit on the scanner bed), arranged into a single 40" × 32" composition. The material of the boards may be foam core, poster board, museum board, or any other stiff sheet material that supports your graphic concept(s).

The scale of your drawings and models may change as necessary to fit onto the boards.

Example:

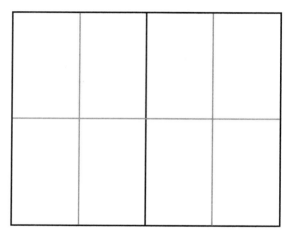

Include the following information (at minimum) on your presentation boards:

Site Context: Typed statements and graphics/photographs.

Concept Statment: Typed.

Site Plan with site section.

Final model of building with local site circumstances: Photograph the model, including shadows and a uniform and nondistracting background.

Local Context Model: Photograph the site model, including shadows and a uniform and nondistracting background. Also include photographs of the actual site, if possible.

Floor Plan(s).

Building Sections: Two, one in each direction, showing site section.

Perspective Views: Interior and exterior.

Project: Courtesy of Professor Steve Temple
School of Architecture
University of Texas San Antonio

REFER TO CHAPTER 11

Three-Dimensional Electronic Modeling and Visualization

Composition and superimposition of three-dimensional models using electronic modeling and image manipulation techniques. A plan was given to students to visualize and to draw in 3D, using both hand drawing and electronic modeling. A hand-constructed model was also created in scale to comprehend the total three-dimensionality of the visualized structure. The 3D electronic model with surface texture and lighting was created using form Z software. Selected views, ranging from two-dimensional plan or elevation to three-dimensional perspective views with varying camera lenses, were saved to compose one integrated presentation. Images were brought into Photoshop to compose, to change scale, and to add filter effects. Final presentation size ranged between 17" × 22" and 24" × 36".

Student: Corey Sengstacken
Professor: M. Saleh Uddin
Course: Design Communications-I
Department of Environmental Design
University of Missouri–Columbia

Student: Kelly Parker
Professor: M. Saleh Uddin
Course: Design Communications-I
Department of Environmental Design
University of Missouri–Columbia

REFER TO CHAPTERS 3,4, 6, 11 and the bonus chapter "Conventional and Computerized Representation in Color" found at www.wiley.com/go/yee.

LEVEL ONE

Fanciful Seating

This assignment is a competition for a chair design that is an expression of an admired architecture.

EDUCATIONAL OBJECTIVE
To recognize a relationship between the scale of architecture and the scale of product design.

ASSIGNMENT REQUIREMENTS
Using technology as an inspiration, transform scale and utility by establishing a geometrical grid into the confines of seating. Juxtapose the extreme scales on a single 24" × 36" board using a single colored pencil, with the composition and the layout as expressive elements.

Project Courtesy of Professor George S. Loli
Department of Architecture
University of Louisiana–Lafayette

REFER TO CHAPTER 11

Format Based on a Rectangular Grid System

For a design solution of a small or medium size building that you may come up with in your design studio, try to use a rectangular grid system to organize the layout of your site plan, plans, elevations, sections, paralines, perspectives, diagrams, and sketches. Scale: ⅛"=1'0"

REFER TO CHAPTER 11

Lake Charles, Louisana, Restaurant Design

This assignment is a post–design studio exercise with the intention of presenting a design in terms of an indiginous Louisiana atmosphere.

EDUCATIONAL OBJECTIVE
To emphasize the need for acknowledging a sense of place as a design generator and using graphic techniques as the means of expression.

ASSIGNMENT REQUIREMENTS
Superimpose an atmospheric condition on a preexisting blueline print with mixed media. The media will be seen as an extension as well as a genesis of the development.

Project: Courtesy of Professor George S. Loli
Department of Architecture
University of Louisiana–Lafayette

REFER TO CHAPTERS 3, 10, and the bonus chapter "Conventional and Computerized Representation in Color" found at www.wiley.com/go/yee.

LEVEL ONE

Assignment: The Bigger Picture

This exercise must include a tonal study and a color study.

On an A3 size sheet of paper, paint an architectural subject (or subject relevant to your discipline), A4 in size. You may need to use a reference photograph and/or sketches. You may choose your own composition either by using part of your photo or, alternatively, by moving or adding elements.

Your painting must be carefully preplanned in order to be successful. Black and white tonal sketches will help you decide on the composition as well as helping you define areas of light and shade. Testing colors before you start the final work will help with color composition.

Hints
• Work from light to dark.
• Render larger areas first and finish with your smallest detail.

You may use a masking agent—masking fluid or magic tape.

Please include your reference photo and rough sketches with finished artwork.

You will be assessed on the following criteria:

• Use of light and shade to define form
• Media technique
• Use of color
• Tonal and color study
• Composition (Composition will not be assessed if you copy format directly from the source, such as a photograph.)

Assignment: Field Sketching

You may use mixed media in this exercise.

You need to be able to quickly record what you see. Use pencils, fine-line felt-tip pens, etc., that allow you to sketch freely. Set yourself a time limit and plan your next sketch accordingly.

When using watercolor, keep it simple. Use only a few colors and try mixing them on the paper.

For this assignment you are required to do a series of sketches of a real-life subject of your choice, as follows:
• Two 30-minute painted sketches, A5 size
• Three 20-minute painted sketches, postcard (A6) size
• One A4 size painted sketch with some preliminary studies

Do not use photographic references for this exercise.

Please note the location, date, and time taken on each piece of work.

You will be assessed on the following criteria:

• painting/sketching technique
• ability to show light and shade
• ability to show nature of subject (to tell a story)

Courtesy of Professor Jane Grealy
Department of Architecture
Queensland University of Technology
Australia, 2000

REFER TO the bonus chapter "Conventional and Computerized Representation in Color" found at www.wiley.com/go/yee.

LEVEL ONE

Observing and Detailing

THE AIM
A defamiliarization exercise to enhance your visual perception and drawing skills. It is an exercise in observation, measurement, and detailing, using basic projection principles and drafting techniques.

THE TASK
You are required to select and photograph five openings, and to graphically describe three of them. You may choose openings that you are familiar with or ones that challenge your familiarity. The most obvious example of an opening is a window, but you may use other examples. Discuss your selection with the tutors. The opening should have a sill and a head, and may be in a glass, masonry, timber, or steel wall. Window details vary in complexity and your attempt to deal with difficult examples will be considered in the assessment.

REQUIREMENTS
1. For the tutorial meeting, bring in your photos of the five openings and sketch detailing of at least three for feedback.
2. For the final hand-in, present for each of the three openings you selected to graphically describe an elevation or part-elevation at a scale of 1:20; two sections at the same scale, one through the head and sill and one through the jambs; and a paraline projection of a vertical (head/sill) section.

ASSESSMENT CRITERIA
Students will be assessed on the following criteria:

- Accuracy of scale and neatness of drafting
- Appropriateness of line type
- Sheet layout and clarity of graphic expressions
- Complexity of detailing selected
- Dimension, lettering, and annotation

LEVEL TWO

Courtesy of Dr. Samer Akkach
Drawing Architecture & Landscape 1
School of Architecture, Landscape Architecture and Urban Design
Adelaide University, South Australia

REFER TO CHAPTERS 4 AND 5

Given: An isometric drawing of a building complex

Required: construct a roof plan and two elevations of the visible sides.

Scale: $^{3}/_{32}$" = 1'0"

REFER TO CHAPTER 5

Problem by Kwok Gorran Tsui, an architecture graduate from the University of Texas at Austin

LEVEL TWO

Plan—Section—Elevation Graphics

Time frame: A one-week project

Locate a piece of furniture that has at least one drawer and another mechanism of movement, such as the leaf of a drop-leaf table. Make sketch drawings of the piece with measurements to use in making the drawings listed below.

Draw the **top, front, side(s), plan, section(s),** and **detail** views in a *projected layout.* Draw all except the detail drawings in 1"=1'0" scale. Draw at least two different details at 3"=1'0" scale. Give each drawing a title and reference number and key the drawing to the original source (for example, show and label cutting plane lines).

Include overall dimensions of your drawings.

FORMAT
Draw in graphite on one sheet of 24" × 36" vellum oriented horizontally or vertically. All drawings should fit on one sheet of drawing paper. The overall layout is up to you. Draw a border on the sheet and a title block with ¾" high lettering with your name, name of the furniture, project number, and the date.

Project: Courtesy of Professor Steve Temple
School of Architecture
University of Texas San Antonio

REFER TO CHAPTER 4

LEVEL TWO

Exploded Isometric

From a project in your design studio related to a small object with components or a small building with component parts, construct an isometric drawing. Then, next to the isometric drawing, construct an exploded isometric showing the overlapping of the component parts. Choose an appropriate scale.

REFER TO CHAPTER 5

Plan and Paraline Shadows for a Structure

Slightly modify the design of the object shown on pp. 354–355 in the textbook (i.e., change the shape and size of the wall openings, etc.). Using the plan and elevation views, manually cast the shadow using the point-by-point method discussed on pp. 338–339. Construct a 45°–45° plan oblique of this object and cast shadows with the light ray parallel to the picture plane (see pp. 352–353).

Combining Horizontal and Vertical Section Cuts

With a design project from one of your design studies, utilize a combination of horizontal and vertical section cuts to reveal the interior of your building.

REFER TO CHAPTER 8

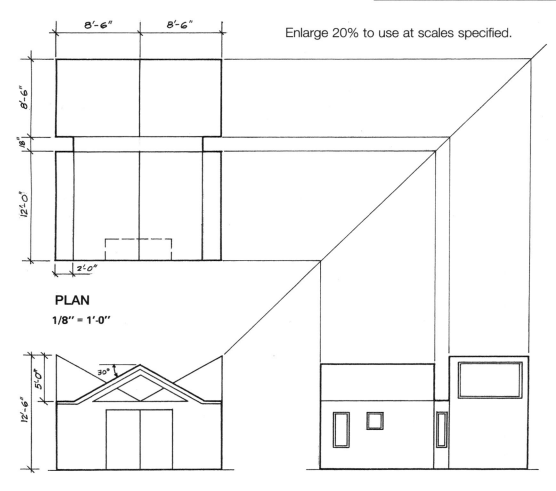

Enlarge 20% to use at scales specified.

PLAN
1/8" = 1'-0"

Given: Three elevations of a building form

Required: Construct a 60°–30° plan oblique. Cast shadows with the light ray parallel to the picture plane. Construct a two-point perspective bird's eye view. Cast shadows with the same condition as above.

Courtesy of Professor Thomas L. Turman
Laney College, Oakland, CA

REFER TO CHAPTERS 5, 6, and 8

LEVEL TWO

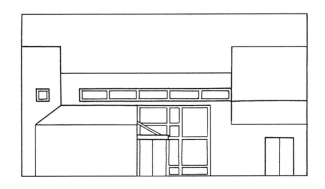
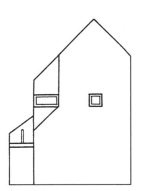

Given: Two elevations of a building form

Required: 1. Construct the missing roof plan.
2. Construct a 30°–30° isometric drawing.

Scale: 1/16"=1'0"

REFER TO CHAPTER 5

Revealing Perspective View

The purpose of this project is to create a single drawing that communicates several kinds of information at once. You have before you information about a building you chose from several options. In this project you will use the information that the orthographic drawings and/or photographs reveal and apply that information to a perspective view that not only shows your building in perspective, but also locates the plan and sectional views in the perspective view.

MAKING THE DRAWING

Use the plan you have, or redraw it, and make a projection in perspective (plan projection) onto a large format such that the resulting view will show the building to maximum effect in terms of overall revelation. That is, you want to make a view that will show as much as possible of your building as well as allow you to locate, *in the perspective view,* the section and plan. The drawing of the building should reveal as much as possible about the building's spaces. You may want to make the entire building, or parts of the building, transparent.

THE RESULT

The more you can show about the building and, in particular, the building space, the better. Therefore, it will be crucial to pay attention to those qualities that create clarity in an otherwise complex image, such as line weight, degrees of contrast, correct foreshortening, and color contrasts. The result should be a complex but clear drawing that reveals the building's essential shape (interior and exterior), as well as the locations of your orthographic cuts.

Projection drawing size: 24" × 36"
Media are negotiable
Color is required but negotiable

Courtesy of Professor Dick Davison
College of Architecture
Texas A&M University

REFER TO CHAPTERS 5 and 6

LEVEL TWO

Floor Plan—Hardline

Using a lead holder with soft and hard leads, draw the floor plan below at ¼"=1'0". The layout lines should be drawn with a 2H lead, and the remaining lines with a softer F/HB lead. Focus on crisp, clear lines. Use 1000H vellum for the final drawing and use trace for initial layout of composition on the final sheet.

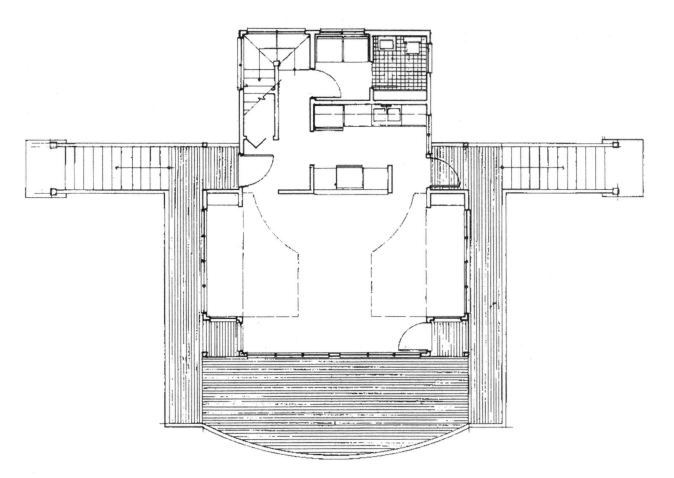

LEVEL TWO

FIRST FLOOR PLAN

Problem: Courtesy of Instructor Daniel K. Mullin, AIA, NCARB
Graphic Communication course
Department of Architecture
University of Idaho–Moscow

James Cutler, Daubenberger residence, 1974

REFER TO CHAPTER 4

LEVEL TWO

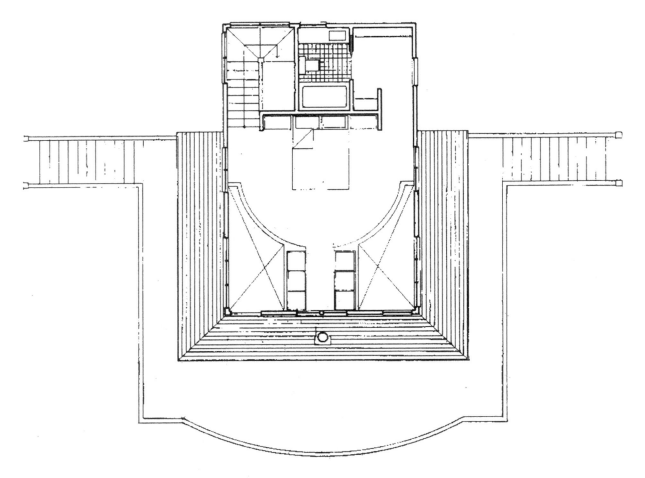

SECOND FLOOR PLAN

James Cutler, Daubenberger residence, 1974

Problem: Courtesy of Instructor Daniel K. Mullin, AIA, NCARB
Graphic Communication course
Department of Architecture
University of Idaho–Moscow

Section Drawing

Enlarge the following **sectional drawings** on pages 100, 101, and 103: the Freeman residence, the Weston residence, and the Barnes House. On the first two houses, replace the solid black section cuts with cuts using dark profile lines. Examine how this change affects the readability of the interior spaces. Do the same with the last house, but instead treat the building section and ground section cut areas with a toned value.

REFER TO CHAPTER 4

Section—Hardline

Using a lead holder with soft and hard leads and the previous floor plan, draw the section AA as indicated below at ¼"=1'0". The layout lines should be drawn with a 2H lead, and the remaining lines with a softer F/HB lead. Focus on crisp, clear lines. Use 12"×18" 1000H vellum for the final drawing and trace for initial layout. Compose final sheet.

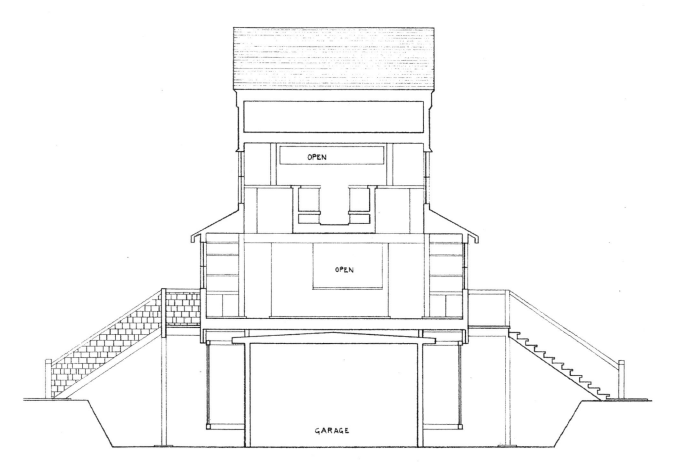

LEVEL TWO

Problem: Courtesy of Instructor Daniel K. Mullin, AIA, NCARB
Graphic Communication course
Department of Architecture
University of Idaho–Moscow

James Cutler, Daubenberger residence, 1974

REFER TO CHAPTER 4

Elevation—Hardline

Using a lead holder with soft and hard leads and the previous floor plan(s) and section, draw the elevation as indicated below at ¼"=1'0". The layout lines should be done with a 2H lead and the remaining lines with a softer F/HB lead. Focus on crisp, clear lines. Use 12"×18" 1000H vellum for final drawing and trace for initial layout. Compose final sheet.

LEVEL TWO

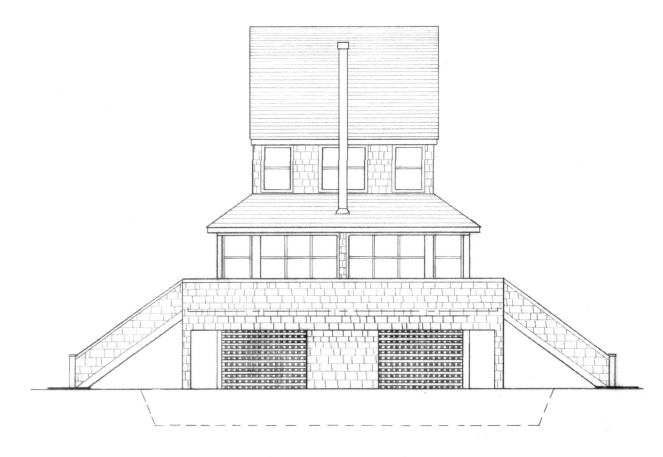

WEST ELEVATION

Problem: Courtesy of Instructor Daniel K. Mullin, AIA, NCARB
Graphic Communication course
Department of Architecture
University of Idaho—Moscow

James Cutler, Daubenberger residence, 1974

REFER TO CHAPTER 4

Paraline Drawings—Isometric/Oblique and Section Perspective

Using lead holders with soft and hard leads, draw the 30°—30° isometric, plan oblique, and elevation oblique for the building indicated below. Drawings should be at ⅛"=1'0" scale. The layout lines should be lightly drawn with a 2H lead, and the remaining lines done with a softer F/HB lead. Focus on crisp, clear lines. Use 8.5" ×11" 1000H vellum for the final drawing and trace for initial layout. Label and date all drawings.

As an additional optional exercise, cut a section through the building just behind the wall of the East Elevation but slicing the window area. Using a measuring point (diagonal vanishing point), construct a one-point section perspective of the interior space (see pp. 251,252, 260, and 261). Construct a plan grid on the floor plane and draw two human figures at different distances in order to give scale.

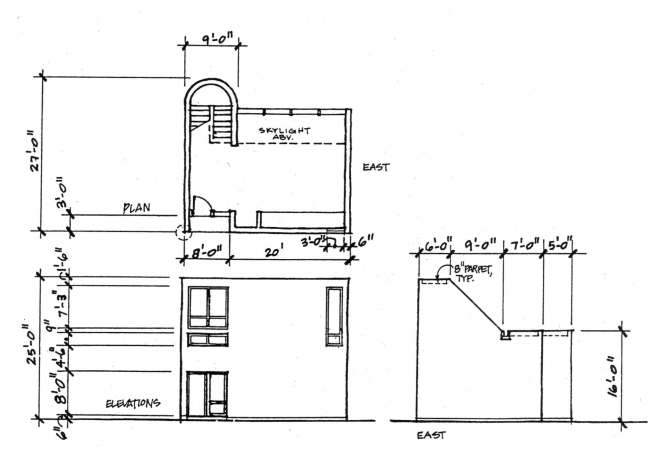

LEVEL TWO

Problem: Courtesy of Instructor Daniel K. Mullin, AIA, NCARB
Graphic Communication course
Department of Architecture
University of Idaho–Moscow

REFER TO CHAPTERS 4, 5, 6, and 9

Axonometric Drawing

Lay out the Cutler house as an isometric or plan oblique drawing with 2H lead on trace. Use ⅛" scale. Show all windows, steps, roof planes, deck, etc., that come into view. Each student may decide which view to illustrate. After completing the trace drawing, transfer to 8½" × 11" vellum for the final drawing.

Problem: Courtesy of Instructor Daniel K. Mullin, AIA, NCARB
Graphic Communication course
Department of Architecture
University of Idaho–Moscow

Drawings and Model from an Architectural Detail

OBJECTIVE
The goal of this project is to have students do research on looking for interesting architectural details. From the available options, he or she will select a detail/section, make a model of this detail, and do drawings of this detail.

PART ONE
Build a model of a slice of the detail.

- Show as many details/layers as reasonable.
- Try to approximate the actual materials in quality and look.
- Select scale as needed.
- As a guideline, the size of the model should be approximately 16" high × 4" wide × 4" deep.
- The base should be 6" × 12" × ¾"

PART TWO
Draw an "assembly" oblique or isometric of the model that you built. Show parts separated as they are built up together. Work on vellum with graphite. The scale varies with each project. After obtaining instructor approval, trace the "assembly" drawing onto a Mylar sheet using technical pens of two different line weights (one for section lines and one for visible lines.) Render according to instructor's requirements and demonstrations if necessary.

REFERENCES
Ford, E. 1990. *Details of Modern Architecture.* M.I.T. Press.
Details in architectural books and magazines.

Courtesy of Arpad D. Ronaszegi, Studio Professor
Division of Architecture
Andrews University

REFER TO CHAPTER 5

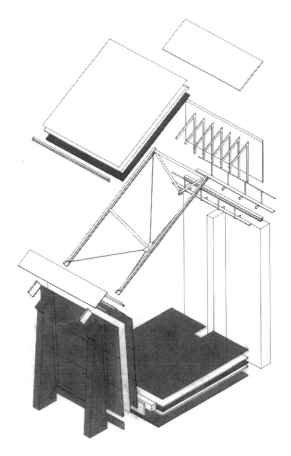

Drawing: Student project by Stephen Zerne
Division of Architecture
Andrews University

Comprehensive Project: Isometric and Exploded View

Time frame: A three-week project

Part One

Locate a piece of furniture that has at least one drawer and another mechanism of movement such as the leaf of a drop-leaf table. Make sketch drawings of the piece with measurements to use in making the drawings listed below.

Draw the **top, front, side(s), plan, section(s),** and **vertical section(s)** in a *projected layout.* In addition, draw two **details** as scaled enlargements of section drawings. (Details may *not* be drawn as axonometric drawings.) Draw all except the detail drawings in 1½"=1'0" scale. Draw at least two different vertical section details at 3"=1'0" scale.

Show and label *all* section cutting plane lines. Give each independent drawing a title and reference number and key the drawing to the original source.

Include overall dimensions of your drawings.

Part Two

Using the piece of furniture for which you constructed orthographic drawings in a previous assignment, construct additional drawings of the piece as follows:

1. An **isometric** at 1½" scale
2. An **exploded isometric** at 1½" scale

Format

Draw in graphite on **one** sheet of 24" × 36" vellum oriented horizontally or vertically. All drawings should fit on one sheet of drawing paper. The overall layout is up to you. Draw a border on the sheet and a title block on the bottom of the sheet with ¾" high lettering. Include in the title block:

1. Your name and the date
2. Title: FINAL PROJECT

Project: Courtesy of Professor Steve Temple
School of Architecture
University of Texas San Antonio

REFER TO CHAPTER 5

Structural Frame/Drawings and Model

Design a structural frame using any kind of cardboard (corrugated, matt, pebble, illustration, etc.) without the use of glue or hinging mechanisms. The frame must span at least three feet and be capable of supporting at least three Sweet's files in the center.

Presentation Requirements

1. Conceptual sketches of your idea
2. Orthographic, isometric, and plan oblique drawings of the solution
3. Exploded axonometric or exploded perspective to show how component parts go together
4. Model of the design solution

Courtesy of the Department of Architecture
City College of San Francisco

REFER TO CHAPTERS 4, 5, 6, and 10

LEVEL TWO

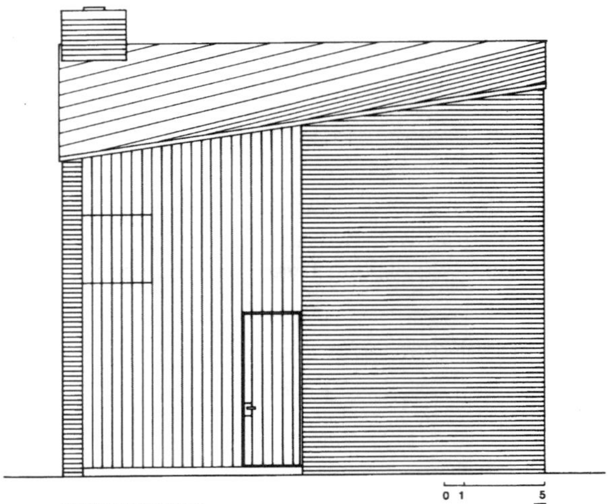

NORTH ELEVATION

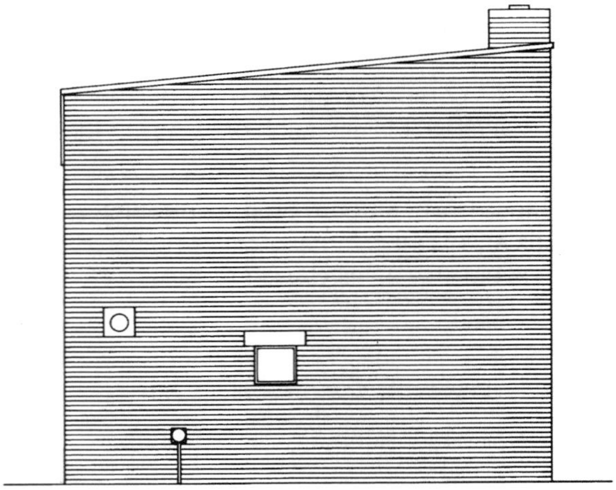

WEST ELEVATION

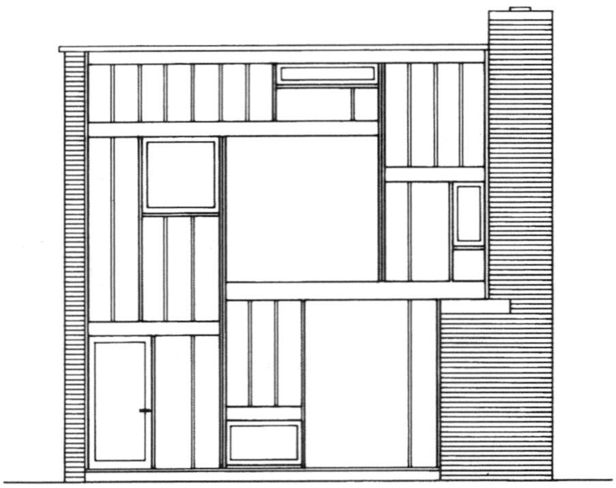

SOUTH ELEVATION

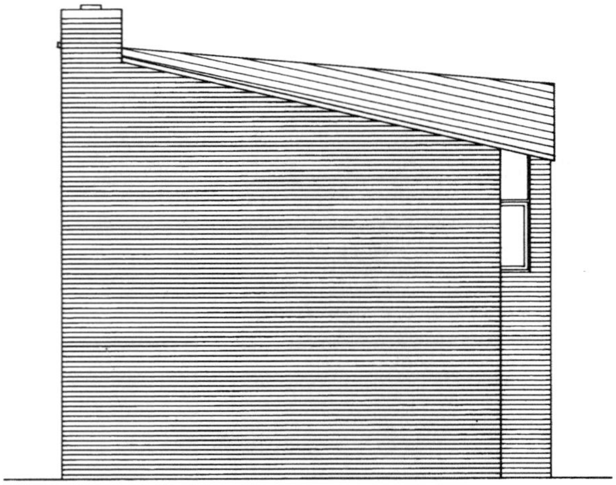

EAST ELEVATION

Drawings: Marking House, Catskill Mountains, New York
Design: 1992–1993
Courtesy of the Architecture Research Office, Adam Yarinsky, partner

Floor Plans, Roof Plan, Section, Elevations, Perspective, Section Perspective—Hardline

On this and the opposite page are drawings for the Marking House. As an exercise in hand hardline drawing, use a scale stipulated by your instructor and redraw these drawings on 12" × 18" size 1000H vellum. Then, using the south and west elevations along with the three plan views oriented 30° from the horizontal, construct a perspective view with the station point 30' above the ground line. As an additional visualization exercise, try to sketch what you think the interior space would look like if you were standing on the stairway platform looking toward the opposite corner of the room (front entrance area).

REFER TO CHAPTERS 3, 4, 6, and 9

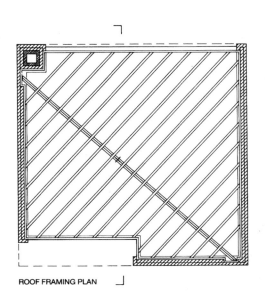

ROOF FRAMING PLAN

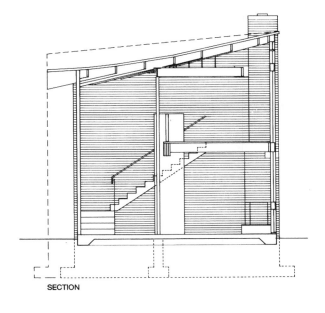

SECTION

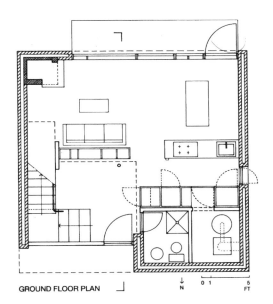

GROUND FLOOR PLAN   N 0 1   5 FT

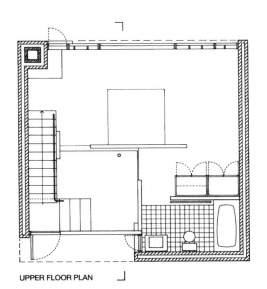

UPPER FLOOR PLAN

LEVEL TWO

Drawings: Marking House, Catskill Mountains, New York
          Design: 1992–1993
Courtesy of the Architecture Research Office, Adam Yarinsky, partner

Use the Ground and Upper Floor plans and place them in the same position (30° from the horizontal) as the Roof Framing plan in order to complete the entire perspective view with the fenestration.

Scale: $\frac{3}{32}$"=1'0"

As an additional optional exercise, use a measuring point (diagonal vanishing point) and construct a one-point **section perspective** (note the shallow depth of field) with the given section looking in the direction indicated. Construct a plan grid on the floor plane and draw two human figures in the interior space.

Revealing Expanded, Exploded or Cutaway View

Find a familiar object (for example, a clock, lamp, piece of furniture, bicycle, etc.) or a set (like a Legos set) that contains between 15 and 30 parts.

Consider how this object (or group) is assembled and how it would be disassembled.

Your goal is to make a single drawing that shows all parts of your object or group, as well as suggesting how it is put together.

Construct either a paraline or perspective drawing in an expanded, exploded, or cutaway view. It may be partially expanded or exploded, and it may have transparency. Convey as much as possible in a single view while still maintaining a high degree of clarity. The medium should be graphite or ink (color is optional).

This problem was adapted, with slight modifications, from a problem given at Texas A&M University.

Drawing: Student project by Paul Paris
Courtesy of Professor Dick Davison
College of Architecture
Texas A&M University

REFER TO CHAPTERS 5 and 6

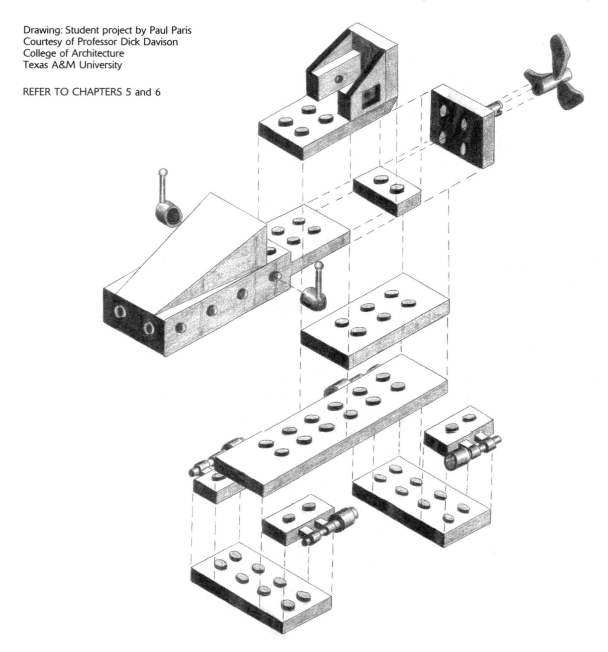

LEVEL TWO

Bionic Model

INTRODUCTION

In this problem architecture and biology are synthesized to create an **archibionic portable bookstand.**
Can one design through nature? Yes. Nature offers a wealth of information for design modeling. In this project,
you are required to study an organic form from the animal kingdom; any living form, including plants, is acceptable. For example, you could study birds, fish, mammals such as bears, reptiles such as lizards, anthropoids
such as insects, spiders, crayfish, and centipedes. The list is endless.

OBJECTIVES

From the living example, you are to extract the structural and functional ideas behind its particular form. You
are essentially abstracting the structural logic of the organism. The problem is to build a bookstand abstraction based on your living organism. The structural and functional principles should be analogous to the same
principles seen in animal form. The archibionic bookstand must be able to hold 3 Sweet's files (or the equivalent) in a vertical or tilted position (cannot lay flat) and the book must be at least 4" off the surface on which the
bookstand rests. It must be made of cardboard of any type (corrugated, mat, pebble, illustration, etc.). Other
materials must receive instructor approval. It must be treated with a minimum of 2 colors (any medium) excluding white or black. The size of the bookstand must not exceed a volume of 2000 cu. in. (10" × 10" × 20",
5" × 10" × 40", etc.).

SOME HINTS ON PROCEDURE

Look at various possibilities that might give you new knowledge of ways to support books. Don't use preconceived ideas of actual bookstands. You will not receive accolades for emulating bookstands found in stationary shops. Use your imagination and think "unthinkable" shapes! Information can be extracted at the micro-
level (you could look at the structure or cross section of a bone) or at the macro-level (the entire skeleton). Try
to develop a metaphorical analogy.

REQUIREMENTS

1. On a 20" × 30" white illustration board (vertically or horizontally oriented), present your use of the organism
    as a bionic model. Indicate the actual shape of the form, the forces acting on it, and how the structure
    responds to the forces. Thus, you must show both the actual organism and its abstraction as an archibion-
    ic bookstand. Label everything important. Use color to clarify and enhance the drawing and diagram. Draw
    the three primary views (top, front, and profile) of your bookstand as well as an isometric or a perspective.
    The text must describe where the bookstand will be used (for example, in a children's library, architect's
    office, etc.) and the rationale behind your choice of colors. Evaluation will be based on the quality of the
    graphics and the clarity of the drawings.
2. A final model of the archibionic bookstand to be tested with 3 Sweet's files (equivalent of at least 30 lbs. in
    textbooks). Evaluation will be based on the design and the workmanship of the model.

REFERENCE

Gates, P. 1995. *Nature Got There First.* New York: Kingfisher.

REFER TO CHAPTERS 5 and 6

LEVEL TWO

The Design-Build-Draw Project

This project, which lasts about seven weeks, is essentially a design project carried out in a drawing studio. It has been taught at the School of Architectural Studies, California College of Arts and Crafts, San Francisco, by Professor Patrick Houlihan in the Design Communications Studio. The work represented is by Nancy Langendorf.

OBJECTIVE

These exercises were devised for beginning students to test their skills in making, measuring, and drawing an object in orthographic, axonometric, and perspective projection. A designed object is the pivot of all the exercises. The project is arranged in a series of discrete steps. Each student makes an object out of a kit of parts that he or she has helped make in a process of mass production in the shop. The object is measured and its multiviews are drawn; these are used to construct an axonometric and perspective.

STAGE ONE. DRAWING THE PARTS OF THE OBJECT

The student is presented by the instructor with a drawing that shows seven or eight solid geometrical forms drawn in axonometric projection; each object is dimensioned. The objective is to prepare views of these for cutting from polystyrene. There will generally be more students than component parts; therefore, more than one drawing will be made of each part. Students will draft the multiviews at full size, dimensioning them so that they can be used to construct the model parts. All drawings can be drafted on 11" × 17" vellum.

STAGE TWO. MAKING THE MODEL PARTS IN THE SHOP

Students will organize themselves into groups to cut the model parts out of a slab of polystyrene. A pattern must be prepared for this purpose. To save time, the cone element is purchased from an arts and crafts store.

STAGE THREE. COMPOSING THE MODEL

Each student is given one of each of the components, which are composed into a sculptural whole. Students are encouraged to organize their models using an orthogonal system. Models should be proportioned to fit on an 11" × 17" sheet of vellum when drawn in orthographic projection and perspective.

STAGE FOUR: FINISHING THE MODEL

The model is finished and painted.

STAGE FIVE: MULTIVIEWS OF THE MODEL

The modeled form is measured and orthographic views are prepared: four elevations (profile views) and one plan view (horizontal view), all at half-size.

STAGE SIX: THE AXONOMETRIC

An axonometric (plan oblique) is constructed at half-size. An overlay drawing of the constructed axonometric is prepared in ink.

STAGE SEVEN: THE PERSPECTIVE

After a thorough examination of his or her model, each student selects an appropriate vantage point by trial and error and sets up a perspective. An overlay of this drawing is made in ink.

REFER TO CHAPTERS 4, 5, 6, 10, and the bonus chapter "Conventional and Computerized Representation in Color" found at www.wiley.com/go/yee.

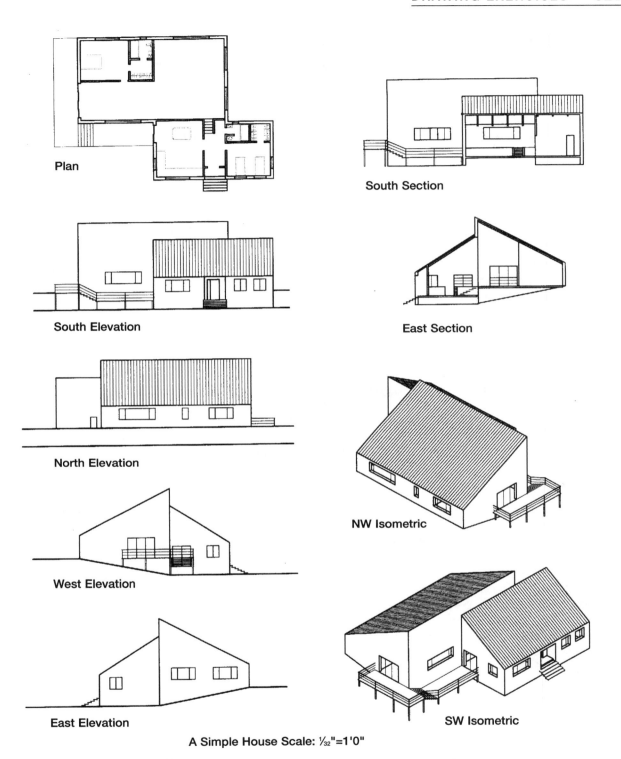

Plan

South Section

South Elevation

East Section

North Elevation

West Elevation

NW Isometric

East Elevation

SW Isometric

A Simple House Scale: ⅟₃₂"=1'0"

Drawn and designed by Kwok Gorran Tsui, an architecture graduate of the University of Texas at Austin

Set up a **composite drawing** presentation for this simple house using the images above. Feel free to add in some other elements like site information, landscape, or color, etc.—anything that is appropriate and can enhance your composite drawing.

REFER TO CHAPTER 11

LEVEL TWO

Geometric Refinement and Construction

This is the first project given to first-semester freshmen in the undergraduate program in architecture at the University of Buffalo—State University of New York. Instructor: Associate Professor Beth Tauke.

INTRODUCTION

As geometers, equipped only with compasses and straightedge, we enter the two-dimensional world of the represen-tation of form. A link is forged between the most concrete (form and measure) and the most abstract realms of thought. By seeking the invariable relationships by which forms are governed and interconnected, we bring ourselves into res-onance with universal order.
[ROBERT LAWLER]

DEFINITIONS

Geometric refinement is the superimposition of a grid system on the predetermined outline of a space and/or form and the subsequent geometric adjustment of the outline to adhere to the limitations imposed by the grid.

Geometric construction is different from refinement in that a form is developed by starting with two points (line) that grow in an order dictated by the rules of geometry and proportion coupled with the maker's thought processes. Unlike refinement, which involves a constant modular order and an external imposition of a grid on a shape, construction involves an organic order and an internal system of growth.

OBJECTIVES

• To study the geometric characteristics and constructs of space
• To compare numeric and geometric systems of measure
• To experience the differences between geometric refinement and construction
• To use various systems as tools to both analyze and develop forms
• To understand the concepts of growth and mapping systems
• To discover the impact that systems can have on the forms within them and vice versa
• To study the principles, purposes, and consequences of perspective projection

STATEMENTS

A. Select an object with the following characteristics: a) interior cavities, b) asymmetry on at least one axis, c) recognizable silhouette, d) less than one cubic foot in size. Document the object with section drawings of all three axes.
B. Using a 45° grid system, a set of limitations, and drafting tools as guides, develop geometric refinements of the interior space of the object on all three axes.
C Using geometric principles and drafting tools as guides, develop geometric constructions of the interior space of the object on all three axes.
D. Develop a constructed perspective representation of the triaxial geometries of the interior space of the object.
E. Develop a drawing that uses/adapts/alters a perspective projection system to suggest movement in the interior space of the object.

REQUIREMENTS AND SUGGESTED METHODS

1. Carefully examine the object to determine the sections that will most fully communicate its space/form characteristics.
2. Cut and measure the object and its interior space on the primary axis. Take enough measurements to accu-rately reproduce the section. Reconnect the sections. Then cut the object on its secondary axis. Again, measure the object and its interior space to accurately reproduce the section. Reconnect these sections. Finally, cut the mold on its tertiary axis and repeat the process.
3. Use geometric tools (triangles, T-square or parallel rule, and compass only) for the development of the drawings.
4. Use the layout of the sections to communicate the relationship that the drawings have to one another.
5. Use line weight to differentiate form from space.
6. Final section drawings should be in graphite on drawing paper specified by your instructor.

7. Preliminary refinements and constructions should be drawn in pencil on trace. All points on the preliminary refinements should be marked with small "x"s or dots.
8. Refinement prescripts include the following:
   - All lines begin and end on grid points. (Grid points are the places where two or more lines intersect).
   - The center of every circle or partial circle (curve) should be positioned on grid points.
   - The endpoints of the beginning and ending radii of every curve should be positioned on grid points.
9. Use the object itself to determine either the width or length of the grid. Consider the grid relationship between each section. Do they correspond with one another?
10. When analyzing the underlying structure of the interior space of the object for the purposes of construction, begin by searching for primary geometric relationships and systems. Locate a line that appears to be central to the development of the form. Using geometric tools, develop from that line a sequence of geometric moves that are logical and related to one another. (No numeric measurements are needed and no arbitrary moves are made in this process.) Consider the geometric relationship between each section. Do they correspond with one another?
11. Although it is painstaking, number and write, on a separate overlay, a description of each move in the development of the construction. This extra step assists in maintaining a geometric sequence devoid of arbitrary moves, and helps in the communication of your process.
12. For Statement D, one-, two-, or three-point perspective may be used. All construction lines should remain in the drawings.
13. For Statement E, consider the introduction of multiple points of view, interlocking spaces, and/or multiple projection systems (paraline and perspectival). Carefully consider your specific intentions for this drawing: What kind of movement and/or movement conditions are you attempting to represent?
14. Final refinements, constructions, and perspectives should be inked. Drawing surface should be double-sided Mylar. Eliminate "x"s and numbers on final drawings.
15. At least two line weights should be used on the final drawings—heavier lines for the outline of the interior space and object silhouette, and lighter lines for grids and geometric structure. Carefully consider the proportions of the line weights.

REFERENCES
Henderson, L. Dalrymple. *The Fourth Dimension and Non-Euclidean Geometry in Modern Art.*
Tauke, Beth. "Geometric Definitions and Formulas."
Yee, Rendow. *Architectural Drawing.*

SUBMISSION
Object, section drawings, preliminary traces, final refinement(s) and construction(s), written explanation of construction process, perspective drawing, perspective movement drawing

EVALUATION CRITERIA
- Object selection
- Comprehension/accuracy of selection
- Comprehension of refinement/construction concepts
- Logic of construction description
- Comprehension of constructed perspective
- Efficiency/complexity of drawings
- Proportion
- Precision/technique

CRITIQUE ISSUES
1. How did you determine the sections?
2. How has the structure within which you are working affected the shape of the interior space of the object?
3. How has the space/shape with which you are working affected the structure/system?
4. How do the systems of geometric refinement and construction vary? Use your drawings to show examples of your main points.
5. How have the geometric systems you are using described three-dimensional space? How are the descriptions different from "actual" three-dimensional space?
6. These geometric systems are often used by designers and architects in the development and production of ideas. Discuss the appropriateness/inappropriateness of these systems in various conditions.
7. Discuss other entities that are affected by the systems in which they exist.
8. Discuss other systems that are affected by the entities existing in them.

LEVEL TWO

LEVEL TWO

Geometric Refinement and Construction

Courtesy of Associate Professor Beth Tauke
Department of Architecture, School of Architecture and Planning
University at Buffalo—State University of New York
Student project by Alberto Rios

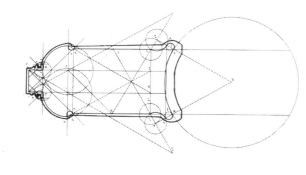

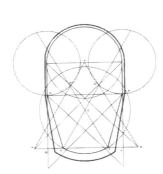

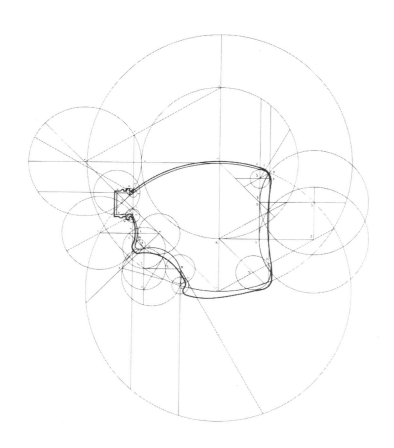

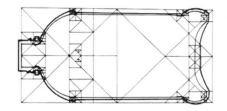

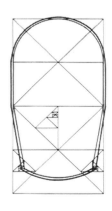

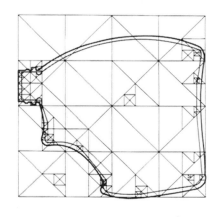

LEVEL TWO

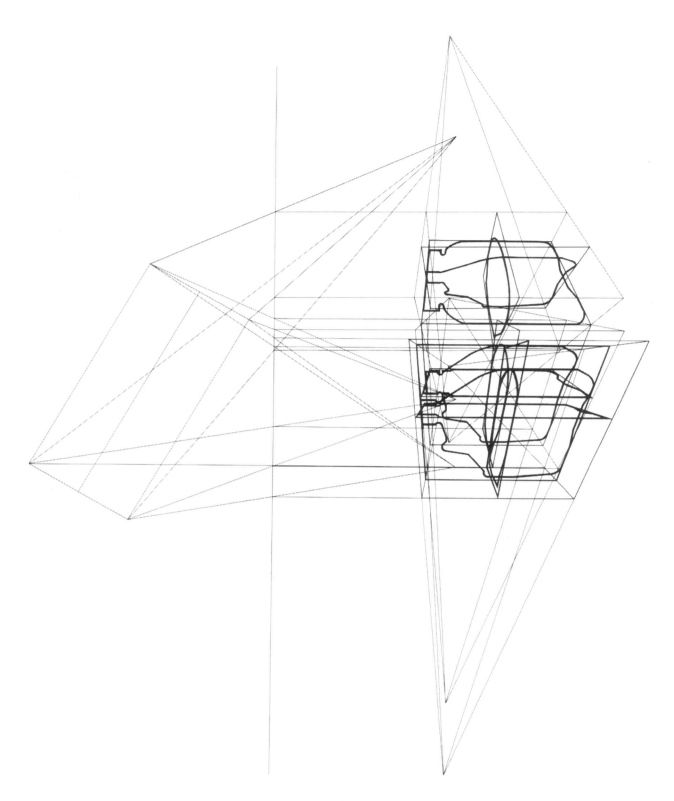

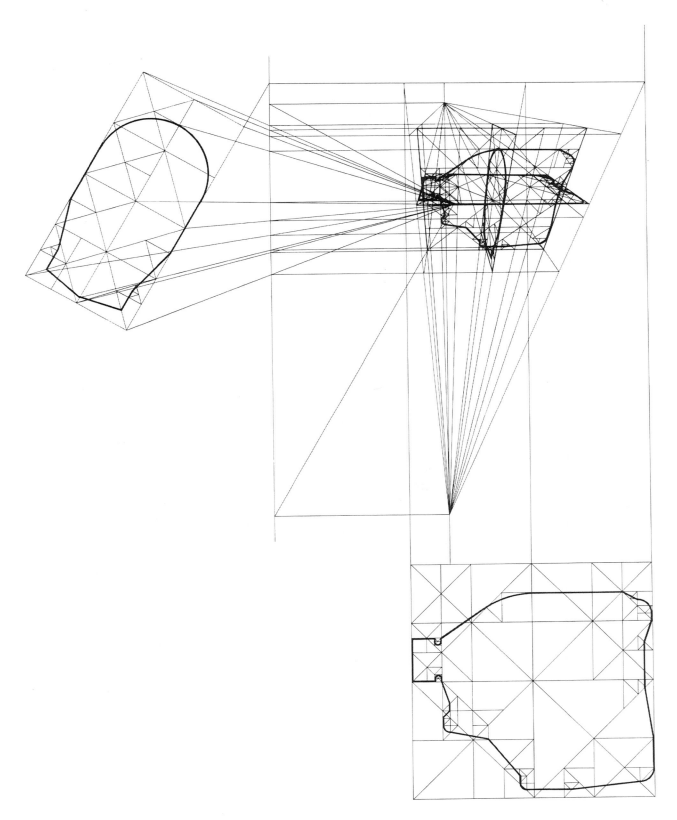

LEVEL TWO

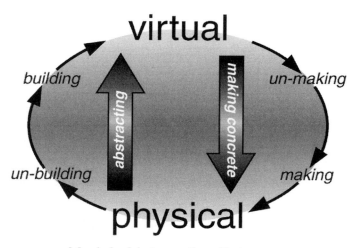

Model of Integration Between
Virtual and Physical Transformations

Figure 1

Building and Making: Unbuilding and Unmaking

Figure 1 illustrates a model of integration between virtual and physical processes as transformations in the design process. The model depicts repetitive cycling from possibility to realization, with the actions of buildng and making fundamental to interaction between the virtual and physical.

Moving clockwise from the bottom of the model illustrates the process of transforming the physical into the virtual. This process can be characterized as abstracting. Within the design process, the designer is transforming tangible substance into virtual representations. The process of abstraction is broken into two components, unbuilding and building. Unbuilding is the discovery of existing and already structured physical systems within physical wholes. Building is the transformation of the physical into the virtual as the representation of the possibilities of those physical systems discovered in the unbuilding process.

Digital modeling (see pp. 458–465, 609, 637–638) is an elemental process of abstraction typically used in the design process for exploring the possibilities of the physical. The raw materials of digital modeling are basic geometries rooted in the physical laws of matter and space. Physical actualities are unbuilt into the possibilities inherent in the geometries of the virtual and become evident in modeling their synthetic likeness. Digital modeling is a form of virtual building.

Moving clockwise from the top of the model illustrates the process of transforming the virtual to the physical. This process, in contrast to abstraction, is materialization. As the designer seeks to transform the virtual into the actual, processes of making are utilized to incorporate conceptual forms into tangible material character. Unmaking is the exploration of the physical for its realization of the virtual. Transformation of the virtual to the material can be characterized as movement toward the concrete — a substantiation of possibilities in a palpable reality. Unmaking/making, as a process, is a mechanism of synthesis utilizing analytic deconstruction of a synthetic likeness in terms of a probable concrete existence derived from qualities inherent to material physicality.

In the context of design activities, systematically linking abstraction and materialiization reveals continuity between them. As the concrete world is the intentional goal of design processes, representations and conceptualizations are empty without physical substance. Without conceptualization, the development of intentionality. in physical substance is limited. In practice, the model functions as a referential structure for dynamic interaction between the virtual and the physical.

Statement by Professors of Design:
David Matthews, Ohio University
Steve Temple, University of Texas San Antonio

Drawing project based on a sketch by Architect Lebbeus Woods
Student project by Melanie Beisswenger
Software: 3D Studio MAX, Premiere
Courtesy of Professors Karen Kensek and Douglas Noble
School of Architecture
University of Southern California

Digital Drawing Based on a Sketch

This project was inspired by a Lebbeus Woods sketch titled "Houses in Tension (reconstruction of the air-space)."
Melanie Beisswenger modeled and rendered the indeterminate form and then used it as a basis for a kinetic transfor-
mation of her own design. She started by digitally reconstructing the architecture from the incomplete drawings that
were available. Many different materials were scanned and edited to achieve the textures she desired. Near the end
of the semester, she remodeled the "flying creature" using NURBS to achieve more fluid contours and shapes. Shown
is a single rendered image and fifteen frames from the Premiere animation.
[PROFESSORS' STATEMENT]

REFER TO CHAPTERS 10 and the bonus chapter "Conventional and Computerized
Representation in Color" found at www.wiley.com/go/yee.

LEVEL TWO

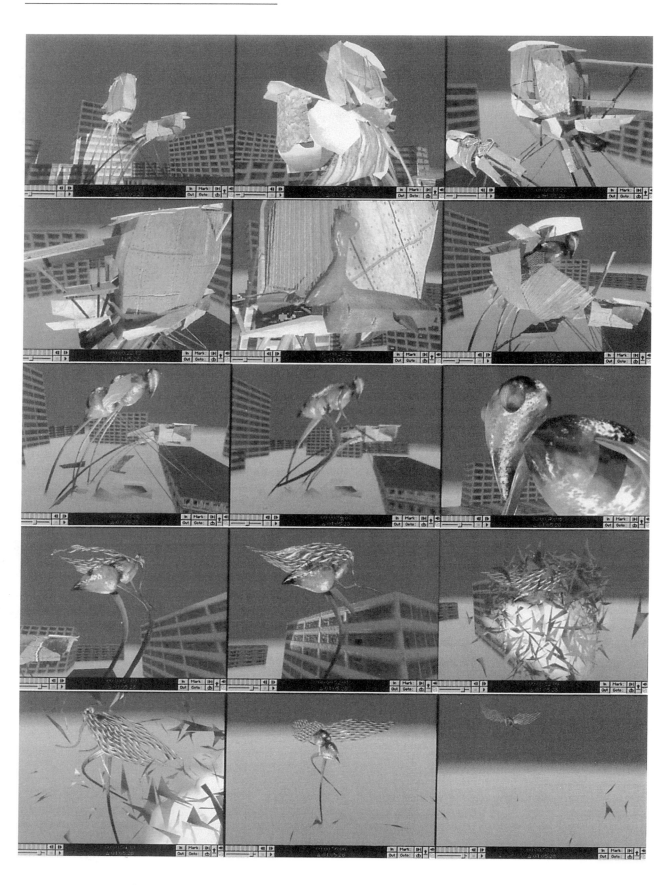

Bibliography

Adler, D. 2000. *Metric Handbook: Planning and Design Data*. Architectural Press.

Allen, G., and R. Oliver. 1981. *Architectural Drawing: The Art and the Process*. Whitney.

Berryman, G. 1990. *Notes on Graphic Design and Visual Communication*. William Kaufmann.

Bertol, D. 1996. *Designing Digital Space*. Wiley. Chapter 12.

Bridgman, G. 2001. *Bridgman's Complete Guide to Drawing from Life*. Sterling.

Brooks, H. A. 1997. *LeCorbusier's Formative Years*. University of Chicago Press.

Buckles, G. M. 1995. *Building Architectural & Interior Design Models Fast!* Belpine.

Burden, E. 1981. *Entourage: A Tracing File*. McGraw-Hill.

————. 1992. *Design Presentation Techniques for Marketing and Project Proposals*. McGraw-Hill.

Burke, M., and P. Wilbur. 1999. *Information Graphics*. Thames and Hudson.

Calle, P. 1985. *The Pencil*. Ingram.

Carter, R., B. Day, and P. Meggs. 2002. *Typographic Design: Form and Communication*. 3rd ed. Wiley.

Carter, R., and P. Meggs. 1993. *Typographic Specimens: The Great Typefaces*. Wiley

Chen, J. 1994. *Architecture in Pen and Ink*. McGraw-Hill.

————. 1997. *Architecture in Color Drawings*. McGraw-Hill.

Chen, J., and W. T. Cooper. 1996. *Architectural Perspective Grids*. McGraw-Hill.

Ching, F. D. K. 1990. *Drawing: A Creative Process*. Wiley.

————. 1998. *Design Drawing*. Wiley.

————. 2003. *Architectural Graphics*. 4th ed. Wiley.

Clark, R., and M. Pause. 1996. *Precedents in Architecture*. Wiley.

Cooper, D. 1992. *Drawing and Perceiving*. Wiley.

Craig, J. 1990. *Basic Typography,: A Design Manual*. Watson-Guptill.

Crowe, P. 1992. *Architectural Rendering*. McGraw-Hill.

Crowe, N., and P. Laseau. 1986. *Visual Notes*. Wiley.

D'Amelio, J. 1984. *Perspective Drawing Handbook*. Wiley.

Dodson, B. 1990. *Keys to Drawing*. North Light.

Doyle, M. E. 1993. *Color Drawing*. Wiley.

Edwards, B. 1999. *The New Drawing on the Right Side of the Brain*. Tarcher.

Eisenmann, P. 1999. *Diagram Diaries*. Universe Publishing.

Ferriss, H. 1986. *The Metropolis of Tomorrow*. Princeton Architectural Press.

————. 1998. *Power in Buildings: An Artist's View of Contemporary Architecture*. H & I.

Fleck, B., ed. 1994. *Alvaro Siza City Sketches*. Birkhäuser.

Foote, C. 2002. *The Business Side of Creativity: The Complete Guide for Running a Graphic Design or Communications Business.* Norton.

Forseth, K. 1980. *Graphics for Architecture.* Wiley.

Fraser, I., and R. Henmi. 1994. *Envisioning Architecture: An Analysis of Drawing.* Wiley.

Friedman, J. *Creation in Space.* Kendall Hunt.

Gill, R. W. 1989. *Basic Perspective.* Thames and Hudson.

———. 1990. *Rendering With Pen and Ink.* Thames and Hudson.

Goldstein, N. 1989. *Design and Composition.* Prentice Hall.

Grimaldi, R. 1990. *R. Buckminster Fuller 1895–1983* (in Italian). Officina Edizioni.

Guiton, J., and M. Guiton. 1981. *The Ideas of LeCorbusier on Architecture and Urban Planning.* George Braziller.

Hanks, K., and L. Belliston. 1977. *Draw.* William Kaufmann.

———. 1980. *Rapid Viz.* William Kaufman.

Hart, R. 1987. *Photographing Your Artwork.* North Light.

Helms, M. E. 1990. *Perspective Drawing.* Prentice Hall.

Herbert, D. M. 1993. *Architecture Study Drawings: Their Characteristics and Their Properties as a Graphic Medium for Thinking in Design.* Wiley.

Johnson, E., and M. Lewis. 1996. *Drawn from the Source: The Travel Sketches of Louis I. Kahn.* MIT Press.

Kammer, G. R. 1996. *Zaha Hadid: Recent Projects 1990–1995.* Nerausgeber.

Kasprisin, R. J. 1991. *Watercolor in Architectural Design.* Wiley.

———. 1999. *Design Media.* Wiley.

Kasprisin, R. J., and J. Pettinari. 1990. *Visual Thinking for Architects and Designers: Visualizing Context in Design.* Wiley.

Kautzky, T. 1960. *Pencil Broadsides.* Wiley.

Kliment, S. 1984. *Architectural Sketching and Rendering.* Whitney.

Knoll, W., and M. Hechinger. 1992. *Architectural Models: Construction Techniques.* McGraw-Hill.

Koplar, R. 1993. *Architectural Studies.* McGraw-Hill.

Laseau, P.. 1980. *Graphic Thinking for Architects and Designers.* Wiley.

———. 1986. *Graphic Problem Solving for Architects and Designers.* 2d ed. Wiley.

Leach, S. 1990. *Photographic Perspective Drawing Techniques.* McGraw-Hill.

LeCorbusier's Sketchbooks, vol. 1–4. 1981. MIT Press.

Leich, J. F. 1980. *Architectural Visions: The Drawings of Hugh Ferriss.* Whitney.

Lin, M. W. 1993. *Drawing and Designing With Confidence: A Step By Step Guide.* Wiley.

Lin, M. Y. 2000. *Boundaries.* Simon & Schuster.

Linton, H., and S. Roost. 2000. *Portfolio Design.* 2nd ed. Norton.

Linton, H., and R. Strickfaden. 1997. *Architectural Sketching in Markers.* Wiley.

Lockard, William. 1994a. *Drawing as a Means to Architecture.* William Kaufmann

———. 1994b. *Drawing Techniques for Designers: Advocating Line and Tone Drawing.* Crisp Publications

———. 1994c. *Freehand Perspective for Designers: Including Shadowcasting and Entourage.* Crisp Publications

———. 2000a. *Design Drawing.* W.W. Norton.

———. 2000b. *Design Drawing Experiences.* W.W. Norton.

Lorenz, A., and L. Lizak. 1988. *Architectural Illustration Inside and Out.* Whitney.

Marquand, E., and M. Weiler. 1994. *How to Prepare Your Portfolio: A Guide for Students and Professionals.* Art Direction.

Martin, C. L. 1968. *Design Graphics.* Macmillan.

Mendolwitz, D., and D. Wakeham. 1993. *Guide to Drawing.* International Thomson.

Metzdorf, M. 1991. *The Ultimate Portfolio.* North Light.

Miralles, E. 1996. *Enric Miralles: Works and Projects, 1975–1995.* Monacelli.

Mitton, M. 1999. *Interior Design Visual Presentation.* Wiley.

Mohrle, J. 1994. *Architecture in Perspective.* Whitney.

Montague, J. 1998. *Basic Perspective Drawing.* Wiley.

Moore, F. 1996. *Model Builder's Notebook.* McGraw-Hill.

Nichols, K., L. Burke, and P. Burke. 1995. *Michael Graves: Buildings and Projects 1990–1994*. Rizzoli.

Novitski, B. J. 1998. *Rendering Real and Imagined Buildings*. Rockport.

Oles, P. S. 1979. *Architectural Illustration*. Wiley.

———. 1987. *Drawing the Future*. Wiley.

Oliver, R. 1979. *The Sketch*. Van Nostrand Reinhold.

Orr, F. 1995. *Scale in Architecture*. New York: Van Nostrand Reinhold.

Paulo dos Santos, J. 1993. *Alvaro Siza Works & Projects 1954–1992*. Gustavo Gili.

Pelli, C. 1990. *Cesar Pelli: Buildings and Projects 1965–1990*. Rizzoli.

Pérez-Gomez, A., and L. Pelletier. 1997. *Architectural Representation and Perspective Hinge*. MIT Press.

Pfeiffer, B. B. 1990. *Frank Lloyd Wright Drawings*. Abrams.

Porter, Tom. 1990. *Architectural Drawing*. Van Nostrand Reinhold

———. 1993. *Architectural Drawing Masterclass*. Scribners.

———. 1997. *The Architect's Eye*. Chapman & Hall.

———. 2000. *Selling Architectural Ideas*. E. + F. N. Spon.

Porter, Tom, and Sue Goodman. 1985. *Manual of Graphic Techniques 4*. Scribners.

Portoghesi, P. 2000. *Aldo Rossi: The Sketchbooks 1990–1997*. Thames and Hudson.

Predock, A. 1995. *Architectural Journeys: Antoine Predock*. Rizzoli

Reid, G. 1987. *Landscape Graphics*. Whitney Library of Design/Watson-Guptill.

Robbins, E. 1997. *Why Architects Draw*. MIT Press.

Roca, M. A. 1994. *Miguel Angel Roca*. Academy.

Ruskin, J. 1997. *The Elements of Drawing*. New Amsterdam.

Sanders, K. 1995. *The Digital Architect*. Wiley.

Shen, J., and T. D. Walker. 1992. *Sketching and Rendering for Design Presentations*. Wiley.

Soleri, P. 1971. *The Sketchbooks of Paulo Soleri*. MIT Press.

Sutherland, M. 1989. *Lettering for Architects and Designers*. Wiley.

Szabo, M. *Drawing File*. Wiley.

Taveira, T. 1994. *Tomás Taveira*. Academy.

Uddin, M. S. 1996. *Axonometric and Oblique Drawing*. McGraw-Hill.

———. 1997. *Composite Drawing*.

———. 1999. *Digital Architecture*. McGraw-Hill.

Vonmoos, S. 1996. *Album LaRoche*. Electra.

Vrooman, D. *Architecture, Perspective, Shadows, Reflections*. Wiley.

Wagstaff, F. 1993. *Macintosh 3-D*. Hayden Books.

Walker, T. D. 1989. *Perspective Sketches*. 5th ed. Wiley.

Walker, T. D., and D. Davis. 1990. *Plan Graphics*. Wiley.

Wallschlaeger, C., and C. Busic-Snyder. 1992. *Basic Visual Concepts and Principles*. McGraw-Hill.

Wang, T. C. 1977. *Pencil Sketching*. Wiley.

———. 1984. *Projection Drawing*. Van Nostrand Reinhold.

———. 1993. *Sketching With Markers*. Van Nostrand Reinhold.

———. 1997. *Plan and Section Drawing*. Wiley.

Watson, E. W. 1985. *The Art of Pencil Drawing*. Watson-Guptill.

White, E. T. 1972. *Graphic Vocabulary for Architectural Presentation*. Architectural Media.

———. 1983. *Site Analysis*. Architectural Media.

Wright, F. L. 1983. *Drawings and Plans of Frank Lloyd Wright: The Early Period (1893–1909)*. Dover.

Wu, K. 1990. *Freehand Sketching in the Architectural Environment*. Wiley.

Zardini, M., ed. 1996. *Santiago Calatrava Secret Sketchbook*. Monacelli.

About the Author

Rendow Yee, Professor Emeritus, received his education at the University of California at Berkeley and at Washington University in Saint Louis, where he received his Master of Architecture degree. He was involved with architectural education for more than twenty years at the City College of San Francisco, and served as chair of the architecture department there from 1982 to 1990. Professional organizations with which he has been affiliated include the American Society of Civil Engineers, the American Society for Engineering Education, the American Institute of Architects, and the California Council of Architectural Education.

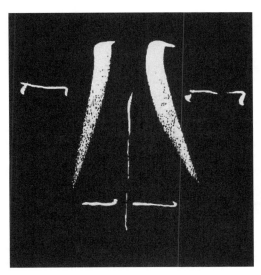

Concept sketch: Sunrise & Sunset Houses
                Sudurhlidar, Kópavogur, Iceland
7 × 7.5 cm (2.8" × 3")
Medium: Staedtler Mars Graphic 3000 pen
Courtesy of Gudmundur Jonsson, Arkitekt, Moval/FAI

Subject Index

Contributor Index

CONTRIBUTOR INDEX

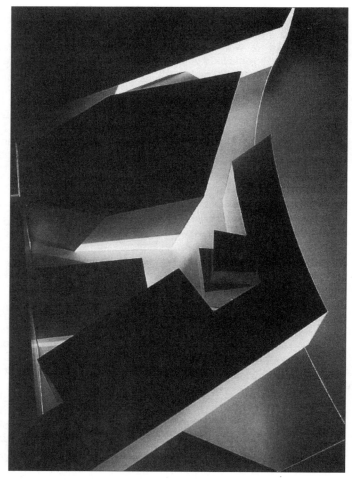

Photo: Cardiff Bay Opera House (1993–2000): Overhead view of opera house
Cardiff, Wales, United Kingdom
Zaha Hadid, Architect
Copyright: Zaha Hadid 1994/Photograph by Edward Woodman